THE
FBI

Other Books by Ronald Kessler

Inside the CIA*
Escape from the CIA*
The Spy in the Russian Club*
Moscow Station*
Spy vs. Spy*
The Richest Man in the World
The Life Insurance Game

*Published by POCKET BOOKS

THE FBI

Inside the World's Most Powerful Law Enforcement Agency—by the Award-Winning Journalist Whose Investigation Brought Down FBI Director William S. Sessions

Ronald Kessler

POCKET BOOKS

New York   London   Toronto   Sydney   Tokyo   Singapore

POCKET BOOKS, a division of Simon & Schuster Inc.
1230 Avenue of the Americas, New York, NY 10020

Library of Congress Cataloging-in-Publication Data

Kessler, Ronald, 1943–
    The FBI : inside the world's most powerful law enforcement agency
/ Ronald Kessler.
      p. cm.
    Includes bibliographical references and index.
    ISBN 0-671-78657-1
    1. United States. Federal Bureau of Investigation. I. Title.
HV8144.F43K47   1993
353.0074—dc20   93-5207
                                                        CIP

First Pocket Books hardcover printing October 1993

10 9 8 7 6 5 4 3 2 1

For Pam, Greg, and Rachel Kessler

Contents

Author's Note and Acknowledgments   ix

Introduction   1

1. New York: Home of the Roast Beef Sandwich   5

2. Criminal Division: Quality over Quantity   29

3. Baltimore: Upholding the Image   46

4. Intelligence Division: The Year of the Spy   64

5. Miami: Super Bowl of Crime   77

6. Inspection Division: Tracking a Hot Dog Cart   111

7. Dallas: My Place, My Rules   140

8. Training Division: Code Red   165

9. Los Angeles: Star Stalking   189

10. Profiling: "Scream, Girl, Scream"   214

11. Atlanta: Watch the Bridges   236

12. Laboratory Division: Stalking the Beast   252

13. Washington: Deep Throat   265

14. Information Division: Secret Files   296

15. Boston: Having a Picnic   311

16. Administrative Division: Pockets of Prejudice   326

17. London: The Best Job in the FBI   352

18. Public Affairs: Selling the Image   362

19. The Director: Perception vs. Reality   374

    Author's Letter to the FBI   439

    Notes   447

    Selected Bibliography   467

    Significant Dates   469

    Glossary   473

    Index   477

Author's Note and Acknowledgments

How does one investigate the Federal Bureau of Investigation? Very carefully.

Fortunately, when I started this book I was no stranger to the bureau. From the late 1960s, I had written newspaper stories about the FBI's questionable wiretapping practices and its compilation of files with embarrassing information about members of Congress. In the late 1970s, I wrote stories about the bureau's training program, the profiling of criminal suspects, and the acceptance of women agents. In the 1980s, I wrote books about the FBI's program for catching spies, including *Spy vs. Spy*, which focused exclusively on the FBI's counterintelligence program, and *Escape from the CIA*, which compared the FBI's sensitive handling of Vitaly Yurchenko, the KGB officer who defected from the Soviet Union and then skipped back three months later, with the CIA's callous treatment of him. In my most recent book, *Inside the CIA*, I revealed that a supersecret joint CIA-FBI squad had recruited a KGB officer inside the Soviet embassy in Washington.

When I finished the book on the CIA, my agent, Robert Gottlieb, head of the literary department at the William Morris Agency in New York, suggested I write a book on the FBI. With Paul D. McCarthy, senior editor at Pocket Books, I decided to focus on the bureau since the death in 1972 of J. Edgar Hoover, portraying how the bureau really works and how it has changed since Hoover was director.

In writing the book on the CIA, I had dealt extensively with William M. Baker. Baker had traveled from the FBI to the CIA and back, heading public affairs at both agencies when William H. Webster was director of the bureau and then of the agency. Webster had authorized the CIA to cooperate to a limited extent on my book about the agency, and I had developed a relationship of trust with Baker, who later became the FBI's assistant director over criminal investigations. I called Baker, who told Thomas F. Jones, then in charge of the FBI's press office, that he thought the FBI should cooperate fully on the project. In a memo to Jones, Baker wrote that the FBI could not get a "fairer evaluation."

While Jones was for the project, his idea of cooperation was not what I'd had in mind. He wanted the press office to arrange all interviews and steer me to the right people. When I asked an FBI agent whom I had dealt with before for his opinion on the racial issues dividing the bureau, Jones's press office told me to direct such inquiries to the FBI's Equal Employment Opportunity office. Moreover, the people in the press office insisted that I clear all such contacts with them. Even if I wanted to call longtime sources and friends who were agents, I had to go through the press office first, I was told. In effect the press office was asking me to break my word to these sources that their identities would remain confidential. When I pointed that out, a press officer said, "Just blame us." It was an invitation to commit professional suicide.

I discussed the problem with Lane Bonner, a retired agent who had been in charge of the press office when Baker supervised it. Still friends with people in the press office, Bonner recommended me as an honest, objective reporter and told them that no self-respecting, independent journalist could accept the conditions the FBI was trying to impose. It was to no avail.

Finally, the press office called me to complain that I had been seen interviewing Baker in his office, and that Baker had not cleared the interview with them. Apparently, they expected me to tell one of the FBI's most important assistant directors to follow FBI directives to clear his interview first. In fact, by writing a memo about me to Jones, Baker had already given them notice that I was interviewing him. But a press officer told me that if I talked with Baker again without calling them first, the FBI's cooperation would end.

I called Baker at home on a Sunday and poured out my frustration. As a sophisticated former public affairs officer, Baker realized that only an objective account of the FBI, with all the warts, would be credible. As he later told FBI executives, I needed to be able to "test" what FBI officials told me, and to do so I needed to have free access to the bureau. Baker said he would take care of it.

The next day, Baker called from his car phone at 6:00 P.M. He said he had talked the matter over with James W. Greenleaf, the FBI's associate deputy director for administration. In the FBI hierarchy, Greenleaf was one rung above Baker. I had dealt with Greenleaf when he had followed Baker as Webster's director of public affairs at the CIA. Also a supporter, Greenleaf endorsed the project. Both men recommended to Floyd I. Clarke, the FBI's deputy director, that the bureau cooperate fully. After Clarke raised the issue with William S. Sessions, then FBI director, Sessions issued a teletype to all FBI employees requesting their cooperation on the project.

"The planned book will be based on the author's own research and observation as well as on interviews with present and former FBI personnel," the teletype said.[1]

According to the ground rules, agents were still supposed to follow FBI regulations and not talk about personnel matters, sensitive techniques, or pending cases. Before granting an interview, they were to obtain permission from their supervisors. They were also to inform the press office that they would be granting an interview. But permission from the press office was not required. Nor did press officers have to sit in on interviews, as was their practice. Most important, I could call anyone in the FBI directly without going through the press office. Thus, if an agent chose to disobey the instructions in the teletype and meet with me without informing the bureau, he or she could still have that opportunity.

Explaining the earlier thinking of the press office, Scott A. Nelson, then deputy chief of the office, said, "We wanted to know what was going on, and we wanted to know if it was going down a negative road, so we could provide the kind of stuff you needed. If it was going to be purely negative, we wanted to be able to say, 'This is a bag of worms. You got it, and we can't provide anything more.' It was our need for keeping track of what you were doing."[2]

Given the restrictions that still existed, FBI officials later said that they were amazed at how deeply I had probed into the bureau. But having a teletype from the director was not enough. Trained investigators, FBI agents are skeptical, independent people. While the director's support helped tremendously, no agent would grant an interview without first making his own inquiries about me and the project.

In some cases, those inquiries were extensive. To my surprise, I found that Sessions himself had been involved in abuses relating to himself, his wife, Alice, and his longtime assistant. Agents familiar with the abuses were not about to discuss them until they had carefully researched my background, veracity, and reputation for protecting my sources.

In each interview, I had to prove myself by the way I asked questions, the kinds of questions I asked, and the amount of knowledge of the bureau I displayed. I had to strike the right balance between being too probing and appearing to accept the company line, between knowing too much and knowing too little, between siding with field agents against headquarters and siding with the headquarters officials who had authorized the project. Most of all, I had to be candid about my project and what I was doing. FBI agents can quickly spot a phony.

As the research progressed, there was a snowball effect. Agents whom I wanted to interview had heard about the project from agents I had already interviewed. While access became easier, I was aware that any misstep could cut me off, not because the bureau might withdraw its cooperation but because agents might decide I was not objective or trustworthy.

When the bureau wants to cooperate, it is a wonder to behold. I was shown FBI facilities that no journalist had ever seen—a monitoring room for listening to electronically intercepted conversations, the Washington area airport where the FBI keeps its surveillance planes, and the top secret building where the FBI develops new bugging and wiretapping devices. Agents took me in bureau cars to the scenes of crimes to help re-create them. At one field office, an agent picked me up at the airport, and the special agent in charge of the office invited me to stay at his home.

I sat in on Sessions's weekly executive conference meeting with the bureau's top officials. I flew with Sessions and his wife, Alice, on an FBI plane to New York, where Sessions handed out awards to agents. At Sessions's invitation, my wife, Pamela Kessler, and I attended the FBI's annual reception for the law enforcement and intelligence agencies of other countries. At FBI headquarters, I shot a submachine gun, a .357 magnum, and a .38-caliber revolver. At the FBI Academy in Quantico, Virginia, I shot a 9-millimeter and the FBI's new 10-millimeter semiautomatic pistol.

At the academy, I sat in on classes for new agents on ethics, sensitivity, and white collar crime, viewed a graduation of new agents, and saw trainees make mock arrests and learn defensive tactics. I visited the "shooting house" used by the hostage rescue team for training in close-quarters combat. At the FBI laboratory, I saw an FBI technician "age" a face with a computer and viewed a videotape that a rapist had made of himself committing his crime. In the FBI's profiling operation, I heard a tape of a serial rapist torturing a teenage girl before he killed her. At headquarters, I visited the operations center where the FBI had coordinated antiterrorist investigations during the Gulf War.

By the time I finished, I had visited the field offices in Los Angeles, Miami, Baltimore, Washington, New York, Dallas, Boston, and Newark, as well as the FBI's legal attaché in Rome, Italy. I had interviewed agents and supervisors who had worked most of the bureau's major cases, from the John Gotti case to fraud in the Defense Department, from the bombing of the World Trade Center to the background investigation of Clarence Thomas, from the destruction of Pan Am 103 to the spying of John A. Walker, Jr., and the Watergate break-in and cover-up.

I made a point of interviewing everyone on the organizational chart—every assistant director and associate deputy director, as well as the FBI's deputy director. Some of the officials spent the equivalent of days with me. I interviewed Sessions four times and Webster—whom I had previously interviewed when he was at the CIA and the FBI—twice. In addition, I interviewed former agents including nearly every former official of the bureau above the level of assistant director. When one last holdout, former FBI official John D. Glover, declined to be interviewed, Webster called him. Saying he believed my portrayal of the bureau would be "fair and accurate," Webster got him to agree to be interviewed.

In all, I interviewed 314 current and former agents and other FBI personnel. The transcripts of the interviews, nearly all on the record, ran to more than half a million words. Documents, newspaper clippings, and hearings filled a filing cabinet. Since agents are constantly being transferred, I have identified them in the position they held when they were interviewed. If relevant, their new position is mentioned as well.

As in any investigative work, there were problems along the way. After I learned how disastrously his office had handled a kidnapping case, the head of the FBI's Birmingham, Alabama, office demanded a leak investigation. He did not get it. The head of the Boston office said he would order his agents not to cooperate after I learned that one of them had, while doing a background investigation, improperly insisted on taking the footprint of a black lawyer who had been nominated to be a federal judge. If the agent in charge ever carried out his threat, it had no effect.

When I requested an additional interview with Sessions about his own abuses, the FBI's public affairs office at first said the matters I wanted to discuss were not important enough to warrant another interview. After higher-level bureau officials intervened, the press office asked me to summarize in writing the issues I wanted to discuss. Without my knowledge, high-ranking FBI officials then turned the ten-page, single-spaced letter over to the FBI's Office of Professional Responsibility (OPR), which investigates wrongdoing by FBI employees. In doing so, FBI officials were following regulations that require them to make OPR aware of any specific allegations of wrongdoing by FBI personnel. Because the abuses related to high-ranking bureau employees, including Sessions's assistant, the FBI's OPR gave the letter to the Justice Department's OPR, which opened an investigation into Sessions and his actions. Sam Donaldson broke the story of the investigation on ABC-TV. The ensuing controversy provided fresh material that illuminated the bureau's inner workings during a uniquely turbulent time.

The FBI hates to give up one iota of its territory. As evidence of that, even though the press office had given me a copy of Sessions's teletype requesting employees to cooperate on the project, when I gave copies of it to several former bureau officials whom I wanted to interview, the press office inexplicably asked me not to do it again. For similar reasons, I had trouble getting elementary statistics. If the bureau did not normally report them publicly, no one wanted to make them available. I decided to ask for documents only when I was sure the request was reasonable and the material could be obtained anyway under the Freedom of Information Act. Once I had made the request, I pursued it if necessary all the way up the bureau hierarchy. In most cases, when I had to bring such requests to Sessions, he approved them.

In the end, Sessions became upset that I had delved into the abuses relating to himself, his wife, and his assistant. He gave me a tongue-lashing, saying he was "offended" and "disappointed" that any embarrassing personnel matters would be included in the book. Sessions's reaction was a reminder that Hoover's dictum, "Don't embarrass the bureau," was alive and well in some quarters of the FBI.

Nonetheless, I am grateful to William Sessions for approving the book project and personally urging agents to submit to interviews. To Bill Baker, Jim Greenleaf, and Floyd Clarke, I owe special thanks for opening the FBI's doors wider than had ever been done before. As the press office told agents who inquired, the director had given me "carte blanche"—an action that some agents thought was crazy. If it had not been for Baker's larger concept of where the public interest lay, I likely would not have had such unprecedented access. Oliver B. (Buck) Revell, the FBI's former deputy associate director over investigations and now special agent in charge in Dallas, also went out of his way to help.

Coming up with the right idea for a book is no easy task, and I am indebted to my agent, Robert Gottlieb, for both the concept and his support.

I am lucky to have Paul McCarthy as my editor. Paul's footprints are difficult to trace. He has a way of giving his opinions without appearing to do so. By tone of voice or offhand remark, he lets me know his reaction. It is up to me whether I take the advice. But I have learned to savor his direction. He is so smart that I know I can go to him with any issue or problem and he will not only understand it but come up with the appropriate solution. His editing of the manuscript added immeasurably to the depth and clarity of the finished work.

My wife, Pam, was a tremendous source of strength and wisdom. Besides sharing her good judgment with me, she read the manuscript and did the initial editing. She also visited some FBI sites such as the laboratory and the FBI Academy and contributed to the book by adding her insights and descriptions. As the author of *Undercover Washington*, on the spy sites of Washington, she lent depth to some of my descriptions of places where spies had serviced their dead drops.

My daughter, Rachel Kessler, now with the Washington bureau of the *Wall Street Journal*, contributed her writing talents by helping to describe FBI agents from photographs. My son, Greg Kessler, contributed by starting a successful career in art, making his father proud. When they were younger, they helped by going with me to Sugar Hill, New Hampshire, to interview William C. Sullivan, a retired FBI official, who let them aim the Smith & Wesson .357 magnum revolver that agent Charles Winstead had used to shoot John H. Dillinger.

My friend Daniel M. Clements read the manuscript and offered helpful advice. Several present or former FBI officials and other experts also read the book and offered corrections, for which I am grateful.

Having taken over the press office after Jones left, John E. Collingwood was the consummate professional, remaining loyal to the FBI by providing invaluable help despite Sessions's later retaliatory and unsuccessful efforts to curb my access to the bureau. Ernest J. Porter, my immediate contact in the FBI's press office until Collingwood took over, was a prince. Even though the Society of Former Special Agents of the FBI knew the book would contain criticism of its idol Hoover, the society helped. Having written the only other book about the changes that were just beginning in the bureau when his book was published in 1975, Sanford J. Ungar shared the experiences he'd had when writing *FBI*, which I appreciate.

Most of all, I am grateful to the FBI's agents, from those on the street to those in the executive suite. Their help and candor made this book. So many went out of their way that I am reminded of the lyrics to Roy Orbison's song "You Got It":

> Anything you want
> You got it
> Anything you need
> You got it

Those who were interviewed or assisted in other ways include:

James M. Abbott; Mark Abramson; Edgar A. Adamson; Milt Ahlerich; Yoshio Akiayama; John (Jay) T. Aldhizer; and William F. Alden.

Robin Baker; William M. Baker; Alice W. Ballard; Sonia Barbara; Bryant L. Barnhart; William P. Barr, Kathy Barrett; Paul Barrett; Donald A. Bassett; Charles W. Bates; William A. (Al) Bayse; John L. Beale; Livio A. Beccaccio; John B. Bellinger III; David G. Binney; Leon H. Blakeney; Thomas E. Bondonza; Lane Bonner; Lawrence A. Bonney; Michael H. Boyle; Homer Boynton; William A. Branigan; William D. Branon; Tron W. Brekke; Tom Brennan; Jack Breslin; Andrew Bringuel II; Jeri Brovey; Russell J. Bruemmer; Robert M. (Bear) Bryant; David Buelow; John J. Burke; James T. Burnett; and Frank Buttino.

Plato Cacheris; John H. Campbell; Dana E. Caro; Jimmy C. Carter; Swanson D. Carter; William D. Carter; Joseph J. Casper; Roger T. Castonguay; G. Norman Christensen; Kelley Cibulas; Don K. Clark; Floyd I. Clarke; Brendan O. Cleary; Daniel M. Clements; John Coleman; Bill Colombell; Lee Colwell; John E. Collingwood; Nancy J. Collins; Richard T. Conroy; Joseph V. Corless; Bill Cotter; Bobbi J. Cotter; and Danny O. Coulson.

Anthony E. Daniels; Richard J. Darragh; Jerome J. Daunt; Joseph R. Davis; Wayne G. Davis; Harold A. Deadman, Jr.; Wilber K. DeBruler; Kenneth E. deGraffenreid; Cartha D. (Deke) DeLoach; Jim Dempsey; Margot D. Dennedy; Roger L. Depue; Susan J. Derk; James

V. De Sarno, Jr.; Phillip Desing; Joseph E. diGenova; Robin Dinerman; Donald S. Donovan; William Y. Doran; John E. Douglas; John M. Dowd; P. J. Doyle; Andrew J. Duffin; Dennis L. Dufour; and the late Thomas E. DuHadway.

U.S. Representative Don Edwards; Lloyd T. Erwin; Salvador Escobedo; Sheriff Van E. Evans; David E. Faulkner; Carlos H. Fernandez; Curtis A. Fitzgerald; Marva Flowers; Chris Flynn; Henry J. Flynn; Kevin D. Flynn; Patrick J. Foran; Carl Richard Ford; Rosalie Ford; James M. Fox; and Robert S. Friedrick.

Neil J. Gallagher; Richard J. Gallagher; Richard T. Garcia; Karen E. Gardner; Theodore M. Gardner; William A. Gavin; Richard Gayer; James H. Geer; Stuart M. Gerson; Brian P. Gettings; Kenneth A. Giel; Michael Giglia; Wayne R. Gilbert; Bobby R. Gillham; Seymour Glanzer; Robert L. Gleason; John D. Glover; Manuel J. Gonzalez; W. Douglas Gow; Stuart R. GraBois; Richard F. Green; James W. Greenleaf; Michael D. Grogan; John E. Guido; John Gulley; Peter A. Gulotta; James Gump; and Howard Gutman.

William E. Hagmaier III; Terrence Hake; Martin V. Hale; John F. Hanlon; Lieutenant Harry M. Harner; William T. Hassler; Robert R. (Roy) Hazelwood; Lawrence J. Heim; Vita Heineman; Richard W. Held; John W. Hicks; William L. Hinshaw; John Hoos; Edison U. (Ed) Horne; Thomas A. Hughes; John P. Hume; Robert W. Hunter; David J. Icove; James O. Ingram; David W. (Woody) Johnson Jr.; Emanuel Johnson, Jr.; David Johnston; Deborah A. Johnston; Ray E. Jones; Robert L. Jones; Thomas F. Jones; Robert J. Jordan; and Edward H. (Ed) Joyce.

Catherine M. Kaiser; Frederick M. Kaiser; James K. Kallstrom; James A. Kavina; Clarence M. Kelley; Thomas C. Kelly; Weldon L. Kennedy; Richard J. Kerr; Allan A. King; Jerry King; Phillip M. King; Dan Kingston; Pat Kirby; Mike Kortan; and Donald M. Koshlap.

Sharon LaFraniere; Larry W. Langberg; Angelo J. Lano; Renée C. Lano; Nicholas Landino, Jr.; Charlene Law; Larry G. Lawler; Jack Lawn; Mary C. Lawton; Edward R. Leary; Marvin Lewis; Thomas Lewis; Robert E. Lill; Carla Liverman; Susan E. Lloyd; Dr. James L. Luke; and Beverley Lumpkin.

Robert J. Mack; Daniel C. Mahan; Charles Mandigo; Walter Mangiacotti; Andrew S. Manning; Belinda Maples; Gary L. Marcus; Mary Jo Marino; Richard A. Marquise; John L. Martin; David A. Maxwell; Jeffrey Maynard; Christopher R. Mazella; Ronald H. McCall; Kathleen L. McChesney; Phillip M. (Mike) McComas; Patrick C. (Mick) McCormick; John J. (Jack) McDermott; Wayne A. McDonald; I. Ray McElhaney; Lawrence P. McElynn; Robert C. (Bud) McFarlane; William J. McGrath; Nancy D. McGregor; John L. McKay, Jr.; James D. McKenzie; William J. McMullin; Gordon G. McNeill; Lawrence McWilliams; Carol Mesheske; Paul L. Miller; Darrell W. Mills; Elaine Mills; Paul K. Minor; Dr. Murray S. Miron; Darvin Moon; James E. Mull; Patrick J. Mullaney; Francis M. (Bud) Mullen, Jr.; Donald Munford; Sarah Munford; Bernard J. Murphy; and Charles E. Murphy.

Scott A. Nelson; Terry L. Nelson; Frances Newby; Gloria M. Newport; Stephen Niezgoda; James E. Nolan, Jr.; Kevin O'Brien; Dennis O'Callaghan; Dr. James A. O'Connor; Gene J. O'Donnell; Ronald J. Ostrow; John E. Otto; Tim Outlaw; Keith Palmer; Phillip A. Parker; Charlie J. Parsons; Mildred C. (Millie) Parsons; Ronald Patton; Gary L. Penrith; Bernardo Matias (Mat) Pérez; James R. Pérez; Hector M. Pesquera; James R. Pledger; Steve Pomerantz; Ernest J. Porter; and Larry A. Potts.

Marion S. Ramey; J. Stephen Ramey; Donald W. Ramsey; James T. Reese; William J. Rehder; Paul C. Reilly; Oliver B. (Buck) Revell; Donald S. Richards; Edward J. Roach; Everett A. (Ed) Robinson III; Hugo Rodriguez; Eileen J. Roemer; Richard M. Rogers; Dr. Susan Falb Rosenfeld; James H. Rowe III; and James Rowley.

Raoul G. Salinas; Michael J. Santimauro; Herbert F. Saunders; Nancy L. Savage; Frank G. Scafidi; Carl A. Schultz; Richard D. Schwein; Alice Sessions; William S. Sessions; Whitney North Seymour, Jr.; David J. Shaffer; Edwin J. Sharp; Thomas L. Sheer; Mike E. Shallenberger; Carl M. Shoffler; James J. Siano; Earl J. Silbert; Robert Siller; Anthony Silva; Robert R. Simmons; Walt H. Sirene; Glenda C. Skinner; William F. Slowinski; Paul South; Nancy Southers; Mary Spaeth; Joseph M. Stehr; Carl Stern; Gregory J. Stevens; Thomas W. Stokes; Gary L. Stoops; Frank J. Storey; Walter B. Stowe, Jr.; Thomas Strentz; Pamela B. Stuart; Cornelius G. Sullivan; Gregg L. Sullivan; Marion Sullivan; and Beverly Sweatman.

George B. (Biff) Temple; Howard D. Teten; Don Thompson; John H. Thompson; Linda C. Thompson; Jerry D. Thornton; Don S. Tokunaga; D. Caroll Toohey; Ralph A. Torres; William E. Trible; Simon Tullai; Joe Ullmann; Sanford J. Ungar; Joe Valiquette; Frederick B. Verinder; Richard B. (Rick) Wade; John C. (Jack) Wagner; Michael M. Wald; Bobi Wallace; Robert E. Walsh; Leonard M. (Bucky) Walters; Kenneth P. Walton; W. Raymond Wannall, Jr.; Steven B. Warner; R. Patrick Watson; Lynda Webster; William H. Webster; Neil J. Welch; William J. White; Michael D. Wilson; Walter A. Witschard; Joseph R. Wolfinger; Joe Yablonsky; Robert E. Yates; Lawrence K. York; Roger S. Young; Norman A. Zigrossi; and James L. Zopp.

THE

FBI

The FBI seal.

The FBI badge.

Introduction

Before new FBI agents met J. Edgar Hoover, Simon Tullai, who was in charge of new-agent training, gave them a lecture on how to present themselves. They were to have neatly trimmed hair, wear white shirts, have shined shoes, look the director squarely in the eye, and shake his hand with a dry palm. There was nothing the director hated more than a clammy handshake. Tullai recommended that agents pat their hands on their pants legs to make sure their hands were dry before entering Hoover's spartan office on the fifth floor of the Justice Department building.[3]

After the meeting, Hoover would question whether certain agents had what it took to be FBI agents. He thought some were too short or too bald. Others, he complained, had protruding ears, bad posture, or eyebrows that were too bushy.

The emphasis on appearance was a metaphor for Hoover's FBI. With his genius at public relations and organization and his stern approach to morality, Hoover turned a corrupt arm of the Justice Department—started in 1908 and named the FBI in 1935—into one of America's most revered and feared agencies. Fueled by brushes with the likes of John Dillinger and "Pretty Boy" Floyd, the G-Men became American folk heroes.

But the image and the reality were quite different. During Hoover's nearly forty-eight years as director, the FBI achieved a string of high-

1

profile successes, bringing to justice the murderers of three civil
rights workers in Mississippi, arresting the kidnapper of Charles A.
Lindbergh, Jr., and finding and arresting Soviet spy Colonel Rudolf
I. Abel. But Hoover's FBI spent much of its time recovering stolen
cars, apprehending military deserters, and chasing down minor government thieves so that Hoover could show Congress how many
arrests the FBI had made. In Hoover's FBI, an arrest of a mafia
kingpin counted as much as an arrest of a car thief. Meanwhile, the
FBI virtually ignored the more serious threats—public corruption,
white collar crime, organized crime, and terrorism. Because he
feared that it might lead to controversy that could embarrass the
bureau, Hoover shied away from undercover and drug trafficking
investigations as well. Instead, he emphasized building statistics.

"When I came into the bureau [under Hoover], we used to go to
the Metropolitan Police Department [in Washington] every day and
check the stolen-car list. If the car was recovered, we took credit. If
it was stolen in Washington and recovered in Maryland, we would
claim that as a stat, interstate theft. We would interview the subject
and try to find out what we could, but we didn't make the arrest or
the recovery," said James V. De Sarno, Jr., an assistant special agent
in charge of the FBI's Washington metropolitan field office.[4]

"Stolen in Washington, D.C., and recovered in Prince George's
County. Contact the police department and claim the credit.
Bullshit. We did good work. We didn't need to waste our time on
that," said James D. McKenzie, a former FBI assistant director of
training.[5]

At the same time, Hoover's FBI trampled on Americans' rights
just as surely as the bureau's nemesis in the then Soviet Union, the
KGB. Under Hoover, the bureau illegally broke into homes and businesses, engaged in wiretapping without proper authorization, collected derogatory information for political reasons, and leaked to
the press damaging information about people like Martin Luther
King. Confusing political dissent with subversion, Hoover's FBI
spied on Americans exercising their constitutional rights of free
expression and tried to disrupt their political movements—often at
the direction of presidents. To preserve his own power, Hoover let
members of Congress and presidents know that the bureau was
aware of their philandering or other indiscretions. Nothing more
had to be said; no one dared to question whether the director had
outlived his usefulness.

The hypocrisy did not end there. Hoover claimed he did not want
the FBI to become a national police force. Yet during his reign, the

bureau became a national thought police, keeping files on the comments and activities of movie and television stars, poets, writers, and playwrights ranging from Thomas Mann, Henry Miller, John Steinbeck, and Ernest Hemingway to Lewis Mumford, T.S. Eliot, William Faulkner, John Gunther, Thomas Wolfe, John Dos Passos, and Charlie Chaplin. Hoover pontificated about cooperating with local police, yet his bureau developed a reputation for appropriating local investigations and taking credit for the FBI. Hoover espoused family values, yet he never married and spent his leisure time, including vacations, with Clyde Tolson, the FBI's associate director. When he heard that a citizen while playing bridge or having her hair done at the beauty parlor had referred to him as a "queer," Hoover sent agents to question and harass the offender.[6]

As an administrator, Hoover was a tyrant. He transferred agents from one end of the country to another for drinking coffee on the job and held back their pay raises for losing their handcuffs. Yet, Hoover and some of his aides engaged in extensive personal corruption. Hoover had FBI employees build a front portico and a rear deck on his home at 4936 Thirtieth Place NW in Washington. They painted the house each year, dug a fish pond equipped with water pump and lights, and constructed shelves and other conveniences for him. Moreover, they maintained his yard, replaced the sod, installed artificial turf, planted and moved shrubbery, and built a redwood garden fence, flagstone court, and sidewalks. FBI employees reset Hoover's clocks, retouched his wallpaper, and prepared his tax returns. Employees were expected as well to give gifts to Hoover such as cabinets and bars, all built by FBI employees on government time.[7] Meanwhile, Hoover had FBI employees write *Masters of Deceit* for him under his name. He then pocketed part of the proceeds.[8]

"Hoover [and some of his aides] would be prosecuted under today's standards. No question of it. And should have been," said Oliver B. (Buck) Revell, the FBI's special agent in charge in Dallas and formerly the bureau's associate deputy director over investigations. "Hoover for the money he kept from the books he supposedly wrote but didn't write. Using government funds and resources for personal gain. And use of government employees to maintain his residence. Again, that is fraud against the government. Taking vacations and putting in vouchers and at the same time those [were] comped. Agents have been prosecuted for that. Those things that were somewhat taken for granted back then would be prosecuted today."[9]

The abuses came to an end with Watergate and the Vietnam war. Watergate led to revelations of misuse of the FBI by the Nixon White House; the government's lying about progress in the war bred mistrust of government in general. In 1975, a committee headed by the late Senator Frank Church, an Idaho Democrat, began an investigation that would profoundly alter the way the FBI did business. Among other reforms, the hearings led to guidelines that limited the FBI to investigating criminal conduct rather than divergent political beliefs.

For all the changes since Hoover's day, the FBI remains a cipher. The FBI carefully guards its image. No institution in America is as powerful. No institution generates as much curiosity, fear, and excitement. No institution holds as many secrets. And few institutions have gone through as many wrenching changes as has the FBI since the death of its creator. Yet, for the most part, the public knows about the bureau only what the bureau wants it to know. As in Hoover's day, it maintains control over the current television series—in this case, *FBI: The Untold Stories*—and vetoes subjects that reflect unfavorably on the bureau's image.

The aim of this book is to depict the FBI as it really is.

1

New York: Home of the Roast Beef Sandwich

● **According to bureau legend,** a New York FBI agent went to lunch at a deli around the corner from the field office, then on Sixty-ninth Street at Third Avenue. The agent thought the deli an establishment that offered a discount or more food to FBI agents and police officers. He ordered a roast beef sandwich and watched as the counterman piled on the slices. The deli man slid the plate toward the agent. To the agent's chagrin, the sandwich looked no bigger than any other roast beef sandwich.

Showing the deli man his credentials, the agent said, "FBI! More roast beef."

Not knowing anything about any special deals, the counterman looked at the agent dumbfounded. The story soon spread to all the FBI's fifty-six field offices, four hundred resident agencies, and twenty legal attaché offices overseas. Probably no story is more widely known within the bureau, and no other story is so sure to send agents into peals of laughter. When they are dissatisfied with anything, agents say, "More roast beef!" When they tell their bosses they showed their credentials, they say, "I roast beefed him."

The story is so appealing because it goes to the heart of what it means to be an agent. FBI agents have awesome power. They are authorized to carry weapons and can shoot to kill. They can deprive a suspect of his freedom and send him to jail for life. They can

5

eavesdrop on private phone conversations, videotape what goes on in bedrooms, subpoena witnesses to testify before a grand jury, open mailboxes and read mail, and obtain telephone toll records and other confidential documents, including income tax returns. By consulting their files, they can find out the most damaging personal information about individuals. With the help of the FBI laboratory, they can turn a shard of glass into evidence of a hit-and-run accident or a drop of semen into evidence of rape. With computers, they can age faces and break codes. In pursuing suspects, they can speed and break other traffic laws. If agents really want to find someone, they can do it in virtually every case, turning for help if necessary to the CIA, Interpol, and foreign governments. By showing their credentials, FBI agents can bypass airport security, take their weapons on airplanes, and get into movie theaters free. But therein lies the rub: Unless an agent is on bureau business, has proper authorization, and in many cases has a court order, he has no more power than any other citizen. Showing "creds," as they are called, to obtain more food at the local deli violates the most basic credo of the FBI.

Very few agents know the identity of the agent who supposedly ordered the roast beef sandwich in New York, or what really happened that day—to be recounted later. Like most bureau stories, the roast beef sandwich story grew and changed shape as it made its way from New York to San Francisco, from Dallas to San Juan. But the fact that it occurred in New York is significant. New York is the office that agents do not want to go to, the place with the highest living costs, the most street crime, the greatest stress. Inevitably, it is where some of the most bizarre incidents involving agents occur, and where some of the tallest tales start.

"Any horror story coming out of any bureau office will end up happening in New York," according to Edward J. Roach, an FBI agent previously assigned to New York.

Because of the high living costs, many New York agents live in remote areas of New Jersey. To beat the rush hour, some try to leave the office precisely on time. One agent got the bright idea of turning ahead the clocks by five or ten minutes. In response, the special agent in charge decided he would have technicians snip off the control levers on the clocks so that they could not be turned ahead. But when a power failure occurred, the clocks could not be readjusted. Nor had anyone thought about the problem Daylight Savings Time would cause. It took months to fix the clocks so they would tell the correct time again.

New York agents are periodically mugged on the way to work or while conducting a surveillance. In a recent case, a man walked up to an agent sitting in an FBI car and demanded his wallet. The agent said he was with the FBI. Meanwhile, an accomplice drove up along the passenger side of the car and yelled, "Shoot him, waste him!"

The agent knocked the gun out of the mugger's hand, pulled his own gun, and shot him dead. The FBI found the accomplice, who has been sentenced to prison for assaulting a federal officer.[10]

One afternoon, New York agents were showing a series of photographs of possible suspects to a teller at a bank that had been held up the day before. Pointing to a photo, the teller said, "That's him." Then she pointed to a man standing in line. "And that's him right there, standing in line."

Roach and other agents chased the robber as he fled the bank, apprehending him after a vicious fight.

David A. Maxwell, another New York agent, found his job a little easier. He noticed two men acting suspiciously and got in line behind one of them as the man waited for a teller at a bank. When the man got to the teller's station, he said, "This is a stickup!"

"No, it's not," Maxwell said, and—with the help of another agent who happened to be in the bank—arrested both men.

One robber held up a car replenishing a check-cashing facility two hundred yards from the FBI's office at 26 Federal Plaza in downtown New York. The robbery occurred in the early morning, when FBI agents and police officers who work at the nearby police headquarters building are in coffeeshops having breakfast.

"When they heard shots being fired . . . the agents and police officers in the coffeeshops and restaurants came pouring out into the street to find out what was going on and to chase these men and capture them," said Donald W. Ramsey, a New York agent at the time.[11]

"Just being in the city is putting you at risk," said James M. Fox, the assistant FBI director in charge of the New York office.

Like New Yorkers in general, New York agents develop a brittle exterior and their own way of doing things. When the rules call for doing a case one way, the New York office will do it another way. If they are busy, New York agents will let their phones ring unanswered. If headquarters wants a survey returned by a certain date, New York agents are the most likely to turn theirs in late. Agents call it the "New York attitude." Yet, some of the bureau's most impressive cases and imaginative techniques have come out of New York, from ABSCAM to the "Commission" case against the heads of all five New York organized crime families.

"New York was always different," said Kenneth A. Giel, a retired New York FBI agent. "Everybody in the field outside of New York was deathly afraid of being sent to New York. You couldn't go any lower than New York. But yet it did the greatest work. It had to do the greatest work."

"They did things in the New York office that were not done anywhere else in the FBI," said Edward H. Joyce, a retired New York FBI agent. "We routinely turned down cases that would have been major cases in other offices."

The New York office is one of fifty-six field offices directed by ten headquarters divisions. Using the analogy of a picket fence, the field offices are the vertical slats that hold up the fence. The divisions are the horizontal rails that bind the slats. Divisions set policy and become involved in cases at critical junctures. For example, the laboratory division may help a field office by analyzing spent shells at a murder scene. The field offices do the actual work of investigating crimes.

With twelve hundred agents, the New York field office is the largest in the bureau, followed by Washington. The field office occupies the twenty-third through twenty-eighth floors of the Jacob J. Javits Federal Building, which has a children's playground in the front and is catty-corner from U.S. District Court. Entry to the elevators to the FBI's floors is blocked by turnstiles and guards who check identification before allowing anyone upstairs. The blue-carpeted reception room is sparse, without the pictures of the FBI director or J. Edgar Hoover found in most field offices.

Over the years, the New York office has been dominated by characters who were larger than life. Under J. Edgar Hoover, John F. Malone ran the New York office. Known affectionately as "Cement Head," Malone fit Hoover's image of an FBI agent—square-jawed, confident-looking, and conservatively dressed. Anyone could have mistaken Malone for the chief executive officer of a Fortune 500 company. But every agent had his own favorite story about Malone.

According to a former New York agent, Malone introduced a black FBI agent in the elevator to a Cabinet officer who was visiting the office.

"This is one of our black agents," Malone said.

"They didn't call him Cement Head for nothing," Joyce remarked.

Thomas L. Sheer, who was appointed to run the New York office by William H. Webster, who was FBI director from 1978 to 1987, was another legend. He took over in 1985 and is credited by many with the bureau's highly successful attack on organized crime in

New York. A handsome man standing six feet one inch tall and weighing 228 pounds, Sheer had attended the University of Florida on a football scholarship and then entered the Marine Corps. An FBI agent whom he had met while in the Marines had persuaded him to join the bureau.

Sheer began on the bank robbery squad in 1966 and became a relief supervisor in 1968. In that job, he helped Joseph McFarlane, the head of the squad, form a task force with the New York City Police Department. In Hoover's FBI, such a marriage was earth-shattering. Traditionally, the FBI wanted full control and full credit for everything it did.

"Hoover didn't want to do dope because he didn't want anybody to go bad. It could also be why we didn't work organized crime. . . . We tended to work clean cases or cases where we would clearly be wearing the white hat, where there was no possibility anything could taint the bureau," Sheer said. "That was one reason we didn't work with cops. We could control our own people. You couldn't control the police."

That attitude hampered the FBI's work.

"There would be a race to the bank, a scramble for the evidence, turf battles time and time again," Sheer said.

After the New York City police refused to hand over a bank robber to the FBI, McFarlane and his police counterparts decided to hammer out a way to cooperate. They formed a task force that became a model for FBI cooperation with local police in cities throughout the country. Under the task force arrangement, the police and the FBI worked the cases together. The FBI even made room for the police in their offices. When it came time for the arrest, the police would claim the credit. Then federal prosecutors would take over, and the FBI could claim the credit for the conviction in federal court. Sheer made sure that headquarters knew nothing about the new idea.

"We didn't know what Hoover's reaction would be, so why make an issue of it?" he said.

Each of the FBI's field offices is headed by a special agent in charge (SAC), except for the New York office, which is headed by an assistant FBI director with SACs reporting to him. Headquarters explains the anomaly by saying that the New York office is too large to be headed by one SAC. Sheer became SAC over criminal investigations in New York in 1982 before taking over as assistant director over the entire office. Together with Frank J. Storey, who was in charge of organized crime investigations in New York, Sheer put in place a plan to try to wipe out the mafia. Until the Apalachin, New York, meeting of organized crime leaders in 1957, Hoover had refused to believe that a national syndicate of organized crime leaders existed.

"Hoover had always recognized that there were individual crime groups carrying out vice activities, and he had gathered intelligence on them," said Oliver B. (Buck) Revell, who discussed the issue with Hoover and worked in the organized crime section at headquarters when Hoover died. "What he did not accept was that there was a national conspiracy. The Apalachin conference showed there was, and we created criminal intelligence squads and began collecting intelligence on the mafia."[12]

At first, the bureau concentrated its efforts on raiding bookies and other minor organized crime figures. Slowly, under Clarence M. Kelley, who was FBI director from 1973 to 1978, the bureau began to take on more significant cases. Instead of merely reacting to crime, the bureau took an aggressive approach that the FBI calls proactive. From informants and wiretaps, agents learned who the important targets were and then went after them with undercover operations.

One of the first major cases was UNIRAC, a Miami-based case that brought indictments in 1978 and resulted in the conviction of Anthony M. Scotto, a longshoreman union leader and reputed organized crime figure. Headquarters was used to arresting suspects the first time they took a bribe. Storey, who was then over the case at headquarters before he was assigned to New York, had to convince his bosses that the FBI would get more out of the case by waiting.

"The assistant director [at headquarters] had to approve the payment," Storey said. "He said, 'We're not going to arrest this fellow?' I said, 'No. We're going to let the money walk.' We wanted to develop initial evidence and find out who he is working for and carry this forward. He said, 'We've never done this before.' That happened several times.

"We changed our whole approach on how we addressed organized crime both from an investigative and management standpoint," Storey said. "That's when it all started. The long-term approach to the problem was new to the FBI. We were more reactive in cases like Dillinger and fighting communism."[13]

Kenneth A. Giel, a New York agent, worked one of the first such cases in New York. Giel started in the FBI in 1970, when Hoover was still in charge and white shirts were mandatory.

"There were fifty people in my class [at training school], and forty-nine had white shirts. I had a yellow shirt," Giel said. "Sy Tullai was the head of new-agent training. He turned around and he said, 'Gentlemen, your appearance is everything.' He went into this long thing about how you have to look. 'That distinguishes you from any other law enforcement agency.' I had a well-tailored three-piece suit on. And he said, 'And that doesn't mean yellow shirts.' He turned around and looked right at me. The entire class, all forty-nine heads, turned around and looked at me. From day one, I got the message that image and appearance were the most important aspects of the FBI," Giel said.[14]

Giel was assigned to a resident agency of the Birmingham, Alabama, field office. Resident agencies are satellite offices with as few as one to as many as fifteen or twenty agents who report to headquarters city, as the field offices are known.

"The first thing I was told by the senior resident agent at the time was we have statistics that we have to uphold. We will always have more stolen cars each year so that each year we will look better and better," Giel said. "They were generated from a wide variety of different things. Cars that were abandoned and found to have been stolen. But there was always an emphasis on statistics. Fugitive apprehensions and things along those lines. A statistic was a statistic. Total number of arrests, regardless. It was on the basis of those statistics that the FBI went to Congress each year and got funded. It meant you were doing something. Convictions, stolen cars, property recovered. Generally it was the Blue Book value of the vehicle. It didn't make any difference if the car had been destroyed."

Meanwhile, Giel said, "We were overlooking some major things. . . . The local sheriff in the county I worked in was absolutely corrupt. There were no meaningful efforts to look into civil rights violations in Alabama."

Giel was transferred to New York when the bureau began the transition to what it calls priority cases. Traditionally, bureau agents had thirty to fifty cases assigned to them. They usually did very little on each one. Because Hoover's FBI required some evidence that each case had been worked on each month, agents would frequently call someone involved in the case and, even if they got no answer, they would report that they had worked the case.

In contrast to working thirty to fifty cases, Giel spent three years working just one labor racketeering case involving New York AFL-CIO trade unions. The case had started with a wiretap that picked up information showing that an air-conditioning contractor was dealing with organized crime. When Giel and another agent confronted him, the contractor agreed to cooperate.

"He said, 'For you to put up any construction work in New York, you have to pay organized crime. It's that simple. In order for you to do that, you have to sit down with the general contractor and OC [organized crime],' " Giel said.

"So we came up with the idea of setting up a consultant business that would act as a go-between between general contractors who wanted labor peace and wanted to pick up nonunion jobs," Giel said.

The FBI whimsically named the phony company James Rico Construction Consultants, after the Federal Racketeer-Influenced and Corrupt Organizations Act, the powerful federal law that has helped the FBI combat the mafia.

"We were right in the middle. We got a kickback of 10 to 15 percent of whatever job we were on. We would get that to mediate it," Giel said. Meanwhile, James M. Abbott, another New York agent, wore a body recorder for each meeting with labor officials and organized crime leaders.

In one poignant tape-recorded conversation, the FBI heard a contractor plead to be allowed to do a job for $1 million *less* than the next highest bidder. It seems the mafia and the carpenters' union had already decided who would do the job, and Vincent Molinari, the contractor who had submitted the lowest bid, was not the right one. So Molinari was told to see Theodore Maritas, then president of the District Council of Carpenters. In the conversation recorded by the FBI, Maritas explained that the project was "being set up" by "very, very heavy people, including myself."

"We steer these things," he said. "You have no idea what goes on in this town. You think things just happen out of the sky?"[15]

Molinari explained how important the job was to him, the fact that he had a son he had to put through college. He said he had turned down three other jobs to do the project, known as Chelsea Walk. But Maritas wouldn't listen.

"Believe me," Maritas said, "if you weren't a friend, you would have problems there right now you wouldn't believe." He said these would include labor troubles and protests by minority groups.

Today's bureau routinely approves paying hundreds of thousands of dollars to run undercover operations, including paying informants. But at the time the case started, undercover operations were relatively new.

"We were working on a shoestring budget, $10,000 for six months," Giel said. "Eventually we ran out of money. This was the bad part of the bureau. They didn't appreciate what we were doing. This was before Webster. When he came in things changed quite a bit."

Giel and Abbott approached the headquarters official over the case. His only previous experience was with bank robberies.

"We went in, and he said, 'Oh, that case.' He pulled it out and wasn't even familiar with it. I remember saying, 'Kiss my ass. Give me that.' "

They took the file and walked into the office of Edwin J. Sharp, who was over organized crime.

"We were furious. But we had the reputation of being bold, brazen. The story in New York was, you can't send me anywhere but New York. I remember the look on Ed Sharp's face."

Giel listed some of the organized crime figures they were recording.

"His eyes kind of went crazy. . . . He said, 'Sit down,' " Giel said.

Eventually, Sharp took the other bureau official off the case. Still, the bureau was slow in sending more money. With the bureau's knowledge, the agents took a loan from a loan shark to keep the operation going—something that would never happen in today's bureau.

As a result of the investigation, Vincent DiNapoli, identified as a captain in the Genovese mafia family, pleaded guilty in 1982 to conducting the District Council of Carpenters through a pattern of racketeering. Maritas, president of the council, was indicted and then disappeared, an apparent target of a mafia hit. Maritas's wallet was found in shallow water near the Throgs Neck Bridge. His body has never been found.[16]

As the chief of the New York office, Thomas L. Sheer decided that this piecemeal approach to attacking organized crime was not enough. He assigned a squad to each of the five organized crime families in the city.

"That was the magic thing about New York," Sheer said. "There was so much good work. You could plan it out. We would strategize. We were planning a ten-year attack on organized crime in New York right up through the indictment of the top five families."

"He was a leader," said Fred B. Verinder, a deputy assistant FBI director who worked for Sheer in New York. "But not because he was the boss. He made you want to work twenty-four hours a day and apologize for not working harder. He taught us about success and how to work toward it. If we had eighteen bank robberies, what is the common denominator? Shouldn't we concentrate on that?"[17]

Despite his skill at conducting investigations, Sheer was known for his absentmindedness.

"He was always running late for everything," said Joe Valiquette, the media representative in New York. "One night he got in his car and drove fifty feet. A cop car came over, and the officer said, 'I think you left your briefcase on the ground.' He had put it on the roof, and it fell off when he drove away."

"Tom Sheer came into the office one day with a trench coat on. He was carrying a bunch of white shirts. He unbuttoned his coat, and there he was in his underwear," said Jim Fox, who replaced Sheer as assistant director in charge of the New York office at the end of 1987.

Kenneth P. Walton, Sheer's deputy, was even more of a legend than Sheer—the sort of Damon Runyon character that is a dying breed in the modern FBI. Walton wore white shirts with gigantic cuffs made by his wife. A chain-smoker, he drew cigarettes from a gold case and wore a gold Rolex watch. While many agents bought their suits at Sears, he bought his at Barney's in New York. Agents called him "The Prince of Darkness."

The son of a truck driver, Walton—like many agents—had been the first in his family to go to college.

"My parents to this day are suspicious about the fact I read. They kind of wonder what happened," Walton said.

After serving in the Air Force, Walton worked in a morgue to help pay his way through the University of Wisconsin. After graduating, he became a newspaper reporter. Then he realized he could make more money as an FBI agent. With a deep, raspy voice, circles under his eyes, a perpetual tan, and bronze hair, Walton still looks more like a truck driver than an FBI agent.

Walton began to make a name for himself in Gallup, New Mexico.

"There was no fear in the man," said Donald S. Richards, an agent who knew him at the time. "I remember he got a call in the middle of the night that some convicts had escaped from a detention center and were on a westbound freight train to California. He rounded up all the law enforcement people he could. He had the train stopped and surrounded by the headlights of the cars of these officers. He personally jumped from train car to train car until he found them and arrested them."[18]

"I was smart enough to realize what the name of the game was, and the name of the game in 1968 to 1969 [under Hoover] was statistical accomplishment," Walton said. "Because of my military background, I was always able to relate to and get along with local law enforcement better than a lot of my peers. So I started the Fifth of the Month Club."

Every month, Walton offered a fifth of Wild Turkey or a box of target ammunition to the state or local police officer or sheriff's deputy who identified the most stolen cars and let Walton know about them so he could claim them as bureau recoveries. Only cars that had been transported from other states counted. But since a major highway snaked through Gallup, that was no problem.[19]

"After I did that for two months, the state police and city police became very competitive. In a very short period of time, I had essentially the city, New Mexico police, and sheriff's office working for the FBI. Before that, they might call the FBI or not. I had more convictions, recoveries than the entire Buffalo field office," Walton said.

With these paper successes to his credit, Walton was transferred to bureau headquarters in 1971. FBI documents had been stolen from the FBI's Media, Pennsylvania, resident agency, and the FBI wanted Walton, as part of a headquarters job, to help improve security at other resident agencies.

The theft of the documents marked a watershed for the bureau, because the documents were sent to newspapers and showed that the bureau had engaged in illegal surveillance practices under a program code named COINTELPRO. The program was meant to disrupt Vietnam war protesters and other political groups by sowing disinformation and dissension within their ranks. In fact, these groups for the most part were exercising their constitutional rights. A review by the General Accounting Office found that of 675 cases studied, 16 had been referred for prosecution. Of those, only 7 had actually been prosecuted. Only four convictions resulted.[20]

Reflecting how confused Hoover was about the distinction between criminal conduct and free expression, *PTA* magazine quoted the FBI director as saying in 1966 that the U.S. was then being confronted by "a new style in conspiracy—conspiracy that is extremely subtle and devious and hence difficult to understand . . . a conspiracy reflected by questionable moods and attitudes, by unrestrained individualism, by nonconformism in dress and speech, even by obscene language, rather than by formal membership in specific organizations."[21]

In New York, as the deputy assistant director over the office, Walton got a reputation as an "agent's agent." He was someone who appreciated the fact that the work of the FBI is, after all, done by the field, not by headquarters, someone who was willing to stand up to headquarters to support his agents.

"Walton was always the first to come in and the last to leave," said Valiquette, the media representative in New York. "His car was always in the garage when everybody pulled in, and it was still there when everybody left. First thing in the morning he'd be going through a stack of teletypes that had been sent in and were coming in. That's the way he kept up on all the cases that were being investigated. But he always had the time to walk around among the agents. He would sit up and put his feet up and talk. He knew everybody on a first name basis. He knew all the cases, he knew all the rumors. People had a lot of respect for him. He really seemed to care.

"Walton was a great one for all these mob nicknames," Valiquette said. "He came up with one for Frank Storey when he was over organized crime. He started calling him Frankie the Beast. Then he started calling me Joey Leaks."[22]

Walton immediately gained the respect of the bureau by successfully supervising cases against a string of radical groups that terrorized New York with bombings in the 1970s. But Walton's style also infuriated bureau officials.

One evening, Walton saw what he took to be a dog in a corridor of the New York office.

"Then I realized it was a rat. I shot it and missed it the first time, to be honest with you," Walton said. "I blew a hole in the carpet. It came back and I hit it. That was the only person I shot in New York. The rat died. I threw it in the incinerator."[23]

One Friday after Thanksgiving, 1982, Walton decided he could free up foreign counterintelligence agents to work on a criminal case. Walton figured they would have little to do because of the holiday. So he assigned three hundred agents from both the counterintelligence and criminal sides of the New York office to find James W. Lewis. Lewis was wanted for attempting to extort $1 million from Johnson & Johnson after cyanide had been found in Tylenol capsules in 1982. Normally, headquarters would have to approve diverting counterintelligence agents from pursuing espionage cases, since Congress allocates money separately to the bureau's counterintelligence program. But Walton decided that no one would know about it if he did it when most high-level bureau executives were taking the day off.

Walton had the agents blanket the city with "wanted" fliers. Three weeks later, Lewis was arrested in the midtown New York Public Library annex after a patron recognized him from the FBI posters.[24]

"Of course, the bureau found out about it, and they said it was another example of Walton subverting the system and doing all the things we know he does all the time," Walton said. ". . . I got my ass chewed by three or four people at headquarters for using FBI agents while everyone was away and could not do anything about it."

Lewis is now serving a ten-year sentence for extortion.[25]

Besides these transgressions, Walton liked to appear on the evening news, claiming that the publicity helped to combat crime.

"The typical and preferable posture for an FBI agent because of the culture of headquarters is to wrap yourself in a trench coat and say, 'No comment,' " Walton said. "What that also means is you don't have to prepare for anything, you don't have to know what the cases are. All you have to say is, 'No comment.' To be able to speak within the confines of the [Justice Department] guidelines, to present a positive, professional, articulate public persona that gives the public confidence and reason to work with the agents requires an effort."

Webster and others back at headquarters became annoyed that Walton was keeping such a high profile.

"Ken Walton had a certain style," Webster said. "He had a lot of color, and he did things in a way that tended to eclipse the people for whom he worked. My recollection is I kept reading about Ken Walton from the New York office, and I didn't read about the assistant director in charge of the New York office. I thought he should be more of a spokesman than Ken Walton."[26]

Webster transferred Walton to be special agent in charge in Detroit, which the director viewed as one of the best offices in the FBI. What that usually means is that an office is located in a city that has a high crime rate. Walton's brash style, his desire to pursue high-profile corruption cases against city judges and officials, and his frequent press appearances brought him into conflict with the U.S. Attorney in Detroit. William Sessions, as the new director, yanked him from that job to headquarters, making him a deputy assistant director in the criminal division.

In 1989, Walton retired, embittered that he had been pulled from Detroit and asked while assigned to headquarters to take a polygraph exam during a leak investigation. Walton refused to take it, saying he did not tell Rita Braver of CBS-TV about an FBI probe of the office of Representative William H. Gray III, a Pennsylvania Democrat.[27]

"It's a cruel organization in that it is highly bureaucratic, rule oriented, rule bound," said Lee Colwell, an associate director of the FBI under Webster. "It's cruel in the sense that it doesn't treat its people very well sometimes, but it's not a conspiracy. It's just the organization—the gears grinding. It can be cruel in transfers, assignments, promotions."[28]

Yet, the fact that Walton was given an important job in headquarters, overseeing white collar crime, informants, witness protection, and other major areas within the criminal division, can be seen as evidence that it is possible to rise within the bureau even with a strong personality and a propensity for taking on one's boss.

Floyd I. Clarke, the deputy director of the FBI who was then chief of the criminal division, had requested Walton as his deputy.

"He was a tremendous asset to me," Clarke said. "He has a tremendous amount of field investigative experience, he is imaginative, aggressive, intuitive, and he is a morale builder among the troops. He always used to bad-mouth headquarters, but within a short period of time here he understood better what all goes on here."[29]

However, Oliver B. (Buck) Revell, who was then executive assistant director at headquarters and had urged creation of the deputy slot for Walton, described Walton as "very bright, capable, totally egotistical, and somewhat foolhardy. His shenanigans showed immaturity and lack of professionalism, and I frankly had lost patience with him by the time he left."[30]

Besides attacking organized crime, the New York office developed a corps of agents who did nothing but conduct surveillance. Under Hoover, agents were prohibited from growing beards or long hair even if it would help them blend into the groups they were infiltrating. Virtually the only exception was in the investigation of the Weather Underground, a radical group responsible for a string of bombings in the early 1970s.

Today, nearly a quarter of New York's agents are assigned to "off-sites," many of them offices behind phony company names. These are where agents assigned to the Special Operations Group (SOG) work. The agents go to work in blue jeans and sneakers and do nothing but conduct surveillance. Another group, the Special Support Group (SSG), is composed of nonagents who follow people in counterintelligence cases. Because they do not work on dangerous criminal cases, there is no need for them to be armed, as agents are, and they can be paid less than agents are paid. In addition, New York has five resident agencies to cover areas such as Westchester County and Long Island.

Because of New York's high density, special techniques are required when following suspects. As in other jurisdictions, the New York office may use airplanes with night-vision equipment to watch a kidnapper who has just picked up ransom money. The New York office will also assign agents to drive along adjacent streets parallel to the kidnapper's route. Agents in a kidnapping case are usually assigned as well to watch each of New York City's bridges and transportation facilities. If a kidnapper decides to hop on a plane, agents already at the airport may be waiting for him.

In conducting electronic surveillance, agents fight a never-ending battle to get clear conversations. Matthew (Matty the Horse) Ianniello, a capo in the Genovese family, insisted on conducting business at an Italian social club that was perpetually noisy.

"So I assigned the agents who worked for me to conduct surveillance at the social club but do it in such a way that they were very visible," said Don Richards, then the head of an organized crime squad. "A male and female agent would have lunch across the street and take pictures. Other agents would walk by and write down license plate numbers. Cars slowly driving by would take photos. One Tuesday we put an agent with a paper bag on his head, with the eyes cut out, in the backseat. He pointed to people inside."[31]

In response, the suspects began conducting all their business in an office building where the acoustics were more to the FBI's liking. Ianniello was convicted of racketeering.[32]

In trying to plant a bug in an Italian social club where mafia members hung out, the FBI found that the sliding steel grate that came down over the door at night made a terrible noise as the agents tried to lift it at 4:00 A.M. So they drove a garbage truck up and down the street and banged garbage cans around as they lifted it.

"Then we picked up on the wire, 'The feds must be around, some garbage truck was driving up and down the street last night,'" according to David G. Binney, then a New York agent.

For some of the major cases against mafia families, the FBI not only had sound but video and still cameras that could zoom in on subjects by remote control.

In the FBI, it is an article of faith that a minor slipup will always occur in an investigation or arrest—an electronic device that doesn't work, an unforeseen obstacle presenting itself at just the wrong moment. Usually, the problems are not fatal. This was the case when

New York agents in undercover roles lured two criminals with $1 million in stolen bonds to the Westbury Hotel. The agents agreed to give them $900,000 for the bonds and brought $75,000 in cash as a down payment.

The agents invited the suspects to their suite, where four other agents had hidden in a closet to help make the arrest.

"The only problem was it was a cedar closet, so it was really sealed airtight," said Walter B. Stowe, Jr., one of the undercover agents. "So Murphy's Law took hold—everything that can go wrong will go wrong."

The suspects went through a long routine as they tried to determine if they could trust the undercover agents. "They wanted us to give them some money, and they would bring the bonds up," Stowe said. "So four hours go by. We have called for room service. We are having beers. The arrest team was in the cedar closet. They must have been really hot. We wanted to get it over with. . . . Finally, we get to the point where we are going to spring the arrest. The signal had to do with counting the money. The closet door pops open and these guys stagger out. . . . The first agent passes out, stumbles, and drops his gun on the floor. The other guys had started in suits, had stripped down, and now only had T-shirts on."

Nonetheless, Stowe said, "We ended up convicting the two guys we were dealing with. We recovered $6 million in stolen securities."[33]

Luck usually plays a role. In investigating the heroin importation case known as the Pizza Connection, New York FBI agents were conducting surveillance of an organized crime figure who wound up going to his pizza parlor in New Jersey.

"A sign on the window says, 'Waitress Wanted,' " said Binney, then the supervisor of the case. "We happened to have a female agent on the surveillance. She said, 'Guess what?' I said, 'Fabulous. Go in and apply.' "

The agent had phony identification with her, making it that much easier to apply.

"She got the job," Binney said. "She was a waitress for six months. She got pinched and the whole nine yards. I was lucky to have a savvy female agent on the scene."[34]

In the end, FBI agents say, it is the ability to get information from people that makes a case. Margot D. Dennedy, the blond, miniskirted supervisor of a squad that tracks stolen art, maintains contacts with art dealers and gets tips about suspicious items. It was an informant who knew about stolen art who started what became known as

ABSCAM, which resulted in the convictions of seven members of Congress for public corruption.

Besides these cases, FBI investigations have brought down the heads of New York's mafia families: John Gotti, who was convicted of ordering the murder of Paul Costellano, the boss of the Gambino crime family, and a string of others. Eight cases were made through the undercover work of Joseph D. Pistone, an agent who posed as a jewel thief for six years and penetrated the mafia.

"We were shutting them down," Jim Fox said. "We put such pressure on the five New York families that we took away their ability to make money."

"We have picked up conversations of long-term organized crime figures who say, 'This thing of ours, it's over,' " said William Y. Doran, the special agent in charge of the criminal division in the New York office.[35]

Unlike murders or burglaries, organized crime activity cannot be measured easily. No one claims that industries like the construction business that are the bread and butter of organized crime families are anywhere near free of shakedowns and kickbacks. Instead, there has been a lessening of organized crime influence, which means that not as many projects require payoffs, and the percentages are smaller. More important, the pervasive political corruption that could occur if organized crime were allowed to flourish has not materialized.

In contrast to the high-profile mafia cases, the FBI's New York office has traditionally devoted as much as half its manpower to counterintelligence cases. These are cases that rarely result in arrests, but when they do, they can be sensational.

It was the New York office that arrested Gennadiy F. Zakharov, a Soviet physicist employed at the United Nations. The arrest was supposed to take place under a utility pole equipped with video monitors that would beam the scene back to the Operations and Command Center on the twenty-sixth floor of the FBI's New York office. This is where major operations are coordinated. Long tables equipped with thirty-four telephones and computer terminals face three giant television screens that can beam closed-circuit or commercial television pictures to the agents, police, and prosecutors who sit at the tables. Other screens show maps where arrests are taking place, and a scoreboard lists which suspects have been arrested.

During the Bicentennial celebration in New York, the FBI had video cameras dangling from helicopters, boats, and a blimp, all transmitting images of the scene back to the operations center. A computer program with all the subway routes in New York and blueprints of possible terrorist targets, such as the United Nations and large banks, is kept in the radio room next to the command center.

In the Zakharov case, however, all the high-tech equipment was useless because, at the last moment, he decided he would pay a thousand dollars to a double agent for three classified documents on a subway platform. A male and a female agent jogged to the subway platform. So as not to appear to be staring, they grabbed each other and began kissing—with their eyes open. As Zakharov was examining the classified documents, they arrested him.

Zakharov's expulsion from the U.S. in 1986 prompted the Soviets to arrest American journalist Nicholas Daniloff and led to other expulsions by both sides.

The New York office also arrested Karl and Hana Koecher, a husband and wife spy team whose methods were somewhat unorthodox. An officer of the Czech Intelligence Service, Karl Koecher orchestrated a phony defection from Czechoslovakia and became a high-level CIA translator, with access to the CIA's highly sensitive operations in Moscow. As the only Soviet bloc mole known to have penetrated the CIA, Koecher achieved a certain distinction. But he was better known for attending sex orgies and wife-swapping parties with his gorgeous wife, Hana, who was also a Czech Intelligence Service officer. At these events, Hana would take on four or five men at one time. It was all for the cause, since they obtained information from other CIA employees who attended the parties. Because the CIA employees had opened themselves to blackmail, Karl and Hana passed along their names to the KGB for possible recruitment as well.

For two years, New York agents listened to their sexual escapades through bugging devices installed in their apartment and at the parties. In 1986, the Koechers were finally traded for Natan Sharansky, the Soviet dissident.[36]

With the cold war over, the New York office, like the rest of the FBI, is beginning to transfer agents from what is known as foreign counterintelligence to criminal investigations. Meanwhile, the successor to the KGB continues to spy on the U.S., and the files of the foreign East Bloc intelligence services have been a treasure trove of possible espionage cases for the FBI. As the head of the office, James Fox is over both foreign counterintelligence and criminal cases. A lawyer who is the son of a Chicago bus driver, he spent most of his career in counterintelligence, supervising spy cases like that of Jack and Morris Childs, two members of the Communist party who were actually working for the FBI in an operation called SOLO.[37]

"Some guys get into FCI [foreign counterintelligence] and it gets in your blood. It got in mine. Others want to break down doors and put handcuffs on people and get scum bags off the street," Fox said.

A man with a paunch and a commanding voice, Fox sits behind a massive oak desk that Hoover used when he visited New York. A color photograph of a fox rests on the desk.

"When you come to work in the morning," Fox said, "you have no idea what will happen."

In February 1989, FBI agents and New York City police officers seized 820 pounds of heroin in Queens, New York, then the largest confiscation in U.S. history. The raid, called WHITE MARE, smashed a major Southeast Asian drug ring.

"One week later, I got a call at 9:15 P.M.," Fox said. The FBI had lost contact with Everett Hatcher, a Drug Enforcement Administration agent assigned to a task force with the FBI. At the time, Hatcher had been meeting with drug traffickers. The FBI and DEA learned he had been murdered. Fox assigned two hundred FBI agents to join the DEA and local police in hunting for Hatcher's killer. Eventually, Costible (Gus) Farace was charged with the crime. But before he could face trial, mob assassins gunned him down.[38]

As an assistant director, Fox is part of the FBI's executive conference, the top executives who meet on Thursday mornings at headquarters in Washington to plan strategy or listen to presentations on new developments. That gives the head of the New York office more access to top FBI officials than the chiefs of other field offices have.

"If you want to get something done in the bureau, there are two ways you can do it," Fox said. "You can send an airtel [bureau jargon for a letter requiring immediate attention], and it might take months. Or I could go to an executive breakfast, make sure I sat next to Bill Baker [assistant director over the criminal division], and, if he agrees with the logic, within days you would have it done. He would extend himself because he spent a lot of years in the bureau and had more field orientation."

Fox was eating swordfish with french fries at Harry's, a restaurant two blocks northeast of the World Trade Center in lower Manhattan, when his beeper went off on February 26, 1993. As he walked to the phone, a friend who happened to be in the restaurant told Fox a PATH train had derailed under the World Trade Center. When he called the office, Fox was told a transformer had exploded at the 110-story complex.

Fox was suspicious that the explosion could have been caused by terrorists.

"I thought, 'If this was a transformer explosion, it's the biggest one I've heard of,' " he later recalled. "In this business, you wonder if it is an accident, or is it terrorist inspired?"

Fox got in his FBI car, turned on the red light, and drove to the scene. The twin towers were already surrounded by fire engines and ambulances. Fox decided he would only get in the way of rescue operations, so he drove back to the office. There, he learned the explosion had occurred at 12:18 P.M. While he still did not know if the blast had been an accident or deliberate, Fox decided to open the command center so the FBI could keep on top of developments. As it turned out, this would be the beginning of one of the most important and successful cases in FBI history.

When the explosion occurred, an estimated 50,000 people were inside the 110-story towers and the Vista International Hotel that separates them. The bomb went off on parking level B-2 and tore through the hotel and the parking garage, wiping out the trade center's emergency operations center. It trapped tens of thousands of frightened office workers in elevators and smoke-filled offices and stairwells. Six people died and more than 1,000 were injured. The damage and loss of business was estimated at more than $600 million.

The next morning, the FBI's bomb squad from the laboratory at headquarters arrived and began examining the scene. David Williams, the FBI's top bomb expert, told Fox he was almost certain the blast had been caused by a bomb. By the following day, he was certain.

"Williams, what makes you such an expert?" Fox asked him.

"I have examined ten thousand bombings," Williams replied.

"That's good enough for me," Fox said.

Indeed, according to Williams, the force of the blast was greater than in any bombing within the U.S. While the loss of life was less than in some terrorist incidents, the prominence of the target and the fact that the bombing placed so many people at risk made the incident perhaps the most dramatic terrorist event in U.S. history.

Fox deployed three hundred agents to work the case, which was codenamed Tradebom. As it happened, it was an explosives technician from the Alcohol, Tobacco and Firearms Bureau (ATF), working with a New York City police detective, who found the critical piece of evidence that made the case start to unravel. The same day Williams declared the incident a bombing, the technician, Joseph R. Hanlin, found the charred remains of part of the chassis of a Ford Econoline van. The blast marks on the metal suggested the bomb had been inside the van. Stamped into the metal was a vehicle identification number.

The FBI traced the number to a Ryder Truck Rental office in Jersey City, New Jersey, where the yellow van had been leased to Mohammed A. Salameh, a twenty-five-year-old Jordanian who had been working as a handyman. After searching his apartment, FBI agents found receipts showing he had rented space in a storage facility in Jersey City. The space contained several hundred pounds of chemicals that, if properly combined, would have produced a powerful blast.

Checking FBI terrorist intelligence files, the New York office found Salameh had demonstrated publicly on behalf of El-Sayid Nosair, an Islamic leader who had been acquitted in the 1992 slaying of Jewish Defense League founder Meir Kahane. Salameh attended a mosque in Jersey City where Sheik Omar Abdel Rahman, a blind Moslem cleric, preached. Rahman advocated violence to overturn the Egyptian government.

Officials at the Ryder office said Salameh had appeared two hours after the explosion to claim his van had been stolen. He asked for his $400 deposit, but the Ryder employees told him to file a police report first. Six days after the blast, Salameh returned to the Ryder Truck office and again asked for his money. This time, FBI undercover agents posing as Ryder representatives were there to help him with his claim. When he left the office, FBI agents based in Newark arrested him. In one of his pockets, they found the business card of Nidal Ayyad, a twenty-five-year-old chemical engineer. Ayyad had a joint bank account with Salameh. By tracing their long-distance calls just before the bombing, the FBI was able to find other possible conspirators, including Mahmud Abouhalima, a thirty-three-year-old Egyptian cab driver who had fled to Egypt just after the explosion. The FBI arrested Ayyad and obtained the extradition of Abouhalima. Four others were arrested and a fifth was being sought.

For weeks, the motive of the bombing remained unclear. But in part by comparing data in the hard drive of Ayyad's computer, the FBI was able to link to the bombing a letter *The New York Times* received four days after the incident. Declaring responsibility for the explosion on behalf of the Liberation Army Fifth Battalion, the ungrammatical note said, "This action was done in response for the American political, economical and military support to Israel, the state of terrorism, and to the rest of the dictator countries in the region."

As in any FBI case, this one had required teamwork to solve. Besides street agents, the New York City police, ATF, Fox's deputies, the counterterrorism section at headquarters, the laboratory, and special units that looked at computer evidence all helped. As the FBI's spokesman on the case, Fox got most of the publicity.

"Clearly finding the vehicle identification number was an early break," said Fox, who had taken to sleeping in a room off his office. "From there, it fell like dominoes. If we were sitting at this point six weeks later without a single arrest, it would be a very frustrating situation."

New York's biggest problem over the years has been the attrition rate. Because of the high cost of living, many agents quit. In recent years the attrition rate has diminished because agents living in expensive areas are given a pay differential that, in the case of New York, amounts to 25 percent of base pay. The average FBI agent is a GS-12, step 6, which pays $45,336. However, in return for working overtime, nearly all agents receive an additional 25 percent of their salary in what is known as Administratively Uncontrollable Overtime. This gives the average New York agent an annual salary of $68,004. In addition, agents who agree to relocate to New York and move within fifty miles of the city now receive a one-time payment of $20,000 as a housing allowance. As an assistant director, Fox makes $116,584 plus the 25 percent differential.

Before the pay differential was put into place, many agents lived in Pennsylvania—three hours from New York—because they could not afford to live in the city. "That affected our ability to respond [to crime]," said William Doran, the special agent in charge of the criminal division in New York.

"New York is different, there's no question about that," Fox said. "But we can't make our own rules. There are plenty of examples where we have been pulled up short. Five years ago, if we missed a deadline or didn't handle something exactly by the book, headquarters would say, 'That's just New York. They are in New York, that's its own punishment.' Now [with the pay differential] New York will do it by the book, the way headquarters says you will do it."

Not quite.

New York continues to be a rat's nest of personnel problems, from the drunk agent who chased a General Services Administration guard around the FBI's underground garage with a gun, to Joseph F. O'Brien and Andris Kurins, who quit after the FBI said they had not followed proper procedures in getting the manuscript of their book *Boss of Bosses*, about mafia boss Paul Costellano, cleared by the bureau.[39]

Which leads back to the roast beef sandwich.

First, according to Kevin D. Flynn, the New York agent who is the subject of the story, it was not a roast beef sandwich; it was a corned beef sandwich. Second, it was not that he wanted *more* meat; it was that he wanted *leaner* meat. Third, the incident occurred at a restaurant, not a deli. As for pulling his credentials, according to Flynn, an engaging man with a light brown mustache and a round head that is almost totally bald, it never happened.

"I . . . mentioned that the sandwich is very, very fatty. I said I would appreciate it if she [the waitress] would take the sandwich back and show the chef. I was very civil about it. I did not identify myself. As a matter of fact, being in New York, and just being myself, I am very sensitive to not identifying myself unless on official business," Flynn said.[40]

Flynn speculated that someone else told the waitress or the manager that he was with the FBI, and that the story grew from there. Not that Flynn is shy about letting people know of his FBI affiliation. Once he gave his FBI business card to a restaurant chef who turned out to be a drug dealer. When the chef was arrested with Flynn's card and his home number written on it, Flynn became the subject of an internal investigation. While Flynn was cleared of being involved with the drug dealer, he was suspended for two weeks without pay for displaying lack of candor during the FBI's investigation of the matter. Two years earlier, another agent overheard Flynn boasting at Donovan's Pub in Manhattan that Flynn worked on Soviet matters. Flynn confided to others at the pub that the FBI knew "all about" what the Soviets were up to. That, too, brought an investigation.

Nor was the roast beef incident the first time Flynn had become the subject of bureau lore. At his first office in Norfolk, Virginia, he was said to have radioed for help from his FBI car, saying he was being shot at. When agents rushed to the scene, they found that gravel from the road had been hitting the floorboards and mimicking the sounds of gunfire.

As in the case of the roast beef sandwich, Flynn said there was some truth to the story.

"The particular gravel incident that I recall is I was [in my FBI car] on a shoulder right across from the office. I was waiting to cross the street to go in the parking lot, and something strikes my glass on the driver's side. It shattered and disintegrated. If it was gravel, it would hit and that would be it. But this actually broke the window. . . .

"I thought, Jesus, I can't bring this back with a broken window without some sort of explanation. I got on the radio," Flynn said. "I said my window is broken. . . . I may have said something about shots being fired."

"Knowing Kevin, he is the kind of guy who likes to immediately tell you he works for the FBI and shows his credentials indiscriminately," said another agent who is a friend of Flynn's.

Despite all the scrapes, Flynn has managed to keep his job, despite at least one attempt to fire him. Meanwhile, he enjoys his celebrity. When agents from other offices visit New York, they often ask to see what he looks like and point him out in the elevators.

"We don't have anything like the roast beef sandwich story here," Robert E. Walsh, an assistant special agent in charge of the Chicago FBI office, said wistfully.

Flynn proudly displays a T-shirt that sells for ten dollars. "More Roast Beef," it says. "NYO [New York office]." As in the question of showing his credentials, Flynn modestly disclaims responsibility.

Pointing to the T-shirt while munching a club sandwich at a New York hotel, Flynn said, "This was not mine. I talked to the guilty one, but he just wasn't in today."

2
Criminal Division: Quality over Quantity

● **For years, Joe,** a homeless man, has railed outside FBI headquarters against J. Edgar Hoover, the FBI, and the ugliness of the bureau's facade. Under Hoover, the bureau would have had local police arrest Joe for disturbing the peace. In the modern FBI, the man agents know only as Joe is allowed to continue his tirades—except when they disturb ceremonies held in the building's inner courtyard. Indeed, when FBI agents arranged a retirement party for Roger T. Castonguay, an assistant director, the FBI laboratory gave Joe a bit part in a video played at the party.

"Roger: good man, good luck," Joe said in the video, then returned to denouncing the FBI.[41]

Joe has a point about the FBI's headquarters building, a 2.5-million-square-foot example of how not to design a building. Located non Pennsylvania Avenue between Ninth and Tenth streets NW in Washington, the J. Edgar Hoover Building is a monstrosity—a monument to Hoover's authoritarian rule.

The building, which was occupied by the FBI in 1974, is a skewed tetrahedron, not quite a square. To conform with local restrictions, the building is seven stories along Pennsylvania Avenue but, to the rear, rises eleven stories. From the side, the grotesque overhang at the rear gives the impression that the building is poised to topple on pedestrians below.

Daunting concrete slabs of uniform size cover the exterior. Each slab is punctuated by an array of small regular holes that suggest bullet holes. A tour guide says that some people assume the building is waiting for marble facing, and that the holes in the concrete are designed to anchor the marble. But in fact the holes are part of the architect's design, a rough look achieved when the slabs' steel molds were removed.[42]

After Sessions had been approached about being FBI director, he and Whitney North Seymour, Jr., a friend and former U.S. Attorney in New York, were strolling by the FBI Building on their way to Ford's Theater. Seymour, an architecture buff who is a member of the Municipal Art Society of New York, looked up at the building and said, "They ought to blow that thing up."

After Sessions became FBI director, he remembered Seymour's remark and said to him, "I want you to know I'll have them looking for you if something happens to that building."[43]

The entrance for employees and expected guests, as distinct from the tour entrance, is on the ground floor at the Pennsylvania Avenue level. The small lobby looks out on a bricked courtyard with a fountain and park benches lined up as if for an outdoor concert. Ivy has been permitted to inch up the cement walls, to relieve their starkness. About twenty feet above the benches is an eight-inch-high carved bronze inscription from J. Edgar Hoover: "The most effective weapon against crime is cooperation . . . the efforts of all law enforcement agencies with the support and understanding of the American people."

The inscription was the gift of the Society of Former Special Agents of the FBI, which fights a never-ending battle to burnish Hoover's image. At first, the society suggested a more militant Hoover quotation: "Law and order are pillars of democracy on which our safety and welfare rest." But Webster vetoed it.

"My thinking on it was I didn't come to take sides over J. Edgar Hoover," Webster said. "I took sides to make sure the agency was staying relevant to the times and the challenges. That included a look at how we did our work as well as our priorities." For that reason, Webster did not agree with some members of Congress who wanted to take Hoover's name off the building once the full extent of his abuses became known. But Webster drew the line over the courtyard quotation, which he thought many would find offensive.

"It was a public courtyard," he said. "There were people who had views one way or the other about law and order and what that meant. Was it a buzz word for something else, like beating up on minorities?

So I asked them to give me a range [of quotes], and the one I selected was the one that put the emphasis on cooperation. . . ."[44]

The building was constructed so that the half a million people who take the tour of FBI headquarters each year can peer through glass windows into the FBI laboratory and other sensitive areas without disturbing employees at work. Visitors learn that since the FBI began publicizing the 10 most wanted fugitives in 1950, 405 of the 434 individuals on the list have been located. Two were recognized by visitors taking the tour.

When he was assigned to the lab, William A. Gavin, later the special agent in charge in Miami, would put tomato juice in a beaker in the serology lab. Then, like a Dracula finding bliss, he would down the tomato juice as visitors looked on, aghast.

"Kids were lined up looking through the glass. He drank tomato juice from the beaker. Kids would say, 'Mom, did you see that?' " according to John W. Hicks, the FBI assistant director in charge of the laboratory.

"They had a table with microscopes on it next to the glass. So he would look through the microscope, [then look up] and cross his eyes. They would run to their mommies."[45]

Because of its emphasis on violent crime, the tour gives the impression that criminals are vicious beasts. But in fact, Floyd I. Clarke, deputy director of the FBI, points out that criminals are a reflection of society.

"You have criminals in the boardroom and in the ghettoes. You could be sitting down to a black tie dinner with a criminal or you could be confronted in an alley by a criminal. . . . Certainly a guy who is a mugger is different from a guy who is committing crimes in the boardroom. You take people like [Michael] Milken and Charles Keating. I'm sure some of the people they associated with at the time didn't realize what they were doing," Clarke said. "They are people that just have a character flaw that causes them to ignore what the prescribed laws or regulations are."[46]

The ground-floor reception area for visitors is like a well-used living room, with coffee tables and comfortable stuffed chairs, though the huge mirror facing the door is two-way glass that allows security personnel to peer at visitors without being seen. Over the sign-in desk are the expected "family" portraits: pictures of the FBI director, the president, the attorney general of the moment—a reminder that the FBI is part of the Justice Department.

Inside, the building is just as stark as it is outside, with charcoal doors and beige walls unrelieved by paintings. This is where 7,500 of the bureau's 23,700 employees—10,300 of them agents and 13,400 support employees—work. Only 925 of the employees at head-quarters are agents. Because of the building's unusual shape, employees require years to learn their way around. "I've been here twelve years, and I still get lost," said Jane Block, a secretary in the criminal division.

The criminal investigative division, which directs the work of 80 percent of the bureau's agents, is on the fifth floor of the J. Edgar Hoover Building. The division is responsible for nearly all of the FBI's publicly known cases. That is because the only other investigative division—misnamed the intelligence division—concentrates on counterintelligence investigations that rarely lead to an arrest or a public expulsion of an espionage suspect.

The office of William M. Baker, the assistant director in charge of the criminal investigative division, overlooks the Justice Department and Pennsylvania Avenue. On the coffee table in his office a gold key lies conspicuously atop a coffee table picture book, *Au Dessus de Paris*. Baker says the key was given to him by the secretaries at the CIA, where he had been Webster's public affairs director. The furnishings are blue and pale rose. Although Baker's office has windows, the plants—a ficus and a palm—are dusty fakes.

Tucked away in a corner is the entrance to a back room where Baker has a white secure phone, a couch, and mementoes of his days at the CIA, including the Distinguished Intelligence Medal. In a cabinet is a bottle of scotch, to be shared on a Friday afternoon with agents who have successfully completed major cases.

Baker is the boyish Ivy League type, with sandy hair and a tanned, smooth face. The son of an American Airlines pilot, Baker graduated from the University of Virginia in 1961 with a B.A. in history. After serving in the Air Force Office of Special Investigations, he became an FBI agent in 1965.

"As an agent he was terrific," said Edward J. Roach, who worked with Baker on the bank robbery squad in New York. "He was quick, he was smart, he was fast. He was a pleasure to work with. He was tough on the street. . . . He could tell the supervisor how an arrest went down, and he had the supervisor in stitches. Yet, it went down quickly and safely, and the guy was in custody, and his paperwork was done. And it didn't look like it was much of a stretch for him. He made it look real easy. He was that good."

Baker came to Webster's attention when he was special agent in charge of the Portland office. At Baker's direction, the Portland

SWAT team had killed a skyjacker. Baker appeared on the evening news looking suave and in control.

Webster chose Baker as his assistant director for congressional and public affairs. When Webster was named director of Central Intelligence in 1987, Baker resigned from the FBI to become his public affairs director. In 1989, Sessions brought Baker back to the FBI as assistant director over the criminal investigative division.

On Baker's desk are color coded briefing books and weekly reports that would make any newspaper reporter salivate. Pointing to a yellow envelope, Baker said, "These are undercover review-board-operation minutes. I review all undercover category-one proposals [for major undercover operations]. We currently have over one hundred category-one cases that go through our undercover review-committee procedure. It's a system to vet all our concerns on third-party liability, all the legal issues, tactical issues, whether we have the resources, the right agents to fulfill the undercover scenarios, and we worry it."[47]

Baker has to decide if a case is worth the expense and risk. "It might be a corruption case, and they want to wire an office. It meets the legal threshold . . . I could say yes, but what are the downsides if it comes out that we put a microphone in a ward politician meeting? How good will we look, and can we possibly get the information somewhere else?" Baker said.

"Another thing I worry about that no one else seems to sometimes is budget matters. It's a great proposal, but it's going to cost $1 million. They'll [agents] say, 'But for $1 million, we're going to get the corruption in this area.' I'll say, 'For $500,000, we could get two operations, one here and one somewhere else.' My budget is $13 million for all undercover proposals. 'You have a good proposal, but you don't have a monopoly on them.' "

On Baker's desk is a blue-covered booklet that is prepared each week for the FBI director. It gives a rundown on major cases. Material on light green paper in the booklet may be made public. The rest must be kept confidential.

An appendix to the booklet shows how the division is using its agents in its seven sections—civil rights and special inquiry, counterterrorism, drug section, investigative support, organized crime, violent crime and major offenders, and white collar crime. Figures show what percentage of agents are working priority cases—cases that, because of their size or the importance of their targets, will have a significant impact. In white collar crime, for example, 96 percent of the 2,152 agents are working high-quality cases.

"If there's a key to all the cases we are working out of these programs, it's the criminal enterprise," Baker said. "That is our target. Obviously the lone criminal gets our attention if he is robbing banks. But we look for the conspiracy-type cases that make use of the real capabilities of the FBI."

Unlike some bureau officials, Baker never forgets that he was once a street agent, to whom headquarters is the natural enemy.

"The cynical comment of a street agent is, 'No good work goes unpunished,' " Baker said. "I see that as the sense of humor that is necessary in the FBI. We want agents who are comfortable with their own abilities yet want support. You want to clearly define their mission, support them in their mission, let them know the parameters where they are going to be out of line, and encourage them. I think that is being done better now than in the past."

Down the corridor from Baker's office is the Strategic Information Operations Center (SIOC), a specially designed suite where the FBI directs major operations such as the investigation of Pan Am 103, the standoff in Waco, or counterterrorism cases during the Persian Gulf War.

Entering SIOC is a little like going through submarine decompression. Someone has to enter the special code and then turn the special lock on the vault door, which is marked with a red Restricted Access sign, a sliding sign that notes IN USE or NOT IN USE, and the name, Operations Center. A TV camera is trained on the entrance. In case the more sophisticated systems fail to keep people out, there's an ordinary padlock on the door frame. The floor of the suite is raised so that technicians can examine its underside for electronic bugs, and it is shielded so that electronic emissions cannot leave or enter it. Material classified beyond top secret can be discussed there.

In a galley inside the entrance, a microwave and coffeepot belie the instructions that there is no eating or drinking allowed.

Four rooms are visible through glass walls. On the far left is a command room, OPS2, where the duty agent sits, then the control room, then OPS1, a command room nearly identical to the first, only larger. The last room visible is a conference room, where men may be seen talking quietly at a long table surrounded by clocks set for various time zones, large-screen TVs, and a map of the world.

Windows separate the rooms but connect them visually. People in one room can look into the next, or across it into the next one, and see one another working or talking, noiselessly. In the carpeted hush, the only noise is the rattle of machines.

In the larger command room, five giant television monitors stand on a shelf near the ceiling. The monitors can be tuned to TV stations or video recorders, or they can project data such as maps, memos, ransom notes, and photo images from satellites. On the wall opposite the televisions, five clocks are set for GMT and Pacific, Mountain, Central, and Eastern time.

Sixteen work stations each have a telephone, computer terminal, and television monitor. The center has secure communications to the White House Situation Room, the CIA, and other federal law enforcement agencies.

The command room feels secure—there are no windows except the ones into adjoining rooms; there are no external surprises to distract one from the task at hand. Thick blue wall-to-wall carpeting muffles the sound of footsteps.

Twelve intelligence research specialists, spread over three shifts, work in the command room. It's deadly dull when they have no crisis to handle. During the day they concern themselves with administrative duties, and at night with sorting teletypes. They answer the phone: Personnel from TV's *Unsolved Mysteries* and *America's Most Wanted* call with tips on fugitives. When citizens call the FBI switchboard at night, they are connected to SIOC.

SIOC was used for the first time during the inauguration of President Bush. Before that, the FBI had a less impressive operations center that kept track of teletypes and overnight communications.

After Iraq invaded Kuwait, Neil J. Gallagher, the chief of the FBI's counterterrorism section, took over SIOC and made it his office. He would come in at 5:00 A.M. and leave at 8:00 P.M. At the time, the section covered both domestic terrorists, such as the neo-Nazi group "The Order," and international terrorists, who are supported by people or countries outside the United States. International terrorism has since been moved from the criminal division to the intelligence division.

"The consensus of the intelligence community was, if there was armed conflict, Iraq would respond with terrorism," Gallagher said. "Sessions gave my immediate supervisor, Bill Baker, our marching orders, that there wasn't going to be terrorism in the U.S."[48]

The counterterrorism section analyzed the threat and concluded that it could come from any of three sources: the Iraqi intelligence service within the Iraqi embassy in Washington or the Iraqi delegation to the United Nations; Middle East terrorist groups; or individual zealots who might react to what they heard or saw in the media.

The section sent warnings to all field offices, which were guarded twenty-four hours a day by FBI agents. Security was also beefed up at headquarters. Cars were not allowed to park adjacent to the building, and the FBI Police—some seventy-five FBI security personnel —patrolled the perimeter of the building.

The field offices identified key pipelines, power plants, and other likely important targets of terrorists. If the FBI got fragmentary reports of a plot to blow up a plant, the inventory of strategic locations would allow the bureau to focus more quickly on protecting it.

Then the FBI took the unusual step of interviewing known terrorists—people the FBI had been silently watching. In doing so, the FBI surrendered an element of surprise. But the bureau decided it was more important to let terrorists know that the FBI knew who they were.

In addition, the bureau interviewed Arab-American leaders, stirring up a wave of protests. Arab groups charged that the bureau was targeting them because of their ethnic origins, just as the U.S. had targeted Japanese-Americans during World War II.

Baker briefed dozens of members of Congress on the effort. "It was more to solicit the cooperation of the leaders and let them know we feared that an ignorant person might strike out at Arab-Americans," he said. "We said when you hear about that, make sure you report it to the FBI."

By intercepting calls to the Iraqi embassy, the FBI learned that Jamal Mohammed Warrayat, a naturalized U.S. citizen from Jordan who was living in New Jersey, had offered to engage in terrorism for the Iraqis. At the time, the State Department had ordered the embassy to reduce its staff, and no one was interested in pursuing his offer.

"[Warrayat] wanted to meet with an Iraqi intelligence officer. So we sent him an Iraqi intelligence officer," Gallagher said.[49]

The FBI agent who met him in New Jersey spoke Arabic fluently and could discuss towns in Iraq both men had visited. Warrayat said he was thinking of planting a bomb in the Holland Tunnel and of blowing up two military installations. The FBI spent more than a month watching him to see if he had any associates. They found he had none. When he threatened to kill the president and other government leaders, the bureau arrested him on November 11, 1990. Warrayat pleaded guilty to one count of threatening a U.S. official and is serving time.[50]

As it turned out, no terrorist incidents occurred in the U.S. as a result of the Gulf War. Overall, terrorist incidents are down dramatically from the late 1970s, when the FBI reported one hundred such incidents a year. In 1990, the U.S. had seven incidents, and the FBI prevented another five.[51]

"But there is a saying in the Middle East that the best revenge is served on a cold plate," Gallagher said. "They don't have time pressure. It could be on an anniversary date. You can't say it's over with."

Indeed, the subsequent bombing of the World Trade Center in New York occurred on the second anniversary of Iraq's expulsion from Kuwait City.

When the FBI began in 1908 as a force of special agents that were to be the investigative arm of the Justice Department, few federal criminal laws existed. Bankruptcy fraud, antitrust crime, neutrality violations, and peonage or compulsory servitude were the extent of the bureau's jurisdiction. Today the FBI has jurisdiction over 271 federal crimes, from kidnapping to espionage, from the Civil Rights Act of 1964 to arms control treaty statutes, from killing a president to discrimination in housing. But the bureau considers counterterrorism, drugs, foreign counterintelligence, organized crime, violent crimes, and white-collar crime to be national priority program targets, a fancy name meaning that they get the greatest attention on an ongoing basis.

While civil rights and background investigations are not normally considered priority work, they can become top priority within a field office if a particular case requires it—for example, the background investigation of Clarence Thomas or the investigation into whether the Los Angeles police violated the rights of Rodney King.

After Hoover's death, "We started to examine ourselves," said Oliver B. (Buck) Revell, who played a role in that examination in the FBI's Office of Planning and Evaluation. "We shed almost entirely our methodologies and our almost obsessive concern with subversion. We started to look at what our real responsibilities should be. We established national priorities: organized crime, foreign counterintelligence rather than domestic security, and white collar crime. . . . Perhaps the most important thing internally was we de-emphasized statistics. If you are driven by statistics, it is much like Vietnam, where you can't measure success any other way, you start using statistical measurements and body counts. What you get is an aberration. You get a lot more bodies than you need to, and they really don't measure the effectiveness of what you are doing because you don't care whose body it is.[52]

"In 1972, when Hoover died, the bureau was probably operating at 50 percent of its potential efficiency because it was saddled with this myth of being all things to all people—that we could thoroughly investigate every case within our jurisdiction and pursue it as required," Revell said. "We spent a lot of time on car thefts and anything that came to our attention. Crimes on government reservations that were petty in nature . . . You had agents investigating a single carton being taken from an interstate shipment."

"We had some stupid rules," said James D. McKenzie, a former assistant director over training. "You had to do something on a case every thirty days. Sometimes you couldn't get to an investigation every thirty days, but you were in trouble if you didn't. So an agent put a memo in the file. A waste of time, a waste of taxpayers' money."[53]

In one bureau memo from 1961, the special agent in charge of the Knoxville office actually warned agents that the office needed to report another forty-seven convictions in order to meet the previous year's "statistical accomplishments." The memo ordered expedited reporting of convictions. It is easy to see how much exhortations would favor quantity over quality when pursuing cases.[54]

The new bureau does keep statistics, but they are hard to find. In fact, the author was required to get a directive from Sessions for them to be released for this book. They show that the criminal investigative division has about seventy thousand cases pending at the beginning of each year and receives seventy-five thousand new cases during the year.

Besides focusing on important cases, the bureau now seeks out information about criminal conduct rather than waiting for allegations to come in.

"Corruption is rarely reported to authorities, particularly public corruption," said Weldon L. Kennedy, an assistant FBI director. "That's the kind of thing you have to determine through source information, business leaders, other law enforcement."

In the old bureau, even unsolicited tips about public corruption were ignored. A turning point came in 1974, when Wilbur K. DeBruler, the special agent in charge of the Oklahoma City field office, took the risk of insisting on talking with Clarence Kelley, Webster's predecessor, about a tip he had received. He told the then FBI director that the state's governor, David Hall, was taking kickbacks on construction jobs. Kelley had already instructed all offices to investigate crime wherever the FBI found it, but headquarters did not take his instruction seriously. An assistant director had ordered DeBruler to drop the investigation.

"Mr. Director, they tell me I shouldn't be doing this, but I think it's what you would want me to do," DeBruler said in explaining why he had called.

After DeBruler had outlined the case, Kelley told him to proceed. The investigation resulted in a prison term for the governor.[55]

An example of the change came in 1982, when Weldon Kennedy became special agent in charge in Jackson, Mississippi, initiating a series of corruption cases against state and local officials.

"To me the principal feature of that [change] was we were encouraged not simply to react to crimes reported to the FBI, like a bank robbery, but rather we should be doing exhaustive analysis of the crime in the territory and focus on that priority whether or not it was being reported to us," Kennedy said.

Using undercover techniques, Kennedy obtained convictions against county commissioners, legislators, and a sheriff—an investigation that started when Kennedy met with the six agents from the resident agency covering Harrison County and asked what their biggest crime problem was.

"They said, 'We have the most corrupt sheriff in the state of Mississippi. . . .' 'What are we doing about it?' 'Well, nothing.' 'What kind of cases are you working?' They had over one hundred stolen-property cases. Typewriters, tape recorders, calculators [taken from the nearby Air Force base]. They had to do interviews on them. I said, 'This is what we're going to do. Close all of them tomorrow. . . . If I catch you working one while that sheriff is in office, I'm going to have your ass. Because your number-one priority is putting that sheriff in jail,' " Kennedy said.

As a result, Howard L. Hobbs of Harrison County was convicted on drug charges.[56]

"We might as well admit it—if it weren't for federal law agencies, Mississippi's future would be to some extent in the hands of a pack of rascals," the *Gulfport Sun Herald* editorialized on June 20, 1985.

"To me that is something that would not, and could not, have been done under the old bureau," said Kennedy, who now heads the FBI's administrative services division.

Nor was the old bureau open to trying some of the innovative techniques the new bureau uses routinely. In the old bureau, anything that brought criticism of the bureau, that caused embarrassment, or that failed was punished harshly. The attitude stifled initiative. When a new approach was taken, it was usually done by individual agents, without the knowledge of Hoover. In doing so, the agents risked their careers.

For example, when he was in charge of the Philadelphia field office in 1966, Joe D. Jameson asked Oliver B. (Buck) Revell, a former Marine pilot who was then a field agent, if he thought the bureau might use planes to watch suspected Soviet spies. Revell said it could be done and spent many weekends successfully tracking several spies. Because they knew Hoover would oppose the idea, Revell and Jameson kept the program quiet.

"Hoover had said he would never have an air force, so they never told him," Revell said.[57]

On the other hand, assassinations such as those of John F. Kennedy, Martin Luther King, and the three civil rights workers in Philadelphia, Mississippi, brought out the best in Hoover's bureau. Despite the proliferation of assassination theories, the FBI investigated each exhaustively and effectively.[58]

In today's bureau, as in the old FBI, nothing is more likely to grab everyone's attention than an assassination. The way the FBI cracked the 1979 assassination of U.S. District Court Judge John H. Wood in San Antonio is a good example of the creative techniques the FBI can bring to bear when it really wants to solve a case.

Judge Wood was gunned down as he walked to his car from his San Antonio townhouse. After a year of seeing no progress in the case, Webster replaced the special agent in charge of the San Antonio office with Jack Lawn. Lawn had come to Webster's attention when he successfully brought under control a spate of violence in the Virgin Islands.

The case agent, Patrick C. (Mick) McCormick, immediately sensed that he was getting more support. For some time, the agents on the case had been reviewing the backgrounds of the defendants who were due to appear before the judge around the time he was killed. They had begun to focus more on Jamiel (Jimmy) Chagra, a high-rolling Las Vegas gambler. The day he was shot, Wood was scheduled to preside over Chagra's trial on drug trafficking charges. Wood was known as "Maximum John," and Chagra may have wanted another judge. By the time Lawn took over, Chagra was at Leavenworth, having been sentenced by another judge.

In the FBI, every field agent is assigned to a squad that concentrates on particular crimes or targets, such as the KGB or a mafia family. An agent may also be assigned to keep in touch with particular agencies or institutions, like the National Security Agency, airports, or prisons. It was the assignment of Walter A. Witschard, an agent at the Kansas City resident agency covering the federal penitentiary at Leavenworth, to develop informants within the prison.

Having previously been assigned to the Kansas City field office, Lawn knew of Witschard's legendary contacts at Leavenworth. Lawn called Witschard and asked if he could find out if Chagra knew anything about the crime.[59]

Plumbing his contacts, Witschard quickly learned that Chagra had become close to Jerry Ray James. Prisons, like the rest of society, have social hierarchies. James wielded considerable power within the prison population. Witschard had dealt with James, and the two had developed a rapport. Now Witschard asked James for a favor—to find out if Chagra knew anything about the killing. James struck up a conversation with the normally close-mouthed Chagra. Chagra not only knew about the killing, he had ordered it.

James agreed to help the FBI further if he received the money that had been offered as a reward for solving the case. He also wanted his freedom. As is typical in such cases, Lawn agreed to write a letter to the parole board citing James's cooperation. He also said he would help him get the reward if his cooperation led to an arrest.[60]

It was one thing to get an admission from Chagra through another inmate and quite another to obtain evidence that would hold up in court. Under the direction of Floyd I. Clarke, then special agent in charge at Kansas City, the FBI developed a strategy for listening in on James discussing the case with Chagra. First, Clarke arranged to have both men moved to the same housing unit in the prison and assigned to work for the prison chaplain.[61]

So that he could record the conversations, an agent posing as James's lawyer gave him a radio that concealed a tape recorder. After several weeks, James managed to record conversations that appeared to show Chagra was involved in the killing. Still, Chagra had not yet divulged enough details. Prosecutors threw cold water on the tapes, saying the conversations were not conclusive.

Clarke decided to bug Chagra's cell and the area where the two inmates worked. This led to unexpected problems.

"We took some techies and went in through the duct work and, between the cells, strung wires and microphones in Chagra's cell and in the area where they were working for the chaplain. They never produced anything significant," Clarke said. "But what did happen is they have inmates who do security checks of the prison. They found a wire and confronted Chagra at the work area with the wires and mikes. They suspected him of bugging the warden's office to run some kind of gambling operation."

To defuse the situation, the FBI, through its sources and informants, put out the word that prison authorities had been concerned about gambling in the prison and had installed the microphones to gather evidence.

Meanwhile, the FBI began monitoring Chagra's telephone calls. By planting rumors, the bureau got Chagra to discuss sensitive points on the phone. Based on those conversations, the bureau planted new rumors that elicited even more information from Chagra.

By then, Chagra had revealed that Charles V. Harrelson had done the killing at Chagra's direction. Back in San Antonio, agents under Lawn's supervision visited every gun shop in Texas. They eventually found out where the rifle that killed Wood had been purchased and who had purchased it: Harrelson's wife. Based on that evidence and Chagra's statements, the FBI arrested Harrelson. But the FBI wanted still more evidence of Chagra's involvement before arresting him.

With Harrelson under arrest, the bureau tricked a friend of Chagra's into thinking that the FBI had tapped Harrelson's phone before he was arrested. Because he was becoming increasingly paranoid, Harrelson had taken to taping his telephone conversations as the investigation proceeded. The FBI obtained one such tape Harrelson had made of himself talking on the phone with another inmate at Leavenworth. With this in hand, an agent told Chagra's friend that the bureau had extensive recordings of Harrelson. To demonstrate, the agent showed the friend twelve tapes.

"Pick any one," the agent said. After the agent played the tape, the friend immediately called Chagra and told him the bureau had been tapping Harrelson's phone.

In fact, the bureau had made duplicates of the one tape Harrelson had made of himself. All twelve tapes were of the same conversation.

When Chagra heard that the FBI had recordings of Harrelson's calls, he called his brother. Even though the brother was an attorney, the bureau obtained court authorization to bug Chagra's conversations when the brother came to visit Chagra in prison.

"We had to develop a way to tape the conversation," Clarke said. "When he comes to the visiting room, there are twenty-five to thirty tables. How are we going to do it? So we got a rush order. We got six tables, sent them to the lab, and in a short period of time they imbedded recording devices by hollowing them out and putting them in."

To make sure Chagra sat at one of the six tables, the bureau covered the other tables in the visiting room with canvas tarps to make it look as if they were being repaired. But the recording quality was poor.

"Every time the Coke machine went on, it interfered with the electronic signal [which transmitted the conversations to the field office in Kansas City]," Clarke said.

So, the bureau turned the visiting room into a recording studio. "We put carpets on the floor, curtains on the walls, a cut-off switch on the Coke machine so we could turn it off from Kansas City."

To make sure prisoners would not suspect anything, the FBI spread the word that Norman Carlson, then director of the Bureau of Prisons, was coming to visit. The refurnishing allegedly was being done for him.

This ruse would work only so long. Eventually, Chagra might get suspicious. So, for the third meeting between Chagra and his brother, the bureau sent in a college psychology class to sit at the tables that were not bugged. For three hours, they peppered the associate warden with questions about the prison. What the associate warden did not know was that the students were in fact FBI agents and support employees. An FBI agent had driven them in a bus from the Kansas City field office. They came complete with books and box lunches.

In the recordings, Chagra discussed how evidence in the assassination was disposed of and other details only the killers would know. The San Antonio field office developed additional evidence, including the amount Chagra is believed to have paid Harrelson—$250,000. Harrelson, Chagra, Chagra's wife, Elizabeth, and two others were convicted in 1982 and 1983 of murder, conspiracy, or other charges. They were sentenced by then Judge William Sessions, who later became FBI director.[62]

If the Wood case was one of the bureau's greatest successes, an obscure kidnapping in Jasper, Alabama, was one of its greatest failures.

On September 11, 1991, Earl Lawson, Jr., a lawyer in Jasper, reported that a masked man had pointed a rifle at him and his wife and had tied them up. The man had kidnapped his twenty-five-year-old wife, Carrie Smith Lawson, and later demanded a ransom of $300,000 for her safe return. Both spouses' parents were wealthy.

As instructed, two days later Earl Lawson left the cash in a dark culvert. Under the direction of Allen C. Whitaker, the special agent in charge of the FBI's Birmingham office, Earl Lawson wore a directional beeper so that agents could follow him as he made the drop. Concealed in the bag containing the money was another beeper so that agents could follow the kidnapper once he grabbed the money.

Because both beepers transmitted on the same frequency, Earl

Lawson was supposed to turn off his beeper after he deposited the money. However, he forgot. The agents unwittingly wound up following the husband rather than the kidnapper with the money.

Since the bureau had the voice of the kidnapper making ransom demands on tape, the FBI was able to determine within a month that he was Jerry Bland, a former president of a mining and land reclamation company. Agents surrounded his split-level home, then went to get a search warrant. Meanwhile, Bland committed suicide, taking with him the secret of Carrie Lawson's location.

Most of the money was found in his home and in the home of his cousin, Karen McPherson, who was charged with kidnapping. To avoid the death penalty, she pleaded guilty and was sentenced to life in prison.[63]

The kidnapping devastated the coal-mining town of twelve thousand people. More than four hundred residents volunteered to search for the victim, who is presumed dead.

"People took vacations to go out in the woods and look for her," said Paul South, who covered the story for the local paper. "Churches were having prayer vigils, and women were cooking dinners. The FBI was overwhelmed that they would bring meals to them."[64]

What never came out is the fact that the FBI had tragically screwed up the case. Not only had the beepers been on the same frequency—a violation of normal practice—but the agents, after identifying him, had left the kidnapper alone. In a later critique, the bureau's criminal investigative division said that since Bland had used the rifle in the commission of a crime, the agents were not required to obtain a search warrant to remove it from his home. Any weapon may be taken if it is believed to have been used to commit a crime. The agents should have confiscated the rifle before Bland killed himself.

On top of that, an FBI plane conducting surveillance at the drop site had radioed that a car was traveling away from the scene, but for reasons unknown, the agents doing the surveillance never got the message. If they had, they might have followed the car as well as following the husband.

Finally, when the kidnapper called Earl Lawson to demand the ransom, an assistant special agent in charge unwittingly answered the phone. He then put Lawson on the line.

In the end, that mistake did not scare off the kidnapper. But the other mistakes most likely did lead to the death of Carrie Lawson, who had just finished the University of Alabama Law School and had passed the bar exam.

"Everyone was sick to death about it," said an agent familiar with the Birmingham office, some forty miles southeast of Jasper.

"I believe that case in Jasper, Alabama, was a very important case that needed a lot of hands-on leadership, and I wasn't sure that had been applied. There were too many screw-ups in the case," Baker said.[65]

Baker wanted Whitaker forced into retirement; Whitaker had previously had a problem when he headed the Seattle office. Instead, the bureau hierarchy opted to downgrade Whitaker's performance rating from "outstanding" to "fully successful." For a special agent in charge, that is the kiss of death: It usually means he will be removed as the head of an office and transferred to headquarters for closer supervision.

Saying that the case is still under investigation, Whitaker, still special agent in charge of the Birmingham office, declined to comment. He later demanded, without success, that the FBI open an investigation into how the author of this book had learned about the screw-ups.[66]

"We're going to have mistakes," said Oliver B. (Buck) Revell, the special agent in charge of the Dallas office who was formerly associate deputy FBI director for investigations. "I think the difference is [that] under Hoover, nobody ever admitted mistakes, they didn't learn from their mistakes, they covered up their mistakes, and they were bound to repeat their mistakes. Under Kelley, Webster, and Sessions, there has been an open willingness on the part of the bureau to accept the fact we are human, we will err, and mistakes will be made. . . .

"You don't get up and write a press release and say, 'Hey! We made a mistake,' " Revell said. "But certainly we try to correct it and improve the system."[67]

3

Baltimore:
Upholding the Image

● **With two hundred agents,** the Baltimore field office is one-sixth the size of the New York office. Only about seventy-five of those agents work in the cream-colored brick building in an industrial park where the FBI has its Baltimore office. The rest are assigned to eleven resident agencies, or RAs, that range in size from one agent to more than a dozen in Maryland and Delaware.

Working in a one-man RA is as far removed from the stresses of working in New York as any agent can get. Usually, an RA is in a rural area hundreds of miles from the field office. Because of the distances, the FBI needs an agent on the scene who can not only respond to a crime quickly but develop and maintain relations with local law enforcement and the community. With RAs, the FBI can cover every inch of U.S. territory through its fifty-six field offices.

For four years, Everett A. (Ed) Robinson III was the FBI's lone resident agent in Cumberland, Maryland. Located 134 miles northwest of Baltimore, Cumberland is a mining community of 23,706 people. Its median per capita personal income is only $11,979. Hamburgers in Cumberland sell for $1.15, and people still order their sandwiches on white. People walk slowly, and no one wears a jacket or tie.

The FBI's RA is a 130-square-foot office on the third floor of the First Federal Savings Bank of Western Maryland on Baltimore Avenue. The street descends from a hill and becomes Cumberland Mall, a tree-shaded brick street that is the main thoroughfare in Allegany County. Because the orange brick bank building has a glassed-in elevator that rises through an atrium, the building is a local tourist attraction. Teachers bring their classes to ride the elevator.

As the FBI's representative in Cumberland, Robinson, a round-faced man with graying light brown hair, was another local attraction. When visitors came to town, local residents would point out Robinson's ranch house as one of the important sites. At community events, Robinson was invited to sit on the dais with the mayor and the chief of police. When local residents wanted information on anything related to the federal government, from Social Security payments to the president's mailing address, they would call Robinson.

"It kind of stroked your ego that you would walk through the shopping mall and people would say hello," Robinson said. "They weren't saying hello to me, but they were saying hello to the FBI. I played the role. I did a good job. Some might say I maintained the myth. But I will admit to trying to maintain the image. I was very professional in my work and personal conduct. If I had an occasion where it would not be appropriate for me to wear a coat or tie, a banker would say, 'Mr. Hoover would not think much of your dress code,'" a jesting reference to the late director's well-known penchant for tidiness. "So I wore a coat and tie and shined shoes. Those Hoover things," Robinson said.

In Robinson's four years in Cumberland, there were only a handful of bank robberies in the territory covered by his RA. A bank robber who was caught in San Diego admitted to doing all of them. That solved most of Robinson's pending cases. But, in February 1988, Robinson investigated a bizarre case that mesmerized the local community. It was the biggest case in anyone's memory and it is still talked about as if it happened yesterday.

In the end, the fact that the community was so closely knit helped Robinson and James L. Zopp, his supervisor in the Baltimore field office, to solve it. The case also illustrates how much discretion the FBI has in pursuing cases. For the disappearance of Catherine D. Ford, a beautiful nineteen-year-old, was a simple murder case that normally would have been handled by local law enforcement.

Ford worked as a waitress and cook at the wood-paneled Old Mill Restaurant in Gorman, Maryland, an area covered by the Cumberland RA. Ford's family owned the restaurant, and she was learning the business. According to her mother, Rosalie Ford, Cathy liked to bake and decorate pastries. She hoped to open a bake shop one day.

But on the afternoon of February 17, Catherine Ford took three calls at the restaurant that would end her life and shatter the community. Claiming he was a magistrate, the caller said he knew of an investigation by the local liquor board into the family restaurant. If she would meet with him, he would give her information about the probe so that it might be stopped. He refused to identify himself.

Ford told her mother and co-workers about the call and said she was going to see the man. Her mother expressed concern, but Cathy insisted on going. Wearing a black leather coat, black sweater, and stone-washed blue jeans, the five-foot-nine-inch-tall woman, with shoulder-length brown hair and sparkling brown, innocent eyes, drove off in her silver 1986 Ford Bronco II toward the neighboring village of Mount Storm in West Virginia. She was never seen again.

When word of her disappearance appeared in the local papers, Sheriff Van E. Evans of Garrett County, which covers the area in Maryland where Cathy was last seen, began hearing about other women who had received similar anonymous calls. Like Ford, the women were unusually attractive, slim, and physically fit. In each case, the caller had posed as an authority figure—a law enforcement official or a doctor—and had tried to lure the woman in question to meet with him. In some instances, the women recognized the caller as a fraud because they knew the information he had given them was incorrect. In other cases, the women simply refused his requests. Eventually, a dozen women reported that they had received such mysterious calls.

Pamela Kitzmiller, a West Virginia woman who did not take the bait, later established that the man who called her six months earlier was Paul W. Ferrell, a thirty-one-year-old sheriff's deputy in neighboring Grant County, West Virginia. Just before she had received the call, her sister received a call asking for Pamela's telephone number. The man did not identify himself, but Kitzmiller's sister recognized the voice as being Ferrell's.[68]

Most of the time, Ferrell, a trim man with a crew cut, lived with his brother above a small grocery store with a tin roof in Gormania, West Virginia. Gormania is across the Potomac River from Gorman, Maryland, where the Fords had their restaurant. Because the Potomac at that point is the size of a brook, Ferrell could see Ford entering and leaving the restaurant each day from his home above the grocery store. Indeed, Ferrell often ate at the restaurant and bowled with Ford's older brother, Richard.

The sheriff's office immediately dismissed Ferrell as a suspect because he was a deputy sheriff in the neighboring county.

"He [the deputy sheriff who interviewed Kitzmiller] wrote that he is a deputy sheriff in Grant County; he's not a suspect because he is a law enforcement officer," Sheriff Evans said.[69]

Meanwhile, Ford's parents received an anonymous letter on March 2 seeking to reassure them that their daughter was safe. The letter said that the family was not to worry, because Ford was with the writer of the letter and needed to get away from some co-workers and her boyfriend. It enclosed two hundred dollars to cover the next payment on Cathy's Bronco.

However, six days later the Bronco was found, burned almost beyond recognition, behind some underbrush along Stony Creek. The vehicle license and identification plates had been removed. The location was just fifteen hundred feet from a mobile home rented by Ferrell.

It was apparent that Catherine Ford had been murdered.

With local authorities getting nowhere, Ford's brother Richard and her boyfriend Darvin Moon, who worked in a local sawmill, began calling the FBI.

"Since she left Maryland and went into West Virginia, and it seemed there were two police forces of different states trying to work together, it seemed confusing," said Ford, an electrical engineer. "I knew the FBI was more expert in that area. I called the Baltimore office and talked to the night dispatcher. The next day they called from Cumberland."[70]

Initially, Robinson and his supervisor, Zopp, agreed to present the case to the FBI's crime profilers, who draw portraits of suspects based on the known evidence and on their experience with similar cases. Zopp and Robinson immediately recognized the anonymous calls as significant. Zopp, a meticulous investigator with a receding hairline and glasses, met with Sheriff Evans and asked him to pinpoint on a map the residences of the women who had received the calls.

Seven of the women lived in Grant County, West Virginia, where Ferrell was a deputy sheriff and had his mobile home. That was also the direction taken by Cathy Ford when she left the restaurant. In fact, Ferrell's mobile home was within a few hundred yards of the location where three of the women had been asked to go.

The profile drawn up by the FBI said that the suspect was a white male in his late twenties or early thirties who lived in the area and knew Cathy Ford. He would follow the case in media accounts and might inject himself into the investigation, according to the profile.

Most of the details turned out to be true, including the suggestion that the murderer would inject himself into the investigation. As a deputy sheriff, Ferrell had played a role in searching for the Bronco. He told Robinson he had seen a strange car in the vicinity, one that turned out to belong to an innocuous salesman.

Then the FBI decided to begin its own investigation. To gain jurisdiction, the bureau proceeded on the theory that Ford had been kidnapped. This was tenuous. Everything indicated that she had voluntarily crossed the state line and met with the caller. The fact is that the case had caught the attention of two agents—Zopp and Robinson—and they decided to tackle it and worry about jurisdictional questions later.

Even though it is a one-man resident agency, Cumberland has the resources of the entire FBI behind it. Soon, a half-dozen FBI agents were working the case, staying at a local hotel and interviewing and reinterviewing everyone involved. Toward the end of the investigation, twenty-five agents were involved.

"It was an example of what happens when you have a one-man RA. When something happens, you have to yell for help. That is what happened," Robinson said.

The fact that the crime occurred in a small community helped bring out the fact that other women had received strange calls.

"You can learn a lot in a short time in a small community," Robinson said. "You ask for Joe Smith, and they say, '[He] works over there.' They would pick up the phone and say, 'I [Robinson] am coming.' They would say, 'He lives all the way across town.' It was three minutes [by car]. Or they would say traffic is heavy. There were three cars at the stoplight."

On the other hand, "In a small community, you have so much gossip," Robinson said. "There was a rumor that every one of the local judges was using drugs. The newspaper said on page one, 'That rumor? We're not going to repeat it, but it's not true.' You can imagine the rumors that would float around on a real case like Cathy Ford. People would sit on the porch and say, 'I wonder if—.' By the end of the day it was being conveyed as being true."

While the FBI's psychological profiles sometimes lead directly to a killer, in this case the agents already had a good idea of where to look. On March 10, an agent interviewed Kitzmiller, the woman whose sister had recognized Ferrell's voice when he called her to obtain Kitzmiller's number. Based on the results of that interview,

Zopp decided to interview Ferrell. Zopp noticed small inconsistencies in Ferrell's story. Ferrell agreed to a search of his gray and white trailer, which he said he had planned to move into with his girlfriend.[71]

But the girlfriend, Kathy Bernard, said she had no plans to move to the trailer. She also said that Ferrell had replaced the carpet in the bedroom of the home two days after Ford's disappearance. In addition, she said Ferrell had confided in her that he was worried about becoming a suspect in the case. She said he even asked her to call the family and pretend to be Cathy Ford, a request she refused.

By then, the FBI had determined that the handwriting in the letter of reassurance sent to Ford's parents matched Ferrell's. The FBI later found that Ferrell was in the habit of posing as a doctor and phoning bookstores throughout the country. He would claim he wanted a patient to pick up a clinical book on sex. To make sure the store had the right edition, he would ask female clerks to read a particular passage describing anal intercourse.[72]

On March 19, Ferrell consented to a second interview with Zopp and Sheriff Evans. He also took a polygraph test, which he failed. As with most FBI polygraph tests, the results never hit the press.

The FBI laboratory had done a second search of the trailer and had found human blood in the bedroom. Several days later, a citizen found a ladies' Timex watch in a pile of burned rubbish near the trailer. Richard C. Ford, Jr., the victim's father, had given Cathy the same kind of Timex watch the previous Christmas.

The FBI subpoenaed the telephone records of the grocery store over which Ferrell and his brother had lived. They showed that long-distance calls had been made to two of the women who said they had received the bizarre anonymous calls. Some of the calls from the grocery store were made on the same dates as those on which the women said they had been called. Other women who had been called lived nearby, so the calls would not have shown up on toll records.

It fell to Robinson, Zopp, and Evans to tell Cathy Ford's parents on March 20 that the FBI believed their daughter had been murdered by Ferrell in his trailer home.

Federal prosecutors did not buy the theory that Ferrell had kidnapped Ford, so they declined to prosecute the case in federal court. However, based on the FBI investigation, the West Virginia State Police arrested Ferrell on state murder and kidnapping charges.[73]

Ferrell was convicted in Grant County Circuit Court in February 1989, in Petersburg, West Virginia.

"I'm not guilty of the three crimes I'm charged with. That's all," he said.

Ferrell was sentenced to life in prison for kidnapping, five to eighteen years for second-degree murder, and one to three years for arson.[74]

At the request of the FBI, Maryland State Police brought in dogs specially trained to find live humans and other dogs trained to find dead ones. Ford's body has never been found.

Ford's parents later split up, in part because of the strains brought on by Cathy's death. "We sort of drifted apart," Rosalie Ford said. "I guess we didn't know how to console each other. He went his way, and I went my way."[75]

Halfway down the rear wall of the Old Mill Restaurant hangs a color portrait of Cathy Ford, who went to her death because she was trying to save the family restaurant. Under the portrait is this inscription: "I have held many things and lost them but whatever I have placed in God's hands, that I still possess."

"She always cared about her family first," said Moon, Cathy Ford's boyfriend. "She was a wonderful girl."

"The FBI came into the case with a lot of professionalism," said Richard Ford, Cathy's brother. "With the type of case it was, I don't think the locals had enough training to go into the detail that they did to solve the case."

Sheriff Evans, too, had high praise for the bureau's work. "When they got involved in the investigation, they worked very closely with my office, with the West Virginia State Police, and the prosecutors," he said. "There wasn't any big hassle over whose case it was. It was more a joint operation to get the case solved. Anything on TV that says, 'I'm the FBI, and it's my case, and to hell with the locals,' that's not the case."

Now assigned to Denver, Robinson finds he is no longer revered. Robinson was doing a routine background check on an individual who had applied for a government job that required a security clearance. Robinson needed to interview a man who knew the applicant in a county sixty miles outside of Denver.

"I went to the door and could see a gentleman seated inside," Robinson said. "I knocked, and he didn't respond. I knocked a few more times. Finally he came to the door. He said, 'Get the hell out of here or I'll call the law.' I showed him my FBI credentials and said, 'I am the law.' He said, 'The only law around here is Sheriff Howard Mann,' the sheriff of Morgan County."[76]

In the end, the man agreed to be interviewed.

In contrast to Cumberland's one-man RA, the FBI's resident agency in Silver Spring, Maryland, has fifteen agents. Located in a cosmopolitan suburb of Washington, D.C., it handles every conceivable kind of case, from foreign counterintelligence—many Russian diplomats live in Maryland—to bank robberies. Indeed, it was a bank robbery that caused the Silver Spring RA its greatest embarrassment.

For twenty years, the FBI office had been located two floors above the Citizens Bank and Trust Company of Maryland at a busy intersection on Connecticut Avenue at Georgia Avenue. On September 10, 1987, the bank was robbed.

"We were embarrassed," said Edward J. Roach, the Silver Spring agent who investigated. "They see the FBI all day, except when they get robbed."

Roach knew all about bank robberies. He had spent six years on the bank robbery squad in New York. A graduate of the University of Baltimore, Roach had requested the Baltimore field office as an office of preference—bureau jargon meaning that he got on a waiting list for a transfer to the office he preferred. In Silver Spring, Roach handles violent crimes, including bank robberies.

A fast-talking Irishman with hazel eyes and gray hair, Roach is one of those agents who is highly respected by his peers and bosses but who has no desire to rise in the bureau hierarchy. When a friend of then Deputy Attorney General William P. Barr reported that his child had disappeared from a home for troubled children, Roach got on the case and found the girl.

No one had to tell William M. Baker, the assistant director over the criminal investigative division, that Roach was the agent who finally got the girl to call her parents. When Baker heard that the agent was in Silver Spring working the case past midnight, he knew it was Roach.

"He [Roach] not only went to the police department but went to the school and family and took a personal interest in it, and within a very short period of time the child had returned," said Floyd I. Clarke, the deputy director of the FBI.

"He [Roach] is a very talented guy. A classic FBI agent. He is a legend around the bureau," said Danny O. Coulson, a deputy director in the criminal investigative division.

Roach was not happy when, on October 1, 1987, the bank below his office was robbed a second time. "It was embarrassing because we were sitting upstairs, and the bank was being robbed downstairs," he said. "But in truth, there is nothing that can be done about it. We don't normally sit out in front of banks with machine guns and say that we are protecting the bank."

In fact, after the second holdup, the forty-three-year-old Roach had a younger agent pretend to be a bank officer and sit in the bank with a two-way radio. The local Montgomery County police also had surveillance cars outside. However, as Christmas approached, the surveillance teams had to cover more important areas. Roach had also checked reports of other robberies in the area, looking for similarities, and had distributed descriptions of the robber to other FBI offices. The surveillance cameras in the bank either had not been working or had not taken a picture at the moment the robber was in their field of vision. Roach had no leads.

On December 22, the bank was held up for the third time. That time, Roach saw the perpetrator. As Roach and his supervisor, Warren Denman, were leaving work at 6:00 P.M., they noticed a man in his late twenties waiting in the lobby of the building outside the entrance to the bank. The man was well dressed, wearing a long green trench coat, a tie, and polished black shoes. Still, Roach decided to check him out.

"I said, 'Excuse me. Can I help you?' He said, 'Oh, no, I am just waiting for my brother to pick me up.' I said, 'We work in the building. Do you need a ride?' He said, 'Oh, no.' Just as nice and polite as can be," Roach said.

When Roach got into Denman's car, Denman asked him what he thought.

"I spoke to him," Roach said. "He's waiting for a ride. He's well dressed, well spoken. If I said anything else to him, I'd be pressing my luck. He would have a reason for a complaint."

"Okay. I'll trust you on that," Denman said.

Roach had just gotten home when an assistant manager of the bank called. "You know that guy you were talking to?" she said. "He just robbed us."

"Oh, God," Roach said.

A police detective who is a friend of Roach's said to him later, "I thought the FBI interviews bank robbers only after they rob banks."

In Hoover's time, Roach would have been transferred to Butte, Montana, and the entire office assigned to do nothing but watch the bank.

"There was a time [in the bureau] when anything that went wrong was totally unacceptable and resulted in action," said Bobby R. Gillham, the special agent in charge of the Baltimore office.

But agents are not superhuman, and the FBI has other things to do besides avoiding embarrassment. Soon, Roach's luck would change.

Around 6:00 P.M. on January 11, 1988, Roach went downstairs to cash a check at the bank, which is where he had his personal account. He saw a man wearing a sweatsuit and white hat. Because the man was turned away from him, Roach could not see his face. But Roach had a hunch that the man might bear watching. As Roach pretended to fill out forms, he saw an assistant manager get up from her desk and start walking toward the teller who was about to help the young man. Roach watched the teller intently. The young man was standing in front of her. If she was being robbed, he thought, she might give him a sign. But the teller was new and didn't know that Roach was an FBI agent.

The teller had pulled the silent alarm. The assistant manager had gotten up from her desk because she saw the alarm blinking, but she thought the new teller might have tripped it accidentally. Then she saw the stricken look on the teller's face. The assistant manager knew Roach.

"Get him, man! Get him!" she yelled at Roach.

By then, the young man was running out the door.

Roach was armed with a .357 magnum revolver. Like most agents, he now chooses to use a 9-millimeter semiautomatic because it carries more rounds and has less recoil. Grabbing his briefcase, which contained his handcuffs, he took off after the robber.

"At the corner at the mailbox, I said, 'FBI. Stop or I'll shoot,' " Roach said. "He hesitated but then split. I said this is going to be a long night. I couldn't give up on this kid because I can't go back to the bank without him."

Just then, a lawyer who worked in the same building drove by in his yellow station wagon. "Roach, who are you chasing?" he asked. When Roach told him about the bank robbery, he said simply, "Get in."

As they approached a shopping center, Roach jumped out, leaving his briefcase on the floor of the car. The bank robber had disappeared, but Roach saw some cleaning women getting out of a van.

"I said, 'Where did he go?' They wouldn't answer me right away," Roach said. "I said, 'Dammit. I'm with the FBI. I'm chasing the kid in the white hat. He just robbed a bank. Now where did he go? One of the ladies pointed to the van."

The elderly driver of the van was just about to pull out. Roach ran to the front of the van and, pointing his gun at the driver, told him to halt. The man stopped the van and ran away.

"He never came back," Roach said. "The company had to pick up the van the next day. He was so scared he never came back."

Roach pushed open the back door of the van. There was Earlington H. Motley, Jr., who had just moved to Silver Spring from Ohio.

"I grabbed him. He had the note and money. I said, 'FBI. You're under arrest for robbing the bank. This is the fourth damn time.' He said, 'No, it's not. It's the first time.' I said, 'This is going to get easier.' "[77]

Then Roach realized he had left his handcuffs in the lawyer's car. He had to walk the suspect a quarter of a mile back to the bank, past a shopping center, his gun pointed at the man's back.

"I said, 'Don't you move or try to do a thing. Because if you try anything, I will definitely blow your brains out right here in front of these people,' " Roach said.

"I remember two women coming out of a dress shop. One of them said, 'Do you think it's the FBI?' The other said, 'No, they don't talk like that.' "

As Roach neared the bank, he heard Montgomery County police sirens. Feigning politeness, an officer said, " 'Good evening, Mr. Roach. Mr. Roach, would you like to borrow my handcuffs?' "

Back at the bank, the teller who had been held up identified Motley as the robber. Other tellers who had previously been held up also identified him. Altogether, Motley had stolen nearly ten thousand dollars.

Before Roach marched Motley upstairs to the RA, he showed him the lobby sign listing the FBI office in the building. Motley—who was subsequently convicted and sent to jail—was shocked.[78]

The Baltimore field office is adjacent to Route I-695, the highway that encircles Baltimore. Traditionally, FBI offices have been located in federal courthouses so that agents will be close to prosecutors and the courtrooms where they testify. But many field offices have found it makes more sense to be located near major highways, so that agents can easily drive to interviews.

Over the years, the Baltimore office has had its share of successes. One was the 1985 arrest of Ronald W. Pelton, the former National Security Agency employee who had been spying for the Soviets. The 1977 General Services Administration scandal started in the Baltimore office, eventually resulting in convictions of more than a hundred GSA officials and suppliers and contractors who were ripping off the government through phony invoices for office supplies and maintenance of federal buildings. During the 1991 war in the Persian Gulf, the Baltimore office determined that bombs discovered on two chemical tanks in Norfolk, Virginia, had been placed there as part of a scam to collect insurance money rather than as part of a terrorist plot.[79]

In one of Baltimore's more memorable operations, agents took over a bar at Baltimore-Washington International Airport. Alice Michelson, an East German national acting as a courier for the Soviets, was to receive tape recordings of classified material from a U.S. Army sergeant pretending to work for the KGB. The FBI replaced the bartender, waiters, and waitresses with agents. Michelson was arrested on October 1, 1984, as she boarded a flight in New York to Czechoslovakia. She was later returned to East Germany as part of a spy swap.[80]

One of the cocktail waitresses at the Baltimore airport was Pat Kirby. Five feet nine inches tall, with blue eyes, blond hair, and a good figure, Kirby is extremely attractive. Her father, Roy Kirby, is a highly successful industrial contractor in Baltimore. She attended Notre Dame Preparatory School, an exclusive Catholic girls' school outside of Baltimore, then graduated from the University of Maryland. Many of Kirby's friends from school are now doctors or lawyers.

Kirby was not sure what she wanted to do. She had vague thoughts of being a social worker. Based on a career aptitude test that she took in college, the Baltimore Corrections Department offered her a job as a probation officer. She accepted.

"I was assigned to an area known as Pig Town, a low-class white and black area," she said. "I started out trying to help these people. After a year, I decided I might do a better job helping society on the other side, locking these people up. There were some people who, no matter what you did, were just not going to see the light."[81]

Kirby quit to obtain a master's degree in criminology from Northeastern University in Boston. Her godfather was a Boston FBI agent, and in 1975 she decided to apply. As acting director after Hoover's death, L. Patrick Gray had allowed the first women to become agents. But by 1975, only 37 of the FBI's 8,441 agents were women, in part because the bureau was hiring few new agents.

"I thought they would be very eager to have a gal with a couple of years' experience in public safety and a master's. They said, 'Why don't you get some policing experience, and then come back and talk to us later?' " Kirby said.

Kirby became a Baltimore City Police officer and was promoted to homicide detective.

"The police don't like the FBI," she said. "They feel, 'I'm the one dealing day to day with these people on the streets. I'm the one who handles these people, talks to these bozos, watching the drug deals go down at two A.M. We really see it. You all sit back and talk about it at school and handle a big case, and the news says the FBI did it. You forget about the people out here doing the grunt work. Then you go back.'

"The other thing they say is, 'The bureau asks for information from the police department but they don't give it back to you.' When agents and police work more closely with each other, they realize they need each other. Singularly certain agents are viewed well by the police. The bureau as a whole is not."

On the other hand, Kirby found that the police respected the bureau's effectiveness.

"I remember when I was a rookie cop, I was told if the FBI comes after you, they're going to get you," Kirby said. "The police department does know that. 'We have just so much time and man-power. Once the bureau starts after you, they are going to get you, and you're not going to get away from the FBI.' "

As a homicide detective, Kirby took courses at the FBI Academy in Quantico, Virginia, in psychological profiling of criminal suspects. She was impressed; several of the profiles led directly to apprehensions. In 1979, Kirby again applied to the FBI.

By then, the climate within the bureau had changed. William Webster had replaced Clarence Kelley as director. Webster was aggressively pushing the hiring of more females and minorities. Recruiters were rated on how many blacks, Hispanics, and women they brought in. Even though budget constraints had reduced the total number of agents in the bureau, Webster boosted the proportion of minorities significantly. Out of 7,800 agents in the bureau when Kirby applied, 197 were female.

Kirby took a test, and three agents interviewed her.

"I remember hearing one of them saying, 'Well, if we have to take women, at least we ought to take this type.' "

Kirby was accepted. At Quantico, she was one of five females in a class of thirty-three.

Because women tend to have less upper-body strength than men have, the bureau had by then modified the push-up requirements for women. Many women had flunked out because their hands were not large enough or strong enough to pull the trigger of a gun dozens of times in succession.

Now the bureau gives hand-strength tests to applicants when they come in for interviews. That way, men and women who cannot meet the standard know it early on. If they wish, they can begin building up their finger muscles so that they can pass the firearms tests.

As a former policewoman, Kirby had no trouble shooting. "When I started police work, I did not like guns," she said. "I didn't think it would be something I would ever get used to. Now I would feel absolutely lost without one. I don't like driving alone late at night. You have a flat tire, and a Ted Bundy comes by. After a while you see so much, and I saw so many sexual homicide cases at Quantico, that I would feel very lost without one."

Kirby thought the bureau, in trying to increase the number of female agents, was taking some women who did not understand what would be required of them.

"I remember one woman was wearing a baseball cap at the range," she said. "It was so obvious she didn't want to mess up her hairdo. She folded her baseball cap and bobby pinned it to the front of her hairdo. I thought, 'Oh, my God. What a laughingstock. Does this woman realize where she is?' "

In the old bureau, agents sometimes used secretaries to help them on undercover assignments that required women. As an FBI agent assigned to Baltimore, Kirby found that she was in great demand to work undercover.

In one case, she played a high class call girl who was offered as bait by a bureau informant to a crooked county commissioner in another state. She crossed the country with a male agent in a tractor-trailer rig as part of a sting to catch thieves who stole truck parts. To assess their intentions, she befriended people who might be spies. Because she and agent Henry J. Flynn did not want to alarm Pelton's former wife, Kirby stood in front of him as they knocked on her door just after midnight.

When she was with the police, Kirby had taken part in the arrest of a man who had kidnapped a gas and electric meter reader, demanding money from the utility in return for releasing him. A year later, the same man had been released from jail and did the same thing. That time, Kirby worked the case as an FBI agent.

"We were driving around in a 1974 Ford Maverick with the muffler falling off," Kirby said of the earlier arrest when she had been a police officer. "We go out to the crime scene, and they send three of us to respond: me, my sergeant, and another detective. We arrive on the crime scene in this dilapidated car. Here is the bureau in 1979 state-of-the-art cars. The bureau must have had fifteen agents there. Everyone said, 'Typical bureau, overkill.' We said, 'Are they going to interview each other?'

"The next year, I handled it for the bureau," she said. "It was very different. From the city-cop point of view, some of it is jealousy. We were lucky to have backup."

Both in the police department and in the bureau, Kirby was the subject of jokes and teasing. Because of the difference in the work, it took longer for FBI agents to realize that she was capable of handling herself.

"It wasn't long before, in the police department, you went into a high rise and people were throwing bottles and shooting. They [the police] realized that you were going to back them up. You weren't going to fall apart when you saw it. You were actually going to be useful in the situation. In the bureau, it could be years before you were in that kind of situation. It was more difficult for the agents to see what you are made of."

The teasing didn't bother her. "A lot of it had to do with your response and the way you handled the situation," she said. "I grew up with two brothers who would just tease the hell out of me. One was two years older, one was eleven months younger. Especially in homicide, everyone teases each other because there is so much stress. Some of the women took it as put-downs and not being taken seriously.

"If somebody made a remark to me, I gave it right back, in a good-natured, kind of a jabbing way. That's the way I grew up, and that's what I was used to," Kirby said. "A male agent would say, 'Nice blouse, Kirby!' I would say, 'Oh, well, you're always on the edge of fashion yourself.' I would always come back like that. If someone wanted to make an obnoxious remark, I think they might be fearful of what the response might be."

"There is a lot of teasing of everyone," said Kathy Barrett, an agent in the Silver Spring resident agency. "It's like hazing. . . . If they figure out something bothers you, they do it to you. I know a guy at one of the other offices is kind of short. It bothers him. They play that song about short people that was popular a few years ago. He took it in stride. It's not the PTA.

"In my first office [in Washington], the guys delighted in blowing up my desk," she said. "It was like firecrackers that they put in the drawers. It got to the point where I'd come in, and they would die waiting until I opened my drawer. I wouldn't, and one guy finally opened the drawer for me."[82]

"I think there is a lot of competition on every level," Barrett said. "I don't care if you are female or black or a white male, you have to recognize what you are into. It's not kindergarten. There is a tremendous amount of stress. Demands are made on you that you never would have imagined before. If you can't handle that, you don't need to be in."

On the other hand, some agents were Neanderthals. "There are blatant remarks that no one can overlook," Kirby said. " 'You women are all alike.' Some said, 'Typical female.' "

Karen E. Gardner, an agent in the Los Angeles field office, said that after two FBI agents accidentally shot and killed fellow agent Robin Ahrens in Phoenix, "An old dinosaur agent said, 'That will teach those female agents to screw up.' " In fact, Ahrens, who was highly respected, had done exactly what she had been told to do.

Female agents become annoyed at being referred to as female agents. When male agents invited Gardner to speak at Rotary Club and other functions, they invariably introduced her as "Karen Gardner, one of our female agents," Gardner said. "I would always hold out the front of my blouse and check and make sure they were still there. There you are at Rotary. Obviously you are female."[83]

For all the annoyances, Gardner said, "This has been one of the most exciting, addicting, enjoyable experiences of my life, being an FBI agent. I would highly recommend it to anyone who doesn't want two days that are the same."

"When I first came in the bureau in 1980, everyone said it's really a man's world and a man's bureau," said Mary Jo Marino, another Los Angeles agent. "You had to prove yourself. Now we have women in management positions and working great cases. They're not relegated to one segment of the bureau. I enjoy it. I couldn't ask for a better job."

Kirby never experienced sexual harassment. But in an internal FBI survey, 13 percent of the female FBI employees and a surprising 2 percent of the male employees said they had been sexually harassed—presumably by the opposite sex.

"Everyone smiled at that," said James R. Pérez, director of the FBI's Equal Employment Opportunity office. "I wish I had been the target of that [sexual harassment]."

Some 40 percent of the employees who said in the survey that they had been harassed were agents, while the rest were support or professional staff. Of the 196 employees who responded in the survey that they had experienced sexual harassment, only 20 percent had made an official complaint.[84]

When the other 80 percent were asked why they had not complained, the responses included: "Management would not handle situation correctly, and I had to work with this person; embarrassment; I advised the supervisor that any more advances would result in an EEO (Equal Employment Opportunity) complaint; SAC (special agent in charge) handled it when I told him; didn't want to get person in trouble; and feared the scales were tipped in favor of supervisor—no witness."

Except for the paperwork—Kirby estimated she spent 80 percent of her time filling out reports—Kirby enjoyed the bureau and the fact that she had the luxury to investigate her cases. But, like some other agents of either gender, she resented the way the bureau tries to consume agents' lives.

"My sense was there was a real idea among a lot of the men that the bureau had been a lifelong ambition for them. Many were sons of former agents. They had wanted to enter the FBI from the age of three or four. Many wanted to go into accounting purposely, not because they enjoyed it, but as a better avenue to get into the bureau," she said. "You're supposed to socialize with FBI agents, you're supposed to live near bureau agents," she said. "I was even criticized for going home and not going drinking after work. I said, 'Well, I have to go home and ride horses. I do have a life of my own. . . .' It was the same with the guys. The guys who didn't socialize with the guys were really thought to be not fulfilling the FBI promise."[85]

"A lot of female agents marry male agents because they understand the job," said Catherine M. Kaiser, an agent assigned to the Silver Spring resident agency. Before she married, Kaiser said, boyfriends would take her to parties and say, "I'm with an FBI agent, and she's carrying a gun. You better be careful." Kaiser said, "That's cute once in a while, but it got to the point where it wasn't. . . . My husband is probably one of the few men I dated who didn't have [a] problem with the fact that this girl he was dating had a gun and might get a call at the last minute and cancel a date [because of a kidnapping or bank robbery], which happened many times in my career."[86]

"Some people have trouble differentiating [the FBI] from who I am," Barrett said. "They think I might see some special meaning in something they say, or might be analyzing what they say. I'm really not. You're not on twenty-four hours a day as a reporter. That's not all you are. There are times when you're having a good time at a party."

After Baltimore, Kirby became a psychological profiler at Quantico. She left the bureau in 1986. By then, she had married David D. Queen, whom she had met when Queen was an assistant U.S.

Attorney in Baltimore. Kirby wanted to live in Baltimore, and the prospects of finding the right kind of slot nearby within the bureau were slim.

"It was a loss. Everyone held her in high regard. She could do it all," said Roger L. Depue, who was Kirby's boss at the unit that profiles criminal suspects at Quantico. "In the bureau, there is only one thing better than being a 'good agent' and that is a 'damn good agent.' Kirby was a damn good agent."[87]

Being on the outside is strange at times.

"I am forever remembering license tag numbers," Kirby said. "We'll go down the street, and I'll say, 'Oh, there goes so-and-so.' Dave will say, 'How do you know?' I'll say, 'Because that is their tag number.' 'Damn!' I just remember minute details. That is maybe why I enjoyed the work."

"When I go down the street and some kid goes down the road at seventy-five miles per hour, I feel I would like to do something about it. I feel stripped of my powers," she said.

Nor has she gotten used to the assumption at retired agents' functions that agents are male, despite the rising number of females. Of 10,300 FBI agents now, 1,167—better than 1 in 10—are women.

"They have the meetings for the agents. Then they have the wives' luncheons. I always want to send Dave," she said. "It's still so chauvinistic."

To this day, Kirby keeps a gun beside her bed at home in a suburb of Baltimore.

"I have to protect Dave," she said.

4

Intelligence Division: The Year of the Spy

● **After William Sessions** became director in 1987, he was fond of expounding on what a diverse agency the FBI was and how little the public knew about it.

"For example," he would say, "I had no idea the FBI has jurisdiction over espionage."

This never failed to enrage bureau officials, who thought the comment made Sessions look, well, less than well informed. After all, they would point out, everyone knew that the bureau caught such spies as Julius and Ethel Rosenberg, Rudolf Abel, and John A. Walker, Jr. As a former U.S. Attorney, Justice Department official, and chief federal judge in San Antonio, Sessions had to know that the bureau was the country's preeminent spy catcher.

Finally, Oliver B. (Buck) Revell suggested to Sessions that he drop the line from his speeches and talks with reporters. Sessions never mentioned it again.[88]

"What that meant was I had no idea when I became director that the bureau had a responsibility for foreign counterintelligence," Sessions said. "I don't know that any of your friends do, either. Very few people have any concept. It is the lead agency charged with FCI (foreign counterintelligence), period. They don't see it in the budget, they don't hear testimony about it."[89]

The fact that Sessions did not associate the bureau with counterspying illustrates how well the FBI has managed to keep its counterintelligence program out of sight. Journalists and government officials who think they are savvy say that there are no secrets in Washington. But there are, and many of them reside within the FBI's counterintelligence program.

Even the name of the FBI's division that carries out counterintelligence—the intelligence division—is meant to confuse. Counterintelligence is the business of tracking and thwarting spying, whether through arrests or other means; intelligence is positive gathering of information, a function normally reserved for the CIA.

The intelligence division has been responsible for most of the bureau's abuses. Yet, under William Webster and Sessions, it has also been responsible for some of its most important successes.

The intelligence division was established in 1919 to investigate suspected anarchists and Communists as potential security risks. Over the years, it has arrested Nazi saboteurs, infiltrated the Communist party, kept watch on KGB spies, maintained files on radical groups, and engaged in the illegal COINTELPRO program to disrupt protesters against the war in Vietnam, the Ku Klux Klan, and black nationalists. In the process, the division has operated wiretaps that were not sanctioned by law and has engaged in illegal break-ins, known as "black bag jobs."

In a July 19, 1966, memo, then FBI Assistant Director William C. Sullivan explained to Assistant Director Cartha D. (Deke) DeLoach, who was over public affairs and congressional relations, "We do not obtain authorization for 'black bag jobs' from outside the bureau. Such a technique involves trespass and is clearly illegal; therefore, it would be impossible to obtain any legal sanction for it. Despite this, 'black bag jobs' have been used because they represent an invaluable technique in combatting subversive activities of a clandestine nature aimed at undermining and destroying our nation."[90]

In acknowledging that some of the bureau's activities had been "clearly wrong and quite indefensible," Clarence Kelley said in an address at Westminster College in May 1976 that the FBI should never again occupy the "unique position that permitted improper activity without accountability."[91]

What the old bureau constantly confused was the difference between constitutionally protected free expression and illegal conduct. Upsetting as it may be to most Americans, an individual who verbally advocates overthrowing the government or aligning with the former Soviet Union is not violating any law. What does violate the law are acts that may further that end, such as plotting to blow up the Capitol or giving classified military secrets to the KGB.

In confusing these issues, Hoover's FBI took a vacuum-cleaner approach to subversion, instead of focusing resources on targets that were legitimate threats. The result was that the bureau was far less effective than it could have been in combatting spying from without—or politically inspired violence from within.

"I think when Hoover died, the bureau was chasing shadows in our intelligence program," Revell said. "There was very little substance because there was so much mythology involved."

To be sure, the bureau reflected the mores of the times and the wishes of a series of presidents from Franklin D. Roosevelt to Lyndon B. Johnson and Richard Nixon. While the bureau was engaging in illegal practices, the CIA was spying on Americans and opening their mail in violation of the law. But Hoover exceeded any presidential mandate in setting up the FBI as a secret police.

After the Church Committee and others exposed the FBI's practices, Attorney General Edward Levi developed guidelines to keep the FBI's eye on the target. The focus of the bureau's intelligence division became spies from other nations and the American traitors who helped them, not American dissidents. Often, that meant Americans with security clearances who worked for the CIA, the Defense Department, and other agencies that maintain secrets. Because it was embarrassing to acknowledge traitors in their midst, these agencies had succeeded over the years in persuading the Justice Department not to prosecute spies. Instead, spies would be allowed to resign quietly from jobs that gave them access to sensitive information.

"Every time, we would present it [for prosecution], and the attorney general would take it up with the secretary of state and even the president," said W. Raymond Wannall, Jr., who headed the intelligence division then. "You'd always go through the procedure [of trying to get a prosecution]. Some years there were none, some years two [such cases]."[92]

In 1977, Attorney General Griffin B. Bell changed that policy and began prosecution of spies to deter espionage. The chief architect of the Justice Department's aggressive policy in prosecuting spies was John L. Martin, who became chief of the Justice Department's internal security section in 1980. Martin, a perpetually tanned, handsome former FBI agent, had one of the toughest jobs in the government. On one hand, he had to withstand pressure from the

FBI to prosecute on evidence that he did not always think was strong enough. When national security is involved, it is easy for people to become hysterical and forget about constitutional rights. FBI agents would then grouse that Martin was too cautious.

"That is a typical FBI or policeman's reaction," said James H. Geer, who was the FBI's assistant director over the intelligence division from 1985 to 1989. "They always believe the prosecutor wants more than he needs to get a conviction." Despite the criticism, Geer said, "John Martin is the most knowledgeable person in this particular area."[93]

At the same time, Martin had to withstand pressure from the intelligence community, which wanted to bury its mistakes and never prosecute a spy.

"The intelligence community often believes that nothing is known unless it originates with them, and that revealing anything previously kept secret helps the other side," Martin said. "That ignores the reality that our adversaries know much more than we publicly admit and that the national interest will inevitably be better served by a public trial revealing and re-creating precisely what took place. Not only does it expose and punish the defendant, it is a way of impressing upon the bureaucracy the ultimate consequences of its oversights, if any. The purpose should be to deter the American who is tempted to spy and to correct within the government the reasons why things have gone wrong."[94]

Martin preached that the government could do both—prosecute spies to deter future espionage and retain any secrets that legitimately needed to be protected. Moreover, he maintained, the government could learn what the spy had given away and protect his rights at the same time.

Despite the pressures, Martin has remained the government's chief spy catcher, presiding over sixty-five espionage prosecutions, all but one of which resulted in a conviction. Throughout this string of successes, no one has claimed that either the FBI or the Justice Department proceeded illegally.

Meanwhile, under Webster, the FBI developed sophisticated techniques for combatting spying. Instead of merely conducting surveillance on KGB officers assigned to the U.S. as diplomats, the FBI took what it likes to call a proactive approach by using double agents to use up their time, learn what they were after, and eventually to help expel them. In what became known as the foreign counterintelligence program, the FBI's intelligence division engaged in a secret and highly effective dance with the KGB and the GRU—Soviet military intelligence—watching, learning, and moving in when necessary to thwart a spy operation.

Because the largest contingents of KGB operatives were in Washington and New York, they were the main cities where spy operations took place. Under the noses of the press, the FBI managed to keep secret the fact that many utility boxes contained video cameras for watching KGB operations. Some stereo equipment stores were operated by the FBI so that undercover agents could befriend KGB officers. Guests at some parties given by neighbors for KGB officers were all undercover FBI agents. Many of the cars driven by KGB officers in Washington were equipped with FBI bugs. And a nondescript office in Springfield, Virginia, was in fact headquarters for a highly effective joint FBI-CIA operation known as COURTSHIP that resulted in the recruitment of at least one KGB officer within the Soviet embassy in Washington. The FBI on its own recruited a second officer within the embassy, giving the bureau a magnificent inside view of the KGB's plans and operations.[95]

In carrying out these schemes, the FBI had the help not only of a supportive Justice Department but of a new law permitting electronic surveillance in foreign counterintelligence. The Foreign Intelligence Surveillance Act of 1978 (FISA) established a court that hears requests for wiretaps in foreign spy or terrorism cases. Located in a sixth-floor room of the Justice Department, the court normally consists only of a clerk. Every two weeks, a judge from one of seven alternating federal district courts sits for as many hours as required in the room, which is shielded to prevent electronic bugging of conversations in the room. There the judge signs wiretap and bugging requests submitted by Mary C. Lawton, a diminutive woman who is the Justice Department's counsel for intelligence policy and review.

Besides requests from the FBI, Lawton handles requests from the National Security Agency (NSA), the CIA, and other intelligence agencies. Under an executive order, any agency wanting to do electronic surveillance abroad of an American, or a physical search for intelligence purposes either in the U.S. or abroad directed at an American, needs to get personal approval from the attorney general. In addition, NSA often works with the FBI in the U.S. to intercept communications in the U.S.—for example, monitoring conversations that take place within foreign embassies.

A secret FBI facility in midtown Manhattan coordinates the work of the FBI and NSA. Code-named MEGAHUT, it operates behind the sign of another government agency. In addition, MEGAHUT has several offices throughout the country, known in FBI parlance as offsites. Altogether, some one hundred FBI agents reporting to the intelligence division are assigned to MEGAHUT. In a typical scenario, FBI agents might break in to a foreign embassy in the U.S. so that NSA can install listening devices.

Over the years, Lawton has had to obtain signatures for surveillance requests from attorneys general on Christmas Day, New Year's Eve, and in the early morning hours.

Today, the court approves six hundred interception requests a year, which include a number of requests that are renewed every ninety days.

"You could have six to eight applications in a year for a target," Lawton said. "If the target travels, and you want to do a hotel room, it's a new application. You have to be very specific."[96]

While Lawton has turned down some requests, the court has approved every request recommended by Lawton. Twelve times, appeals courts have upheld the legality of FISA orders.

In a chilling episode, one of the FBI's electronic bugs approved by the FISA court picked up the sounds of a father murdering his sixteen-year-old daughter. For two years, the FBI had listened to the activities of Zein Isa, a Palestinian-American, and his wife, Maria, in their tiny apartment in St. Louis. The bureau believed Zein Isa was involved in terrorist activities.

Isa disapproved of the fact that his daughter Tina had gotten a job at Wendy's and, without his permission, was seeing a young man. When Tina got home from work on the evening of November 6, 1989, her mother asked in Arabic where she had been.

"Working!" Tina shot back, according to the FBI tape.

"We do not accept that you go to work," Isa interrupted.

"Why are you doing this to us?" Maria asked angrily.

"I am not doing anything to you," Tina said.

"You are a she-devil," hissed her father.

Isa then asked about Tina's boyfriend and accused her of engaging in "fornication."

Her parents threatened to throw her out of the apartment. Tina challenged them to do it.

"Listen, my dear daughter," Isa said. "Do you know that this is the last day? Today you're going to die?"

"Huh?" said Tina, bewildered.

"Do you know that you are going to die tonight?"

Realizing that he was serious, Tina let out a long scream. There was a crash, and Tina's screams became muffled.

"Keep still, Tina!" her father yelled.

"Mother, please help me!" she cried.

Instead of helping her, her mother held her down as Isa began stabbing Tina in the chest with a seven-inch boning knife.

"No, please!" Tina cried.

"Shut up!" her mother said.

"No! No!" Tina shrieked.

"Die! Die quickly! Die quickly!" her father shouted.

Tina screamed one more time. By then, Isa had punctured her lungs. Only the sound of air being expelled could be heard.

"Quiet, little one!" her father said, stabbing her the last of six times.

"Die, my daughter! Die!"

Then there was silence.[97]

"We translated it the next day from Arabic," said Neil Gallagher, the chief of the FBI's counterterrorism section. "It [the investigation] wasn't so active that you had to have people listening live. We were always one day behind because of the limited number of agents who speak Arabic."

The agent who came to work the next day to translate the tape heard the tragedy played out. The tape even picked up Isa calling the police the night of the murder and claiming he had killed his daughter in self-defense.

There was never any question that the Justice Department would inform the police and local prosecutors about the recording.

"As soon as we learned about it, we knew we would hand it over," Lawton said. But, because the monitoring had been done secretly through the FISA court, Attorney General Richard Thornburgh had to approve turning over the tape.

FBI agents presented Thornburgh with a paper to sign at a formal dinner the day the FBI learned of the killing. The next day, St. Louis police arrested the couple. Based on the tape, Isa and his wife were convicted of first-degree murder and sentenced to death by lethal injection.

In a stunning conclusion to the story, based on FBI evidence, Zein Isa and three others were indicted in St. Louis in April 1993 for allegedly plotting to kill thousands of Jews, blow up the Israeli embassy in Washington, and smuggle money to members of the Abu Nidal terrorist organization. According to the indictment, the four were members of the Abu Nidal group, considered by the State Department to be the most dangerous terrorist organization in the world. And contrary to the impression given by the transcript of Isa killing his daughter, the true motive for killing her was that she knew too much about the group's activities and might expose them.

The indictment was the first of Abu Nidal members in the U.S. Already on death row, Isa pleaded not guilty to the charges.

Since the abuses of the Hoover era, the only program in the intelligence division that got too close to violating individual rights was the Library Awareness Program. Under the program, agents asked New York scientific and technical libraries to keep the bureau informed about patrons who perused certain technical publications. The bureau was looking only for real spies—KGB and GRU officers who may have been engaged in espionage and who consulted technical books as part of their work. But it was a ham-handed approach that showed no sensitivity to the fact that libraries are symbols of Americans' First Amendment rights. The idea of government agents scrutinizing lists of the reading material of library patrons was abhorrent. Moreover, the program produced very little useful information. Headquarters rejected the idea of extending the program to other cities, saying it did not produce enough to justify the effort.

Webster deserves the most credit for turning the FBI's counterintelligence program into a tool that is both effective and lawful. Spurned by many agents because of its tarnished reputation, the counterintelligence program under Webster and later Sessions had a waiting list of agents who wanted to transfer to it from the criminal side.

"The thing that brings you credibility is not standing up and saying, 'I'm the best,' " Geer said. "The thing that can turn it around are the kinds of cases and the impact these cases are having. That is what overcame the problems left after Hoover."

The zenith came in 1985, called "The Year of the Spy," when eleven spies were arrested. Among them were John A. Walker; Jonathan J. Pollard, the Israeli spy; Pelton, the former NSA employee; and Lawrence Wu-Tai Chin, a spy for the Chinese. All pleaded guilty or were convicted.[98]

Not included on that list was Edward Lee Howard, a former CIA officer who escaped FBI surveillance in 1985 and fled to the Soviet Union. An inexperienced FBI agent conducting the surveillance of Howard's home in Santa Fe, New Mexico, simply did not notice Howard leaving. The agent was suspended for forty-five days and then left the bureau.

"It was the wrong agent at the wrong place and the wrong time," said Oliver B. (Buck) Revell, then executive assistant FBI director for investigations. "He was a very young agent, very new. He really didn't understand at all what was going on."

On the other hand, said R. Patrick Watson, deputy director for operations in the intelligence division, "I've watched a front door and found out the guy walked out the front door, and we had five guys watching the front door. After you watch it for four or five hours, people lose their attention."[99]

The Howard incident underscores a perennial problem. At the time, the bureau did not have probable cause to arrest Howard. Even if it had, as part of his preparation by the CIA, Howard had been trained by the FBI in evading surveillance.

"My personal opinion is there was no way we could have ever put a surveillance on Howard in a way that he couldn't escape, short of arresting him. If he didn't beat us then, he would have beaten us the next day," Watson said.

In contrast, when the FBI began trailing State Department official Felix S. Bloch, the agents did it openly and were prepared to arrest him if he tried to leave the country. At the time, Bloch was still under active investigation.

"The Bloch case was done openly," Watson said. "It was the only way we could keep track of his activities."

Many newspapers criticized the FBI at the time for turning the Bloch case into a circus. For months, reporters followed FBI agents following Bloch. But the criticism was misguided. As a State Department employee with a security clearance, Bloch was obligated at the least to report contacts with a national of a Soviet bloc country. After meeting with Reino Gikman, who was working for the KGB, Bloch failed to comply with that regulation. Under State Department rules, that alone can be a firing offense. If Bloch thought Gikman to be a Finnish citizen, as he later claimed, then he had an obligation to report that the man had warned him elliptically in a phone conversation of an investigation into his activities—an event that suggested Bloch knew precisely with whom he was dealing.[100]

Ironically, the newspapers that raised objections to the FBI's approach criticized the FBI for allowing Howard, the former CIA employee, to escape to Moscow.

What never came out is that when FBI agents interviewed Bloch on June 22, 1989, at the State Department, they warned him of his rights when they had no obligation to do so. After some preliminary questions, the agents felt they had gotten Bloch to the point where he might confess.

"What are my options?" Bloch asked.

According to a later bureau critique, the agents should have said he had only one option: to cooperate. By engaging in such sleight-of-hand, FBI agents David E. Faulkner and Dudley F. B. Hodgson had gotten Pelton, the former NSA employee, to confess, resulting in his conviction. Because espionage cases are so difficult to make, a confession is often the only way to obtain a conviction.

In a bank robbery, for example, "Normally you have physical evidence. The individual hands over a demand note. He has written it in longhand, and there are fingerprints on it," said J. Stephen Ramey, who has worked counterintelligence at the Washington metropolitan field office and at headquarters. "Sometimes they touch the countertops. You have a dye pack that explodes as they run down the street. You have surveillance cameras taking their photographs. Even though they may wear a mask, you can pick out an unusual feature or type of clothing."[101]

In contrast, Ramey said, the only physical evidence in an espionage case is usually documents that are already in Moscow.

Instead of letting him continue to talk, the agents who interviewed Bloch warned him of his rights. Since the FBI did not go into the interview expecting to arrest Bloch, there was no need to give him a Miranda warning.

"It was terrible," said a lawyer familiar with the case.

No one—perhaps not even Bloch—knows if Bloch would have talked more if the agents had not warned him of his rights. The State Department eventually fired Bloch.

"I think there might have been criticism of the way it was handled, but not in the sense the case hinged on that," Geer said, meaning he did not think Bloch would have confessed in any case. "These were all experienced people, and they have a good sense about when that is necessary. It wasn't necessary. But the point I'm trying to make is, I don't view that as the thing that turned this around."[102]

With the cold war over, the intelligence division scrambled for things to do. While the Russian Republic continued to spy on the U.S. much as before, the countries that comprised the Soviet bloc ceased their intelligence activities against America and turned their attention to their immediate neighbors. Countries such as Czechoslovakia and Poland that had once been targets of FBI counterintelligence operations began receiving training in law enforcement from the FBI. Even representatives of the successor to the KGB met with the FBI to discuss cooperation. As long as the Russian intelligence agency continued to spy on the U.S., the FBI would not help the Russians.

In 1992, Sessions appointed Wayne R. Gilbert, a former special agent in charge of the Philadelphia field office, to head the intelligence division, which is on the fourth floor of headquarters. Gilbert had little experience in counterintelligence, but he was highly regarded in the criminal end of things and had supervised the bureau's counterterrorism investigations.

Within the FBI, there is constant debate about whether counterintelligence gurus should run counterintelligence programs or whether agents from the criminal side should run them. Those from the counterintelligence end have the experience, knowledge, and patience; those from the criminal side are thought to bring a more focused approach to cases: Their inclination is to look for criminal activity and bring cases to a head with an arrest. On the other hand, few objections are raised when a former counterintelligence official assumes a position over criminal cases. They are thought to have greater knowledge of the special organizational skills needed to solve crimes and build prosecutable cases.

When a case involves the KGB or the mafia, it is necessary to gather intelligence on their activities before moving in. But in the past, the intelligence division lost sight of the fact that its goal was to prevent espionage rather than to gather intelligence for the sake of it. It is precisely that kind of unfocused mentality that led to some of the abuses during the Hoover years.

"My criticism of all of us was we studied things too long and waited too long to act," Geer said. "Analysis is a wonderful thing, but analysis for the sake of analysis is questionable."

Based on a previous in-house study, Gilbert began a reorganization that focused on protecting key types of information and armaments—such as corporate proprietary technology or biological or nuclear weapons. If the FBI became aware that any country was trying to get this kind of information or technology, it could open a case even if a friendly country such as France was behind it.

This approach recognized that the list of countries trying to obtain such information was expanding beyond those that are simply adversaries of the U.S. At the same time, under the program, called the National Security Threat List, the FBI continued to focus on traditionally hostile countries such as Russia, which spies on the U.S. despite the end of the cold war.

"They are still working their agents and trying to recruit," Gilbert said. "They don't sit around watching TV all day. But there is uncertainty. 'Am I going to be here tomorrow?' Every intelligence service in the world is trying to reach out to them."[103]

Even if successful, spying by the former Soviets does not carry with it the threat it once did.

"We know there is not a clearly articulated threat in terms of a military power out there," said W. Douglas Gow, the FBI's associate deputy director over investigations, who supervised development of the FBI's new approach. "They still have a nuclear capability, of course. There are concerns. But not to the degree there was before."[104]

In response to the end of the cold war, Sessions transferred three hundred agents who had been working counterintelligence into investigating violent crime. Another fifty agents—half from the counterterrorism section and half from the criminal investigative division—were assigned to combat health-care fraud, expected to reach $100 billion by 1995.[105] But these changes were trivial. The FBI still had 20 percent of its agents—some twenty-six hundred— assigned to foreign counterintelligence, many of them poring over intelligence files of the former Soviet bloc countries to obtain leads on Americans who had committed espionage in the past. The counterintelligence program has a budget of almost $500 million that is appropriated separately by Congress and is classified.

"Because of the intelligence services [of former bloc countries] going out of existence, there is a lot of information available that was not before," said Patrick Watson, the deputy director for operations in the intelligence division. "We have a lot of cases going on as a result to address historical things."

In the midst of the changes, Howard slipped out of Moscow and wound up in Sweden. When Sweden expelled him, he returned to Moscow.

In a harbinger of things to come, the FBI's Newark office helped the successor to the KGB solve the kidnapping of Daniel Weinstock, an Australian computer-company executive who had been taken hostage along with his wife by Russian kidnappers in Moscow. In exchange for their freedom, the kidnappers demanded $1.6 million from a New Jersey doctor who is a relative of Daniel Weinstock. By getting the kidnappers to call a number in New Jersey and persuading them to leave their telephone numbers, the FBI determined where they were in the Moscow area. Through the American embassy in Moscow, the FBI passed along the information to the internal successor to the KGB, which arrested the kidnappers and freed the Weinstocks. Since the FBI did not deal directly with the KGB, the bureau could still say it does not cooperate with the Russian service.[106]

Despite the changes, the intelligence division remained almost as secretive as it was during the cold war. Not only did it refuse to say how many agents it has, it even insisted that the total numbers of FBI agents in each of the bureau's field offices should not be divulged for this book, regardless of whether they work criminal or counterintelligence cases.

"I had three hundred agents in Philadelphia. There is no reason not to give that out," Gilbert said.

But a briefing book given to top FBI executives states that the FBI does not disclose such numbers. FBI officials from other divisions insisted the figures could not be given out because of objections by the ever close-mouthed intelligence division.[107]

5

Miami: Super Bowl of Crime

● **Miami is the Super Bowl of crime,** an international city where pro-Castro and anti-Castro forces battle each other, where cocaine taints most of the currency, and where drivers who flick on their headlights to get the car in front to move over risk being mowed down by machine-gun fire. In Miami, anything from plastic pipes to bottled beverages may conceal smuggled cocaine, and a $1 million drug buy is hardly worth bothering with. Usually crime is where the money is, and Miami has that in abundance.

"It's a smorgasbord out there. You just walk down the table and take off a case, and it's going to be a big one if you put the effort in," said William A. Gavin, the special agent in charge of the Miami field office.

With 380 agents, the Miami office is the fifth largest in the FBI. As a key transhipment point for Colombian drugs entering the U.S., Miami is considered the FBI's number-one office in the drug field. Because Miami is so swamped with work, the office turns down lesser drug cases that other field offices eagerly grasp.

Miami is the place where the most tragic shooting of FBI agents in the history of the bureau took place. It is where the first FBI agent to be convicted of taking payoffs from drug sales was based. And it is the city where two agents who were husband and wife got caught going to a sex club together.

The FBI likes to think that it aims at the highest levels of the drug world, that its drug cases are the most imaginative and effective at stanching the flow of illegal drugs into the U.S. To a large extent, that is true. Not that anyone thinks law enforcement by itself will make a major dent in the drug trade. But by waging a constant battle against the drug lords, law enforcement can prevent the underworld from taking over.

"The Drug Enforcement Administration (DEA) does have success against major traffickers, but essentially they go after transactions, whereas we go after an organization," Buck Revell said. "It is the same approach we use against organized crime. We attempt to take out the hierarchy and obtain forfeitures of all their assets."

An example of the FBI's approach is CAT-COM, the code name for a Miami undercover operation that resulted in the indictment of ninety-two people, including two top Medellin cartel operatives. CAT-COM was the idea of Richard T. Garcia, a Miami agent, and his informant, Alvaro Meisel. A native of Colombia, Meisel grew up with people who would become major cocaine traffickers. Angered by the violence spawned by the drug traffic, Meisel called the FBI in 1985 and offered his services.

As an agent of Mexican descent, Garcia spoke Spanish fluently. At the time, he was on a drug squad. After other agents talked with Meisel, Garcia got the assignment. One morning, Garcia met with Meisel at a coffeeshop on Biscayne Boulevard. In evaluating informants who volunteer their services, FBI agents have to be careful that they are not being taken in by operatives from the other side or by people who simply want money. Meisel gave Garcia information on drug traffickers that Garcia was able to corroborate.

"You never fully take him in and trust him totally," Garcia said of informants in general. "I'm not saying he is not trusted. But you always have some caution to make sure he is not a double agent." In this case, he said, "Everything checked out."

Garcia and Meisel decided that the service drug shippers most needed was cellular phones, and they decided to provide it. People in the drug business use cellular phones for the same reason legitimate businessmen do—they make it easy to make appointments and arrange deliveries. Moreover, from the standpoint of criminals, cellular phones have a special advantage: As a rule, they are safer to use than regular phone lines; it is harder for the FBI to zero in on numbers to intercept. But cellular phone companies, like regular phone companies, want Social Security numbers and credit histories. These are things drug dealers are not eager to provide.

The FBI was glad to help. After Garcia and Meisel worked out the strategy, the Miami field office opened R.A. Communications & Computers at 7547-A West Twenty-fourth Avenue in Hialeah, in August 1987. R.A.—for Richard and Alvaro—not only offered cellular phones without asking questions, it maintained a bank of phones in the one-story office for making calls to foreign countries such as Colombia. All the while, the FBI was eavesdropping from a nearby computer company. And, because the FBI knew what frequencies the cellular phones transmitted on, the bureau could easily intercept the drug dealers' conversations on them. Thus, the code name: CAT, for catch, and COM, for communications.

Like any good company, the bureau insisted that the traffickers pay their bills. If they did not pay for a month, their cellular phones were shut off.

To find customers, Meisel would meet planes arriving from Colombia. Pretending that he knew traffickers, he would greet them and give them his business card. Word spread, and, almost immediately, the business was successful. Using the FBI's intelligence base on drug traffickers, Garcia knew in most instances the entire backgrounds of the cartel operatives who came in to do business.

One of the first customers, Luis (Tico) Linares, took Meisel into his confidence, telling him that he was arranging to ship ten thousand kilos of cocaine from Honduras. Within months, R.A. became a major communications point for drug traffickers from all over south Florida. Listening in on earphones, agents learned the precise locations of dozens of planes and ships bringing cocaine into the U.S. Another customer, Javier Mendez, confided as he sat on a sofa at R.A. that he was not worried about law enforcement authorities recording his voice.

"You can always say it's not your voice," he told Garcia. Looking straight into the concealed lens of a video camera, he added, "When they really get you is when they get you on videotape."

"Yeah, that's right," Garcia agreed.

At one point, a brother of Jorge Ochoa, one of the top leaders of the Medellin cartel, called R.A. to compliment the company for doing a good job in providing his people with communications and connections to other drug traffickers.

Garcia learned firsthand that the drug cartels operate just like any other business. Indeed, listening to their calls, Garcia was reminded of the way FBI headquarters and field offices interact. Every proposal had to go through a layer of bureaucracy. The cartels also keep a tight rein on inventory. If a shipment is lost or part of a shipment is missing, the cartels have their own internal inspectors who investigate thoroughly. If necessary, they hire lawyers to obtain the court records listing the quantities of drugs seized by law enforcement authorities. If there is a discrepancy, the cartels assume the shippers took a cut. They then dock the next shipment by the same amount, expecting the shippers to make up the difference. If the shippers don't come through, the cartels don't report them to the credit bureau. They kill them.

In the same vein, if a vessel sinks, the cartels launch an investigation to see if the traffickers purposely sank the boat and kept the drugs. If the Coast Guard becomes involved in investigating the sinking, the cartels obtain records from the Coast Guard to see what actually transpired. Although the FBI has sometimes gotten the Coast Guard to doctor records to make it appear that a drug shipment has been lost because the vessel sank, too many sinkings would create suspicion.

"You need documentation for the [cartels'] investigative team," Garcia said. "Otherwise, they whack you. If you lost it at sea or it is taken by law enforcement, you have to account for every kilo. . . . It's a business."

In operating the cellular phone company, Garcia traveled with Meisel, his informant, to Panama and Caribbean countries to meet with members of the cartel. Besides offering cellular phones, Garcia was glad to help cartel members determine if their phones were wiretapped or their boats bugged. In checking out their phones, Garcia determined what kind of security their homes had in case the FBI had to install eavesdropping devices. He used a checklist with headings like W/E. If a trafficker asked what the heading meant, Garcia would say it meant "wire evaluation." In fact, it meant weapons: Under the heading, Garcia listed any weapons found during his bogus sweep for electronic listening devices. Garcia never did report finding a bug, which pleased the drug merchants.

With Garcia's success came a problem: The FBI wanted the operation to go on indefinitely. Yet, the bureau could not very well close its eyes while tons of cocaine hit the country for distribution all over the U.S. If the FBI began arresting drug dealers transporting the stuff, the bureau would have to produce in court all the evidence against the traffickers. That evidence would include recordings of conversations made through the good services of R.A., tipping the bureau's hand.

"Anyone who was recorded we did not arrest," Garcia said. "That would cause discovery problems. It would go to trial, and we would have to give up evidence. So we had to do a lot of finessing to avoid exposure."

The first challenge came when Robert Lubberger, the captain of a sailboat called the *Velda Marie*, began making plans through R.A. to bring in a shipment of cocaine then worth $28 million on the street. Lubberger worked for R.A.'s early customer Linares, who headed a group of cocaine shippers.[108]

Garcia instructed the Coast Guard to intercept the boat near Jamaica. From listening in on the captain's calls, the FBI knew exactly where inside the sailboat the cocaine would be stashed. But the FBI did not want the Coast Guard to find the cocaine. If it did, the FBI would be obligated to prosecute the drug dealers immediately. So the FBI told the Coast Guard where the drugs were but asked the agency not to look there. As prearranged, the Coast Guard told the drug dealers they could not find the cocaine and would have to take apart the keel of the boat. To take apart the keel would require the Coast Guard to escort the boat to shore. Garcia figured that the FBI could quietly remove the drugs from the boat, and no one would be the wiser. When it came time to close down R.A., the traffickers involved would be arrested.

It took three days for the Coast Guard to pilot the boat to Florida. Meanwhile, they fished with the drug traffickers, who were still on board.

"They got in [to Key West] at 3:00 A.M.," Garcia said of the drug traffickers. The FBI told the Coast Guard to inform the drug traffickers that they could wander on shore until the boat could be examined at daybreak. The FBI was sure the captain and his first mate would not return. The bureau wanted them to escape. The FBI could arrest them when CAT-COM closed its operations. That way, the traffickers would not know that the FBI had been pulling the strings all along. The traffickers might think it strange that they had been told they could go ashore, but probably they would think they had been lucky and not jump to the conclusion that they were being manipulated. But when the traffickers got off the boat, they called Meisel from a coffeeshop with some startling news.

"These guys [the Coast Guardsmen] are so dumb," Lubberger, the captain, said. "They couldn't find the drugs. They said to come back. We're going to go back and get our boat back."

Garcia called Carl P. Florez, a co-case agent who was at the boat dock in Key West.

"We have a problem," Garcia told Florez. "They are coming back to find the boat."

"They are what?" Florez gasped.

Florez dispatched a male and a female Customs agent to sit down in a booth next to the drug dealers in the coffeeshop. The agents posed as a couple in love. The male agent said in a voice loud enough for the captain and his first mate to hear that he had just left the dock and had been struck by the commotion.

"They had this cocaine on the dock, and they are looking for two guys," the agent said.

The drug dealers took off and called Meisel.

"It's a freaking miracle," the captain said. "We overheard this couple saying what happened on the dock. We need help."

The FBI arranged for Meisel to dispatch money from Linares, the owner of the drugs, for the captain and first mate so they could hide from the FBI. Finally, now that the traffickers were gone, the Coast Guard could remove the drugs. The FBI preserved them as evidence.

When Garcia got word that another boat, called the *Naut-For-Fun*, would be bringing in drugs from an island off Colombia, the FBI decided that the best way to dispose of the drugs without having to arrest those on board was to make it appear the vessel had sunk. But that would have to be done very carefully.

In this case, Garcia arranged for the FBI to transmit phony distress signals from the boat. He also arranged for phony Coast Guard reports saying the boat had sunk at sea. The FBI had placed an undercover agent on board the ship. Two other crew members were cooperating with the FBI.

Unfortunately, between Colombia and Cuba, the forty-seven-foot schooner ran into a storm. The mast broke, the fuel tanks split, and the *Naut-for-Fun* started taking on water. At the Miami field office, an agent monitoring the shortwave radio received a faint message from the agent.

"Help! We are sinking!" the agent said.

"Oh, come on!" the radio operator said.

"No, we *are* sinking," said the agent on board the boat.

The Coast Guard figured it would take three hours for their nearest cutter to reach the sinking boat. So, they sent a helicopter from the cutter to rescue the crew members. Because of the storm, the helicopter could not drop a rescue line. Instead, it dropped rafts and other emergency equipment. The cutter eventually reached the vessel, which was still afloat.

A few months later, Garcia wanted the Coast Guard to find the fifty kilos of cocaine that were supposed to be hidden in compartments in the stern of a $50,000 boat called the *Pic-N-Ga*. In this case, the FBI did not have the traffickers on tape, and the bureau wanted to arrest them. The Coast Guard took apart the stern and could not find the cocaine. The FBI insisted the boat had cocaine on it, so the Coast Guard ripped the entire boat to shreds. Still no cocaine was found.

"The boat captain was irate," Garcia said. "He said he would sue. He showed up at R.A., and we recorded him saying, 'We threw it overboard before they got to the boat.' "

The government used delaying tactics to stall the progress of the captain's litigation. When the case finally was ready for trial, the FBI got the suit dismissed by presenting recordings of the captain boasting that he had thrown the drugs overboard.

In the middle of the operation, Garcia was driving the undercover black Corvette convertible he had been given for the case when he got a call from the Miami field office congratulating him on having been promoted to a job supervising international cocaine investigations in headquarters. Riding with the top down and feeling Miami's balmy breezes, Garcia was not sure he wanted to go.

To ease him out of the R.A. operation without arousing suspicion, Florez, the co-case agent, decided that Garcia would die in the next appropriate plane crash. But in the coming months, no plane crashed in the U.S., so the bureau could not spread the word that he had died. Instead, the FBI decided that Garcia would say he was moving to Chicago to help some Mexican drug traffickers. To authenticate the story, the Chicago field office mailed to the drug dealers in Miami postcards Garcia had written in Washington.

To replace Garcia, the FBI chose Gloria M. Newport, an attractive and curvaceous agent of Mexican and Irish descent. Newport had never worked an undercover operation before but had volunteered for the job and passed muster. When Garcia and Florez were interviewing her for the job around the pool at Florez's house, the chair Newport was sitting in gave way, and she fell to the ground. Although embarrassed, she quickly composed herself, and the two male agents were impressed. They decided she had the poise needed for the job.

Garcia introduced Newport as his cousin and said that in his absence, she would help Meisel run the business. For a time, Garcia and Newport worked together until she was ready to take over.

Because of her looks, Newport had to fend off drug traffickers who wanted to date her. She told them she was not dating anyone because she was recovering from a broken romance. But one trafficker, a self-proclaimed killer, started pawing Newport whenever he thought she was alone. The agents listening in to the encounters were afraid they would have to rescue her, thereby blowing the operation. While that never happened, Newport had to fend off more polite advances from another man who was taken with her. Carlos Mario Echeverra dealt at the upper echelons of the drug cartels. The best man at his wedding had been José Rodriguez Gacha. Until he was killed in Colombia in 1989, Gacha was one of the three top leaders of the Medellin cartel.

Garcia and Newport knew that Echeverra used his home as a stash house, but the FBI had been unable to locate it. Then one day Echeverra invited both agents to his home in south Miami for dinner.

"He liked Gloria, 'my cousin,' " Garcia said. "He was a gentleman, too. He really did like her. But he was dumb as a rock."

Echeverra busied himself in the kitchen making ceviche. As he served the dish, he poured wine for the two agents and talked about how he needed someone to front for a company that would import cocaine and engage in money laundering. Would the two agents start the company with him?

"That sounds like a good idea," Garcia said. "Do you mind if Gloria takes notes on it?"

No problem.

Echeverra started bragging about his contacts in the drug world and describing how the front company would work. Meanwhile, Newport was taking notes in shorthand on an eight-by-eleven-inch pad. When Echeverra finished, Garcia said Newport's notes would be the charter of the new company.

"Why don't we sign it and date it, and I'll hang it in my office," Garcia said.

So all three signed Newport's notes—evidence to be used, if needed, at trial.

Then Garcia suggested that they photograph each other holding the charter. Garcia got his camera and a tripod from his Corvette. Using the timed release, he photographed himself, Echeverra, and the micro-mini-skirted Newport sitting around a table and holding the charter. It was, in effect, a confession.

A year and a half after R.A. began, the FBI decided it was time to close it down. The Medellin cartel was planning to import seven tons of cocaine, and this time it would be impossible to let the bad guys escape. On the day of the arrests, December 6, 1988, one of the drug traffickers scurried into R.A.'s office, thinking he could hide out there.

Because of the overwhelming evidence, nearly all of the ninety-two people who were arrested—including Echeverra, Mendez, and Lubberger—pleaded guilty to cocaine-trafficking charges. Linares was convicted after a trial. Two of the top leaders of the Medellin cartel—Pablo Correa Rodriguez and Blás Fernando Canedo, who worked directly for Ochoa—are fugitives. During the operation, the FBI seized 5½ tons of cocaine and 105 tons of marijuana.[109]

The Miami field office is a two-story building surrounded by lush green grounds just a few blocks from Interstate Route 95 in north Miami. It was on Route 95 that local toughs robbed Special Agent Eugene J. Flynn. He and his wife were on their way to a party. Youths had thrown debris on the road so that cars would get flat tires and have to stop. The agent's car got a flat, and while he was changing the tire, they robbed him at gunpoint and took his credentials. As they left, he chased them. One of the youths fired at him and missed.

Flynn plastered the area with "wanted" posters. He eventually caught the young men and retrieved his credentials.

"I tell kids [agents] who come here one of the most dangerous things you can do is get on 95 and flash your lights to get someone to move out of a lane," said William A. Gavin, the special agent in charge. "It's a territorial imperative. Give them the lane. Do you want to get into a shootout over a lane? It's not worth it. People have been shot because someone flashed their lights and went faster than they were."

Outside the front entrance of the Miami field office, a flagpole is anchored in a marble base that bears the names Benjamin P. Grogan and Jerry Dove, a memorial to the two agents who were killed in a shootout on April 11, 1986. Grogan and Dove were the twenty-sixth and twenty-seventh FBI agents to be killed in the line of duty as a result of adversarial action. Given the number of agents who have passed through the bureau since the first agent was killed in 1925, the number of deaths has been unusually low.

The key to the FBI's success has always been its ability to outman and outmaneuver the other side. A police officer in a patrol car has little idea what he will face when responding to a call or stopping a driver for speeding. He will quite naturally be unprepared for some of the threats he encounters. The FBI, on the other hand, has the luxury in most cases of planning ahead—of choosing the exact time, place, and circumstances of an arrest. The bureau's philosophy has always been to smother the opposition with agents and equipment. For example, the bureau deployed fifty agents and support personnel to watch John A. Walker, Jr., as he left classified documents for his

Soviet handler in Potomac, Maryland. Then, agents wearing bulletproof vests lured him out of his Ramada Inn room at 3:30 A.M. with a pretext call. There was no way Walker, who was armed, could have escaped. FBI agents manned the stairwells, elevators, and lobby, and surrounded the hotel.

"What we teach is superiority of manpower and firepower to prevent incidents," said James R. Pledger, who heads the FBI's firearms training unit, which sets firearms policy for the bureau and trains new agents. "We have an advantage over most law enforcement, because 90 percent of the time, we know who we are going after, their name, their address, how they think, whether they are likely to be armed. We usually pick the time and place of the confrontation. When they [suspects] are looking down the barrels of fifteen guns, which is not an unreasonable number for a very dangerous fugitive, most of the time they won't opt for 'suicide by cop.' That's why you don't hear much about the FBI getting involved in shootouts. We have the luxury of picking the time and place."[110]

The Miami shootout began as fourteen FBI agents in ten cars were on their way to stake out banks over a five-mile area in southwest Dade County. The agents hoped to catch Michael Platt and William R. Matix, who had been robbing banks and armored cars in south Florida. Lately, Platt and Matix had been focusing on the area where the surveillance was about to take place.

On their way to one of the banks, Grogan, a twenty-five-year veteran, and Dove, who had been an agent for four years, spotted a black Monte Carlo with the Florida plate NTJ-891. The car belonged to the victim of a recent attempted killing by Platt and Matix, the same men who were the targets of the FBI's planned surveillance that day.

Grogan and Dove radioed to the other nine cars going to the surveillance points to converge on the area. As they followed the Monte Carlo north on South Dixie Highway, Dove radioed, "We're burned. They know we're on them."[111]

The Monte Carlo turned off the highway, where heavy traffic would have made a shootout particularly dangerous.

"Let's stop him. Felony car stop. Let's do it," Grogan said over the radio.

Four other FBI cars converged on the Monte Carlo on SW Eighty-second Avenue near One Hundred Twenty-second Street. They forced the Monte Carlo off the quiet, tree-lined residential street. In doing so, they became involved in violent collisions with the Monte Carlo and with one another.

The agents were not as prepared for a shootout as they would have been had they already "set up"—FBI jargon for conducting surveillance—on the banks. Most of the agents who confronted the men were armed only with Smith & Wesson .38-caliber revolvers. Besides the fact that they did not have the stopping power of heavier-duty weapons, the revolvers had to be reloaded after only six shots. Few of the agents on the surveillance had 9-millimeter semiautomatic pistols, which fire a more deadly round, are loaded with fifteen shots, and can be reloaded easily by replacing a magazine rather than by tediously dropping individual bullets into a cylinder.

Most of the agents' shotguns—which are highly effective in a gunfight, especially against moving targets—were either in the trunks of their cars or had slid from the backseats onto the floors during the collisions. In the ensuing melee, the agents did not have time to grab them. Another agent with a submachine gun had not yet arrived. Only two agents had time to don their bulletproof vests. During a collision, one agent's revolver slid from the front seat and fell outside his car. Grogan's glasses fell to the floor and lodged under the brake pedal. He was never able to retrieve them. A deadly shot who had headed the SWAT team in Miami, Grogan could see little without his glasses. As a result, he was effectively out of commission during the ensuing gun battle.

In contrast to the poorly armed agents, Platt and Matix had a Ruger Mini-14 semiautomatic carbine and a Colt AR-15 assault rifle. Unlike a machine gun, the trigger of the Ruger Mini-14 has to be squeezed for each shot. But the weapon has a thirty-bullet clip and is extremely accurate up to 375 yards. Its bullet travels at devastating velocity and can penetrate a car door. Against this weapon, bulletproof vests would have been useless.

Forced off the road, Platt and Matix began firing from the Monte Carlo, then emerged and began firing at the agents from closer range. In the next five minutes, they killed Dove and Grogan and wounded five other agents, including Edmundo Mireles, Jr., the only agent with a shotgun. Mireles's left arm had been shattered, but as he sat on the ground behind a car, he reached for his shotgun. With one arm, he racked the action of the shotgun and, balancing the barrel on the car's bumper, fired at Platt and Matix, who were in Dove's car trying to get away. Again he cocked and fired, five times in all.

Already severely wounded by Dove, Platt staggered out of Dove's car to finish Mireles off. With sirens screaming nearby, he fired at him three times from point-blank range. Miraculously, he missed each time. Thinking the FBI agent was dead, Platt got back into the car and tried to start the engine. Bleeding profusely, Mireles then got up and began firing at Matix and Platt with his revolver as he moved closer to their car. Still firing, he moved within several feet of the driver's side and finished them off.

"If you give up, if you lie down to die, you *will* die," Mireles said later.

The FBI agents had fired eighty rounds, while Platt and Matix had fired sixty. The smoke from the gunfire was so thick that it was difficult to see. Their voices quavering, terrified residents called the 911 emergency police number, not knowing if the FBI agents were law enforcement officers or gangsters.

Devastated, William Webster wrote a statement that he gave to Lane Bonner, who was in charge of the press office at headquarters: "Today's tragedy is a severely felt loss to the FBI. It is difficult to recall so many agents killed and injured in a single incident. . . . This is a violent world, but it would be much worse without their fidelity, their bravery, and their integrity"—the FBI's motto, whose first letters are FBI.

There were those, like Buck Revell, who said the agents' supervisor should have insisted on waiting until the agents had armed themselves better, had regrouped, and were ready to confront the two suspects, who were known to be heavily armed and volatile.

"My only criticism is that, knowing of the potential for danger and violence, and having prepared for that with the number of people and equipment they had, there should have been a pause for more of the agents to prepare themselves for this confrontation, so they would have shoulder weapons and vests on," Revell said. "It obviously would have been better to have had a pause while other agents maintained a surveillance."[112]

Others, like James D. McKenzie, who was assistant director over the training division at the time, said it was difficult to second-guess the agents' decision to confront the suspects when they did. For some time the bureau had been looking for the suspects, who had already killed a security guard, and they might have gotten away if the agents had waited, according to this argument.

"Nobody is ever in a position to second-guess what they did in Miami unless they got the bullets flying at them," said McKenzie, meaning that agents have to make snap decisions on the scene based on their instincts.

"We could not have waited. They would have been gone," said John F. Hanlon, one of the wounded agents. The suspects knew they were being followed, Hanlon said, and would have either opened fire on the agents or tried to get away.[113]

"To have waited any longer would have put a lot of innocent civilians at risk," said Gordon G. McNeill, the supervisor on the scene who spent three years out of work recuperating from his wounds. "I'll take six agents against two anytime. We had a veteran crew out there. What I am most proud of is we went out there together, we fought together, and we all went down together."[114]

While a headquarters inquiry found that the agents had acted properly, one lesson was clear: The bureau was going to have to arm agents better. Several of the agents, their shooting hands shattered, were pathetically trying to reload six-shot revolvers as Platt shot them. Against Platt's firepower, the revolvers were toys.

"All the injuries that occurred to our people were a result of not being able to load weapons—all the people who were wounded," said Chris R. Mazella, the Miami agent who headed the investigation of the incident until headquarters inspectors arrived on the scene. "John Hanlon was shot in the hand, so he could not put a bullet in his gun. Gordie [McNeill] was also shot and could not load his weapon. With the nine-millimeter, you just throw those cartridges in."[115]

Since the shooting, the bureau has installed racks designed to hold shotguns under the roofs of bureau cars. The racks extend from the front of the car to the back, so an agent can reach up and remove the shotgun while driving. But the bureau has been slow to equip agents with semiautomatic weapons, which load more easily than revolvers and which most police departments now use routinely. The reason is that the FBI, being the FBI, must have the best. Simply issuing existing 9-millimeter weapons to all agents would be too simple. So, the FBI embarked on an extensive research program to determine what round would be most lethal.

After consulting experts, the firearms training unit within the FBI's training division decided that the standard test used for determining how much damage a round of ammunition inflicts was flawed. Simply firing into gelatin did not re-create what really happens when a bullet enters a human body.

"People have done that for years [fired into gelatin], but what people didn't think to do was to add clothing, the windshield of a car, a door," said Pledger, who later took over the unit. "Nobody had stopped to think of what a bullet does in those conditions. So we developed a test with a T-shirt on it . . . and denim and down clothing. Different bullets do totally different things."

Using the FBI's new testing method, the 10-millimeter round came out the best—which in this case means it is not only more accurate, but more lethal.*

"The theory we believe in is the heavier [10-millimeter] bullet provides more penetration," Pledger said. "All the pathologists we talked to said you can't predict what a bullet will do when it hits someone. All you can do is try to poke the biggest hole you can. . . . The only way is to lose a lot of blood. Some [suspects] get mad. Some give up. Some are on drugs. A larger, heavier penetration will make them bleed more."

Or, as explained by James Greenleaf, who was then assistant director over the training division, "When an agent fires his weapon, he is doing it to defend himself or an innocent person. So what you try to do is, when you shoot somebody, you shoot them basically to prevent them from returning fire. It's to shoot the center of mass to knock the person down. An unfortunate outgrowth of that is death."[116]

The diameter of the 10-millimeter round falls between a .45-caliber and a 9-millimeter bullet. Thus, it is wider than either the standard .38-caliber bullet or the 9-millimeter bullet that many police departments had begun using around the time of the Miami shootout. No one had made extensive use of the 10-millimeter round until the FBI selected it as its bullet of choice.

But a better bullet was not good enough for the FBI. The bureau also wanted to design its own gun to deliver the round in the most effective way. That was the FBI's undoing. After seeking bids, the FBI let a contract to Smith & Wesson to develop a special 10-millimeter pistol. From William Sessions, who approved the contract, to the agents in the firearms training unit, who recommended it, everyone now wishes he had never heard of a 10-millimeter gun.

The bureau ordered 250 test guns, which worked well. Then, in 1989, the FBI ordered 12,000 guns for all its agents.[117]

"The problems came when full production started," Pledger said. "We've had a half-dozen instances of agents in the field with guns that have totally locked up unpredictably." In addition, he said, "[We had] parts breakage problems and functioning problems, meaning jamming. We are seeing too much jamming. We attribute that to quality control and some other things."

---

* The diameter of long bullets is given in millimeters, while the diameter of shorter bullets is given in calibers.

Because the problems were detected early, most of the guns had not yet been sent to the field, and the rest were recalled.

"We are deciding whether to continue with it or terminate the contract and try something else," said Greenleaf, now deputy director for administration.

Meanwhile, the FBI has issued 9-millimeter weapons to agents who want them. Besides the issue of how minorities are treated and promoted in the FBI, no issue evokes as much passion and debate within the FBI as which gun the FBI should use. Each weapon has its opponents and detractors.

"People who are gun nuts are very emotional people, and all have their own ideas about which way it should go," Greenleaf said. "You have to be careful about what they tell you, because they get so wrapped up in the issues. I'm trying to get people to stand back and take an unemotional view of it. They all think they do that. But they're all so close to their own agenda, and that wisdom gets washed out."

"It actually got nasty," said one agent. "They [opposing groups] were pissed off at each other."

The result is that seven years after Dove and Grogan were killed, many agents are still armed with six-shot .38-caliber revolvers which can take longer rounds, known as magnum cartridges. For years, only new agents and agents who worked violent crime, or who were assigned to SWAT teams, got 9-millimeter weapons. Agents such as Pledger purchased semiautomatic pistols with their own funds. Meanwhile, the DEA got 9-millimeter pistols in 1988, as did the District of Columbia police. The FBI has begun issuing 9-millimeter semiautomatics to all agents, and 60 percent of the FBI's agents now have them.

If the 10-millimeter pistol ever is issued, many agents have no intention of using it.

"Agents have to have confidence in their weapons," said Michael Giglia, the supervisor of a drugs and organized crime squad in Buffalo. "I wouldn't want to go into a gun battle with any weapon that I do not have complete confidence in."[118]

Because of the violence in Miami, most agents there carry semiautomatics, and security is unusually tight. In the late afternoon when many FBI employees are leaving work, two agents patrol the area. In separate incidents, gunmen have held up three female clerks as they were going home, and the agents are there to see that it doesn't happen again.

Recently, two agents returning from lunch saw a man running through the yard behind the field office. He was carrying a gym bag. Suspecting that he might have stolen the gym bag, Anthony M. Gonzalez, one of the agents, yelled, "FBI! Halt!"

The man pulled out a revolver and began firing at the agents as he continued to flee. Gonzalez shot him dead with his 9-millimeter semiautomatic. It turned out that the man had just stolen a car and had left it three blocks away. Paul L. Miller, the FBI's longtime media representative in Miami, often goes to the scene of an arrest to brief newspaper and television reporters. This time, he only had to step out the front door of the field office.

The entrance to the field office on the first floor is nothing more than a bare passageway scanned by video cameras. An elevator takes visitors to the second floor, where receptionists behind bulletproof glass retain driver's licenses of visitors before allowing them inside.

In one area of the second floor, investigative assistants take complaints over the phone and obtain credit bureau and corporate records. Among other records, they have on computer all forwarding-address notices sent to post offices in the U.S.

The first floor houses the organized crime, white collar, bank robbery, and drug squads. A white collar squad is working the Bank of Credit and Commerce International, the notorious international bank that regulators closed down in July 1991. As far back as 1986, the CIA began to report to other government agencies on BCCI's criminal activities and secret control of First American Bank of Washington—reports that were ignored. The FBI did not launch a full-scale investigation until after the bank had closed. William Baker, assistant director over the criminal division, attributed the delay to a lack of coordination.

"If one analyst had had access to all of it from the FBI, CIA, Customs, it might have stirred something," he said.[119]

The first floor has one squad that just focuses on obtaining forfeitures of assets of criminals—everything from BMWs to airplanes. While the new bureau has deemphasized statistics as a measure of success, they are not totally ignored. Nancy L. Savage, the head of the squad, is proud to tell you that in the most recent year, the forfeiture squad seized $150 million in assets.

"I look at total arrests. I'm not foolish," said Gavin, the special agent in charge of the office.

During a recent inspection, the Miami office received kudos for seizing sixty-seven tons of cocaine in the two years covered by the inspection. And the fugitive squad caught five hundred fugitives in the six months ending in May 1992. With the shift after the death of Hoover to quality over quantity, the FBI deemphasized catching fugitives. Now the bureau has come full circle and is again in the business of apprehending fugitives who are believed to have crossed state lines.

"If you don't have a way to bring people before the bar of justice who leave a state, then you don't have a criminal justice system," said Danny O. Coulson, the deputy assistant director in the criminal investigative division over violent crime. "The system can't work if the people who are supposed to be participants aren't there."

Like a stockbroker watching his stock plunge in value, Steven B. Warner, the bank robbery coordinator on the bank robbery task force in Miami, worries that bank robberies—up to 346 in a year—lately have been down.

"While I don't like to see the number of banks that got robbed last year robbed this year, I certainly would like to have a little bit more to justify our existence, so to speak, so we don't start picking up some other violations that other squads can't keep up with in Miami," Warner said.[120]

Besides recovering a kidnap victim alive, nothing makes FBI agents quite as proud as uncovering political or police corruption. Lately, the Miami office has been successful in taking down a mayor of Hialeah and most of the members of the Sweetwater city council. Working with the local police, the Miami office has also convicted a number of police officers for taking bribes.

"We're the only office that has a squad devoted to nothing but police corruption," Gavin said. "We also have a corruption squad. It's difficult here. The way we manage is by being partners with the [police] department if that is doable. It doesn't serve us well, I don't think, unless the corruption is pervasive from top to bottom, to go into a department and do a police corruption case without the department's knowledge. I don't like to do that."

One of Miami's more impressive police corruption cases resulted in the convictions of Bureau of Customs officials in Florida for giving drug smugglers inside information on law enforcement efforts to catch them. The drug smugglers hoped to control trafficking in all of south Florida, using information they obtained from Customs officials on the location of radar used to track their boats and planes and the timing of planned raids.

Charles Jordan, a Customs supervisor who was a fugitive, was caught when his case appeared on *America's Most Wanted* and tips came in that gave the FBI probable cause to search the home of

Jordan's parents. There, agents found a videotape Jordan had made when his wife gave birth to a baby, according to John H. Thompson, the FBI case agent. The videotape showed the couple's license tag number. It also showed the name of the hospital imprinted on a pillow case at the hospital where Jordan's wife gave birth.

"We called each state and determined there was a hospital outside Denver by that name," Thompson said.[121]

In Miami, as in other cities, agents who once worked foreign counterintelligence are being switched to criminal cases at a rate even faster than that mandated by headquarters.

"The strength of the FBI is that we are a diversified investigative agency," William Baker said. "The investigative prowess we get from our agents working foreign counterintelligence can be translated effectively to other major programs as needed."

Agents who make counterintelligence their life's work tend to have different personalities from those who like criminal work. The counterintelligence types are more cerebral. They enjoy studying the KGB and the GRU, the Soviet military intelligence, and they relish the prestige of working cases that involve national security and relations among major powers. Those who like criminal work —for example, bank robberies—like action and quicker results.

"They [bank robberies] have all the makings of what I came into the FBI to do: Point guns at people, scream and yell at them, put handcuffs on them, put them in jail, get them off the street, and see some results from the investigations that I conduct," said Warner, the bank robbery coordinator.

For the most part, criminal and counterintelligence agents do not mix socially. Criminal agents tend to view counterintelligence agents as lazy and timid. Counterintelligence agents look at criminal agents as dumb and low-class.

Michael D. Grogan is one of those agents who has switched from counterintelligence to criminal cases. When he was based at the Washington metropolitan field office, Grogan handled some of the most important and sensitive espionage cases the U.S. has ever seen. Now in Miami working organized crime, Grogan looks back at the old days somewhat wistfully.

"It was an extremely interesting time," Grogan said of the cold war. "I don't know if we'll ever see those times again. I feel really fortunate that I was assigned to Washington during those times."

But Grogan enjoys his new work.

"Organized crime is almost like FCI [foreign counterintelligence] with a gun. You have to get to know your adversary or target extremely well, to get into their heads so you can take appropriate countermeasures. The transition was easy."[122]

The criminal side has welcomed former FCI agents.

"The reason these people [former FCI agents] are successful is they are good at talking to people. They can comprehend and analyze material," said Manuel J. Gonzalez, Miami's assistant special agent in charge over drug investigations.

The primary focus of the Miami office is drugs, which a third of the agents work. While many agents enjoy the fast pace, it is frustrating and often repetitive work. If there is a war on drugs—which FBI agents question—it is being lost. The street price of illicit drugs is going down rather than up. The size of shipments and number of seizures are soaring, meaning that drug traffickers are becoming more brazen and supplying even more drugs than before. Usually the U.S. Attorney in Miami will not handle a drug case unless it involves at least five kilograms.

"In another division [field office], three kilos of cocaine may be the biggest thing they've seen in the history of that program," Gavin said. So, if a case has a nexus with another field office, "We give it to them and give them support. 'You take this product home. I don't want it.' Destroying it is such a pain in the neck."

Because cocaine burns at very high temperatures, it destroys incinerators. To minimize damage, the government burns cocaine in small quantities.

Often, working drugs is like trying to keep afloat in a tidal wave. The seizures get bigger and bigger, the cases are more impressive, and the targets are ever higher in the drug chain. Progress is hard to discern.

"One of the problems with the drug world is how do you measure success?" said Gonzalez, the assistant special agent over drugs. "Everyone is trying to figure out how to do it. Some agencies count arrests. Others count convictions and indictments. Are they measures? No one knows. Today we are hearing more and more that the southwest area of the country is a major importation point. Everything you see here is the opposite. We don't see activity decreasing. Does anyone have a handle on it? By the time we finish analyzing it, we would have missed the point anyway."

Anyone in the office will tell you that in Miami, $1 million in illegal transactions means nothing.

"Just about all the money in Florida is tainted with cocaine," Gonzalez said. "The money flowing through here is phenomenal. It is the northernmost city in South America. It's easier to fly into

Miami to go from one point to another than to go through South America," he said.

Meanwhile, the drug cartels have become as sophisticated as IBM.

"It's a business to them," Gonzalez said. "They have become cellular. One cell doesn't know who the other cell is. They are intelligent. They send people here to get engineering and chemistry degrees. They might need that one day. They train them to detect law enforcement. They hire attorneys here to find out how they got caught. They look at the affidavits, the presentations in court. They look for the vulnerabilities."

The U.S. government continues to take a piecemeal approach to the problem, using dozens of law enforcement agencies that often get in one another's way. For most of its history, the FBI did not work drug cases because of Hoover's fear that drugs might corrupt agents. It was part of Hoover's no-risk policy that put the fear of embarrassment to the bureau ahead of the welfare of the country. After Webster and Attorney General William French Smith agreed on the need, the FBI began working drugs in January 1982. In August 1987, drugs became one of the FBI's priority programs.

"My personal view was that the most serious domestic problem was drugs, and the FBI could not stand aside and say we will not help," Webster said. "We had to have enough confidence in the integrity of our agents and the way we selected and trained and appointed them that we could accept that minimal risk that we might occasionally lose out on an agent."[123]

It made as much sense to have two major federal law enforcement agencies battling drugs as it would to have two police departments with overlapping jurisdictions in a city. As part of the original plan, the DEA would eventually be merged into the FBI after the bureau gained jurisdiction for drugs. Until the merger, the DEA administrator would report to the attorney general through the FBI director. But none of that came to pass.

All kinds of excuses were found to put off a merger: How would the education and training of DEA agents meld with that of FBI agents? All FBI agents must be college graduates; 20 percent of DEA agents had not gone to college. Jack Lawn, a former FBI agent who was DEA administrator at the time, posed another question: "Would they [DEA agents] become FBI agents? Would they be sent out to investigate 271 violations, or would they be kept in the drug arena?"

Fundamentally, many DEA officials, including Lawn, did not want to give up their territory.

"Jack went over to facilitate the consolidation, and he got an extreme case of egotism," Revell said. "Jack had worked for me. I recommended him as SAC in San Antonio. I did not anticipate that his ego and personal ambitions would take over. He did not sell it to DEA. It would have enhanced their opportunities. Would you rather be an FBI or DEA agent? Their concern was they would be shunted aside in the bureau. That wasn't the case at all."[124]

But it was not Lawn who made the final decision. In the end, a Justice Department committee that included Webster recommended against a merger.

"I felt that eventually, if we were successful in bringing the standards [of education] together and getting the right kinds of people, the FBI could eventually take it all on," Webster said. But he said he thought a merger should proceed gradually.

In retrospect, the delay was a mistake. The idea of merging became a dead issue. Instead, to coordinate investigations better, the head of DEA was to report to the FBI director, but he never did. Now, by order of the attorney general, the head of DEA reports to the deputy attorney general in the Justice Department.

While the FBI officially recognizes no problem, the fact is that the FBI and DEA are always at each other's throat, to the detriment of the public. As the official responsible for drug investigations in the FBI's number-one office for drugs, Gonzalez should know. He finds the overlapping jurisdiction frustrating.

"We have every agency involved in the drug war," he said. "It's ridiculous. Should it be one agency? No. Should it be a few involved in it? I would say so."

One Miami agent, Chris Mazella, does nothing but coordinate the drug investigative activities between the FBI in Florida and the Caribbean and the other federal, state, and local agencies.

"There is a tremendous amount of friction [with DEA]," he said. "DEA is supposedly the premier agency in drugs, but they work what I would consider to be midlevel and low-level drug targets." According to Mazella, "We should have one drug agency. We have twelve hundred agents working drugs [compared with thirty-five hundred DEA agents], but we still are like a stepchild. If we want to go overseas to do investigations, we have to clear it with DEA. That's bullshit. . . . The effort [against drugs] is significantly hampered by the inability of the agencies to really work together."[125]

"I think it's a waste," said Floyd I. Clarke, the deputy director of the FBI. "I think we spend inordinate amounts of time on interagency issues that is not productive in terms of accomplishing goals. I don't know what kind of funding goes into the office of the drug czar, the office of National Drug Control Policy. But why was that ever created? It was created because there wasn't a single entity to control the federal law enforcement drug concept."[126]

Lawn, the former FBI agent and former DEA administrator, acknowledged that the FBI aims for higher targets than does DEA, but he said drug cartels do not work like organized crime families and must be approached differently.

"It took the bureau several years to recognize that drug investigations could not be conducted the way a normal criminal investigation would be conducted," he said. "In drug syndicates, they are less structured. Even in penetrating to the heart, you never got to the heart. It was a many-headed dragon. The dragon will develop four or five other heads."[127]

Gavin, the special agent in charge of Miami, dismisses the reports of friction by saying he is friends with Tom Cash, the head of the DEA office in Miami.

"Do we disagree on things? Of course we do," Gavin said. "But when we disagree, the first part of the conversation might not be pretty. But it works out because we all understand each other. We work it out and laugh and joke about getting excited at first."

Known for his sense of humor and leadership abilities, Gavin weighs 210 pounds and is six foot one. He strides around the Miami office wearing a flowery tie and a 9-millimeter semiautomatic, his biceps bulging out of his shirt. Gavin bench presses 300 pounds. In his free time, he skis and cycles on a twelve-speed touring bike, taking thirty-two-mile trips.

Another of Gavin's pastimes is poking fun at Buck Revell, who is known throughout the bureau for his collection of plaques and trophies.

"There are no pictures here to show how important I am shaking hands with someone," Gavin said, pointing to the Waterford crystal, a print of a Colorado scene, and the fedora worn by Hoover that decorate his office. "I'm not into that kind of stuff. I have a theory that by the time they get through the front gate and past my secretary, if they don't know where they are, I'm not going to give them any clues."

A native of Revere, Massachusetts, Gavin became an FBI agent in 1967.

"I call it the Irish mother syndrome," he said. "If you're an Irish Catholic from Boston, you had to be either a priest, a cop, or a fireman. I didn't like heights, and celibacy disappeared with puberty. The only other choice I had was to be a cop."

Gavin is one of those agents who can't imagine a better job, who would like to pay the bureau for the fun he has had.

"I don't think there were two mornings in twenty-five years I didn't want to get up and go to work," he said. "Every day is a challenge. This is a dynamic place."

Working in a place with the stresses of Miami, agents must strike a balance: They must not let work impinge on their personal lives or begin to take themselves too seriously.

"People here have the ability to laugh at themselves, which I think is all important," he said. "Every morning when you shave that ugly face, you realize you have some strengths and weaknesses. You can't do it all."

"I always tell the kids [new agents], 'Look, that set of credentials will get you in the door the first time [to interview witnesses and suspects]. Whether or not you get in the second time will depend on your performance when you were there.' People aren't going to care about those credentials the second time. They'll say, 'This guy was a jerk when he came here, this gal was a jerk when she came here. They don't come back in.' If you are professional about it, you will get back numerous times. You are the salesman. The credentials are just the initial key. They'll change the lock on you if you're not good."

Some SACs tend to be remote and communicate with the troops through layers of management. Gavin is a hands-on man.

"I'm in squad rooms every single day sitting down, making supervisors very nervous," he said. "I start shooting the breeze, and they are looking out of their offices. 'What is he doing now, what are they telling him?' They learn it's not a challenge. I want to hear it from them, and from supervisors. I want to see what the real problems are. I want to know that they have a dog named Teddy and a daughter named Amy. To me, that makes a difference in trying to understand maybe why someone didn't perform one day."

Gavin encourages agents to tell him and their supervisors when they think they are on the wrong track. One of Gavin's first lessons in that regard was when he was a squad supervisor in St. Louis. One of the squad members clearly did not like the plan he had outlined on an undercover case but would not say so.

"I said here's what we are going to do. I got a lot of head shakes. All the body language you could possibly want to see told me he [the squad member] didn't like it. So I said to him, 'Obviously you don't agree.' 'No, do whatever you want to do.' I said, 'You are going to go out there and tell everyone how dumb I am for doing it this way. If you were a real man, you'd bring your way up now, but I guess you're not, because you don't have that in you.' That will bring the best out of most guys. He let me have it with both barrels right there.

"The minute he disclosed it, it was clear to everyone in that room it was much better. It was a way to not become too involved with someone and have him take you to the stolen property. . . . If we had done it my way, we would probably have had a 60 to 65 percent chance of success. With his way, we had a 95 percent chance. It worked.

"That's what management is all about. There is a difference between being a manager and a leader. If you can't figure it out, you are probably a manager," Gavin said.

Gavin's role model was Thomas Sheer, who was assistant director over the New York office and later Gavin's boss in the inspection division. Part rogue, part brilliant theoretician, Sheer motivated agents like few other bureau officials have. He was one of those bureau officials who generated both admiration and affection within the bureau.

"His briefcase always looked like an unmade bed," Gavin said. "But when the SWAT team was leaving the New York office when they had the Atlanta [prison] uprising, as they got in the buses with the blue lights to go to the airport, he was down on the street and patting them as they went out the door of the field office." Gavin, who was inspecting the New York office at the time, said Sheer would say to the agents as they climbed in the bus, "You're the best I got, Ralph. You go down and do us all proud and don't get hurt." Then he would repeat the same litany to the next agent.

"They each heard him say it, but they thought he lied to the other one. That was his style," Gavin said. "If the laboratory division had a clone machine, I would stick Tom Sheer in it."

Given the temptations and pressures, it is not surprising that Miami has had more than its share of agent misconduct and internal investigations. Just as Hoover feared, the bureau's involvement in drug investigations finally corrupted an agent.

Dan A. Mitrione, Jr., was the son of an Agency for International Development official who had attended the FBI's National Academy, a training school for police officers within the FBI Academy. After a left-wing guerrilla group in Uruguay tortured and killed him in 1970, the father's name went up on a wall of the academy in Quantico, Virginia, as a graduate who had been killed in the line of duty.

Now the story of what happened to the younger Mitrione, an

unusually handsome and likable agent, is an object lesson for new agents at the FBI Academy. As Walt H. Sirene described him to a class in ethics at Quantico, Mitrione Jr. became frustrated with the FBI's bureaucracy as he was working an undercover drug case. At the same time, an informant began to manipulate him and give him expensive gifts.

"He [Mitrione] was trying to get things approved," Sirene told a recent class. "They [the bureau] said, 'No, you don't do it that way, you have to do it this way.' The informant gave him a Rolex watch, many other gifts. He told a fellow agent with a tear in his eye that this informant was the father he barely knew. Somewhere along the line, the informant suggested they steal some cocaine off a shipment, which they did. Dan's share was $850,000.[128]

Mitrione pleaded guilty on March 14, 1985, to possessing and distributing ninety-two pounds of cocaine and receiving cash as a payoff for allowing distribution of cocaine in Florida, Pennsylvania, and other states. He was sentenced to ten years in prison.[129]

Friends of Mitrione attribute what happened to him to the pressures of working undercover. Without a firmly developed sense of self, it is possible to become subsumed in the world one is infiltrating.

Undercover investigations pose particular problems for female agents, who are often used in such operations because of their sex. In one well-known example in Miami, Linda C. Thompson was assigned to pose as a paralegal and as a girlfriend of Michael Guibilo, a violent criminal then in the Metropolitan Correctional Center in South Dade. A longtime government informant, Guibilo was awaiting action on bank robbery charges.

Seeking a lighter sentence, Guibilo offered information on another prisoner's plans to knock off an assistant U.S. Attorney. The bureau wanted to debrief him and obtain evidence from him without arousing the suspicions of guards and other prisoners. So Thompson, a pretty thirty-nine-year-old with shoulder-length blond hair and a quick laugh, was asked to meet with Guibilo in prison and get him to tape record conversations of the fellow prisoner who was plotting to kill the prosecutor.

Thompson played her part very well—some would say too well. But the real problem lay with Thompson's supervisors, for the plan was ill-conceived from the start. At the time, Thompson was on a white collar crime squad and had had no experience with organized crime or undercover work investigating crimes. She received none of the training the bureau normally gives agents who work undercover. Initially, she was to meet with Guibilo only a few times. But eventually she wound up meeting with him as many as four times a week. It is one thing to play girlfriend occasionally. It is another to spend weeks playing that role with a man in prison who is both manipulative and dangerous.

Trouble started when the guards complained that during their meetings, Thompson and Guibilo were kissing passionately. The prison authorities knew that the FBI had an interest in her meetings with him, but they did not know that Thompson was an agent.

The complaints filtered back to the Miami office, which removed Thompson from the case and told her to break off her relationship with Guibilo. However, according to the prison's computerized records, Guibilo subsequently called Thompson's direct line several more times in the spring of 1991. One call lasted thirty-eight minutes.

Concerned that she might have disclosed bureau secrets or made promises to Guibilo about his prosecution, the bureau began an investigation of Thompson by the Office of Professional Responsibility (OPR), the bureau's internal gumshoes. As part of that inquiry, she underwent a polygraph test.

Thompson admitted to kissing the prisoner, saying that that was exactly what she was supposed to do to play her role convincingly. She passed the test when she denied having made promises to Guibilo or given away too much information. But it appeared that she was afraid of Guibilo and did not act firmly enough in cutting off contact with him.

In deciding how male or female agents may behave with informants, the bureau draws the line at kissing.

"They are not allowed to use drugs, they are not allowed to have sex with anybody," said David Binney, the chief of OPR. "There are a lot of restrictions on what they can do. If they are in an undercover role, probably kissing is okay. You have to maintain that distance to conduct a good investigation."

With justification, Thompson, who is originally from Huntsville, Alabama, said the problem was that the bureau had set up a scenario that could lead only to trouble.

"They seemed to have the opinion that any woman can play the girlfriend," she said in a southern drawl. "It can be a pretty intense situation sometimes. They didn't give me any training or guidance. . . . The bureau never would have sent a man in there to play a homosexual lover, but in a heartbeat they will send a woman."[130]

Originally, Thompson said, her supervisors wanted her to see Guibilo once or twice a week. Then she was told to see him more often and see some of his friends as well, some of whom were murderers.

"I didn't start to fall for him, but he did for me. But he had been there [in jail] for six months and had not had any visitors at all, and then they send me in there to play his girlfriend. So what do they expect is going to happen?" she said.

Thompson said she only kissed Guibilo. "He did not feel me up. Absolutely not. Number one, he never tried to do that, and number two, I wouldn't have let him. That was over and beyond anything I had to do. . . . He didn't push. I think he is from the old Italian school. I think he really cared about me, and I think he really respected me. . . . He fell for me, but I'm sorry. It was work for me. I had never played that role before. I had never worked organized crime before. It was some scary stuff."

Thompson said she continued to talk with Guibilo after she was told to break it off partly because she was afraid of what some of his friends might try to do to her if she did not go along and partly to make sure he continued to cooperate with the bureau.

"He was not getting along well with the case agent. He would call me," she said. "I did what I thought I had to do for the case. . . . I was told to play a paralegal and his girlfriend, so I did that the best way I knew. . . . I felt this guy [one of Guibilo's friends] was trying to kill me," she said, referring to another prisoner on whom she was gathering evidence. "The bureau didn't care. Not only didn't they care, but they turned this OPR inquiry on me after I did all this. It was a nightmare."

Thompson said that because she was afraid, she asked her supervisors to delay revealing her true identity to the man who was eventually convicted in the case.

"They just laughed at me," she said. " 'I'm overreacting.' There were comments about being female."

As is common during internal investigations, false rumors began to reverberate throughout the bureau about Thompson and what she had done with Guibilo.

"It's all over the bureau," Thompson said. "It's not just Miami. Friends called me and said, 'Are you okay?' "

Karen E. Gardner, an agent in Los Angeles, said the rumor mill in the bureau works overtime when female agents are involved.

"If it's a female agent, it's, 'Jeez, did you hear the latest female agent story out of New York or Dallas?' " Gardner said.

When she was a new agent in Sacramento, Gardner and eight other female agents decided to make up a story about one of them and see how long it took to get around.

"We said what we should do is say we had a Bucar accident," Gardner said, using FBI jargon for a bureau car, "and the reason was she [the agent who was the subject of the story] had taken an antihistamine and had had a beer at lunch, and she wrapped the car around a tree. It wasn't just any car, it was the SAC's car. We made up this whole story. Within two hours, we heard it back. We made one call to one field office, and two hours later it made it to New York."

Thompson said she has learned that the bureau is not the "family" it likes to portray itself as being. "The bureau moves you around and tears you from your family and support group, so you become very dependent on the bureau. I bought into the myth of the bureau as a family. I went to them and asked them not to identify me. I said, 'Don't do that to me.' I had a listed number. It was a harsh reality for me. The bureau is not what I thought it was.

"I have learned some hard lessons," Gardner added. "I took my work too seriously. I did whatever I was asked to do, and I would work endless hours just because I wanted it done right. It came back to haunt me."

As a result of Guibilo's help, James R. Monaco was convicted of drug conspiracy and plotting to kill Assistant U.S. Attorney Barbara Petras, who had prosecuted him on the drug charges. He got a prison term of fifty years.[131]

Thompson filed a complaint under Equal Employment Opportunity laws, claiming that she had been targeted because she is a woman. That only delayed the OPR investigation, which continues almost two years after it started—testimony to a truism within the FBI that the bureau discriminates against everyone.

"Every agent in the bureau thinks he is being discriminated against," said Mazella, the Miami agent. "It doesn't matter whether you are white, black, Hispanic, male, or female. . . . There is a great deal of animosity in the sense that many years of extreme disciplinary action and hardship have always existed. Under Hoover, there was never any recourse."

As part of the OPR investigation, the bureau is looking at the conduct of Thompson's supervisors as well as her actions. Meanwhile, she is still investigating white collar crime, which she enjoys because of its complexity.

"I'm still here, and I'm still kicking," she said.

If the Thompson case drew a lot of attention in the Miami field office, it was nothing compared with the amount of interest generated by Frank and Suzanne Monserrate, the married FBI agents who were held up at gunpoint after leaving the Playhouse in Perrine, a suburb south of Miami.[132]

Paul Miller, the media representative in Miami, first learned that there was a problem when the office called him just after 2:00 on Sunday morning, January 4, 1987.

"They said there had been a shooting of one of our agents, Sue Monserrate, whom I knew," Miller said.

To Miller, the Playhouse sounded like a dinner theater. He had no idea it was a sex club. Miller turned on his siren and flashing blue light and raced to the scene at 9551 SW One Hundred Sixty-eighth Street. There, he noticed that national network reporters, not just local television stations, had already arrived. Miller wondered why the networks would send reporters to cover a shooting of an off duty FBI agent in Miami.

From police on the scene, he picked up the basic facts: The Monserrates had left the club at 2:05 A.M. when Chester Williams confronted them and demanded their money. Williams, who had an extensive criminal record, began ripping the gold chains off Sue Monserrate's neck. Frank Monserrate was not carrying his gun, but he knew his wife had hers in her purse. When Williams demanded money, Suzanne Monserrate reached into her purse to get her wallet. At that point, Frank Monserrate grabbed his wife's .38-caliber revolver from her purse and shot Williams several times, fatally wounding him. Meanwhile, Williams had shot and wounded Sue Monserrate in her back.[133]

"I saw Bill Johnson, the media person for the police department," Miller said. "I asked, 'How is she doing?' He said, 'I can tell you don't know what this is about. Do you know what this Playhouse is? It's a swingers' club.' "[134]

Like other agents who knew Suzanne Monserrate, Miller was shocked. Pretty and blond, Monserrate was a respected agent who had a fresh, midwestern look. She was the principal relief supervisor on a squad that handled background investigations and coordinated the work of three of Miami's resident agencies or satellite offices.

Frank Monserrate worked on a terrorism squad. Both agents had received performance appraisals of "superior." The only higher rating is "exceptional."

"She acted very professionally," Miller said. "I always thought she was very prim and proper. The last thing in my mind was that she might be involved in swinging."

Miller sees his job as getting out news as quickly as possible. "That's the challenge of my job, to articulate what occurred," Miller said. "They [the media] expect it. If you don't give it to them or do something, they'll say whatever they can and grab someone on the street."

Miller appeared on all the newscasts. On Channel 4 in Miami, he said, "She is hopefully recovering quickly. An agent can carry a weapon at any time. They are not required to do so while off duty."

Miller adroitly sidestepped the fact that the Playhouse was a sex club by saying honestly that he did not know if the Monserrates had, in fact, engaged in swinging there. But the club's brochure left little doubt that anyone who did not swing at the club would feel like a person wearing a golf shirt at a black tie affair.

For an annual membership of $150 and an additional nightly charge, the club offered "a blending of today's sounds, cozy conversation, light dancing, rapturous coed hot tubs, sophisticated movies . . ." At the Playhouse, ". . . your activities are limited only by your imagination," claimed the brochure, which was illustrated with drawings of scantily clad women and men.

The club's calendar of future events included "The Big Pillow Fight! Wear your favorite pajamas through the front door and get a $5 discount"; "Exotic Sexy Treasure Hunt: Hunt for sexy things and win sexy things"; and "Big, Big Easter Hunt: Come and Hunt for your favorite bunny or buns."

Every Friday, the club had a wet T-shirt and wet jock-strap contest. On Saturdays, which was when the Monserrates attended, only couples were allowed.[135]

The *Miami Herald* dispatched a male and a female reporter to the club and reported that its facilities included the Orgy Room, an adult movie room, the Oral Room, and the Mattress Room, where large mattresses were lined up side by side.[136]

As is standard in any shooting, the bureau's inspection division began an investigation. While the inspectors found that Frank Monserrate had acted properly in shooting the robber, they determined that the club does indeed cater to swingers. The inspectors carefully defined the practice as spouses or couples who engage in "swapping for sexual purposes." An agent who went to the club reported that "open and essentially uninhibited sexual activity between consenting adults was accepted practice" there. The agent saw coed locker rooms, coed showers, hot tubs, and rooms that contained wall-to-wall beds. A sign at the entrance to one section warned that all clothing must be removed before entering.

The investigators found that the Monserrates had been at the club under fictitious names, that there were reports of illegal narcotics use at the club, and that the media had covered the incident extensively—in other words, the bureau was red faced. Based on these factors, the inspectors referred the case to the FBI's OPR within the inspection division.[137]

When interviewed at the hospital by a supervisor from the Miami field office, Frank Monserrate volunteered that he and Suzanne—who recovered fully from her wound—had been to the club on only one prior occasion. He said they had gone to the club on the evening of the robbery attempt only because another couple whom they knew had suggested they join them there.

In a signed, sworn statement given to investigators from OPR on January 8, 1987, Frank Monserrate said that he and his wife had joined the club to enhance their sexual relationship and had never exchanged partners at the club. However, he said, they had been members of the club for two years. In contrast to his earlier statement, he said he had gone to the club at least fifteen times.

That evening, Suzanne Monserrate gave a signed, sworn statement to OPR saying that their interest in joining the club was primarily voyeuristic. She acknowledged that while at the club she and her husband had engaged in intercourse, but only in the privacy of a cubicle.

"At no time during our two-year membership at the Playhouse did I ever pair off with any other couple or person for sexual purposes," she said.

Their stories quickly fell apart. Both Monserrates had denied having sex with the couple who supposedly had invited them to the club that fateful night. Frank said he had never met with the couple outside the club, and Suzanne said they had been to their home on one occasion. Yet, later that evening, OPR interviewed the other couple at their home. Describing themselves as "dedicated swingers," they said they had met the Monserrates at the club two years earlier and had entertained them at parties at their home five or six times. They declined to say if the Monserrates had engaged in swinging.

The following morning, FBI agents told Frank Monserrate they had developed information that contradicted what he had said in his sworn statement. He then admitted that he had not been entirely truthful in that statement.

At that point, Frank "disclosed that he and his wife did, in fact, fully participate in sexual activities at [the club], to include swapping spouses," according to the OPR report. The swapping was both with the other couple who had been interviewed the night before and with "several other couples whose identities he does not know and whose names he could not now recall."

It was downhill from then on.

On January 18, Frank gave another signed, sworn statement. As he had earlier, he admitted that he had not been truthful in his previous statement. This time, he said he and Suzanne had regularly attended parties at the other couple's home and had had sex with them and with other couples there.

Two days later, Suzanne Monserrate admitted for the first time that she and Frank had "engaged in sexual intercourse with other people" at the club during their two years of membership. Retracting other information she had given previously, she said that she had "also participated in oral sex and engaged in sexual activity with other females at the club."[138]

In July 1987, the FBI fired both Monserrates. What it came down to was that FBI agents simply don't go to sex clubs. The Monserrates might have received only suspensions, except that they lied about it as well. Moreover, Suzanne Monserrate had committed a sin almost as bad as going to a sex club—by checking her handgun and FBI credentials with an employee of the club. Clearly, it would be difficult to have sex while wearing a gun and a badge. But FBI agents are never supposed to relinquish their guns and credentials. Nowhere in the OPR report did the FBI give Frank Monserrate credit for quick thinking when he grabbed his wife's gun from her purse.

In their defense, the Monserrates and their lawyer told the bureau that they had the right to associate with anyone they wanted. They said the fact that they used an alias at the club only supported their contention that they were sensitive to their position of trust when attending the club. Suzanne said her lack of candor had been caused by her medical condition as she recovered from her wound.

A year later, the *Miami Herald* quoted Frank Monserrate as saying he was angry because William Wells, then the special agent in charge of the Miami office, had fired him for off-duty actions.

"He [Wells] didn't care what the facts were. He wanted us out,"

Frank said. He refused to say what he and his wife had been doing in the club.

"If it's legal, they have no right to bother you," he said.[139]

Indeed, just what they were doing in the club, and the fact that they had lied about it repeatedly, never came out. As is common in internal discipline actions, only one part of the story circulated within the bureau—the fact that the Monserrates had been caught going to a sex club. Agents thought that was the sole reason for their firing.

In fact, "It was more than going to a sex club," said John E. Otto, who approved the dismissal as acting FBI director. "There was lack of candor. There were a variety of other things that were tied up in that. There was no justification for the whole conduct situation from beginning to end."[140]

In commenting for this book, Frank Monserrate said that others who had displayed lack of candor during OPR investigations were not fired.[141]

In analyzing the case, the OPR noted that defense attorneys in future criminal cases investigated by the Monserrates could point to their lack of candor to undermine their testimony. The OPR inquiry found that no illegal drugs were used at the club. In fact, the club had signs warning against use of drugs. But because of their untruthfulness, their poor judgment in exposing themselves to potential blackmail, and their "loss of effectiveness" because of the public attention focused on their membership, it was felt that the Monserrates should be dismissed. Shortly after they were fired, they divorced.

In supporting its conclusion that the agents had lost their effectiveness, the OPR appended to its report a newspaper clipping on the case. Mailed anonymously to FBI headquarters, the clip had Suzanne Monserrate's name circled in red. An arrow pointed to a scribbled notation at the top of the page: "I f—— her in the ass!! ha! ha! ha!"[142]

In a surprise ending, the Monserrates appealed their dismissal to the Equal Employment Opportunity Commission, claiming that Suzanne had been fired because she is female and Frank had been fired because he is Hispanic. In 1992, the EEOC sided with the Monserrates and ordered them reinstated with back pay and interest.[143] Furious bureau officials vowed to appeal, but they lost.

The EEOC decided the Monserrates' lack of candor was insignificant. True, the agents had not falsified evidence or given false testimony against a defendant. But they had repeatedly changed their stories under oath to cover up their own activities. The thought of such agents being entrusted with investigating others was not reassuring. Moreover, a defense attorney, faced with testimony from either of the agents in a criminal proceeding, would rightly be able to call into question their credibility based on their previous performance. Nonetheless, in accordance with the EEOC decision, the bureau began the job of retraining the two former agents before again placing them on the rolls.

"If we can't fire agents for lying as they did, we might as well forget about discipline in the bureau," said one high-ranking FBI official.

Within the bureau, it is an article of faith that J. Edgar Hoover, who never wanted female FBI agents in the first place, will return to settle scores over the direction the bureau has taken since his death. If there were ever a reason for his return, this case was it.

6
Inspection Division: Tracking a Hot Dog Cart

● **If there is one thing FBI agents** hate about the bureau, it is the inspection division and particularly its Office of Professional Responsibility (OPR), which investigates FBI employees' misconduct. In the Hoover era, the inspection division was used arbitrarily as a tool to control agents. No matter what they found, the inspectors were to finger a respectable number of agents.

"The inspection staff used to walk in and say, 'Who can take a hit?' " said David G. Binney, who now heads the OPR. " 'Who can take a letter of censure and it won't affect his pay for the year?' They would come every year, and it was very haphazard. If you had just received your promotion to GS-13, and you were not due for another increase for two years, they would say, 'Dave Binney can take a hit this year. But don't get Joe Jones because he is coming up next month for his promotion.' They would go through your files and say, 'On this case, you didn't put something in the files for forty-five days.' 'Okay. You got me.' This was under Hoover and spilled into the Kelley days."[144]

In 1967, members of the inspection staff saw Phillip M. King, an agent in the Washington metropolitan field office, drinking coffee on the job at what was then the Holloway House cafeteria on Fourteenth Street NW.*

---

* The Washington metropolitan field office was then called the Washington field office.

Under Hoover, clerks could drink coffee in the office, but during work hours agents could not drink coffee in or out of the office. Apparently, drinking coffee did not comport with the image Hoover wanted to convey of hardworking supermen who never took a break. As a result, agents took more time off from work in search of coffee-shops than they would have spent just drinking coffee at their desks.

The inspectors demanded to know the identities of the other two agents drinking coffee with King. When King refused, the inspectors said they would review photos of the several hundred agents in the field office looking for the suspects. King finally agreed to ask the other two offenders to get in touch with the inspectors, and they did.

"In my signed statement I admitted drinking coffee, I said I had done it before, and I would do it again," King said.

All three agents were transferred, put on probation for six months, and given a letter of censure. While letters of censure can temporarily put a crimp in a bureau career, they are forgotten after a year or two.[145]

When King left Washington, the field office gave him a party and presented him with a coffee cup that said "Holloway House" on it. The office also gave him a cartoon that depicted him leaving Washington. Sticking out of his back pocket was the butt end of a pistol. In his hand he clutched a coffee cup from Holloway House.

"The amount of hours saved by allowing coffee [after Hoover died] was incredible," said Andrew S. Manning, the media representative at the Baltimore field office. "Agents couldn't go across the street to have coffee because they would get caught. Some did. I was in Boston once when the SAC got word that some agents were drinking coffee across the street. He walked over there and caught them. So consequently they went farther away [to drink coffee]. It was another one of those ridiculous things that needed to be changed—a lot of little irritants that made it difficult to do your job."[146]

Hoover's FBI left no room for agent misconduct, so the bureau simply denied it existed. If an agent got into trouble or cheated on his expense vouchers, he was quietly fired or told to resign. In most cases, no one ever knew that misconduct had occurred. Since everything tended to be covered up, it is difficult to pinpoint how prosecutions were handled. If an offense occurred outside of work, an agent might be prosecuted after he left the bureau. If an agent committed a crime in connection with bureau work, he would be severed but—because of the embarrassment it would bring to the FBI—not prosecuted.

"Sometimes managers in the bureau in the old days were measured by how many problems they had in their office," said James Greenleaf, the FBI's associate deputy director for administration. "The way to solve that was to push it under the table. In today's bureau, it's important that managers address those problems, and we measure them by the way they handle them. They get in real trouble if we find out they swept them under the table."

"The bureau used to brag that no agent was ever convicted of a crime while in the bureau," Binney said. "The reason was he resigned, and the next day he got arrested. That was the approach Hoover used. In a more open society, we take our lumps."

Yet today, as before, very few cases of employee misconduct become public. Even statistics on discipline, as opposed to the details of actual cases, are a closely guarded secret. The FBI's quarterly report on disciplinary matters specifically warns special agents in charge of field offices not to share the figures with members of the news media. If quarterly reports are shown to supervisors or squads, "a charge-out procedure must be instituted to ensure proper accountability for all copies," the cover sheets warn.

For this book, successive layers of FBI management up to the level of assistant director refused to reveal the figures. Only after William Sessions interceded did the bureau release the statistics. Those figures show that in one recent year, the bureau investigated 1,304 of its 23,700 agent and support employees. Of these investigations, 775 resulted in disciplinary action, ranging from censure to dismissal. In that same year, 25 employees were dismissed, 12 were demoted, and 13 were suspended for fourteen days or more. Of the employees dismissed, 21 were clerks and 4 were agents. Another 67 employees—56 clerks and 11 agents—resigned while under investigation. Those who either were dismissed or resigned represented 0.4 percent of the total employees.[147]

Citing privacy concerns, the FBI will not disclose details of individual cases, even though misconduct by law enforcement officers is a matter of legitimate public concern. Nonetheless, some of the incidents have become public through court cases, and the details of others have been learned through sources. The cases range from the funny to the tragic, from drinking in bureau cars to misusing information from FBI files, from becoming too friendly with informants to making up reports of investigations, from misusing FBI credentials to lying before grand juries, from taking drugs to taking a cut of drug sales, from sexual misconduct to espionage and murder. What they show is that, contrary to the image the bureau conveyed under Hoover, FBI agents are human, subject to the same frailties as the rest of society.

Besides the story of the New York agent who was said to have flashed his credentials to get more roast beef on his sandwich, probably no story of employee misconduct is more widely told than the tale of the hot dog cart. According to the legend, an agent in Indianapolis had a side business of selling hot dogs from a cart. Every morning, he would hitch the hot dog cart to his bureau car and pull it to a local fairground. His girlfriend would go with him, and she would sell hot dogs at circuses or carnivals until the agent picked up the cart at night.

One morning, the agent was driving to the fairground when he heard a report of a bank robbery over his FBI radio. He could not very well drive to the scene dragging a hot dog cart. So he got out of the car and nonchalantly called the field office from a pay phone.

"Anything cooking?" he asked.

"We have a bank robbery," he was told.

The agent told his girlfriend to drive the FBI car to the fairground. Meanwhile, he hopped in a taxi and went to the scene of the robbery. On the way to the fairground, the car got a flat tire. The girlfriend got on the car radio and asked the FBI dispatcher for help. When the agents saw the hot dog cart attached to the car, they reported it to the field office. As a result, the agent was fired.

It was a good story, but the facts are a little more complicated. According to the agent who investigated the case for OPR and his supervisor, the agent in Indianapolis had gotten over his head financially. One way he was trying to recoup was by selling corn dogs on the side. Corn dogs are cornmeal-dipped hot dogs that are deep fried.

It was true that the agent drove the cart to the fairground every day and that his bureau car got a flat tire. But the agent's girlfriend was driving the FBI car when the flat occurred, and the agent was not with her. Nor was the cart hitched to the car. However, the hitch for the cart was attached to the rear bumper. When the bureau mechanics arrived, they saw the hitch for the hot dog cart but did nothing about it. Nor did they report the fact that the agent's girlfriend was driving the car.

"It gives you an indication of the leadership of the office," said Binney, the agent who did the OPR investigation.

The agent, who was married, had several girlfriends. Six months after the flat tire incident, two of the girlfriends found out about each other. It was then that the women told the bureau about the agent's activities, including his use of a bureau car to tow the hot dog cart. During the ensuing investigation, the agent resigned.[148]

Over the years, the bureau has had difficulty in dealing with marginal employees—people who really should not be agents but who never do anything quite bad enough to get them fired. That was the case with Richard W. Miller, who eventually did do something bad enough to get him not only fired but convicted of espionage.

Before he became involved in espionage, Miller was "a terrible agent," said Weldon Kennedy, who worked with him briefly in Puerto Rico and later became an assistant FBI director. "I hope there are not a lot like that. But I'm sure there are. There are probably a lot of agents that shouldn't be there. There are no doubt some in every field office in this country."

While FBI agents would not hesitate to turn in another agent who had clearly done something illegal, they have trouble dealing with an agent who merely shows poor judgment or is eccentric.

"As wacky as he was, he was still an FBI agent," Kennedy said. "He had done some good things. He didn't come up to the standard I thought an FBI agent should have. Would I then dime him out? I didn't know of anything he did that was illegal."

"Probably 20 percent of the agents are real go-getters, just dynamos," said Robert E. Lill, who headed the bureau's undercover program at headquarters. "Sixty percent are pluggers. Day in and day out, they do a good job. They are there when you need them. They work on the big cases and keep other balloons in the air also. Then probably 20 percent are on the downside who are dogging it."

"I think there has been an institutional reluctance to cashier them," William Webster said of marginal FBI employees. "They try to find something for them to do, especially if they have a family and are getting close to retiring. Unless they have done something morally or criminally unacceptable, there has been a reluctance. We tried to have people work with them."[149]

All FBI employees are in the excepted service, meaning that they are outside of normal civil service rules and can be fired and disciplined more easily than can other government employees. Yet, they still can appeal personnel decisions through the courts, and usually do.

"It's very difficult even in an excepted service, when you consider the rights of a person, to terminate an employee," said Baker, the assistant director over the criminal investigative division. "You have to have a very strong case to do that. You hear grousing from others that the guy is worthless, but the investigators may not have been able to verify all that. Even with Miller, the allegations of selling Amway products on the job could not be pinned down, even though it was common knowledge."

In most cases, the agents who get in serious trouble were considered model employees before their transgressions came out. Dan A. Mitrione, Jr., a Miami agent, was highly regarded before he pleaded guilty in 1985 to federal charges that he had accepted $850,000 in bribes and payoffs from a Florida cocaine ring. Likewise, Mark S. Putnam had had no previous apparent problems, before he pleaded guilty in 1990 to strangling to death an informer with whom he had been having an affair and had impregnated in Kentucky.

To agents, the most shocking case of a well-regarded agent going astray was that of H. Edward Tickel, Jr. A stocky man with brown hair, Tickel was the FBI's top break-in artist, a man who could pick almost any lock, crack any safe, and enter any home or embassy without creating suspicion. Because of his specialty, some of the bureau's most precious secrets were entrusted to Tickel, including the fact that the FBI had bugged certain Soviet bloc embassies, as well as the homes of leading mafia figures. It was Tickel who was chosen to change the locks on William Webster's home in Bethesda, Maryland, after Webster became FBI director.

"He was exceptional," said William A. (Al) Bayse, assistant director over the technical services division.

The son of a former FBI agent, Tickel graduated from Henderson State University and obtained an M.S. in forensic sciences from George Washington University. Tickel became an agent in 1969 and was assigned to the technical services division. Among other things, the division installs wiretaps and electronic bugs.

Tickel was widely admired within the bureau and had many bureau friends, including James Greenleaf, who was then assistant director over the laboratory and later became associate deputy director of the FBI. Tickel gave lavish parties and had a collection of Porsches and horses at his house on a five-acre lot in Virginia. He owned a ten-thousand-dollar boat as well.

"He was so highly regarded and so highly respected," Greenleaf said. "He was living a little above his means, but we thought it was from royalties from inventing a lock."

Then, around 5:30 P.M. on April 16, 1980, Earl Thornton, an FBI janitor, opened the door to the FBI Federal Credit Union on the eighth floor of headquarters, next to the FBI's cafeteria. Thornton turned on the lights and was about to start vacuuming when he saw Tickel crouched behind the counter, the safe open behind him. In it was $260,000.

"Tickel jumps up and says, 'Halt, FBI!' " said Paul K. Minor, the FBI polygrapher who later tested Tickel's veracity. "Tickel said he was called because the door was unlocked. He checked it and saw a black man come in. He crouched down and arrested him," Minor said.[150]

But Thornton said that the door was locked when he came in. Moreover, no one could find the person who supposedly had called Tickel for help.

"His [Tickel's] story wasn't believed because the door was locked, the safe was open, and he waited too long to jump up," Minor said. Ultimately, Tickel failed a lie detector test on whether he was trying to burglarize the credit union.[151]

"I polygraphed him, and he failed," Minor said. "There were no admissions. Except when he left [the polygraph room], he said, 'From the beginning, I knew this might come down to a contest between experts. I respect you very much.' We shook hands, and he left. In my mind, it was a way of confirming that I was right: 'I can't tell you anything, but you are good, and you did good.' "

After an investigation by the OPR, the bureau referred the case to the Justice Department. John P. Hume, then a prosecutor in the U.S. Attorney's office in Washington, was placed in charge of it. Hume found that the OPR had previously investigated Tickel because he had used his authority as an FBI agent to help a friend who was being investigated as a suspect in a theft of $200,000 in jewelry in North Carolina.

Hume obtained Tickel's credit card records and found that he had lied when he denied having been in North Carolina when the theft took place. Ultimately, Hume found that Tickel himself was involved in selling the rings and loose diamonds that had been stolen. He also found that he was involved in selling stolen cars and stealing two-way FBI radios for friends.

Tickel was acquitted in federal court in Washington of breaking in to the credit union. However, he pleaded guilty to having taken the radios. After a nine-day trial, Tickel was also convicted in Alexandria, Virginia, of charges connected with the jewelry theft—interstate transportation of stolen goods, making false statements, obstruction of justice, and tax evasion. For these charges, he received a prison term of eight years. And he was convicted in Loudoun County in Virginia of receiving $120,000 in stolen cars and other items.[152]

During the trial in Alexandria, a half-dozen FBI agents agreed to testify to Tickel's good character.

"He was the type of guy who would schmooze everybody," Hume said. "He couldn't wait to do a favor for you. He was always quick to impress people with gifts, parties."

But Tickel lost the agents' support when he claimed that the charges against him had been concocted by then FBI director William Webster. Webster was out to get him, according to Tickel, because he had reported to him illegal entries by the FBI in organized crime cases.

"I said to these guys, 'Your friend Tickel said Webster is a liar. Does that change your testimony?' They said yes," Hume said.[153]

In an affidavit filed in court, Webster said that he had no recollection of having met or talked with Tickel.

Generally suspicious, FBI agents often lose their objectivity when it comes to one of their own. When an agent is suspended or fired for breaking rules, they often take up a collection to help him out. Sometimes the agents do not know all the facts in the case. Other times they simply believe that one way or another, the bureau was unfair and contributed to the agent's malfeasance—often a perception left over from the Hoover era, when discipline was meted out arbitrarily. Yet, those same agents turn a deaf ear when people they have arrested claim that their employers' actions contributed to their criminal conduct.

"It's not so much whether he did it or deserved it, but the individual usually has family and other commitments," said D. Caroll Toohey, assistant director over the inspection division, who has himself contributed money to agents who were suspended. "I think a lot of times they don't know the facts. They are friends, and they hear one side of the story. The other side is not made public. The individual has the right to privacy. He may say they didn't treat me fairly. In many cases, agents know there is a problem. But he still may be a friend even though he got in trouble. Perhaps he drank too much and wrecks his [FBI] auto. I differentiate that from someone who willfully does something wrong like taking money. I don't think there would be any question on those types of incidents."

"It is, 'There but for the grace of God go I,' " said Weldon Kennedy, who heads the administrative services division. "I mean we have manuals full of rules. You can break those rules without even knowing you broke them. They are three to four inches thick. I'm not talking about criminal acts or violating rights. I'm fairly certain that no one took up a collection for Miller or Mitrione."

One person who did not agree to testify on Tickel's behalf was Greenleaf.

"The day that credit union thing went down was the last time I talked with him. I felt there was something wrong," he said. "I lost a friend."

At the end of the proceedings, Tickel was charged in Prince George's County with having sex with a daughter of one of his many lawyers. The daughter, who was twenty at the time, had a learning disability and epilepsy. Tickel pleaded guilty to a second-degree sex offense—having sex with force or the threat of force. His twenty-year sentence for that crime ran concurrently with federal sentences he was already serving.[154]

"He [the lawyer whose daughter Tickel victimized] was generous in dealing with people like Tickel," said Hume, now with a Washington law firm. "Tickel took advantage of him."

An even more bizarre case that never came out involved Harry L. Peel, an unusually well-liked FBI polygraph examiner in Jacksonville, Florida. Peel committed suicide after the OPR began investigating his work and lifestyle. Most field offices have a polygraph examiner, but the polygraph unit at headquarters reviews the work. Before the results of a polygraph exam are considered valid, the polygraph unit must certify them correct.

As the FBI's senior polygraph examiner at the time, Paul Minor was the highest-ranking examiner in the unit. He first learned that something was amiss when he got a call in 1983 from the special agent in charge of the Jacksonville office, where Peel was based.

"He [the SAC] said he was retiring, and he would like me to keep Harry close to home. He said there had been an incident where Harry had been traveling on the road. . . . He had been arrested in a shopping center and had allegedly solicited another male who was an undercover person, possibly a police officer," Minor said.[155]

"I mulled it over and told the section chief," Minor said. "I thought he probably should have been returned to regular investigative duties. Polygraph probably was not where he should be. That was my recommendation. . . . Ultimately, it was decided not to do that, not to do anything. I thought that was pretty amazing. I thought it was a big mistake. That was probably responsible for what did happen."

In 1985, claiming violations of local ordinances, police again picked up Peel, this time at a beach in Florida frequented by homo-sexuals. As in the earlier incident, Peel, a balding man with a gray beard and a gravelly voice, had no identification on him. When the police found out that he was an FBI agent, they called the field office in Jacksonville.

"I got to thinking then about the tests he had been doing," Minor said. "We kept up closely with polygraph examiner statistics: how many confessions, how many were lying, how many telling the truth. I noticed that his truthful rate was higher than average. I was thinking about it. I asked a secretary to get a bunch of Harry's charts. The thought was maybe there was a trade-off for sex. I knew there would be a lot of questions, and they weren't going to go away."

Minor found serious anomalies. In giving polygraph tests, poly-graph examiners start by asking control questions to see how sub-jects respond. They may, for example, ask for the subject's birthdate. When the subject tells the truth, few physiological reactions are noticed. Then the examiner may ask if the subject has ever cheated on his income taxes or on his wife. Knowing that many people have done so, the examiner can detect a much greater response if the subject lies in response to the question.

Peel's charts showed an unusual pattern. When Peel asked ques-tions that the subject could be expected to answer truthfully, he drew out the questions, as if trying to make them seem more sig-nificant. That could be seen on the charts because they show the time that elapses between a question and a response. Sensing that the examiner considered them important, the subject would show a greater response. By comparison, heightened responses to ques-tions that the subject was lying about would not appear as lies because the peaks they created on the charts were not any higher than the peaks from control questions.

By then, the OPR was investigating Peel over his encounter with the police. When Minor told the OPR about the charts, the office called Peel in for questioning. Meanwhile, Minor confronted Peel with his discovery.

"Harry admitted he had falsified the charts," Minor said. "He said the reason he falsified the charts was to make sure they were very clear. Once he decided they were telling the truth, he wanted to make sure the charts had no trouble at headquarters when they came through for review.

"By pausing," Minor said, "he created reactions at control ques-tions rather than at the relevant questions. It was an artificial creation. It was readily apparent. The examiners should have seen it, but, quite frankly, the review officers were fairly inexperienced."

Peel's apparent motive was simply to look better to his superiors. If the polygraph results were exaggerated, there would be less chance that he would be questioned about them.

"Now I realize that his secret life may have made him feel defensive and inadequate," Minor said.

Whether Peel, in the process, may have passed subjects that he should not have passed is not known.

"What he said was he wanted to make sure they came out truthful if he thought they were truthful," Minor said. "But how does he know they are truthful until he tests them? He is coming up with an opinion. Someone walks in, and he says, 'Well, I think they sound good. I'll make sure they pass.' That's what he was doing."

When Peel was in Washington, the OPR assigned agents from the Washington metropolitan field office to conduct surveillance of him to see if he went to homosexual bars. He did not. When he returned to Jacksonville on May 2, 1986, Peel shot himself with his service revolver. His daughter found his body in his car in a shopping center. In his desk at work, agents found a note.

"I was just trying to be fair," Peel had written.

The case still tortures Minor and others involved in it.

"I regret we didn't spend more time with him the day he confessed, to make sure we didn't take everything away from him and leave him with something," Minor said. "Leave him with some feeling of well-being, that everything wasn't lost. That we still like you. Maybe if we had taken him out to have a beer afterward, that would have been good."

Invariably, what gets FBI agents into the most jams is lying during an internal investigation. The classic example was Robert S. Friedrick, a Cleveland agent who for five years was the bureau's contact with Jackie Presser. At the time, Presser was president of the Teamsters Union. Since 1974, he had been a bureau informant on mafia infiltration of the Teamsters. When the Labor Department started investigating Presser for paying $700,000 in union funds to bogus employees, the FBI could do nothing to stop it. In 1975, Presser was indicted in connection with the employees, and Friedrick took it upon himself to claim that the bureau had approved Presser's actions. In fact, the bureau was aware that Presser had placed some ghost employees on the payroll; it had taken no action because Presser insisted that his credibility with the union would be diminished if he did not approve some of the requested payments. But the bureau was not aware of the phony employees on whom the Labor Department was focusing.

Friedrick not only lied about the bureau approvals, he tried to get Presser and other FBI agents to do the same thing. Friedrick was indicted for perjury, but the charges were dropped because he had not been advised of his rights. However, while taking a polygraph test administered by Paul Minor, Friedrick confessed to lying and trying to cover up in order to protect Presser.

"He said that he had spoken to two other agents, and had inspired and made up that story [that the bureau had authorized the ghost employees]," Minor said.

In 1986, Webster fired Friedrick for not being truthful and for removing a file on the case from the field office.[156] Because of the confusion, the government dropped the case against Presser, who died in 1988.

Agents collected ninety thousand dollars for Friedrick. Understandably, many felt that Friedrick had been placed in a terrible position. On one hand, he was appreciative of the information Presser was giving the bureau and wanted to protect him. On the other hand, he had an obligation to tell the truth to his superiors, to investigators, and to the grand jury.

"That one is a tragedy, it really is," said Oliver B. (Buck) Revell, who was in overall charge of the Presser operation. "He's a fine man, and a fine agent, who simply made the wrong choice. To try and protect an informant, he lied. You can't do that."

Today Friedrick does not want to discuss in detail what happened. "I don't trust anybody," he said. "People say, 'Are you bitter?' I say, 'No.' Because I have buddies in the police department who have been hammered, and they focus on that and ruin their lives. I've seen good guys turn into prunes."

The Office of Professional Responsibility is one part of the inspection division, whose function is to evaluate how well the FBI does its job. Essentially, it combines the roles of a police internal affairs unit, office of inspector general, and audit staff. Established by Hoover within a few years of his appointment as director in 1924, the inspection staff, as it was then called, was a response to the corruption that had plagued the bureau in its early years and was well ahead of its time.[157]

Roughly every two years, the division examines each field office and headquarters division. Besides inspectors assigned to the division, agents from other offices are temporarily assigned to help out on an inspection. It's a way to teach agents how other offices work and to bring fresh ideas to the offices being reviewed. The temporarily assigned agents refer to themselves as "rent-a-goons."

In order to advance in the FBI, agents must serve as inspectors' aides and later as inspectors. Generally, agents are not put in charge of a field office until they have served as the inspector in charge of a review team.

An inspection of a large office such as New York requires sixty or seventy agents working a month. The smaller offices require ten or fifteen agents working three weeks.[158]

In the course of an inspection, agents review every case and interview nearly every employee. They also perform a financial audit and interview outsiders who deal with the office—the U.S. Attorney, police chief, community and business leaders, and the media. Among other areas, inspections focus on the use of autos, procedures for handling evidence, undercover operations, violations of regulations, personnel problems, and the accuracy of expense vouchers.

In the end, the inspection team writes a report citing deficiencies and suggesting improvements. For example, after a recent inspection, the review team suggested that Los Angeles focus more on Asian organized crime. The team rates each agent, squad, program, and the office as a whole on whether they are "effective and efficient." In rare cases, an office may be rated "very effective and very efficient."

"A division or a field office has never been inefficient and ineffective," said D. Caroll Toohey, a short man with graying hair and gleaming white teeth who is the assistant director over the inspection division. "We have had parts of a field office or division rated ineffective and inefficient, like the white collar program in one field office. They would have to be pretty screwed up [to be rated ineffective and inefficient overall]."

The findings are presented to the director, and the offices have fifteen days to correct any deficiencies. As a result of an inspection, agents may be censured, suspended, or dismissed. Some employees take the news too seriously. Upset at a negative inspection, James T. Rich, the office services manager in the Boston field office, committed suicide in 1992 by jumping off a bridge near his home in Lowell, Massachusetts.

To protect the independence of the inspection division, the assistant director over the division reports directly to the director of the FBI. The only other division that reports directly, instead of reporting through an associate deputy director, is the legal division.

Two offices—the office of public and congressional affairs and the quality-management office—also report to the director.

"One reason the FBI is so effective is the inspection process. It's human nature to let things slide," said Charlie J. Parsons, who heads the Los Angeles office and previously headed the inspection division.

While the inspection division is good at making sure the FBI is well run, it often misses the larger picture. None of the problems perceived as major issues in the FBI since Hoover—the investigation of the left-wing CISPES organization, the Library Awareness Program, or the problems in dealing with minority agents—was flagged during an inspection.

A recent inspection of the FBI's office of public affairs rated it "very effective and very efficient," with no major recommendations for improvement. Yet, members of the media who regularly cover the FBI, as well as many of the FBI's own media representatives in field offices, say that the public affairs office under Sessions operates far less effectively than it did under Webster.

According to Toohey, none of the media or field-office public affairs agents who were interviewed expressed an unfavorable opinion of the office. But the reporter who is most respected for his long-term coverage of the bureau—Ronald J. Ostrow of the *Los Angeles Times*—was never asked for his opinion. In fact, the inspectors interviewed a reporter for only one of the four major papers that cover the FBI—the *Washington Post*, *New York Times*, *Los Angeles Times*, and *Wall Street Journal*. They did not interview any of the reporters who regularly cover the bureau for the three major television networks—NBC, ABC, and CBS. In the cases of Rita Braver of CBS and Sharon LaFraniere of the *Washington Post*, the inspectors called but insisted they had to see them right away.

"There was a message on my machine [from an inspector]," Braver said. "They wanted to see me that day. I called him back at six. He was gone for the day. That was the end."

LaFraniere said that when she told the FBI agent who called that she would be away for several days, he said that the inspection team had already talked with enough reporters.

Braver and LaFraniere, like other reporters, said they were not sure how candid they would have been in any case. Like others who deal with the FBI on a regular basis, reporters do not want to diminish their access to the agency unless there is a good reason. Helping the inspection division by giving honest opinions about the office of public affairs is not necessarily one of them.

While people who are interviewed by inspectors can request confidentiality, few reporters took that step. Instead, many of those who were interviewed by the inspectors said that they had not revealed their true opinions. A reporter from one of the major newspapers who was interviewed said that he only gave the inspector "gloss."

"I don't feel they had any feel for what the public affairs office is supposed to do, or what press people need," said the reporter, requesting anonymity. "I wouldn't say anything to them I wouldn't tell the public affairs office—which is not a lot. My opinion is fairly negative. In some cases, they have been helpful in giving a heads-up. In terms of presenting what the bureau is doing on important cases, it's tough to get what you need. . . . They seem to have no idea of what a story is. Sometimes they are not anchored to reality."

Another reporter who covers the FBI for one of the networks and was not interviewed said that while some public affairs officers are good, the office overall has been in decline since Webster left.

"What you get now is these people who seem to know about as much about the FBI and what is really going on as the greeter at Bloomingdale's knows about how decisions are made at Bloomingdale's," the reporter said. "My biggest criticism is if they are doing something interesting, I'm not going to hear about it."

One of those who was not asked her opinion, Beverly Lumpkin, who has covered the bureau for ABC since 1976, said that if she had been asked, she would have said the office has gone downhill since Webster left.

"[Under Webster] I would get guidance on things that were ongoing," she said. "One of the people there [then] would say, 'We work the edges. To the extent we can, we will try to help you. If we think you are going down a wrong path, we will get you off that wrong path.' There is no one there now I can count on for that, as compared with the way it was under Webster."[159]

Agents in field offices, like people from the media, are often reluctant to rat on their bosses or on other agents. Good investigators can gain agents' confidence and learn what they need to know. However, too often the inspection interviews are done by rote, following a script prepared at headquarters. The process produces reams of paper and the appearance of a rigorous examination, but in the end, important problems are overlooked.

"You are really dealing with an awful lot of duties," said an agent who has been on five inspections. "You have to review all the pending files, all the informant files, you have to go through all the administrative files, tons of paperwork that has been created over the past two or three years, write a product, then defend that product, which is a hell of a process. It tends to make it very difficult for you to focus on any [major] issue unless it is brought to you by somebody."

In evaluating the effectiveness of an office, the agent said, the inspection process does a good job. "It doesn't take a genius to come into a squad and see who is working and who isn't. The problem is when you write a Schedule F, which is a schedule of findings, basically they are negative; they are intended to be criticisms. So when you write a critical document, you are basically in an adversarial role with the field office. You have to document it. You have to make sure you are totally accurate. If one minor fact is found to be deficient, the whole Schedule F goes down the drain, you eat it, the inspector is pissed at you, and your whole career is gone," he said with some exaggeration. "So there is an enormous problem. You are sitting there and saying, 'Oh, my God, I don't want to know this.' I wouldn't count on the process to detect major flaws in a program."

"I think the role of the inspection division as a training ground has subordinated its role as an analyzer of policy," said James J. Hogan, a certified public accountant and an FBI agent who was one of Sessions's special assistants from 1988 to 1992.[160]

In contrast to the office of inspections, no one thinks the Office of Professional Responsibility is anything but effective. Since Clarence Kelley started the OPR in 1976, there have been no charges that the FBI has been involved in any cover-ups of its internal discipline problems.

"Any problems [in the Hoover era] they did not want publicized," Toohey said. " 'You leave and you won't be prosecuted [for crimes committed while on official business].' Now we prosecute agents."

Indeed, Hoover himself would have been prosecuted under today's standards.

"The improvements to the homes of Hoover and his aides would be prosecuted today. Any kind of misuse of bureau funds [would be prosecuted]," David Binney said.

"What tended to happen [under Hoover] is it [an offense] would be handled locally, as opposed to at the headquarters level," said John C. (Jack) Wagner, a former special agent in charge in Norfolk. "A lot fell back to the SAC. It would reflect on him if it ever came to headquarters, so they handled it in house. Who knows how they did it?" If an SAC thought that disciplining an agent might make him look good with Hoover, he might take action, Wagner said. If it would not, he might not take action. The offenses often were not criminal in nature. Yet, Wagner said, "In a sense, you could say it was being covered up."[161]

In the new bureau, several FBI agents have been prosecuted for expense voucher fraud. In Kansas City, the FBI uncovered and presented for prosecution a case against two agents who became involved with an informant in stealing shipments of tires, air conditioners, and bicycles from rail boxcars. The FBI even installed wiretaps on the office and home phones of the agents, Alan H. Rotton and Stephen S. Travis.

"I called Rotton into the office and gave him his notice of dismissal," Revell said. "He had been indicted. He gave me a disdainful stare and said, 'I hope you don't think you have heard the last of me.' I said, 'No, I'm sure we haven't heard the last of you, and I'll be looking forward to seeing you in court.' Two days later, he committed suicide."

Travis pleaded guilty in 1980 and received a prison sentence of four years.[162]

More recently, OPR aggressively investigated a complaint against an agent in San Antonio who had been assigned to help break in a new female agent there. Instead, according to the woman, in August 1991 he raped her in her apartment, where they had stopped during an assignment. Because she was still new and unsure how the FBI would respond, the female agent did not report the incident until the summer of 1992.

During an investigation, the FBI found that in 1990 an FBI clerk had accused the same San Antonio agent of harassing her, repeatedly patting his groin in front of her. The FBI ordered him to stay away from her, but after a year he again began harassing the clerk. As a result, the clerk quit the FBI. Another woman who worked at the Wyndham San Antonio Hotel said that when she showed the San Antonio agent a suite at the hotel in 1990, he forced her against a wall and began fondling her. She reported the incident to the FBI, and the agent was disciplined for it.

During the FBI's rape investigation, the San Antonio agent admitted he had used "some" force in getting the new agent to have sex with him, but he said she then began to enjoy it. He claimed she subsequently twice consented to have sex with him. But he flunked an FBI polygraph exam on that question.

As a result of the investigation, the FBI quietly fired the San

Antonio agent in the fall of 1992—the first time in history an FBI agent has been fired for rape. The FBI then presented the evidence to local authorities for possible prosecution.

Besides not showing up for work, the most common infraction in the bureau is misuse of FBI property, usually cars. While driving bureau cars, agents have killed themselves and other drivers and demolished the FBI cars assigned to them. Agents have been caught using bureau cars for taking kids to Little League games and buying liquor at the local liquor store. One assistant special agent in charge from Memphis gave his kid in college a car being used in an FBI undercover drug operation.

In one widely told but probably apocryphal story, an agent who had been drinking in upstate New York saw troopers stopping cars on the road ahead. He parked his bureau car on the shoulder, relieved himself in the bushes, then turned his car around and drove home, taking a different route. At 3:00 A.M., two state troopers knocked on his door.

"Do you mind if we look in your garage?" one asked.

Inside the garage was a state highway patrol cruiser. The agent had mistakenly driven it home instead of his FBI car.

In avoiding speeding tickets, agents like to take advantage of what they call "professional courtesy." It must be accomplished adroitly. Simply flashing FBI credentials would be improper use of FBI authority. Instead, "Some guys put their badge inside their wallet so when they open it, there is the badge," an agent said. But that approach can backfire.

"The word will go around the office not to get stopped for speeding in Chicago because we're indicting officers there," another agent said. "I had to go to the Chicago airport with a first-office agent [an agent just out of training] who was driving. We were flying down the freeway." When stopped, "I said, 'This is my fault. I'm in from headquarters in the FBI, and I have—'

" 'FBI!' the officer says. 'You goddamn sons of bitches! All you want to do is indict Chicago police.' I thought, 'What a great time to bring up FBI.' I said, 'You know that we're just doing our job like you are. We haven't singled out the Chicago police. We haven't made up any evidence on anybody. You're probably angry because those people embarrass you. It's nothing personal.'

"So he grits his teeth. He motioned the other guy out of the car. All I saw was finger pointing and rage. The young agent came back and said, 'He didn't give us a ticket.' "

The biggest complaint of agents and supervisors in the new bureau is that the OPR takes too long to do its investigations. Meanwhile, an agent's professional life may be hanging in the balance. This is exactly the same complaint as that voiced by suspects in FBI criminal investigations, except that by the time a suspect knows he is being investigated, chances are good he will be prosecuted. In contrast, half of all OPR investigations bring no action because the allegations cannot be substantiated.

"We are desperately trying to get OPR cases completed sooner. Cases would take a year or more to be resolved. It is simply unfair to leave a person spinning that long, not knowing if he has a job or not," said James Fox, assistant director over the New York office.

Often, wild rumors circulate about an agent under investigation. A pretty blond agent who was accused of becoming too close to a male informant was said to have had sex with the informant. When confronted, according to the rumors, she confessed that she was a nymphomaniac and threatened to reveal that she had slept with most of her bosses if OPR did not drop its investigation. The entire story was untrue. She had not slept with the informant or her bosses. Nor had she made any threats, which would have been the surest way to get fired. Yet, agents from Los Angeles to New York heard the story and repeated it with glee, embellishing it still further with the detail that the informant was infected with the HIV virus—also false.

"As soon as OPR is called in, you are stigmatized," said Gary L. Penrith, special agent in charge of the Newark field office. "It's all secret-secret stuff. As soon as they get to the office and do their first interview, we have a rumor. No matter what the outcome is, everyone remembers that OPR came out and interviewed Gary Penrith."

Although rumors can become vicious when they involve individuals, they can be seen as a way for agents to express themselves.

"I think the rumors are a healthy kind of safety valve to allow them to get rid of gripes and concerns and frustrations," said William Baker, assistant director over the criminal investigative division.

Unless they involve high-ranking bureau officials, allegations of misconduct are investigated for the OPR by agents in the appropriate field office and are assigned by the OPR to conduct specific interviews. Agents within the OPR at headquarters then write the final report. Beyond a two-day orientation, these agents are not given any special training. When allegations are made against assistant special agents in charge and above, the head of the OPR personally investigates them.

Besides complaints from management, the OPR receives complaints from police departments, irate spouses or former spouses, citizens, and agents. Some agents have been known to make anonymous complaints about other agents competing for the same promotion. By anonymously touching off an OPR investigation, the agent neutralizes his competition, since an agent cannot be considered for promotion if he is under OPR investigation.

"A lot of us believe that if somebody doesn't have hair on his chest and the ability to write his own name down, we're going to be chasing our tail with anonymous letters and calls," Penrith said, referring derisively to agents who place anonymous calls to the OPR. Penrith said that if he were competing for a position, "I can make a phone call and put you under OPR in one day. You are out of the competition. It doesn't mean I'm going to get it, but your competitor is gone."[163]

Yet, anonymous tips produce solid leads, particularly on higher-ranking agents. About 5 percent of disciplinary actions begin with anonymous letters or calls, according to David Binney.

If the OPR recommends disciplinary action, the administrative summary unit in the administrative services division decides what action to take. In addition to OPR matters, the unit disciplines agents for poor judgment or poor performance. For example, the FBI fired an agent, and another agent resigned, after they accidentally shot to death fellow agent Robin Ahrens in Phoenix on October 5, 1985. Ahrens, who was tremendously well liked and respected, was the first female FBI agent to be killed in the line of duty. According to the FBI's investigation of the shooting, the two agents were near panic as they tried to arrest a suspected armored car robbery fugitive and exhibited "faulty and atrocious judgment."[164]

"Webster asked me for my view on the Ahrens shooting," said James D. McKenzie, then assistant director for training. "I said, 'Regardless of the circumstances, anybody involved in shooting another FBI agent should not be an FBI agent.' I don't care what the circumstances are, for any number of reasons: their reputation in the future, trust, other agents working with them, as well it's just a good rule to have. If you shoot another agent, you don't belong here. Look for something else to do."[165]

Recognizing that agents consider the slowness of the OPR process to be one of the bureau's greatest problems, Sessions added more agents to supervise OPR cases. While only appeals of disciplinary actions are reviewed by high-level bureau officials, the director is aware of the more sensitive ones.

"It would take a long time for OPR investigations to get to him

[Sessions]," said John E. Collingwood, a former Sessions aide who heads the FBI's public and congressional affairs office. "That drove him [Sessions] bonkers. It affects the agents, his family, and everyone around him. So he said we have to do better."[166]

"OPR is critical," Sessions said. "Sometimes you say, 'Why don't we let go of this? Why don't we get through with it?' . . . It's tough. It's no fun. . . . If you ever had a circumstance where your integrity has been questioned, you know what I mean."[167]

But the average duration of an OPR investigation is still four months. Then, it takes another three to four months for the administrative summary unit to make its decision. Additional time usually passes before high-level bureau officials sign off on disciplinary actions.

For all the attention the OPR gets, "Serious misconduct is really small, given that there are twenty-four thousand employees," said Binney, the deputy assistant director over OPR. "Maybe twenty or thirty get serious disciplines. That's a minor number. I keep having to remind myself of that. You get bogged down in what you see coming in every day, and you begin to get a little jaded."

While agents in the field must serve as inspectors to be promoted, agents who take more permanent jobs in the OPR or the administrative summary unit at headquarters do so with some trepidation.

"Why would you want to judge your fellow employees and take action against them?" asked Edward R. Leary, who is over the section that includes the administrative summary unit. "When you first think of it, you say, 'I don't want to be involved in this.' I deal with it by saying, 'The best thing I can do for my fellow employees is to ensure they get a fair shot.' "[168]

However, there is a widespread perception in the FBI that internal discipline is not fair—that, for the same offenses, management is not disciplined as severely as field agents.

"One of the things that continues to grate at a lot of agents is the perceived difference in discipline between management and street people who break the rules," said James T. Burnett, vice president of the FBI Agents Association, a professional organization that represents two thirds of the agents. "They always tend to get the little guy."[169]

The most frequently cited case is that of Frederick B. Verinder. The special agent in charge of the Columbia, South Carolina, field office, Verinder was driving home after going to a bar after work when a state trooper stopped him for driving while allegedly intoxicated.

Since coming to South Carolina, Verinder had made impressive cases against state legislators. When he took over in 1988, the field office lacked informants and a knowledge of local criminal activity. Verinder quickly found that one of the biggest problems in South Carolina was public corruption. As a result of the investigations Verinder initiated, State Representative Robert B. Brown, one of the state's most influential legislators, pleaded guilty to taking a two-thousand-dollar bribe to push a bill to let voters decide whether to allow parimutuel betting in South Carolina. State Senator W. Richard Lee also pleaded guilty to taking a bribe.[170]

In addition to these probes, Verinder was working on an undercover operation with the state police—the agency that stopped him on March 23, 1990. The officer, John Osborne, said he was swerving. Verinder said he had been talking on his car phone. The officer asked him to repeat the alphabet. According to the officer, Verinder failed the test.[171]

"I said, 'I beg to disagree with you. Do you mind if I find your colonel so we can adjudicate it at the highest level?' " Verinder related.

Colonel J. H. (Red) Lanier, the state highway department's director of law enforcement, came out to the scene. He said he did not think Verinder had been drinking excessively.

"Lanier said, 'Fred's a friend, we have some operations going on, it's your call,' " Verinder said.

In the end, Osborne gave Verinder a speeding ticket. Lanier then drove Verinder home.[172]

"I was drinking spritzers. In my opinion, I was a long way from intoxicated. My concern was I was being set up," Verinder said.

Verinder's claim is hard to follow. Since he had been working with the state police, there would appear to be no reason why that agency would have been interested in setting him up. Clearly, he had used his position to try to beat a charge of driving while intoxicated. Since his blood alcohol level was never tested, no one knows if the charge would have stuck. A state investigation found no evidence that he had been drinking excessively.

"Probably in perspective it may not have been the right thing to do," Verinder said. "But I was thinking clearly, and I thought, at that point, something is wrong, and I will nip it in the bud. As a result of all the publicity, it would have been better to let the officer, if he was going to write me, write me, and then resolve it in a courtroom."

The story hit the local papers, giving Verinder more reason to believe the entire episode had been retribution for his aggressive investigations of state legislators. After the OPR investigated, Verinder was removed as SAC and transferred to a headquarters job at the same pay level. A year and a half later, he was promoted to deputy assistant director of the criminal division. In that position, he is in overall charge of white-collar-crime investigations, informants, undercover operations, and support functions.

Agents in the field say that a street agent would have been fired for such an offense. Bureau officials such as Revell and Greenleaf, the associate deputy director for administration, say that is not true.

"A field agent would not be fired for that," Revell said. "It happens all the time, and they are not fired. In fact, I've had three such incidents since I've been here [in Dallas]. They all got suspensions."[173]

"He was transferred, he was demoted, he was suspended without pay three weeks," said Greenleaf, the associate deputy FBI director who hears appeals on discipline. "What more can you do? If that happened to an agent, he would be suspended and not transferred. He was brought here for a year. He had an outstanding attitude and did an outstanding job."[174]

Verinder had another thing going for him: His work up to that point had been exceptional. Before being assigned to South Carolina, Verinder had supervised major public corruption cases in New York, including the one against New York Congressman Mario Biaggi. Biaggi was convicted of fifteen felony counts in the Wedtech case, which involved corruption by a government contractor. He subsequently resigned from Congress.

"There wasn't a public corruption program when we got there [to New York]," said Tom Sheer, who was over Verinder then. "Fred Verinder came up with some brilliant strategies."

"There is more discipline of SACs than people realize," Revell said. "A number have been demoted, a number moved, a number brought into headquarters, a number who have retired rather than be brought back to a lesser position. Agents in the street say SACs get away with things. They really don't. They really are held to a higher standard."

"I've been here eight months," Binney said. "We've had four SACs and three ASACs [assistant special agents in charge] disciplined."

In fact, over the years there has been inconsistency in bureau discipline, but it has not been in favor of management. Rather, it is an inconsistency that has applied across the board to all agents. Admittedly, no two cases are exactly the same. But it is possible to see patterns. Agents are fired routinely for drug convictions. Yet, a female agent was suspended for thirty days after being arrested entering the U.S. with marijuana and drug paraphernalia in her possession.[175]

Lee Colwell, who was a high-ranking bureau official at the time, said that he believes the fact that the agent was female and black played a part in the light punishment.

"It was when we were developing a meaningful affirmative-action program," he said. "The bureau was trying to define what its policy was [on marijuana use]. You had a lot of imbalances in punishments, just like you do in the court system."[176]

Sessions took a tougher stand on discipline than did Webster, who emphasized taking into account an employee's entire record. But employees still are not necessarily fired for lying or for other serious breaches of trust.

"Let's say you get an allegation that an agent is having an extra-marital affair with a neighbor," said Floyd I. Clarke, the deputy director of the FBI. "You can't really verify it. You interview the agent, and he says it's not true. Later on you find out it is true. You go back and confront him. He says, 'I don't know what I was thinking about. The impact on my wife, my stature in the neighborhood. I did it, and I'm sorry I wasn't forthright.' Should we fire that agent? I'm not saying we would not. But you might not. You take a look at how long this individual has been an agent, what is his track record. Is this a single emotional time? Denial may be a human instinct. On the other hand, if he has a pattern of this kind of activity in trying to manipulate the system and use deceit as a means of defending himself, he'll probably be fired."[177]

A review of the FBI's quarterly reports of disciplinary actions illustrates the range of trouble that agents and support employees can get into and how easily the power that comes with the job can be abused. It also shows how easily agents get off for misuse of that power.

In the second quarter of 1988, an agent falsified official investigative reports. He was censured, which means that a letter of criticism is placed in an agent's file and may be taken into consideration when promotions are given out. The agent was also given six months' probation and was suspended for thirty days. Another agent who drew a revolver and openly displayed it during an off-duty domestic dispute was censured. In the third quarter, an agent divulged to someone outside the FBI the fact that an individual was a bureau informant. He was censured. An agent who was already on probation assaulted another agent. He was suspended for twenty-one days, received a censure, and was continued on probation for another six months.

Another agent during this period backdated memos to cover up the fact that he had delayed an investigation. He was censured. An agent made improper inquiries of another government agency on behalf of a friend. He was censured and placed on probation.

In the first quarter of 1989, an agent was placed on probation for one year for attempting to mislead an aide to an inspector by instructing subordinates to backdate written reports of interviews. A support employee queried bureau records for personal reasons. The employee was reprimanded, which is a verbal censure. An agent who made a false statement during an administrative inquiry was censured and placed on probation.

In the second quarter of the same year, a support employee used FBI computer records and indices to obtain information for personal reasons. The employee got a verbal reprimand.

In the third quarter of 1990, a support employee made an unauthorized query on the bureau's computer system to obtain official records regarding a friend. The employee was verbally reprimanded. A special agent was censured for becoming involved in a verbal and physical altercation with a private citizen. A support employee gave information from a closed investigative file to the subject of the file. The employee was censured, given probation, and suspended for fourteen days.

Discipline meted out during the same period shows that the punishment for misuse of bureau files or lying was about the same as for being overweight or making sexually harassing or racially derogatory remarks to another employee. For example, an agent who refused to comply with supervisory instructions to report to monthly weight monitoring was censured. Another agent was censured and instructed to attend sensitivity training for use of obscene language and gestures in the presence of four female agents. A third agent who failed to comply with the bureau weight program was censured and placed on probation.

In general, agents are fired for lack of candor during an administrative inquiry only when it is combined with other offenses. In the first quarter of 1989, an agent was already on probation when he failed to conduct assigned interviews, falsified official documents to conceal this fact, and was charged with a lack of candor during the administrative inquiry. He was fired.

What these and other reports show is that field agents and support employees often get off with far lighter punishment than the public has a right to expect. Considering how much trust the public places in agents, it is surprising that falsifying reports of interviews, obtaining information from bureau files for friends, and lying during administrative inquiries are not firing offenses.

Revell, the former associate deputy director, said that in his opinion, any agent who lies should be fired. "Every case I got hold of, that was my recommendation. I think we made a fundamental mistake, and much of it occurred under Webster," Revell said. "He tried to differentiate on each case and look at mitigating factors. There are certain standards you shouldn't do that with, and that includes integrity. There should be a bright line that you simply don't cross. You don't make false statements. You do not lie. You do not give false testimony. If you do, you will not be employed. That bright line should always be there, because that is a standard everyone can understand. If we mitigate that, it becomes blurry."

Under the present standards, "Lack of candor in and of itself is not a firing offense," said Edward Leary, who is over the unit that makes the decisions. "In any case, you have to learn more. Is it is a white lie or a critical lie? If someone demonstrates a significant lack of candor in handling their responsibilities, we weight that heavily because the agent who is testifying can be impeached on the basis of deficiencies in that area."

According to Weldon Kennedy, the assistant director in overall charge of disciplinary actions, the bureau has felt constrained from firing some people because the FBI has treated agents more leniently for the same offenses in the past. If the FBI fired agents now for those offenses, he said, they could successfully challenge the actions in court.

For example, an agent fabricated an interview during an applicant investigation to show that he had performed his assignments when, in fact, he had not. After reviewing precedents, Kennedy decided he could not fire him and have the action sustained in court. Instead, he censured the agent, placed him on probation for six months, and suspended him from duty without pay for seven days.[178]

Anthony P. Rezza, a Philadelphia agent, received a settlement from the government after he filed suit challenging his firing because he was a compulsive gambler. The settlement followed two rulings by U.S. District Court Judge Edmund V. Ludwig favoring Rezza's claim that his firing violated a federal law banning discrimination against the disabled.[179]

Another agent, Fernando E. Mata, has challenged his firing in court even though he failed two FBI lie detector tests on whether he thought he was authorized to give information—including locations of CIA bugging devices sent to Cuba—to Cuban intelligence officers. After being suspended from the FBI and given immunity from prosecution, Mata answered truthfully when he said he had given classified information to the Cubans, according to one of the tests conducted on January 9, 1990. Mata, who worked foreign counterintelligence in Miami and was highly regarded, said that he was trying to recruit the officers to work for the FBI.[180]

"He failed the polygraph. That wasn't the basis of the concern. The concern was what we could establish on what he had done," Revell said. "I finally, when I was down there [in Miami] on a trip, probably exceeded my authority. I told the SAC to remove his [Mata's] badge and bar him from the office and place him on administrative leave. He [the SAC] agreed to that."[181]

Acknowledging that Mata had been fired for compromising national security, Mata's then lawyer called a press conference to claim that the real reason Mata had been fired was that he had participated with other Hispanic agents in a racial discrimination suit against the bureau.[182]

On November 1, 1990, Greenleaf sent a memo to all bureau employees expressing concern about misconduct and stating that the bureau was upping the ante on punishments. For example, an infraction that brought a forty-five-day suspension before would now bring a sixty-day suspension.

While bureau officials such as Greenleaf, Kennedy, legal counsel Joseph R. Davis, and Deputy Director Floyd Clarke would like to make punishment more severe, they say they are constrained by precedents that have been used successfully in court to challenge harsher penalties. In one example, an agent working on background investigations fabricated reports showing that he had verified information with references. He also attributed to the references information they never gave.

As the assistant director over administrative services, Kennedy ordered the agent fired. The agent hired a lawyer, who found precedents that Kennedy's division had overlooked. The precedents showed that the bureau in the past had not necessarily fired agents for similar offenses. Moreover, the agent in this case was black. He could claim he had been singled out because of his race. After Davis pointed out that the FBI would have serious problems defending the firing in court, Kennedy reversed his decision. Instead, the agent got a thirty day-suspension and a reduction in pay grade from GS-13 to GS-12.[183]

The bureau is trying to ratchet up punishments gradually. The courts will accept tougher standards if they are applied across the board in response to a rising number of infractions. But the modifications that have been made are so minor, and the internal investigation process is so slow, that no change is yet perceivable. Agents continue to receive relatively minor discipline for abuse of their positions and for lying.

In the third quarter of 1991, an agent improperly interceded in a local police matter. He was censured. Another agent attempted to review an investigative file that he was not allowed to see because of restrictions on access. He was reprimanded. A third, who interceded with local law enforcement on behalf of a friend, was censured, placed on probation for a year, and suspended without pay for fourteen days. A support employee who failed to accurately report limited use of marijuana before employment and was not candid about it during the internal inquiry was censured, placed on probation for a year, and suspended for five days.

As FBI officials are the first to point out, law enforcement officers must be held to a higher standard than is the rest of the population.

"We don't have a product that we make. Our product is information," said D. Caroll Toohey, the assistant director over inspections. "The public thinks the bureau can solve any crime, that we are omnipotent and know all. Because of the public's trust in us, they give us the information. They tell us who the bank robber is. We use that to solve crimes. Every agent understands that if we weren't respected and didn't have a high degree of integrity, they wouldn't provide us with this information, and we wouldn't be as successful as we are."

It is a federal offense to lie to an FBI agent. While prosecutors exercise discretion in prosecuting such cases, the law does not distinguish between "white lies" and other lies. If ordinary citizens can be put in jail for lying to an FBI agent, then FBI agents who lie to other agents during the course of an internal investigation should at least be fired.

Some agents who worked under Hoover say that the rules were more clearly defined then.

"One of the critical changes [since the Hoover era] is the lack of discipline," said David Faulkner, one of the two agents who arrested Ronald Pelton in Baltimore. "For all the criticisms of Hoover, and a lot are true, we had discipline." At the same time, he said, the discipline "intimidated people so they were afraid to do anything, because they were afraid to make mistakes."

What is needed is a balance between the arbitrary and harsh discipline of the Hoover era and the slap on the wrist that is too often meted out today for lying or for abusing the FBI's awesome power.

7

Dallas: My Place, My Rules

● **From the assassination** of John F. Kennedy to ripoffs by savings and loan associations, the Dallas field office has had some of the FBI's most important cases. With 240 agents, the twelfth largest field office in the FBI also has had the modern bureau's most embarrassing case—the investigation of CISPES. Dallas is home as well to Oliver B. (Buck) Revell, who became special agent in charge of the office after serving as the FBI's associate deputy director for investigations at headquarters.

Since the death of Hoover, Revell has been a major force in leading the FBI into the modern era. He can claim credit for dozens of innovations, and he often does. For if Revell's intellect and drive are legendary, so are the plaques on his wall. No retirement dinner for top FBI officials is complete without a few jokes about Revell's plaques, which line his office walls and spill out onto the walls in adjacent corridors.

When Revell left headquarters to take over in Dallas, William A. (Al) Bayse, the FBI's assistant director over the technical services division, sang, "Oh Lord, It's Hard to Be Humble When You're Perfect in Every Way," at the J. W. Marriott Hotel in Washington. Strumming his guitar, he adapted verses to depict Revell's career.

Before Revell got to Dallas, one of the biggest problems facing the office was the Bandidos, a motorcycle gang that deals in drugs, stolen weapons, and other stolen property. The Bandidos live primarily off the earnings of young women whom gang members induce to be prostitutes or topless dancers. Each Bandido has four or five women who are considered his girlfriends. Generous to a fault, the Bandidos pass around the women to their friends as sexual gifts.[184]

The Bandidos menaced Lubbock, Texas, in particular. Because members of the gang were terrorizing residents, the Lubbock police had taken to stopping gang members on their motorcycles and searching them simply because they wore jackets with the colors of the Bandidos—on the back was a picture of a Mexican bandido with a sombrero, a gun, and bullets. Because of the harassment, a local court had banned the police from investigating the gang, which was getting increasingly out of control.

In 1984, the FBI sent Dennis L. Dufour, a New York agent, to Lubbock, where the Dallas field office has one of its eleven resident agencies. Dufour was to pose as the owner and operator of a bar where the gang hung out. Dufour became friends with gang members, who offered him shapely young women and discussed their murders and thefts while the FBI secretly videotaped and tape recorded them.

Called the Sidebuster, the bar was taken over by the FBI after the woman who owned it had been assaulted and threatened by gang members. In choosing an agent to work a particular undercover operation, FBI headquarters consults a computer data bank listing every conceivable characteristic of FBI agents who want to work undercover—their tattoos, work experience, hobbies, and languages. Dufour, who stands six feet two inches tall and weighs 235 pounds, was perfect for the job. As a teenager Dufour owned a Triumph motorcycle and later raced dragsters in California, where he learned to fix engines. Before joining the FBI in 1978, Dufour had owned and operated several bars in New Orleans. He then became a New Orleans police officer working drugs. Dufour knew about motorcycles, drugs, and bars. But more than that, he was quick-thinking and had the gift of gab—attributes that would save his life on more than one occasion.

Before taking the job, Dufour had to pass muster with Thomas C. Kelly, then the special agent in charge of the Dallas office. Kelly was a self-proclaimed Hooverite, a man who unabashedly admired the former director's values and method of operating. At the time, he was not used to undercover operations.

"I came with rather long hair, a full beard, and a mustache," Dufour recalled. "He was very adamant about not having facial hair and having very short hair. I said, 'With all due respect, if you can get someone to walk in with that choirboy look, and walk in on these guys, God bless you.' I said, 'I sure wouldn't want to do that. They would either kill him or totally ignore him.' "

Dufour convinced Kelly of the need for long hair, and the SAC became an enthusiastic supporter of the operation.[185]

Using the name Dennis Donovan, Dufour posed as a drug dealer and murderer who was associated with organized crime figures in New York. The FBI established a phony history for Dufour with credit bureaus and entered an arrest record for him in police data banks. The Lubbock police department participated in the operation, and some police officials knew about Dufour. To protect Dufour, the FBI programmed the department's computers so that if anyone inquired into Dufour's background, the FBI would know who had made the request. The bureau could then investigate the individual to see if he or she was working with the gang members.

While Dufour posed as the owner, the real owner of the bar leased the bar to the FBI, which assumed the insurance. She introduced Dufour, dressed in cowboy boots, jeans, and snakeskin belts, as an old boyfriend. The bureau gave Dufour a Chevrolet pickup truck instead of a motorcycle; it would be too difficult to conduct surveillance of him on a motorcycle. And, if he was unprotected in the wilderness, gang members who might have decided he was a cop could choose that moment to beat him up or inject him with cocaine. Instead, the bureau wanted Dufour to stay as much as possible in the bar, where agents could rescue him more easily if he was threatened, as happened several times.

About thirty members of the gang belonged to the Lubbock chapter, and they included several of the Bandidos' national officers. They induced young women who had been abused or were runaways to be prostitutes or topless dancers. The topless bars would not allow the gang members in, so they needed a place to go after their women—called "old ladies"—finished their performances.

Dufour was more than willing to accommodate them. After the bar had been wired for sound, he not only let the Bandidos hang out at the bar but took in their Harley-Davidsons—which they prized above all else—overnight during inclement weather.

"It would be snowing, and I would put their bikes on the hardwood floor," Dufour said. "They would say, 'It leaks oil.' I would say, 'Don't worry. We'll put a towel on the floor. Your bikes will be here in the morning. They will be as safe as in your own house.' The next morning they couldn't say enough thank-you's."

During the night, FBI agents would examine the bikes and note their serial numbers.

"When the bikes were parked in there, we could get the numbers, see if the frames had been ground, parts of the engines had been stolen," Dufour said. "They would steal a Harley-Davidson and put the parts on their bikes. . . . No other bar in Lubbock would allow the Bandidos to come into the bar, much less leave their motorcycles there."

Soon, gang members from other parts of Texas and as far away as Louisiana began flocking to the Sidebuster.

"I had a barmaid there who was friends with them but wasn't one of them," Dufour said. "She knew them all. She advised me that two were having their birthdays coming up. One was Wild Willie, a Vietnam veteran who experienced flashbacks. He stayed at what they called the Pig Pen, which was an old hog pen with razor wire and Cyclone fences and house trailers. He would wake up in the middle of the night and start shooting up the campground with an M-16, yelling, 'The Vietcong are coming.' "

Dufour threw a birthday party for Wild Willie, serving half a barbecued goat and a large birthday cake decorated with alligators, his favorite reptiles.

"They brought members from God knows where. They were posing for pictures, not knowing the bar was wired for video and sound," Dufour said.

Dufour refused to accept any money for the party, so the gang members passed around a hat and gave him a thousand dollars. The money went into the FBI's bank account. Soon the bar had gone out of the red and was making money.

To establish Dufour's credentials as a drug dealer, the FBI had Joe Pistone, the legendary undercover agent from New York, fly in one day with $250,000 in cash in a briefcase.

"I told one of the guys my truck was overheating," Dufour said. " 'Would you take me to the Lubbock airport to meet him?' We picked him up. He wanted to know who he was. I said, 'He is okay. He's one of the guys. He knows what's happening.'

"We went back to the bar, locked the doors, opened the briefcase. He said the old man in New York wants you to take care of this. I said okay. The idea was it was drug money that I had been involved in before. These people sat a little way away at a table. But they saw me take it and got a look at me counting money. Then we returned him to the airport, leaving them with the impression that this guy had just given me several hundred thousand dollars."

In fact, it had all been a show. Pistone flew back with the money.

In front of the video cameras, the gang members discussed business, including thefts of explosives and a murder one said he had committed. After closing the bar at 2:00 A.M., Dufour would take a roundabout route to his apartment to make sure he was not being followed. Then he would meet with Rick Harris, the case agent, and dictate his 302s—the government forms the FBI uses for reporting information that might be used in court. Dufour matched and verified the information the FBI was getting from the electronic and video surveillance.

In the morning, Dufour had to buy liquor and beer from distributors who came to the bar. He got three or four hours of sleep a night and worked seven days a week.

Occasionally, James J. Siano, who was in charge of undercover operations in Dallas, would secretly meet with Dufour and slip him out of town. Dufour would tell the gang members he had to close the bar so he could meet some associates who did not want to be seen.

"We would shut it down and tell them a couple of days in advance," Dufour said. "At two Saturday morning, I would leave and get a couple of days to call my family, talk to my kids."

During the ten-month operation, Dufour never saw his wife or children back in New York.

"I told my wife originally I was leaving for three weeks. Ten months later I came back. She was not real happy," he said.

The bureau's original plan called for Dufour to be unarmed. In case of trouble, the agents watching the video monitors were supposed to rescue him. But all of the gang members carried guns, and they would sit at the bar and take them apart. Dufour decided he needed a gun, too.

"The bureau finally issued a gun, a .32-caliber. I laughed. I gave the weapon back. I said, 'I shoot one of these three-hundred-pound individuals with a .32-caliber, I'm just going to piss him off,'" Dufour said. "I got a 9-millimeter, which I am now authorized to carry, from a friend of Mr. Kelly [the SAC]. If I'm going to go through administrative inquiry, I would rather do that than be crippled or killed," Dufour said.

"It was tense all the time because you were constantly being tested," he said. "They had a variety of tests. They would ask you questions and then they wouldn't. You didn't know if they truly believed you or they were watching you. You were constantly wound like a watch spring. You never let your guard down. You couldn't. The slightest miscue, anything you said out of character. You had to be what you portrayed and yet you could not forget what you represented and what you were. So it was a very fine line. That more than anything was the biggest strain. You constantly had to keep that in the back of your mind. You couldn't dishonor what you were and what you really represented.

"A guy would take out a gun and lay it on the bar and look at you. One of the big things was to always look them in the eye. You never look away from a person. You are talking to a guy and he takes out a gun or sticks a Crocodile Dundee or Rambo knife in the bar, you look right back at him. If you start looking at the knife and you get nervous, your voice starts trembling, you come up with an excuse to leave the area. You sit right there. You say now I got another hole in the bar. Why don't you stick it in that hole that is already there. People have a thing about other people who can't look them in the eye.

"If a guy accuses you of something while talking business, you look right back at him and tell him he is an asshole or stupid. 'I didn't ask you for anything. I don't want to know your business. If you want a drink here, fine. You don't want a drink here, that's fine too. There's the door. Don't let it hit you in the ass on the way out.' "

Dufour laid down strict rules. Because the police could close down the bar he told the gang members, he did not want drugs used in the bar. Nor did he want any fights.

One evening, a gang member known as Earthquake got in a scuffle with another member.

"I said, 'Take it outside,' " Dufour said. "Earthquake pulled a large knife and started to walk behind the bar. I pulled the gun out. I said, 'One more step, and it will be your last. . . . All bullshit aside, it's my place, my rules. I like you all. The day you threaten me and step behind my bar is the day they carry you out.'

"He stopped, put the knife back, went outside, and they finished their fisticuffs outside. That was the first time they knew I carried a weapon. . . . End of discussion. That was it. They fully respected me from that day on," Dufour said.

Another gang member known as Mack invited Dufour to his trailer home. The surveillance team knew Mack kept a python at his trailer but had not told Dufour.

While drinking a beer in the trailer home, Dufour noticed a large white rat crossing the kitchen floor.

"Oh, yeah," Mack said. "That's Spot's plaything."

"I couldn't believe a dog would play with a live rat," Dufour said.

"At about the second can of beer, I felt this large snake crawling up my leg. It was a six-foot python. That was Spot. About that time he offered me tequila. I'm not a big drinker. I can drink and stay sober for many hours because I pace myself. But I immediately started drinking straight shots of tequila because this snake had wrapped itself around my left arm, around my neck, and had its head laying on my shoulder. Mack said have you been a good boy today and kissed the snake on its head. He suggested I kiss him on the head so he would get to know me. I did."

Another hazard was the women whom the gang members constantly offered Dufour as a token of friendship.

"The bikers thought it was a great honor to offer a female to you for sexual services. You had to figure a way to refuse and not insult them and still maintain you were a bad guy. Most bad guys would say, 'Great. I got a good-looking woman there.' They didn't worry about gonorrhea, syphilis, and it was prior to when AIDS was big. They didn't care," Dufour said.

"You would go to a house and three or four women in their early twenties would be sleeping on mattresses. The guy would say, 'Go and take care of Dennis or Ron.' It could be all the women, or they would say, put on a show for us. It would be female-female or whatever.

"You had to figure a way to continue conducting business or say you had to take care of something and would take a rain check. You had to still maintain that relationship, because a cop would say I can't do that.

"It's quite natural for them to offer females," Dufour said. "If you have a female or I have a female that I am taking care of, and the organization protects their women, and the woman displeases me, I can say, 'You are out of here, you go to Joe. You are Joe's property.' She becomes a chattel of Joe. Joe can turn her around and say, 'We are going to have a party. My five buddies are going to share you.' They are physical property that they deal. The girls would come up at birthday parties or barbecues and offer you sex."

One gang member offered to have a scantily clad woman strip for Dufour and put on a show at the gang member's home.

"I figured that would lead to something else," Dufour said. "I said, 'I have to meet this guy to discuss some stolen money orders.' I mentioned who I was going to see so he could check. But this same girl he offered me became a pain after that. She would come into the bar half naked with no panties on and put her knees up on the bar and say, 'I'm still waiting for that rain check.' I would say, 'Yeah.'

It was uncomfortable from that time on. She would say, 'Anytime you are ready.' She was a blond, very chesty young girl. She was one of the topless dancers at one of the clubs. You have to walk away from it. Any red-blooded American male would say, 'Wow!' "

Refusing sexual advances was difficult, but mixing drinks for the gang members was easy.

"It was either opening a can of beer or it was Crown Royal on the rocks," Dufour said. "The other customers drank beer or vodka or a scotch and water. If someone said, 'Scotch and water,' you knew they weren't a biker. A biker would say, 'Give me Crown Royal or a shot of Wild Turkey.' I would give them a double shot. They would say, 'I appreciate that.' The next time they came in they would leave you twenty or fifty dollars on the bar. That's the way it was. You took care of them, and they didn't care.

"Occasionally, when they were getting wound up because they were, as they say, upset or pissed off about something, they would drink Wild Turkey 101. When I saw them drinking that, I knew I had problems, because they were either upset with their girls or having other problems. It's one-hundred-one proof and would burn if lit with a match," Dufour said.

"I had a barmaid by the name of Madonna. She had a habit, if I said, 'We are out of Crown,' she would say, 'Don't worry. I'll mix this bottle in.' Grrrr. I really couldn't say yes or no. The minute I started protesting too much she would say, 'Everybody in the bar business does it.' I would say, 'Do what you got to do. I'll go grab a couple of bottles anyway.' If I got paranoid about adding cheap liquor, a normal person wouldn't do that. You have to do what a normal person in that quality establishment would do. I would watch her short the customers. If I gave the guy ten dollars back, she would say, 'What, are you crazy?' I'm supposed to be a bad guy from New York.

"Probably the toughest time I had was when the liquor authorities came in and started pushing me around. One guy said he was with the Lubbock police department and he would kill me if my back was turned," Dufour said, explaining that the officer didn't like long-haired bikers.

The FBI decided to bring the operation to a close when it got word that some gang members in Canada were plotting to kill Dufour. Dufour announced that he was going on vacation, and he closed the bar. In the early morning hours of February 21, 1985, Dufour met with some two hundred law enforcement officers from agencies that had participated in the operation, including the Texas Rangers, the

DEA, and the IRS. Several of the officers apologized to Dufour for having given him a rough time when they came to check the bar.

"I said, 'You don't have to apologize, because you did the greatest service. The look in your eyes, the hate you had, probably saved my life.' Things like that you can't plan," Dufour said.

The FBI brought in an armored military carrier to mow down the fence surrounding the gang's compound on the outskirts of Lubbock. Dufour warned the FBI's SWAT team from Dallas that the gang had two Rottweilers. Also, the gang kept money and cocaine in an aquarium with a rattlesnake in it.

"When the SWAT team entered, they had to shoot the dogs," Dufour said. "They shot one, and the SWAT member stepped over him. He wasn't dead and got up and tried to bite the next agent. They had to shoot him again."

In the melee that followed, the armored vehicle ran over three of the gang members' motorcycles. "That created a good bit of controversy because their bikes are more precious than their wives or children," Dufour said.

The FBI arrested more than eighty members of the gang on narcotics, firearms, and racketeering charges not only in Lubbock but in eight states. Nearly all pleaded guilty to narcotics, firearms, and racketeering charges. The Sidebuster never reopened. In the meantime, the bureau had rung up a profit of sixty thousand dollars on the bar's operation.

In contrast to the success of the Bandidos investigation, the CISPES investigation blackened the FBI's reputation and raised troubling questions about whether the new bureau was really that different from the old bureau. The investigation began in June 1981, when Frank Varelli, a native of El Salvador, met with Dan Flanagan, an agent in the Dallas field office, and gave him a wild story about right-wing Salvadoran death squads targeting people in the U.S.

The Dallas office knew nothing about El Salvador or its politics. But Gary L. Penrith, then an assistant special agent in charge in Dallas, thought it was worth checking out.

"If half of what he was saying was true, we had something super," Penrith said. "He said they were murdering people, setting up hits in the U.S. for anyone who defected from the administration there. I said let's work it, see if other agencies have heard of him, and see if it's true."[186]

The FBI checked with the CIA, which thought that Varelli knew what he was talking about, Penrith said.

"Then he started talking about CISPES," Penrith said.

CISPES—the Committee in Solidarity with the People of El Salvador—is an amorphous left-wing group that raises money in America for humanitarian aid to El Salvador. Varelli claimed that it, too, was targeting Americans.

"Once again, I had never heard of it," Penrith said. "It [the investigation into CISPES] went on for six months. I read some of the pamphlets. It looked like people who were worried about the government there. I never read we should bomb AT&T. I said let's close it."

Two years later, the Dallas office, with the consent of headquarters, reopened the CISPES case as a terrorism investigation. This time, the investigation was directed by headquarters and got out of control. In trying to establish criminal activity, FBI agents attended political rallies, conducted surveillance of nuns, took notes on what people said in exercise of their constitutional rights, and opened files on 2,375 individuals.

According to U.S. Representative Don Edwards, a California Democrat and former FBI agent who heads the House Judiciary Committee's subcommittee on civil and constitutional rights, agents "took thousands of photographs at peaceful demonstrations, surveilled rallies on college campuses, attended a Mass at a university, surveilled churches and church groups, sent informants to numerous meetings, rummaged through trash, collected mailing lists, took phone numbers off posters opposing intervention in Central America, recorded license-plate numbers of vehicles parked outside public meetings, and obtained long-distance billing records from telephone companies."[187]

Unlike the bureau's activities under Hoover, the investigation had no political motive. No one from the White House even knew about the investigation, the purpose of which was to gather evidence of violations of law. But a later review by the FBI's inspection division determined that there were two major problems with the CISPES investigation: Varelli's information was false, and even if it had been correct, the techniques used were too broad, unfocused, and chilling—a fact that some agents in the field noted at the time.

For example, a July 1984 memo from headquarters specifically instructed field offices not to monitor political activity. But the special agent in charge of the Denver office sent headquarters a memo saying that "in spite of attempts by the bureau to clarify guidelines and goals for this investigation, the field is still not sure how much seemingly legitimate political activity should be monitored."

Since the days of COINTELPRO and the abuses of the Hoover era, the bureau had established elaborate procedures and guidelines for high-level review of the legality of opening sensitive cases. But these reviews came into play only if intrusive techniques like wiretapping were to be used. In the CISPES investigation, no one was wiretapped, no homes were broken in to. In fact, nothing illegal happened. For that reason, the case did not get the kind of scrutiny it would otherwise have received.

The bureau started its own review of the CISPES investigation only after members of Congress and the media began asking questions about the investigation, according to D. Caroll Toohey. Then in the inspection division, Toohey headed an internal probe of the CISPES investigation by twenty-five agents over a period of four months.

"I had been in Hawaii," Toohey said in describing how his review of the CISPES investigation had started. "When I came back, there was a note on the door saying, 'I hope you had a good time, because it's over.' " The note was from William Gavin, then assistant director over the inspection division.

Toohey's report with appendixes fills an entire filing cabinet.

"There was proper predication for the inquiry, but a lot of it, unfortunately, was furnished by Varelli," Toohey said. "Had we looked closer at him and discovered a little more about him and his motives and veracity, perhaps we wouldn't have gone into the case. Once we got into the inquiry, it got out of hand. The scope was too wide. I didn't find it to be so intrusive, but it was more of a waste of time. We spent a lot of time checking people's driving records and seeing if they had an arrest record. . . . I didn't find any indication really that they were interested in political opinions. They didn't care. They were trying to see if they were involved in terrorism against the U.S. Agents did show up at public meetings. The interpretation was it was a First Amendment problem. They were there to see if an overt [criminal] act was committed. If someone stood up and incited them to bomb something, that was the purpose, and to identify the leaders of the organization."[188]

"We found an unreliable informant and a case agent who was inept and a supervisor who didn't do his job," said Revell.[189]

Eventually, Daniel Flanagan, Varelli's case agent, resigned from the bureau after admitting he had withheld FBI payments meant for Varelli. He also paid one thousand dollars in restitution to the FBI.[190]

If Webster, who was then director, had known the extent of the investigation, he would have seen it as a problem, said Russell J.

Bruemmer, who was one of Webster's assistants at the FBI and later Webster's general counsel when Webster headed the CIA.

"His antennae would have gone up," Bruemmer said. "He would have said, 'Why are we doing this? Where are we going with it?' He might have said, 'You have thirty days to show that somebody violated something.' But it just kept going."[191]

As it turned out, the CISPES investigation continued until 1985. After the FBI's internal investigation started, Varelli failed an FBI polygraph test on the veracity of his information, according to Paul K. Minor, who was the FBI's senior polygraph examiner at the time.[192]

Sessions, who never failed to point out that when he became director in 1987 the CISPES investigation had already begun under Webster, suspended three FBI employees for two weeks and reprimanded three others—including Penrith—for mishandling the investigation. He also improved procedures for reviewing such investigations before they begin.

"Varelli's background was not checked, he was not properly and thoroughly reviewed, and there was just negligence all the way along the line," Sessions said.[193]

The Dallas field office is in the West End, an area that once was filled with warehouses but now is the trendy part of the city, with restaurants, boutiques, shops, and bars. The FBI occupies the first, second, third, and sixth floors of Landmark Center, an orange-brick building with green awnings. On the third floor, receptionists sit behind bulletproof glass in a waiting area that has maroon carpeting and red leather chairs.

Everyone in the FBI has to contend with a certain number of calls and visits from nuts. Some callers say that the Russians brainwashed them or that they have become robots. What is the FBI going to do about it? Some agents accommodate them by pushing a few keys on their telephone keypads. Hearing the tones, the callers think they have been deprogrammed.

The investigation of the Kennedy assassination brought out unstable people from all over the country. A Cleveland man told the FBI that Jacqueline Kennedy was a Communist, and that the president had been shot with her permission.

A Newark woman said Kennedy had made her "chief" so that she could investigate a master spy ring. She said Hoover had agreed that she was "chief." Deadpan, the agents who interviewed her wrote in their report: "Although with difficulty, she was admonished, and told never again to refer to herself as being associated with the FBI in any manner. As the agents departed, she said, 'It is always good to see my men.' "[194]

The Dallas office has had its share of unusual visitors. Around lunchtime one afternoon, an agitated man went to the office and demanded to see an agent.

"George has no business out there!" he ranted as an agent politely showed him the elevator. "Abba is no kin to me. Peggy is no kin to me. All them people are no kin to me. I'll get the military after you all."

To enter the locked door of the FBI's Dallas office, agents must punch in a code and peer into a scanner. Every eye has a unique pattern of blood vessels, and the device stores in its memory the pattern for each FBI employee. If the patterns match, the retina scanner unlocks the door, storing the time of the entry and the name of the employee who entered. This is one of several unusual security devices the FBI has installed at field offices since a gunman held ten employees hostage at the Atlanta field office in 1981.

Regardless of its size, each field office in the FBI has the same basic components. For example, the Dallas office, like every other office, has a firearms vault, a telephone-monitoring room, and a secure vault for coded telecommunications. It also has a media representative, a SWAT team, and a surveillance team. Some offices may have one or even two media representatives who do nothing but deal with media requests. Because of its size, Dallas has a fraction of a media representative—an agent who handles media requests but also investigates crimes.

If a survey were taken of why FBI agents like their jobs, the reason most commonly cited would be their diversity. As Donald W. Ramsey, the media representative in Dallas, explained it, "All of us are professional people, but we don't have to spend all our time in an office. We get to talk to diverse people of different education levels with diverse occupations. There's always that element of excitement, too. You might have to go and make an arrest. You might have to pull your gun. There's always that little element of danger in what we do regardless of whether it's a white collar crime case or a bank robbery."[195]

The second most commonly cited reason would be that agents do something they consider worthwhile.

"We are fortunate enough to do things that novels are written about, that we all kind of fantasize about," Ramsey said. "The James Bond kind of thing, even though the work is not nearly as romantic

as that, or as dangerous. But it's exciting—it sounds like a cliché—
to protect this way of life. . . . This [America] is a great place. I really
do think it's something that is worth defending, and this is one way
to do it."

The third reason might be the prestige of being an agent.

"There is an awful lot of authority and responsibility that goes
with the job," said Ramsey, who has a boyish grin and graying light
brown hair. "I think all of us have an ego that is at least partially
fulfilled by the fact we do have a tremendous amount of authority,
that we are kind of awesome. Most people don't know an FBI agent.
When they hear the words 'FBI' or meet an FBI agent, it's an impressive thing."

At the same time, he said, "It carries a lot of responsibility because
we are responsible for not damaging the organization or its image.
So much of the information we are able to gain that other agencies
maybe are not able to gain is based on the impression that the FBI
[is] a cut above the other organizations. Whether it is true or not, if
that is the public perception, that helps us to gain people's confidence so that we gain information from them. Because the absolute
bottom line on what our profession is about is talking with people
and gaining information from them, whether it is detrimental to
them or to others."

FBI agents see some of the worst of society and some of the best.
As in any law enforcement job, that tends to generate some cynicism.

"I don't know if we become FBI agents because we are suspicious
people, or if we become suspicious because we are FBI agents,"
Ramsey said. "I guess it's an occupational hazard. We see so much
of the bad sides of people that we tend to become a little cynical
and suspicious of everything we see. Not everything. I really can't
say that. But I guess we become more attuned. We become better
observers."

But, for all the power, some people are not impressed. Several
years ago, two Dallas agents were pursuing a fugitive as he drove
into the private parking garage at his apartment house.

"The attendant lowered the gate after the man went through,"
Ramsey said. "They [the agents] said, 'We are from the FBI. We need
to arrest this man.' She said, 'I'm not going to open the gate for you.'
They said, 'This is not a request. This is the FBI, and we have a
legal right to go through here.' She would not let them through.
Ronald Patton, who was a passenger, gets out and walks up to the
wooden arm, snaps it off, and they drive on through."

After that, Dallas agents put up a sign in the office to commemorate the event—a broken gate inside a red circle and a slash across the gate.

"We called him the gate-buster. We made up a tune, which can't be repeated, to the tune of *Ghostbusters*," Ramsey said.

"Most of the time, the last thing you want to do is show your credentials," said Andrew J. Duffin, the special agent in charge of the Houston field office. "More often than not, it gets you in trouble. We have agents who are criticized because we went to the receptionist and said, 'We're with the FBI, and we want to talk to somebody to check references.' People [executives] get mad at that."[196]

As for showing credentials at airports, Duffin said, "I'd like you to come here and go through airport security with me and see the forms that I have to do, and the people who will stand around and want to know who are you holding things up for? The pilot comes back and creates a commotion. We cannot get into the airport without going through a lot of red tape."

The head of the SWAT team in Dallas is George B. (Biff) Temple, a beefy man who speaks with a nasal twang and keeps a color photo of John Wayne over his desk. Before becoming an FBI agent, Temple was a police officer in Kansas and then in New Mexico. Most of the time, Temple works on the squad that deals with bank robberies, fugitives, and extortions. The team trains once a month on mock hijackings or hostage takings.

If suspects have high-powered weapons or are particularly violent, Temple and his team jump in a specially made van and drive to the scene. The team keeps a range of weapons from submachine guns to shotguns in a vault on the third floor. In addition, they keep urban assault suits and body armor in their FBI cars.

"I like going out and making the arrests and taking the bad guys off the street," Temple said. "Most of the agents who try out for SWAT are former police or people with military backgrounds. Others don't have that background, but they are can-do people. . . . Their psychological makeup is they like to go out and do things."

Field agents are supposed to carry their weapons when on duty outside the office. When off duty, it is up to the agent.

"We [on the SWAT team] just don't feel comfortable going anywhere without a weapon," Temple said, raising his voice over the squawk of the FBI dispatcher announcing that a bank robbery is in progress. "I think because of the crime wave, a lot of people would like to carry weapons. We are authorized to, and it makes it nice for us. You just never know, when you go to a grocery store or a restaurant. At the restaurant down in Killeen, Texas, a guy comes in and goes crazy and starts killing people. I would hate to be in a situation of that nature and not have a gun."[197]

The head of the surveillance squad is Ralph A. Torres, a man with gray hair and glasses framed by transparent rims. On his desk on the second floor, Torres keeps a nameplate that says "R.A.T." Because his initials spell RAT, agents in the San Juan office, where Torres was previously assigned, called him "Rat" on the radio.

"Everyone had a nickname on the radio. One was Preacher, another was Wimpy, and I was Rat," he said.

Torres's squad is the Special Operations Group (SOG), the agents who conduct surveillance, pilot surveillance aircraft, and make sure it is safe for technical agents to install wiretaps and bugging devices. Monitoring of calls is done by agents working in a small, blue-carpeted room on the third floor. The room is crammed with tape recorders and has five monitoring positions. If the people begin talking about matters not related to a case, the agents turn off the tape recorders.

A sign on the wall says, "The floggings will continue until morale improves."

Besides wiretaps in foreign counterintelligence or counterterrorism cases, the FBI has authority under Title III of the Omnibus Crime Control and Safe Streets Act of 1968 to engage in electronic eavesdropping in criminal cases. Typically, three hundred such interceptions are authorized each year on the federal level, and most of them are carried out by the FBI.[198]

"In movies, they say, 'Let's tap his phone,' and within hours they are on the phone and getting great sound," Torres said. "In reality, under normal circumstances, it takes at least a month to get Title III court authority on criminal cases."[199]

Most of Torres's squad works out of an offsite, a nondescript office in a warehouse behind a phony consulting-company sign in northwest Dallas. But Torres keeps his radio on to hear operations as they occur. While he is being interviewed, squad members are "taking" a subcontractor to a lunch with a contractor. In FBI parlance, that means they are discreetly watching him. They expect him to pay off the contractor to get a federal building contract.

"There is a skill to surveillance," Torres said. "Part of it is working together. Part is the equipment you have. Part is the training. All will go to a one-week driving school in New York, which we call the Emergency Vehicle Operation Course. It's pursuit driving. They'll feel a little safer and more confident [after taking it].

"We're the only squad in the office where everyone knows everyone else's bladder capacity. They'll advise they'll be out of the car for five minutes. The team leader will keep that in mind and anticipate it.

"Normally, I like to have five cars on a surveillance," Torres said. "It gives enough flexibility. We have worked it with four. On a kidnapping or extortion, we'll get as many people out there as we can.

"The worst day is when nothing happens, or the subject makes a couple of insignificant trips. When he is doing stuff or looking for surveillance, those are great days. It's a beautiful day when you have the plane working, and the plane says, 'He is making a U-turn, or going into a dead end.' They'll park and wait. Those are great days.

"Most of the time in the summer the agents dress in shorts. But you have to have another set of clothes in the car to go to a nice restaurant. You try to sit next to them, hear what they are saying, see who they are with," Torres said.

In following suspects on a street, agents communicate with one another through walkie-talkies. They may wear stereo headsets to give the impression that they are listening to rock music when instead they are receiving instructions on where to go next. Meanwhile, FBI agents in cars or trucks may pass the suspect or move with him along parallel streets. The agents may switch vehicles to further confuse the suspect. The vehicles themselves may be Corvettes, old rattletraps, bulldozers, buses, or ice cream trucks.

"The best surveillance agent doesn't get noticed and doesn't flash credentials. Guys try to avoid parking near schools. You're going to get called in. 'Why is that old man sitting in the field near that school?' A lot of times when we follow someone into a building, if you are challenged, you have to have an excuse. We ask to go to a restroom," Torres said.

When agents follow suspects on planes, they must declare their guns before boarding. Pilots often come out to greet the agents, blowing their cover. In some cases, agents travel on planes without their guns so that they will not be singled out.

"In one situation, we had a guy sit next to him [a suspect] and start talking to the bad guy," Torres said. "He gave them a lot of information on his intentions. It was a terrorist investigation. He was basically saying, 'I'm nuts. I've had a lot of problems these days. I'm under a lot of pressure. I say things I don't mean.' "

Headquarters decided the man did not have the means to carry out his threats, which were not specific enough in any case. Agents openly interviewed the man, scaring him so that he would stop making threats.

In any field office, agents and SACs come and go, but certain support employees tend to remain forever, providing an institutional memory. One of those is Nancy J. Collins. Now secretary to Buck Revell, Collins has been secretary to seven Dallas SACs over the past sixteen years. A leggy, stylishly dressed redhead, Collins began working for the FBI at the age of seventeen and has worked in the Dallas office for thirty-four years.

Collins remembers staying up every night to get out the first report on the assassination of John F. Kennedy a week after the shooting, which took place just down the street from where the field office is now.

Working for Revell is quite different from working for other SACs.

"Anytime you've walked in here, you've seen I have three calls at one time. When this man came to Dallas, the work, the mail, the calls tripled. He is unique unto himself," Collins said.

"I picked up the phone, and a man said, 'This is Tom Clancy.' I said, 'Yeah, right.' He said, 'I am.' "[200]

Indeed, many people—including Revell—believe that the character Bill Shaw, a high-ranking FBI official who becomes FBI director in Clancy's novels, is patterned after him. Clancy insists the character is entirely fictional.

"There may be some accidental similarities, but they are indeed accidental," Clancy said. "Buck is a friend, but I have not immortalized him in that way."

Six feet three inches tall and weighing 250 pounds, Revell wears black-rimmed glasses and looks more like a stocky college professor than an FBI agent. He has thinning hair and a very round face. Revell's memory for detail is legendary, and his globular head seems to be extra large to carry all the information.

A native of Muskogee, Oklahoma, Revell received a B.S. from East Tennessee State University and an M.A. from Temple University. Revell's full name is Oliver Burgin Revell III. His maternal grandfather's name was William, but everyone called him Buck. In high school, people started calling Revell "Buck."

Revell served in the Marines as an aviator. The FBI likes to say it has a close association with the Marines—many of its top officials have been former Marines. In addition, the FBI's training academy is on the Quantico Marine base. However, because the Marine Corps is far smaller than the other services, the representation of former Marines is far lower than that of the other services.

After the assassination of John F. Kennedy, Revell acted as the Marine liaison with the FBI on Lee Harvey Oswald's record in the Marines. Bill Pearson, then a senior FBI resident agent, suggested he join the bureau, and Revell's wife, Sharon, a registered nurse, urged him to do it. Revell started in Kansas City in 1964 and quickly rose through the ranks. In 1980, Webster appointed him assistant director over the criminal division, but after six months, Webster moved him over to the administrative services division.

That was punishment for leaking to a Dallas newspaper the FBI's BRILAB investigation into labor racketeering. As Revell tells it, the reporter, whom he knew and trusted, merely wanted to know if running the story then would cause any harm.

"I said give me what you have. He outlined what was basically correct. I said, 'If you publish that at this point, it will jeopardize the case.' He said he won't. He said, 'Will you tell me when it would be okay?' I said, 'I can't assume that responsibility, but if you call me when I am in Washington, I will check on it," Revell said.[201]

Revell reported the conversation to his superiors. But, during the leak investigation, he failed an FBI polygraph test given by Paul K. Minor, the FBI's senior polygraph examiner at the time. Moreover, Minor said that Revell admitted, near the end of the session, having told the reporter more than he had initially claimed.[202]

"What Buck did was, he got lulled into carelessness because he assumed I didn't know much about the case," Minor said. "That I hadn't been well briefed and didn't understand the ins and outs of the case. That is a ploy I use all the time. I tell people, 'I don't know much about the case. I haven't been very well briefed. But I understand this is the issue. If it's not, tell me. If you previously said something different from this, let me know.' That's what he did. He denied the facts before the test but he made the little admission afterward. I told him he had a problem with the test, and if there was something there, let me know. . . . That is when he said what he did. That ultimately got him in trouble. It had to do with confirmation of what the reporter had. It led the director [Webster] to believe that Buck had been less than candid in the beginning. But it did not show he had been the leak. He did not go that far."

Revell vigorously disputes Minor's account, saying he would not be so stupid as to admit something to Minor that he had not already told the Justice Department, which was conducting the leak investigation.

"How do you defend yourself?" Revell asked. Referring to himself and Minor, Revell said, "There were only two parties to the conversation. On the basis of that, they were ready to trash my career."

As a result of the internal investigation, Webster moved Revell from the coveted position over criminal investigations to the administrative position.

"Webster didn't want to take the heat," Revell said, explaining why Webster had disciplined him. "He knew they didn't have any evidence."

Revell was in the doghouse for a year and a half. Webster then transferred him back to head the criminal division and later promoted him to executive assistant director over investigations. In July 1989, Sessions changed the name of the position to associate deputy director over investigations.

While the titles keep changing, the FBI generally has two officials who report to the director and are over the assistant directors. One of these officials is over the investigative divisions, while the other is over the noninvestigative divisions such as training, administration, and the laboratory.

As the deputy over investigations, Revell helped develop policy and served on a dizzying array of interagency and international committees that deal with intelligence, counterintelligence, terrorism, and the like. From organized crime to terrorism, from counterintelligence to undercover work, Revell has been a visionary, bringing the bureau into the modern era. Under Revell, the FBI built its operations center, known as SIOC, and started a hostage rescue team. It also started its own air force.

"When I went to Washington in 1970 [just before Hoover died], I had never been in an atmosphere of such fear and intimidation," Revell said. "I hated it. I was happy with the work I was doing. It was the organized crime section. But I hated seeing professionals who were so intimidated by the process. . . . When I came into the bureau as a young agent, I had very idealistic expectations. They were severely diminished by the reality of the organization. Not the people or the work but the system. It's been my crusade over twenty-eight years to make the reality live up to the ideal. We're not there, but we're close. Probably as close as a public institution can be."[203]

Like many other agents, Revell missed working in the field and asked to return to it after twelve years at headquarters. Most agents consider special agent in charge to be the best job in the FBI because an SAC is totally responsible for the work produced in his area and does not report on a daily basis to anyone.

Revell asked to go to Dallas, which is near his family, and became SAC there in the summer of 1991. Just after his arrival there, construction near the field office required him to drive his FBI car through a parking lot to get to the FBI's underground garage. A rainstorm had filled in a trench between the parking lot and the street. As Revell drove his car into the trench, the wheels sank, immobilizing the car. Before a tow truck came, an agent photographed the scene, and the office held a contest to see who could come up with the best caption.

"The Buck Stops Here" is the inscription that made its way around the field office under a print of the photo.

On taking over, one of the first things Revell did was to slash by almost half, to fifty, the number of agents who could take their FBI cars home. According to Revell, he was following Justice Department guidelines that allow cars to go home only if agents are likely to have to respond to crimes when they are off duty. But the decision caused unhappiness among agents, who dearly love their FBI cars and come to depend on them as second cars.

Like every other SAC, Revell gets to take his FBI car home. It is a 1992 Mercury Grand Marquis. Like the rest of the FBI's fleet, it has no markings that would distinguish it as a bureau car, or Bucar in FBI jargon. Outfitted with extra-heavy-duty suspension and a high-horsepower engine, it has a flashing red light that can be taken from under the front seat and placed on the dashboard, a siren and public address system, an encrypted radio, a cellular phone, and a shotgun rack under the ceiling. The shotgun is kept locked in the trunk. When an arrest is planned, it is taken out of the trunk and placed in the rack.

"SACs are like anybody else," Revell said when asked about his encounter with the ditch in front of the field office. "When you don't see a ditch, you go in."

Since coming to Dallas, Revell has expanded his empire, adding four resident agencies and erecting a section at the field office to display employee awards. To the left of Revell's desk are hats, mugs, and plaques received from all over the world. To the right are photos of him with various presidents. A glass case displays more mementos. Behind the sofa are more plaques. On a coffee table are the scales of justice in brass.

If there is a foreign intelligence agency or national police force that has not recognized Revell with a plaque or trophy, it is probably an accident. Revell is especially proud of the National Intelligence Distinguished Service Medal he received in 1991 from Webster when Webster headed the CIA.

The top priority in the Dallas office is bank and savings-and-loan frauds. The FBI receives an average of 2,346 referrals from financial institutions of fraud cases each month, and the bureau has 8,678 such investigations in progress at any one time. The greatest focus of the effort is Dallas, where 100 of the 240 agents are assigned to bank frauds. The increased emphasis began in 1987, when Bobby R. Gillham, then special agent in charge, asked for a meeting at headquarters with FBI and Justice officials.

"I asked for fifty additional agents immediately," Gillham said. "Institutionally, you don't ask for fifty FBI agents. After the laughter in the room died down, it turned out we got twenty approved in six weeks."[204]

The second priority in Dallas is violent crime. The office successfully investigated members of the Juan Garcia Abrego gang, who were major traffickers for the Cali drug cartel. Revell formed a task force with local law enforcement to work the cases.[205]

"Dillinger and Bonnie and Clyde, even Pretty Boy Floyd, by today's standards would be minor bit players," Revell said. "We have kids in south Dallas that have killed more people than they ever thought about. . . . Even the old mafia had a reason to kill. They may be reasons we didn't accept. But the mafia didn't kill just for the hell of it. We have a number of groups that do that. A number of individuals have no hesitation about killing if someone looks at them the wrong way."

Revell's attractive wife, Sharon, who is widely admired within the bureau, has largely banned plaques from their four-bedroom home in a suburb of Dallas. One wall, however, displays an aerial photo of Revel, France, taken by the French government. Since coming to Dallas, "the police commissioners from Germany, Norway, Denmark, Sweden, Italy, France, Spain, Israel, Peru, Colombia have maintained contact," Revell said. "We have gone there or they have come here. Also Korea, Japan, Thailand."

Revell said he is not bothered by the jokes about his plaques. "As long as people say, 'He's competent, he's professional, he has integrity,' I don't care what they say," Revell said.

Being married to Revell has had its advantages and frustrations, according to Sharon Revell. "In our thirty-three years of marriage, this is our twenty-second house," she said. "So we have moved twenty-two times. It's tough on the kids. Russ [their oldest child] was in five schools from seventh to twelfth grade."

"After a thirteen- or fourteen-hour day, he [Revell] would come home and watch the eleven o'clock news and read more papers from his briefcase, then get up at 5:30 A.M. That was typical," said Russ Revell, now in the Air Force.

But Sharon Revell said she has had "the kind of life that I could only fantasize about as a young girl growing up in a small town in North Carolina. I've been able to travel the world to meet wonderfully interesting people and to be actually a part of history in the making."

Having begun his career as liaison to the FBI on the JFK assassination, Revell recently completed the circle in Dallas by instructing agents to try to find the three so-called tramps said by some assassination buffs to have had something to do with the killing. Prompted by the controversy created by Oliver Stone's movie JFK, Revell's decision thirty years after the event illustrates the discretion that FBI agents have.

The two tramps who are living had nothing to add to the debate.

"I haven't done anything," John Gedney, now sixty-seven, told the Dallas Morning News. "I finally settled down and got a job." In Dallas, his activities were easy to summarize: "Came to town, went to jail, left town. That's the story," he said.[206]

Revell again made news during the 1992 presidential campaign when he appeared on 60 Minutes to confirm that the Dallas field office had tried to determine if Jim Oberwetter, the Texas chairman of the Bush-Quayle campaign, had been planning to wiretap the office of third-party candidate Ross Perot. Scott Barnes, a purveyor of tall tales who has claimed to be a former military intelligence officer, had told Perot that Oberwetter had asked him to help install the wiretaps. Perot, in turn, had alerted the FBI. While the FBI knew that Barnes lacked credibility, the bureau was able to obtain corroboration for his story, including a statement from a BBC-TV reporter. In retrospect, the corroboration may have been cooked up by Barnes. But there was enough support to convince the bureau that the allegation should be checked out by getting Oberwetter's reaction to it. The Dallas office assigned an undercover agent to meet with Oberwetter. When the agent broached the idea of wiretapping Perot, Oberwetter said he was not interested. After the matter became public, Oberwetter charged that the bureau had tried to "entrap" him.

Some newspapers editorialized that the FBI had gone too far and was injecting itself into a political campaign. But the bureau had handled it exactly as it should have. Having checked into the story as much as it could, the bureau had no other way to verify the allegation without using an undercover operative. If the FBI had received a tip before the Watergate scandal of a plot to bug the headquarters of the Democratic National Committee, and had caught the individuals before they had broken in and installed wiretaps, newspapers no doubt would have commended the FBI. While it is possible to take sting operations too far—as postal inspectors did in barraging Keith Jacobson, a fifty-six-year-old farmer, with solicitations to buy child pornography—this operation had been approved by high-level FBI and Justice Department officials and conformed with Justice guidelines for FBI undercover operations. A succession of attorneys general have approved the guidelines, and as long as there is sufficient reason to believe a crime has been committed, the courts have repeatedly upheld the operations themselves. To look the other way—as Hoover's bureau did in politically charged cases—would have opened up the FBI to an accusation that the bureau was part of a conspiracy by Bush to penetrate Perot's campaign.

"We have developed an ethic in the bureau that we are going to follow these cases wherever they go, we are going to be totally apolitical, and the chips are going to have to fall where they fall," Revell said. "We've done that with federal judges, with members of Congress, with Cabinet officers. That's the only way to do it. If you try to skew these things, you are aiding and abetting the illicit process. You take them wherever they lead you."[207]

Even though Revell was no longer at the top of the bureau hierarchy, Sessions continued to call him for advice. When the Los Angeles riots broke out over the verdict on the beating of Rodney King, then Attorney General William P. Barr assigned Revell to coordinate federal law enforcement efforts in Los Angeles. Revell is one of the few FBI executives Webster would have recommended as director. Of the bureau's directors, only Clarence Kelley had been a former agent.[208]

For all the joking about Revell's plaques, no one has claimed that his ego actually interfered with his work or his relations with people. Because of his contributions to the modern FBI, Revell is one of the most admired bureau officials.

"Revell was a driving force in the new bureau," said Robert E. Lill, who headed undercover operations at headquarters. "He had the personality, intellect, and stamina to do it."

"Buck Revell is one of my heroes," said Dana E. Caro, who headed the Washington metropolitan field office. "He really cares about the FBI."

"Everyone can kid about his ego and being a bull in a china shop, but there is a tremendous amount of substance to Buck," said James W. Greenleaf, the FBI's associate deputy director for administration. "Quite frankly, we miss a lot of his insights back here. He was good."[209]

8
Training Division: Code Red

● **Bryant L. Barnhart,** a twenty-four-year-old with a light brown ponytail, lights up a Drum cigarette from Holland at the All-Med Drugstore in Quantico, Virginia.

"I've done everything from bank robberies to kidnappings," he boasts, then launches into an animated description of how he poisoned a federal judge.

Just then, an FBI car, siren screaming and tires burning, screeches to a halt outside. Another FBI car pulls up in front of the Bank of Hogan next door.

The air is filled with shouted commands over loudspeakers mounted on FBI cars as agents leap from their vehicles.

"Halt! FBI!" an agent calls out from behind a shotgun.

But Barnhart need fear neither arrest nor conviction. He is being paid eight dollars an hour to act out a life of crime. The Bank of Hogan is not at risk, either. If it is *not* robbed twice a week, it may as well go out of business. Indeed, says Patrick J. Foran, the FBI agent who is the mayor of the town, "The only way I stay in office is to have the highest crime rate in the United States."

His "town" is Hogan's Alley, a $5 million training ground for new agents, located at the FBI Academy in Quantico, Virginia. In sixteen weeks of intensive training, the academy takes men and women who generally have no previous law enforcement experience and turns them into agents who carry a gun and credentials. The academy, part of the FBI's training division, also plays host each year to 989 local police officers who enroll at the FBI's National Academy within the FBI Academy, 748 new Drug Enforcement Administration agents, 672 new FBI agents, and 3,988 current FBI agents studying everything from management to working undercover. Finally, the academy's 150 full-time instructors conduct research and field special teams that help agents deal with stress after a shooting incident or cope with other work-related problems.

The early bureau had no formal training courses. For that reason, the FBI considered law enforcement experience or a background in law desirable. In January 1928, Hoover established the first formal training course for new agents. He also began recruiting lawyers and accountants. However, it was a myth that agents had to be accountants or lawyers. Most were not.

Until the FBI Academy opened at Quantico in 1972, the bureau conducted training in a handful of classrooms on the sixth floor of the Old Post Office Building in Washington and in a classroom and gym at the Justice Department. Trainees spent just three weeks on the Marine Base at Quantico, learning to fire weapons and make arrests.

For all his competitiveness with local police departments, Hoover recognized the value of developing the police as information sources. In 1935, he conceived of the National Academy—a place where police could learn the latest in crime-fighting techniques— as a way of seeding local law enforcement with officers who could be called on to help the FBI. In the process, local police became far more effective.

"Hoover really professionalized law enforcement," said Richard J. Gallagher, an assistant director over the FBI's criminal investigative division under Clarence Kelley. "When I was an agent in the field, most of these departments had no training programs."

Together with a rigorous training program for new FBI agents, the National Academy was one of Hoover's greatest legacies. Just before Hoover died on May 2, 1972, he saw his vision take shape in concrete form. The academy opened its doors three days later.

The FBI Academy is off Interstate Route 95 some forty miles south of Washington. It is reached by a long, wooded, two-lane road through Quantico Marine Base, from which its 385 acres are carved. Signs like "Danger—Government field reservation—Firing in progress" pepper the roadside.

The complex of twenty-one tan-brick buildings that comprise the academy looks like a comfortable, well-kept community college. At the entrance to the administration building, an inscription on a pillar on the overhang over the driveway reminds visitors that construction was started in 1970 during Hoover's reign. Inside, high up on the walls of the sunny atrium the expected exhortations are carved, relating to the letters FBI and its slogan. For fidelity, "Prosperity asks for fidelity; adversity exacts it"—Seneca. For bravery, "Courage is resistance to fear, mastery of fear—not absence of fear."—Mark Twain. For integrity, "Integrity without knowledge is weak and useless, and knowledge without integrity is dangerous and dreadful."—Samuel Johnson.

Once an FBI trainee steps through the entrance to the academy, he or she need never leave. There's a student cafeteria where the food is free, laundry service, a swimming pool, a student store that sells everything from greeting cards to FBI mugs, a pub that doubles as a cafeteria during the day, a trainer for athletic activities, and a nurse for related injuries or sickness.

Glass-walled corridors interconnect all the buildings. The configuration of the buildings produces a quad in the middle. Like high school, there is mayhem in the halls when classes change. Everyone wears a T-shirt with appropriate insignia and khaki pants. Each FBI class chooses its special T-shirt color and class slogan.

Under Hoover, trainees wore white shirts, jackets, and ties to class. As soon as he died, the standards began to loosen up.

"One day we would go into class, and the instructors would say, 'You have to wear coats and ties to class," said Steve Ramey, whose class was the first to be sworn in after Hoover's death. "The next day, they would say, 'We have thought about this. You can take your jackets off.' Then it was, 'You can wear sport shirts.' Then on Thursday they would say, 'It's back to coats and ties.'"

By the time James Greenleaf became assistant director over the training division in 1986, the pendulum had swung the other way. Greenleaf decided that the academy had become too much like *Animal House*. There were wild parties in the dorms, and women wore halter tops without bras in the cafeteria. There was even a rumor—which was not true—that a male agent had been caught having sex with a female trainee on a dice table. The tables are used to train agents how to gamble.

Greenleaf established tougher disciplinary standards and required uniforms. He banned jeans from the campus and required students to dress up in coat and tie for dinner on Wednesday nights. For the first such dinner, a Drug Enforcement Administration class given to state and local law enforcement officers showed up wearing T-shirts with ties painted on them. After consulting with DEA management the next morning, Greenleaf dismissed them, giving them three hours to pack their bags.[210]

"I was concerned about their lack of discipline. If they behaved like that in an academy environment, I wondered how they would actually behave on the street," he said.

To become FBI agents, candidates must be U.S. citizens between the ages of twenty-three and thirty-seven. They must hold a degree from a four-year college. They must pass a background check and receive a top-secret security clearance.

The FBI seeks applicants who have had significant work experience in fields ranging from law to banking. The average age of new agents is roughly twenty-nine. Close to 15 percent have law degrees and 15 percent have accounting degrees, proportions that roughly apply to existing agents as well. Competition for the new slots the FBI has each year is keen. In recent years, only 300 to 500 agents have been accepted each year out of a total of 5,000 to 11,000 who take the test. Typically, only about one in twenty applications is accepted. Turnover—now down to 2 percent a year—keeps dropping, so the number of openings keeps dwindling.

Of the existing agents, the greatest number—665—come from New York State, followed by 486 from California. The greatest number of agents—209—went to the University of Maryland, followed by the State University of New York with 139 agents, and the University of Texas with 131. A total of 3,860 agents served in the military, including 1,877 in the Army, 753 in the Marine Corps, 607 in the Navy, 581 in the Air Force, and 42 in the Coast Guard.

"I am very positive about the future of the FBI," William Baker said. "We are getting a very strong cadre of investigators. The selection system for agents is strong. I am pleased at their caliber and the work they are doing."

A class of thirty-two students, including eight women, two blacks, and two Hispanics, was sworn in at 8:15 A.M. one recent Monday. All the new agents were well dressed, the men in business suits, the women in jackets with skirts or pants. At long tables arranged in tiers like a small amphitheater, they sat in assigned seats. Each trainee's name was written in large letters on a label taped on the table edge in front of him, where the instructor could see it. On top of each desk was a navy-colored notebook with the letters FBI on it and an inch-thick sheaf of paper—class assignments, evaluation sheets, applications, list of requirements, student handbook—just the sort of things you'd find on the first day of school anywhere.

Lawrence A. Bonney, chief of the special agent training unit, stood in the front of the room. Including the salaries trainees receive at the academy, the FBI spends an estimated thirty thousand dollars to recruit, check out, and train each new agent. The bureau does not want its investment wasted.

"If you're here as a résumé filler to stay three or four years and go out and get yourself a high-paying job, with a little moniker at the end that says former FBI agent, don't waste our time, don't waste your time," he said. "We want folks who are committed to the United States of America and believe in what it stands for, and in its ideals. We want people who will make a difference, who have a sense of mission, and we want people who believe in truth, justice, and the American way, as hokey as that sounds."[211]

A gray-haired woman went to the front of the room to instruct the students—designated class 92-3—on registration. Her long red fingernails stood out. By contrast, to project their seriousness, the new female agents wore no nail polish. They wore light makeup or none at all.

The woman doing registrar duty said that the bureau has strict rules about agents' names. "If you are a junior and your father is living, you have to retain junior in your name," she said. "You may use your middle name if you like and use the first name as an initial."

She told a black student that there was already a John E. Lewis in the FBI. "You're going to have to drop the E or use your middle name."

"That would be interesting," an instructor noted from the back of the room, in that the man's middle name is Edgar, and that would make him J. Edgar. "We're never going to let him die," the instructor said.

Despite his classmates' encouragement, the new agent decided on John Edgar, rather than J. Edgar, as his official bureau name.

Anthony E. Daniels, the assistant director over the training division, came in and automatically scanned the faces of the class. Daniels is small in stature, with intensely blue eyes and black hair with distinguished flecks of gray in it. He continued to scan the class, as if picking through a crowd for a suspicious-looking person, or as if to memorize the faces. Daniels asked each student to give his or her background.

The new agents seemed to have been chosen for diversity in accents. A man with a southern accent was a former Louisiana state trooper: "I wanted to be part of the pride and integrity of the bureau," he drawled. A man from Puerto Rico with a Spanish accent said he wanted to use his language abilities in his new job. A black man who gave the impression of great physical strength became suddenly vulnerable, recounting how as a kid he "watched *The FBI* on TV, and it's been a childhood dream."

One new agent had just spent twelve months in the Persian Gulf. Another man had an M.A. and a law degree. A woman with curly blond hair had just graduated from law school. An athletic-looking man "worked for the Yankees" and was the son of a former agent: "I wanted to be with the best," he said.

The decision to join up is often based on happenstance—on having gotten to know FBI agents, for example. Among the countless other factors that decide them, one new agent enjoyed his investigative experience with his Marine battalion while serving in the Persian Gulf. A fair-haired young man from Utah said that his father is an agent. He said twice in the three sentences he used to introduce himself that joining the bureau was what he has always wanted to do. A former Lehman Brothers paper trader from New York said that his brother is an agent. An attractive blond woman from Phoenix said, "Every family member had been in law enforcement," and she's just carrying on the tradition.

Many were influenced by television shows such as *The FBI*. The show premiered on ABC on September 19, 1965, and featured Efrem Zimbalist, Jr., as FBI Inspector Lewis Erskine. For many agents already in the bureau, the 1959 movie *The FBI Story*, starring James Stewart, had been their inspiration.

Many of the new trainees bring special expertise that will likely be used in future assignments. A buttoned-down New Yorker did internal audits for E.F. Hutton. Another man did forensic engineering. One of the women previously worked for the Ohio state treasurer.

The introductions finished, Daniels asked the students to raise their right hands and repeat after him: *I do solemnly swear that I will support and defend the Constitution of the United States against all enemies, foreign and domestic. . . .*

Over the next sixteen weeks, the trainees would receive instruction in such diverse subjects as interviewing techniques, development of informants, legal principles, physical fitness, operation of an emergency vehicle, forensic science, foreign counterintelligence, the use of computers, background investigations, the polygraph, and the history of the FBI.

In classroom instruction, as at Hogan's Alley, the academy makes heavy use of role-playing. Secretaries, agents, and cooks are all enlisted to play the bad guy—or gal. A typical classroom is amphitheater-style, with mustard-colored chairs behind five semi-circular tables that rise on tiers. Each position is labeled with the student's name on a large card. The students keep the same seats at these tables through their training; teachers who are FBI agents come to them.

A class in white collar crime began one afternoon with a problem outlined by Philip Desing, the instructor: It seems that seven thousand dollars was missing from the day's receipts of Helen Powell, a bank teller who was actually a secretary at Quantico. "It is hard to accidentally give away seven thousand dollars," Desing noted. "Maybe five or ten dollars . . . What do we want to do? Anyone have any suggestions?" he asked.[212]

"Contact headquarters and see if we have anything on the teller," a student suggested.

"We have done an indices check," Desing said. "It is negative. Whom should we interview? What about the branch manager? There is some missing information. Let's get as much information on her background as we can. We need proof to verify the story."

Desing said that the FBI does not need a subpoena to obtain bank records that may implicate officers, directors, or employees in a crime. But he recommended bringing one to the bank anyway, just in case.

"The financial institution may not be aware of the law," he said.

Two students volunteered to play agents who would interview the bank manager, Mr. Porter. Another instructor at the academy, Porter played his role with flair.

"Thank you for getting over here so quickly," Porter said. "It's an unfortunate situation. Tellers keep twenty thousand dollars on hand. Quite frankly, she [Helen Powell] had no legitimate explanation for what happened to it."

Just then, there was a loud banging on a door. In a loud voice, Fred Sloan, a bank customer, said that the bank had just bounced one of his checks. In tracing what happened, he had found that Helen Powell had endorsed a check he had written to someone else. Now his account was overdrawn.

"What kind of bank are you running here?" he demanded. As he spoke, one of the agent trainees peered over Sloan's shoulder to catch a glimpse of the records he held in his hands.

Quickly, the agents learned that on her teller's meager salary, Powell had been trading heavily in commodities. Bringing subpoenas with them, they tried to interview an officer at the commodities firm. He was reluctant.

"Can I call my attorney and ask him?" he asked.

"Actually, I don't see any reason for you to contact your attorney," one of the agent trainees said. "You're not a focus of our investigation."

"I don't even want to be involved in the investigation at all," he said.

Eventually, the agents confronted Helen Powell. After they read her rights to her, she gave a long-winded explanation of what had happened, blaming it on her ex-husband. Her story did not check out. However, before she was arrested, she excused herself. It was the end of her shift at the academy.

Desing critiqued the new agents' performance. Overall, he said, they did an excellent job.

"Everyone in the class might have done something, or asked questions, slightly differently. That's okay. You want to run it your way," he said reassuringly.

But there was no need to read Helen Powell her rights.

"She's not in custody. That's [reading rights] a big turn-off. You need to establish rapport," Desing told the class. "Good questions on the ex-husband," he said. "I was impressed that you got his date of birth."

By pinning Powell down about her former husband, the agents were able to get enough information to refute her story that it was all his fault.

"When Fred Sloan jumps into the room, don't be afraid to say, 'Excuse me, we are conducting an investigation,'" then ask to see his records, Desing said. "I wouldn't stand behind the person and look over his shoulder," he said to laughter.

Advising the commodities broker not to get a lawyer was also out of bounds.

"Saying, 'Don't get an attorney' is a no-no," he said. "Say, 'You can do whatever you feel like doing.' Then explain why you are here."

Even though Helen Powell was excused, her name will pop up again. Hers is the name used whenever a woman has committed a crime at Quantico. Even the academy's attractive public affairs representative, Kelley Cibulas, has played Helen Powell.

"They gave me a script," Cibulas said. "They told me what I had done. They gave me a few options on how I should explain it, but at no point was I to confess. I didn't, and managed to cut short the interview by saying I had a daughter in school, and I have to pick her up. That was my debut."[213]

Each class receives four hours of training in ethics, which has been taught for five years by Walt H. Sirene. One afternoon, the ethics class began with a review of the case of Dan Mitrione, the Miami agent who had begun taking a cut of cocaine from the traffickers he was supposed to be arresting.

"There will be temptations," Sirene told the class. "You will have to make judgments. That's why an organization like ours creates rules and regulations to discourage the development of habits that lead to what Dan Mitrione did. As the small gifts build up, we don't know for sure that the slippery slope works. But it probably does. Pretty soon you make bigger and bigger rationalizations."

Then Sirene launched into a series of scenarios designed to test the new agents' judgment. He said that Ted Bundy, the serial killer, was going to have to be set free unless the agent on the case stretched things a little, perhaps concealing some evidence or exaggerating in his testimony.

"What should you do?" Sirene asked the class.[214]

"I'd like to hear whether you will get caught," said Brad, a man with brown hair and glasses who was obviously the class clown. His comment was greeted with laughter.

"Let's say you won't get caught. You don't think you will get caught."

"You don't compromise yourself," another student said.

"What happens if a prosecutor were to tell you to go ahead and stretch it a little bit?" Sirene asked.

In response, a student cited a statute dealing with obstruction of justice: "It's a new case. Obstruction of justice. Suborning perjury."

But Brad was not convinced. "I deal every day with the U.S. Attorney. He is the one who will make me look good or bad," he said.

Sirene went on to another problem: An agent was too aggressive in handcuffing and handling a prisoner. "What do you do?"

"I would ask why he did that," a student said.

"Does management need to know this?"

"Not from me," Brad said to more laughter.

"Think of it from the point of view of the public trust," Sirene said. "Why might management need to know this? What I'm reminded of is the [Rodney] King situation in Los Angeles. There were twenty-plus officers who were watching that. What did they assume

the other officers would do? What you learned is someone took
a swing, everyone had to take a swing. What has happened in
that organization? The chief of police has fired people, trying to
change the culture of that organization. What level of force do we
use?"

"Just what is necessary," a student said.

"You should bring it to the attention of the U.S. Attorney, who
is his [the agent's] boss," another student said, misstating agents'
chain of command.

"To whom are we obligated?"

"The public."

"To the accused and the public as a whole to assure that equal
justice is provided for everyone," Sirene said. "We have an obligation to the accused to search out every bit of evidence. Isn't that
what our obligation is? Our obligation is justice."

Then Sirene made a point made by many FBI agents: "The greatest
satisfaction you will someday get is when you will see all the evidence pointing to one individual or group of people and, by getting
to the bottom of the facts, you will prove their innocence. That is
our obligation to the justice system as a whole, to find out the facts,
find the truth, wherever it lies."

Sirene dimmed the lights and played a video on the classroom's
two monitors. Called *I Used to Be a Cop*, the movie began with
scenes of New York.

"This is the Seventy-seventh Precinct in New York," the narrator
said. Referring to an investigation of seventeen officers who were
investigated for corruption, the narrator said, "Seven officers were
indicted and suspended, and/or terminated. Fourteen of the seventeen were dismissed or resigned."

A cop who was arrested in 1986 for taking bribes appeared on
the screen. "People on the streets don't want to talk to you," he
said. "You find yourself alone. You do crazy things. Your life as
you knew it is over with. Your family life is over with. You feel you
want to die."

The class was transfixed, caught up in the tragedy. But Brad
yawned, looked at his wristwatch, and shuffled his papers as if he
was bored. As the movie made its point—that becoming a dirty cop
is not worth it—Brad shook his finger at other students sitting in
front of him.

After class, Sirene said he had noticed Brad's behavior and was
troubled by it. On one hand, he said, he tries to allow dialogue to
take place freely. This is a classroom, and everyone should feel free

to express his or her opinion. At the same time, the academy has an obligation to weed out agents with poor judgment.

For that, the academy has a special review committee called the New Agent Review Board (NARB). Started in 1980, the NARB was designed to replace the previous rigid rules that governed whether a student graduated.

"It was an attempt to design a process whereby we could learn from the trainee and do an evaluation of the trainee if there was a problem," said Robert E. Yates, who developed it. "Prior to that, we had a pass-or-fail system. There was no appeal process. They had limited retesting."[215]

The NARB process is triggered by grades below certain levels or indications of unsuitability. Some agents resign before their cases get to the NARB. For example, one agent kept firearms in his dormitory room in violation of regulations. He also confided to roommates that he "couldn't wait to get out there." The implication was that he couldn't wait to kill someone. The other agents reported his strange behavior. Before the case got to the NARB, the trainee was allowed to resign.[216]

James D. McKenzie, the assistant director over training before Greenleaf, said he was walking through the academy one day when he saw a trainee buy a candy bar from a vending machine, rip it open, throw away the candy, and eat the wrapping.

"I go, 'I didn't see that. I've been here too long,'" McKenzie said, "I went to the new agent's counselor. I said, 'I thought I just saw . . .' He said, 'I thought I saw him do that, too.' I said, 'Let's call him in and see what he has to say.' The kid is before us, just as innocent and sincere and honest as you'll ever find anybody. I said, 'I was walking down this hall, and I saw you buy a candy bar, throw the candy bar away, and eat the paper.' 'Yes.' I said, 'What did you do that for?'"

The trainee said that when he was a small child, his parents would not let him have candy in his room, so he would sneak it.

"I would eat the candy, and then I would eat the paper so there wouldn't be any evidence. After a while, I started to like the paper," he told McKenzie.

"I don't believe this guy," McKenzie said. "He's sitting there telling me that. Now can you imagine this guy being an FBI agent? Now this guy is out on a surveillance and gets hungry and eats the surveillance log. The guy is a couple of bubbles off center. Naturally people like that don't become FBI agents. He resigned based on that."[217]

"The joke was he would eat the evidence," said Roger L. Depue, who was aware of the case as the head of the behavioral science unit at Quantico.

Other agents decide that they really could not bring themselves to kill someone, or they realize that the FBI requires more commitment than they are willing to give.

"About 5 percent do not graduate," said Walter B. Stowe, Jr., the assistant section chief over training and administration. "The reasons are flunks and voluntary withdrawal, deciding this is not what they want to do, deciding they didn't want to be transferred all over. It's about half withdrawals and half flunks."

In the past two or three years, only one trainee has been dismissed for cheating. But in the early 1980s, the FBI had a major cheating scandal on its hands when the bureau discovered that clerks who wanted to become agents had the answers to the entrance tests. They were given a choice of taking the test over or taking a polygraph test on whether they had cheated. Dozens of clerks who had passed the test failed the retest or the polygraph.

In Brad's case, Sirene reported his seemingly insolent attitude to others at the academy. Asked about Brad after he had graduated, Stowe said that Brad had been given more scrutiny.

"There was counseling of Brad, and hopefully he saw the point," Stowe said. "He had a wrong notion of this organization, that we're not very ethical. He was not an FBI agent yet. That's the goal: To make them into FBI agents."[218]

Stowe has a thick head of salt-and-pepper hair, bushy eyebrows, a thick mustache, blue eyes, and round tortoiseshell glasses. He is athletic-looking, tall, and always stands with his feet planted squarely, at the ready, whether on the shooting range or at a formal reception.

A graduate of the College of William and Mary and its law school, Stowe is smart and intellectually curious. When projecting his FBI personality, like most other agents he is sensitive to the image of the bureau. It comes with the territory. But when he does not feel he is onstage, he is funny, direct, and informative.

"It is important that the public perceive us with a high degree of respect," he said. "If we don't have support, we're not going to be successful. If the public perceives us as an organization with a high degree of integrity, they will give us that support."

Agents get five hours of sensitivity training. The instructor of this class, James A. Kavina, began by asking the class what the FBI is all about.

"Information," a student said.

"The FBI is in the business of information," Kavina agreed. But he was trying to make another point. "Would you not agree that if you would sum up what our business is in, it would be people? Think about it. We're in the people business—302s, OC [organized crime] investigations, physical surveillance, arrests, drug investigations, FCI. What's it all about? *People*.

"I submit to you," Kavina said, "that the better you understand people, the better you will be able to do your job. The better you understand yourself, the better you will be able to understand other people."[219]

Indeed, the FBI is known for its smooth way with people. That is the way the bureau gets its man, by treating people with respect and lulling them into telling all.

Kavina cited factors that may influence people's personalities and attitudes: what sex they are, where they are from, what their education has been. "My high school had 1,054 graduates. Do you think I had a different perspective on education than a guy in Cedar Rapids, Iowa?" he asked.

Kavina's point was that race is but one of thousands of elements that go into the makeup of people's personalities, including the size of the schools they attended and where they are from. There is no more reason to think of it as significant than is the fact that a person grew up in New York rather than Kansas. Stereotyping by race is just as foolish as stereotyping by height or weight. To drive the point home, Kavina played an *Oprah Winfrey Show* featuring Jane Elliot, who was introduced on the show as an Iowa schoolteacher.

"The most shocking thing I learned over the years is the inability of blue-eyed people to achieve academically," Elliot said, as people in the television audience smirked.

"Now, these people find that amusing," she said. "Blue-eyed people are not as clean as brown-eyed people. As they came into the studio, the blue-eyed people were acting as I am describing them. They were belligerent. I asked them to go to restrooms for either brown- or blue-eyed people. The blue-eyed people don't have to follow the rules, because they make the rules."

Soon, Oprah's phone lines were jammed. Some viewers found some way to agree with Elliot's diatribe. Most did not.

What was happening? Kavina asked, turning off the video.

"It was a scenario to demonstrate what prejudice is," a black trainee said.

Turning on the video again, Kavina let the spoof run its course.

"Jane, we have been doing an exercise for the past half hour on this show in prejudice," Oprah said.

"Eye color, the amount of melanin in your eyes, does not make you a better or worse person, any more than the amount of melanin in your skin does," Elliot agreed.

Compared with the 5 hours devoted to sensitivity training, new agents receive 198 hours of training at Hogan's Alley and an emergency vehicle operations course, 113 hours of firearms training, 76 hours of legal training, and 73 hours of physical fitness and defensive tactics training. According to the academy, physical fitness includes eating properly and dealing with stress. Trainees are told to avoid sugar, salt, animal fat, and processed white flour.[220]

"Sugar brings your blood sugar up. It makes you tired. After you get off the high, it makes you feel low," according to Livio A. Beccaccio, who has been in charge of physical training at the FBI Academy and now directs the National Academy. "Besides making agents tired, it is more empty calories. If they substituted whole wheat for white bread, they would be getting a food that is much better for them; it's high-fiber stuff."

New agents are told to "talk out your worries" and to "learn to accept the things you cannot change." And they are told they must clearly distinguish between their roles as FBI agents and private citizens. If another car cuts in or someone on the street is obnoxious, FBI agents may not abuse their authority by pulling out their weapons or showing their credentials, James T. Reese, who teaches stress management, told a class of new agents. "You have no right to react that way," Reese said. "You can elect to be mad or not be mad."

At the same time, agents must keep in mind that they represent the FBI at all times and must behave accordingly. "When you mow the lawn, you're still the FBI," Reese said.

Agents may be asked by neighbors to intervene in situations they should avoid. "You should tell them to call the police," Reese said. "What you do is give them a logical explanation for why we are not Batman."[221]

In coping with the stress of the job, agents receive support from their colleagues. Agents refer to the FBI as a family, and—with the exception of family members under internal investigation—there is a lot of truth to that. In any organization, employees feel a kinship with co-workers and their families. When a child of a colleague dies, everyone is devastated. But in the FBI, agents go beyond expressing sympathy. They routinely take up collections for families of agents who have been killed or injured or for agents' children who have developed problems. For example, a son of Mel Jeter, who works in the criminal investigative division, was paralyzed from the waist down after a car accident during a visit home from college. Spurred on by Joseph R. Davis, the assistant director over the legal division, FBI employees collected money to buy him an Epson computer and printer so that he could work more easily at home. When forty FBI employees in Miami were driven from their homes by Hurricane Andrew, agents from all over the bureau took up a collection to help them out.[222]

"Anywhere you go, the FBI will help," said Catherine M. Kaiser, an agent in Silver Spring, Maryland. "Anytime you need help, they're there for you."

Many companies nurture the idea that their employees are part of a family, then lay them off at the first sign of hard times.

"Americans look at the Japanese and see their companies make these long-term family commitments," said Roger Depue, the former head of the behavioral science unit at the academy. "Americans say the right words, but at the drop of a hat, they lay off eight hundred people. I can't remember when I got my kids together and said, 'Times are tough, so, René, you're going to have to hit the road.' When you look at organizations from a behavioral science standpoint, they don't treat the members as families. They are hollow words."

In fact, the FBI has never laid off employees. In 1989, Sessions closed the infamous field office in Butte, Montana. It was an idyllic spot for hunting and fishing that Hoover, for unknown reasons, chose as purgatory for errant agents. So that support employees could continue their FBI employment, the FBI chose Butte as the site for a new processing center for FBI records.

To enhance the family concept, the FBI Academy set up a program for counseling the victims, families, and colleagues of agents involved in shootings. The academy also instigated a program to teach agents about to retire how to adjust to their new lives.

"What happens when you are involved in a life-threatening event is you may have a lot of normal stress reactions," Depue said. "If you don't know they are normal, they can be very fearful. Your family can be very concerned. Waking up at night with flashbacks. Failure to concentrate. Sweating. You feel you are going back on the street. The literature said the earlier you can intervene and help someone with that, the greater the likelihood they can deal with it."[223]

In one example, Lieutenant Fred House, a state corrections officer, assisted FBI agents involved in a shootout on January 28, 1988, outside of Salt Lake City, where a polygamist clan had split from the Mormon Church and were believed to have bombed a Mormon chapel. A close friend of some of the agents, the officer brought his German shepherd to the scene to help out, then was killed as he tried to urge the dog on.

"The dog came back and is now standing over the officer and wouldn't let anyone go near him," Depue said. "It was just a horrible thing. The bureau had asked his assistance. The following Friday night, the officer and his wife were going to come to one of the agents' homes for dinner. The office felt tremendously bad."

So, the academy sent agents to talk to all employees at the Salt Lake City field office, as it did after the shootout in Miami that took the lives of agents Jerry Dove and Benjamin Grogan.

"There are a lot of people you don't normally think about," Depue said. "The dispatcher had to listen to these Miami agents in serious trouble and needing assistance. The dispatcher is trying to get help to them. He realized these agents are dying, and he can't get help out to them quickly enough. Secretaries come to work and these desks are empty."

New agents are taught about the psychological impact of shootings as part of firearms training. The academy has both an indoor and an outdoor firing range. As the visitor approaches the academy's outdoor range, there is the intermittent pop of rifle fire, like the straggling last cherry bombs late at night on the Fourth of July. Then, suddenly, a barrage. Sounding somewhere in between the barrages, a stray rat-ta-ta-tat bounces off a building. This goes on all day, five days a week. Snap, snap.

Someone makes an announcement over the loudspeakers—something about reloading—and the illusion of war is thoroughly shattered. But from one end of the yard to the other, there are rolling volleys of semiautomatics. The indoor and outdoor ranges use a million rounds a month.

To graduate, agents must qualify twice with the bureau's new Smith & Wesson Model 1076 semiautomatic 10-millimeter pistol and demonstrate proficiency with the Remington Model 870 shotgun and 9-millimeter carbine.

Like a football coach, James R. Pledger, the chief of the firearms training unit, doesn't want to speak directly about the sort of violence that can happen on the field, or in this case, in the field. When the agents shoot, they are told to go for the "center of mass," he said, using his euphemism for the stomach and other vital organs.

"We want them [the criminals] to stop what they are doing. Many times that results in death. We don't have a military objective, which is to wound," he said. "It takes three support people to take care of every wounded person."[224]

When James D. McKenzie became assistant director for training in 1978, he revised the qualifying standards for firearms training. As the chief of the academy for nine years, McKenzie had more impact on training in the modern bureau than did anyone else. McKenzie joined the bureau as a clerk. Within the bureau, agents who started as clerks are often referred to as "clagents" and treated with some disdain. But agents like McKenzie—as sharp a man as you would ever want to meet—show that the attitude is merely prejudice.

While working as a clerk, McKenzie obtained a law degree. Just after Webster was appointed director, he was making a plane connection in Miami. As acting special agent in charge of the Miami office, McKenzie met him at the airport. Because of late flights, Webster ended up spending three hours with him. Called "Jimmie Blue Eyes" because of his striking blue eyes and roguish style, McKenzie impressed Webster with his straight answers to the new director's tough questions.

"He said, 'What do you think of our informant program?' " McKenzie recalled. "I said, 'I don't like it.' I thought it was a program that produced quantity over quality. I didn't think agents were adept at developing informants. That was the program Hoover had. Everyone had to do everything. There was a lot of pressure to have them. It was almost a job requirement. So you may get an informant that you really shouldn't be dealing with."

At a later conference for special agents in charge, Webster asked for opinions on the informant program. The SACs said it was a good program.

"He said, 'The other day, I was in Miami and talked with Jim McKenzie, and he said . . .' They said, 'Well, Jim McKenzie is right,' " McKenzie said.

Not long after that, Webster transferred McKenzie to the number-two position at the FBI Academy. In 1978, he named him an assistant director over training.

"I felt we were running a vocational academy," McKenzie said. "The theme was highly academic. To me, it wasn't real world."

Among other changes, McKenzie built a more elaborate version of Hogan's Alley and changed performance standards to make them less arbitrary. While they do not relate directly to agent training, he also pushed for a hostage rescue team and got more money for profiling crime suspects, a function that the academy houses.

"I had a bunch of agents arguing about whether a bullet cut the seam of the target," he said. "If it was in, he would have been an FBI agent. If it was out, he was out."

McKenzie changed the standard so that agents had to qualify two out of three times instead of once. "If you failed to qualify, you would have one more chance after a remedial session," McKenzie said.

One afternoon, McKenzie saw a male firearms instructor walk up to a woman trainee, put his hand in her front pants pocket to get out some shells, and hand them to her.

"I walked up to him and said, 'If you want to keep your job at the FBI Academy, you will walk down the line and put your hand in the pocket of every new agent and hand him some shells,'" McKenzie said. "And there were some new agents who didn't take too kindly to this. It was probably an overreaction on my part, my temper. The guys didn't think he was too cute when he started sticking his hand in their pockets. I thought he was going to get decked about twice. I stopped him after ten agents. Someone was going to kill him, and they were carrying guns at the time."[225]

Bureau officials such as Buck Revell thought McKenzie relaxed conduct standards too much. But McKenzie believed that FBI trainees were adults who should not be treated as college freshmen. If they wanted to have affairs with one another, that was their business.

McKenzie said that one evening he walked into a bar at a Sheraton Hotel halfway between Quantico and Washington. As he turned his head, it seemed to him that two women and two men sitting at a nearby table had disappeared.

"A waitress walked over to me and said, 'If you'll go into the men's room, somebody in this room would like to buy you a drink.' I said, 'What?' She said, 'Please, just do it.' So I went into the men's room, came back, and, working on the waitress a little bit, I said, 'What was that about?' She said, 'I guess they go to your school, and they are married, but not to one another. They saw you walk in, and they crawled under the table, all four of them.'"

"Jim McKenzie took a sort of very laissez-faire attitude," Revell said. "He said, 'They are adults, and I'm not going to baby-sit them.' That's true, but you also need to maintain standards of your institution and academy."

"I tell them the very first night that we do not allow holding hands, any kind of hanky-panky, here at the academy," said Ray E. Jones, a class counselor. "Anything you do is your own business, but don't bring it to the academy."[226]

Like the firearms training requirements, the physical training requirements at Quantico are complicated and based on a point system. Because of differences in physique, women must meet less rigorous standards in each category except sit-ups. The academy changed the standards for female agents after Christine A. Hansen, then an FBI agent, filed a complaint with the Equal Employment Opportunity Commission. In 1981, the commission ordered the FBI to recruit women more vigorously, to modify the physical training requirements for women, and to give women exercises when they apply to give them an idea of what will be required of them during firearms training.[227]

Brains have always been more important than brawn in the FBI. Nothing is more important than the art of eliciting information from people who may have every reason in the world not to want to divulge it.

"We tell them to treat everybody like they would like their mothers to be treated," said Edward Tully, who has taught interviewing.

"Our concern is not physical strength alone," McKenzie said. "The first way to solve a problem is with your brain. The defensive tactics are next. The last resort is deadly force."

In defensive tactics, psychology and brain power are critical. Robert F. Rogers, who teaches the course, is a trim fifty-one-year-old whom you wouldn't want to mess with under any circumstances. He's got the physique; moreover, he's got the psychology of defensive intimidation down cold.

Rogers explains that "defensive tactics" is a misnomer: "It is only defensive until we make our first move, and then it becomes offensive."

Rogers told a class, "You can do something that's different as long as it's aggressive. You're generating that commitment. . . . Be positive, be forceful, control your aggressiveness, and let it escalate professionally as you need it."

He grabbed one of the students by the forearm. "Think about the commands you're going to use." There was no smile or pleasant expression from the "subject," whose hand was now being twisted away from his thumb.

"When I am exerting physical control, I am reinforcing psychological control," Rogers said. As he twisted the trainee's arm, he said, "I want you working this, and then I want you working right here." The man was experiencing moderate pain in his hand.

The students crowded around the two, folding their arms in front of themselves as they listened attentively. Then they chose partners and grappled with each other's forearms—one person being the agent, the other playing the role of the assailant or suspect.

By one arm, Rogers whipped around the agent who was helping him demonstrate. Caught off balance, the man grabbed at Rogers's shirt.

"Don't pull my shirt," he warned him wryly. "If you rip my shirt, then we gotta do the rest for real." The class laughed. "Out there in the field I don't mind—they rip my shirt, the bureau buys me a new one. In here, I buy a new one."

Rogers put himself face to face with the trainee, who was now holding a demonstration gun in Rogers's face. He showed how it is possible to prevail even then. "Get the gun, move the muzzle up, get the gun where you can control it," Rogers said.

The point that Rogers kept dramatizing in a very physical way is that an agent can exert much more power when the object—such as someone else's hand holding a gun—is at the center of the agent's body rather than at arm's length. ". . . We know our body now. We know where we are stronger, where we are weaker. Watch his elbow. When he is out like that he is weak; when he is in like that he is strong.

"Fitness is ability to resist panic, maintain composure, exercise judgment, all those things," Rogers told the class. "Commitment in this endeavor is a synonym for speed. Commitment is speed. It's action versus reaction, even here with a revolver."

From the academy it's a short walk across Hoover Street and up a hilly dirt path to a small town. On the outskirts of the town is a sign that reads: "Caution: Law enforcement training exercises in progress. Display of weapons, firing of blank ammunition and arrests may occur. If challenged, please follow instructions."

Hogan's Alley has all the comforts of small-town America—the Co-Op Laundromat, the All-Med Drugstore, the post office (zip code 22135)—while at the same time being a little seedy and down-at-the-heels with its billiards parlor and pawnshop. If the town were more like a pristine New England town with clapboard houses and church steeples, it would be hard to believe the crime wave that comes over it five days a week; or that the Pastime Lounge conceals a casino where FBI agents who will work undercover learn the ins and outs of playing blackjack, roulette, and craps.

Down the street, the Biograph is screening *Manhattan Melodrama*, with Clark Gable and Myrna Loy. This movie was showing when

FBI agents gunned down John H. Dillinger as he left the Biograph Theater in Chicago on July 22, 1934. In the center of town is a no-tell motel with about thirty rooms behind orange doors. The Dogwood Inn takes Visa and MasterCard, and guests don't have to check their guns.

In Hogan's Alley, no one's identity is certain—except for that of the mayor, Patrick J. Foran, who has gray hair, a mustache, and a smile that reveals his upper gums and very white teeth. Foran, who is actually chief of the practical applications unit, has his office in a room in the Dogwood Inn. Other rooms are used for teaching and for other academy offices.

Occasionally, suppliers, construction workers, and other innocents wander too close to Hogan's Alley and are challenged as suspects.

"If you walk over there fifteen minutes after a bank robbery, they'll start interviewing you," said Michael J. Santimauro, the section chief over the training and administrative branch at Quantico. "We say, 'No, you screwed up. Now go find the real guy.' "

But trainees, being suspicious, do not always take no for an answer. Until Hogan's Alley was built, trainees chased FBI agents who posed as criminals. One day, Vincent P. Doherty, then the academy's feisty comptroller, was showing the facilities to official guests. Doherty happened to match a description given to a training class of the perpetrator of a bank fraud. A trainee spotted Doherty and gave the usual warning: "Freeze! FBI!"

Saying that he was giving a tour, Doherty told the agent to "get lost."

Whereupon she flipped Doherty, who found himself lying on the carpet.

Now everyone is given a code word—like Code Red—that means time out, stop the action. Instead of using FBI agents as the bad guys, the academy hires Day-by-Day Associates to provide actors like Bryant Barnhart. Barnhart loves the action. "Where else can you go and do this kind of thing?" he asked. When asked what he means, he replied, "Harassment."

One actor took it a little too seriously. Because of his erratic hours, he was fired from his job. Six months later, he robbed a real bank.

As Barnhart waited to commit his next crime, a typical scenario was going down outside the All-Med Drugstore. "Ray Sweet" had been fired from his job. He wanted a hundred thousand dollars or he would blow up his former employer's factory. He had already driven to a street corner and picked up the money, only to be surrounded by FBI cars. Trainees pointed shotguns at him and his girlfriend.

Over an FBI car's public address system, a trainee commanded the suspect to get out of his car. "Put your hands on your head, interlace your fingers," he told the mock suspect. Then he told him to pull his jacket down over his elbows so that he could not move his arms. Other agents barked mostly unintelligible orders at him, the overall message being that he was not to move. They got him to lie down on his stomach so that they could handcuff him.

Foran frowned. "They're confusing them. They're telling them to turn around, to move ahead. They're not attaining their goal. They're going to be judged on that."[228]

A Marriott truck that was not part of the scenario quietly drove around the knot of cars in the intersection and left town. Meanwhile, an agent ordered the woman out of the car and attempted to cuff her.

"You are going to break my damn arm," she snarled.

Having subdued the suspect, the trainee tried to stick his gun in the holster on his back. When he could not get it into his holster fast enough, he clumsily tried to stick the gun into his waistband under his belt. He got it on the third try. He handcuffed her with one hand. Then he combed through her hair and, despite the fact that it may sound like an impropriety, did his duty by feeling her blouse. While the FBI prefers to have agents of the same sex search for hidden weapons, that is not always possible.

"She's got a gun!" a female trainee called out from behind her shotgun. Trainees' shotguns are plugged so that they won't work. The girlfriend's gun was hidden around her ankle. The trainee grabbed it. Meanwhile, other agents called in the bomb squad to disarm the bomb the suspect had left on the floor of his car.

Foran said the trainees had been told to alert the local police that an arrest would be going down. "If they haven't told the police, they [the police] might arrest them. With Dillinger they didn't tell the police. Today, we would," he said.

Although the trainees needed some lessons in people moving, they managed not to stumble into the two major booby traps of this "event." Were they to miss the woman's gun during their body search, she was under instructions to "use it" and escape. And if they touched the box in the station wagon, the "bomb" would have gone off in the form of an alarm.

Watching it all was an evaluator who would critique their performance. "The plan was good, the plan was excellent," he told the trainees later. "It can always be better, but you only have so many hours to do it, and I think this was a pretty good plan."

Then he explained as nicely as he could that the way they had set up, they had had crossfire—if they'd had to shoot the suspect, they could have shot each other instead.

Foran seemed unperturbed. He has seen it all. "We've seen new agents jump out of the cars, lock the keys in, and leave the engine running," he said. "I've seen them leave the car in gear, and the car starts rolling. Generally, they have been brought to a stop. The trainees stop them."

Just then, a new crime wave started. Three cars appeared from nowhere, two with sirens wailing. A weather-beaten gray Oldsmobile was in the lead. The car behind it passed it and nearly jumped the sidewalk, in order to block the Olds, now in the middle. Trainees in the car behind the Olds got out, holding their guns and yelling at the driver with an anger far out of proportion to the situation.

"Do exactly as I say! Reach your left arm out the window and open your door from the outside." The trainee had not made allowances for the possibility that the door could be locked, but apparently it wasn't, because it opened.

When the suspect left the car, a trainee barked, "Drop to your knees right now!"

"Driver, face forward," someone else yelled.

"There's someone in the car," a surprised trainee called out.

"Open the right rear door. Open it all the way," a trainee said. When there was no response, he said, "If there's someone in the car, get out with your hands up."

As the visitors left, a sallow-faced man lurking outside a motel room looked hopefully into their faces, then quickly lost interest when he realized they were not trainees about to hassle him.

After sixteen weeks, it was over. Camera bulbs were flashing and parents were crying as a class graduated in the academy's first-floor auditorium. This class had thirty-one new agents, including two black males, four Hispanic males, and six women. As a baby shrieked, the class spokesman, Joshua Ben Mayers, walked to a podium.

"It was in the gym that this group really came together as a team for the first time," he said. "We realized early on that in order to make it, we had to work together and help one another."

Weldon L. Kennedy, the assistant director over the administrative services division, presented the agents with their badges and credentials. He talked about the changes he has seen since he joined the bureau in 1963.

"The class composition is totally different," he said. "In 1963, they were all white males, and it remained that way for many years. That has changed. I could go on and talk about changes in terms of applying science. For example, DNA. The application of computers to investigative techniques. Increased jurisdiction has been phenomenal. For example, we did not have narcotics."

Afterward, the new agents ate a rectangular chocolate sheet cake decorated with "Good Luck, 91-18," the number of the class.

By now, the new agents had received their first assignments all over the country. They would begin as GS-10s, making $29,511 a year. With the overtime that comes with the job, they would get $36,888 a year. At least a quarter of the agents had taken a pay cut to join the FBI. For their first year, they would be on probation and receive further training on the job.

"I wanted to do this for a long time," said Pamela S. Butcher, a graduate who had been a security analyst for General Dynamics. "I wanted to work for the best law enforcement agency in the world and put the bad guys in jail. It's not fair that they are making all the money and hardworking people do it the hard way."[229]

"The training was very, very good," she said. "It was the hardest thing I've ever done. It was extremely challenging. You have to really want it or you're not going to make it here."

Katherine M. Andersen graduated first in defensive tactics and physical training. Formerly an officer in the U.S. Army, she has a B.S. in general engineering from the U.S. Military Academy at West Point. Andersen said she could not have done it without help from others.

"I worked out with some good people who helped me," she said. "You can't do it by yourself."

Bryan B. Wallman graduated highest in academics. Before he joined, he was an attorney in Detroit, where he was "fixing traffic tickets" for companies.

"I wanted to do something important," he said.

Already the agents' minds were elsewhere—on cities from Washington to Los Angeles, where they would try to live their class slogan: "Win Every Fight, Every Time."

9

Los Angeles: Star Stalking

● **After Charlie J. Parsons** had been special agent in charge in Los Angeles for a week, he told his wife, Chris, that there had already been sixty-seven bank robberies in his jurisdiction.

"You mean sixty-seven during this year," Chris corrected.

"No, sixty-seven this past week," he said.[230]

With 570 agents, Los Angeles is the third largest field office in the country. Besides being the bank robbery capital of the world, Los Angeles has problems such as "star stalker" crimes and gang warfare that are unique to the city. Los Angeles is the field office that investigated the police beating of Rodney King, and it is the place where Richard W. Miller, the only FBI agent ever convicted of espionage, worked and was arrested.

Because of the city's aggressive newspapers and broadcast media, Los Angeles is the only field office in the FBI that requires two media representatives to handle the daily deluge of calls.

"This has been the capital of bank robberies for as long as I can remember," said Parsons, a handsome man with a tanned, pear-shaped face and receding hairline. "Each day someone tells me something else that we have more of than anybody else: money laundering, white collar crime, drugs, health care fraud. . . . I'm going to start a chart like you see in a fair with six wheels. I'm going

189

to put a blank in after 'Los Angeles is the capital of' and spin it and
see what comes up.''

"They could probably double the office and still keep agents
busy," said Larry G. Lawler, the former special agent in charge in
Los Angeles. "It has about everything anybody would want to put
his priorities into."[231]

William J. Rehder, a professorial-looking agent in his tortoiseshell
glasses, keeps track of all the bank robberies and coordinates their
investigation with local police.

The walls of Rehder's office are papered with bank surveillance
photos of robbers in the act and charts that demonstrate Los Angeles's dubious claim to fame as the bank robbery capital of the
world.

"From our chart, you can see we broke all records for the seven
counties that compose our division [field office]," Rehder said. "It
was 2,355. The previous record was in 1983 with 1,833. We broke
that by more than 25 percent. We took over as bank robbery capital
of the country in the mid-1970s."[232]

Photos on the walls depict bank robbers shooting customers or
police officers. In one photo, a customer standing before a teller's
window is smiling as he looks at a robber brandishing a revolver.
At that point, the robber had already fired two shots. Rehder explained that it is not unusual for bystanders to react inappropriately.

"The reactions of people inside vary from panic to, in this case,
this guy is of the thought that, 'If I do not acknowledge this, it's not
really happening.' I've seen that in a number of takeover robberies,"
Rehder said. "He wants to continue on as if nothing is happening."

Rehder pointed to a photo of a robber wearing a skeleton mask
and said that the man had held up the bank as a way of committing
suicide.

"He did a robbery but spent much too much time in the bank,"
Rehder said. "By the time he went out, the bank was totally surrounded by police. They were in pursuit by helicopter after he got
in his car. He made a U-turn and put the gun in his mouth and
pulled the trigger."

In the robber's car, police found a note saying that this would be
his "last day on earth."

Rehder focuses on serial bandits—repeat bandits whose robbery
spree extends for months and sometimes years before they are located and arrested.

"Each time I see a bandit a second time, he becomes a serial
bandit," Rehder said. "I will track him through all the robberies in

this division [field office]. My job is to keep track of these individuals."

To make his job easier, Rehder appends a nickname to each suspect. The nicknames—which are the code names used by the FBI for each case—are based on some distinguishing feature about the suspect, or the way he or she committed the crime.

For example, there was the *Budweiser Bandit*, who wore a Budweiser baseball cap; the *Bug Eye Bandit*, who had bulging eyes; and the *God Bless You Bandit*, who would force everyone to lie on the floor and who would say "God bless you" as he left the bank.

The *Pervert Bandit* got his name because a teller said he looked like one; the *Count-to-100 Bandit* would order bank employees to count to 100 before they called the police; the *Miss Piggy Bandit* was a huge white woman who looked like the famous Muppet; the *Tabloid Bandit* carried a newspaper under his arm; the *Shit Happens Bandit* wore a T-shirt that said SHIT HAPPENS; and the *Bonny and Clyde Bandits* were a man and woman team with tommy guns. The *Benihana Bandit* brandished a ten-inch kitchen knife, while the *Shadow Bandit*, who has robbed since 1984, disappears for a time, then comes back to rob again. The *Postgraduate Bandit* has trouble spelling in his notes demanding money.

Actually, few bank robbers would win any literary awards. "Give me all the money starting from 100's, 50's, 20's, and if you must give me differant [sic] I must kill you so no tricks or games," said one note. Another robber wrote, "Don't pannick [sic]. Empty out your drawer and you won't get hurt. Put the money in the bag." A third robber scribbled, "I want your money top and bottom drawer. Don't press alarm. There is a hooked bomb to it. System screwed me now I screw system." But Postgraduate's spelling was unusual. He wrote, "This is a robbeey [sic]. Put all the monty [sic] on counter."

Certain themes recur. "Give up all the money or die," one robber wrote. Another wrote, "I have a gun. Give me all the money or die."

Many robbers are fussy about how they want their bills. "This is a holdup," one wrote. "I want 100's, 50's, 20's. I have a gun!! So hurry."

There are polite robbers, like the one who wrote, "Hello, this is a holdup. Empty all your drawer into this bag and do not touch the funny money. Thanks for your cooperation." And there are threatening robbers, like the one who wrote, "This is a robbery. Don't make it a murder. Give me all the money now."

One robber wrote a tearjerker:

To whom it may concern: Please understand I'm not a bad person nor do I make a habit of this. I'm just a depositor and have no choice. I've tried to borrow and can't. I tried to beg with no results. I am about to lose what I have left, my pride and dignity, my car and house. I've already lost my family. So please just place $2,500 in envelope and let me get outside. I don't want to harm anyone or be harmed. So please understand I'm scared just like you. You can sound alarm when I have left.

Also my mother passed away, 84 years old, and I need to get to the funeral. I'll pay you back as soon as I get on my feet. Oh and I don't use drugs. Thank you. I'm 60 years old. Merry Christmas. Say a prayer for me, please.

"All of this is bogus," Rehder said of the robber's claims. "It's all a bunch of crap. He's in custody."

Some 80 to 85 percent of bank robberies in Los Angeles are solved, demonstrating that bank robbery is one of the stupidest crimes one can commit. Each field office has its own store of bank robber tales. In Philadelphia, for example, a bank robber wrote a note demanding money on the back of the computer punch card that came with his telephone bill. Tracing the number, Caroll Toohey, now assistant director over the inspection division, got the man's address. Armed with a bank surveillance photo that showed him wearing a bright red checkered shirt, Toohey and other agents knocked on the robber's door.

"He still had on the same shirt," Toohey said. "And we looked over, and he had half the money shoved under the couch."[233]

Just before four robbers held up one bank, one of them sprayed the lens of a surveillance camera with black paint.

"We got a beautiful picture of one of them," Toohey said. "Sometimes the cameras didn't work or didn't focus on some areas. But now we had the optimum focal length. So we got the film developed and put it on the six o'clock news. It was solved at nine that night."

Another robber smashed the surveillance camera with a short sledgehammer.

"He beat it to death," Toohey said. "It went blank. But we got the film in the canister and got the whole scene."

To make it easier to catch robbers, bank tellers are given marked bills that conceal dye packs that explode. Often, the packs explode while robbers are trying to escape in a car. As police and FBI agents arrive on the scene, they can easily spot the getaway car if it is still in the area because it has a stream of red dye spewing from it. They can also spot robbers fleeing on foot because they are covered with red dye, as are the bills they have stolen. The serial numbers of the bills are listed in the FBI's National Crime Information Center (NCIC), the computerized data base that police use when they stop cars to see if they are stolen or the occupants are fugitives. When arrests are made, the suspects' money is routinely checked with the NCIC system to see if it was stolen.

In Philadelphia, Toohey got a warrant to search the home of a suspect in a bank robbery. Trying to remove the dye from the bills, the robber had put them through the washing machine and hung them to dry. When Toohey and other agents searched the home, they saw pink bills hanging on a line.

Another robber sauntered into a bank, held it up, and stuffed the dye pack into his pants pocket.

"It blows up a block later, nearly emasculating him, and he strolls into the nearest bar," said Richard D. Schwein, the special agent in charge in El Paso who was then Toohey's partner. "We walked in. The bar was choking now with tear gas [detonated by booby-trapped bills]. He is sitting there casually with a beer at the bar with tears running down his face and a big hole and a red mark on his pants. We said, 'Excuse me,' and took him away."[234]

In Atlanta, a disorganized robber held up a bank without bringing a bag to hold the money.

"He has the gun in one hand and the money in another hand," said Toohey, who was then assistant special agent in charge in Atlanta. "Now he starts to go outside, and while the cameras are on him, he drops the money. He reaches to pick up the money and shoots himself in the foot. We get there, and there is a trail of blood. We followed the blood for a block."

The blood led the FBI to a housing project, where the agents arrested the robber the next day.

Not all bank robbers are bunglers. Sometimes the bureau has to use extraordinary means to catch them, even if that entails paying them *not* to rob banks. That happened after Terry Lee Conner and his partner Joseph W. Dougherty, who were serving time in Oklahoma for robbing a bank of $700,000, escaped from U.S. marshals. The two held a bank security officer in West Allis, Wisconsin, hostage, telling him, "We despise banks, and we despise insurance companies." The next day, they stole $550,000 from the man's bank, Central Bank, after locking ten employees in a vault.

By then, the FBI had put both suspects on the top-ten-fugitives list. Figuring they would keep in touch with Robert B. Butcher, one of their friends from prison, the FBI conducted surveillance of Butcher. As it turned out, Conner and Dougherty would call Butcher in Albuquerque at a designated bank of pay phones at prearranged times, letting him know in code of their plans. To make it easier to intercept the calls, the bureau got permission from the telephone company to disable the remaining phones in the bank of pay phones. By listening to the calls, the FBI learned that Butcher was going to meet Conner and Dougherty in Chicago to rob another bank. Meanwhile, Butcher was short of cash, so he planned to hold up a bank in Albuquerque.

"Well, we can't let him rob a bank," recalled James D. McKenzie, who was special agent in charge in Chicago at the time. "We got an Albuquerque patrol car to sit outside the bank with a radar gun the day he was going to rob the bank so he would be discouraged from that. The next problem is how do you get him some money? We had one of our Hispanic agents get on the phone Butcher was about to use and leave his wallet at the phone booth. He left $302 in it."

Butcher found the money and kept it.

"The next time Conner says, 'Do you have enough money to get to Chicago?' Butcher says, 'Yeah, I got lucky. I found $150.' "[235]

Butcher had trouble following directions and never did meet up with Conner and Dougherty in Chicago. But, knowing that the two fugitives were coming to town, McKenzie distributed their photos to every hotel, motel, and bank in the area. In response, a clerk at a Red Roof Inn in Arlington Heights, a suburb of Chicago, phoned the FBI and said that a man who looked like Dougherty had just checked in. When agents checked the register, they realized the man was actually an official of the Chicago Fire Department who was there with his girlfriend. However, in looking for Dougherty, George Spinelli, the agent who went to the motel, also checked the names of other guests for Conner. By amazing coincidence, he found an alias he knew Conner had used. Spinelli made a copy of the registration form and took it back to the field office.

"We had a photocopy of his registration form," said Robert E. Walsh, the assistant special agent in charge. "The driver's license on the registration form was the same as one he had used before. Plus it appeared to be the same handwriting."

The next morning, the FBI arrested Conner in his room. The following week, the bureau captured Dougherty in California. Butcher was also arrested and charged with conspiracy to rob a branch of Bank of America.[236]

What FBI agents like about bank robberies is the feeling of immediate accomplishment.

"There's less paperwork compared with organized crime or white collar cases that you work on for two years without seeing results," Toohey said. "With bank robberies, you get immediate gratification, immediate results."

"I like this squad because there is constant action, from the time you get in in the morning until the time you leave at night," Rehder said. "There is always something going on. There are very few dull moments around here."

Rehder and other FBI agents say that banks with Plexiglas or bulletproof glass barriers between tellers and customers are held up far less than are banks with open spaces between tellers and customers. However, most banks do not use the so-called bandit barriers because, besides the extra expense, they think customers don't like them. Yet, those same banks think nothing of offering impersonal automated teller machines (ATMs).

"Banks are loath to use it [a bandit barrier] because it is expensive, and they are reluctant to give up the press-the-flesh customer relations," Rehder said. "The ones that have bandit barriers are robbed much less. It's night and day. Every now and then you have someone who slaps a note against the Plexiglas. Usually the teller crouches behind the counter, and that's the end of it."

The Federal Deposit Insurance Corporation, which insures nearly all banks, requires banks to have alarms and secure places for storing money. But FDIC regulations say nothing about bandit barriers.

"There's no doubt that banks that have bandit barriers have fewer robberies," said Don S. Tokunaga, a Los Angeles banker who is the American Bankers Association's vice chairman for security and risk management. "The cost has the most to do with it. A lot of the banks in California like the open look."

A typical holdup nets only a few thousand dollars. A total of $66 million is taken in bank robberies nationally each year. By comparison, some savings-and-loan failures have cost taxpayers billions of dollars. But there is more than a dollar cost from bank robberies. In a typical year, 27 people were killed and 132 injured in the nation's 9,810 bank robberies.[237]

Jerry D. Thornton, the Los Angeles assistant special agent in charge over bank robberies and other violent crimes, thinks one reason why Los Angeles has so many bank robberies is that the area has many small bank branches close to freeways where robbers can escape easily.

"It's a combination of the warm weather year round, 2,550 branch banks, the freeway system, and the narcotics problem," Thornton said. "Eighty-five percent are drug related."[238]

"If you were to pick a criminal enterprise [to engage in], you wouldn't pick bank robberies," Charlie Parsons said. "You would pick white collar crime. Bank robbery is high risk, low gain. The real sophisticated criminals will pick some other line of endeavor. With burglaries, you have much less chance of getting caught. People don't think it through. People who were robbing 7-Elevens and gas stations now are robbing banks."

Parsons's office is on the seventeenth floor of 11000 Wilshire Boulevard, a white building surrounded by a velvety green lawn, benches, and a vast, free parking lot. The building is catty-corner to the University of California at Los Angeles.

Before taking over in Los Angeles, Parsons was a deputy assistant director over inspections in Washington, headed the San Antonio field office, and ran the organized crime program in Las Vegas. Originally from Tennessee and then Texas, Parsons speaks in a soft drawl. Besides collecting old cars—he has a 1961 Lincoln Continental and a 1968 Mustang convertible—Parsons is a consummate gambler. It's all in his line of work: When assigned to the FBI Academy at Quantico, Parsons taught gambling. In Las Vegas, Parsons used his knowledge of gambling when investigating organized crime penetrations of casinos.

On Parsons's wall is a photo that appeared in many papers throughout the country with stories on Sessions's confirmation as director. It shows Parsons, who was then special agent in charge in San Antonio, appearing to whisper something to Sessions, who was then chief federal judge in the same city. An inscription from Sessions reads, "Best wishes to Charlie Parsons. Only you, I, and the lip readers know for sure."

"I have no idea what we were talking about," Parsons said.

Across the corridor, in a position of importance, is the media office. Each SAC has his own style in dealing with the media. Some love the attention, while others feel uncomfortable with it. But SACs are rated on how well they deal with the media, and on that score Parsons has done exceptionally well. Since coming to Los Angeles, his name has appeared in the *Los Angeles Times* an average of once a week in connection with favorable stories.

Karen E. Gardner is one of the office's two media representatives. A savvy, attractive blonde who is married to Theodore M. (Ted) Gardner, the former special agent in charge of the Washington metropolitan field office, Gardner knows how to walk the fine line between revealing too much and making the media feel they are being stiffed. She also knows which agents are more apt to overcome traditional bureau restrictions on talking to the press and so will give an interesting interview.

"I think you have to understand that according to the unspoken rules and sometimes the spoken rules, the things that get you into trouble fastest are misuse of the Bucar, drinking on duty, probably fooling around inappropriately, and the media. Not in that order," Gardner said. "There are agents who have been in a lot of hot water because of remarks they have made, or things that have been attributed to them, in the press. The organizational response is not only administrative [punishment], but if there is a pending case, you might get in trouble with the judge. So, people tend to err on the side of saying less rather than saying more."[239]

"It's [talking to the press] always something we have shied away from," said Mary Jo Marino, a blue-eyed brunette who is an agent on a white collar squad. "It's the office policy not to talk to the press. If you are told to, it's still in your mind not to talk to the press."

Like most media representatives in field offices, Gardner is relaxed about dealing with the press, a contrast to the bureaucratic and formal approach of many media representatives at headquarters.

"Bu-ease spoken here," Gardner said. "There are Bucars, Busteeds. Actually it's Buc's. The lingo varies from division to division."

As she spoke, press calls began flooding in. A man who resembled fugitive Amando Garcia, one of the FBI's Top Ten fugitives, had been seen running down the street with a revolver in his hand. Garcia, a former Miami police officer, was wanted for his alleged role in the 1985 Miami River massacre. In that incident, uniformed Miami police officers confronted drug traffickers and stole from them cocaine worth $7.5 million to $10 million. To avoid being caught, three of the drug dealers jumped into the river, where they drowned.[240]

By now, some three hundred FBI agents and police officers had surrounded the apartment house where the man who looked like Garcia had fled.

Parsons stuck his head into the media office.

"They think he might be Amando Garcia, a Top Ten," Gardner said.

"They pretty sure they have a lead on him?" Parsons asked.

"It looks real good," Gardner said.

Gardner then told each caller from the press that the FBI could not confirm that the man was Garcia.

"You never say 'no comment'," she said. "They say, 'Can you tell me if it is Amando Garcia? Well, can you tell me if it is a Top Ten fugitive? Can you tell me off the record? Well, what can you tell me?' We could say no comment all day long, but we're in a better position if we say, 'Our fugitive guys are out there. It's a breaking case, they've set up a perimeter, and we'll call you as soon as we have something.' That's not the whole ball of wax, but at the same time, it's not saying no comment."

A breathless television reporter broke in to regular coverage to report that the man had been arrested and had been identified as Garcia. Now a new flood of calls began coming in. Gardner, an agent since 1983, took them calmly and patiently, but she was irritated.

"The TV stations are calling me and screaming at me because I won't confirm it's him," she said. "He is an FBI Ten Most Wanted fugitive. It's an FBI case, and the FBI is not confirming it's him. We're going to have to wait until we get some fingerprint results. It's going to take a while."

One reporter told Gardner that the Los Angeles police were saying the FBI had confirmed the man was Garcia. She called the police.

"We're working a joint operation," she told the police, keeping her anger in check. "It's an unknown quantity at this time, but [reporters] are quoting LAPD that we are confirming it is a Top Ten fugitive. Someone has made a quantum leap, because we're not confirming it. Someone has been detained. We believe it's the same person who ran down the street a couple of hours ago with a revolver in his hand. We are not confirming it is Amando Garcia."

Mark Llewellyn, the supervisor of the squad in charge of the case, kept Gardner informed by car phone from the scene. Besides keeping the press apprised, he counted on her to pass along information to Charlie Parsons. It is a tradition that the SAC is on the scene for the apprehension of a Top Ten fugitive. If the man was Garcia, Parsons would need to know it immediately. If not, there was no point in Parsons going to the scene. By now, agents had seen the man the police had arrested, and Llewellyn said he did not appear to be Garcia.

"They're 99 percent sure it's not him," Gardner said. "The agents have looked at him, and he doesn't have the right scars."

"Are we going to say that?" asked Joanne Wilfert, another agent in the media office.

"No," Gardner said. "Until Llewellyn calls in and says, 'It's not him,' we're not going to."

"They're quick to confirm sometimes, and then they say, 'We were wrong,'" Gardner said of the Los Angeles police. "We're a little slower and try to be right."

The phones in the small office were now ringing off the hook. One caller wanted to know about a pending investigation of a health care company.

"Basically, all I can do is take down the name of the company and at such time as criminal charges are filed or there is something we can talk about publicly, I'll call you back and say, 'Hey, Larry, remember when you asked me about this company?'" Gardner said.

Would Gardner tell a reporter that he is on the wrong track?

"It depends on the individual relationship with the reporter," she said. "The first time I ever really get in trouble, I'll be out of here. You take a risk."

Another reporter cut in to the regular programming on another station.

"The FBI says they'll have to check the man's fingerprints before they can say who he is," the anchorwoman said.

"Great," Gardner said, pleased that she had won a small battle.

The media office keeps a log of calls. So far, 210 calls had come in, most of them about the man thought to be Garcia. As it turned out, the man was not Garcia, who remained at large.

"He was a local guy wanted for some traffic warrant," Gardner told Parsons later in the day. "He had some coke in the house."

"Probably by now he's wanted for dope and personal firearms violations and all sorts of things," Parsons joked.

Two months earlier, the Wave, a local weekly, had run a story claiming that a concrete-block building struck by a jetliner at Los Angeles International Airport was the West Coast command post of a "secret FBI anti-terrorist organization." The Los Angeles Times picked up the story and ran with it. What gave the story some credence is that Steve Yee, the airport manager, had said on the record that the facility was a command post where surveillance was conducted.

"It has special equipment," Yee said. Then, to make sure the story would get good play, he said, "I can't tell you exactly what is in it. I don't want to make it a bigger target than it is."

In fact, the facility was an abandoned fire station where the FBI had a room for assembling a SWAT team. Should an airline hijacking take place, pilots would be instructed to pull up to the old firehouse instead of to a gate. There, the SWAT team could more easily over-whelm the hijackers away from other planes and passengers. The only "equipment" in the room was telephones and antennae for two-way radios. There was nothing sinister about the room; its pur-pose was to save the lives of innocent airplane passengers.

In part, the story was based on a misunderstanding. Part of the role of SWAT teams is to take out terrorists who have hijacked planes. To make a good story, that can be translated as a "secret FBI anti-terrorist organization," which sounds more like a terrorist group than an anti-terrorist unit of the government.

"We don't have a supersecret counterterrorism control center hid-den anywhere in the U.S.," said Neil J. Gallagher, who heads the FBI's counterterrorism section at headquarters. "You are seeing it here."

Another problem was that the *Los Angeles Times* story had been written by local reporters rather than Ronald J. Ostrow, who covers the bureau nationally for the paper and is known for his accuracy.

"There is a guy I really respect in your profession, Ron Ostrow," said John E. Otto, who was acting FBI director after Webster left to become director of Central Intelligence. "That little son of a bitch. He [Ostrow] knows his business, he's tough, he's got wonderful sources, but I never once saw him write something that was not accurate, that was not verified, no matter how hard-hitting it was or whom it affected. You deal with many in the press, and he will always stand out in my mind. He is a consummate professional."[241]

Gardner saw the "secret counterterrorist" story as an example of the inexperience of many Los Angeles reporters.

"What happened is the airport manager confirmed it, that it was an FBI secret blah-blah-blah," Gardner said. "It was Christmas Eve. The media called the office on Christmas Day. The agent on duty said John [Hoos, another media representative] was off, it was Christ-mas Day, and he'll call him back tomorrow. They went with the story."

Hoos said that the field office would have connected the reporter from the *Los Angeles Times* to his home if the dispatcher had thought it was a breaking story that had to be dealt with right away. After the story appeared, Hoos convinced the local media that the story was false. But meanwhile, distributed by the *Washington Post–Los Angeles Times* News Service, the *Los Angeles Times* story about a "secret FBI anti-terrorist organization" had appeared all over the country, including in the *Washington Post*.[242]

"The FBI has never officially acknowledged existence of such a unit," the *Los Angeles Times* reported, making it sound even more ominous.

"This is a very aggressive media market, second only to New York," Gardner said. But, she said, "the media are much more sophisticated and more professional in D.C. You don't have to spend as much time laying pipe, as I call it—groundwork."

Gardner said that a young *Los Angeles Times* reporter had called her a few days earlier and asked if the FBI was investigating a shooting by a Los Angeles police officer under the Civil Rights Act of 1964. Under the Justice Department guidelines for dealing with the press, the existence of only two kinds of investigations—civil rights and antitrust—may be disclosed to the press.

"So I said, 'The investigation was opened in November incidental to the shooting,' Gardner said. " 'What does that mean?' I said, 'Well, we opened the case at the same time the shooting happened.' 'Oh, okay. Well, how come you're only telling me about it today?' I said, 'Because you only called to ask about it today. We don't pick up the phone and call you.' Then she said, 'Well, does this mean the FBI will sue?' I said, 'This is a criminal case, not a civil case.' She said, 'You just said it was a civil case.' I said, 'It's a civil rights case.' She said, 'Well, that's a dumb name for the law. Why do you call it civil rights if it's a criminal case?' I said, 'That's the name of the law passed by Congress in 1964.' I had to explain to her about police brutality and how these cases are filed and how we investigate. She wasn't even alive in the 1960s and had no concept of what I was talking about."

Gardner said that some reporters "couldn't even tell you what branch of government we are in. . . . You don't see that with the national press corps, with the New York or D.C. press corps."[243]

Because the Los Angeles office has two media representatives, Los Angeles reporters try to squeeze information out of the media office by talking with more than one media representative about the same subject.

"If there are two of us in here, they'll play one against the other," Gardner said. "They'll talk to John, and then they'll call back and talk to me to see if I give the same responses. On days like today, they'll do what I call human wave. If they have four or five reporters from a news channel, they'll have four or five of them call, which just jams up the phones and makes it difficult for anybody else."

"There is a difference between the New York media and someone calling from west of the Hudson River," agreed Joe Valiquette, the media representative in the New York field office. "For example, if we were to have captured a person who is wanted in Colorado, invariably I'll get press calls from the *Denver Post* or whatever. They'll say, 'How did you know that he was in such and such a location?' The answer usually is because somebody told us, a neighbor told us. But we don't usually answer questions like 'who gave up a fugitive?' So I'll just give a pat answer that that is not a question that I can answer. Very often the reporter almost apologizes for asking. He goes into this long explanation. 'I'm sorry I asked, but I had to ask, and I knew you would give that answer.' Whereas here in New York, they ask, and I give that answer, and they say, 'Well, come on, everyone knows what the answer is, why don't you just give it to me?' It's a little more aggressive. But by the same token the New York media hasn't screwed us at all. By and large, I've had very good experience."

Gardner enjoys the press job because she learns about the work of the entire office. "You are exposed to just about everything that is going on," she said. "You're not confined to just the violent crime or white collar areas. You interact with all the supervisors and a lot of the agents."

Nonetheless, Gardner hopes to return to the street. "I wanted to be an investigator," she said. "I wanted to kick doors and take names and all that."

Before she was assigned to the press office, Gardner was the case agent on star stalker crimes—people who follow and harass celebrities and sometimes kill them. Until 1989, the FBI generally had left such cases to local authorities.

"It was a largely ignored problem," Gardner said. "No one took it seriously."

Then there was a series of tragedies involving stars and models, including the killing of Rebecca Schaeffer from the television sitcom *My Sister Sam* by a viewer who had been outraged by a love scene. The bureau decided to combat the problem by using a federal statute that prohibits sending physical threats through the U.S. mail.

"Usually if you have a couple of big FBI agents who lay their creds on them, and they realize they are looking at a criminal case, most of them stop," Gardner said. "But about 2 percent of them don't. Some are trying to get attention, and in a way, we are reinforcing what they are doing [by talking to them]."

Gardner became the star stalker expert after solving a case involving threats against actress Stephanie Zimbalist, who starred in the TV series *Remington Steele*. Over a period of two years, Zimbalist received 212 intimidating letters from a man who identified himself only as "Your Secret Admirer." Several letters mentioned the FBI, and Gardner concluded that the mystery man had selected Zimbalist because she was a daughter of Efrem Zimbalist, Jr., who played Inspector Lewis Erskine in the long-running ABC series *The FBI*.

"From the beginning, I felt he [the letter writer] was playing games with us, and he had picked her as a vehicle to communicate with us," Gardner said. "He picked her because of the relationship with the bureau, and we had to deal with it because of that. He thought she had a special relationship with the FBI."

In fact, Efrem Zimbalist continues to show up at retirement dinners given by the Los Angeles field office. But his thirty-three-year-old daughter initially did not tell her father about the threats because she did not want to worry him. Instead, she called the Los Angeles office of the FBI on her own.

"Your Secret Admirer" followed Zimbalist all over the world. His notes afterward cited details he could have picked up on only by watching her, even sitting next to her in restaurants. At first, the man sent the letters to Zimbalist's agent. Then he began sending the mail to her home in Encino, California, enclosing photos of it to show he had been there.

"I matched her travel schedule from 1987 on," Gardner said. "When he said, 'You were in Dallas on June 13,' she was in Dallas on June 13. Even in pulling the hotel records, when he said, 'You were on the fourteenth floor,' she was. It was very real."

Zimbalist became so frightened that she stopped making public appearances. That only brought more mailed threats:

Dateline: Ann Arbor 8/5/89

Dear Stephanie,
   . . . I am disappointed that I have not been able to find you doing any plays this summer. Contact with you on the road, following you around different cities, waiting for you at the hotel, seeing you at the theater, looking for you late at night; these have become the most important things in my life. You had better do another play soon. My continued patience depends on at least being able to see you on the road.

In another note, he said, "You can run, but you can't hide." Finally, the man wrote that he was coming to visit Zimbalist again at her home in Encino.

Dateline: Plymouth, MI 12/15/89

Dear Stephanie,
I am coming back to Encino. I will be staying at the Valley
Hilton March 2–5. (I have in mind some mischief.)

Gardner turned the letters over to Dr. Murray S. Miron, who heads
Syracuse University's Psycholinguistics Center. Miron's relationship with the FBI dates back to 1974, when he called the bureau to
see if it would be interested in his opinions on the taped messages
Patricia (Patty) Hearst's kidnappers were sending to radio stations.
On the tapes were the voices of members of the Symbionese Liberation Army and the newspaper heiress herself. By studying the
way written or spoken phrases are constructed, Miron could make
amazingly accurate guesses at the types of people who had expressed
them.
   "I called the [FBI] public relations office," Miron recalled. "This
SOB gives me a dance. 'We always like our citizens to be concerned.'
I was so angry. He said send it along. I thought bullshit. It would
drop into an abyss. But I sent it [his report]."[244]
   Since Hoover's death, Clarence Kelley had made it clear that he
wanted the FBI to explore new ways of doing things.
   "Kelley's mandate to me was how can we improve it. Even though
it seems to be working, let's check and see," said Richard J. Gallagher, the assistant director who then headed the criminal investigative division. Gallagher wound up getting Miron's report on the
Hearst tapes. He took it very seriously.
   "He [Miron] said the shots were being called by middle-class,
highly educated women who didn't really know what they wanted
but they were against the system," Gallagher said. "They were running the show. He said Patty Hearst is going to go across to the other
side [and join her kidnappers]. . . . He said these people are going
to commit suicide, not by their own hand, but would put themselves
in that position. It turned out that is what happened."[245]
   "She was identifying with the aggressor," Miron said. "All the
indications were that she was afraid the FBI would come in and
shoot her."
   Gallagher passed Miron's report along to Charles W. Bates, the
case agent on the Hearst kidnapping.
   "I was impressed with his [Miron's] analysis," Bates said. "I talked
to him a number of times on the phone."[246]
   The analysis did not lead to Hearst's arrest on September 18, 1975,

on bank robbery charges. Instead, the FBI learned where Hearst was hiding by conducting surveillance of associates of Hearst's friends, according to Larry Lawler, who supervised the investigation from the San Francisco field office. But Miron's work has helped the FBI narrow the list of suspects in dozens of other cases.

In the Zimbalist case, Miron confirmed to Gardner and later to prosecutors that the mystery man posed a serious threat.

"His explicit taunting of the authorities, his avowed compulsions and erotomanic fantasies, in the clear language of sadistic enjoyment, represent precisely those content features which both research and experience associate with real and imminent danger of violent actions," Miron said in his report.

Another longtime FBI consultant, Dr. Park E. Dietz, came to a similar conclusion.

By the time the mystery man had arrived in Encino, he was no longer a cipher. He had made the mistake of referring in his letters to too many specific dates, airline flights, and places. In a letter mailed from the Detroit area, he would say he was arriving in New York on a Northwest Airlines flight. He also said that he had stayed on the fourteenth floor of a particular hotel on a specific date. Matching names from flight manifests, hotel registers, and other sources, Gardner decided "Your Secret Admirer" was Michael L. Shields.

Gardner found that Shields had mailed more than one hundred anonymous threatening letters to a professor at a community college he had attended. Shields had pleaded guilty to prowling after the professor accused him of mailing the letters, slashing her tires, and throwing rocks through her windows. Gardner had her man.[247]

When Shields arrived in California, members of the Special Operations Group tailed him. They saw him mail two postcards, and they got postal inspectors to open the mailbox. Addressed to Zimbalist, the cards warned her that he had arrived.

When Shields checked in to the Valley Hilton in Encino, Gardner and seven other agents were in the lobby and halls. The agents did not think Shields had a gun. Moreover, "he was a huge, sloppy guy," Gardner said. "He would probably have hurt himself before he hurt any of us." Nevertheless, as a safety precaution, the agents waited to arrest him until he had entered the elevator and emerged on his floor.

Shields, forty-two, lived with his seventy-two-year-old mother, Cletus Shields, a retired elementary-school teacher. After his arrest, she said her son had taken care of his room and the laundry and often had cooked for them, not to mention paying for his trips.

"He's always stood by me and, in fact, he's been one of those kids that has worried more about me than himself, I guess because he always felt I was alone and needed help," she said.

Gardner and John R. Trimarco, another agent, interviewed Shields in the hotel.

"We did a good guy, bad guy," Gardner said. "I was the dumb blonde."

Shields told them that he wanted to cause Zimbalist "angst" but would not have harmed her. He also denied having any guns. However, in the Shieldses' apartment, the FBI found eighty videotapes of *Remington Steele*, twenty-seven magazine clippings on Zimbalist, and a Marlin semiautomatic carbine rifle.

With some trepidation, an assistant U.S. Attorney in Los Angeles agreed to prosecute the case.

"One of the frustrations was he [Shields] never came out and said, 'I'm going to kill you,' " Gardner said. "You had to look at the totality of what he had written. We convinced the AUSA [assistant U.S. Attorney] that this was a case that could make some new case law. She [the prosecutor] is a risk taker. She thought it was a 70 percent case. But the determination of whether there was a threat would rest with the jury. If nothing else, it would teach him that he was engaging in criminal behavior."

As it turned out, Shields pleaded guilty to seven counts of mailing threatening communications. He was sentenced to two years in prison, ordered to undergo psychiatric counseling, and prohibited from approaching or trying to contact Zimbalist or her family.[248]

As Parsons sees it, star stalker and other crimes are a growth industry in Los Angeles. The latest example is gang violence. After the May 1992 riots that followed the acquittal of Los Angeles police officers for beating Rodney King, the incident became national news. But the Los Angeles office—and the FBI in general—had been working the problem for some time.

Going back to Hoover's refusal to let the FBI become involved in drug investigations, the FBI traditionally has been an organization that keeps its hands clean. But, spurred by political concerns of the Justice Department, Webster and Sessions changed that attitude. Webster began by taking on drug investigations, and in June 1989, Sessions declared violent crime another priority for the FBI.

What that meant was that a range of violent crimes traditionally worked by the FBI—kidnappings, bank robberies, fugitive apprehensions, assaults on federal officers, aircraft hijackings, and interstate transportation in aid of racketeering—would be elevated to higher priority. In addition, in a program called Operation Safe Streets, the FBI would assist local law enforcement in combatting violent crimes not normally within federal jurisdiction. For example, the federal antiracketeering statute can be used to prosecute drug dealers. In some cases, the FBI even helped local police develop murder cases and then gave them to local district attorneys to prosecute.

"Crime is unfortunately a very strong byproduct of the success of our American culture," William Baker said. "To the extent it is organized at the enterprise level, it needs to be addressed by an agency that has the intelligence base, communications ability, and investigative strength to deal with it."

"This is the FBI's response to what really has turned out to be the number-one crime problem in the U.S," said Danny O. Coulson, the deputy assistant director in the criminal investigative division over violent crime. "If you are going to have a democracy and have the Constitution that applies to everyone in the U.S., then you have to have an environment that gives an opportunity for all those freedoms to flourish. With the type of crime we have now, the things we have come to expect as part of the freedoms of this country are in fact lost."

When Larry Lawler took over in 1988, the Los Angeles field office was not working gangs.

After Lawler had been named to head the Los Angeles office, he called from the Minneapolis field office, where he was then assigned, and asked what the Los Angeles office was doing about gangs.

"The ASAC [assistant special agent in charge] said, 'We are not doing anything about it,' " Lawler said. "I said, 'I have Crips in St. Paul. We have a national problem, and we are going to start working it.' "

Once Lawler took over in Los Angeles, he named Robert L. Jones to head a thirteen-agent squad that focuses on gangs. Gangs are a phenomenon in Los Angeles that goes back to the 1920s. Today there are two primary gangs, the Crips and the Bloods, with an estimated combined membership of fifty thousand. Both black, they claim different territories in the city and have their own colors— red for the Bloods, blue for the Crips. The gang members distinguish themselves by wearing blue or red scarves, caps, or jackets. An innocent bystander who wears the color of an opposing gang in the wrong territory stands a good chance of being killed.

"We've had a lot of people who have been murdered who were

not gang members and were standing on the corner wearing red or blue," Jones said. "It's an invitation to be shot. If you're in south central LA, and you have a knowledge of which gang is claiming what turf, it would behoove you not to wear the rival color."[249]

"They may not blast a white person wearing blue in a red area," said Jones. But even whites may get shot. "If you're flying the wrong color, you're probably going to catch a bullet," he said.

Jones found that most of the violence associated with the gangs had its roots in distribution of cocaine. So, using traditional FBI methods—informants, wiretaps, and surveillance—he focused on one ring within the Crips that had distributed fifty tons of cocaine over the past decade. The drug network got its supply from the Medellin cartel in Colombia. It then shipped the drugs to Mexico and brought them into Los Angeles by car. From there, the gang members distributed them to Anchorage, Dallas, Detroit, Honolulu, Houston, and Seattle.

Called LA COLORS, the case began when an informant identified a drug dealer as a midlevel broker within the ring.

"He was our central focus," Jones said. "He was arrested, but we didn't publicize it. He is cooperating. We used undercover agents, wiretaps, conventional investigative techniques, analysis with the computer. There are people you would never link up because of the voluminous paperwork you would have to go through."

The wiretaps—a technique rarely used by the police—were critical. "They picked up information relating to murders, drive-by shootings, drugs, distribution points, who they are networking with, who their suppliers are," Jones said.

In January 1992, the FBI arrested three of the ring leaders, while three others remain fugitives. Jones expects more arrests. For his work, Jones received an award from then Attorney General William P. Barr.[250]

After the beating of Rodney King on March 3, 1991, the Los Angeles field office quietly began an investigation under the Civil Rights Act of 1964 of the Los Angeles police officers involved. Unlike the jurors who acquitted the officers, FBI agents almost universally saw the beating as unprofessional and a violation of law.

"The tape [of the beating] was pretty dramatic," Charlie Parsons said.

At one point, Parsons had one hundred agents working on the case. But only the Justice Department could decide whether to prosecute the police officers involved, a step taken after the local verdict in the case.

"The civil rights program is a backstop for Justice," said Tron W. Brekke, who is over civil rights and applicant investigations at headquarters. "Local authorities in a lot of cases will take action against the perpetrators either administratively or by prosecution. We will actively monitor that situation, and once a decision is made by the local authorities and reviewed by Justice, if they feel the punishment equates to the crime, then they will close the case. If not, they may come in with a civil rights investigation behind the local action."[251]

Each year, the FBI conducts 5,500 civil rights investigations, most of them based on complaints from the victims or from civil rights groups. Some 70 percent of the investigations involve allegations of police brutality. In a recent year, these investigations resulted in 138 convictions.

"The problem with civil rights cases," Brekke said, "is they are so sensitive in the community and in police departments that we work with that it's very difficult to sift through what happened."

After the acquittal of the police officers charged in the beating of Rodney King, the field office moved into high gear to obtain further evidence for a prosecution. As a result of the FBI's investigation, four of the officers involved in the beating—including Laurence M. Powell and Stacey C. Koon—were indicted for using "unreasonable force" under color of law.[252] In April 1993, Powell and Koon were convicted; two other officers were acquitted.

The Los Angeles office also contributed agents to a 120-member task force to investigate the violence during the ensuing riots, much of it perpetrated by gang members. The FBI participated with the Los Angeles police in arresting three men who allegedly beat truck driver Reginald O. Denny—an attack that was broadcast throughout the world in the first hours of the riots.

During the riots, then Attorney General William Barr placed Buck Revell in charge of federal law enforcement in Los Angeles, including law enforcement activities of the military. Revell operated out of the Los Angeles field office, coordinating assistance to the Los Angeles police and reporting to Barr and Sessions in Washington.

After the riots, Parsons formed two additional squads to work on gang violence. "One very loud message—one heard all the way back in Washington—is that citizens consider gangs and their violence to be near or at the top of their list of concerns," Parsons said.[253]

Meanwhile, the Los Angeles office expanded its white collar crimes program by starting a new squad to work on health care fraud—ripoffs by doctors, pharmacies, and other health care providers that fraudulently bill the government.

"When you think of a white collar squad, you think of digging in paper," said Mary Jo Marino, who, as the principal relief supervisor on one of the squads, takes over when the squad leader is out of town or on vacation. "But we have a lot of arrests, search warrants, as well as looking at paper trails. You're out day to day talking to people. There is something different every day."[254]

Over the years, the Los Angeles office has played a major role in apprehending spies who worked for California aerospace companies. Los Angeles agents helped catch Christopher J. Boyce, a TRW Inc. employee who sold material to the Soviets in Mexico City and was the falcon of the book *The Falcon and the Snowman*; James Durward Harper, a free-lance engineer, and his wife, Ruby Schuler, who sold documents on the Minuteman ICBM and ballistic missile research to Polish intelligence officers for $250,000; and Thomas P. Cavanagh, who tried to sell the plans to the Stealth fighter plane to two Soviets who turned out to be Russian-speaking Los Angeles FBI agents.[255]

But for all the successes, Los Angeles also is where the most embarrassing incident in the history of the FBI occurred—the arrest of Special Agent Richard Miller for espionage.

Weldon Kennedy, now assistant director for administrative services, worked with Miller when they were both assigned temporarily to do a special background check on a man who had been nominated as a federal judge in Puerto Rico. Miffed that her husband had been sent to Puerto Rico without her, Miller's wife decided to have a vacation as well and showed up with three of their young children, according to Kennedy. One afternoon, Miller was in a police chief's office dictating a report on the phone. Meanwhile, Miller's children were scurrying around the room. The police chief and another agent came back to see Miller trying to pacify a screaming child while dictating.

"Here are two kids running around the office. He is holding this baby. The baby has a pacifier. The baby spits it out. 'Wait a minute.' He feels around on the floor and sticks the pacifier back in his mouth," Kennedy said. "Miller was the sloppiest human being I have ever known. He stank."

In Los Angeles, Miller drove to work in a car pool with an agent who was known for his neatness. The other agent regularly got mad at Miller because his car was so littered with food and garbage. Miller weighed 250 pounds and snacked on Twinkies.

"One morning they rode in Miller's car," Kennedy said. "They start walking to the office. Stuck on the back of [the other agent] is half of a peanut butter sandwich. He [the other agent] had to be physically restrained. He wanted to kill Miller. Miller was summarily dismissed from the car pool."

"I talked to him on the phone on a bank robbery," said Brekke, who was assigned to the Los Angeles office when Miller was there. "He called me fifteen times asking what to do. Here is an experienced agent who should know these things."

When William Baker was an assistant special agent in charge of the Los Angeles office, he recommended that Miller be transferred from a resident agency to the field office for closer supervision. His reports were badly written and often late. Traditionally, the repository for marginal agents is the squad that does background checks on applicants for government positions. But because Miller was so often late, the field office decided to put him instead on a squad that dealt with foreign counterintelligence. The idea was that counterintelligence investigations often come to no conclusive end, and Miller's tardiness would not be as much of a problem if he was assigned to conduct them. It was then that Miller got into much more serious trouble.[256]

Miller became sexually involved with Svetlana Ogorodnikov, who, it turned out, was working for the KGB and routinely visited the Soviet consulate in San Francisco. On his annual salary of fifty thousand dollars, Miller was constantly strapped for cash. By then, the twenty-year FBI veteran had eight children. So, Miller decided to get some help from the Soviets. In return for classified documents, Miller demanded from Ogorodnikov and her husband fifty thousand dollars in gold and fifteen thousand dollars in cash.

When the FBI got wind of what was happening, the bureau dispatched headquarters officials from Washington to work in a secret office established in Los Angeles just to coordinate the case.

"Miller was going to leave the country with her and meet with the KGB in Europe," said R. Patrick Watson, one of the headquarters officials on the case. However, at the last minute Miller decided against going. On September 28, 1984, he confessed to an assistant special agent in charge that he had been seeing Ogorodnikov without authorization.[257]

After Miller failed a polygraph test on whether he had given away classified documents, the bureau sent Paul K. Minor, the senior polygrapher at headquarters, to work on him. If Minor could get Miller to admit a small part of what he did, Miller might open up further. Minor focused on Miller's trip to San Francisco, where he admitted he waited at a restaurant three blocks from the Soviet consulate while Ogorodnikov told the KGB about him.

"I said you would have to give her something to tell them who you were," Minor said. "That was a ploy on my part to get him to admit something simple, something nonincriminating that was innocuous. Once you get that, you can use it to pry into something else."[258]

After getting nowhere, Minor suggested that they continue the next day.

"I was getting ready to leave," Minor said. "He said, 'Look. You're right. When I went up there, I gave her the credentials because she said she needed something so she could say who I am.' "

The next morning, Minor probed Miller on whether he had given any documents to Ogorodnikov to give to the KGB. Again, Miller clammed up. But after lunch he said, "You know, I was thinking while I was at lunch. You're right. There was a document."

Miller identified the document as a classified 1983 FBI foreign counterintelligence manual. He said he felt hurt because Ogorodnikov appeared not to appreciate its importance.

That night, Webster ordered Miller's arrest. After three trials, Miller was convicted of espionage in 1991 and sentenced to twenty years in prison.[259]

Miller was the first FBI agent ever to be convicted of espionage. It devastated fellow agents.

"I don't think anybody would have been surprised to hear anything about him, except that he committed espionage," said Larry W. Langberg, a Los Angeles agent who is president of the FBI Agents Association and knew Miller at the time. "That floored everyone."

There was much talk within the FBI about the existence of a "Mormon mafia" and whether it contributed to the bureau's tolerance of Miller's slovenly work. Miller was a Mormon, as were Richard Bretzing, the special agent in charge at the time, and Bryce Christensen, the assistant special agent in charge over Miller.[260]

Convenient as it was, this excuse deflected attention from a more serious problem: failure to confront marginal employees and discipline them severely or fire them if they do not measure up. Yet, as demonstrated by the case of the two Miami agents who went to a sex club and lied about it, even when agents are caught covering up, the American legal system may work to prevent the bureau from firing them.

Even with the cold war over, the counterintelligence investigations to which Miller was assigned continue to be important. Los Angeles companies are a target not only of Russian intelligence officers but of agents of other countries, such as France, China, Iraq, Pakistan, and India, that try to steal American technology.

"There is no shortage of work here," Parsons said. "I could take a thousand agents and put them to work very productively. That may happen someday. This office by the year 2000 may be larger than New York. That's the way I see the crime problem here."

10

Profiling: "Scream, Girl, Scream"

● **When John E. Douglas** played it for Scott Glenn, who was preparing for his role in *The Silence of the Lambs*, it made the actor cry. Douglas, whom Glenn portrayed in the Academy Award–winning movie that depicted the work of the FBI's crime profilers, didn't want to hear again the pitiful shrieking of a thirteen-year-old girl being tortured. But reluctantly he left his office, got a cassette tape recorder, and placed it on his desk at the FBI Academy. He pushed the Play button. The sound was the same, over and over: repeated screaming, a teenage girl's screams. Sometimes she cried "no" in a tremulous wail.

Douglas, a tall, good-looking man with even features, smoothed-back light brown hair, thick brown eyebrows, and ruddy cheeks, looked unhappy. He rewound the tape toward the beginning, where Lawrence S. Bittaker, one of the two assailants, taunted the girl, telling her that she wanted to give him oral sex, then saying sadistically, "Scream, girl, scream." It is very clear that Jacqueline Lamp was suffering excruciating pain and sheer terror. The tape goes on for hours, unrelieved screaming, shrieking, over and over.

The real thing is so much more devastating than in the movies. Sounds one never forgets.

Douglas explained that while Bittaker's accomplice, Roy L. Norris, drove the van near Redondo Beach, California, Bittaker was in the back with the girl, squeezing her nipples with pliers and applying a coat hanger to her vagina. So that they could later relive the girl's torture, the men tape recorded it. Soon, Jacqueline Lamp's terror would end. She would become another of Bittaker and Norris's murder victims, strangled for the two men's pleasure.

"Killing is one thing, but there are people who are just interested in inflicting pain and punishment," Douglas said. "They enjoy seeing those tears streaming over the faces."

Of the two killers, Douglas said, "They got life. Big deal. The idea that this person is still living, and this [tape] goes on for hours. I'd be lying to you if I said it doesn't affect you. It does."[261]

Douglas's job requires some relief from the daily emotional assault. When he goes to a shopping center and sees unattended children, he thinks of his cases and the possibility that a serial killer could be stalking them. So, in the FBI's profiling unit, black humor serves a purpose.

Displayed on a table next to Douglas's desk is a three-dimensional layout of a murder scene that invites solution. This glass-enclosed room from a dollhouse was the parting gift of an employee who left after she'd had enough of the grim job of learning more than anyone would want to know about heinous crimes.

Lying on the floor of the dollhouse room is a "dead" clay animation doll with a rope around her neck. She's a female "Gumby" in lace, her eyes crossed out. It doesn't take an expert crime solver to see that the crime scene has been staged. Rifled drawers make it look like a burglary attempt. The room has been too carefully ransacked—black panty hose draped from a dresser drawer, the telephone taken off the hook, eyeglasses thrown on the magazine rack, tiny beer cans tossed about. Closer inspection reveals small bits of hay on the victim's body, and a suspicious-looking clump of horse manure on the floor. And so the murderer is: Pokey, the horse.

Douglas's office is relegated to a dungeonlike basement. There are no windows. The grim work Douglas and his FBI colleagues do begs for the light of day, but the FBI has quartered them in what amounts to a bomb shelter.

This is where the FBI's profilers solve serial murders, rapes, and other macabre crimes using a modern version of Sherlock Holmes's techniques. Since the profilers also teach at the FBI Academy, they are considered part of the training division. Much of their work product will eventually be distributed to local law enforcement through a new FBI division called criminal justice information services. The new division consolidates all the services the FBI offers to local law enforcement. Included is what used to be the fingerprint identification division as well as the National Crime Information Center (NCIC), which lists 23 million items of interest to law enforcement that can be identified by serial number—stolen vehicles, guns, license plates, boats, securities, and cash—as well as fugitives, missing or unidentified people, and people who have threatened the president. As a result of NCIC checks, 169,000 vehicles were recovered in a recent year. Police identified and arrested 136,000 people. They also located 36,000 missing children and 9,000 missing adults.

Even though fingerprint identification is the most tedious work the FBI does, it is one of the bureau's most important responsibilities. Each year, this division—the largest in the bureau, with 2,800 employees—identifies 42,431 fugitives by their fingerprints and receives another 9 million new sets of fingerprints. Altogether, the bureau has the fingerprints of 196 million people—107 million of them criminals and the rest applicants for military, teaching, police, or other sensitive jobs.

It was James Earl Ray's latent fingerprint on the rifle that killed Martin Luther King that allowed the FBI to identify him as the killer and apprehend him. A key piece of evidence linking Lee Harvey Oswald to the assassination of John F. Kennedy was a palm print taken of Oswald. It matched a print found on the rifle that killed Kennedy, according to Lawrence K. York, who was the assistant director over the identification division before it was merged into the new criminal justice information services division.[262]

In 1988, the FBI began using laser and other lighting devices to pick up latent fingerprints from Styrofoam cups and old documents. In one case, a man who, as a pro-Nazi youth, had made speeches in Germany leading to the slaughter of hundreds of Jews, was deported from the U.S. after the FBI matched fingerprints on letters he had written forty years earlier to the Nazi hierarchy pledging his loyalty. In another case, the FBI's identification of a fingerprint on the body of a murder victim led to the conviction of the murderer.

To process prints is a massive undertaking. While an indexing system helps to narrow the search, identification in the end is done by the naked eye. The FBI is planning to automate the process by storing the existing fingerprint records in digital form on computer at a new facility on 986 acres in Harrison County, West Virginia, near Clarksburg.

In effect, the new $185 million building was the gift of Senator Robert C. Byrd, the West Virginia Democrat, who said he would get the FBI the money if the bureau would move the division to his home state.

"There was no way to get it done until Senator Byrd came along and said, 'I will help you. Please consider West Virginia,'" Sessions said. "We did consider West Virginia. It is a fully justified site, a perfect site for us."[263]

For all the publicity about John Douglas—Jodie Foster thanked him when she accepted an Academy Award for best actress for her role as an FBI agent in *The Silence of the Lambs*—the father of FBI profiling is Howard D. Teten. In contrast to Douglas, who is a natty dresser, Teten is indifferent to clothes. A beefy, six-foot-tall ex-Marine, Teten has a Marine Corps tattoo on his right arm—skull and crossbones over the letters U.S. EMBASSY.

No one singlehandedly develops anything in the FBI. Everything is done by teamwork. But Teten, a man with a strong nose and chin between big ears and soft gentle eyes behind glasses, stands out as the pioneer. Although Teten began what has turned out to be the sexiest technique in the FBI's arsenal of crime-solving tricks, he has eschewed publicity. Indeed, with the exception of interviews for this book, the soft-spoken Teten has never granted an interview on the subject. Nor does Teten maintain a typical FBI agent's views on such topics as drug abuse. He thinks drugs should be legalized.

Teten began developing his ideas on profiling when he was an evidence officer in the San Leandro, California, police department near Oakland. At the same time Teten was examining murder scenes, he was finishing a bachelor's in criminology at the University of California at Berkeley. There, he was heavily influenced by such world-famous teachers as Douglas Kelly, Paul Kirk, and O. W. Wilson.

"Being very influenced by a criminal psychiatrist and having a background in criminalistics, and having worked as an evidence officer, you're going to be thinking along these lines: This is physical evidence. What does it mean?" Teten said.[264]

Teten began to see a correlation between what he saw at crime scenes and the people who committed those crimes. In effect, he concluded, criminals leave their signatures at the scene by the way they commit their crimes. Generally, the patterns are more pronounced in sex-related crimes, which account for most serial murders. These are defined by the FBI as three or more killings in separate incidents. They differ from spree killings, such as Richard Speck's, when killers mow down a number of people over a period of a day or two without any cooling-off period. A mass murderer kills many people all at once.

As is the case with any discovery, the correlation between the crime scene and the killer seems obvious: Anyone who performs a task—whether it is writing a book or playing golf—does it in a certain way. Because of their mental abnormalities, serial killers are especially apt to leave telltale signs that form a distinctive pattern. Once that pattern is recognized, it can be compared with patterns from other cases and used to narrow down the list of suspects and ultimately find the murderer.

For example, FBI profilers found that a person who is careful enough to dispose of a body in a river is usually an older person. If the body is dumped in a remote area, the killer is probably an outdoors person with a knowledge of the area. When the slashes on the victim's body are vicious and directed at the sex organs, the assailant usually knows the person. If there is no sign of forced entry to the victim's home and the assailant stayed around to have a snack after the murder, he probably lived in the neighborhood and knew the victim. In contrast, killers who don't feel comfortable in an apartment leave immediately.

Thus, based on a few elementary facts about a killing, the FBI can draw a profile of the killer as an older man who likes the outdoors, is familiar with the area where the body was left, knows the victim, and lived in the neighborhood. In many cases, armed with the profile, police can focus on one or two suspects and solve the crime.

Police have always used clues at crime scenes to guess at the identities of perpetrators. But homicide detectives as a rule do not have the time, inclination, or vast store of cases from all over the country to systematically amass data that would truly prove helpful in solving crimes. Ironically, it was Sir Arthur Conan Doyle, the British author of the Sherlock Holmes detective mysteries, who came up with some of the techniques used by profilers long before Teten and his FBI colleagues perfected them.

After joining the FBI in 1962, Teten began teaching police management at the National Academy. In 1969, he suggested a course in what Teten called applied criminology. It focused more on crime scenes than did the traditional criminology course.

Because Teten and his supervisors feared that Hoover would veto such an innovative idea, they never told him about it. This was part of the mystery of Hoover's bureau, a place that in many ways was tightly controlled by the director but at times went in its own direction. Agents who took it upon themselves to try new techniques in defiance of the director knew that, if caught, they would be punished if the idea had failed. If the idea had succeeded, they might escape punishment with the help of FBI officials who helped one another when in trouble with Hoover.

Teten taught the new course by asking police to bring him their unsolved homicides.

"Law enforcement officers have psychological baggage," said Roger Depue, a brilliant agent who began working with Teten in 1973 and later headed the unit that does profiling at the FBI Academy. Boyish-looking, with an almost mischievous smile, Depue wearing a baseball cap would look like he belonged in Little League. "If you've ever worked a case, a kidnapping for instance, and you've done everything you could possibly do, and you sleep at your desk, and you try as hard as you can with everything you possibly know, and the child is found killed anyway, you carry that around. It bothers you. I've known law enforcement officers who are still working a case ten years after retiring."

As officers described the cases in class, other officers recalled cases they had worked on with similar characteristics. They would conduct brainstorming sessions, trying to analyze the similarities and the strategies that had worked best in previous cases. It wasn't long before officers were coming to class carrying briefcases crammed with records of their unsolved cases.

By now, Teten had associated crime-scene patterns with particular mental disorders. Mental disorders are constantly being renamed and reclassified. One such disorder was referred to at the time as simple schizophrenia.

"Simple schizophrenia is a form of mental disorder that comes on usually about puberty," Teten said. "It results in an individual becoming more and more of a loner, distancing himself from the family. A true recluse. The simple schizophrenic never went out of his way to do something. But if things were put in his way, particularly sexually oriented potentials, like a woman who was pretty and might flirt with him, he seemed to retreat from reality at puberty because of a fear of this type of contact. He would act defensively. His method of defensive action was to kill."

Most schizophrenics are harmless. But when they do kill, they do it in a particular way.

"The simple schizophrenic will always kill first, and then, because he is so curious, he's going to look it over. It's almost as if the sexual organs are magic. The way he does it depends on his age. If he is younger, he will touch, but as he gets older, he will somehow try to remove them or change them to make a woman a man. He will place a stick in the vagina. He might cut off the breasts, something like that. In spite of his actions, he is not an ogre looking for people to kill. He doesn't do that. He is defending himself against what he believes to be a threat."

Teten found that because killers' behavior changed with age, he could predict their ages based on the way they had killed. A younger person, Teten said, "will take part of the clothes off, expose the breasts and maybe feel them, examine the vagina. Often you can see that because they have killed them, they have blood on their hands, and you can see the marks of the blood. They don't damage anything. They remove the danger so to speak, but they are fascinated by it."

On the other hand, to an older person, the danger appears greater. "They try to remove the evidence and change the sex," he said.

Teten saw these patterns in one of the earliest cases brought to him by his students at the National Academy—a murder in Amarillo, Texas. By the way the victim had been mutilated, it was clear that the killer was a younger simple schizophrenic. Because the simple schizophrenic tends to kill people in his own geographic area or people with whom he may have had contact, the police usually have already interviewed him.

"I said, 'Did you interview anybody or did you hear of anyone who is a real loner, hardly talks at all, won't look you in the face, and is probably fifteen to nineteen?' " Teten asked the police. "They said yes. After that, they went back to him and he confessed."

In contrast to the simple schizophrenic, a person known then as a psychopath is outgoing and articulate.

"A psychopath will actually kill someone and then sit where the police drink coffee and sit and listen," Teten said. "He gets a great thrill about the police discussing how this crime happened. This gives him a sense of superiority, that he knows something they don't know, and they'll never figure it out. If they stop investigating, he may commit another crime to get the police going. He may even write them a taunting letter.

"Psychopaths will often go back to the crime scene or the cemetery," Teten continued. "So will some schizophrenics, for different reasons. . . . A simple schizophrenic may kill a woman but under no circumstances will he ever rape her after she is dead. A psychopath would probably never rape one *after* she is dead. A schizo-phrenic would never torture a woman. He would just never do that. A psychopath, on the other hand, might enjoy torturing his victim. He would take pliers and squeeze the nipples of a woman before she is dead. This power over her is his sexual stimulant."

Besides the preservation of the crime scene, good autopsies are a must in helping profilers do their work. An autopsy can determine if cuts occurred before or after death. It a cut produces little or no blood, it was inflicted after death.

"Everything at the crime scene is important," Teten said. Because maggots come from the eggs of flies, and flies do not lay eggs at night, the presence of maggots on a body means that the body has been dead at least a day, Teten said.

By 1972, Teten had found that Dr. James A. Brussel, a New York psychiatrist, was doing essentially the same thing as he was. Brussel, who had written *Case Book of a Crime Psychiatrist*, had served as a consultant to local police on several serial killings, including the case of the "mad bomber" in New York in 1956. In that case, Brussel said, the bomber was an Eastern immigrant in his forties who lived with his mother. He even said the man usually wore a neatly but-toned double-breasted suit. When arrested, the bomber, George Me-tesky, was wearing a double-breasted suit and fit the profile in most other respects.

Teten asked Dr. Brussel if he would tutor him.

"I said, 'The FBI will pay to have you tutor me. How much do you charge?' " Teten said. "He said, 'You can't afford it. But I'm a patriot, and I cannot reduce my rates. So I'll have to do it for free.' "

By then, Patrick J. Mullaney, a New York agent with a degree in psychology, had become interested in Teten's work. Teten helped to get him transferred to the FBI Academy so that they could both teach and conduct research. Teten and Mullaney began offering their conclusions on particular cases to their police students. They were careful not to put anything in writing on the letterhead of the FBI.

"When we first started, we were in the period when the bureau didn't like to be 'embarrassed' was the word," Mullaney said. "It was a whole different era. My personal belief is if you make a mistake or don't have the answers, you show more strength by admitting it than if you don't have the answers and are unwilling to admit it."

Teten and Mullaney were afraid that if some of the profiles were wrong, as they inevitably were, Hoover or his loyalists who remained in control after his death would find out and stop the profiling program.

"This was something new and chancy," Mullaney said. "We always felt we would rather do it on a personal basis rather than having to go through four or five layers before it went out of the organization."[265]

As the word spread that the profiles had actually solved some of law enforcement's most intractable cases, "Graduates would call in and say they have a case similar to one we had talked about," Depue said. "So we got heavily into the consultation business. It was on a time-available basis. The FBI was not involved very much at this time. By and large the FBI was the last to recognize we had a contribution to make.

"By 1976 or 1977, we had more questions than answers," Depue said. "How does the criminal gain control of his victim? How does he manipulate the victim? How does he maintain control? How does he select his victim in the first place?"

The agents found nothing in the academic literature. By and large, academics study crime from afar. They generally focus on theories and would not think of asking criminals how they did their crimes.

As the FBI Academy began adding more academic courses to its training program, the bureau formed a research unit with Teten as its chief. By then, John Douglas and Robert K. Ressler had joined the academy and were being trained by Teten and others in the unit. Douglas and Ressler began supplementing the data the other agents had amassed by interviewing criminals in jail for committing serial rapes, murders, or assassinations. In this way, they hoped to learn more about the criminals' thinking so that they could use it to solve serial murders and other crimes.

The agents began with assassins, interviewing as many incarcerated assassins and would-be assassins as possible, including Sirhan B. Sirhan, Sarah Jane Moore, James Earl Ray, Arthur H. Bremer, and Lynette (Squeaky) Frome. After asking them fifty-seven pages of questions, the agents noted similarities and differences in the responses. They confirmed that assassins generally are unstable individuals looking for attention. In many cases, assassins keep diaries as a way of enhancing the importance of their acts.

"The assassin in this country frequently is a person who is screaming for attention and recognition," Depue said. "As soon as you realize that, you become aware of what that kind of person would do. He'll keep records, take photographs, make recordings, leave a record for posterity on why he's doing it. Once you know that, you can design your investigative strategy to take advantage of it. So now the Secret Service investigates threats, and you have a profile of the kind of person who would do this."[266]

The behavioral science services unit, as it is now called, went on to conduct research into serial killers, serial rapists, and child molesters. The assailants—including David Berkowitz, Richard Speck, and Charles Manson—actually enjoyed sitting down with professionals who had conducted research on their crimes. It gave them a way of reliving what they had done.

"They are very egotistical," Douglas said. "They want to be the best. They think they are the best even though they are still in jail."

At one point, Ressler, who had joined the profilers in 1974, was interviewing Edmund E. Kemper III, who had killed his mother, grandparents, and six other people. When he was finished, Ressler rang a buzzer to summon a guard to let him out of the interview room in the California prison where Kemper was serving multiple life sentences. When the guard didn't come, the 295-pound prisoner told Ressler to "relax" because the guards were changing shifts and feeding prisoners.

"If I went ape-shit in here, you'd be in a lot of trouble, wouldn't you?" Kemper said menacingly. "I could screw your head off and place it on the table to greet the guard."

Hannibal Lecter, the serial killer in *The Silence of the Lambs*, was a composite of serial killers like Kemper, who removed people's heads and saved them as trophies; Edward Gein, who decorated his home with human skin; and Richard T. Chase, who ate the organs of his victims.[267]

Ressler was able to cool Kemper off by suggesting that he might have a concealed weapon.[268]

After that, agents interviewed inmates only in pairs. Contrary to the impression created by Foster's role in *The Silence of the Lambs*, the FBI never sends trainees to interview anyone. But inaccuracies like that didn't matter.

"That movie did more for the FBI than any real case," Douglas said. "It was tremendous."

From the interviews with serial killers, a clear pattern emerged. Most of the perpetrators lived a fantasy life that included enacting and reenacting the crimes they had committed. With their understanding of the killers' behavior, the agents were able to develop more in-depth profiles of suspects for whom the police should be on the lookout. In a current project, Richard L. Ault, Jr., is interviewing convicted traitors to learn more about the types of people who commit espionage.

"The interviews help us to understand motivation and how they were able to elude law enforcement," said John H. Campbell, who now heads the behavioral science services unit, which does some of the profiling along with the investigative support unit. "We learn how they planned the events and got rid of evidence."[269]

Many times, these profiles conflicted with the leads police had gotten or what appeared to be common sense. For example, the profilers said that a man who had killed a series of black children in Atlanta was himself black. Everyone had assumed that since all the victims were black, the killer must be a white man who hated blacks. In fact, Douglas concluded, "There was no way a white person could go in these areas and not be spotted." In addition, serial killers as a rule turn on people of their own race. The killer turned out to be Wayne B. Williams, who is black and is now serving two consecutive life terms.

"Because that [the conclusion that the killer was black] did not fit the preconceived notion, there was a clamor down there," Buck Revell said. "It was bad enough they were being killed."

The fact that agents in the field often accept the profilers' advice over the recommendations of headquarters officials sometimes ruffles feathers.

"Headquarters says, 'You mean SACs listen to you guys?' " Douglas said. "That sometimes is upsetting to the criminal investigative division at headquarters."

For all the skepticism, police and FBI agents have found over and over that the profiles are usually accurate, leading not only to apprehensions but to convictions. While the FBI provides the majority of profiles to local law enforcement as a service, about 40 percent of the profiles are done for FBI cases. Usually, the profiles consist of eight or twelve double-spaced pages. On occasion, the profilers consult with investigators over the phone.

When he was special agent in charge in Salt Lake City, Robert M. (Bear) Bryant called Douglas for advice. Two federal fugitives had killed at least five people. When confronted by a sheriff's SWAT team in a small town in Montana, they had gotten away.

"We had been looking for these guys for five or six days," Bryant said, "We were getting weary. So we called Douglas. I said, 'Are they mountain men or what?' He said, 'These guys aren't mountain men. They're dopers. They'll be in a house.' The sheriff got mad at me because they had already searched these houses."

Within an hour, the FBI and the local sheriff found the fugitives, who opened fire from a cabin with M-16s. In the ensuing shootout, the cabin caught fire and the fugitives burned to death.

"If it were not for those guys at Quantico, we would literally still be looking for them," said Bryant, who now heads the Washington metropolitan field office.[270]

In addition to profiling criminals, the profilers began suggesting ways of trapping them.

"Most of these successful violent criminals are caught by accident, by fluke, as in David Berkowitz, the Son of Sam killer," Depue said. "He was caught because of a parking ticket. Had he parked somewhere else that day, he might still be out there. It was good police work but it wasn't narrowing the focus of the investigation to the most likely suspects."

Since the FBI's research found that some types of killers carefully follow details about their crime in the papers, the profilers suggested planting stories in local papers pointing out the anniversary of an unsolved crime. The story might also describe where the victim was buried. A killer reading the story might decide to visit the grave of his victim on the anniversary of the crime. By videotaping the grave site, police have actually heard assailants confessing to a tombstone. In some cases, they have enumerated details of the crime that no one else knew.

"They will even say, 'You bitch! The reason you're here' is such and such," Depue said.[271]

Police who have ignored the FBI's advice have done so to their sorrow. Police from an Illinois town lay out all day in a cemetery, hoping that an assailant would show up. Because the weather was nasty, they finally gave up but left their video camera running. Sure enough, the killer showed up. However, because the police could not follow him, they do not know who he is.

"They have a videotape of a man, and they have no idea who he is. All they have is the videotape," Depue said.

"Are we revealing investigative techniques that are so unique? The answer is no," said Douglas, who wears crisp white shirts with monogrammed cuffs, a natty white handkerchief in his vest pocket, large-print ties, and black wingtips. "This stuff has been around for years, the subject returning to the scene of the crime. That's the kind of thing Sherlock Holmes did. We just verified it. Not just serial killers but arsonists and bombers go back to see their handiwork. That is their work, their accomplishment. If a killer sees a book that says killers return to the scene of the crime or to the cemetery, that will not prevent him from going back. He may be more cautious. But he is driven to go back."[272]

In profiling serial killers and rapists, Douglas and Robert R. (Roy) Hazelwood, both of whom joined the profilers in 1977, came up with a simpler, more objective way to categorize perpetrators. They divided them into "organized" and "disorganized" personalities. In part, this was a way to simplify the profiling art for the benefit of police officers who have no training in the subject.

The organized killer, who resembles the individual previously classified as a psychopath, has fairly high intelligence and is socially and sexually competent. He lives with someone, is controlled and calculating during the crime, and is likely later to follow news of his crime in the media.

The disorganized murderer, who resembles the individual previously classified as a simple schizophrenic, has average intelligence, is socially immature, and has a poor work history. He lives alone and is sexually incompetent. He does not follow his crime in the news media.[273]

"The disorganized personality can be either young and therefore careless or inexperienced, not smart, or mentally disturbed," Depue said.

These personal characteristics exhibit themselves in the way killers commit their crimes. The organized killer plans his offense and targets a stranger. The crime scene shows that this killer maintained control over his victim. He may use restraints such as ropes, chains, tape, gags, or blindfolds to maintain control and prolong the victim's agony. He may engage in aggressive acts before the murder to create even more fear. In one example, a murderer tightened and loosened a rope around the victim's throat so that he could watch the victim fall into unconsciousness, then revive him. After the crime, the organized killer removes the body from the scene and hides it. He may also take souvenirs of the crime, including body parts.

In contrast, the disorganized individual engages in murder spontaneously and knows the victim or is familiar with the location. With this type of killer, the crime scene is sloppy and disorganized. There usually is evidence of sudden violence. The murderer uses no restraints or very few. He nearly always engages in sexual acts with the body after death and may mutilate it. The body is left in view at the scene, and the weapon is usually found there as well.

Some offenders, like Jeffrey L. Dahmer, have a mixture of traits. Dahmer confessed to murdering seventeen young men, cutting them up, and in some cases cannibalizing them after having sex with their dead bodies.[274]

"Jeffrey Dahmer would be a mix, but he would be more in the disorganized category," Douglas said. "The method of disposing of the bodies using acid was very clever. He had a job and planned the way he picked up these people. Toward the end, he became more sloppy and disorganized. Often they start to break down."

In 1986, the FBI changed the name of the primary unit that develops profiles to the "investigative support unit." Headed by Douglas, this unit within the FBI Academy does profiling through the National Center for the Analysis of Violent Crime (VICAP) in the training division. The FBI also began calling profiles "criminal investigative analyses." However, as is the case with many bureau names, the new term was too unwieldy. Most investigators prefer to continue to call them profiles.

Each field office has an agent who coordinates the work of the profilers with agents or police who need their help. Before drawing up a profile, the profilers generally meet with the coordinator and the police or agents working the case to go over all the facts, including the medical examiner's reports and photographs of the crime scene.

Such a meeting occurred in July 1988, after county police from New Castle, Delaware, and the Delaware State Police asked the FBI's help in solving two murders that appeared related. Both victims, Shirley Ellis and Catherine A. DiMauro, had worked as prostitutes. Both lived in cheap hotels in an area of adult bookstores and fast food outlets in the New Castle area south of Wilmington. Both women walked along U.S. Routes 40 and 13 at night to negotiate tricks with passing motorists.

Ellis was found lying beside the road on her back, her breasts exposed, her bra cut, and her slacks pulled down to her knees. The medical examiner said she had died from strangulation and a skull fracture caused by three blows by a heavy tool like a hammer. Her left breast had been cut, and the nipple had been pinched with a tool like pliers.[275]

The material used to strangle Ellis was not at the scene. However, there were remnants of black tape in her hair, and adhesive from the tape remained on her face. Marks from some kind of restraints were found on her wrists.

DiMauro's nude body was found near a construction site. She too had died from strangulation and three blows to the head. Her right breast had been mutilated, and part of the nipple had been removed with a tool. Her buttocks had been beaten with a paddle as well. Duct tape similar to the one used on Ellis was found on her body, as well as red and blue fibers.

Working with James L. Zopp, the profiling coordinator from the Baltimore field office, Douglas drew up a profile that said the killer was an organized offender who lived or worked in the area. He was in a construction trade. He was said to be a white male in his late twenties to early thirties. He would be driving a van or a pickup truck with high mileage. According to the profile, he had a regular relationship with a woman. During the crime, he would be emotionally flat. The man would have a history of assaultive behavior, including arrests for assault and robbery. He would also be a police buff, someone who follows law enforcement. If not caught, he would continue to kill.

Douglas drew his conclusion on the man's age from previous experience with offenders of this type and the fact that the crimes had been well planned and executed. This level of organization and expertise meant that the killer was more experienced than would be a man in his late teens or early twenties. The restraints and other methods of control indicated that the killer was an organized offender. Douglas knew that typically, these types of crimes are committed by men who drive vans or pickup trucks, which make it easier to conceal the act. Killers in such cases generally cruise for hours waiting for the right opportunity, accounting for Douglas's prediction that the vehicle would have high mileage. Because they like to control, these offenders are likely to gravitate toward the authority represented by police.

Douglas said the man would be in a construction trade because "one of the victims was dumped near a construction site." Because some of the tools were quite specialized, their use indicated that the man was familiar with them.[276]

Douglas and Zopp suggested using a woman as a decoy to lure the man. Initially, the police resisted the idea. They were not convinced that the man would return. Nonetheless, they assigned Renée C. Lano, a New Castle police officer, to walk the highways in the area at night as police watched from afar. Lano, dressed in sneakers, jeans, a tank top, a flannel shirt, and a brown wig, wore a hidden transmitter so that the surveillance team could listen to her conversations. She also carried a gun in a hidden pocket of her handbag.

Over a period of two months, more than a hundred men stopped her as she walked along the highways two to four times a week.

Meanwhile, Douglas's prediction that the killer would continue to strike proved correct. On August 22, 1988, Margaret L. Fenner, who also lived in motels in the area, disappeared. Her body was found in November. On September 10, Cathleen A. Meyer disappeared. Her body has never been found. On September 18, Michelle A. Gordon disappeared. Her nude body turned up two days later in the nearby Chesapeake and Delaware Canal. All the women were prostitutes or in the habit of taking rides from strangers at night.

Finally, on September 14, Steven B. Pennell stopped to negotiate for oral sex with Officer Lano. Pennell fit the profile in almost every respect. He was a white male, was thirty-one years old, driving a van that had high mileage on it. He was an electrician, was married, and had applied twice for police jobs in Delaware and had been turned down. While he had not been arrested for assault or robbery, as the profile had indicated, he had been arrested for theft and breaking and entering. As he negotiated with the decoy, Pennell seemed emotionally flat, just as the profile had predicted. The other fact Lano developed while talking with him was that he was an electrician, making him a dead ringer for the suspect Douglas had described.

"I was talking to him, and he fit the profile," Lano said. "His age, he was a white male, where he worked, the van."[277]

Because he fit the description, Lano singled him out from the other men who had stopped her. She talked with him at length. Admiring his van, she noticed that it had blue carpeting. As she ran her hands over the carpet, she snatched a few fibers for later analysis. The FBI laboratory would later confirm that it was the same carpet as had been found on Ellis's body.

"I told him my price was thirty dollars, but I said I would do it for twenty," Lano said. "He said he only had ten dollars." Lano suggested that Pennell go to a bank cash machine and get the rest, but Pennell said that his wife kept all the ATM cards.

"At the end, I said I had been stoned all day and really had a headache and would be out later that night," Lano said.

The police put Pennell under surveillance. When they saw him buy new tires for his van, they recovered the discarded tires and had the FBI laboratory compare them with a tire imprint found next to Ellis's body. It matched one of Pennell's tires.

The police arrested Pennell on November 29, 1988. A jury found him guilty of murdering Ellis and DiMauro. Pennell later pleaded nolo contendere to murdering Gordon and Meyer, meaning that while he would not concede his guilt, he would not contest it either.

Although Meyer's body was never found, the FBI lab, using DNA analysis, concluded that blood found in Pennell's van was Meyer's. On March 14, 1992, Pennell was executed by lethal injection.[278]

By interviewing serial killers like Pennell, the FBI profilers learned that they invest as much time and energy in killing as normal people do in their occupations or hobbies. Pennell, for example, would put 130 miles on his van in one night looking for the right opportunity to strike. Ted Bundy, who killed thirty to fifty people, would go on what he called a "kill," as if hunting deer.

Bundy and other serial killers told FBI profilers who were interviewing them to close their eyes.

" 'Okay, you and I now. We're going to go on a hunt today,'" Douglas said. " 'Let's get prepared.' Your eyes are closed, and the killer will talk about the selection process. He has the murder kit ready. 'We'll ride around to preselected areas where we'll take the victim. Make sure it's still a safe place because we want to spend some time with her.' They'll talk about spotting the victim, almost like she is a wild animal in a herd. They are able to look at that child in that video arcade and are able to determine which one is vulnerable, based on the body position, the clothing, being timid."

As he waited for three and a half years to be executed in Florida, Bundy told FBI profiler William E. Hagmaier III how he had committed his crimes. Hagmaier said that Bundy attributed his urge to kill to a biological clock.

" 'You know you are hungry without looking at the clock,' " Hagmaier quoted Bundy. " 'You wake up angry one morning. You don't know why.' He perceived that there are criminal cycles."[279]

According to Douglas, "[Edmund] Kemper said, 'When hitchhikers reach out for my doorknob, they are like butterflies. They are fragile butterflies that land in my hand, and I squeeze them and crush them. Once they touch that doorknob, they are mine.' "

Norris and Bittaker, the two killers who made the tape that John Douglas played for Scott Glenn, met in prison and decided to rape and murder teenage girls "for fun," Norris told the police. So that they could relive their pleasure, they tape recorded or videotaped the murders. Norris said that they had approached girls at random, photographed them, and offered them rides, marijuana, or modeling jobs. Most turned down the offers. Some were abducted forcibly, raped, and murdered. Lamp had been hitchhiking along Redondo Beach when the killers offered her a ride.

The FBI had nothing to do with catching them. After having been raped, a victim got away and identified the two killers in 1980. The arresting officers discovered drugs in their possession and held them for parole violations. Ultimately, the victim failed to make a positive identification, but meanwhile Norris—trying to shift the blame to Bittaker—began confessing to the crimes.

Norris led sheriff's deputies to a shallow grave where one of the victims was buried, an ice pick protruding from her skull. In a van the killers had dubbed the "Murder Mack," police recovered a tape that the two killers had made of themselves torturing Jacqueline Lamp to death.[280]

Besides profiling, the behavioral science services unit began working on a number of other techniques for helping FBI agents solve crimes, such as how to confront suspects during interviews. This advice has been particularly useful in espionage cases, where often the only way of getting a conviction is with a confession. Based on an evaluation of the suspect, the unit tells agents whether they should interview him in the morning or at night and whether to use a hard or a soft approach.

Another technique is evaluating language—including body language—to see if suspects are lying when they are interviewed.

"If someone says my wife and I and our children went out shopping, and the kids got a little bit unruly—in other words we went from our kids to the kids—he is unconsciously distancing himself from the kids," Teten said, "You would listen for that where there was no logical reason for distancing, perhaps suggesting that the father killed his own children."

The FBI teaches agents that when a right-handed person looks to his left when asked a question, it may mean he is genuinely trying to remember the answer and attempting to tell the truth. If such a person looks to his right, he may be trying to create information—in other words, to lie.

"If we are talking about memory, you shouldn't be creating," Teten said.

Conversely, left-handed people usually look to the left when they are lying.

Training given by the behavioral science services unit extends to how to negotiate with criminals who have taken hostages. Agents are warned to look for evidence of the Stockholm Syndrome, when hostages begin to identify with their captors and even protect them. That training, by Thomas Strentz, who taught terrorism courses at the FBI Academy, helped Carl A. Schultz, a St. Louis FBI agent, solve the kidnapping of Dr. Hector Zevallos, who ran an abortion clinic, and his wife, Rosalie. The kidnappers—calling themselves the Army of God—took them from their home in Edwardsville, Illinois, in 1982. In a rambling forty-four page letter, the kidnappers demanded that then President Reagan give a speech against abortion.[281]

When Dr. Zevallos agreed to stop giving abortions, the kidnappers released him and his wife after holding them for eight days. Simply because he was not good at describing things, Hector Zevallos had trouble remembering facts that would have helped the FBI identify and locate the kidnappers. His wife clammed up entirely.

Schultz recognized that she was suffering from Stockholm Syndrome. As part of the FBI's hostage negotiations program, Strentz had taught Schultz what signs to look for—signs that Patty Hearst exhibited after she had been kidnapped. Indeed, Strentz had interviewed Hearst after she was released from prison and pronounced her a classic victim of Stockholm Syndrome. Schultz told Zevallos's wife what she was feeling.[282]

"I said, 'You are scared to death that these people who took you captive and held you might walk in the door this minute, yet you would also like to invite them to Sunday dinner and make the best Sunday dinner you could,' " Schultz said.

"Her features and eyes changed, and she said, 'You're absolutely right. How did you know that?' I said, 'Mrs. Zevallos, what you are going through is a very common phenomenon. Let me explain it to you.' We went off, and I explained it. She just opened up."[283]

As a result of her help, the FBI found the room where the kidnappers had hidden the couple, and agents located three suspects. At the trial of one of them, Rosalie Zevallos broke down in tears as she described her fear of the kidnappers. Nevertheless, Schultz said, "She was a phenomenal witness. The entire case was broken because of her."

The three kidnappers were convicted or pleaded guilty.

The FBI profiling program received a setback when profilers Ault and Hazelwood, in response to a request from the Navy, offered their opinion that Clayton M. Hartwig had deliberately caused a blast that took his life and those of forty-six other sailors on board the battleship *Iowa* in 1989. While the profilers usually describe unknown suspects, they may also be called in to try to reconstruct the personality of a dead person. The issue became a cause célèbre when the Navy began leaking stories that Hartwig was a homosexual who might have blown up the ship because he was despondent over the end of a relationship with a shipmate.

What was overlooked in the controversy was the fact that when the Navy asked the FBI to profile Hartwig, it said it had already determined that the explosion was deliberate and not the result of an accident. The profilers are always at the mercy of investigators and the facts they develop. If the investigators say that a crime happened in a particular way, the profilers are usually circumscribed by that. Nor had the profilers been given the FBI lab's conclusion that from the physical evidence it was impossible to determine whether the explosion was an accident or deliberate. If the explosion had indeed been set deliberately, it made perfect sense to conclude that Hartwig was the most likely suspect. When Hartwig was in the eleventh grade, a friend saw him running the blade of a knife across his wrist. The friend snatched it away. Later, the friend said he believed Hartwig was about to commit suicide. He quoted Hartwig as saying he had made pipe bombs and thrown a Molotov cocktail into a field. More recently, a shipmate said Hartwig had shown him how to make pipe bombs and other explosives.

Another shipmate told the Naval Investigative Service that he and Hartwig had ruminated about committing suicide. The sailor quoted Hartwig as saying he had thought about killing himself with an explosive device because "he wouldn't feel a thing." Another shipmate said Hartwig had said he wanted to die in the line of duty and be buried at Arlington National Cemetery. He said Hartwig had talked of dying in an explosion in the gun room, which is where the *Iowa* explosion occurred. Hartwig's sister said he had talked to her about the possibility of an explosion occurring in the gun room, saying that no one would live to tell what had happened. Finally, among Hartwig's possessions, the Navy found *Improvised Munitions*, a manual on how to get even with people by blowing them up.[284]

Ultimately, the Navy decided that the blast could well have been accidental after all. Ironically, that was what the FBI laboratory had said all along. As a result, there was no "clear and convincing evidence" to support the Navy's earlier accusations against Hartwig.[285]

But FBI profiles never purport to be evidence. They are merely highly educated guesses, hunches that turn out to be right in an impressive number of cases. It is up to investigators to gather the evidence that may implicate people in actual crimes. In concluding that Hartwig had blown up the *Iowa*, Ault and Hazelwood said it was their *opinion* that he had done it.

Assuming that the explosion was deliberate and not accidental, "Nothing has occurred to change our opinion," Hazelwood said.[286]

The FBI accepts only the most difficult cases to profile, crimes that have gone unsolved in most cases for years. Yet, in about 5 percent of the cases, the profiles lead immediately to a solution. In another 5 to 10 percent, the suspects are later found after the profiles helped refocus the investigation. In response to a survey, investigators who used the profiles said that in 77 percent of the cases that were later solved, the profiles helped focus the investigation.[287]

Today the FBI does about 800 profiles a year, a pitiful number compared with the 7,688 unsolved murder cases in a recent year. Each year, the profilers turn away 100 to 150 cases for which they do not have sufficient staff. Most of the country's unsolved murders are never presented to the profilers.

"We're doing all we can to keep our heads above water," Douglas said. "We should be doing written profiles. Instead, we have to do it verbally just to keep up with the demand. If this were a business, we would have a lot more resources."

Indeed, Teten and Depue, who also helped develop the program and are both retired from the FBI, now offer profiles to private companies faced with extortion and other threats. Based in Manassas, Virginia, their Academy Group Inc. includes former agents who did profiling at the FBI Academy.

For profiles, most police departments have to rely on the FBI, which employs only twelve profilers. Together with a travel budget of $180,000 a year, the FBI's total annual expenditure on profiling is less than $1 million, or about 4 percent of what the Navy spent to investigate the *Iowa* explosion.

On the walls of Hazelwood's tiny, windowless office are dozens of plaques recognizing his help in solving crimes. They are from the U.S. Secret Service, New York State police, Pennsylvania State police, Baltimore County police, U.S. Air Force, New York City police, and on and on—testimony to the fact that profiles work.

Tom Brennan, formerly a Pennsylvania State police detective and now working with the profilers, said that the profiles helped solve more than thirty homicides in Pennsylvania alone from 1988 to 1991.[288]

"I've used [the profiles] in four sex crimes where it helped tremendously," said John Decker, who formerly headed a New York City police task force. "It's worked in many homicides as well."[289]

For several years, according to James Greenleaf, the associate deputy director for administration, the FBI has asked the Office of Management and Budget for more money to expand the profiling program.

"We have asked for more profilers, and it's been cut out of the budget," Greenleaf said.

If more money had been made available, perhaps an FBI profile would have caught Bittaker and Norris before they abducted and killed Jacqueline Lamp, delighting in her torture.

11

Atlanta:
Watch the Bridges

● **The fifteen largest field offices** in the FBI are
known as major offices. Because of their importance, only agents
who have previously headed other offices are named to run them.
As the fourteenth largest office in the FBI, the Atlanta office, with
192 agents, barely makes it into that league. Yet, the Atlanta office
solved two of the biggest and most difficult cases in modern bureau
history—the killing of federal appeals court Judge Robert S. Vance
and the serial killings of black Atlanta schoolchildren. Atlanta is
also the first field office to have been invaded by a gunman who
took employees hostage.

When a bomb killed Judge Vance at his home outside of Birmingham, Alabama, on December 16, 1989, only two federal judges
had previously been assassinated. The FBI had solved the first
case—the killing of Judge John H. Wood—ten years earlier. In the
second case, the assassination of Judge Richard J. Daronco of the
Southern District of New York in 1988, the murderer killed himself.
Because the bomb that killed Vance was sent anonymously through
the mail, and because bombs usually obliterate most of the evidence,
solving the case was at least as difficult as solving the Wood case.[290]

It is human nature to suspect someone who has an obvious motive
for committing a crime. In the Vance killing, drug traffickers from

236

Miami, whose appeals are heard by the appeals court in Birmingham, were automatically suspect; perhaps the bombing was revenge for upholding a conviction. But often the people who commit crimes are not the most obvious suspects.

Two days after Vance was killed, a bomb in Savannah, Georgia, killed civil rights attorney Robert E. Robinson, who was an officer of the NAACP. The same day, another bomb was discovered undetonated at the federal court in Atlanta. Another undetonated bomb was found at the NAACP offices in Jacksonville, Florida.

The incidents appeared to be related, and the new wave of episodes suggested that right-wing extremists rather than drug dealers were behind them. That theory seemed confirmed when an Atlanta television station received a letter from Americans for a Competent Federal Judicial System claiming responsibility for the two killings and saying that the judicial system was too lenient toward blacks who attack whites. Similar messages were found in the bombs that did not go off and were pieced together from the ones that did.

But the truth proved far more complicated. It would take more than one hundred FBI agents working jointly with a task force of a dozen other law enforcement agencies to unravel the bizarre tale and develop the evidence necessary for a conviction. As did the assassination of Judge Wood, the Vance case, called VANPAC, immediately became the FBI's highest priority.

"When we have a major case like the Vance slaying, we go all out," said William Baker, who directed the investigation as assistant director over the criminal investigative division. "This is what the bureau does the best."

Because the Vance bombings involved four FBI field offices—Atlanta, Birmingham, Jacksonville, and the former Savannah, Georgia, office—Baker and Buck Revell, who was executive assistant director, installed an inspector in charge of the case. *Inspector* is an old bureau term that gives an agent a status equivalent to that of a deputy assistant director. For the purposes of investigating the Vance case, the inspector would supersede the SACs and report directly to Baker. That step had not been taken in recent bureau history. But Revell was not happy with the friction that developed among field offices during the investigation of Judge Wood's assassination. That case, like this one, had involved more than one field office. Nonetheless, Revell and Baker took the action with some reservations, knowing it would ruffle feathers.

"Agents in charge don't like to be told an inspector is coming in to take over a case," Baker said. "But it involved four U.S. Attorneys, four FBI field offices, crimes committed in four of our field offices."[291]

As inspector over the investigation, Baker and Revell recommended Larry A. Potts, who was one of Baker's deputy assistant directors, and Sessions accepted the recommendation. Originally from Loudoun County, Virginia, Potts had graduated from the University of Richmond and served in the Army, where a fellow company commander said he was thinking of applying to the FBI.

"I laughed at him," Potts said. "I couldn't imagine anyone wanting to be in the FBI. It seemed like a good job, but there was so much travel. I wanted to settle down."

Potts became a probation officer but later thought better of his decision and applied to the bureau after all. He was accepted in 1974 and rose quickly through the ranks. Exceptionally bright, direct, and easygoing, Potts was highly regarded not only within the FBI but within the Justice Department.

Under Hoover, such an endorsement by Justice would have been the kiss of death. Organizational charts aside, the old bureau regarded itself as a separate agency, not under the control of anyone but the president. In the modern FBI, not only is it recognized that the director reports to the attorney general, but the best managers make it a point of working closely with the Justice Department and local U.S. Attorneys because they realize that without their cooperation, their cases will not be prosecuted.

At the same time, the FBI keeps in mind that attorneys general are political appointees who have been known in the past to abuse their positions of trust. As a result of an FBI investigation, Attorney General John M. Mitchell was convicted in the Watergate scandal, and Attorney General Edwin Meese III was constantly being investigated for his role in the Wedtech Corporation scandal.

Once Potts joined the FBI, he realized that, just as he had feared, being an agent meant that his time was not his own. Having made the decision to appoint an inspector, headquarters told Potts on a Wednesday to report to Atlanta three days later, on April 1, 1990. Potts was not told when he could leave Atlanta.

" 'You are to stay there until it is solved,' " he said he was told. "The next day [Thursday] was my wife's birthday. I went home to tell my wife to tell her I'm going on TDY [temporary duty] for unknown duration. It could be a year or two years. That was traumatic."[292]

Because of the many geographical areas involved, Potts and his superiors at headquarters urged the Justice Department to appoint special prosecutors for the case. Potts then asked the Justice Department to quarter Louis Freeh and Howard Shapiro, the special prosecutors who were appointed, on the fifth floor where he had his office at 77 Forsyth Street in Atlanta.

"That's the new bureau," Potts said. "We used to have the attitude, 'We investigate, you prosecute.' We still look at ourselves as the investigative experts. But we also feel it is important to have prosecutors who are involved all along. They may have investigative input."

Immediately after Vance's assassination, the name Walter Leroy Moody, Jr, appeared on an FBI list of dozens of suspects because he had previously been convicted of a bombing in the same geographic area. A man with a mop of dark hair and hypnotic eyes, Moody was a high school graduate who had served in the Army and the Air Force. He was a loner who was always tinkering with machines of some kind.

Back in 1972, Moody had been convicted of possessing a bomb that exploded in his first wife's hands, wounding her severely. Moody had intended to send the bomb to an Atlanta auto dealer who had repossessed his car. But Hazel, then his wife, saw the package containing the bomb in the kitchen and opened it. It tore up her hand, thigh, and shoulder, sending scrap metal into her eye. She needed six operations. After the conviction, he and his wife divorced.[293]

Overturning that conviction, for which he served only three years, became Moody's primary occupation, along with enticing people to send him money for services he never delivered. Moody formed the Associated Writers Guild of America, which supposedly trained aspiring writers. The Better Business Bureau of Metropolitan Atlanta found the guild to be one of its most troublesome businesses, with inquiries from forty-eight states and numerous complaints from people who said they had paid money to the company and gotten nothing in return. In June 1990, postal inspectors closed the business, returning letters sent to Moody's post office box.

Moody also claimed to be developing a revolutionary boat motor and propeller. On a frigid day in December 1982, he took three of his employees for a ride on a boat equipped with the new motor. The employees were to take underwater photographs of the propeller. As soon as they were in the water two miles off Grassy Key, Florida, Moody took off, the three later told police. Moody refused to pick them up or throw them life preservers. When they tried to climb back on board, he pried their fingers from a ladder. Moody threw an anchor at one of them, hitting him in the head, the employees said. Another boat happened to be passing by and rescued the employees. They later learned that Moody had taken out $750,000 in life insurance on each of them.

Moody was charged with three counts of attempted murder, but the trial ended in a hung jury.

Moody then filed suits against the three employees, the deputy sheriff, and the prosecutor in the case, claiming that they had maliciously prosecuted him. When Moody lost the case, he appealed to the Eleventh Circuit, where a three-judge panel that included Judge Vance heard the case and denied his appeal.

By the time Potts got to Atlanta, Moody had become a prime suspect. Lloyd T. Erwin, a forensic chemist with the Alcohol, Tobacco, and Firearms Bureau (ATF) in Atlanta, had worked on Moody's 1972 bombing case. Erwin was not assigned to the Vance case, but three days after the killing, he attended a gathering of explosives experts at a Ryan's Steak House in Atlanta. The informal monthly meeting is a way for technicians from different agencies to exchange information on the latest incidents and techniques. Another ATF employee displayed photographs of the remains of the bombs in the most recent explosions. Erwin immediately spotted similarities between the type of devices used in the most recent occurrences and the bomb that exploded in the hands of Moody's wife in 1972. For one thing, some of the bombs used bolts to strengthen them. To illustrate to the others, he drew a picture of the 1972 device on a napkin. Moody had been on a list of thousands of known bombers. Without the critical link between his techniques and the most recent devices, the case would likely never have been made.

"They [criminals who use explosives] start with something and stick with it. If he had changed, he would still be running around today," Erwin said.[294]

"It was good fortune really, as happens in a lot of police work," said John W. Hicks, the assistant director over the FBI laboratory. "Had he [Erwin] retired or not been there, it might have been a different situation."

Analyzing the more recent devices, the FBI laboratory found that all four were pipe bombs packed with nails. All had been mailed through the U.S. Postal Service using the same type of stamps. All came packed inside corrugated paper boxes with hinged lids. The boxes were wrapped in brown paper secured with the same type of white string and tan plastic tape. All the red mailing labels were from the same commercial supplier. The devices used the same electrical and booby trap systems. They used the same kind of detonator. Finally, they all used Hercules Red Dot double base smokeless powder as the main charge.[295]

In investigating Moody's past, the FBI started focusing on a witness Moody had used to claim he had new evidence that would exonerate him in the 1972 case. The witness, Julie L. West, testified in 1988 that she was riding with a man who dropped off a package at Moody's home in Macon, Georgia. As they left, she said, they heard on the radio that a bomb had gone off in Moody's home. The man supposedly said, "Oh, no. The package went off."

"Our investigation developed evidence that she had been in the hospital in Wisconsin flat on her back and suffering paralysis as a result of a car accident at that time," Potts said.

When FBI and ATF agents confronted her, West admitted that Moody had paid her two thousand dollars to make up her story and lie on the witness stand. She said that Moody had threatened to kill her mother if she did not testify on his behalf.[296]

After West agreed to cooperate, the FBI wired her wheelchair so that agents could listen to Moody coaching her on lying. Because he suspected the FBI might be monitoring his conversations, he wrote notes to her. The hidden microphones picked up only the shuffling of paper. The next time, the bureau videotaped their encounter. The cameras picked up what Moody was writing in his notes to her. They then showed Moody burning the notes after West had read them.

With that hook, Potts decided to attack the case on three fronts. He would try to obtain an obstruction-of-justice charge against Moody for concocting evidence in the 1988 appeal of his 1972 conviction. He would try to obtain evidence against Moody on the Vance case. And, because he was now convinced that Moody had done it, he would try to prevent Moody from striking again.

Potts found that William L. Hinshaw, the SAC in Atlanta, and other FBI field offices had made substantial progress by the time he got there. But, as headquarters had suspected, Hinshaw and the other SACs were constantly in one another's hair. In addition, as Hinshaw saw it, headquarters wanted him to focus on the Ku Klux Klan rather than Moody.

Baker said that headquarters wanted the investigation to remain broad enough to cover any stray leads.

Both the FBI and the ATF conducted surveillance of Moody. The surveillance had two purposes: to make sure he did not mail another bomb, and to find out where he bought his supplies, who his associates might be, and where he kept his materials. As much as possible, Potts wanted to associate each component of the bombs with Moody. The FBI also obtained court authorization to install eavesdropping devices in Moody's home in Rex, Georgia, fifty miles southeast of Atlanta.

After a month, the bugs had picked up nothing useful, and Potts decided to shut them down. The manpower was needed elsewhere. But Potts knew how easy it is to miss something when intercepting conversations, so he had John Crisp, an agent with extremely good hearing, review all the recordings again.

"After a few weeks, Crisp said, 'We have something,' " Potts said. "What we had was Roy Moody in a whisper saying to himself, 'Now you've killed two. . . . Now you can't pull another bombing.' "[297]

"It was obviously a pretty devastating statement," Potts said. "We assumed he was referring to himself."

The bureau and the ATF searched Moody's home and a rented storage compartment. Moody had kept voluminous journals and other records that the FBI entered on computers. They would help link Moody with the components used to make the bombs.

Since his home had been searched, Moody was aware that he was a suspect and even went on television to defend himself. When he detected surveillance, he would drive one hundred miles per hour on the highways. The FBI decided it was not worth the risk to pursue him. Instead, they notified state troopers in the area so that they could arrest him for speeding. The troopers never caught him either.

The ATF gave the bureau a list of firearms dealers in the region. Along with the ATF, the Internal Revenue Service, and state and local police officers, FBI agents interviewed each one. After he was shown a picture of Moody, one dealer said Moody had come to his store, and he had referred him to another dealer in Georgia. There, a clerk said, Moody had purchased four pounds of Hercules Red Dot double base powder, the type used in the bombs.

After Moody was subpoenaed to appear in a lineup, the store clerk identified him as the man who had bought the powder.

The FBI had found that Susan McBride Moody, Moody's second wife, had helped her husband coach West on her perjured testimony. Now the bureau had a second hook. She was indicted along with her husband for obstruction of justice. But, in exchange for her cooperation on the Vance case, the prosecutors would let her plead to a lesser charge and would let the judge know of her cooperation at sentencing.[298]

As it turned out, Moody had assigned his wife to buy the components he needed for the bombs.

"Susan said he became very secretive in the summer of 1989," Potts said, "giving her lists of things to buy and locking a room and telling her not to go in. She was to pay cash, use a phony name when she ordered something, park away from the buildings so the license plate could not be connected. . . . She didn't know what she was buying it for. She bought tape, the boxes, the wrapping paper."

In the end, Moody's paranoia was his undoing. To make it more difficult for law enforcement to match his typewritten threats to his typewriter, Moody asked Susan to photocopy the notes. He told her to drive for twelve hours and use any copying store she saw. So that her fingerprints would not show up on the paper, he told her to wear gloves. Susan Moody wound up in Covington, Kentucky, where employees at a copying store later vividly remembered seeing her because she was trying so hard to be incognito.

"She goes in disguised, wearing gloves and acting suspiciously," Potts said. "She wore sunglasses, a scarf, and a coat. We put her in a van and said, 'Take us to this place.' These people recalled the incident. She acted so suspiciously that they recalled her."

Verifying that Susan McBride had gone to the store not only corroborated her story. It also solved the mystery of a latent fingerprint found on a piece of copying paper rolled up in the package containing the Jacksonville device. After taking fingerprints of every employee, past and present, of the copying store, the FBI found that the mystery print belonged to a young man who swept the floor. Before Susan used the machine, the young man had refilled the copier machine with paper.

Despite extensive efforts, the typewriter Moody used to write his bomb-threat notes was never found. Susan Moody said she thought her husband probably had thrown it in a lake.

Trying to match every component of the bombs to Moody, Potts became obsessed with the boxes. A box made by a company in Chicago was similar to the ones used in the bombings, but the FBI laboratory said there were minute differences.

"The more I was told it was just a box, and the more we couldn't find it, the more I felt there was something special about it," Potts said. "I didn't know if that was my ignorance on how many kinds of boxes there are."

Susan Moody took the agents to the store in Kentucky where she had bought the boxes. One looked exactly like the one used in the bombings. It turned out to have come from the company in Chicago that had been eliminated as the source. When agents began focusing on the box, the store owner said he had made up two thousand of his own boxes and had made minor alterations in the design. He did not want to infringe on the patent of the company in Chicago. He even gave the agents the name of the man in Indiana who had made the die for the boxes. The man still had the die in his barn.

"He [the agent] put it in the bureau car," Potts said. "He calls me at every step. I am getting more and more excited. We were able to say this die made the bomb box."

Still unanswered was where Moody had obtained the nails with which the bombs were packed. Susan Moody said that her husband had not asked her to buy them. By coincidence, Andrew Bringuel II, an agent from Birmingham who was working on finding the nails, happened to be visiting his family in Atlanta. While his wife was buying glue at a Kroger's, Bringuel, who had been with the FBI two months, decided to check out the nails. He spotted exactly the kind that were used in the bombs. Susan Moody independently recalled that her husband had shoplifted some nails at Kroger's.

"We had been looking for the nails for months," Potts said. "The lab said they are the same kind, made by the same manufacturer, and were made within seconds of the nails on the bomb."

With Moody awaiting trial on obstruction-of-justice charges, the FBI arranged to bug his jail cell at the Atlanta penitentiary, hoping to pick up more incriminating statements as he talked to himself.

"Bob Matthews, the regional director of prisons, said, 'Can we get together for lunch?' " said Hinshaw, the SAC in Atlanta. "He said, 'We're going to help you with this bug, but you got to be straight with me. Who on my staff do you suspect? Moody is by himself.' I said, 'No, Bob, this is not your people. This guy talks to himself.' "

In his cell, Moody said, "Kill those damn judges . . . I shouldn't have done it, idiot."

Agents assigned to the case typically came in at 7:00 A.M. and left at 11:00 P.M. "You had to kick people out at night," Potts said.

Sessions called repeatedly to ask about progress in the case and offer encouragement.

"Talk about pressure on a case," said an agent who did some work on the Vance case. "It's relentless. Everything in the FBI stops. Full court press. No lead is too small to be covered by two agents. Bang like that. When we get rolled up on one of those, we're going to get the guy. There's just no doubt about it."

"One pressure was knowing there is nothing you can ask for that you won't get," Potts said. "It was almost frightening. I'll probably never have that again. The turnaround on that was this better work. . . . This was not a case you would want to lose."

Because of the local publicity in the case, the trial was held in St. Paul, Minnesota. In June 1991, a jury convicted Moody on seventy-one criminal counts, including first-degree murder, transporting explosive materials with intent to kill, and other charges relating to the deaths of Vance and Robinson. One of the pieces of evidence was the tape of Moody appearing to say he had already killed two people.

Moody was sentenced to seven life terms plus four hundred years with no possibility of parole. He had previously been convicted on the obstruction-of-justice charge. Because of her cooperation, Susan Moody, who had no idea that her husband was making bombs, received probation.[299]

Just why Moody chose to single out Vance from the other judges on the three-judge appeals panel that heard his case, and why he targeted civil rights organizations, remains hazy.

"There are all kinds of theories," Potts said. "There were some civil rights decisions that the court decided around the same time. They said it doesn't matter how long ago a wrong had been done, it must be righted. On his appeal, the Eleventh Circuit said there has to be some finality. He interpreted that as being in conflict. He didn't necessarily see that minority groups had never had their hearing over wrongs from the past."

While nothing is so squarely within the FBI's jurisdiction as the killing of a federal judge, nothing could be more outside it than a series of murders of children in Atlanta. Yet, as occasionally happens, the FBI found a way to enter the case.

The nightmare began on July 28, 1979, when an old woman hunting aluminum cans stumbled across the body of Alfred James Evans, age thirteen, who had been strangled. Over the next weeks, there were more grisly finds: Milton Harvey, fourteen, who had been strangled; Yusuf Bell, nine, also strangled. All the victims were black.[300]

It took many months for Atlanta police to begin to see a pattern. As the murders continued, blacks became transfixed with fear. Armed with baseball bats, residents of predominantly black areas formed neighborhood "bat patrols" in an effort to protect their children. Youngsters brought knives and guns to school in case they met the "Snatcher." Some mothers accused the police of ignoring the children because they were poor. A reward of $150,000 was offered.

Atlanta Mayor Maynard Jackson appealed to Griffin Bell, then the attorney general, who was himself from Atlanta. While the FBI has no jurisdiction in investigating murders unless they entail crossing state lines, the FBI can always find a way to gain jurisdiction if it wants to. The body of one of the missing children had not been found. Theoretically, he could have been taken over state lines. In fact, Buck Revell said, "The governor asked Griffin Bell, and he said, 'Can't you fellows find a way to work on it?' I said, 'Yes, if you order it.' He said, 'Okay, I order it.' The grounds were we assumed a missing boy had been transported interstate. We never had any indication they were taken out of the state."

At first, the bodies were found in the woods or in alleys. Then, in February 1981, word leaked to the press that the FBI was building a case based on fibers. The bodies then started showing up in rivers around Atlanta. Before, the bodies were generally clothed. Now, they were either nude or clothed only in undershorts.

"We were distraught when this information [that the FBI was building a case on fiber evidence] was printed," said D. Caroll Toohey, who was the assistant special agent in charge. "We thought, 'Now he'll be careful.' "[301]

Phillip M. (Mike) McComas, a first-office agent assigned to the case, was walking to work one morning when the idea popped into his head to stake out the bridges. The idea was that the killer might throw bodies from them into the rivers. Since it was his idea, McComas was put in charge of the operation. But after four or five weeks, no bodies had turned up. The operation was to be shut down at 6:00 A.M. on May 22, 1981. At 2:00 A.M., a team of four FBI agents and Atlanta police officers—including, by chance, McComas— heard a splash beneath the James Jackson Parkway Bridge over the Chattahoochee River in northwest Atlanta. They stopped a man driving slowly across the bridge. He was Wayne B. Williams, a self-styled music promoter who had more cheek than talent. McComas asked Williams where he was heading.

"This is about those boys, isn't it?" Williams asked nervously.

Williams, who lived with his parents, claimed he was going to a nightclub to meet Cheryl Johnson, a singer he was planning to promote. But there was no Cheryl Johnson at the address or the phone number he gave them.

McComas immediately sensed that Williams was the killer. "His story wasn't working," McComas said. "He was saying things that didn't fit."[302]

McComas also realized that Williams fit a profile that John Douglas had drawn up. Douglas had said that the offender would be black, single, and between the ages of twenty-five and twenty-nine. He would live in the area, sometimes pose as a police officer, show extreme interest in media coverage of the case, and have difficulty relating to members of the opposite sex. In fact, children who lived near Williams thought he was a policeman because he drove cars that looked like police cars, showed them a badge, and ordered them around. Williams was black, single, and twenty-three years old.[303]

McComas noted that when he stopped Williams, he talked incessantly about the media coverage of the case. But, at that point, the FBI was dealing with only circumstantial evidence. McComas wanted to take no chances by arresting Williams and raising false hopes that the tragic nightmare was over. He decided to investigate him further. After all, the FBI had no body to associate with the splash they had heard on May 22. However, two days after Williams had been stopped on the bridge, the nude body of Nathaniel Cater was pulled from the river a mile downstream from the bridge. He had yellowish green nylon carpet fiber in his hair.

On June 3, the FBI obtained warrants to search Williams's home and automobile. Despite the fact that Williams had washed out the inside of his car, the FBI found enough fibers there and in his home to link him to the bodies. Williams was arrested on June 21, 1981. But catching Williams and proving that he was the killer were two entirely different matters. While Williams had been seen with two of the victims, the FBI had no witnesses to the murders. The case would have to be made almost entirely on fiber evidence.

Harold A. Deadman, Jr., the FBI laboratory agent who did it, tracked dozens of kinds of fibers all over the country. As often happens, a certain amount of luck was involved. Deadman was trying to determine the source of a yellowish green carpet fiber on most of the bodies.

"Over lunch at Du Pont, a researcher said, 'The FBI was looking for that fiber. The other guy said, 'I think I have that.' He kept track of competitors' products. It was made by Wellman Corp.," said John W. Hicks, the assistant director over the laboratory. "West Point Pepperell Corp. had used it for two years ten years earlier. They said we sold this amount in the Atlanta area."[304]

Deadman then tracked the carpet to dealers in Atlanta. Some of the dealers were no longer in business, but agents found and interviewed the former employees. As a result, Deadman established that the probability of finding the same fibers in any home in Atlanta was one in seven thousand.

Eventually, Deadman was able to associate Williams with twenty-eight fibers found on the bodies of twelve of the twenty-eight children and young men who had disappeared or had died under suspicious circumstances during a twenty-two-month period beginning in July 1979. Deadman matched the fibers on all twelve victims to Williams's violet and green bedspread and connected ten of the victims to the green-yellow carpet in his bedroom, eleven to the hair from Williams's German shepherd Sheba, five to blue rayon carpet fibers in Williams's home, and six to the carpeting in Williams's 1970 Chevrolet. Other fibers found on the bodies came from Williams's porch bedspread, trunk liner, bathroom carpet, a glove, blue throw rug, and kitchen carpet. In all, the FBI analyzed and identified more than seven hundred individual microscopic fibers found on the bodies.[305]

Before the trial, John Douglas and Roy Hazelwood of the FBI's behavioral science services unit coached the prosecutors on how to get Williams to show his true character.

"I wanted him [the prosecutor] to physically touch him, talk in a low voice, ask him what it was like when you wrapped your hands around his throat. 'Did you panic?' First there was a weak response. Then he starred screaming," Douglas said.

"You must be a fool," Williams ranted, his respectful demeanor cracking.

As soon as Williams had been accosted, the killings stopped. After a ten-week trial, a jury on February 27, 1982, convicted Williams of murdering two of the victims, Nathaniel Cater and Jimmy Payne. Williams was sentenced to two consecutive life terms.

Ever cocky, Williams gave a number of interviews professing his innocence. Just before his trial, he said in Fulton County jail, "I would compare the FBI to the Keystone Kops and the Atlanta police to *Car 54: Where Are You?*[306] What never came out is that Williams had consented to taking an FBI polygraph test and, when asked if he had committed the murders, had failed the test.[307]

In solving the case, McComas's idea of watching the bridges was of critical importance.

"That was going to be the last night we were going to cover the bridges," said William J. McGrath, the agent who was the case coordinator, a position sometimes created under the case agent to keep track of all leads on big cases. "We had covered them for four or five weeks."

McComas never received any publicity on his contribution. "Publicity is something no agent worth his salt seeks out," he said. Instead, he attributed the successful conclusion to John D. Glover, the SAC in Atlanta at the time, who met with the agents on the case twice a day to plan strategy.

"Glover was a prince," McComas said. "There was probably no one in the FBI who could have done it. He was fair and open. He was an agent's agent."

"I tried never to transmit to the troops the stress that I was under in the entire case," Glover said. "There was pressure from everywhere. This had worldwide attention. We had kids dying. Toward the end of the case, almost every ten days we were getting a new victim. We had a lot of ideas and theories, but we had no real live suspect. My style was to absorb all that external pressure to the extent I could so the agents would be free to do the investigation."[308]

Just after Williams had been arrested, on Sunday morning, June 28, 1981, Morris E. Roberts, Jr., a twenty-six-year-old golf course keeper who had been in and out of mental hospitals, pulled a gun on a security guard at the federal building in downtown Atlanta where the FBI was then based. Armed with two handguns, an automatic pistol, and a sawed-off shotgun, Roberts got the guard to take him to the FBI office on the tenth floor. There, he had the guard ask the support employees on duty to open the door. Roberts rounded up all ten support employees in the office and held them hostage. Roberts, who worked for the DeKalb County Parks and Recreation Department, made no specific demands other than that he wanted to see a chaplain, whom police could not locate.[309]

"Agents were calling the office to get information, accessing indexes. Nobody was answering the phones," said Susan E. Lloyd, an agent working on the Williams case at the time. "Someone decided something was wrong."[310]

FBI agents tried to negotiate with Roberts over the phone, but he only became more bizarre and agitated as calls started coming in from news organizations asking for his comment. The FBI's Atlanta SWAT team was called in, but, because the emergency exit doors on that floor were locked and barred, the agents could not enter the office.

"At that time the bureau didn't survey their own buildings for such an event," said Leon H. Blakeney, who was in charge of the SWAT team. "It was unthinkable that anyone would have come into a field office. No one knew how to break in to their own offices. It was like getting into a jail."

A building engineer told the SWAT team that by climbing through an entrance on the roof, they could enter an air-conditioning utility room on the tenth floor, where Roberts was. SWAT team members and local police entered the room and, through louvers, saw Roberts across a hall in an adjacent room. They could aim their guns at him through the slats.

Twice, Roberts forced the hostages to walk with him down a corridor to make sure no one was sneaking in through one of the rear exit doors. When Roberts returned, he herded the hostages in front of him without pointing a gun at their heads.

Blakeney advised Glover, the special agent in charge, that the best time to shoot Roberts was when he was returning from one of these missions. Glover, who had been directing the Wayne Williams investigation, decided that the negotiations were going nowhere. He said it was "necessary to terminate the hostage situation."[311]

"John Glover was an agent in charge who would make a decision," Blakeney said. "I've seen others say, 'We're not going to go.' We would have the guy dead to rights, and we could kill him without any problem at all to the hostages. They would say, 'No, let's wait.' That's not making any decision."

When Roberts again returned from checking the rear doors at 2:30 P.M., one of the SWAT team members said, "Now!" Two agents and an Atlanta police officer shot Roberts more than a dozen times. Ricocheting bullets wounded two FBI employees.

After that, the FBI revamped its security plans to take into account the possibility of snipers entering a field office. Rather than store all the machine guns and shotguns in a gun vault at the field office, the bureau now instructs SWAT team members to keep them in their cars. The bureau also obtained building plans for FBI offices.

In the FBI, solving highly publicized, major cases such as VANPAC and the Atlanta child murders usually leads to bigger things. For John Glover, who was in charge of the Williams case, it meant a promotion to assistant director over the inspection division. Later, Webster promoted him to executive assistant director, making him the highest-ranking black in the history of the FBI.

For Larry Potts, who had been the inspector in charge on the Wayne Williams case, it meant that when William Baker retired as assistant director over the criminal investigative division, Sessions would appoint him to the coveted position. It was only the second time since Clarence Kelley was director that an agent who had not first served as an SAC over a field office became an assistant director. The first was when Jim Greenleaf became head of the laboratory division. When the announcement came, there was no grumbling about the fact that Potts had not gone through all the hoops, not even from the SACs he had coordinated during the Vance investigation.

Hinshaw, the Atlanta SAC, called Potts "a magnificent human being, someone I really admire."

"If it had not been for Larry Potts, the whole thing [Vance investigation] could have fallen apart," said Thomas W. Stokes, who headed the ATF office in Atlanta.

12

Laboratory Division: Stalking the Beast

●Witnesses are notoriously unreliable. Documents can lie. Skillful defense lawyers can twist videotapes of crimes to cast doubt on a defendant's guilt. But physical evidence found at a crime scene—a spent bullet, a shard of glass, a drop of semen or blood—is the surest kind of proof, one that is least susceptible to differing interpretations. It can cut either way, sending a suspect to jail for life or exonerating an innocent person.

If dealing with certainty is one of the joys of working in the laboratory, one of the drawbacks is that the five hundred agents and technicians who work for the division are constantly in direct contact with the reality of crime. The laboratory occupies 145,000 square feet on the first basement level and the third floor of headquarters. Nowhere is the presence of crime more palpable than in this featureless maze. The employees who work there have made their peace with the beast of crime only because they have to, in order to stalk the brute and get the job done.

The beast is present in the videotaped evidence played for the visitor in the control-room-like chambers of the video support unit—in the deranged laughter of the drunk on a driving spree, videotaping himself just before his car crashes into another car and wipes out a family. It lies in wait—for the pretty young girl being videotaped by her rapist.

An examiner wearing a plastic shower cap, a lab coat, and gloves holds a woman's bra over a table and uses a dull knife to scrape off a dark brown encrustation on the fabric. The bra is beige lace, the style that hooks in the front. On a table nearby, bags of other things wait to be processed—tablecloths and towels, a pair of men's long pants, a child's blanket. It is these simple objects that rivet one's attention—a ribbon, a button. The victim's things are never comforting to see, even if one doesn't know the victim.

On the wall is a copy of a highly circulated flier about Melissa L. Brannen, a five-year-old missing child from Lorton, Virginia. The lab analyzed fibers in a suspect's car and successfully linked him to her abduction. She has never been found. Success stories in the lab don't presume happy endings.

The solution of a puzzle—that's how it's presented to the employees of the laboratory division. Underscoring this philosophy are the puzzle pieces with fragmented photos of FBI offices that appear on a few corridor walls. Ideally, each department provides a piece of the puzzle. Intellectualizing the activity is necessary. If the employees obsessed on the raw reality, they might feel paralyzed, angry, vulnerable. They may turn it around to, "Let's get the bastards." But even this motivation can't be dwelled upon. Emotion gets in the way.

Each year, the lab handles 20,000 cases, about two-thirds for the FBI and the rest for state and local law enforcement. In handling those cases, the lab receives as many as 170,000 pieces of evidence and performs 900,000 examinations.

Besides analyzing evidence, the lab runs the FBI's polygraph program, supervises the bureau's language specialists and photo labs, and builds exhibits for trials and special operations. For example, before FBI hostage rescue and SWAT teams stormed inmates at the federal prison in Talladega, Alabama, the lab built a model of the prison so that agents would be familiar with the place. The lab's special projects section makes retirement plaques and phony birth certificates and drivers' licenses to help in FBI undercover operations. Finally, the lab runs the Forensic Science Research and Training Center, a 45,000-square-foot facility that conducts research and trains state and local law enforcement at the FBI Academy in Quantico, Virginia.

Another of Hoover's legacies, the FBI lab started in 1932 with a microscope, some ultraviolet light equipment, a drawing board for firearms identification, and a Packard sedan agents called "Old Beulah" for going to crime scenes. After scientific crime analysis had been used successfully in several cases, including the kidnapping of Charles A. Lindbergh, Jr., Hoover decided to incorporate it into the bureau's operations. In the Lindbergh case, local police were able to show that a ladder that Bruno Richard Hauptmann used to climb into the Lindbergh baby's bedroom had been fashioned from struts from Hauptmann's attic.

"They determined the wood was the same," said John W. Hicks, the assistant director over the laboratory division. "Also there were unusual square nails used. The positions of the holes with respect to the holes in the attic were the same. An outside expert determined that. That generated interest and the need for the FBI to have this scientific approach."[312]

Today the lab is recognized as the most comprehensive and objective forensic laboratory in the world. With encouragement from Sessions, the lab pioneered DNA analysis, the biggest advance in scientific crime-fighting since fingerprints.

The lab can take anything physical—a tire impression, a pill that has been tampered with, a watermark, a photocopy, a bite mark, semen, dandruff, a piece of tape, a mark from a tool—and turn it into silent testimony of events at a crime scene.

On the third floor of headquarters is the scientific analysis section, where the nitty gritty of forensic examination takes place. There are the traditional lab scientists in white lab coats bent over their tables, signs on the wall that note the necessity of eye protection, a single white mouse scampering in a cage. Along with the tried and true methods, the section is also on the cutting edge with the latest in computers, the mass spectrometer, and the scanning electron microscope.

In the inner sanctum of the DNA analysis unit, the slides are nothing like the ones from biology class. On the slides are series of red dots that can be very incriminating when lined up and compared with the configuration of dots from samples taken from the criminal or the victim.

DNA—deoxyribonucleic acid—is present in the cells of every organism, including human cells most likely to be found at a crime scene, such as hair, sperm, or blood. The lab estimates that, with the exception of identical twins, the chances of one person having the same DNA typing as another are no greater than one in 100 million. So far, virtually every court has upheld the method.

"If you look at a crime scene and you look at it as a transaction, there may be soil left from the shoes, a bullet, a bank robbery note, a trace of the explosive used, and traditionally the forensic role has been to have the investigators find this," said Hicks, a six-foot-two-inch agent who has spent most of his FBI career in the lab. "But our techniques can be used to direct investigators and show a link with other crimes in other jurisdictions. Serial rape is repeat activity and mobile. We can detect it in real time based on DNA typing of semen or hair samples from the rapist's hair. It's a fingerprint of the offender."

When Sessions took over in 1987, the lab was only beginning to explore DNA and did not have the full support of the bureau in developing it as a crime-fighting technique.

"I credit him with providing the support that influenced other elements of the FBI," Hicks said. "In many police organizations, the things that get the greatest interest are officers on the street, cars, things that people can see and feel. He [Sessions] took an interest in it right from the start."

Now DNA typing is a powerful tool. Besides using it for FBI laboratory cases, the FBI has taught technicians from local and state police and private labs how to use it.

"We feel lucky if we can recover fingerprints 20 percent of the time in most violent crimes," Hicks said. "In a rape case, you are likely to recover blood, semen, or hair virtually 100 percent of the time. It gives us other capabilities. We can now take a cigarette butt that has been left at the crime scene or an envelope that was licked by an extortionist. There is enough cellular material very often in the saliva so we can use the DNA."[313]

Robert L. Gleason, a section chief in the lab, is quick to point out that DNA analysis exonerates 36 percent of rape suspects. "It makes you wonder what was happening before DNA typing was used," he said.

Spurred on by its success with DNA typing, the lab is developing DNA data banks to keep track of individual DNA analyses, much as the FBI keeps track of individual fingerprints. So far, sixteen states have passed laws requiring criminals who have been convicted of sex crimes to provide blood for DNA typing as a condition of parole. It is common for such people to commit similar crimes again, and now the FBI will have an easy way of matching potential suspects with sperm, hair, or other human cellular material found at crime scenes. Other files will include DNA data recovered from the scenes of serial killings or rapes. The data bank will also be used to identify missing children who are too young to talk and thus cannot identify themselves.

Almost as soon as the lab was opened, it began processing film of crime scenes and suspects. Then it began producing sketches of suspects. Now, in the latest twist, the lab ages faces with computers. These are the photos used to apprehend suspects decades after they committed their crimes, or to help find older children whose non-custodial parents snatched them when they were much younger. Many of the photos appear on *Unsolved Mysteries* and *America's Most Wanted*.

According to Gene J. O'Donnell, the man in charge of aging faces, people age in predictable ways.

"What people don't realize is that lines that you will get in your face as you get older were there when you were young," he said. "I'm not inventing this stuff. All I'm doing is pronouncing those lines, adding weight where we know it will appear or the muscles will become flabby. You start packing the pounds on, the muscles start giving out, and your face takes on more of a square rather than a triangular appearance. But there is nothing major. You are basically the same person you were. Your face structure is the same. There are little crevices. The skin gets more fleshy-looking. The coloring of your face changes. It doesn't look as pink-looking and fresh."[314]

Photos of relatives can help, because the way they have aged may suggest how the subject has aged. If someone has seen the subject recently, O'Donnell asks for help from that person. If O'Donnell has no photograph of the subject, he asks people who knew the individual to pick out different features from a "face kit." He then punches in to his computer the file number of the feature.

O'Donnell uses a mouse shaped like a pen to move features around on his computer screen or to select new ones. He moves the eyes farther apart or up and down. He creates a raised iris, "average" lids, flared nostrils, a pointed chin. He can produce different mustaches, different hat styles, even different styles of glasses. Generally, the process takes two hours.

"If I wanted to alter the length of the nose, I can set this grid to the face. I can move the grid points and shorten or lengthen it," he said, demonstrating. "Unless he had an operation, the nose would look the same. If he lost fifty pounds, I would get rid of this flab here."

O'Donnell applies some commonsense assumptions to his art.

"A seventeen-year-old kid with long hair doesn't have it at forty-three," he said. "If they lived on the street, they would look different. I just did one for *Unsolved Mysteries* like that. It's coming up. A lady was photographed at seventeen. She is in her late fifties. She has mental problems so she probably lives on the streets. She wasn't that attractive originally. I don't make someone look better for stylishness. If she has been on the street for forty years, the results will be nasty."

When O'Donnell first started aging people three years ago, he tried it on friends at work.

"I didn't have one person say that's pretty good," he said. "They said I never would look like that. One got irritated. They never believed they would look like that. One said, 'That is my father.' "

O'Donnell, thirty-eight, has not aged his own face. "God is doing that for me," he said.

O'Donnell aged the face of John E. List, the man who slaughtered his entire family, including his mother, in Westfield, New Jersey, in 1971. Sixteen years later, in Denver, Wanda Flanery, a neighbor of List's, recognized him from the photo O'Donnell had prepared. She showed the photo, which had appeared in a supermarket tabloid, to List's wife, Delores, and dared her to show it to her husband. Apparently Delores never did, and Flanery forgot about it.

Two years later, Flanery was watching *America's Most Wanted* and saw a plaster bust of List prepared by Frank Bender, a commercial artist who specializes in such work. The bust was similar to the photo O'Donnell had prepared. By this time, List—posing as Robert P. Clark—had moved to Midlothian, Virginia. Flanery asked her son-in-law to call the FBI and give the bureau List's new address.

Eleven days later, FBI agents from the Richmond office visited List's home. His wife told them where he worked. When they interviewed List at his accounting firm, he denied that he was List. But the agents noticed a distinctive birthmark and arrested him. Fingerprints did the rest. He was returned to New Jersey, convicted of murder, and sentenced to life in prison.[315]

Down the hall from O'Donnell, in the video support unit, TV monitors never sleep. Day and night, VCRs record every major network show—the soaps, the sitcoms, and everything in between—just in case. Should anyone ask, a program or news bulletin can be fished out of the day's catch.

The unit also reconstructs tapes that criminals want to destroy and compares television images with the real thing to help identify people. When Lebanese television showed a partly decomposed face said to be that of Lieutenant Colonel William R. Higgins, an American hostage slain by his captors in 1989, the unit electronically lined up the facial features of the image with a file photo of Higgins. Visual inspection determined that the man was Higgins.

A Washington, D.C., man videotaped himself raping a woman in Dundalk, Maryland. He later killed her mother. As the police came to arrest him, he cut up the tape, immersed the fragments in lighter fluid, and burned them. The lab reconstructed the tape enough to make a positive ID of the man. At first, the tape shows the figure of a man lying on a bed, where a young woman is seated. Then briefly the static lines clear, revealing his face in the lower left corner of the screen. The man was convicted.

Undamaged tapes have presented other challenges to the lab. One such challenge was to figure out how fast a train or a car was traveling while it was being filmed just before an accident. This serendipitous, objective evidence can help the court decide to what degree a driver was at fault.

The results are not always to the government's liking. During a demonstration against U.S. intervention in Central America on September 1, 1987, Brian Willson sat with other demonstrators on a train track in California in an effort to stop a Navy munitions train. Willson's daughter had set up a video camera to film the confrontation. As it became clear that the train would not stop in time, the other demonstrators ran from the track. But Willson remained riveted to the track, apparently frozen by fear. His legs were severed as his daughter screamed helplessly—all recorded on videotape.

Willson sued the Navy, claiming that the train could have stopped and did not. In defending the suit, the Justice Department asked the lab to analyze the speed of the train from the videotape. The lab determined that the train was going seventeen miles per hour when the limit was ten miles per hour. That evidence helped the plaintiff, as did testimony that the engineer failed to apply the brakes even though he had a clear view of the demonstration from 600 feet away and could have stopped in 143 feet. In addition, a supervisor had commented that a confrontation with the demonstrators was inevitable, "so we might as well have it now." The Navy settled the case for $920,000.[316]

As more criminals store evidence of their deeds on computer, the lab has had to start a group known as the Computer Analysis and Response Team (CART). Not only white collar criminals but serial rapists and murderers have been known to store data on their activities on personal computers. Much of the seized evidence is encrypted and booby trapped on hard disks, diskettes, magnetic tape, or optical disks. The team examines evidence at the lab and goes out to the field as well, training agents in how to preserve and extract computer data. For the lab, prying open the "locked" files in personal computer word-processing programs is as easy as recovering deleted files is for the average user.

In other parts of the lab, analysts compare handwriting, typed or photocopied messages, paint, tape, minerals, adhesives, and glass.

In Baltimore, a suspect was convicted of raping and murdering a woman after the lab matched glass fragments found on his jogging suit to a pane of glass he broke when he reached inside and opened her door.

"The examiner asked, 'Were there any other similar crimes in Baltimore? Because I'm picking up five other types of glass,' " Gleason said. "He identified him as the perpetrator of five other murders."

Because paintings do not come with serial numbers, they cannot be entered on the NCIC computer when they are stolen. So, the lab set up the National Stolen Art File, which stores in a computer information about stolen works of art, including photographs of them. The data bank lists seven thousand pieces.

The document section includes bank robbery notes sent in by field offices. Individual bank robbers tend to stick with the same language. "Don't be foolish," says an example on the wall. The author of this note was more sophisticated than the average bank robber. The notes are on file in a computer, and an investigator need only enter the key word "foolish" to come up with evidence of a possible repeat offender.

The FBI's collection of guns is under the aegis of the lab, which uses them to make firearms comparisons. Besides more modern guns, the collection includes Pretty Boy Floyd's .45-caliber Colt and John Dillinger's .45-caliber Smith & Wesson. The lab's ammunition file has samples of each of the 13,792 kinds of ammunition recently manufactured in the U.S.

Because polygraphing uses scientific instruments that require centralized quality control, the lab supervises the program. This has the added benefit of insulating polygraphers from investigators, whose opinions on a suspect's guilt or innocence may not be accurate.

The polygraph unit is located in rented quarters at Seventh and D streets NW, two blocks east of headquarters. There, five supervisory agents who are examiners review the polygraph charts and findings of the polygraph examiners in each field office. No chart is certified accurate until it has been reviewed by the unit, which is part of the lab's documents section.

No one can fully explain why suspects who are guilty consent to taking polygraph tests. Suspects are not required to submit to the tests. While the results cannot be used against them in court, a failure means that the FBI's investigation of the suspect will intensify. On the other hand, many suspects do not want to appear guilty by refusing the tests. Others are so used to getting away with their lies that they do not consider the possibility they might fail.

Even FBI agents who are under internal investigation are not required to take polygraph tests. Nor can failing a test be used as conclusive evidence of guilt in an internal investigation. But for an agent, refusing to take the test—and failing the test itself—is considered a "negative inference" that can be used along with other evidence to fire the agent.

The FBI does require applicants to submit to polygraph tests when certain security concerns arise. For example, an applicant who previously had a security clearance or who traveled to the former Soviet Union would be required to take the test. Existing agents who are being cleared for highly sensitive classified information also must take the tests. But, unlike the CIA, the bureau does not routinely polygraph all new applicants or every employee on the rolls, even on a random basis.

"There is a lot of debate about the value of the polygraph internally," said Floyd I. Clarke, the deputy director. "It's a valuable tool when used in the right situation and the appropriate amount of weight is given to it. I think polygraphs are valuable in a prescreening interview. No one has a vested right to a job they are applying for," Clarke said. But, he said, "I have a big problem when you have gone through a background on an individual, he has been hired, he develops a reputation, and after five or ten years has established himself or herself as a competent employee, and unless there is an articulable basis for doubting that, I have a serious problem with checking on people's honesty with the polygraph. From a personnel standpoint, you run the risk of putting a tarnish on people's reputations with a false reading from a polygraph that is difficult to change."[317]

To evaluate the polygraph's reliability, the inspection division reviewed all the FBI's polygraph examinations—some twenty thousand in all—going back to 1973. To determine if the polygraph test had been right, the inspectors asked all current agents to report on whether later developments proved the tests right or wrong. As the study pointed out, this method was not foolproof, but it was the best available method for getting at the truth. The National Academy of Sciences, when asked to review the approach, concluded that it would be useful.[318]

The study found that only ninety-one tests—fewer than one percent—were probably wrong. Of these ninety-one cases, the greatest proportion—sixty-four—were false positives, meaning that people who were telling the truth about their innocence had registered as liars. The rest—twenty-seven—were false negatives, meaning that the polygraph tests had failed to detect that people who were guilty were lying.

The study concluded that the incorrect determinations could have been due to examiner error, including, in one case, an examiner who had not adjusted the instrument properly. Some subjects learn to fool the polygraph. The KGB and its successors have long taught its officers to overreact to control questions by thinking exciting or repulsive thoughts. On the critical questions, officers are taught to will themselves into believing they are telling the truth.

In some cases, the study found that errors occurred because subjects had been "contaminated" by information that misled them. In investigating the assassination of Judge John H. Wood in San Antonio, the FBI polygraphed members of the Bandidos motorcycle gang. A number of them failed when they said the gang had not shot the judge. As it turned out, the Bandidos knew that Jamiel (Jimmy) Chagra, who was later convicted of the killing, wanted Wood killed and had offered to pay the Bandidos to kill him. That was enough to create the physiological reactions that FBI examiners interpreted as deception.

"Most of the Bandidos believed that gang members were involved [in the shooting]," the FBI study said. "As a result, polygraph tests showed deception to questions on knowing about and participating in the shooting."

In another example, the FBI polygraphed 141 employees of the Sentry Armored Courier Corporation in the Bronx after $11.2 million had been stolen from the company in 1982. Charles Edger, one of the employees, confessed after failing the test. He was later convicted of participating with two outsiders in what was then the largest cash theft in U.S. history. But another employee also failed. As it turned out, she had been involved in separate thefts amounting to $343,000.

The employee "was indeed involved in stealing company money, but the polygraph could not determine if her involvement was related to the robbery in question," the study said.

In an example of an error in the other direction, the Federal Reserve Bank in Cleveland reported that fifteen coin bags, each containing one thousand dollars in quarters, were missing. The FBI polygraphed an employee who had access to the cash, and he passed. The employee later confessed to stealing the coins and was convicted.

In some cases, the truth remains elusive. Robert C. (Bud) Mc-
Farlane twice failed an FBI polygraph test on whether he leaked to
the *New York Times* an October 24, 1982, story saying that the
British in effect had covered up the fact that a Soviet agent, Geoffrey
A. Prime, had learned British security secrets and divulged them to
the Soviets. McFarlane offered President Reagan his resignation
from the National Security Council, but he also arranged for Arthur
O. (Punch) Sulzberger, Sr., the publisher of the *Times*, to verify to
Reagan that he was not the leaker.

Paul Minor, who performed the test as the FBI's senior polygraph
examiner, said McFarlane could have told someone on his staff to
leak the material. In that case, Sulzberger would have been telling
the truth when he said McFarlane was not the leaker, and McFarlane
still would have failed the test because he felt guilty.[319]

For a polygrapher, detecting leakers is one of the most difficult
jobs because so many government officials deal with the press and
disclose some information in the process.

"Everybody reveals information," Minor said. "You get along with
the press. They want a story. They pick up something, and you want
them to hold it, and you've got to give them something to make it
worth their while."

A good polygrapher knows how to hone his questions so that they
focus on the pertinent issues and are not clouded by extraneous
matters that might produce a false reading. A polygrapher who is
not skilled at his art may produce incorrect results simply by asking
questions clumsily.

Testing the credibility of witnesses and informants is one of the
best uses of the polygraph. Armed with knowledge of whether an
informant or witness has passed the test, the FBI is in a better position to evaluate whether to pursue an allegation. A classic example
occurred when Tawana Brawley, a black teenager, claimed she had
been assaulted and smeared with excrement in Wappingers Falls,
New York. Joyce Lloray, a neighbor, said she saw Brawley jump
into a trash bag. Because she was acting suspiciously, she called the
police. When an ambulance arrived, Brawley pretended to be com-
atose. At the hospital, she responded to questions enough to assert
that four white men had sexually assaulted her and left her in the
trash bag.

Despite all the publicity about the case, what never came out is
that early on, the FBI gave a polygraph test to Lloray. She passed
when she said she had seen Brawley put herself in the bag, showing
that Brawley had concocted her story. After Lloray passed, the FBI

resisted tremendous political pressure to investigate the case as a kidnapping. The bureau could then devote the manpower that might be used on the Brawley case to investigate real crimes. A New York State investigation, helped extensively by the FBI laboratory, later concluded that Brawley had made up the story and smeared herself with feces to avoid punishment for not going to school for four days.[320]

In another example, the FBI's counterterrorism section was considering paying twelve thousand dollars a month to an informant. The man flunked a polygraph test, ending his relationship with the FBI. Another man walked into the Albany field office claiming that a shipment of cocaine was about to be flown in by drug dealers from New York. He flunked the polygraph and admitted that he had made up the story for reasons that were convoluted.

Polygraphs are often used to clear innocent people, which frees up investigators to pursue more promising leads. That happened in May 1979, when six-year-old Etan Patz disappeared after leaving for school from his parents' SoHo apartment in Manhattan. A polygraph test cleared a member of his family who was briefly a suspect. The case is still unsolved.

Very often, when told that they have failed, people confess, or they give enough details to obtain a conviction. That happened with Richard Miller, the Los Angeles FBI agent who was convicted of espionage after he told Paul Minor that he had given the Soviets a classified document. It was also the way the FBI solved the December 31, 1986, fire in the Dupont Plaza Hotel in San Juan, Puerto Rico, which killed 96 people, injured 150, caused $10 million in damage, and left 400 employees without jobs. The fire started in a room that had just been used by a Teamsters local to call a strike against the hotel. After a union member who was a suspect failed a polygraph test given by Salvador Escobedo, an FBI polygraph examiner based in San Antonio, he confessed to torching the hotel and implicated two others in the crime.

"He began by explaining that he did not mean for the fire to get out of hand," said Escobedo, who at the time was the only Spanish-speaking polygrapher in the FBI.

All three men pleaded guilty and were sentenced to prison terms ranging from seventy-five to ninety-nine years.

In the latest twist, the FBI is experimenting with a computerized polygraph that analyzes a subject's responses and tells the operator if they mean he is being deceptive. In part because they track a subject's pulse rate more accurately than a human operator can, they are believed by the FBI and other agencies such as the CIA and the National Security Agency (NSA) to do a better job of detecting lies than conventional machines.

Each year, the laboratory adds to its arsenal of other tests. A man in Miami lapsed into a coma after drinking Poly Malta de Bavaria soda that had been mixed with cocaine. The FBI developed a way to test entire shipments of the beverage with a machine that detected contamination in unopened bottles. In this way, the lab found at least forty-five more bottles that had been laced with cocaine as a way of smuggling the drug in a thousand-bottle shipment from Colombia.[321]

The lab's biggest problem is evidence that it never sees. The lab estimates that only a fifth of crime-scene evidence that should be submitted by local and state police ever makes it to a crime lab.

"It isn't until after the fact that you realize that it was important to retain certain material," said John W. Hicks, the assistant director over the laboratory. "The technology is happening so rapidly that keeping the line people aware of it is a problem. A lot of times officers say, 'We can't give it a hundred percent in every case because we don't have the resources.' "

Because of lack of funds, the lab is not able to handle promptly all the cases it does receive.

"We don't turn down many cases, but we are backlogged," Hicks said. "There are some cases that we don't complete the work on for four or six months. That means the family of a victim who has been murdered or raped is waiting for the results of lab tests so the perpetrator of the crime can be identified and brought to justice. Sometimes the investigation is stalled because of the delays."

Delays do more than affect the families of victims. If a perpetrator is not identified quickly, he may go on to kill other victims.

The annual cost of running the lab is about $56 million, out of the FBI's $2 billion annual budget. When one considers that the funds for one Stealth bomber could run the lab for forty years, the backlog of cases points to a need to reallocate resources.

13

Washington: Deep Throat

● **For the FBI, Watergate began** when a supervisor from the Washington field office called Angelo J. Lano at home in Hyattsville, Maryland, at 8:00 A.M. on June 17, 1972. The supervisor told Lano, who was assigned to a miscellaneous crime squad, that international jewel thieves had broken in to the Watergate office building in Washington around 2:30 that morning.

Since Maryland and Virginia encircle Washington, any jewel thieves are presumed to have crossed state lines and thus fall into the FBI's jurisdiction. Who came up with the idea that the thieves operated internationally is not known. But whoever the intruders were, the theft would fall in Lano's bailiwick. It was one of Lano's jobs to keep track of thefts at the Watergate, one of Washington's posh addresses.

A man of medium height with black hair and a mustache, Lano had started in the bureau as a clerk in 1960. He worked his way through college and the law school of what is now the University of Baltimore. He became an agent in 1966, and was assigned to Washington in 1968. Known for his easy way with people, Lano could be counted on to get to the bottom of any jewel theft.

"The SAC wants you to get to the Watergate because you're familiar with it," the supervisor told him.[322]

It was Lano's day off, and he was about to leave for Little League

265

practice. The field office rotated weekend duty. This weekend, the office had a criminal agent and a counterintelligence agent on duty to handle matters like this.

"I'm not going down there," Lano said. "You have a criminal guy working. I have Little League practice."

Lano then got a call from Robert G. Kunkel, the special agent in charge.

"What's the problem?" Kunkel asked.

"There is a criminal guy working down there," Lano repeated. "I have Little League practice."

"I want you to go there because you're the only person who knows the place," Kunkel said. "You won't be there long. Just check it out and come right back."

For the next three years, Lano worked on nothing but the Watergate break-in. As the case agent, he was more responsible than any other individual for breaking the case and bringing to justice those involved in the later attempt to cover up the involvement of the White House and the Committee for the Re-Election of the President.

For the Washington field office, Watergate meant a break with the past. Opened in 1924, the office was known as a quiet one because roughly half its agents were assigned to counterintelligence cases that never became public. Suddenly, the Washington field office— the first field office in the bureau, and the FBI's second largest— was handling one of the hottest cases in the bureau's history.

After receiving the call from Kunkel, Lano called Peter Paul, another agent on his squad, and asked him to ride with him to the Metropolitan Police Department's second-district headquarters, then at Twenty-third and L streets NW. The police said the burglars had been caught in the sixth-floor offices of the Democratic National Committee. They had two Minolta 35-millimeter cameras, rolls of high-speed film, walkie-talkies, Mace, and Playtex rubber surgical gloves.

When questioned, two of the suspects had used the same phony names. The police were checking their identities through fingerprints. Eventually, they would be identified as Bernard L. Barker, Virgilio R. Gonzalez, Eugenio Martinez, Frank A. Sturgis, and James W. McCord, Jr. All had a connection to the CIA. McCord, for example, had retired from the CIA's Office of Security two years earlier.

At the station house, Lano emptied a carry-on bag containing the articles the police had seized from the suspects. He found bugging devices concealed in rolls of toilet paper. The police had not yet noticed the devices. Lano called in a technical agent, who confirmed that the devices were indeed for bugging and wiretapping.

In a later search of two of the burglars' rooms at the Watergate Hotel, the police found four packets of hundred-dollar bills and two address books with a notation suggesting that E. Howard Hunt—who, it later turned out, was also involved in the break-in—worked in the White House.

Back at the field office, then at the Old Post Office Building on Pennsylvania Avenue at Twelfth Street NW, Lano called an agent he knew at the Secret Service. Since the bills were new, they could be traced. He asked the agent to find out through the Federal Reserve System what bank had received them. He then sent a teletype to Miami, where four of the suspects lived, asking for assistance on the case:

> At approximately 2:30 A.M. security guard, Watergate complex, 2600 Virginia Avenue NW, notified Metropolitan Police Department (MPD) that he discovered tape around two doors on offices located at above address on sixth floor. Guard reported that on earlier security check, he had removed the tape not knowing that an apparent burglary was in progress.[323]

By Monday, the Secret Service and Miami FBI agents had traced the bills to a bank account in Miami maintained by Barker. In turn, the agents traced the money through Barker's account to Kenneth H. Dalhberg, who had used funds collected for Nixon's reelection campaign.[324]

Later that morning, Kunkel asked Lano what he thought about the case.

"I said, 'If you want my honest opinion, the agency [CIA] is involved in it somehow. Look at all these guys. McCord had worked for us and then for them. Then the other four guys. They had been contract people,' " Lano said.

Lano said he needed help. Within two days, two dozen agents from the squad were assigned to work the case. Agents from the rest of the office were assigned to work the remaining cases on the squad, which was known as C-2.

Usually when the bureau has a major case, it gives it a code name such as VANPAC or UNIRAC. That way, agents can refer to it easily. If many defendants are involved, reports do not have to list all the suspects at the top. But Lano, who often worked from 7:30 A.M. to

11:00 P.M. on the case, never slowed down long enough to come up with a code name.

"We never applied for it," he said. "The title was so long. It was all the names, the Democratic National Committee, burglary, interception of communication. It went on and on." But the scandal popularly became known as Watergate.

As the FBI began to develop suspects in the White House, agents found themselves stymied because the bureau had a rule that no one in the White House could be interviewed without permission from headquarters. It would take four or five days for headquarters to give the okay. So, Lano told headquarters that he needed to conduct interviews at the White House without prior approval and received permission to do so.

Almost every field office in the FBI became involved in checking leads. But when critical interviews were held, Lano wanted them conducted by agents from Washington who were familiar with the case. Only rarely had Hoover permitted this kind of freedom. To travel into the jurisdiction of another field office required headquarters approval. But Hoover had died almost two months earlier. Moreover, Watergate clearly was an unusual case. Lano got permission for agents on his squad to interview key subjects in other cities.

"What was different was we handled our own leads," said Robert E. Lill, one of the agents on the case. "Almost all of it was done by people here [in Washington] flying out to other cities, which was a vast departure from what had been done before. Before, you did a teletype, and field offices did the interview. This was considered so sensitive it should be done only by the squad."[325]

Only once did bureau headquarters try to put the brakes on the agents. That was when L. Patrick Gray III, the acting FBI director, deferred to a request from the Nixon White House to avoid delving into money funneled to the break-in through Mexico. Nixon claimed he was trying to protect CIA operations in Mexico. In fact, he had invented the excuse to help cover up the involvement of his own reelection committee. The delay lasted only a week.

Gray later destroyed files that E. Howard Hunt had collected on the Kennedy family before Watergate. When this fact came out, Leonard M. (Bucky) Walters, then an assistant director over the inspection division, led a palace revolt that never became public. Saying that he planned to resign if Gray did not leave the bureau immediately, Walters invited the FBI's other top executives to join him. When they all said they would, he informed Gray of their

Posing as owners of a cellular-phone company in Florida, Special Agents Gloria M. Newport and Richard T. Garcia, right, got drug trafficker Carlos Mario Echeverri to sign Newport's shorthand transcript of the trafficker's account of his drug-smuggling operation. Because she continues to work undercover, Newport's face is obscured.

An FBI profile accurately described Catherine D. Ford's killer.

Unless noted, all pictures are from the FBI.

In an exercise in close-quarters combat, the hostage rescue team shoots to either side of a team member (seated, with his back to the team) in the team's "shooting house" in Virginia.

FBI Special Agent John E. Douglas, who profiles serial killers and rapists at the FBI Academy in Quantico, Virginia, posed with Scott Glenn, left, who played him in the movie *The Silence of the Lambs*, and Jonathan Demme, the film's director, right. In front row, from left, are two of Douglas's children, Erika and Lauren, who had bit parts, and Jodie Foster, the star. © *1991, Orion Pictures*

Howard D. Teten, the father of FBI profiling.

Pat Kirby crossed the country with another agent in a tractor-trailer rig as part of an undercover operation to halt fencing of property from interstate truck shipments.

Agent trainees learn defensive tactics at the FBI Academy. *Ronald Kessler*

Having just made a mock arrest of an extortionist, agent trainees show their stuff at the FBI Academy's Hogan's Alley. *Ronald Kessler*

Agent trainees arrested the "girlfriend" of an extortionist during exercises at Hogan's Alley, a fake town at the FBI Academy.
Ronald Kessler

If Patrick J. Foran, the "mayor" of Hogan's Alley, does not have the highest crime rate in the country, he is fired.
Ronald Kessler

William S. Sessions and his wife, Alice, flew to New York in February 1992 with the author, right, to give awards to agents there.

The author shot a submachine gun, a .357 magnum, and a .38-caliber revolver at FBI headquarters, as well as a 9-millimeter and the FBI's new 10-millimeter semiautomatic pistol, shown here, at the FBI's firing range in Quantico. *Pamela Kessler*

After Ashley Weiskotten's noncustodial father abducted her in 1982 at the age of five, left, the FBI laboratory produced a computer-aged photo of her, right, which resulted in her recovery and the arrest of her father in 1990.

Ashley Weiskotten after she was found.

Special Agents Jimmy C. Carter, right, and Roger L. Depue surveyed racism within the FBI. Carter is now the bureau's chief recruiter.

William M. Baker, left, headed the criminal investigative division; Floyd I. Clarke is the FBI's deputy director.

The J. Edgar Hoover FBI Building.

James M. Fox, assistant director in charge of the New York field office, left, and John Walsh, host of Fox-TV's "America's Most Wanted," got some target practice when Walsh addressed an FBI conference in upstate New York.

William S. Sessions modernized the FBI's personnel and administrative side.

William H. Webster restored the FBI's credibility with Congress and the media and improved investigations.

After Hoover's death, Clarence M. Kelley began the transition to the modern FBI.

J. Edgar Hoover dominated the FBI from 1924 to 1972.

By 12:20 P.M. on April 19, 1993, the Branch Davidian compound
occupied by David Koresh and his followers near Waco, Texas, was a
mass of flames.

Oliver B. (Buck) Revell, the special agent in charge in Dallas, posed in
the gun vault.

FBI Headquarters Functional Organizational Chart

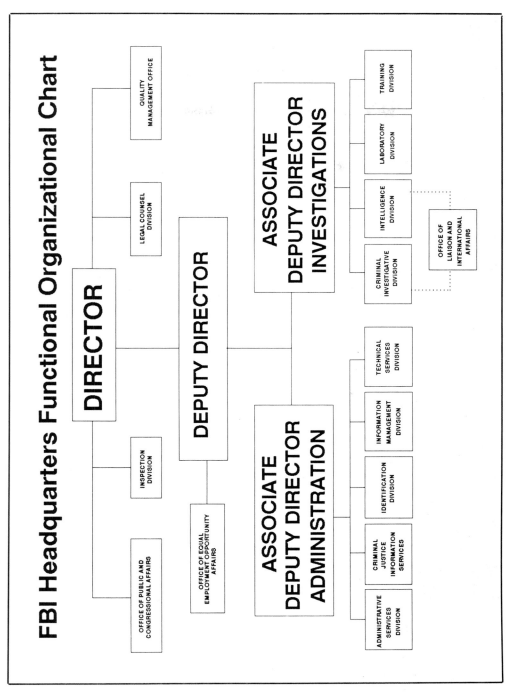

The FBI organization chart temporarily shows eleven divisions. Eventually, the criminal justice information services division will absorb the identification division.

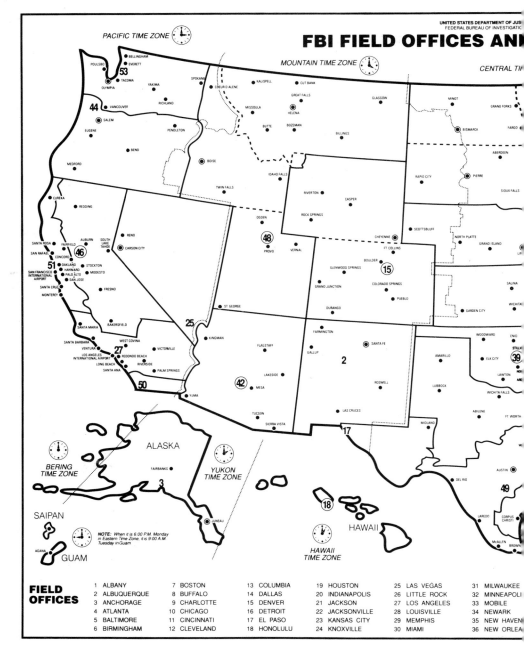

UNITED STATES DEPARTMENT OF JUS
FEDERAL BUREAU OF INVESTIGATIC

FBI FIELD OFFICES ANI

PACIFIC TIME ZONE

MOUNTAIN TIME ZONE

CENTRAL TIM

BERING
TIME ZONE

ALASKA

YUKON
TIME ZONE

SAIPAN

NOTE: When it is 6:00 P.M. Monday
in Eastern Time Zone, it is 9:00 A.M.
Tuesday in Guam

GUAM

HAWAII

HAWAII
TIME ZONE

FIELD OFFICES									
1	ALBANY	7	BOSTON	13	COLUMBIA	19	HOUSTON	25	LAS VEGAS	31	MILWAUKEE
2	ALBUQUERQUE	8	BUFFALO	14	DALLAS	20	INDIANAPOLIS	26	LITTLE ROCK	32	MINNEAPOLI
3	ANCHORAGE	9	CHARLOTTE	15	DENVER	21	JACKSON	27	LOS ANGELES	33	MOBILE
4	ATLANTA	10	CHICAGO	16	DETROIT	22	JACKSONVILLE	28	LOUISVILLE	34	NEWARK
5	BALTIMORE	11	CINCINNATI	17	EL PASO	23	KANSAS CITY	29	MEMPHIS	35	NEW HAVEN
6	BIRMINGHAM	12	CLEVELAND	18	HONOLULU	24	KNOXVILLE	30	MIAMI	36	NEW ORLEA

The FBI has fifty-six field offices and four hundred satellite or resident agencies.

RESIDENT AGENCIES

37	NEW YORK	43	PITTSBURGH	49 SAN ANTONIO
38	NORFOLK	44	PORTLAND	50 SAN DIEGO
39	OKLAHOMA CITY	45	RICHMOND	51 SAN FRANCISCO
40	OMAHA	46	SACRAMENTO	52 SAN JUAN
41	PHILADELPHIA	47	ST. LOUIS	53 SEATTLE	55 TAMPA
42	PHOENIX	48	SALT LAKE CITY	54 SPRINGFIELD	56 WASHINGTON, D.C.

FBI/DOJ

Defiant after Attorney General Janet Reno told him he would be fired by President Clinton if he did not resign, William Sessions told reporters outside his Washington home that as a "matter of principle" he would not resign. A day earlier, Sessions had broken an elbow after stumbling over a curb following his meeting with Reno. Clinton fired Sessions and named Deputy FBI Director Floyd I. Clarke acting director on July 19, 1993, the day after this photo was taken. *AP/WIDE WORLD PHOTO*

President Clinton chose Louis J. Freeh, a federal judge and former FBI agent and federal prosecutor, to succeed William Sessions as FBI director. *AP/WIDE WORLD PHOTO*

ultimatum. Gray resigned from the FBI the same day and withdrew his name from consideration as FBI director.[326]

"They didn't try to suppress what I did," said Daniel C. Mahan, another agent on the Watergate case. "It was one of the FBI's finest hours. There was tremendous pressure. Gray was trying to be director so bad and ingratiate himself with the White House. The people who did the job, day in and day out, did a tremendous job. There was tremendous personal and professional pressure."[327]

"There was no attempt in the FBI to slant what we were doing," Lano said. "It was like a freight train running wild. We didn't know where we were going, but we were rolling. We had fifty-five field offices working on it."

"Whenever we did an interview," said Lill, "it was exhaustive, and we wrote them up so we wouldn't miss a thing. We double-checked them with each other. It had to be right, accurate, because we would all wind up testifying. And almost everyone did."

The agents were blessed with unusually tough and aggressive prosecutors—Earl J. Silbert, Seymour Glanzer, and Don Campbell. Neither they nor the agents worried much that President Nixon might simply fire them all in his effort to cover up his own involvement in the scandal. Since they were protected by civil service regulations, it would have been difficult in any case.

The fact that Bob Woodward and Carl Bernstein of the *Washington Post* were breaking stories on the investigation helped to ensure that it would not be suppressed. The agents were amazed to see material in Woodward and Bernstein's stories lifted almost verbatim from their reports of interviews a few days or weeks earlier.

What Lano and others involved in the investigation resented was the public perception that the two newspaper reporters solved the case. As far as Lano was concerned, Woodward and Bernstein were the enemy, reporters trying to obtain leaks from an ongoing criminal investigation that was supposed to remain secret until indictments were returned by a grand jury. Each time a leak appeared, the agents had to prepare affidavits certifying that they were not the source.

At one point, Mahan recalled, Gray called all the agents on the squad into his office to try to ferret out who was leaking the material. Because a story that had just appeared had come from Mahan's report, Gray singled him out for censure. Later, when Gray was subpoenaed to appear before the grand jury, Lano selected Mahan to help him serve Gray with the subpoena.[328]

"I considered Woodward and Bernstein thieves," Lano said. "It wasn't their story. It was the government's story."

Other agents, however, saw value to the press reports.

"The media served a significant purpose," said Edward R. Leary, an agent on the case. "On the one hand, it was a pain in the neck to us because what would be published in the paper was generally one day to two months behind where we were. We would have to go up the chain with information to explain or critique what was on the street. Why should we be bothered telling whoever wanted to know whether an article was accurate? On the other hand, through media involvement, clearly public focus was placed on the incident, and the glare of the public spotlight eventually opened some doors that would have been closed to us. Did the media solve Watergate? No. Their contribution was focusing a spotlight and causing things to be done in the light of day."

Both police at the scene and the prosecutors credit Lano and the other agents with aggressively pursuing the case to the end. Carl M. Shoffler, one of the police officers who arrested the burglars, said of Lano, "He was a hero because of the actions he took and the effective way he went about doing his job. He immediately traced the information we got from the search warrant. That left little room for maneuvering. When you have someone like a Lano, and he has fingers all over the clues, there is just so much covering up you can do."[329]

"The FBI's field agents did everything we asked," said Silbert, who was then first assistant U.S. Attorney. "Anything we asked for, we got."[330]

"Watergate was an example of what I refer to as agent power," Leary said. "There is no book that tells you how you go about this. It's the individual investigator's imagination, ingenuity, and willingness to go the extra mile to make the case."[331]

On Leary's wall at headquarters is a letter from Harold Titus, Jr., then the U.S. Attorney, commending the "outstanding efforts" on the case by him, Mahan, and "especially Angelo J. Lano."

As for the identity of Deep Throat, the FBI is as much in the dark as anyone else. Many FBI agents, such as John J. McDermott, who took over as head of the Washington field office in October 1972, thought Deep Throat was a composite meant to fuzz up the identities of Woodward and Bernstein's sources. That was a misunderstanding of how the name evolved. From Woodward and Bernstein's *All the President's Men* and from the editors who handled their stories, it is clear that the reporters had a number of sources. With little fanfare, two of them have since come out—Hugh W. Sloan, Jr., the treasurer of the Finance Committee to Re-Elect the President, and Judy Hoback, a bookkeeper for the Committee for the Re-Election of the President.[332]

In discussing the stories with editors at the *Post*, Woodward would refer to one of his sources, who was knowledgeable but not always forthcoming, as "my friend." Possessed of a wry sense of humor, Howard Simons, then the managing editor of the *Post*, dubbed the source "Deep Throat" after the X-rated movie then in vogue.

Because of the notoriety attached to the name, this source took on mythic status well beyond that of the other sources, who were also important and to this day remain anonymous. When guessing sources, people typically focus on individuals who have access to information, who have motives for leaking, and who are visible. In fact, very often, because they know they will be suspected first, people with obvious motives are least likely to leak information. Because no one has heard of them, people tend to forget that dozens of agents, prosecutors, secretaries, and aides may have access to sensitive information and may be willing to leak it for reasons they consider altruistic.

Not only had the FBI never before taken on a president, it had rarely investigated any branch of the government. In Hoover's FBI, if local sheriffs and politicians were off limits, members of Congress and Cabinet officers certainly were. That change, and the fact that the Justice Department in 1977 began prosecuting spies, meant that the Washington field office was no longer the quiet office. From John A. Walker, Jr., to Jonathan Pollard, from Ronald Pelton to Larry Wu-Tai Chin, counterintelligence cases became sexy, and the Washington metropolitan field office, as it is now called, became involved in almost every one.

As the bureau became more sophisticated, the Washington metropolitan field office, or WMFO, as it is now called, began developing major cases on the other side of the house—the twenty-four squads that do criminal and background investigations. Besides Watergate, WMFO was responsible for the FBI's first sting operation and the investigation into contract fraud and bribery at the Defense Department. As the office that does most of the background investigations of high government officials, the Washington office conducted the investigation of Anita Hill's allegations about Clarence Thomas's conduct. It also probed allegations about Senator John Tower's drinking.

Because WMFO is responsible for dealing with federal agencies, most cases of any consequence go through the office at some point. Being near headquarters, the Washington office also is responsible for programs such as the hostage rescue team and an international response squad that worked the Pan Am 103 crash in Scotland.

"Anything that was going on in this country, WMFO had a piece of," said David G. Binney, a former assistant special agent in charge.

In pursuing counterintelligence cases, WMFO agents made extensive use of airplanes—known as Buplanes or Bubirds. Ever since Buck Revell founded the program in 1984, the bureau has been expanding its air force.

Ronald H. McCall, who was the first to head the aviation unit, said, "He [Revell] was very innovative. He rented planes long before the FBI had planes. He conducted aerial surveillance long before it was a recognized investigative tool. He was an innovator and on the leading edge. He gave us the energy and support we needed during the initial stages of the unit."[333]

In closing in on John Walker, FBI airplanes were critical. Initially the FBI had screwed up. An agent from the Boston office had interviewed Barbara Walker, his former wife, who claimed she had seen him engage in spy activity—leaving classified documents in dead drops in the woods and picking up cash. As she rambled on, she downed one glass of vodka after another and slurred her words. Her story seemed dated. She had not lived with Walker in ten years. And she made no secret of her hatred for her ex-husband, who was living with a pretty blonde young enough to be her daughter.

The FBI had slipped up by sending an agent with no experience in counterintelligence to interview her. He failed to recognize that the details she cited were genuine signs of a Soviet spy operation.

The agent wrote off her story as an attempt at revenge by an embittered former spouse. But, after three months, his report made its way to the FBI's field office in Norfolk, Virginia, where Walker lived. Joseph R. Wolfinger, who was in charge of operations under the SAC at the Norfolk office, jumped on the case and notified headquarters officials in charge of monitoring the GRU—the Soviet military intelligence—that he would be pursuing it. Because Walker was a military man, Wolfinger initially assumed that the GRU would be handling him.

When Phillip A. Parker, deputy assistant FBI director in the intelligence division, read the report, he also recognized it as real. Barbara Walker's description of the drops made by her former husband in northern Virginia contained details of spy operations that she could not have picked up by reading spy novels.

Parker assumed that Walker, if still active, would continue to make his dead drops in the Washington area. He called William

Warfield, then assistant special agent in charge of the Washington field office for counterintelligence, and requested support for the Norfolk office.

"We've got a hot one," he told Warfield. "Whatever you want, you've got it."

Wolfinger assigned Robert W. Hunter of the Norfolk office to handle the case. Besides reinterviewing Barbara Walker, the agents ordered an interview with Laura Walker, his daughter. On March 7, 1985, she corroborated many of Barbara Walker's allegations. After both women passed polygraph tests, FBI counterintelligence officials were convinced that the case was for real. But the FBI still needed proof. To trap Walker, they drew up a plan called WIND FLYER, one of the many code names that headquarters makes up randomly and assigns as the need arises.

Walker had retired from the Navy in 1976. Then forty-eight, he ran his own private detective agency. Because of his new occupation as a detective, Walker was likely to be on the lookout for surveillance. Above all, the agents assigned to WIND FLYER did not want to tip their hand. So, instead of watching him constantly, they obtained approval from the Foreign Intelligence Surveillance Court to wiretap his home phones at 8524 Old Ocean View Road in Norfolk and his business phones at 405 S. Parliament Drive in Virginia Beach. Meanwhile, Beverly Andress, an agent assigned to Norfolk, talked Barbara Walker out of confessing to her ex-husband that she had ratted on him.

"It was a love-hate relationship," said John C. (Jack) Wagner, who was special agent in charge of the Norfolk office. "We were afraid she [Barbara Walker] would spill the beans about telling the FBI."[334]

"Bev developed excellent rapport with her," Hunter said.

After six weeks, the agents had turned up no hint of Walker's spy activities. Then, during the week of May 13, 1985, the agents heard Walker chatting about a business trip planned for Sunday, May 19. To some, he said he was going to Charlotte. For others, he manufactured other stories. When his favorite aunt died that week in Pennsylvania, Walker insisted that he could not attend the funeral. His business trip could not be postponed, nor could his partner in the detective agency handle the assignment.

To the agents assigned to the case, Walker's activities indicated that he might be planning a drop. On Saturday, they placed him under constant surveillance. The next day, they watched as Walker, wearing blue jeans, a dark blue pullover shirt, and a black nylon windbreaker, got in his blue-and-silver 1985 Chevrolet Astro Van and began driving into and out of driveways and dead ends. Clearly, he was about to go operational. Overhead, an FBI pilot in a single-engine FBI plane radioed scrambled reports to the command car manned by Wolfinger. At 2:00 P.M., the pilot radioed that Walker was driving north along Interstate 95 toward Washington.

Some twenty FBI cars followed him. Never looking directly at Walker, the agents would pass him, turn off the road, then come back and pass him again. In case they were observed during that time, individual agents changed disguises en route.

Because the FBI was betting that Walker would continue dealing with the Soviets in Washington, a special surveillance plan had been devised in case he should head toward the capital. Now Wolfinger called the Washington field office to activate the command center—a cluster of secure phones, television screens, radio transmitters, and blackboards on the tenth floor of the Washington field office on deserted Buzzard Point overlooking the Anacostia River. The location is enough to depress the most aggressive agent, having been chosen by the General Services Administration (GSA), the government landlord, because the owner of the building submitted the lowest bid. Apparently it never occurred to GSA that the bid was lowest because the location was atrocious. Agents have to drive over rutted roads and railroad tracks to get to the office, wreaking havoc on their personal cars and FBI cars. Because the area has no restaurants, agents frequently bring submarines for lunch from Mangialardo and Sons, a favorite haunt that specializes in the G-Man Special, an Italian cold-cuts sub.

The Washington field office had a command center for just such purposes as the Walker arrest. After Wolfinger called the command center, it notified another forty agents and members of the Special Support Group (SSG). Known as G's, they are the support employees used in counterintelligence cases. As they rushed to pick up Walker on I-95 in northern Virginia, some of the agents and G's changed into camouflage so they could blend into the woods better. Typically, the Soviets designated dead drops in the woods if they could.

By now, the Walker case was considered a "special," meaning that it took precedence over any other case. The Norfolk office was the OO—office of origin—while the Washington office was the auxiliary office. A case may require investigations by many auxiliary offices, and each one places a case agent in charge of that case for the office.

At 4:00 P.M., Walker's van crossed the Potomac River on Route 495 heading into the Maryland suburbs outside of Washington. To blend in, many of the agents changed their license plates from Virginia to Maryland tags. Walker began traversing the countryside in Potomac, Maryland, just off River Road, slowing down at certain intersections and peering at utility poles.

The lush area has long steep hills and million-dollar homes equipped with lighted tennis courts and swimming pools. Ponds dot the front yards, and golden retrievers romp near the swing sets. It is hunt country, and the residents groom their horses on the lawns. The site was not only beautiful; it was perfect for the Soviets' purposes. Because it was nearly deserted, Walker could easily detect anyone following him. Walker was careful to dry-clean himself—turning into dead ends, speeding up and then slowing down, looking around for surveillance. But he never looked up, where the FBI plane was tracking his moves.

Nonetheless, at 4:45 P.M., the agents and the plane lost him. The agents later learned that Walker had gone to check in at the Ramada Hotel in nearby Rockville. He registered as "Joe Johnson." Crestfallen, the agents regrouped behind the Safeway at the shopping center at River and Falls roads. There, more than fifty agents and G's wrung their hands until William P. O'Keefe and A. Jackson Lowe, the supervisors of the two Washington counterintelligence squads on the case, came up with a plan. Figuring that Walker would return, they ordered the agents to conduct "picket surveillance" at choke points—a fence of stationary surveillance at every key intersection leading to the area. At 7:48 P.M., they were rewarded.

Over the radio, the agents heard the voice of a female G. "Hey, I've got him!" she exclaimed.

Walker was driving up River Road again near the shopping center. Now that Walker had turned on his headlights, a second FBI plane from National Airport had a bird's-eye view from four thousand feet.

A good intelligence officer under no circumstances meets with his asset—in this case, Walker—after the first encounter. So, the KGB had instructed Walker to communicate by placing 7-Up cans in particular locations. If, for any reason, Walker could not leave his documents where he was supposed to, or if his Soviet handler could not leave the cash payment, the instructions included alternate sites.

Over the next four hours, Walker performed an intricate dance as he left off classified documents and looked for his money. While the drop points were all within an area of twenty square miles, it took him two hours of driving to hit all of them.

At midnight, Walker headed back to the Ramada Hotel. By then, a third plane had taken over the surveillance. Walker entered the hotel at 12:17 A.M. and went directly to his room on the seventh floor. O'Keefe, as the head of Washington's two GRU squads, would be in charge of the arrest. At the time, the FBI still assumed that Walker, as a military man, would be handled by the GRU. O'Keefe wanted to take him off guard, away from other guests. Under no circumstances was he to get away.

At 3:30 A.M., after Walker was presumably asleep, O'Keefe had Special Agent William Wang pose as the hotel clerk and call him on a house phone. Wang was a coordinator of the G's. His name is pronounced "Wong," prompting the joke, "If it's Wang, it's Wong."

Wang apologized to Walker for waking him and said that another guest had smashed into his van, causing considerable damage. Would he mind coming down to look and exchange insurance information?

Warily, Walker opened the door. He saw no one. He closed the door again, walked to his window, and looked out. From that angle, he couldn't see his van. Nothing seemed amiss.

Shoving a .38-caliber Smith & Wesson revolver under his belt, he opened the door and walked into the hallway. As he approached the elevators, Hunter, the case agent from Norfolk, and Special Agent James L. Kolouch, the case agent in Washington, accosted him, their guns drawn.

"FBI. Freeze!" Kolouch said.

Walker drew his gun and pointed it at the agents, who were both wearing bulletproof vests. There was no way out. There were agents outside, and other agents had blocked off the stairways and elevators. Still others waited in nearby rooms.

If Walker shot one agent, the other one would kill him. He hesitated a moment, then dropped his gun, along with a manila envelope that turned out to contain instructions from his Soviet handlers. If Walker had hesitated another moment, the agents later said, they would have killed him.

Throwing him against a wall, the agents searched him and, to make sure he had no concealed weapon or suicide pill, they ripped off his toupee. Placing handcuffs on him, Hunter told him, "You are under arrest for violation of the espionage laws of the United States."

Stunned, Walker was still thinking of the desk-clerk ploy. "An old trick," he called it, grinning.

When O'Keefe saw the drop instructions Walker had been clutching, he realized immediately that the KGB, not the GRU, had handled him. The GRU never includes photographs of drop sites in its instructions.[335]

For eighteen years, Walker had given away the codes to top-secret U.S. naval communications. Later, Vitaly Yurchenko, the KGB spy who defected to the U.S. in 1985 and then returned to the Soviet Union three months later, would say of the Walker case, "It was the greatest case in KGB history. We deciphered millions of your messages. If there had been a war, the Soviets would have won it." Walker was sentenced to life in prison.

In the Walker case, as in most other surveillance situations, the FBI used a single-engine Cessna 182 RG with high wings. That way, agents could easily peer down with no obstructions. The plane that watched Walker flew at night without lights. The FBI has a special exemption from the Federal Aviation Administration for this.

"We have the capability and authority to fly without lights," said Robert J. Mack, the FBI aviation program manager. "But in most urban areas, it doesn't make any difference. The average person in a city will see lights in the sky anyway. In 99 percent of the cases, the planes fly at night with lights."[336]

Today the bureau has one hundred planes and two hundred FBI agents who are pilots. Many of the planes were seized in narcotics busts. Some are equipped with infrared night-vision equipment that allows agents to see in the dark. Besides planes at each field office, headquarters operates its own planes and helicopters out of an airport in the Washington area. Some have special equipment for taking high-quality photographs for use in planning operations or presenting evidence of a crime in court.

For all the high-tech methods, nothing beats the human touch. At that, the FBI has excelled. When Yurchenko defected from the Soviet Union in 1985, he had information in his brain that billion-dollar satellites could not obtain. Among other things, he gave up the fact that Edward Lee Howard, a former CIA officer, and Ronald W. Pelton, a former NSA employee, were spying for the Soviets. Yet the CIA treated him coldly, even confining him like a prisoner. Despite Yurchenko's wishes, the agency under William Casey leaked to the press the fact that he had defected. The CIA did not even bother to assign Russian-speaking intelligence officers to debrief him.

In contrast, the Washington metropolitan field office assigned two Russian-speaking counterintelligence agents to debrief Yurchenko. Because he treated Yurchenko with respect and showed compassion, Michael T. Rochford, one of the agents, won his confidence. Rochford and his partner, Reid P. Broce, tried to improve

Yurchenko's treatment and stop the leaks, but they were unsuccessful. Yurchenko redefected to Moscow after staying in the U.S. only three months.[337]

During his stay in the U.S., Yurchenko told the agents and his CIA debriefers that he had heard that a KGB officer had paid one thousand dollars to Dusko Doder, the *Washington Post*'s Moscow bureau chief in the mid-1980s, as a way of getting him to work for the KGB. Yurchenko cautioned that he had not learned of the alleged payment in the course of his work. Rather, the payment had been mentioned in office gossip. He did not recall who had told him of the alleged payoff, nor was he ever told the name of the officer who supposedly made the payment.

Checking this out, Rochford, Broce, and other agents assigned to the case concluded that the allegation was false. First, they knew that it is not uncommon for KGB officers to claim they have paid off well-known individuals as a way of impressing their bosses. Second, Yurchenko had honestly characterized the information as rumor. As anyone who works for a large organization knows, rumors are as plentiful as fallen leaves in October and often turn out to be untrue. Finally, looking at Doder's work, the agents concluded that the reporter was objective and certainly not a toady for the KGB or the Soviet government. They attributed the fact that Doder often scooped the competition to his track record as a good reporter, not to any sinister theory that tied him to the KGB. Indeed, in an undercover operation, the FBI verified that Doder was not a Soviet plant by offering him classified documents that would whet the appetite of any spy. Even though he was then covering national security issues, he showed no interest in them. Back in Moscow, Doder would have been of little use to the KGB in any case. He was a straight news reporter, not a columnist. If the KGB had wanted to pay a journalist to sway Americans' opinions, Doder would have been of little value.

As then FBI director, William Webster felt impelled in the fall of 1986 to inform Ben Bradlee, then executive editor of the *Post*, that the FBI had received the allegation but had found no evidence to support it. At the time, Doder had just been assigned to cover national security issues, and the FBI had not yet completed its investigation.

The FBI never goes so far as to say an allegation is untrue. Rather, the bureau says it has found "no evidence" to support an allegation. But by the time the FBI closed its investigation, the agents on the case believed that the allegation was, in fact, untrue. Yurchenko's tip was the kind of allegation the FBI and newspapers receive every day. They check them out and find that many have no basis.

Nonetheless, in a classic example of journalistic irresponsibility, *Time*, under then managing editor Henry Muller, published a story on Yurchenko's tip in its December 28, 1992, edition. The story never said that the claim was based on office gossip or that KGB officers often make up stories of payoffs to make themselves look good. Instead, *Time* suggested that Doder owed his scoops to the KGB and that the U.S. government believed his reporting was "too good"—a claim that was the opposite of what the FBI, which was in charge of the case, had concluded. The article quoted Doder as denying the charge, but the damage to his reputation had been done.[338]

While the FBI's Washington office has the reputation of being the bureau's premier counterintelligence office, Washington has pulled off a number of major criminal investigations as well, including the bureau's first undercover sting operation. Called PFI Inc., it was a phony company whose acronym stood for "police fencing incognito." Run jointly with the Metropolitan police, the company was a fencing operation that solved dozens of crimes in the Washington area in 1976. To enhance its attractiveness to criminals, Robert E. Lill, the case agent, presented the company as having mob connections in New York.

"We were in Washington as an outpost of New York to buy up stolen property," Lill said. "They [criminals] would become part of the organization and maybe get to go to New York. The police loved it. We were solving local and some federal crimes, but we were working with a concept that was different. We were able to show headquarters that we were able to do this. The police departments had been doing it forever, but Hoover didn't want it."

As soon as Hoover died, Joe Yablonsky, a supervisor at headquarters who had played limited undercover roles when he was in Miami, began to propose more extensive operations.

"The idea of an agent portraying a bad guy was out of character for the image," Yablonsky said. "Hoover was a strong authoritarian, and anyone undercover was not under the everyday controls. He was out there and not subject to the same everyday discipline."[339]

In 1978, Howard Teten, who had pioneered profiling within the FBI, began research on undercover work.

"There are unique problems in undercover work that result in losing agents," Teten said. "Sometimes they start committing crimes or have severe mental problems." At the time the FBI asked Teten to look into the problem, the divorce rate among undercover agents was rising.

By informally asking who were the best and worst undercover agents, Teten began to develop profiles.

"Very introverted people are not good," he said. "Being introverted doesn't mean you can't interact on a daily basis with people. You will find people who will work every day and be friendly and happy, but they have to be home and alone to recharge their batteries. . . . A person who worries and tends to blame himself is also not good for undercover work. What happens long term is certain kinds of people blame themselves and will become prunes, and when the person is arrested will have guilt feelings."[340]

Successful agents, Teten found, are extroverts who excel scholastically and tend to be creative, relaxed, and adventurous.

In teaching agents to do undercover work, Yablonsky and later others gave them clues on how to read body language and how to respond if a criminal accused them of being cops.

"If you're caught, and someone says, 'You are lying, and I saw you at a place you shouldn't have been, and they tell me on good information you are an FBI agent,' and you sit there, and your world crushes in on you, and you do nothing, that confirms it," said Lill, who later headed undercover operations at headquarters. "If it's a dangerous situation, it could be your life. If it's not, it could be the operation. So you say, 'Why you son of a bitch!' You scream and counterattack and say, 'I don't have to stand for this.' You go on the offensive."[341]

The bureau learned that families of undercover agents need almost as much support as the agents themselves. By keeping in touch with them, supervisors can learn of signs that agents may be under too much stress.

"I used to make a point of every two weeks meeting with each undercover agent," said David G. Binney, who was an assistant special agent in charge in Washington. "Every two months, I met with his wife and him. She may say everything is fine, but you can tell by the look on her face that problems are developing."

In 1978, the bureau formed an undercover review committee within the criminal investigative division to pass on proposals from field offices. Bureau officials, lawyers, and prosecutors take the proposals apart and look for weaknesses before the ideas are approved. The committee is critical to keeping bureau investigations proper and legal.

Besides ABSCAM, which brought convictions of members of Congress for taking bribes, one of the FBI's most successful undercover operations was GREYLORD, which resulted in some ninety-one convictions of judges, lawyers, sheriffs, and police officers in Chicago's Cook County. The Chicago field office was able to pull off the ruse because Terrence Hake, a Cook County prosecutor who became disgusted with the corruption he saw, agreed to cooperate with the bureau. First as a prosecutor and then as a defense attorney, Hake pretended to be corrupt and participated in bribing Cook County Court officials. In the meantime, he had become an FBI agent.

The FBI brought in agents from all over the country to pose as defendants who had paid off judges. With some misgivings, Webster approved the first bug placed by the FBI in a judge's chambers. With the knowledge of top Illinois officials, the bureau also arranged for the first time to permit agents to testify falsely under oath, in order to carry off the ruse.

"I was always concerned about getting into privileged territory," Webster said. "Unless the judge invited an undercover agent back to his chambers, I had concern about it. I had a sense of privacy, that we could not be indifferent to privacy interests. I usually looked to be sure that there were exclusions from putting audio capability in bedrooms, particularly in view of the history of the Martin Luther King episode. I don't believe we should be in the bedroom unless there was some overriding reason that could be documented and then controlled. They should turn it off when they were not getting things they were supposed to be hearing. . . . Anytime you deal with ultrasensitive techniques, you have to have thought through the reality and perception of your actions. It must not only be legal but also not be seen to be so offensive that we might lose the technique because of outrage. Nor must it be seen as an attack on one separate but equal branch of government by another one."[342]

The case had a devastating impact on the city and the people involved. Holding a Father's Day card and his war medals, one judge committed suicide. The father of a judge had a heart attack and died the day his son was convicted. The wife of a lawyer who was indicted left him.

One of the toughest moments for Hake came when a close friend who was a lawyer confided in him that he had bribed a judge to fix a case for a client.

"When I told my mother about it, I cried," Hake said. "I cried because I had lost a good friend." But Hake overcame his feelings to help convict his former friend. "Six weeks later, he passed me a hundred-dollar bribe, which I took. I had my tape recorder on."[343]

So convincingly had Hake "gone bad" that other friends who were honest lawyers began to shun him. He was left out of social functions, and a colleague commented, "Isn't it too bad what's happened to Terry?"

Today, the FBI has one hundred major undercover operations going at any one time, and two hundred to three hundred minor ones. Of the major ones, the Washington office works two or three. A recent operation focused on allegations that District of Columbia officials were receiving bribes for awarding contracts. That led indirectly to the conviction of Washington mayor Marion Barry on cocaine possession charges.

"There was an attitude [within the Washington field office] we shouldn't do it because it is too politically explosive," recalled Norman A. Zigrossi, an aggressive agent who headed the Washington office when the FBI began the probe. "After discussions with Joe diGenova, the U.S. Attorney, I was convinced that it was not only our responsibility, but we would be derelict if we didn't get involved. So we did."[344]

A few years earlier, in 1977, twelve Hanafi Muslims took 149 hostages at three Washington buildings, including the headquarters of B'nai B'rith's Anti-Defamation League. Although the Metropolitan police were in charge, the FBI gave tactical advice and offered FBI pilots so that the police could land helicopters atop the B'nai B'rith building. By then, each field office had a SWAT team, a response to the massacre by terrorists at the 1972 Olympics in Munich. But the SWAT teams, which were started in 1973, consisted of agents who were marksmen only part-time.

Donald A. Bassett, one of the tactical advisers, said that if the Hanafi Muslims had not agreed to leave the buildings peacefully, "It would have been a bloodbath. These [police] officers had never been trained to do airborne assaults."[345]

That same year, GSG9, a German hostage rescue team, succeeded in liberating hostages taken during the hijacking of a Lufthansa airliner going to Mogadishu, the capital of Somalia in Africa. As a result of the two events, Bassett and others in the FBI's firearms training unit at Quantico proposed an FBI hostage rescue unit that would train full-time and respond to hostage takings and other extremely dangerous threats all over the country.

Meanwhile, Buck Revell had attended a demonstration by Delta, a military special unit. He saw the need for an FBI force, but one that would take a more surgical approach.

"They [Delta] might well rescue every one of the hostages, but there would have been bodies all over," Revell said, explaining that the military tends to decimate their targets. The FBI, on the other hand, aims to take suspects alive if at all possible. "So I came back and said we need to develop a law enforcement team based on our principles: minimum use of force with whatever is necessary to get the job done. The ability to use maximum force if necessary, but one that would minimize the risks at hand."

Revell asked Jim McKenzie, who was over the training division, about starting such a force, and McKenzie said that the firearms unit had been working on the idea. Webster approved it, and, by 1983, the team was operational.

In naming the new force, the bureau did not want to create the impression that it was an elite group. "Super SWAT" was proposed and shot down for that reason. "Hostage rescue team" sounded less elitist and more benign.

"I wanted it to be invisible until it's needed by the bureau," said Danny O. Coulson, the first team commander. "I didn't want them to have this high-profile image that would cause jealousies or resentment."

Despite Coulson's misgivings, Revell arranged for a demonstration by the hostage rescue team for the press. Revell said that the demonstration would warn off would-be terrorists. As part of the demonstration, Coulson had team members using night-vision equipment shoot in the dark at targets within two or three feet of Revell's head. This is a standard training exercise, one that secretaries in the unit and team members participate in. But when Revell's wife, Sharon, heard about it, she called Coulson and bawled him out.

"She said, 'You did this to my husband and turned the lights out and shot around his head,' " Coulson said. "I said, 'Sharon, he's a tough guy. He's an FBI agent. Everyone on that team does that.' She said, 'Yeah, but he's a grandpa. Don't you ever do anything like that again.' "[346]

"That is absolutely a part of the necessary level of training," Revell said. "I have complete confidence in them. It's just like when you fly in an airplane. You have to have confidence in the pilot."

The HRT's only casualty occurred in April 1986, when James K. McAllister, an original member of the team, died in a fall from a helicopter during a training exercise at Quantico.

Today the team consists of fifty-one members, who train in Virginia. To practice at close range, the team shoots inside a specially constructed pen that resembles a crude house. To make sure bullets don't leave the practice area, the pen is encircled by layers of tires. In a week, the team might spend two days practicing entry tactics —methods for getting control of a building, a bus, or an aircraft. Another two days might be spent on the range with shoulder weapons and pistols.

"Our approach is there is no room for failure," said Richard M. Rogers, the commander of the team. "If you get the mission, you do it, and you succeed. To have that mind-set requires being on a sharp edge all the time."

Each year, about fifty agents apply for the six or eight openings on the team. Each member stays on the team for five or six years.

Besides rescuing hostages, the team may supply groups of four or five sharpshooters to take down a sniper or to help out in a particularly dangerous arrest. In Sperryville, Virginia, for example, the team took out a man as he marched his wife through a field with a carbine at her head.

Rogers is an assistant special agent in charge of WMFO. However, the team operates nationally and even internationally. It was the hostage rescue team that arrested Fawaz Younis after he had been lured to an eighty-one-foot yacht off the coast of Cyprus.

Younis, a Lebanese used-car dealer who reported directly to the leadership of the Shiite Amal militia, had commandeered a Royal Jordanian jet at Beirut International Airport on June 11, 1985. He brutalized its armed guards and demanded that the plane fly him and his henchmen to Tunis, Tunisia, so that he could deliver a message to a meeting of the Arab League. When the plane was denied landing privileges, Younis had the pilots fly him back to Beirut. After allowing the passengers and crew to leave, Younis had his fellow terrorists blow it up as he read a ringing statement on the need to expel Palestinians from Lebanon, his embattled homeland. Three Americans were among the passengers who were released unharmed.

When Younis stepped on board the yacht on September 13, 1987, he saw two attractive female agents clad in bikinis lounging on deck. But they were not there to accompany him on a cruise. Other agents slammed him to the deck and arrested him. It was not the first time the FBI arrested suspects in international waters. But it was the first time the FBI arrested a terrorist under a new law that allows the bureau to arrest perpetrators of terrorism against Americans regardless of where the acts occur. Younis was advised of his rights in Arabic. During the arrest, Younis sustained hairline fractures to one of his wrists. Whether he broke his wrist when the agents threw him to the deck or when he became seasick and was throwing up while handcuffed is unclear.

"Maybe we were too rough," said David W. (Woody) Johnson, Jr., who was then commander of the team.[347]

"He [Younis] confessed in the first thirty minutes we talked to him," said the omnipresent Revell, who was on a larger naval vessel commanding the operation. "We debriefed him over three days."

Younis was convicted of conspiracy, hostage taking, and air piracy. He is serving a term of thirty years at Leavenworth Federal Penitentiary in Kansas.[348]

More recently, on August 30, 1991, the hostage rescue team, along with regional SWAT teams and Bureau of Prisons teams, stormed the federal prison in Talladega, Alabama, where 121 Cuban inmates had taken hostage nine employees of the Bureau of Prisons and the Immigration and Naturalization Service. The inmates, who were trying to avoid deportation to Cuba, had held the hostages for nearly ten days. Armed with submachine guns and 9-millimeter pistols, the teams rescued the hostages after a three-minute raid. No shots were fired. One inmate received a minor cut on his head.[349]

It was another success for the HRT, one that William P. Barr, then the acting attorney general, could claim credit for because he was closely involved in calling the shots. On the night he gave the order to strike, Barr was in the FBI's operations center at headquarters with Sessions and with Floyd Clarke, the deputy director, and Bill Baker, the assistant director over criminal cases.[350]

"I don't think there is any question that the bureau's actions at Talladega gave him the attorney generalship," Revell said. "He supported it, made the right call, he showed he had guts. It came out exactly right, and I think that raised his stature with the president to the point that he wanted him as attorney general."[351]

If the HRT is the sexiest part of the work of the Washington metropolitan field office, background investigations are the dullest. Because of the federal presence in Washington, three of the office's forty-one squads are devoted to checking the backgrounds of applicants for sensitive government jobs. Yet, as the Clarence Thomas hearings demonstrate, background investigations at times can be the bureau's most important cases, dominating the news for weeks on end. They can also get the bureau into a lot of trouble, as happened when Raymond J. Donovan was confirmed as secretary of labor.

In that case, Francis M. (Bud) Mullen, Jr., who was executive assistant director over investigations, wanted to conceal the fact that the bureau in New York was wiretapping the home telephone of William Masselli, a member of the Genovese mafia family. Donovan's name had been mentioned six times during the interceptions, which occurred in 1979. Mullen felt that the references to Donovan, who was in the construction business in New Jersey, were not significant. He did not want to jeopardize the taps, which were producing evidence about bribes to members of Congress.

In testifying before Congress on the bureau's 1981 investigation of Donovan, Mullen said that Donovan's name had not come up in any New Jersey wiretaps. The fact that his name had come up in a New York wiretap later came out, boomeranging on Mullen and the FBI. A staff report of the Senate Labor Committee charged Mullen with deliberately withholding the information. When Mullen was nominated to head the DEA, Congress delayed his confirmation over the issue for more than a year. He blamed the delay on Congress's alleged hostility to the bureau because the FBI had targeted members of Congress in ABSCAM.

"As far as I know, to this day no one has ever shown any evidence or hint of organized crime connections to Donovan," Mullen said.[352]

But Mullen's handling of the issue left a lot to be desired and contravened Webster's instructions on dealing with Congress. "Ordinarily, and I'm not talking about Bud, I always preached that one should try to understand what the person wants to know, regardless of how well they have asked it," Webster said. "Then if you don't want to answer it, decline to answer it for a reason you give. You can debate it later or negotiate it or try to figure out how you can give them the information if there are good reasons for not waiting to make a statement on the public record. You try not to be in a situation where you are saying, 'He didn't ask the right question.' "

After the Donovan episode, Webster changed the system so that, rather than summarize its investigation, the bureau gives the White House any interviews or other reports containing derogatory information. Favorable material is summarized. Congress then receives the reports from the White House and comes to its own conclusions about the significance of the information. While the system provides more direct disclosure, it places more responsibility on Congress to evaluate raw information gathered by the FBI. In the case of the nomination of former Senator John G. Tower to be secretary of defense, Congress became mired in dozens of allegations about his drinking and sexual activities and had to assess their credibility. Inevitably, background investigations produce a lot of conflicting information that may or may not be credible.

"In a background investigation, you are asking people questions about someone they may like or despise," said James V. De Sarno, Jr., who supervised the Tower investigation at headquarters. "A lot of times you'll get two different views. You really are reporting. You draw no conclusions. In a criminal case, you draw conclusions on probable cause based on the evidence. But in a background investigation, you ask, what is their opinion of this person's character, attitudes, and loyalty? You get lots of different opinions. A lot of times it's based on what side of the aisle they are from."

Issues such as drinking or smoking marijuana pose even more problems.

"When someone says he views this person as having a drinking problem, we ask, 'What do you mean by a drinking problem?' " De Sarno said. "They explain what they mean. 'Have you ever seen him drink to excess? Where and when?' All we do is then report it. Someone else says, 'I was at that party, and he wasn't drunk.' You don't ever resolve that. The public asks why didn't we resolve that? You can't resolve that."

In a situation like the Tower or the Clarence Thomas nomination, the bureau receives pressure from all sides—from the White House to speed things up, from Congress to probe more deeply.

Tower's nomination ultimately was rejected amid criticism of press leaks and claims that the allegations against him would not hold up in a court of law. But that is not the standard when confirming a Cabinet officer or granting a security clearance. If it were, there would be little point to reviewing a candidate's qualifications and character. Almost everyone would be confirmed or granted clearances, since few candidates for high posts are convicted felons. The derogatory information on Tower was so great that he would not have been given a security clearance as an FBI agent or a military officer, according to De Sarno. Yet, some thought that Tower should be secretary of defense simply because the charges were not proven as clearly as they would have to have been for a criminal proceeding.[353]

That same mind-set led Congress to confirm as a U.S. District Court judge Robert F. Collins, a New Orleans magistrate, even though the FBI reported that as a local judge Collins had traded the services of prostitutes for favorable court decisions.

"He [Collins] was involved in prostitution, sexual favors for decisions," said Mullen, who was then special agent in charge of the New Orleans office. "This was when he was a state judge. We reported it, and he was appointed anyway."[354]

Senator Dennis DeConcini, the Democrat from Arizona who presided at closed hearings on Collins's nomination, publicly alluded to the allegations, but he said he believed there was no basis for the charges.[355]

After Collins became a federal judge, the FBI received more allegations that he was corrupt. As a result of an FBI investigation, Collins was sentenced to six years and ten months in prison for taking a bribe of $100,000 from a convicted marijuana smuggler in exchange for giving the defendant a lighter sentence in federal court.[356]

In investigating nominees to be Cabinet officers and senior White House aides, the FBI normally conducts twenty-five to thirty background interviews with people who know them. In the case of the nomination of Clarence Thomas to the Supreme Court, those interviews did not include Anita Hill, the law professor who formerly worked for him at the Equal Employment Opportunity Commission.

"What happened is that, at the urging of other people, she contacted the congressional staffers and later furnished a statement that was sent to the committee that made allegations [against Thomas]," said Tron Brekke, who supervised the inquiry at headquarters. "That was brought to our attention, and a request was made for us to interview her. She had not been interviewed by the FBI before that. We don't interview everyone who ever worked with the individual. We interview people who are there, people they list, people about whom others say, 'You ought to talk to so and so.' "[357]

Hill later passed a polygraph test paid for by her pro bono lawyers and administered by Paul Minor, who by then had retired from the FBI. To make sure that extraneous issues did not cloud the results, Hill first disclosed to Minor that, although she had come across during the hearings as embarrassed by the sexual comments she said Thomas had made, she was more offended than embarrassed.

"She said, 'The only thing I want to tell you that has gotten kind of off track in the hearings is, I wasn't really all that embarrassed,' " Minor quoted her as saying. " 'I've been around. I've lived. I wasn't raised under a tub. I wasn't all that embarrassed. It made me mad when he would say that.' "[358]

The FBI looked inept when Douglas H. Ginsburg had to ask that his name be withdrawn from nomination to the Supreme Court after the press had disclosed his marijuana use.

"I think we took a bad rap in the Ginsburg case," said Floyd Clarke, the FBI's deputy director. "People lied to us. When you go to professional people at some of our most respected institutions of learning, you expect them to tell the truth. They knew he took marijuana and lied about it or withheld."[359]

After the incident, the FBI changed the forms it gives to people when they are nominated or appointed to high-level government positions. Before, the forms asked general questions about conduct that would disqualify the candidate. Now, they specifically ask about prior drug use—questions previously thought to be too demeaning.

"He [Ginsburg] was not asked, 'Have you ever used marijuana?' " Clarke said. "He was asked questions that would have elicited a response that should have revealed that. The form is now very specific."

To help in conducting background investigations of applicants for government jobs, the bureau has begun paying retired agents twenty-one dollars an hour to do the checks. This saves money and produces excellent work by veteran agents, many of whom held important positions in the bureau before they retired. The three applicant squads, based at a resident agency in Tysons Corner, Virginia, continue to check on presidential appointees and other higher-level applicants.

The other eight squads at the Tysons Corner RA are devoted to white collar crime, much of it involving fraud against the government. Before it was folded into the Washington office in 1988, the FBI's Alexandria office undertook one of the most massive white collar crime investigations in bureau history. The investigation began on September 6, 1986, when a vice president of a company told the Naval Investigative Service that he had been offered information on a competitor's Defense Department bid. Called ILLWIND, the ensuing joint investigation with the NIS relied extensively on the computer.

"Without the computer, we could not have done this case," said Richard B. (Rick) Wade, the FBI agent who directed the case for five years. "Fairly early on, we would have had to shut down the case because if we had gotten any more information, we wouldn't have been able to prosecute it."

At one point, the bureau had three hundred agents working the case. They intercepted ten thousand telephone calls, did two thousand interviews, and issued two thousand subpoenas. In one search alone, the agents obtained a quarter of a million documents. Altogether, the agents obtained 1.2 million documents.

The wiretaps and bugs enabled agents to overhear a contractor planning to destroy evidence.

"We heard him calling some friends to help him destroy the evidence," Wade said. "We were able to get a search warrant based on that.

"The agents were phenomenal," Wade continued. "Extremely dedicated, extremely bright. During the years we were covert [before the case became public], there were five or seven snow days. All the agents came to work. One ran five miles. She couldn't drive to work. Almost everybody worked six days a week. Many worked seven days a week."

The investigation resulted in the conviction of fifty-four Defense Department and private defense contracting officials on bribery, fraud, and other charges. Unisys Corporation paid a fine of $190 million, while United Technologies Corporation paid $6 million in penalties. To this day, Wade is pleased that the operation is referred to in the press as ILL WIND instead of ILLWIND. To him, it means that the first leaks to the press about the case did not come from FBI agents, who knew that the case's code word—derived from Shakespeare's "Ill blows the wind that profits nobody"—is one word rather than two.[360]

A new squad focuses on computer crimes such as the one for which Robert T. Morris was convicted. A Cornell University graduate student, Morris developed a computer virus that paralyzed or slowed six thousand government and research computers in November 1988. As part of an "academic experiment," Morris said, he intended the virus to make one copy of itself in each computer that is part of Internet, a collection of computer networks. However, because of a programming error, the virus copied itself hundreds of times in each computer. The experiment, Morris said, was a "dismal failure." Morris made no secret of his culpability, and, as a result of an FBI investigation, he was charged with creating the virus. He was given three years' probation and ordered to pay a ten-thousand-dollar fine and perform four hundred hours of community service.[361]

Like the hostage rescue team, the new squad is based in WMFO but responds to computer crimes anywhere in the country.

"The technology is advancing so rapidly that the skills you get in school are overtaken in three or four years," said Floyd Clarke, the FBI's deputy director. "So we have developed a capability much like the HRT. . . . We will have people stay in touch with the industry and educational institutions. They are experts in all aspects of computer technology."

Besides such white collar cases, the Washington office has investigated every political scandal involving presidents, from Debategate to the Iran-Contra affair. It was Debategate that resulted in the removal of Theodore M. (Ted) Gardner, then head of the WMFO. He had met with Bob Woodward in 1983 and discussed the bureau's plans to use lie detectors in investigating how Ronald Reagan's campaign aides had obtained documents from the Carter White House during the 1980 presidential race. A day after meeting with Gardner, Woodward ran a story on the FBI's plans in the *Washington Post*.

"I had lunch with Woodward the day before the article," Gardner said. "The issue of polygraphs was discussed in a generic sense. I told him what the procedure would be."[362]

William French Smith, then the attorney general, had specifically prohibited any outside discussion of the case. Gardner told Webster he hadn't discussed it specifically.

"He didn't buy that," Gardner said.

Webster transferred Gardner to head the Portland office, which then had only fifty-six agents. What did not come out was that Webster was sure Smith would ask that Gardner, who was highly respected, be fired.

"There was a lot of hate in the department," Webster said. "A number of people sent signals, not including the attorney general, that he [Gardner] should be fired from the FBI. Make an example of this fellow. There was some concern on my part that someone might persuade the attorney general to go along with it. . . . So I owed it to him to protect his job because I thought he was a good man. I did not want him fired."[363]

Ultimately, polygraphs were not used in the investigation, which failed to determine who was responsible for obtaining the documents. Gardner, whose comments had not affected the outcome of the investigation, later retired from the Portland office.[364]

Today, half of the six hundred agents in the Washington office work criminal and background investigations, and more and more agents are being transferred from counterintelligence to violent crime cases. So far, thirty have been assigned to work with local police in a program developed by Sessions known as Operation Safe Streets. Under this program, the WMFO has participated successfully with District police in sweeps against two violent drug gangs, known as the P Street Crew and the R Street Gang. Having worked in Washington, the safe-streets program has been expanded to thirty-nine other communities. Almost immediately, the FBI announced arrests under the program of street gang members involved in drug trafficking in Los Angeles, Omaha, and Portland.

The WMFO also moved against the latest twist in crime, carjacking. Rather than try to steal parked cars, thieves hold up people in their cars, threatening them with guns and then driving away with their cars. In cooperation with the local police, the Washington office announced that it would use agents as decoy drivers in an effort to catch carjackers. But the agent who was returning home with his wife one evening in September 1992 was no decoy. As he pulled into the parking lot of his apartment complex in Largo, Maryland, Anthony Tyrone Brown, an eighteen-year-old man, pulled a gun on him and ordered him and his wife out of their car. As Brown was about to drive away, the agent shot him dead.[365]

It was, as WMFO agents would later say, a "clean shooting." Since Brown had pulled a gun on the agent, he was presumed to be a threat, and the agent was justified in shooting him in self-defense. Before the shooting, the agent had identified himself as such. If the agent—who was assigned to a gang squad—had not killed him, Brown might have killed the agent as he drove away with his car.

Robert M. (Bear) Bryant, the special agent in charge of the WMFO, keeps a sign in his office overlooking the muddy Anacostia River. YOU LIED, it says. Bryant, who has big blue eyes and a broad forehead, explained that when the bureau transferred him to headquarters from Salt Lake City, "My wife [Beth] didn't want to move. My daughter was in high school. She was an all-state athlete. You really don't want to come back here [to Washington]. You come back to an environment where you are a subordinate, and it is expensive. She is not a great fan of the bureau. She thinks we move too much. You redo five to six houses. I told her I would stay three years at the bureau [headquarters] and go back and practice law and make a lot of money. She said I lied. That's the reason I have that plaque."[366]

As the head of the Washington office, Bryant has special status. Although he is not an assistant director, he and the head of the New York office are the only field executives who are part of the FBI's executive conference. Consisting of the bureau's top management, it meets every Thursday morning in the executive dining room for breakfast.

Bryant, who was over the bureau's drug and organized crime programs at headquarters before becoming SAC in Washington, has little patience with those who question why the FBI is working gangs and other violent crime cases.

"We have thirty agents working with the police," Bryant said. "Why? Because there will probably be five hundred murders this year. Sixty percent result from crack cocaine. People are afraid to come out of their houses here. Does the FBI have a responsibility? Can we say, 'It's not our problem? Let the police handle it?' When they kill four hundred eighty-seven people in one year, that's an issue I think we ought to be involved in.

"When I first came to the FBI," Bryant said, "I arrested one hundred fugitives in ten months. But the thing we didn't do is attack a lot of the major issues. Today, I'm not looking for *numbers* of drug convictions. We want to know what impact we're making on the problem."

"We're the Washington metropolitan field office," said James De Sarno, the assistant SAC over violent crime and terrorism. "If we're not serving the needs of the Washington area and addressing the problems that the people of Washington see as problems, I don't think the people paying taxes to pay our salaries are getting their money's worth."

As part of that, the Washington office is trying to improve the image of the FBI among minorities.

"One thing I learned early on when I came out to the field was the FBI in the minority community does not have a very good image," said De Sarno, whose office wall is decorated with a copy of a *Washington Post* recap of the victims of homicide during the past year. "We worked a case against the mayor [Marion Barry, who is black]. In some respects we were seen as targeting him. 'Was the FBI involved in the murder of Martin Luther King? What about the civil rights era? What did the FBI do? Were they helpful or were they part of the problem?' Generally the minority community doesn't like law enforcement anyway because their first contact with law enforcement officials is often negative. We're making a real effort to get out and let people know who we are. That has been part of the problem. We have been a real mystery to the minorities in Washington. I don't think they really know us, and maybe we don't know them very well."

Like many other offices, the Washington office participates in the Drug Demand Reduction Program. Started by Sessions in 1988, it sends agents into the community to talk about the dangers of drugs. In addition, under Operation Safe Streets, the Washington office started adopting inner city schools. Fifteen agents and support employees from the field office—most of them minorities—tutor students at Savoy Elementary School in southeast Washington or take them on trips, acting as role models. In a Junior G-Man Program once a week, they talk about the FBI, law enforcement, and the importance of taking responsibility for one's own actions. Another twenty-five agents tutor students at Hendley Elementary, also in the southeast section.

"They have established a bonding with the young people here at the school, not only with the children they are tutoring but with the schools," said Marsha Semlar, the principal at Savoy. "We are very impressed with the program."

Besides accepting female agents, this development is the one that would most likely have amazed and enraged Hoover were he alive today. Putting aside the fact that it does not contribute to the bureau's arrest statistics, it conflicts with Hoover's rigid view of the FBI's role.

"When Hoover was alive, no one participated in anything anyone else was doing," Buck Revell said. "An SAC never left his office and was not really involved in the community."

Mildred C. (Millie) Parsons, Bryant's secretary, has seen it all—when agents could not drink coffee, when they had to wear white shirts and fedoras, and when the bureau used secretaries like her for surveillances because Hoover would not allow female agents. Parsons has been an FBI secretary for fifty-three years—and never had a sick day, she will tell you. She has been secretary to the head of the Washington office since 1948. In that time, she has worked for twenty-six SACs, eight of whom—including Robert G. Kunkel, who was SAC when the Watergate investigation began—are no longer living.

"When I came in, agents always wore white shirts and hats," Parsons said. "You could tell an agent the minute you saw him. The female employees wore dresses. No slacks or shorts. There were no female agents. The dress code changed when Clarence Kelley became director. We could wear pant suits.

"It was no coffee at your desk under Mr. Hoover," Parsons continued. "The agents could not drink coffee outside, either. If you had a break and went to the break room, support people could drink coffee. If agents drank coffee outside, they could be censured or transferred."[367]

Parsons is known as a "Betty Bureau," an affectionate bureau-wide term that describes a female support employee who, in effect, is married to the FBI.

"I have no children," said Parsons, who is seventy-eight. "No immediate family right here. I just look forward to coming to work. I like my work. I like the people. They have been wonderful to me. Since I began working for the bureau, I lost my mother, my husband,

and both my sisters. If it hadn't been for the bureau, I don't know what I would have done. They are just like family. They treat me just like family."

When Parsons had been with the FBI fifty years, 280 people attended a party given for her by the WMFO. Former SACs and ASACs flew in from all over the country—Zigrossi from Tennessee, Gardner from California, Warfield from New York, Parker from Norfolk, Virginia. McDermott, who took over the Watergate investigation from Kunkel, and Nick Stames, another former head of the office, came from Washington. The bureau's highest-ranking officials—Sessions, Floyd Clarke, and John E. Otto—attended either the party at Fort Myer in Virginia or a coffee for Parsons at the field office.

Otto, who was executive assistant director, read a letter of congratulations from President Bush. Nick Walsh, then an assistant special agent in charge, narrated a humorous slide show depicting what Parsons was doing when hula hoops were the rage. Sessions presented Parsons with a specially made FBI pin with five diamonds to represent her five decades with the FBI. Douglas Gow, who was then the special agent in charge of the WMFO and later became an assistant director and then associate deputy director, presented Parsons with a diamond-studded gold watch, a gift from the office.

"They always say I train them, and they go on to bigger and better jobs," Parsons said. "Of course, a lot of them *have* become assistant directors."

14

Information Division: Secret Files

● **Under Hoover,** the secret to the FBI's success was its legendary files. With information on millions of people, most of them criminals, the files were so well indexed that an agent often could solve a case without leaving his office.

The files also guaranteed Hoover's job. For, as any taxi driver in Washington knew, the director maintained files that could be used to blackmail members of Congress, presidents, and their aides. Defenders of Hoover maintained that he did no such thing—that he kept sensitive information about politicians and celebrities in his office because he did not want young clerks in the file rooms reading the material. These former Hoover lieutenants have challenged anyone to show an instance when the bureau actually threatened a member of Congress with exposure for not going along with the director's wishes.

"The biggest canard and distortion is the fact the FBI kept blackmail files or wiretaps on congressmen," said Cartha D. (Deke) DeLoach, who was assistant to Hoover in charge of investigations and congressional and public relations. As for the bureau's leaks of information from the FBI's tapes of Martin Luther King's sexual activities, "I doubt if Mr. Hoover knew about divulging the information," DeLoach said.[368]

However, in 1975 testimony before the House Select Committee on Intelligence, retired FBI Special Agent Arthur Murtagh testified about a comment DeLoach had made to agents receiving in-service training at the FBI Academy. Asked what headquarters did with memos passing along information that might be of interest to Hoover, DeLoach said, "The other night, we picked up a situation where this senator was seen drunk, in a hit-and-run accident, and some good-looking broad was with him. We got the information, reported it in memorandum, and by noon the next day, the senator was aware that we had the information, and we never had trouble with him on appropriations since."[369]

"That is absolutely false," DeLoach said recently. "No such thing ever happened. I would not have made any statement lecturing to agents like that."

Of course, the FBI never directly threatened a member of Congress or a president with exposure. There was no need to. Everyone in Washington knew—or thought they knew—that Hoover maintained derogatory information and would leak it if necessary. Hoover had a way of subtly informing his subjects. As a "courtesy," Hoover's aides would let politicians know that the bureau had picked up scurrilous information about them. But even if Hoover did not go out of his way to inform a congressman that the bureau knew of his indiscretions, the *perception* that Hoover had dirt on everyone was enough to assure Hoover lifetime tenure and passage of his annual budget requests.

Hoover's defenders have tried to obfuscate the issue through semantics—quibbling about whether the files were *blackmail* files or *secret* files. Most of them were contained in Hoover's Official and Confidential files maintained in his suite. But what they were called and whether they were kept in Hoover's suite or in the general files is irrelevant. Reading those files that survived makes it clear they could have been gathered for no other purpose than as potential blackmail material.*

For example, on June 13, 1958, the head of the Washington field office informed Hoover that, prior to marrying a member of

---

* According to Athan Theoharis, editor of *From the Secret Files of J. Edgar Hoover*, Ivan R. Dee, 1991, Hoover wrote a memo on June 4, 1971, recording a conversation he had had with then Attorney General John Mitchell. To avoid leaks, Hoover said he told Mitchell, he filed especially sensitive memos in his Personal and Confidential file. Upon Hoover's death, Helen Gandy, his secretary, destroyed these files according to Hoover's instructions. However, eight of the files had been transferred to Hoover's Official and Confidential file, which remained intact. Those files relate to the bureau's "black bag" jobs and other illegal acts.

Congress, the member's wife had been "having an affair with a Negro . . . [and] also at one time carried on an affair with a House
Post Office employee." More recently, the report said, the congressman's wife "endeavored to have an affair with [an] Indonesian,
who declined. . . ."

In response to this tidbit, Hoover wrote back on June 25 that it
was "certainly thoughtful of you to advise me of matters of current
interest, and I am glad to have the benefit of this information."[370]

On August 8, 1958, the head of the Washington office advised
Hoover that a senator "prepares a personal check each month in the
amount of $500, payable to [name withheld]. [The FBI's source]
stated that he had heard that [name withheld] is a 'party girl' and
that she may be living with Senator [name withheld] at the Shore-
ham Hotel, Washington, D.C."

Another memo, on October 21, 1958, told Hoover that a married
senator "has been frequently in the company of [name withheld] of
the public relations staff of the Sheraton-Park Hotel. The relationship between the senator and [this woman] appears to be much more
than casual. . . ."

On June 9, 1959, the head of the Washington office informed
Hoover that a prostitute said she had had sexual intercourse with
a senator in the afternoon "on the couch in the senator's office."

"I have received your note of June 9, 1959, and I want to thank
you for bringing this data to my attention," Hoover wrote back.

When Representative William R. Anderson of Tennessee, a World
War II hero and former *Nautilus* skipper, attacked Hoover on the
floor of the House for abusing his office and using "tactics remi-
niscent of McCarthyism," the special agent in charge of the Memphis
office sent Hoover a memo alleging that Anderson had consorted
with prostitutes.

"This shows what a whore monger this old reprobate is," Hoover
wrote on the bottom of the letter.[371]

Hoover's intrusions into politics extended to the political beliefs
of members of Congress and even to the inner working of the Supreme Court. It is tempting to excuse Hoover's prying as a product
of a different era. But as far back as 1924, Attorney General Harlan
F. Stone had limited the bureau's activities to investigations of "violations of law."

In written guidelines, Stone told Hoover that the bureau is "not
concerned with political or other opinions of individuals. It is concerned only with their conduct and then only with such conduct
as is forbidden by the laws of the United States." He stated that a

police force that passed beyond these limits was "dangerous to the proper administration of justice and to human liberty, which it should be our first concern to cherish."[372]

Contrary to the claims of Hoover's defenders, there is ample evidence to show that Hoover provided damaging information to the press, to political adversaries, and to the subjects of the allegations to make sure *they* knew that *he* knew. On January 26, 1971, Hoover wrote to H. R. Haldeman, President Nixon's assistant, forwarding the allegations about Representative Anderson. He added, "The information concerning Congressman Anderson's alleged extracurricular activities has also been furnished to the Attorney General [John Mitchell] and to the vice president [Spiro Agnew]."

On May 18, 1970, Hoover wrote a memo to his assistant directors, including DeLoach, informing them that he had told Agnew that he had "briefed the [House] Appropriations Committee about his [Martin Luther King's] background, and it had been effective recently because they had been trying to make a national holiday of his birthday, and many of the congressmen who know the facts are opposing it."

Hoover made similar information about King's sexual activities available to the press and provided Senator Joseph McCarthy with information from the bureau's files for use in McCarthy's witch hunts against alleged Communists.[373]

On November 22, 1961, Hoover wrote a memo recounting a conversation he had had with Robert F. Kennedy, the brother of John F. Kennedy, who was then attorney general. Hoover said he told him that rumors were being circulated that John F. Kennedy, then the president, had been secretly married to another woman before Jacqueline Kennedy.

"The attorney general expressed appreciation for my concern . . ." Hoover wrote. "I stated I just wanted him to be alert to this."

On August 20, 1962, Courtney Evans, an assistant FBI director, wrote that he told Robert Kennedy that the bureau had received information that he was having an affair with a girl in El Paso, Texas. "He said he had never been to El Paso, Texas, and there was no basis in fact whatsoever for the allegation," the memo said.

"Our men were always on the lookout for anything they could dig up on the personal lives of public figures to send to Hoover . . ." wrote William C. Sullivan, an assistant to Hoover who presided over the COINTELPRO abuses. When an FBI agent in Hong Kong wrote Hoover that Richard Nixon had been friends with a

Chinese girl before Nixon became president, Hoover immediately showed the letter to the future president.

" 'I know there's no truth to this,' " Sullivan quoted Hoover as telling Nixon. " 'I'll never speak of it to anyone,' Hoover concluded with great solemnity. It was one of his favorite speeches, one he gave often to politicians."[374]

Lawrence J. Heim, who was in the crime records division, which handled public and congressional affairs, confirmed that the bureau sent agents to let members of Congress know when Hoover had picked up derogatory information on them.

"He [Hoover] would send someone over on a very confidential basis," Heim said. As an example, if the Metropolitan police in Washington had picked up evidence of homosexuality, "He [Hoover] would have him say this activity is known by the Metropolitan police department and some of our informants, and it is in your best interests to know this. But nobody has ever claimed to have been blackmailed. You can deduce what you want from that."[375]

Of course, no one ever claimed to have been blackmailed because that would have made public the embarrassing material Hoover had on him. The fact that no one complained was further testimony to the effectiveness of Hoover's leverage. If there is any doubt about that effectiveness, it is dispelled by the tapes of President Nixon's conversations in the Oval Office. In them, Nixon stated bluntly in November 1971 that he was afraid to remove Hoover as FBI director because Hoover would "pull down the temple" by releasing damaging information about him.[376]

Today, the FBI's files are still a key to the bureau's success, but not because they are used for blackmail. As a result of the Church Committee hearings, strictures imposed by Attorney General Edward H. Levi, and policies developed by Clarence Kelley and William Webster, the FBI limits its investigations and its files to information relevant to possible violations of criminal law.

"Information we collect has to be relevant to investigations," said G. Norman Christensen, the assistant director over the information management division, which maintains the FBI's files. "We teach that the agent is the first level of filter of information. It used to be that anything we got, we kept. Even during an interview the agent does not take down verbatim what is said. We don't collect dossiers on people just out of curiosity. The person receiving it has to decide if it is pertinent."[377]

Occasionally, a bureau employee improperly gives out information from the files for personal reasons or for money. For that, they are disciplined or fired. Especially sensitive criminal files and all counterintelligence files are maintained in special rooms with restricted access on the fifth floor of headquarters. Today's FBI officials would no more use information in the files for blackmail than they would give up their pensions.

While the problem of improper use of information may have been solved, the method of storing information has not. The carefully cultivated image of the FBI is that of an efficient agency on the leading edge of technology. From the laboratory's leadership in using DNA typing to the bugging devices used to eavesdrop on John Gotti, that image is deserved. But when it comes to communicating and storing information—the foundation of the FBI's work—the bureau is shockingly behind the times.

Since the early 1980s, all the Central Intelligence Agency's reports and messages from all over the world have been transmitted and stored electronically by computer. From newspapers to airline reservation offices, virtually every office in private industry uses computers for writing reports and transmitting and storing data. Yet, for the most part, the FBI still labors with manual files and indexes. Only high headquarters officials and selected officials in field offices have electronic mail for transmitting internal messages. Very few field agents have personal computers or terminals. As a rule, reports of interviews are still dictated to secretaries. With the exception of a few pilot projects, the reports are still on paper and filed manually.

The files in headquarters alone would equal the height of 275 Washington Monuments if stacked on top of one another, which represents a massive waste of paper. The index to the bureau's files contains 75 million names. Each year, it grows by 830,000 names. In any year, the bureau makes 2 million checks of its files for outside agencies. On any given day, as many as 30,000 files are in transit within headquarters. Each file has to be pulled by one of the information management division's 1,100 employees from an endless array of gray filing cabinets and placed on a conveyor system that takes it to its destination. Every field office has its own set of files, some of which duplicate files at headquarters. Most of these are still retrieved through the same three-by-five index card system Hoover developed.

William A. (Al) Bayse, the assistant director over the technical services division, is in charge of automating the bureau. With unruly sandy hair and hazel eyes, Bayse—whose name is pronounced "bays"—likes to play the role of technical genius. If he can use a technical term to describe a new computer development, he will.

Piles of computer books and technical papers cover every square inch of table space in his office. Charming and smart, he plays Mozart and Bach on his stereo and reads a quote from Rachmaninoff that he has typed on an index card: "Music is enough for a lifetime, but a lifetime is not enough for music."

"My favorite piece in the world is his second piano concerto," Bayse says, and begins humming it as he passes out another index card, this one with a quote from Winston Churchill.

After obtaining a B.S. in physics from Roanoke College, Bayse studied graduate engineering and mathematics at the University of Virginia and obtained an M.S. in technology of management from American University. The only assistant director who was never an agent, Bayse was hired by Webster in 1978 from the National Aeronautics and Space Administration and the Army. In 1979, Webster named Bayse an assistant director over technical services, which is responsible both for the FBI's computer systems and automation and for developing bugs and other highly sophisticated means of intercepting communications. Among themselves, Webster's special assistants referred to Bayse as "Q," after the inventor of James Bond's technical gizmos.

Bayse is in his element showing off some of the artificial intelligence systems his 1,026-employee division has developed. These are designed to help investigators keep track of complex investigations and to suggest new avenues to explore. Bayse has developed some powerful systems, such as the one used by counterintelligence agents to track intelligence officers from opposing services. Simply by entering details like descriptions of scars and tattoos and height and weight, the Intelligence Information System can often come up with the name of an intelligence officer who is an "unsub"—unknown or unidentified subject. Other systems display mug shots of suspects on the screen. Moreover, the engineering section within his division has developed ingenious and sophisticated devices that are more than a match for any mafia figure.

A new, $50 million building near the FBI Academy at Quantico houses the supersecret Engineering Research Facility, which develops the devices. Low-slung, with sloping lines and attractive landscaping, the tan and brown building is a contrast to the forbidding J. Edgar Hoover FBI Building in Washington.

The engineering section is headed by James K. Kallstrom, who is a legend in his own right. While working organized crime cases in New York, Kallstrom supervised installations of several wiretaps and was not impressed by the way they were done.

"I was a critic of the technical program," Kallstrom said. "It didn't seem to be that effective. It didn't seem like they had the right level of competence. It didn't seem to work quite as well as it should, and didn't have the support of the organization. They said, 'We'll shut this guy up,' and they put me in technical."[378]

When he was based in New York, Kallstrom started the Special Operations Group (SOG). Those agents conduct surveillance in criminal cases, install wiretapping devices, break in to homes and offices to install bugs, bypass alarm systems, place tracking devices on cars, break in to computers, wire undercover agents for sound, command suspects' answering machines to play back messages, and pilot surveillance planes. Besides these nefarious duties, the agents take care of the bureau's two-way radio systems and make sure bureau offices are not bugged.

In larger offices like New York, the technical agents—called soundmen—who install bugs or wiretaps are assigned to separate Technical Support squads. In smaller offices they are on the SOG squads. Because they help each other, the SOGs and the techies usually work together. By the time Kallstrom left New York, the office had fifteen SOG and Technical Support squads.

"Anything that is audio, visual, imagery—however they are communicating—we have the methodology to be there and collect that covertly," Kallstrom said, referring to his section. "We are the wiretappers, and we are the people who put microphones in."

The technical people are much in demand. In Washington, the Technical Support Squad (TSS) is known as the Tough Shit Squad because it turns down so many requests for help.

As part of an operation called SPIDERWEB, this squad in the WMFO and the engineering section near the FBI Academy developed devices that agents in the Washington metropolitan field office implanted in cars driven by KGB and GRU officers attached to the Soviet embassy in the mid-1980s. A beam installed at certain intersections recognized the devices and transmitted to monitoring agents the fact that the cars had just passed them. In this way, the FBI hoped to pinpoint the intelligence officers' activities without implanting devices that would themselves transmit signals that could be detected or that required batteries.

The FBI obtained the keys to the cars from the dealers who had sold them to the Soviets; or they would pick up the code to the keys from the sales agreements and have the keys made. At night, when the officers were usually asleep, technical agents installed the devices in the headrests of their cars. One of the cars did not have headrests, so the agents installed the device above the glove compartment. That was the bureau's undoing. When the KGB put the car up on a lift for a regular inspection for bugs, a mechanic noticed that all the bolts to the glove compartment were rusted except one. Apparently the rust had rubbed off when the FBI agents took out the bolt to get at the glove compartment. The mechanic found the FBI's device and removed it. Soviet mechanics then located the devices in the twenty other cars that had been fitted with them up to that point. After only six months, the FBI program—which cost hundreds of thousands of dollars—had to be abandoned.

An effort to bug a KGB officer's car in Washington was more successful. While the KGB officer was asleep in his apartment, technical and counterintelligence agents from the WMFO entered the underground garage where he kept his car. They unhooked the speedometer so that the odometer would not register any miles. They then drove the car to the underground garage at FBI headquarters. Meanwhile, the agents left a replacement car in the KGB officer's space. It was the same make, model, year, and color as his car. The mileage had been altered to make it conform to his car's.

In three hours, the agents had wired the officer's car for sound. They then reswitched the cars. When the KGB man sat down in the driver's seat, the seat activated a tiny tape recorder concealed in a tail light. Wires under the floorboard connected the tape recorder to a microphone in the passenger compartment. By removing the tail light reflector, agents could easily change the tapes every few days.

The KGB officer had been trying to recruit a Pentagon official, and the bug enabled the FBI to keep track of the relationship. It did not lead to anything, so the bug was not useful. But in other counterintelligence cases—and in organized crime cases such as the one involving John Gotti—ingeniously disguised bugs have produced critical evidence.

By engineering such devices, Kallstrom's section saves time and money. For example, the bureau needed a microchip to coordinate electronic interceptions in a foreign counterintelligence case.

"Three or four years ago, we would have had to go through a bidding process that would have taken a year," said Floyd Clarke, the FBI's deputy director. "It probably would have cost a hundred thousand dollars. We developed it in two weeks for five thousand."

In counterintelligence cases, the engineering section has obtained help from the CIA, which continues to be the premier electronic snooper.

In general, "They don't need to be as sophisticated as the CIA is in the bugging business because their target is primarily here in the States," said Herbert F. Saunders, former deputy director of the CIA's Office of Technical Service, which provides the agency with lock-pickers, installs bugging devices, and makes spy equipment ranging from disguises and speech-altering devices to paper used for secret writing.

"Criminals aren't likely to be able to detect a listening device unless it's dangling from a light fixture," Saunders said. "Like anyone else, the FBI gears its capability to the threat level. I would say it is more than sufficient to handle the normal threat level. Going up against Mossad, the Israeli service, might be a horse of a different color."[379]

In its latest project, the FBI's engineering section is trying to persuade Congress to pass legislation to require telephone companies to alter their software so that the FBI can tap in to calls made on digital phones. Without such alterations—which the section estimates would cost the companies $200 million—the FBI finds it virtually impossible to pinpoint the calls it is trying to tap at telephone switching stations. The alternative—placing wiretaps on lines near homes or offices—can be detected. Eventually, nearly all phones will be digital, and the bureau wants the phone companies to alter their technology before that happens. Once the changes are made, they will be incorporated into future software, and no further extra costs will be incurred. Without the changes, one of the FBI's most effective tools—one that has led to the convictions of terrorists, kidnappers, murderers, and traitors—will be virtually lost.

"We have known about the problem for four or five years," Kallstrom said. "We got the bureaucracy interested in the issue two years ago. The director and the seventh floor [where top FBI officials have their offices] saw the light two years ago. In the last two years, we have gone hot and heavy [on the issue]."

The engineering section now occupies 400,000 square feet and employs 350 agents, scientists, engineers, and support people, compared with 100 employees and 40,000 square feet ten years ago. In addition, the section deploys 300 technical agents in field offices.

But for all the successes of the engineering section and a few glitzy programs, Bayse's technical services division has been better at giving dog-and-pony shows than at automating the bureau.

"The average agent does not have access to computers to the degree necessary to do the job efficiently," said Michael Giglia, who is over a drugs and organized crime squad in Buffalo. "There is one computer for a squad of twelve to fourteen agents. It hampers the office's efficiency. You have to wait for the computer to write a report, or you dictate it."

"The agents today are computer literate," said Manuel J. Gonzalez, the assistant SAC over drugs in Miami. "They started using computers in grammar school. When they get here, they don't have a computer."

"Our level of computerization for the agents is absolutely atrocious," said Larry G. Lawler, who headed the Los Angeles office. One reason the problem has been allowed to exist is that few agents know the level of computerization achieved by the world outside the bureau. As a rule, agents have no reason to learn this. As the self-proclaimed genius, everyone looks for answers to Bayse, who tries to impress with his index cards and does not seem to grasp the problem.

While budget cuts have been a factor, "Al [Bayse] doesn't have the slightest idea of what's going on in the bureau," Lawler said. "He thinks he does. . . . He has gotten a lot of press on artificial intelligence, and it doesn't work worth a shit. It doesn't help us, and they keep putting money into it."[380]

Lawler said that he showed Sessions the pitiful state of computer technology when the director came to visit the Los Angeles office.

"I would bring Sessions into a white collar squad with fifteen agents and say, 'See this computer? That's all we have.' With forty on terrorism, they had one computer."

As one of the five SACs on an advisory board to Sessions, Lawler made sure that the level of computerization was a high priority on the board's agenda of things to fix in the bureau.

"Al Bayse knows how to sell programs," Lawler said. "He needs to be put in charge of getting money from Congress. He sold the director [Sessions] and he sold Webster. He computerized their offices. They think this whole bureau is computerized. It's not. The level of computerization is atrocious. If the public knew, they would say, 'What the hell is going on?' "[381]

Ever the showman, Bayse will acknowledge only when pressed that the bureau as a whole is still working in the precomputer age.

"We are short on work stations," Bayse said when it was pointed out that computers are a rare commodity in the bureau. "That has been a funding limitation. Originally we were going to have one computer for two agents. Now we don't even have that. Eventually we should have more."[382]

In seeking more funds for computers, the bureau has run into resistance from some members of Congress, such as Representative Don Edwards, the California Democrat, who view computerization as a threat to privacy. Edwards has no jurisdiction over the CIA and therefore has not raised objections to its state-of-the art systems.

"There is kind of a lingering uncertainty about just how automated the Congress wants us to be and, in some instances, I suspect the administration as well," said Richard W. Held, the special agent in charge of the San Francisco field office, who formerly headed Sessions's SAC advisory committee. "We are not as efficient as we could be, and in some sense, I think it's almost calculated to be that way. I think some people who pass on our budget don't know how efficient they want us to be."

"There's some degree of truth to that," said John E. Collingwood, who heads the bureau's public and congressional affairs office. "More important is the fact that people always come before equipment."

But sufficient funding will never be forthcoming if the bureau does not recognize the need. It is clear that Bayse is more interested in showing off esoteric programs at headquarters than in computerizing the field. Even the FBI's mainframe computers are a wreck. In a scathing report, the Justice Department's inspector general said that the FBI's program is "fragmented and ineffective." The report said that the bureau's programs for managing investigations are "labor-intensive, complex, untimely, and non-user friendly."[383]

The answer to privacy concerns is not to hobble the bureau with inefficient and ineffective machines but to insist that they be used properly and within the law.

Sessions, who has a special interest in technology, worked to bring the bureau into the twentieth century. Through electronic mail, he peppered Bayse with questions. On December 19, 1991, he saw a story in the *Washington Post* about a new and more powerful computer chip.

"What will this mean to us in the FBI?" Sessions typed on his computer, sending the message to Bayse, typos and all.

When Sessions first learned about a computer system called the Field Office Information Management System (FOIMS), he found out that Bayse was installing a more advanced form of the system in many offices before the initial stages had been installed in all field offices. Claiming that it would create a paperless office, the FBI first tested FOIMS in Richmond in 1979. But FOIMS allows only secretaries and specially trained personnel to perform word processing and administrative functions such as keeping track of cars and expenses. Agents are still left without computers.

"They showed me baseline FOIMS," Sessions said. "Then they told me they were going to advanced FOIMS. They said they were going in major offices. I said, 'Have you completed baseline FOIMS?' 'No.' I said, 'Do not do anything until we have the basic system in every office.' "[384]

Sessions said that all field offices and all but thirty resident agencies have FOIMS—thirteen years after the system was first tested.

Even the bureau's agency-wide internal communications are slow and not easily retrievable.

"We have a history of recording facts," said Andrew J. Duffin, who heads the Houston office and is chairman of the SAC advisory board to Sessions. "That's what we do for a living. . . . But by the time we communicate to employees issues that affect them, they've already been on the news or front page of the *Wall Street Journal*."[385]

In contrast to Bayse, G. Norman Christensen, as the assistant director over the information management division, has been making progress in modernizing the bureau—if only by cutting the amount of material the FBI retains.

"We no longer process 50 percent of the material," he said. "We have a lot of interagency material coming in. Some is current intelligence information. It keeps us up to date, but there is no reason for this organization to retain it. So that's an example of a category of information that we did not need to hold.[386]

The bureau has also stopped saving slips that the field offices use to transmit film to the laboratory for processing.

"We received fifty thousand to sixty thousand of those forms a year," said James Greenleaf, the associate deputy director for administration. "We asked the supervisors, 'Do you need this?' 'No, we just assumed you threw it away.' Nobody cared about them. So now we throw those away. That's fifty-five thousand documents that no longer need to be filed because we asked the person at the end of the chain whether you need that, and he said no."

Gary L. Stoops, a deputy assistant director, cited another example of paper that the bureau could do without: "Every time there is a pay raise, every person gets a sheet, and it goes in his or her personnel file. Eventually the person will get the paper copy, but it will not be in his or her file," meaning that no copy is kept in each employee's file. "We already have that information. Why handle it again?"[387]

"Before, there was an attitude that, 'We've always done it this way, it's working well, leave it alone,'" Greenleaf said.

However, the bureau continues to be a giant paper mill.

"We were basically, and still are, a manual operation," Christensen said. "Our investigative files are paper. We constructed a system that was so efficient. There is probably nothing that parallels our ability to retrieve information. The indexes worked wonderfully well." But, as a computer executive told Christensen, "Progress has passed you by."[388]

Now, the bureau's goal is to report and store most data electronically by 1995—something the CIA was doing fifteen years ago.

Besides cutting down on paper, Christensen wants to get rid of FBI jargon. Like many law enforcement agencies, the FBI, when given a choice, always opts for the longer and more bureaucratic term. Agents do not *call* suspects. They *contact* them *telephonically*. They do not *give* them documents or *read* them their rights. Instead, they *furnish* them with documents and *afford* them their rights. The FBI does not *do* work. It *accomplishes* its *responsibilities*.

From the NCAVC (National Center for the Analysis of Violent Crime) to the SOARU (Special Operations and Research Unit) programs, the FBI has assigned acronyms to programs that could be given simpler labels. Over time, the verbiage grows. What was the Washington field office is now the Washington *metropolitan* field office. What used to be the behavioral science unit is now the behavioral sciences *services* unit. Now that its functions have been expanded, the identification division is now the *criminal justice information services division*—a title so long that no one can remember it. Ironically, Sessions placed Christensen over the newly named division.

Meanwhile, the bureau perversely continues to misname the division that does counterintelligence the "intelligence division." As if purposely to confuse, the FBI refers to the territory covered by a field office as a "division," even though headquarters divisions cut across those same divisions.

The reasoning behind some of the terminology has been less than impressive. For example, the term *metropolitan* was added to the Washington field office so that the Alexandria field office, which was being merged with the Washington office, would not feel that its identity would be lost. Since the office never covered Washington's Maryland suburbs, which come under the jurisdiction of the Baltimore field office, the Washington metropolitan office does not cover metropolitan Washington in any case. Efforts to change the name of the intelligence division to the counterintelligence division have met with the objection that then the abbreviation for the division—CID—would be the same as the abbreviation for the criminal investigative division.

New agents learn bad writing habits on the job, according to Christensen. "The FBI Academy reviewed the writing skills of new agents," he said. "They were good writers. They were concise. What happens is they leave the academy, they get in our environment, and they learn they have to conform. They eventually abandon their practices and conform with our practices. The supervisors change it to bureau style. We say we have to change this from top to bottom."

Besides keeping the files and running the Uniform Crime Reporting Program, which collects crime statistics from sixteen thousand law enforcement agencies, the information management division processes requests for copies of files under the Freedom of Information Act. This is the function the FBI loves to hate, one that takes up tremendous resources that the bureau would like to devote to fighting crime.

Each year, the bureau receives 17,570 such requests for headquarters or field office files. The greatest proportion—13 percent—come from prisoners. Four percent come from the media and 5.5 percent from scholars. The rest come from individuals, companies, and organizations. The FBI has twelve agents and two hundred support employees who sit in brown and orange cubicles handling the requests at a cost of $15 million a year.

"I'm working on labor organization files from the 1940s," said Gloria Ruddick, an FBI analyst poring over old files. "It's interesting to see what kind of information we obtained."

The FBI claims that it takes an average of 429 days to complete requests. But that includes material that requires only a few months to process because it was sent out to someone previously. Major requests take many years to process. Requests to Congress for more money to reduce the backlog have been turned down.*

Yet, it was only through the Freedom of Information Act that many of the bureau's abuses under Hoover—including his compilation of blackmail files on members of Congress—came out.

---

* A request by the author in September 1989 for material on several deceased spies had not been received three years later.

15

Boston: Having a Picnic

● **Brendan O. Cleary,** a beefy agent in the Boston field office, looked up at the sky and felt miserable. Cleary had arranged a picnic for sixty-five people at a leafy highway rest stop near West Wellington, Connecticut. Everyone had brought picnic lunches. They were about to occupy all but four of the picnic tables on either side of Interstate Route 84 at State Highway Route 32. Those four tables had been bugged by the FBI.

As a result of some clever detective work, Cleary was sure that one of the bugged tables would soon be occupied by two men who were procuring electronic components to help the Provisional Irish Republican Army (PIRA), the international terrorist group spawned by the Irish Republican Army, to blow up British helicopters. To force the two to sit at one of the bugged tables, Cleary had arranged for agents from the Boston and New Haven offices to bring some of their family members to have picnics at the other tables that Saturday, May 27, 1989.

Just before noon, when Richard C. Johnson, an electronics engineer at Mitre Corp., and Martin Quigley, a member of the PIRA, had planned to meet at the rest stop, the sky darkened. Rain began to fall, lightly at first, then torrentially.

Cleary and the FBI's Boston office had a lot riding on recording this meeting. With 259 agents, the Boston office is the tenth largest

311

in the FBI. Located on the ninth floor of the JFK Federal Office Building in downtown Boston's Government Center, the office is spartan, with old wooden desks that are constantly being pushed around for renovations. Through undercover work, the Boston office was the first to record the mafia inducting four new members in a secret rite. It exposed widespread corruption within the Boston police department, and it played a major role in apprehending vicious terrorists known as the United Freedom Front. The Boston office was also the scene of one of the more embarrassing incidents in the modern history of the FBI—one that led to complaints directly to Attorney General William P. Barr and that brought the suspension and transfer of an agent.

The FBI first began to receive clues about the PIRA case in 1984. British authorities informed the bureau that they had been finding electronic switches inside bombs in Northern Ireland. The PIRA, which works to unify Ireland, was using the device, called a tone frequency selector switch, to detonate bombs remotely. The electronic switch, model FX-401, responded to tones that the PIRA transmitted at critical moments to detonate bombs. Many of the bombs had killed innocent civilians, including infants and children. The size of a small box of wooden matches, the component evaded countermeasures that the British had been using to neutralize the bombs.

Through a manufacturing date code of 8308 found on the switches, the FBI traced the devices to a subsidiary of a British company in Winston-Salem, North Carolina. The subsidiary had made only 430 switches with that date code. It had sold 50 of them to a company in Walnut, California, which had sold them to Richard Johnson. Then a Northrop Corporation engineer, Johnson had ordered the switches in May 1983. In September 1984, agents from the Los Angeles office questioned Johnson about the switches. Over the phone, he told them that he had bought the switches to experiment with them in burglar alarm systems he was developing on the side. While he said he may have sent electronic components to relatives in Ireland, he said he had never sent them the FX-401 switch. Johnson's attorney later told the FBI that he had advised Johnson against any further interviews.

As the British kept turning up the switches, the FBI decided to try to interview Johnson again, in February 1986. This time, he agreed to meet with the agents at his home in Irvine, California. His story was similar to the one he had given a year and a half earlier, with one difference: This time, Johnson said he might have sent a few of the FX-401 switches to relatives in Ireland.[389]

More evidence developed the following year when Republic of Ireland authorities searched the home of Peter E. Maguire, a member of the PIRA, in Clondalkin, a suburb west of Dublin. The national police suspected Maguire of heading the southern command of the PIRA's engineering section, a unit that made explosive devices. In a stove in his garage, the authorities found a series of letters signed "Tom," "TC," or "Tom Clark." While the letters were elliptical, it was clear that they referred to detonation devices. One said, "Inquiries being made here about chips sent to you."

Searching their records, the Garda Siochana, the national police, discovered that Johnson had been in Ireland in November 1978. During a traffic stop, the police had found he was driving with a PIRA recruiter. At that time, Johnson told the authorities that his name was Thomas Clark. Questioned further, he showed his American passport and admitted his true identity.

Having tied the letters to Johnson, the Irish authorities sent copies of them to the FBI. By then, Johnson had left Northrop and was working for the Mitre Corporation in Bedford, Massachusetts. As an agent who specialized in counterterrorism cases, Cleary got the case. Then a twenty-year FBI veteran, Cleary had worked counterterrorism much of his career.

Cleary noticed that one of the letters seized in Dublin said that certain material should be sent to "18721." Cleary deduced that this referred to Johnson's previous address, which was 18721 Portofino Drive in Irvine. Cleary was also troubled by the fact that Johnson had given differing stories to the FBI about whether he had sent the switches to Ireland.

"With the material contained in those letters, it was evident that Johnson was engaged in some serious activities in assisting the PIRA in a bombing campaign," Cleary said.

Mousy in appearance, Johnson had never married and had no friends. Now that he was working for Mitre, he was living in an apartment in Nashua, New Hampshire, but spent nearly every weekend with his parents at their home in Harwich, Massachusetts. Johnson's American-born mother was of Irish descent, and she had visited Ireland. But Johnson seemed to have no more motive for working for the PIRA than did Cleary, who was also of Irish heritage.

In July 1988, Cleary obtained permission from the Foreign Intelligence Surveillance Court to wiretap and bug Johnson's apartment on Casco Drive in Nashua and his parents' home on Oak Street in Harwich. Nothing interesting came up until the evening of November 16, 1988, when a woman who identified herself as Chris called

Johnson at his apartment in Nashua. Chris said that "Michael," who was a friend of "Ed," wanted to meet him. She also said that "Michael" would tell Johnson "some things . . . so you know who he is." Johnson said that he was nervous because the FBI had interviewed him.

Having analyzed the letters from Maguire's Clondalkin residence, Cleary suspected that "Ed" was Maguire, the PIRA member whose home had been searched by the Irish national police. "Michael" was Martin Quigley, a bomb expert for the PIRA.

In her call to Johnson, Chris mentioned that she was calling from San Francisco. Stockton Buck, a San Francisco agent who worked counterterrorism, surmised that Chris was likely Christina L. Reid, who was involved in activities supporting the PIRA. A student of electrical engineering at San Francisco State University, Reid was a member of the Irish Republican Socialist Party, part of the Irish National Liberation Party, which was a spinoff of the PIRA. Examining her telephone credit card records, Buck confirmed that she had placed the call to Johnson that particular evening.

A week later, Chris placed another call to Johnson at his parents' home in Harwich to firm up plans for him to meet "Michael." To evade surveillance, Johnson told Chris to call him at his home in Nashua on a given evening. Johnson would then give her a number of a nearby pay phone to call. Johnson would proceed to the pay phone and wait there for "Michael" to call fifteen minutes later.

Wiretapping every pay telephone within fifteen minutes of Johnson's apartment in Nashua would not be easy. Since this was a foreign counterterrorism case, the FBI would have to apply for permission from the Foreign Intelligence Surveillance Court to conduct the surveillance. But the court would not give blanket permission to tap the 950 pay phones in question. Cleary thought that the bureau would have to use the emergency provisions of the act that set up the court. Under this rarely used provision, once the bureau knew which phone Johnson was using, a judge from the FISA court would grant permission over the phone. Then, within twenty-four hours, Mary Lawton, the Justice Department attorney who deals with the FISA court, would have to submit written justification signed by the attorney general and the FBI director.

"We must be to the judge in twenty-four hours with the completed package and all the signatures," Lawton said. "It's a struggle. We don't use it very often for that reason."

Rather than use the emergency clause, Lawton suggested a way to limit the request. The bureau could still apply for authorization to tap the 950 phones, but before an agent could begin listening to a line, bureau agents in a surveillance van would have to see Johnson actually using that phone. In Lawton's opinion, this procedure would appropriately balance the FBI's need for flexibility with the need for specific limitations imposed by FISA and the Fourth Amendment. At the same time, it would avoid the frantic rush to obtain signatures from government officials who could be halfway around the world at the time their approval was needed.

As planned, Chris called Johnson at 10:00 P.M. on December 15, 1988. Johnson gave her three pay phone numbers to call. He said "Michael" should dial each number in sequence until he reached him. Ten minutes later, in subfreezing weather, FBI agents conducting surveillance of Johnson saw him park his car in front of the Market Basket Supermarket at South Gate Plaza in Nashua. At 10:15, Johnson walked to a public phone on the outside northern wall of the supermarket. At 10:27, the phone rang, and Johnson picked up the receiver. Meanwhile, at a telephone switching station, an FBI technical agent relayed the call to Cleary, who was at a nearby apartment house used as an offsite post.

Thinking they had prevented interception of the call, the two men talked freely. "Michael"—who was really Quigley—said that he needed Johnson's help in developing a new surface-to-air missile system "to counteract kinda low-flying helicopters." Because many roads in Northern Ireland are mined, the British use low-flying helicopters to supply their troops. The PIRA had been trying to shoot down or blow up the helicopters. Quigley, who was a PIRA technical expert, said that he wanted Johnson to design a proximity fuse capable of working at low altitudes. The fuse would fire rockets at helicopters as the rockets came within thirty or forty feet of them. Johnson said that a system using radar would be the best approach.

"I'll start working on something immediately," Johnson promised.

In February 1989, through intercepted calls at Johnson's parents' home, Cleary realized that "Ed"—who was really Maguire—would be visiting Johnson soon. The FBI bugged the meeting that month in Johnson's apartment. The two men launched into highly technical discussions about British jamming techniques and ways of detonating a remote-control bomb without risk of hostile radio interference.

Johnson told Maguire that the FBI had visited him in 1986 to ask about the switches he had bought three years earlier.

"It was all for those stupid little parts," Johnson said. "But I told the guy, 'No, I had them in my basement.' And they never bothered to look."

Through coded messages mailed to Johnson's parents' home, the two began arranging another meeting. On May 17, 1989, Quigley called Johnson at his home. Quigley mentioned the numbers 27-32 at 12. Based on some previous experience and interceptions of calls, Cleary and other Boston agents interpreted the numbers to mean that Quigley would meet Johnson at 12 noon on May 27 in Connecticut at the rest stop at the intersection of Interstate Route 84 and State Highway Route 32. Cleary arranged for the FBI's technical agents to bug two tables at either side of the rest stop. The bugs were concealed in wooden crosspieces nailed to the undersides of the tables and painted to blend with the tables. The agents and their adult family members sat at the remaining tables, ready to begin their barbecue.

Just as Johnson and Quigley drove up to the clearing, the downpour started. Cleary was afraid that the FBI would miss the conversation. Given the elaborate security precautions the two men had taken, he believed the discussion would be more detailed than at previous meetings. Lives hung in the balance.

"We were looking for basic intelligence that would break down the cells they were using to conceal their activities," Cleary said.

Because of the deluge, Johnson and Quigley drove down the interstate to a McDonald's. Cleary and his supervisor, Richard Watson, who were coordinating the operation, followed them. Cleary and other agents sat near the two men but had trouble hearing what they were saying. Then Cleary got the break he needed. After lunch, Johnson and Quigley sat in Johnson's Subaru station wagon in the parking lot. In preparation for just such a possibility, Cleary earlier had had the technical agents install a remote-controlled tape recorder in the dashboard.

Now, with the skies still opening up, Cleary got a perfectly clear recording of their conversation with the sound of rain as a backdrop. The two men discussed Johnson's progress in making the proximity fuse and other methods for downing helicopters with machine guns and missiles. Quigley said that he had been thinking about releasing balloons tied to high-strength Kevlar rope. The rope would become entangled in the helicopters' rotor blades and draw grenades or bottles filled with gasoline up into the bodies of the helicopters.

Cleary's luck was about to run out. As a rule, Cleary ordered a tape recorder installed in Johnson's station wagon only when a significant meeting was expected. Therefore, after the meeting, agents removed the tape recorder from the vehicle. However, another important meeting was coming up in mid-July. In anticipation of that, while Johnson was at work at Mitre on the morning of July 12, 1989, two agents began installing another tape recorder in the dashboard of his station wagon. They never thought Johnson would come out to the company parking lot once he was at work. But Johnson happened to notice the agents tampering with his vehicle as he walked between two of the company buildings. He immediately notified Mitre security.

With guards converging from every direction, Johnson approached his car. A quick-thinking agent pretended he was a technician who had been asked to install a new stereo system in the car. But Johnson, an electronics wizard, saw that the device on the front seat was no stereo system. There was no point in carrying the ruse any further. The agents could have allowed themselves to be arrested, but Johnson would still know that the agents were no car thieves trying to steal his radio. So, the agents showed their credentials, forestalling their arrest. Meanwhile, one of the agents called Cleary at the field office on the car phone.

"What shall we do?" he asked.

For advice, Cleary called Richard G. Stearns, the assistant U.S. Attorney who was handling the case.

"You can either arrest the two agents for car theft, or you can arrest Johnson. I recommend the latter," Stearns said facetiously.

When the agents brought Johnson to the garage at the field office, Cleary met him for the first time. Trying to ease Johnson's obvious stress, Cleary joked, "America is a great country. You catch two guys breaking in to your car, and you get arrested."

Cleary had hoped the case would go on longer so that more conspirators would be identified, but now the bureau's hand had been forced.

"We had to take the rest of it down," said Neil Gallagher, who was assistant special agent in charge in Boston during most of the case. "Time was of the essence. We initiated SIOC operations [the headquarters command center] because we had to get search warrants prepared."

In the basement of Johnson's parents' home in Harwich, agents found a bomb-making laboratory, complete with a detonation system and radar and rudimentary proximity fuses.

"It stopped their ability to shoot down low-flying British helicopters," Gallagher said. "It saved untold numbers of innocent lives." Gallagher, who later was placed in charge of counterterrorism at headquarters, called Cleary "one of the best FBI agents I've met."

Johnson, Quigley, and Reid were found guilty of conspiracy to destroy the property of a foreign government and of exporting arms illegally. Because of the types of charges, the Justice Department's internal security section supervised the prosecution. Johnson was sentenced to ten years in jail, while Quigley got eight years. Reid was sentenced to three years and five months. Maguire is a fugitive.[390]

"It was a good case, and the bureau did it right," said Lawton, the Justice Department attorney who arranged for the approval of the wiretaps.

The cases that save lives are the ones agents find most satisfying. Allan A. King, an agent in Chicago, kept dropping in on an individual he suspected was involved with Serbian nationalist terrorists.

"Most of the time they don't cooperate with you. They don't give you the information you want. But most of the time they'll meet with you, they'll parry back and forth," King said.[391]

Finally, the man, Bogoje Panajotovic, had had enough. He noticed that money raised for Serbian nationalist cases was being diverted for personal use. Then three Serbians working on explosives in Toronto had blown themselves up. Panajotovic called King and told him that the Serbians were planning to blow up hundreds of people, including children, who would be attending a reception the Yugoslav consulate was holding at a hall in south Chicago on November 29, 1977. Under the direction of John E. Otto, who was then special agent in charge, the FBI outfitted Panajotvoic with a transmitter to use when meeting with the terrorists. Over a period of months, the FBI obtained twenty-five hundred single-spaced pages of transcripts of their conversations, all of which had to be translated from Serbian into English.

"On one of the tapes," Otto said, "one of them was laughing and said, 'Half of them will break their bones and be smashed on the concrete. They'll be crushed at the door.' Another said, 'They'll jump out through the windows—that will be even more dramatic.' "

For the reception, the Serbs were planning to ship thirteen sticks of dynamite on an Amtrak train from New York to Chicago. However, before they could put the explosives on the train, the FBI arrested six Serbs, including their leader, Stojilko Kajevic, a priest in a dissident faction of the Serbian Orthodox Church. Despite objections from prosecutors, the judge in the case allowed the defendants out on bond. On his way to Chicago for sentencing, Nikola Kavaja, one of the Serbs, hijacked an American Airlines plane and demanded to be taken to Shannon, Ireland. Each of the terrorists received prison terms of ten to twenty years on bombing charges. After Irish authorities turned him over to the FBI, Kavaja got an additional forty years for hijacking the plane.[392]

Otto, who later became the FBI's executive assistant director, called the case the most rewarding one of his career. "It was because of the diligence of an agent," he said, referring to King's repeated visits to the Serbian nationalist. "He was polite and professional. That's what did it."

In the middle of the PIRA case, the Boston field office had two other major cases going: one into corruption in the Boston police, the other into the mafia family of Raymond J. (Junior) Patriarca. While attending the New England School of Law in the late 1970s, Robert J. Jordan had worked in the Boston police department's internal affairs unit, which was supposed to investigate corruption within the department. But Jordan was struck by the fact that the unit seemed to focus only on trivial disciplinary matters.

"The fact of the matter is, they were chasing police for not having their hats on while in uniform or for wrecking cars—not corruption," Jordan said. "I remember thinking to myself, 'What the hell is this? This is a major police department. You know there is something out there.' But I was not in a position to prove it."

Later, as an agent assigned to the Boston field office, Jordan was. The case started in 1982, when Jordan got court permission to bug the office of a drug dealer and bookmaker who was selling cocaine to players on the New England Patriots football team. The surveillance revealed that the drug dealer had been paying off a Boston police detective for protection.

"We decided that rather than put him in jail for drugs, we would get much more interesting cases if we pitched him," Jordan said. "He agreed to cooperate. Twenty-four hours later, we had a tape of him paying off a Boston police detective."

To explore corruption on a larger scale, Jordan went undercover. An informant who was cooperating with the FBI introduced Jordan as an entrepreneur interested in buying gay nightclubs. After meeting club owners a few times, Jordan would ask, "What is the story with the cops? What is the overhead here? Are they friendly?"

Every club but one said they were paying off the police. In the one exception, the owner said his wife was a police officer and he would have to know more about Jordan before talking about it.

"We went to twelve clubs," Jordan said. "We got all these club owners to tell us what they were doing."[393]

The clubs, most of them in Boston's Back Bay section, were paying the police to overlook a series of liquor board violations, from serving liquor to minors and overcrowding to remaining open after legal closing hours. If the clubs received too many violations, they could be closed.

Over a period of ten years, the case resulted in twenty-eight convictions, including thirteen of police officers. Using the provisions of the Racketeer Influenced and Corrupt Organizations Act (RICO), the government seized $2.7 million in club owners' assets.

More recently, the Boston office infiltrated the Patriarca mafia family and tape recorded a mafia induction—the first time this had ever been done.

Consigliere Joseph A. (J.R.) Russo conducted the ceremony on October 29, 1989, for four inductees in a two-story frame house at 34 Guild Street in Medford, Massachusetts. With lines taken straight from the movies, he told them, "This thing you're in, it's gonna be the life of the heaven. . . . It's a wonderful thing, the greatest thing in the world."[394]

As Patriarca and fifteen other mobsters from Rhode Island, Connecticut, and Massachusetts watched, Russo turned to Carmen A. Tortora, one of the inductees. He explained that as consigliere, he resolved family disputes.

"In order to belong to us, to be a part of this, Carmen, you have to have trust, truth and trust," Russo said. "Do you have that? If I told you your brother was wrong, he's a rat, he's gonna do one of us harm, you'd have to kill him. Would you do that for me, Carmen?"

"Yes," said Tortora, who had once told a loanshark customer that he would "split [the man's] head open with an ax and slit [his] throat" if he didn't pay up.

"Any one of us here asked for that?" Russo persisted.

"Yes," Tortora replied.

"So, you know the severity of This Thing of Ours," Russo said, referring to La Cosa Nostra, which is Italian for "this thing of ours" and is more commonly known as the mafia or the mob.

Tortora pricked his trigger finger and, repeating after Biagio DiGiacomo, a captain in Patriarca's family, vowed in Italian to "enter into this organization to protect my family and to protect all my friends. I swear not to divulge this secret and to obey, with love and omerta."

Omerta refers to the mafia's code of silence.

"We get in alive in this organization, and the only way we gonna get out is dead," DiGiacomo explained. "It's no hope, no Jesus, no Madonna, nobody can help us if we ever give up this secret to anybody.

"You become a member for life," DiGiacomo added. He smeared a holy card bearing the image of a saint—the FBI does not know which one—with the blood from Tortora's finger. Then, igniting the card, he instructed him to juggle it in his hands until it turned to ashes. Chanting in Italian while flames licked the saint's picture, Tortora repeated: "As burns this saint, so will burn my soul. I want to enter alive into this organization, and I will have to get out dead."

Noting that the new "made men" all came highly recommended, Patriarca, whose father, the late Raymond L. S. Patriarca, ran the organization before he took over, said, "You've all done everything you hadda do, and everybody likes you, and everybody's been watching you for a long time. Stay the way youse are, don't let it go to your head, don't because a lot of people, they get into it, and it's not to be used to make money, it's not an advantage, a ticket to abuse people. It doesn't make you better than other people. The thing is you have all of us to protect you. If [you] don't let it go to your head, and you don't abuse it, you'll have a happy, happy, happy life."

Again warning the new soldiers not to reveal any of the organization's secrets, Russo said, "To the rest of the world, this does not exist."

As the five-hour ceremony came to a close, one of the mafia members locked the doors to the two-story frame home.

"Only the fuckin' ghosts knows what really took place here today, by God!" he remarked.

"We were salivating, of course," said William Baker, the assistant director over the criminal investigative division, who heard the tape shortly after it was made.

Attorney General Richard Thornburgh and Sessions flew to Boston to announce the indictments of Patriarca, his top lieutenant, and more than a dozen other members of his mafia family on RICO and other violations. When played at their trials, the tapes put to rest the mafia's claim that it does not exist, or that it is a social club.[395]

"What was said is just classic stuff," said Thomas A. Hughes, special agent in charge of the Boston office. "Never accomplished before, and will be in demand for years in other prosecutions of organized crime people who claim there is no organized crime."

"It just confirmed everything we've been trying to tell people," said Dennis O'Callaghan, an assistant agent in charge who was one of the agents eavesdropping on the conversation from a nearby command post. "There are still doubters who say the mafia is a figment of the government's imagination. I knew as soon as we heard the oath we'd never have to listen to doubters again."

The Boston office began selling T-shirts with Casper on the back and ONLY THE GHOSTS KNEW WE WERE HERE on the front.

U.S. District Court Judge Mark L. Wolf took the glow off by sentencing Patriarca to only eight years and one month in jail. He fined him $50,000 and ordered him to pay $122,344 for the cost of his confinement. Although Russo had admitted murdering Joseph Barboza Baron, he received only sixteen years. Tortora got thirteen years. The sentences were the lowest for any mafia figures convicted in New England in the previous decade.[396]

Wolf said that he was following sentencing guidelines, which took into account the fact that Patriarca had no previous criminal record. Prosecutors argued that the fact that Patriarca was boss of the family and had knowledge of the murders of Vincent J. Limoli and Theodore Berns was relevant under the guidelines. But by Wolf's interpretation, since the murders had nothing to do with the acts Patriarca was charged with—loansharking, narcotics violations, and gambling—they should not be taken into account. When U.S. Attorney A. John Pappalardo criticized the decision, Judge Wolf admonished him for not paying attention to the reasoning Wolf had set forth.

Regardless of how the guidelines are interpreted, judges have considerable discretion in sentencing defendants. The prosecutors had asked for a sentence of sixty-five years for Patriarca. The sentence Wolf handed down was more appropriate to a drug dealer or bank robber than to someone who had been found guilty of running an enterprise that had committed murders and terrorized people.

Trying to put the best light on it, Hughes said, "The upper echelon of this family is out of commission and away. You can't run an OC [organized crime] family from prison. Raymond couldn't be a chambermaid for an LCN family because he allowed this to happen, including being taped at a La Cosa Nostra induction ceremony. He's done and finished."[397]

Next to his desk, Hughes keeps an assistant fire chief's hat. When he left his previous assignment as special agent in charge of the San Diego field office, agents gave it to him as reminder of one of his first days heading the office. He and another agent had walked into a government building to meet the police chief of nearby Calexico, California.

"I went into this building," Hughes recalled. "I said, 'Is the chief in?' The receptionist said yes. We sat and talked to him and said, 'We are here to help.' He said, 'It's nice of you guys to come out here. We don't have much arson work here.' There I was, talking to the fire chief."

Hughes never told the fire chief that he had meant to meet with the police chief. The hat, with a Calexico Fire Department patch on it, says, YOUR LIAISON IS THE KEY TO OUR SUCCESS.[398]

Unlike most FBI agents, Hughes, an accountant, is taciturn, almost cold, and not known for his people skills. But he has a reputation for doing a professional job.

In contrast to Hughes, James Greenleaf, one of his predecessors, was smooth and sharp. When he headed the Boston office, agents figured out the location of members of the United Freedom Front, a small group that advocated overthrowing the U.S. government and claimed responsibility for ten bombings and one attempted bombing from 1982 to 1984. The group was also implicated in the wounding of a Massachusetts state trooper and the murder of a New Jersey state trooper. Greenleaf, who was also in charge when the Boston police corruption case started, put together a task force of local, state, and federal law enforcement agencies to hunt for the United Freedom Front's members.

"As in all good cases, you need a little bit of luck," Greenleaf said. "One of the subjects had rented a storage space and never returned. The owner discovered some radical literature and cash bags from bank robberies. He called the FBI."[399]

With the help of a Connecticut state trooper who was a member of the task force, through a letter the FBI traced the owner of the material to Connecticut and then to Ohio. In Cleveland, the FBI arrested Raymond Luc Levasseur and other members of the gang in November 1984. In their effects, agents found a receipt showing that Carol Manning, the wife of Thomas W. Manning, one of the gang's other leaders, had purchased a gun through a rented box at a Mail Boxes Inc. in Norfolk, Virginia.

"We went to the box, and it was still active, which we couldn't believe," said John C. (Jack) Wagner, who was special agent in charge of the Norfolk office. "We made a fast and hard decision that we were going to watch it. These were the most wanted people in the FBI at that time."[400]

On April 24, 1985, Carol Manning came to get her mail.

"Our guy observes her," Wagner said. "He says, 'God, it sure looks like her.' It was her. We had surveillance teams in the area ready to go. We also had a plane up in a short period of time."

Carol Manning drove to a two-family home where she was living with her husband and children on the first floor. Agents identified the family on the second floor and called the husband at a restaurant where he was the manager.

"He is scared out of his wits," Wagner said. "He says, 'My wife and kids are there.' We said, 'Can you get them out of there?' He says, 'Well, my wife is pretty savvy. Let me call her.' Somehow in a nice way he tells her, 'Come meet me. You have to get out of there.' He doesn't panic her. Lo and behold, she goes, and on the way out sees Carol Manning and says, 'I'm going out for a while.' "

Wagner deployed thirty agents to surround the house. At one point, Tom Manning went into the backyard with his three children to read a book in the sun. As Wagner was rushing to the scene, his two-way car radio went on the blink. He had to run to a pay phone at a 7-Eleven to supervise the case. Marty Houlihan, the case agent, told him he wanted to arrest Manning.

"I said, 'You can take him down, but I don't want the kids in the picture,'" Wagner said. Finally, the children went inside. "Fifteen seconds later, fifteen agents descended on him," Wagner said. "The only thing he said was, 'Ah, shit.' "

In the meantime, Robert Hunter and Beverly Andress, who were watching Soviet spy John Walker, happened to be driving in the area when they heard the call on the radio to converge on Carol Manning. With the help of a third agent, they arrested her as she left a grocery store.

Manning, his wife, Levasseur, and other members of the group were convicted and sentenced to long prison terms.[401]

Today, the biggest problem facing the Boston field office is fraud against banks. In the four states covered by the Boston office—Massachusetts, Rhode Island, New Hampshire, and Maine—Boston agents are investigating fraud cases that have caused more than $1 billion in losses.

"It's just one scam after another," said Hughes, the head of the Boston office. "We have thirty-five agents for that type of work. That has become the top investigative program of this division [field office]."

Whatever the great work of an office, no story circulates faster within the bureau than an embarrassing internal-personnel case. Of all the stories in recent memory, none is quite so mortifying as the one involving Paul M. Dimura. A Boston agent who had been in the FBI for five years, Dimura was assigned to conduct a background investigation of Walter B. Prince, a Boston lawyer who was about to be nominated by President Bush to become a federal judge. As Dimura explained it later, Prince was slow to return the agent's calls. When Prince finally came into the field office for an interview, he seemed impatient with Dimura's questions.

"Is that all?" Dimura quoted the lawyer as saying as the agent was wrapping up the interview.

Frustrated, Dimura said, "Well, we need a footprint."

The agent later said that he had meant it as a joke. Unless it is relevant to a particular crime, the FBI does not take footprints. But Prince, who represents the Boston School Committee and has lectured at the Boston College School of Law, assumed that Dimura was serious. He had no way of knowing that a footprint is not a requirement of a background investigation. Once Prince took him seriously, Dimura did not want to admit that he had been toying with the lawyer. He felt compelled to follow through. After the lawyer took off his shoes and socks, Dimura got a roller and inked his feet with it. He then made an impression of his feet on a sheet of paper.

Dimura later boasted about what he had done to other agents and showed them the prints of the nominee. One of the agents anonymously complained to an assistant special agent in charge. Meanwhile, through friends at the Justice Department, Prince learned that footprints are not required—that he had been had.

Charging that the act was racially motivated, Prince, who is black, demanded that then Attorney General William Barr fire Dimura. In response to the anonymous complaint, the ASAC had taken little action.

After an investigation by the FBI's Office of Professional Responsibility, Dimura was suspended for forty-five days in July 1992, reduced in pay grade, and transferred to another office for "loss of effectiveness," meaning that he had to be transferred because he could not continue to perform his duties effectively in Boston. The ASAC was disciplined for failing to take firm enough action.[402]

For unknown reasons, Bush never did nominate Prince.

Claiming that he wanted to protect the judge, Hughes became furious when asked about the incident.

"If it wasn't for you, this wouldn't have come out," Hughes said. "I'm concerned about the judge. . . . I would rather the book didn't come out at all than to have this in it."[403]

"Don't embarrass the bureau," Hoover always said. The Boston footprint case was one time when that maxim would have come in handy.

16

Administrative Division: Pockets of Prejudice

● **While assigned to the FBI Academy,** Roger L. Depue spent much of his time profiling serial killers and rapists. But at a meeting of the FBI's top executives in Virginia Beach in January 1988, Depue described a different kind of suspect: FBI agents who engage in racist or sexist behavior. The reaction from the FBI hierarchy was shock.

"There is a certain amount of resistance in the FBI to the idea that there is prejudice," said Depue, who then headed the behavioral science unit. "A lot of our leaders didn't want to believe it."

In preparing that talk, Depue had made an informal study of racism and sexism in the FBI. Along with Jimmy C. Carter, a black agent who taught cultural diversity as part of a course in sociology at the academy, Depue had selected twenty-five of the most outstanding minority and women agents at five field offices. These agents were highly respected by both their supervisors and their peers. They were not malcontents or slackers. Depue and Carter had purposely weighted the study in this way. If these agents reported racism and sexism, there would be no way to minimize what they said.

Depue and Carter asked these blacks, Hispanics, American Indians, Asians, and women if they had ever experienced discrimination in the FBI. As Depue related it at the executive conference, the agents did not perceive the FBI as a racist organization. But nearly every one of the agents reported prejudiced remarks or putdowns that made them feel uncomfortable, if not angry.

"There were several agents going out to lunch," Depue told the conference. "Three white, an Hispanic, and a black agent. The black agent, as he approached the group, was putting his coat on. His collar was turned up, and his tie was askew. The white agent straightened it. Then the black agent said, 'I forgot something. I'll be right back.' The white agent said, 'You can take the boy out of the jungle . . .' and laughed. The Hispanic agent, who told us the story, didn't laugh."

In some cases, Depue said, minority and women agents had experienced clear-cut discrimination in addition to offensive remarks.

"A woman agent, an excellent agent, was the only female on a squad," Depue related. "The squad members were suiting up to go on an arrest on a case she had worked on. She was just coming in. She said, 'What is going on?' One agent told her they had gotten a tip on the case. She said great. So she starts suiting up. The case agent looked at her and said to her, 'We're not taking any broads along on this.' "

Depue's talk was a defining moment for the FBI, one that Sessions used to further his goal of transforming the bureau into an agency that not only enforces laws against discrimination but promotes equality in its employment practices. A year earlier, Bernardo Matias (Mat) Pérez, an Hispanic agent, had filed suit alleging discrimination against Hispanics. Donald Rochon, a black agent, had just filed a suit, alleging that he had been discriminated against and harassed because he was black. Then as now, agents had differing opinions on the merits of those suits. But what Depue and Carter portrayed that day to the executive conference—and repeated again two months later to the SAC conference—was incontrovertible.

In some respects, the bureau was reaping the consequences of Hoover's policies, which left no room for females and very little room for blacks. Because Hoover's management style was so harsh and arbitrary, nearly everyone felt discriminated against in the sense that they worked in an environment where unfairness was the norm.

"I was the subject of those very poor personnel policies," said Weldon Kennedy, the assistant director over the administrative services division. In that capacity, Kennedy is responsible for the bureau's personnel, budget, and buildings, including a force of security guards, incongruously called FBI Police. Together with the FBI's equal employment opportunity affairs office, Kennedy sets FBI hiring and promotion policies.

After graduating from the University of Texas, Kennedy had been a Navy intelligence officer. In November 1963, Kennedy became an FBI agent assigned to Portland, Oregon. Seven months later, the bureau transferred him to Washington to attend Russian language school.

"The day before my arrival in Washington, Hoover changed my orders," Kennedy said. "This was on a Friday. 'Monday report to Newark.'"

Apparently, Hoover had seen a list of the agents going to language school and had become angry, saying that too many agents were doing that.

"I had a houseful of goods en route from Portland to Washington," Kennedy said. "I reported in and tried to find my household goods. I had never been to Newark or heard of it. I'm from Texas."[404]

Two years later, headquarters decided that Kennedy should attend language school after all, but this time to learn Spanish in Monterey, California.

"By then I had two children, a wife," Kennedy said. "I had to sell the house and move in nine days. You received absolutely no assistance on your house. That was your problem. You had no financial consideration for temporary quarters. That was your problem. Back across the U.S. I go for the third time. We don't do things like that anymore. We were inhuman."

Six months after that, the bureau transferred Kennedy to Key West, Florida.

Hoover's inconsistent discipline policies fostered an atmosphere of cynicism. For the same offense, one agent might be fired or transferred to Butte, Montana, while another might receive a letter of censure. Agents who flattered Hoover or gave him gifts might get off scot-free.

In his book, William C. Sullivan, former assistant to Hoover over intelligence, recounted getting a call at 2:00 A.M. from the Baltimore field office. It seemed that Hoover's driver had been arrested for drinking and for hitting the arresting police officer. Sullivan assumed that the driver was reacting to the shabby way Hoover usually treated him. A few hours later, an agent reported to Sullivan that he had seen the driver in his cell.

"He's still drunk and cursing Hoover like I've never heard anyone speak about the old man," the agent reported.

To try to save the driver's job, Sullivan and other headquarters officials told the Baltimore office to submit a memo stating that when Baltimore agents saw the driver in his cell, he was on his knees praying.

"Good Lord, I'll always condemn myself as long as I live for embarrassing Mr. Hoover," the memo quoted the driver as saying. "I don't care what happens to me, it's Mr. Hoover I'm concerned about."

The ruse worked. Hoover said he would overlook the infraction that one time. "That's how we protected ourselves, playing on his ego," Sullivan said.[405]

Clarence Kelley, in his book, said that when the agent gave him a wristwatch, Hoover forgot about lecturing one SAC whose statistics were below par. Another agent avoided censure over his statistics when he brought him a coconut cake.[406]

Hoover occasionally showed his human side by canceling transfers of agents who were suffering personal hardships. Any employer might take such actions, but because they stood in such contrast to the bureau's normally unfeeling practices, many agents took them as signs that Hoover was a magnanimous man.

"In the past, Hoover was the organization," said Lee Colwell, an associate director under Webster. "It was his child. He was married to it. With that went all the parental intrusions into personal lives."

While punishment has become more consistent and personnel practices more enlightened, the bureau still displays the kind of unfairness inherent in bureaucracies.

"The organization still protects itself," Colwell said. "It always will. That's the nature of it. There is nothing unusual about that. . . . It has a tendency to put the blame on someone. If something happens, someone has to be accountable within the bureau, thereby protecting the rest of the bureau. . . . That's where some of the horror stories start. The bureau sets out to make examples of some people."[407]

Expressing a widespread feeling, Chris Mazella, a Miami agent, said, "If you are in the FBI, you are going to be discriminated against in one way or another by the nature of the job."

Everyone in the bureau felt discriminated against under Hoover, but minorities had even more reason to feel that way. Although police departments had been hiring female officers for decades, Hoover refused to admit female agents. Before John F. Kennedy became president, the bureau had only a handful of black agents. According to Weldon Kennedy, they drove Hoover around when he visited field offices.

"At one point under Hoover there was criticism there were no black agents," Kennedy said. "He rectified that. He had a black employee who was kind of a driver and gofer and several others scattered around the U.S. in Los Angeles, Chicago, New York, and Washington, D.C. So he made them all special agents of the FBI with no training. I met all of them because my first in-service [training] in 1965 had them in my class. They had not gone through the training course."

As a result of pressure from John F. Kennedy and his brother Robert, who was his attorney general, Hoover began accepting more blacks. But in 1972, when Hoover died, the FBI had only 70 blacks and 69 Hispanics out of 8,659 agents.

Within the FBI, the only official action that L. Patrick Gray is remembered for during his year as acting director is that he began accepting female agents. But it was not until Webster became director in 1978 that the FBI began actively recruiting women and minority agents. In doing so, Webster had to overcome the stereotypes that Hoover—and to some extent society in general—had fostered.

To Hoover, image was all. In testimony before the House Appropriations Committee in 1966, he spoke about the qualifications he looked for in agents.

"I will not appoint any man merely because of the color of his skin," Hoover said. "We have some employees who are full-blooded Chinese. We have white and Negro employees. I will not lower the qualifications. I must insist that appointees be above average in intelligence and reputation, of good character, and be above average in personal appearance."

In that regard, Hoover cited Efrem Zimbalist, Jr., who played the FBI inspector in the television series *The FBI*.

"In other words," Hoover said, "there is an image that people have of the FBI. I want our agents to live up to that image."[408]

To Webster, Efrem Zimbalist, Jr., was no more an example of what an agent should be than was Bill Cosby. There was a need for FBI agents to reflect society in general. That was not only the right thing to do, it was the practical thing to do. Black agents might have a better chance of gaining the confidence of black informants or witnesses than white agents. Undercover operations demanded agents of all races and both sexes. Whatever their race, agents were more likely to obtain information from minorities if the FBI as a whole had a reputation as an integrated agency.

Drawing on his experience as a judge, Webster devised an ingenious way to accept more minorities and women without running afoul of laws that ban preferential treatment. He divided applicants into seven categories—minorities, women, lawyers, accountants, applicants who spoke needed languages, and applicants who had scientific or engineering backgrounds. Known as "diversified," a seventh category was for white males. Saying that the bureau might need more of one category than another at any given time, Webster then weighted applicant test results. A white male had to score at least 34, while a minority applicant had to score 31, an attorney or accountant 31.5, a female 32, and an applicant who spoke a critical language 29.5.

If this was an early form of affirmative action, it did not necessarily bring in less-qualified agents. While women, minorities, and applicants with special skills had an edge in getting into the FBI's training program, in the end each had to pass the same tests before graduating from the academy. The only exception to that was women, who had to pass less rigorous physical tests at the academy.

At the same time, Webster tried to put an end to the old boy network—the tendency of the bureau's career boards, which pass on promotions, to promote people they know. While he was director, Webster also named two outstanding blacks—John D. Glover and Wayne G. Davis—as executive assistant director and an SAC, respectively. Glover was the highest-ranking black agent in the FBI's history.

"It helps a person's chances for promotion if someone on the career board knows them," Webster said. "If you are talking about women, blacks, or Hispanics, the chances of their having a rabbi on the board are lower. I had to keep reminding the people who had those responsibilities that they should be looking beyond their own personal acquaintances."[409]

Webster kept a card in his wallet showing the numbers of minority and women agents. During his nearly ten years as director, the number of minority agents more than doubled, from 413 to 943. The number of women increased fivefold, from 147 to 787. By the time Webster left the FBI to become director of Central Intelligence, 10 percent of the FBI's agents were minorities and 8 percent were women.

When Sessions took office on November 2, 1987, he was immediately confronted with problems related not to hiring but to the promotion and treatment of minorities. Symbolized by the Pérez and Rochon lawsuits, these were the problems Depue addressed in his talk to the executive conference just after Sessions took over. The idea of an agent filing a lawsuit against the bureau would once have been unthinkable.

"Back in Hoover's day, if someone said they were unhappy, they could go someplace else to work," said D. Caroll Toohey, the assistant director over the inspection division. "The discontent did not rise to the management level because the management had a different way of dealing with it," meaning that management ignored it.

But these were different times. A well-regarded agent, Pérez zeroed in on the fact that the bureau tended to assign agents of Hispanic descent to work in areas populated by Hispanics or to translate Spanish. While this may sound perfectly reasonable, it meant that Hispanic agents were unintentionally being denied the opportunity to participate in programs that might advance them faster.

Praising the bureau as "arguably the best law enforcement agency in the world," U.S. District Court Judge Lucius D. Bunton ruled for Pérez and the class of Hispanic agents he represented. More disturbingly, the judge found that Pérez's supervisors in Los Angeles had retaliated against him. Because he had complained, he had received negative ratings. Bunton ordered Pérez and others promoted.[410]

The Justice Department and the FBI's legal counsel advised Sessions that an appeal would probably be pointless. Moreover, Sessions had already put into effect many of the remedies the judge ordered. In September 1990, Sessions accepted the judge's decision and said the bureau would promote eleven Hispanic agents involved in the suit, including Pérez.

To Sessions, it was the right thing to do and a way to communicate his determination to change the way things had been done in the past—to show that he was serious about making sure minorities were treated equally. Many agents and bureau officials were outraged.

"I think we should have appealed it," said Buck Revell, who, as executive assistant director at the time, was asked for and gave his opinion to Sessions. "Judge Bunton clearly ignored compelling evidence of Pérez's poor performance and statistics showing this was not institutional discrimination against Hispanics."[411]

Given the response to his decision, it would have been easier for

Sessions to appeal. Nevertheless, agents began calling him "Consessions" for having accepted the court's decision.

"There was a hard core of white agents who told the director he was a knee jerk liberal," said Pérez, now SAC in Albuquerque. "In their anger, they said they wanted him to appeal the case. These are supposed to be trained investigators. They didn't realize that the Justice Department had advised the FBI not to appeal."[412]

The same outcry greeted Sessions's decision to settle Rochon's lawsuit. Formerly a Los Angeles police officer, Rochon began working for the FBI in Los Angeles in 1981. In 1983, he was transferred to Omaha, where other agents began harassing him and his then wife, Susan, who is white.

According to findings by the Equal Employment Opportunity Commission, a picture of a black man and a white woman was placed in Rochon's interoffice mail slot. Rochon received invitations to office functions with the words "don't come" scribbled on them. Bogus telephone messages were left for him. When he called the numbers, he heard black preachers delivering sermons. Other numbers were those of unsuspecting blacks who became alarmed when they learned that an FBI agent was calling. After Rochon discussed taking scuba diving lessons, he found on his desk a mechanized toy scuba diver, its skin blackened with a felt pen. He found a photo of his two children on his desk with a gorilla's face pasted over them.

Rochon complained to his supervisor, Michael J. Santimauro, who talked with some of the agents involved. Rochon also complained to the field office's EEO officer, Charles R. Wylie, who also is black. Wylie had no use for Rochon, whom he considered a slacker and complainer. Indeed, most of the agents who worked with Rochon or supervised him—white or black—rated him a substandard agent.

Wylie considered Rochon an "embarrassment to this organization" who, when confronted with his "ineptness and incompetency, immediately assumed that this was an attack on him because he was black."[413]

Wylie and other black agents who had worked in Omaha said they had never experienced any problems.

"I have been in the bureau for fifteen years, and I've never had a racial problem," said Ray E. Jones, a black agent who is a counselor at the FBI Academy and worked in Omaha with some of the agents who harassed Rochon. "In Omaha, there was only one other black agent. Never a problem," he said.[414]

Washington attorney Carl Rowan, Jr., the black son of the columnist and a former FBI agent, roomed with Tom Dillon, one of Rochon's antagonists, when they were going through training. He described Dillon as a "class guy, a terrific leader, just a quality guy in all respects. . . . In my experience, in my opinion, Tom Dillon does not have a racist bone in his body."

But it was clear that the perception of Rochon as an incompetent whiner had brought out racist behavior.

After Santimauro warned other agents to leave Rochon alone, a more subtle campaign began. Agents circulated rumors that Rochon had burned out an auto engine by idling it all night to keep it warm in cold weather; that when he jogged in the rain, he carried a lightning rod; that during a surveillance, Rochon slept in the backseat of a bureau car.[415]

No formal action was ever taken against Rochon's harassers. Herbert L. Hawkins, Jr., the SAC in Omaha, called Rochon a "cry baby" who had "poor work habits." He said he considered the pranks to be "healthy" and a sign of "camaraderie."

In 1984, Rochon sought a transfer to Los Angeles or San Francisco but was sent instead to Chicago. The EEOC ruled that since all twelve agents who left Omaha during the same period received transfers to the areas they had requested, Rochon's transfer to Chicago was another act of discrimination. In supporting a complaint that he should have been transferred to California, Rochon said that both Omaha and Chicago discriminated against minorities. In Omaha, he claimed, he had been denied rental housing because of his race. But the facts established by the FBI were quite different.

"What Rochon alleged had nothing to do with race," said Robert Siller, a black agent who investigated Rochon's complaints for headquarters. "It had to do with the fact that Rochon had a big dog. One person he was trying to rent from did not want him there because of the dog. Another location [that turned him down] also had nothing to do with race."[416]

No one saw the larger picture. If Rochon was incompetent, he should have been fired. If not, he should have been helped. In either case, his harassers should have been disciplined. Blindly, headquarters looked at the fact that Rochon had apparently made up a story about being discriminated against in housing and came up with a bureaucratic—which is to say stupid—solution.

"We either had an agent lying or one who failed to file notice he had been discriminated against," Revell said. "They [the administrative services division] decided they did not want to ruin his career, so they simply gave him the lesser penalty of failing to file a report, rather than calling him a liar. That would have been a much more serious offense. That act of forgiveness turned out to be what they called retaliation, which was absolutely bullshit. It was an attempt by the people involved to give him the benefit of the doubt. . . . That is the kind of thing that alienated everyone he worked with. He wove everything into a conspiracy."

For failing to report that he had been discriminated against, Rochon was censured, the first time an agent had been disciplined for failing to report a violation of law against himself. The EEOC ruled that that, too, was an act of discrimination.

In Chicago, the harassment continued. By coincidence, Dillon had been transferred there as well and sat within twenty feet of him. Rochon began receiving calls at home and when he arrived at his office. The callers would hang up, breathe heavily, or refer to interracial sexual relationships. Some threatened him with mutilation or death. One letter received in Rochon's interoffice mail began, "Asshole, look at your future reward for your deed. You made yourself a nigger and shall pay the price. . . ." Another letter said, "Your wife is a cheap whore and we can fuck her anytime in your secret Niggerville house."

Rochon received bills at home for life insurance policies he never applied for and one thousand dollars in other items he never requested, including a fee for membership in a dating service for white women. In April 1986, he received a bill for an ad in the *Chicago Tribune*. Referring by name to Rochon and his wife, it said, "Mr. EEO, We thank you and your wife for visiting us. You will be missed."[417]

Most of the perpetrators were never identified. But Chicago agent Gary Miller, who admitted filling out a coupon that led to Rochon's receiving a life insurance policy, told Phil McCombs of the *Washington Post* that filling out coupons is "one of the oldest practical jokes in the bureau. You get someone on a mailing list. It's just for yucks. I'm not a racist. I have good relations with black people."

Jerry Webb, the agent who put the blackened toy scuba diver on Rochon's desk, said, "It was never meant as a racial joke. It was funny. The fact that he was black had nothing to do with it."

In response to Rochon's complaints, the Chicago office took strong action that eventually led to a grand jury investigation to see if Rochon's civil rights had been violated.

"I have always been disappointed that the bureau was lambasted for that case when, in fact, we got to the bottom of it," said Milt Ahlerich, who, as an assistant special agent in charge in Chicago, took Rochon's complaints. "We found an agent who had sent insurance letters and forms anonymously to Rochon. That was different from what happened in Omaha."[418]

Siller, the black agent who investigated the Rochon case for headquarters, said, "My opinion is it started out unintentionally, and it just got out of hand. It did not appear to be outright discrimination from the outset. But at some point it could be interpreted that way. There was behavior that was not tolerable."

"When he started having problems [performing his job], his problems should have been dealt with, and the problems eradicated," Revell said. "The problems should not have been the basis for being harassed. The agent in charge in Omaha said, 'These are guys being guys. Don't worry about it.' "[419]

In 1986, Rochon was transferred to Philadelphia, where Wayne Davis, the black SAC, did not consider him a stellar agent.

"If I had to rate him, I couldn't rate him among the better agents in the office," Davis said. But, Davis said, the previous experiences probably had had a negative impact on Rochon.

Some thought that Rochon had been subjected to pranks rather than harassment. Carl Rowan said that when he was an agent, he went on a diet of bananas. "I always had a couple of bananas in my briefcase," he said. "One day the guys in the squad filled my desk with bananas. I got a good laugh out of it . . . but if I'd wanted to make the bureau look bad, I'd say it was racial."

Thomas F. Jones, a black agent who served most recently as chief of the FBI's public affairs office, pinpointed what had happened much better. He said that pranks cross the line into harassment when the joke "ceases to draw humor" from the intended target. Clearly, that had happened with Rochon.

In August 1990, Sessions settled the case. Rochon left the bureau, and the FBI agreed to give him disability payments with a differential that would bring him to full salary assuming that he could continue to show he was emotionally and mentally disabled and could not be gainfully employed elsewhere. He also received attorneys' fees. While the settlement was widely reported to total one million dollars, in fact, said Joseph R. Davis, the assistant director who heads the FBI's legal division, "How much it costs depends on a number of factors. It was tied to a disability claim with the Labor Department. If it was one million dollars, it would have been a good deal for the FBI. The facts were bad for the FBI in certain areas. Some of the things the FBI was accused of were not valid. There was some truth there."[420]

Sessions disciplined eleven agents for harassing Rochon or ignoring his complaints, suspending them without pay for up to twenty-one days. Having ruled that the Omaha office had discriminated against Rochon, the EEOC ordered agents there—including Hawkins, who had been Rochon's SAC in Omaha—to undergo sensitivity training. It also ordered censure for failing to report discrimination expunged from Rochon's record. Nothing came of the criminal investigation in Chicago.[421]

If Rochon's civil suit against the bureau had gone to trial, "It would have been very embarrassing for the public to hear that the FBI has agents who are that stupid," said Larry Lawler, a former member of Sessions's SAC advisory committee. "There was good reason to get rid of that case."

Again, many agents criticized Sessions for caving in. Their criticism demonstrated that the bureau still had a lot to learn about racial sensitivity. As in the Pérez settlement, Sessions not only wanted to put such divisive issues behind him, he wanted to make it clear that whether purposeful or not, discrimination—or the appearance of it—would not be tolerated.

"I think he has used the Rochon and Pérez suits to bring about change in the FBI," said John L. McKay, Jr., a White House fellow who was one of Sessions's assistants at the time. "I think the reason he didn't appeal them was so he could use that to create change," meaning Sessions would send a message to agents that way.

If nothing else, in the wake of the lawsuits, pranks have became a thing of the past.

"Because of the possibility of harassment complaints and the heightened awareness, the pranks that used to be done are just not done," said Donald Ramsey, an agent in Dallas. "You never know when you might really offend someone. Most agents have cut it out unless they do it with a friend."

Long before the Rochon or Pérez lawsuits, Roger Depue, who studied racism and sexism in the bureau while teaching at the FBI Academy, knew that the FBI had a problem, and he was trying to do something about it. No one could accuse Depue of being a bleeding heart liberal. The son of a deputy police chief, Depue had served as a police officer and police chief in Clare, Michigan, before joining the FBI in 1968. Boyish and personable, with a big, white-toothed smile, Depue had been an agent in New Orleans, where he worked civil rights investigations. In doing so, he developed an appreciation for what blacks were experiencing as well as what the FBI was doing about it. Despite Hoover's well-publicized harassment of Martin

Luther King, it was Hoover's bureau that helped bring justice to the South. The FBI successfully investigated the killings by Ku Klux Klan members of Viola Liuzzo, a civil rights worker from Detroit, and civil rights workers James E. Chaney, Andrew Goodman, and Michael Schwerner, who were murdered near Philadelphia, Mississippi.

"I really don't think the black community knows or appreciates the work the FBI did," Depue said. "If you arrested a Klansman, there were certain parishes [counties] where the sheriff wouldn't take the prisoner. You had to take the prisoner in the back of a bureau car, and you would have to drive through several parishes before you found one that would take him. Sometimes you had a parade of pickup trucks following you. There was a tremendous effort to intimidate agents."

Depue later went to the Washington metropolitan field office and served on its SWAT team. He became an instructor at the FBI Academy, where he received training from Howard Teten in profiling criminal suspects. In 1980, Depue became chief of the behavioral science unit, responsible not only for profiling but for a range of research projects and instruction to new and on board agents.

One of the things Depue taught the new agents was a sociology course that included instruction on cultural diversity. In the early 1980s, Depue taught that racial jokes are not funny and must not be tolerated; that FBI agents, of all people, must be free of prejudice; and that in response to racial and sexist incidents, agents and supervisors must take an aggressive stand.

Jimmy C. Carter, the black agent who later helped Depue study prejudice in the FBI, was one of his students.

"I was impressed," Carter said. "I decided when I grow up, I'm going to be like him. I never forgot it."

A similar experience when Carter was in the sixth grade in Memphis had gotten him interested in the FBI. An agent had visited his class looking for future FBI support employees—not agents. But Carter, whose mother was working three jobs, saw being an agent as a way out of the life most of his classmates would have, working in the cotton fields.

Carter confided his ambition to his sixth-grade teacher, who derided his goal. "She said, 'What you ought to do is major in agriculture so you can work on a farm,'" Carter said. " 'You'll never be successful as an agent. You're not smart enough.' " The teacher was a light-skinned black, and in the South, Carter explained, "If you were a dark black person, there was segregation among your own. The light-skinned blacks tended to get more positive reinforcement."

Despite his teacher's discouragement, Carter read up on the FBI in the library. "I learned there were blacks in the FBI," he said. "There weren't a lot, but there were some."

As Carter got older and obtained a B.A. and an M.A. from the University of Louisville, his ambition to join the FBI never wavered. "People said, 'Why would you want to go to the other side?' But I never gave up, even though beatings of blacks by the police commonly occurred."

In 1971, Carter joined the Louisville police department and became a sergeant. In 1980, he applied to the FBI and was accepted. In Depue's class at the FBI Academy, Carter learned how to deal with discrimination—how to take a stand and face down comments that had racial overtones.

"I know what discrimination is about," Carter said. "I've been there. I sat at the back of the bus. I was twenty years old when [Martin Luther] King got killed. I lived in that era. I was part of a police department that had to ride the bus with kids who were being bused from one end of Jefferson County to the other. One of the officers got his eye shot out by people shooting at us with ball bearings and slingshots. Having gone through that, I didn't have all the answers, nor do I have all the answers now. But a lot of my finesse, if I have any, in dealing with these matters I learned from Roger Depue."

After Carter had been in the bureau for five years he asked to work with Depue, and so they became partners in teaching the class and doing research in the behavioral science unit. When Carter and Depue started picking up hints from new agents that some instructors at the academy had been making prejudiced or sexist remarks, they got approval from Jim McKenzie, then the assistant director over training, to give the instructors sensitivity training.

"New agents would tell us of instances where there might be a problem," Depue said. "Maybe a firearms instructor on the range made a remark about a woman not being able to shoot. Jim McKenzie said, 'We ought to have our own class clean. If there are problems in the bureau, you can't have those problems.' "

Depue and Carter began with the firearms and physical training instructors, the most macho agents in the academy. As former firearms instructors and SWAT team members themselves, Depue and Carter knew how to handle them.

"We figured we could match them, macho for macho," Depue said.

In meeting with the firearms instructors, Depue and Carter asked them about their goals. When they said it was to get agents to hit the target, Depue and Carter would point out that offensive remarks get adrenaline going and affect fine motor coordination.

"So with the firearms guys, we demonstrated that if they are insensitive to anyone, they would defeat their own goals," Depue said. "They pretty much bought it."

James Greenleaf, who took over from McKenzie as head of the training division, asked Depue to talk about prejudice at the meeting of the FBI's executive conference in Virginia Beach. Depue wanted to be prepared with the facts, so he proposed visiting five offices and interviewing the most outstanding minorities and women to obtain their experiences. Greenleaf supported him.

Depue chose Carter to work with him. As they told the executive conference, they found "pockets of prejudice" and a reluctance by management to deal with it.

"One of the biggest problems was management's perception that it's okay," Carter said. "It's okay to tell the jokes or do whatever. Because management would laugh at the jokes, and management never addressed areas where there were problems, and management never took a stand."

"What they [the agents who were interviewed] told us surprised us," said Greenleaf, now associate deputy director for administration. "They told us the same things the so-called malcontents were telling us. They said they were satisfied with their careers and the bureau. But they had been subjected to racist remarks that in the 1970s were considered kidding but now were not. It showed we had some pretty dumb people out there who didn't appreciate what these sensitivities were all about."

In December 1988, Carter was transferred to New Orleans. He was placed in charge of a squad that investigated government applicants and civil rights violations. Now he had a chance to carry out Depue's teaching. Carter had heard that New Orleans had had some racial problems. At his first meeting with the twelve-agent squad, Carter made it clear where he stood.

"I let people know that being the investigators of such, we were not only going to *look* right but *be* right in the area of civil rights," Carter said. "We would not tolerate any violations of law within the squad. Also we would not tolerate any sexual harassment. This was unusual because very few supervisors take the time to take a position. I said, 'We're not going to put up with the jokes. You joke and make racial remarks, and I will do whatever I have to do administratively to take care of it.' "[422]

Greenleaf saw Depue's talks to the executive conference and later to the SAC conference as a turning point.

"I look at that as the beginning of our drive to sensitize the organization," Greenleaf said. "If some of our best people are telling us this, we better start listening. A lot of practices needed to be reviewed."[423]

Following up Depue's work, the training division conducted an extensive survey of agents. In December 1990, the study reported that 26 percent of the FBI employees who responded said that they had been personally offended on the job because of their race, national origin, religion, handicap, color, sex, or age. Nearly half of those employees said that they believed the person who offended them had done so intentionally. Roughly half of the employees said that they had witnessed such incidents. Finally, 40 percent of the black and Hispanic agents said that management was at least sometimes insensitive to acts of discrimination.[424]

FBI managers learned that arguing about whether there was or was not discrimination was pointless. Echoing Depue's findings, William Baker, as head of the criminal investigative division, would tell agents in his division and in field offices that the bureau has "pockets of prejudice" that need to be eliminated. Rather than arguing about whether discrimination exists, the bureau needs to eradicate the perception that it exists by seeing if accommodations can be made.

"Our product should not be a lot of EEO cases," Baker would say in these talks. "Our product is investigative cases we bring to court."

Sessions moved on a number of fronts. In March 1989, he hired James R. Pérez, a California native of Mexican descent, to take over the FBI's equal employment opportunity affairs office. Pérez, who is no relation to the Pérez who brought the Hispanic lawsuit, had worked for the Justice Department's Community Relations Service in San Antonio. As the U.S. Attorney there, Sessions had been Pérez's titular boss. Known for its long delays and lack of action, the FBI's EEO office was essentially useless and had been criticized by Judge Bunton in his ruling on the Hispanic lawsuit. Sessions had Pérez report directly to Deputy Director Floyd Clarke and gave him final authority to resolve complaints.

Sessions gave him carte blanche, said Pérez, who has a gray mustache and wears turquoise ties with light blue suspenders. "He said,

'I want you to look at all facets of the FBI for any EEO implications. Everything is open to you. You can go to a classified briefing, see an operation, anything.' "

At the time, the average EEO complaint took 800 days to resolve. Pérez cut that to 150 days.[425]

To make sure the FBI tests new applicants fairly, Sessions scrapped the FBI applicant tests and commissioned outside consultants to develop a new test. While it was being devised, the FBI stopped giving tests and selected new agents from existing applications.

Inevitably, the changes created resentment among white male agents, who thought the bureau was going too far. Gary Penrith, the SAC in Newark, said that his performance is rated in large part on his actions on behalf of minorities.

"I think we all try," Penrith said. "But it gets beaten into your head. I have to submit a quarterly EEO report. A minority agent comes in to do the report. 'Let's see your calendar for the last three months. What have you done about this? Do you realize that you only have one full-time relief supervisor who is a minority? What are your plans to bring up more agents so they can be primary relief supervisors?' "[426]

Penrith resents what he sees as an emphasis on advancement of minorities regardless of merit.

"These are management calls that are not going to necessarily be based on ability and work performance but on getting the right faces in the right places," he said. "I think that's a shitty way to do business." He said that what is expected is "jumping people with lesser performance and ability."

Another item on which Penrith is rated is how many minorities his office has recruited to be agents.

"It ain't easy to hire minorities for this job, and particularly blacks," he said. "Number one, they don't grow up liking law enforcement in the first place. The director says that's an old issue. It's not an old issue. It's a true issue."

Penrith said that well-qualified blacks can get better salaries elsewhere.

"I have a regional recruiter here who is black and really works hard," he said. "Our rating is based on what he does. I'm out on boards and trying all the time. If he doesn't try and get rated well, that means I don't get rated well. You get tired of that. That's why I say it's time for the younger guys to come in," said Penrith, who is fifty.

Meanwhile, Penrith said, the white agents are taking notes, ready to spring their own lawsuits because they feel discriminated against. What this amounts to, he said, is a policy of affirmative action in an administration—then the Bush administration—that is against affirmative action.

"We are the only agency I know of that does it," he said. "You go to the Senate office building, and you tell me how many minorities they have. Yet, that in my opinion is Director Sessions's number-one concern. It is a concern of everybody, but it is not the primary concern of the FBI as a whole. We are not a bunch of racists."

In April 1991, 230 black agents met in Washington to discuss filing a class action suit against the bureau alleging discrimination. When Sessions heard about it, he asked the agents to meet with him.

In a highly unusual move, Sessions agreed to let the black agents and their organization, called BADGE, see bureau documents that they would be able to obtain through discovery proceedings if they filed a lawsuit. The leader of the group, Emanuel Johnson, Jr., who headed an applicant squad that does background investigations at the Washington metropolitan field office, recounted an early experience with discrimination at his first office in Indianapolis, where he was the only black agent.

"One day we had an employee celebrating his anniversary," Johnson said. "As I was standing there, another agent walked up to me and took a pair of scissors and clipped my necktie off. I said, 'Why did you do that?' He said, 'I don't like your necktie.' I said, 'I don't consider that to be a justification for cutting it.' I surveyed the situation and decided I was the only black agent, and I had to take my stand."

Johnson gave the other agent two hours to come up with twenty-five dollars to replace the tie.

"In about thirty minutes, I had my twenty-five dollars," he said.[427]

After a year of intense negotiations with BADGE and its lawyer, David J. Shaffer of Arnold & Porter in Washington, Sessions announced an agreement in principle—later ratified by a federal court—that would promote six blacks to supervisory positions and thirteen blacks to relief supervisory positions. In addition, Sessions said he would take other steps to train and help advance blacks in the organization. Although Johnson felt that after ten years as the head of an applicant squad he should have a better assignment, he was not personally affected by the agreement.

As expected, there was a backlash, this time from the FBI Agents

Association. Another development that would have been unthinkable under Hoover, the agents association was formed in 1981 to promote the interests of on-board FBI agents. The organization was formed after agents found themselves being investigated and prosecuted for carrying out bureau orders to engage in illegal break-ins. Called "black bag jobs," the break-ins were to plant electronic bugging devices in the homes of leaders of the Weather Underground, a radical group that had carried out a number of bombings in the late 1960s and early 1970s. In November 1980, W. Mark Felt, former acting associate FBI director, and Edward S. Miller, a former assistant director, were convicted of authorizing such break-ins. In March 1981, President Reagan pardoned them.

"When the Weather Underground case surfaced, we had agents for the first time in jeopardy because of what their sanctioned job was," said Larry W. Langberg, the president of the association. "We had agents being advised of their rights from the Justice Department. That was a shock. Hoover was gone, and there wasn't anyone to safeguard us. . . . Hoover might have been tough at times on people within the bureau, but he was out there fighting for us against people who were taking pot shots against us."[428]

Not a union, the group is a professional association that cannot negotiate wages. But with a membership of two-thirds of the bureau's agents, the association can make itself felt. Among other things, it helped get Congress to change the way the FBI computes overtime. Overtime pay is now based on agents' actual salaries, rather than on a lower cutoff. For the average agent, that means an extra six thousand dollars a year.

The bureau has not officially recognized the group. While Sessions has met with the association, Floyd Clarke, the FBI's deputy director, has refused to do so. In explaining his position, Clarke said he was in his first office in Birmingham, Alabama, when he received orders to transfer to Boston. His father had just died, and his mother, who lived in Phoenix, had just had a back operation. He wanted to be near her and considered leaving the FBI. The SAC told him he should write a letter to Hoover asking to be transferred to a city closer to Phoenix. Clarke wouldn't do it.

"I made a decision at that point that I either had to leave the FBI or I was going to stay in it and live by the integrity of the organization and do what I could in those areas that I felt were wrong to change it," he said, explaining that the agents' association is not part of the bureau.

While Clarke has not met with the association, he spends hours talking with individual agents to find out their concerns. Don K. Clark, a black agent who is an assistant special agent in charge in New York, told the deputy director that the FBI could alleviate perceptions of discrimination by being more open about agents' performance.

"If you tell people what you like and what you don't like, what they are doing good or bad, they may not like it," Clark said. "You still may get sued for it, but you don't leave people in suspense."

Like many black agents, Clark said he has not experienced prejudice in the FBI.

"As a minority agent, I have a responsibility to become part of the organization when I come on a squad," he said. "Who is to say I should wait for you to come over and ask me to lunch? Maybe I should also walk over to you and introduce myself. You would be amazed how that brief conversation changes attitudes and perceptions."[429]

"My door is open," Floyd Clarke said. "But I don't need someone to represent a group of employees and try to back me into a position based on numbers."

"These are strange times for the bureau and the association. I don't think the bureau knows how to deal with us, and we don't know how to deal with the bureau," Langberg said.

The agents association says it stands for fairness in hiring and promotions.

"We have made overtures to the leaders of the black agents group [BADGE] to sit down with us and exchange ideas," said Susan E. Lloyd, the national secretary of the agents association, which includes blacks. "So far they haven't wished to sit down with us. Our position is that we believe in hiring, promotions, and transfers based on merit and merit alone. We don't subscribe to affirmative action, to goals, or quotas. None of these buzzwords for hiring or for promotion."

In response to the agreement in principle with the black agents, the agents' association sought permission from the courts to intervene and question whether the agreement impinges on the rights of white agents. The request was denied.

Perhaps because it has more minority agents, the Miami office has had more racial discord than any other office. William Gavin, the SAC, dealt with it by holding a conference for all of Miami's agents. He told them, "Nobody gets out. We either are going to end up in a bloody war and punch each other out, or you're going to get it out of your systems."

At first, no one at the meeting spoke. But eventually, over the next four and a half hours, agents vented their emotions.

"It was amazing," Gavin recalled. "All that tension dissipated. I haven't heard word one since that meeting."

One of the agents who spoke, Manuel J. Gonzalez, an Hispanic who is an assistant special agent in charge over drugs, said he has never seen discrimination in the FBI.

"I don't think any minority in this organization is kept down," he said. "I sometimes feel that some of the minorities might feel because they are minorities, they have an edge. To me, all opportunities are open to everyone. At the same time, you have to measure ability. I don't say minorities are getting more or less."

Michael H. Boyle, a white supervisor in Miami, said that the factionalism along racial lines has chopped the FBI into little pieces.

"We all came to the FBI for the same reasons," he said. "We came because we thought we could make a difference in the problems out there. I think the longer we continue to focus on the differences among its employees, the more we set them against each other. It's very divisive and self-destructive."

The lawsuits and negotiations have generated lots of business for Joseph R. Davis, the assistant director who has headed the legal division since 1985. A native of Mobile, Alabama, Davis received a B.S. in business administration from the University of Alabama and his LL.B from its law school. He thought he would stay in the FBI a few years and then return to Alabama and practice law. Initially assigned to the Kansas City and Washington field offices, Davis became a legal adviser and found he could be involved in the FBI's work and still practice law.

With fifty-six attorneys and seventy-two support people, the legal division helps the Justice Department when it litigates cases involving the FBI. The division advises bureau agents on legal issues, such as whether an undercover operation would expose the bureau to civil liability if something went wrong. As assistant director, Davis, a sharp, mild-mannered man who is often at work at 6:30 A.M., is the FBI's chief lawyer.

"A lot of people think it's the worst job in the FBI," Davis said. "No matter what happens that is bad, it usually has some legal ramifications. But I view it the other way. Whatever happens that is hot, you are involved in it. It's usually interesting and usually positive. It's not always negative."[430]

As the legal adviser to first Webster and then Sessions, Davis has been in the unusual position of giving legal advice to two former federal judges.

"I've been very fortunate, because both Webster and Sessions have been very good about doing what is right," he said. "They don't have any hesitancy about following legal advice. They seek it out.

"People accuse us of race norming or having quotas," Davis said. "I don't think we do. Is there an effort to have some diversity? Hell, yes."

"As part of the new FBI, we are trying in every possible way to change the organization and be much more sensitive to our people than we ever were before," Weldon Kennedy said.

Homosexuals are the one group that has been left out. Officially, the FBI says homosexuality is but one negative factor that may be taken into account when deciding whether to hire or retain an agent. In practice, despite growing scientific evidence that homosexuality is an inherited genetic trait, like skin color, the bureau always finds a way to reject or fire homosexuals.[431]

Frank Buttino, an agent in San Diego, found that out. In his twenty years as an agent, Buttino had an unblemished record and had won several incentive awards.

"Buttino was an excellent agent," said Thomas Hughes, who was his SAC in San Diego.

Five years into his career, Buttino recognized that he was a homosexual. Knowing the bureau's attitude, he kept his orientation hidden. Early in 1988, he responded to an ad in a gay publication. Although he did not reveal that he was an FBI employee, someone sent a copy of his letter to the FBI and to his parents. Asked by an assistant special agent in charge if he had written the letter, Buttino said he had not. Buttino also checked driver's licenses and criminal records to try to trace the person whose name appeared on the envelope's return address. That person denied sending the copy of Buttino's letter. Who sent it remains a mystery.

As part of an OPR inquiry, Buttino was asked to undergo an FBI polygraph examination at headquarters. Before the examination, Buttino admitted to OPR investigators that he was gay, that he had written the letter, and that he had checked driver's license and criminal records. In his effort to find out who had sent in the letter, he had disclosed the results of his inquiry to a few friends, which was considered giving bureau information to people not authorized to have it.

"They [OPR] wanted names of other homosexuals in the FBI,

names of homosexuals I had had sex with outside the bureau," Buttino said. "What kind of sex had I had, details going back to day one. Oral sex? Anal sex? Masturbation? Are you the active or passive partner? What kinds of things don't you do? Are you into bondage?"

Buttino passed the polygraph on whether he had given any classified information to unauthorized individuals or had otherwise been compromised. But the FBI suspended Buttino and, claiming that he was a security risk, lifted his top-secret clearance in February 1990. In a letter, the FBI cited his lack of candor and "your past and present conduct and association with unknown individuals in the homosexual community."

Without a clearance, Buttino could not be an agent, so, in June 1990, the FBI fired him.

"You really are in a catch-22," Buttino said. "They find out you're gay, you keep it a secret, they hold it against you. If you come out and become public, they'll use that against you, and you get fired. If you apply as a homosexual to be an agent, they won't take you."[432]

Like any other organization, the bureau has homosexuals who have not come out. Buttino said he always knew he might be fired if the bureau found out he was gay.

"I knew the bureau doesn't exactly love gay people," he said. "I had heard they had pressured others to resign. But when it's you personally after twenty years in the outfit, and to be trusted as I was. I was part of this family, the FBI family. Loyalty works both ways. I would think you would say, 'This guy is one of our outstanding agents.' All of a sudden, I'm a threat to the national security."

In fact, after studying all the cases, the Defense Department has admitted that homosexuals are no more likely to turn to espionage than are heterosexuals. In the modern history of the U.S. government, there has been no known case of a homosexual becoming a spy under the threat of blackmail.[433]

Within a few weeks of his firing, Buttino sued. In a preliminary ruling, U.S. District Court Judge Saundra Brown Armstrong in San Francisco denied the government's request for a dismissal of the suit, clearing the way for it to proceed. In her ruling, the judge said, "The court cannot help but wonder . . . whether there is anything to indicate that Buttino's lack of candor would *ever* have been an issue but for society's prejudice against gays and the FBI's history of anti-gay discrimination. . . ."[434]

Ideally, lack of candor or misuse of files should be a firing offense.

In fact, it is not. Having found out about Buttino's transgressions, the bureau likely would have given him a suspension and a reprimand if it had not been for his homosexuality.

For all the problems, nothing that is going on in the FBI is any different from what society as a whole is experiencing. Unlike the FBI, the Defense Department openly banned homosexuals until President Clinton put a stop to it. Until the incidents that occurred at a meeting of the Tailhook Association, the Navy tolerated sexual harassment. The Drug Enforcement Administration had its own black and Hispanic suits. From the *New York Times* to the *Washington Post*, private companies have been hit with complaints of discrimination based on race or sex.

"I think we tend to think the whole world is watching us as we deal with this," said Richard Held, the SAC in San Francisco who formerly headed Sessions's SAC advisory committee. "The rest of the world is watching their problems where they work. I think we have a tendency in the FBI to engage in self-flagellation. But we'll come through that."

For every employee in an organization, there is another opinion on the performance and qualifications of every other employee. When asked if they know of unqualified white agents who have been promoted unfairly, agents who complain about the promotion of unqualified minorities invariably say they do. With little complaint, agents have put up for years with marginal white employees like Richard Miller, the agent who ultimately committed espionage. Yet, because of racial stereotyping, some agents tend to focus on minorities who may have been promoted unfairly, ignoring the larger good that comes from fully integrating the bureau.

"It is absolutely essential that the bureau, which has the heaviest law enforcement investigative responsibility in this country, be perceived as fair and not discriminatory, for the good of the bureau, for the good of the country," Sessions said.[435]

For the most part, it is. Raoul G. Salinas, an Hispanic agent based in the Laredo, Texas, RA, said he has never felt discriminated against or seen it in the bureau.

"The biggest thing in my life was when I received my credentials, making my family proud, making my mom proud," he said. "Being an FBI agent has been the greatest thing in my life."

"If you were to ask me, 'Is the FBI a racist organization?' " I would say no," said John D. Glover, the agent who, as executive assistant director, became the highest-ranking black in the FBI. "If you were to ask if there were certain individuals who harbor certain discriminatory perceptions, the bureau drawing as it does from the larger society, I would say probably yes to that."[436]

Today 1,167—or 11 percent—of the bureau's 10,300 agents are women. Of the male and female agents, 505 are black and 597 are Hispanic, representing 10 percent of the total number of agents. Including Asians and American Indians, 12 percent of the bureau's agents are minorities.

While the minority population of the U.S. as a whole is about 20 percent, the proportion of minorities in the FBI is about the same as the proportion of the population qualified by degrees and age to be agents. The FBI comes out ahead of newsroom staffs at newspapers that responded to a survey by the American Society of Newspaper Editors, which reported that 9 percent of the staffs are minorities. The bureau also exceeds the minority proportions among partners at major law firms. In cities such as Chicago, Cleveland, Houston, and Baltimore, only 2 percent of the partners are minorities.[437]

The FBI has only two minority SACs—Pérez and, subsequently, Thomas F. Jones, who is black—and one female SAC, Burdena G. (Birdie) Pasenelli, who heads the Anchorage, Alaska, office. Kennedy said that many minorities and females have not been in the bureau long enough.

"While I look at those candidates and they are qualified, when you look at someone who has twenty years in the FBI and has had many assignments, as compared with someone with fewer years, it's a matter of degree," Kennedy said.

In September 1990, Sessions placed Jimmy Carter in charge of FBI recruiting. In that headquarters job, Carter often speaks to minority groups on the director's behalf. But he never forgot that hurt he felt when his sixth-grade teacher tried to discourage him from aspiring to join the FBI.

"I went back to her and said, 'I am an FBI agent, and I'm working on my Ph.D., and I want you to know I do public speaking in my work for the bureau,' " Carter said. " 'I speak for the director.' "

The teacher was not impressed. "When I told her, she didn't say anything," Carter said.

In his talks, Carter tells what he likes about being an agent:

"I enjoy being an investigator and putting the pieces of the puzzle together, and coming up with what you need to effect an arrest. It's a rewarding thing to help society. If you catch a bad guy who has done something wrong to someone else, think what you have done for that victim. The victim will never know, but you know in your heart what you have done. If you catch a rapist, think what you have done for the victim's family. Or the bank robber who scares the heck out of the bank teller by pointing a weapon at him, going out and bringing this person to justice. The terrorist, the bomber who sends explosives through the mail. The spy who tears at the thread that holds our American society together. I have the ability to send evidence to the FBI lab and use that to convict someone, to protect America."

Carter talks about how FBI agents will put their lives on the line to protect a witness, to apprehend a serial murderer, or to find a kidnapper and return the victim to his or her family. Speaking of these agents, Carter says, "They will put themselves between you and the adversary. What else can you do to prove loyalty? That is more than some people put into their marriages. This organization will put their lives on the line for you and the public. That means a lot, to be a part of that."

And sometimes Carter talks about Roger Depue and the way he influenced him. "I learned a lot of answers about race, culture, and understanding from Roger Depue, a white guy from Detroit," he said. "He took a stand a long time before it was popular for white guys to take a stand."

17

London: The Best Job in the FBI

● **When Pan Am 103 crashed** on December 21, 1988, Darrell W. Mills, the FBI's legal attaché in London, and his assistant Richard F. Green were at the Old Bangkok restaurant in Kensington toasting Mills's son, Kyle, who had just graduated from college. At 7:30 P.M., the restaurant owner called Green to the phone. FBI headquarters in Washington said the Boeing 747 had disappeared from radar screens thirty minutes earlier. Bodies had been raining down from the sky over Lockerbie, Scotland.

"We had a gut feeling from the get-go it was sabotage," said Green, who was placed in charge of the FBI's efforts. "Within two days, we knew it was a bomb."[438]

Mills rushed to the American embassy, where the FBI's office is on the fourth floor, and set up a command center in the ambassador's conference room. As the FBI's representatives in London, Mills and Green would coordinate with British and Scottish authorities the ensuing FBI investigation into the cause of the crash and the identification of the 259 passengers and crew members.

The FBI's London office is one of twenty foreign offices—known as legal attachés or legats—that coordinate FBI investigations with foreign police and security services. The legat program goes back to 1940, when Franklin D. Roosevelt authorized the FBI to establish a Special Intelligence Service to counter Nazi intelligence efforts in the Western Hemisphere. It was Hoover's dream to expand the FBI's jurisdiction all over the world, and conducting spy operations was a way to do it. Agents assigned to SIS served in overt and covert capacities. Rather than engage simply in counterspying, which is normally the FBI's mission, they gathered what is known as positive intelligence. To conceal their true roles, they were given the innocuous-sounding title of legal attaché. Under the program, FBI agents in 1942 intercepted radio messages of Josef Jacob Johannes Starziczny, a German spy in Brazil, and prevented a submarine attack on the SS *Queen Mary.*

With the founding of the CIA, the FBI lost its overseas intelligence-gathering function. The CIA spies overseas and may not spy on Americans in the U.S. Conversely, the FBI investigates violations of law in the U.S. or, in some cases, against American citizens. It may not spy overseas. However, the FBI still had to exchange information with foreign police and security services and coordinate investigations that involved activities in other countries. That is the function of the legat program. While the FBI, as part of its counterspy role, occasionally sends agents overseas in covert capacities, these agents report to the bureau's intelligence division and have no connection with the legats.

With the end of the Cold War, international crime as it affects Americans has become the new focus not only of the FBI but of all American federal law enforcement and intelligence agencies. Now that international travel and communication have become commonplace, terrorism, organized crime, drug trafficking, money laundering, arms dealing, and securities and banking fraud increasingly transcend national boundaries. Once tightly controlled by the state, many former Soviet bloc citizens, spurred on by capitalism's promise, have become accomplished criminals. The unification of Europe is expected to bring even more crime as borders dissolve and customs inspections within Europe become a thing of the past.

"There has been an explosion in international crime," said Lawrence P. McElynn, who heads the drug division of Interpol's U.S. office. "The police in the Eastern European countries have ceased to exist as institutions for the most part. The criminal elements have become a lot stronger. The Eastern Europeans are emerging as very well organized, strong criminals. With the borders being removed, it is a great event for the international criminal."

International crime syndicates have started cooperating with one another. The American mafia, known as La Cosa Nostra, and the Cali cartel in Colombia have forged an alliance. So have La Cosa

Nostra and the Sicilian mafia, which traditionally have worked separately. Meanwhile, entire South American countries have been held hostage by the drug lords.

Countries themselves have taken on the role of international criminals, engaging in economic espionage to gain trade secrets. French agents have been caught using hotel chambermaids to steal papers from the briefcases of IBM employees in Paris. Japan has obtained secrets more adroitly by buying U.S. companies outright. The successor to the KGB has continued to spy on the U.S., focusing more on economic than military secrets. These are the spies of the twenty-first century.

A joint FBI and DEA money-laundering case demonstrates the scope of the problem. Known as Polar Cap, it closed down an operation that handled $1.2 billion in cocaine funds from 1987 to early 1989. The money was delivered to precious-metals brokers in Los Angeles, then laundered through accounts in Panama, Uruguay, Great Britain, Luxembourg, Austria, and Switzerland. After Colombian drug lords pocketed most of the money, they wired $350 million of it back to the U.S. to finance more drug operations.[439]

Each country has its specialty.

"The Colombians do the narcotics," Mills said. "The Nigerians recently began transporting narcotics. Indians do millions of dollars in airline ticket schemes. The Russians have become involved in organized crime. The Australians go all over the world and pickpocket. The French government sanctions economic espionage. Japan has organized gangs. The Italians have organized crime with kidnapping, extortion, and violence."[440]

U.S. agencies have responded in kind. New laws have expanded the jurisdiction of the FBI and other federal law enforcement agencies. While the laws are complicated, they allow the FBI to investigate certain crimes anywhere in the world as long as the targets of the crimes are Americans. Because of these new laws, the FBI in recent years arrested Fawaz Younis, the Lebanese plane hijacker, on a yacht in the Mediterranean; lured Arturo Durazo, a former Mexico City police chief who had been selling millions of dollars in drugs to the U.S., to the Caribbean island of Aruba so that he could be arrested; and even arrested members of the Sicilian mafia for shipping thirteen hundred pounds of cocaine from Colombia to Sicily. While the shipment never touched U.S. shores, the planning of the crime took place in Florida.

In September 1992, DEA and Italian police arrested 150 drug traffickers from all over the world. Meanwhile, the Defense Department has been sending planes into the jungles of South America, spending $1.2 billion a year to rout out drugs and drug traffickers. Finally, the CIA, trying to remain relevant after the Cold War, has devoted more and more resources to obtaining intelligence on terrorists and drug traffickers. The agency secretly funnels the information to the FBI, the DEA, and other law enforcement agencies. The Justice Department's Office of International Affairs arranges extraditions of more than 300 people a year from foreign countries, compared with about 153 in 1984. The number of attorneys assigned to that office has grown to 46 from 16 in 1984. Even private investigative agencies have gotten into the act, working for foreign governments to trace Saddam Hussein's assets and the Communist party's millions.

In attacking international crime, each country goes it alone. Interpol serves as a clearinghouse of information for law enforcement agencies in 158 countries. But it has no law enforcement powers. Because of its broad jurisdiction, the FBI is the primary American law enforcement agency that focuses on global crime, and legats are critical to that effort.

In all, fifty agents are assigned to legats—one or two to the smaller offices and four or five to the larger ones such as Bonn, Rome, London, Mexico City, and Paris. The legats report to John E. Guido, an inspector in charge at headquarters who heads the office of liaison and international affairs and reports to the criminal investigative and intelligence divisions. Professorial and low-key, Guido looks at the bureau's overseas operations as a growth industry. Although the new laws have broadened the FBI's jurisdiction, they do not mean the FBI will necessarily operate in a foreign country without the permission of that country.

"We are not empowered to do anything in these countries," Guido said. "Everything we do is with their advice and consent. If we have a criminal conspiracy in the U.S. that has impact in another country, it probably is a violation in that country, so that country will be very cooperative. Law enforcement cooperates and works against the bad guys. It's the white hats and the black hats. The cops can pretty much find ways to cooperate."[441]

However, in 1989, the Justice Department issued an opinion saying that the FBI may seize fugitives in other countries even without those countries' permission. Usually this authority—called extraterritorial jurisdiction—is reserved for terrorism cases. Under this jurisdiction, suspects have been arrested overseas either with the consent of the country involved or on international waters, as when the FBI arrested Fawaz Younis on the Mediterranean.

The FBI had asked the Justice Department if it could seize a suspect in a country such as Libya, which, not having friendly relations with the U.S., would not agree to such an arrest. Two years later, the press reported that the Justice Department had secretly issued an opinion saying that the FBI could do so. This created the impression that the FBI was gearing up to invade friendly countries and arrest suspects unilaterally.

"That caused all kinds of uproars all over the world," Guido said. "We had people batting down our legat doors, we had calls in here from the diplomatic community in Washington saying, 'Don't you dare do anything unilaterally.' We said, 'We have no intent of doing anything without your knowledge.' It took us a number of months to undo the concern."

Guido pointed out that the FBI never has, in fact, invoked the opinion. It was intended to apply only to countries such as Libya, Panama, and Lebanon that are either hostile to the U.S. or do not have control over their own territory. Further, if the U.S. were to approve such a venture, it would be done with the recognition that the U.S. was breaking international law and, in effect, declaring war on another country.

"The only situation where we would do it is where there is no law or no cooperation and we had an unlawful regime and a state of anarchy," said Buck Revell, who testified before Congress on the issue. "Lebanon would be an example, where you had warring factions."

Meanwhile, Guido is trying to open more FBI legats.

"Our view is international crime is a growing business, and we need to be posted in the right place to carry out our responsibilities not only here but also in the extraterritorial area," Guido said. "So we are in there slugging. We are bigger than in 1987. We're not looking to be five times bigger than we are. But right now, if given a free hand, I would open four or five more legats with another ten agents."

The key to success is cooperation with foreign police and security services, so not the least of Guido's duties is throwing the FBI's annual party for these services. Even services such as MI-6—which purportedly does not exist—have been known to attend the bash, given in late winter. Bureau officials are quick to point out that the party is the bureau's only lavish affair, reciprocating invitations to dozens of parties given by the services of other countries at their embassies in Washington.

At a recent party, Sessions and his wife, Alice, presided over a spread of shish kebab, stuffed grape leaves, fajitas, and a seafood bar with raw oysters and clams on the half shell, crab claws, and shrimp. Both Sessions and his wife are teetotalers, so wine is a concession and hard liquor has been removed from the menu. During the party, guests could shoot at the FBI's indoor range and pose for photographs to be inserted in a plastic key ring souvenir that says, "Wanted by the FBI—A Drug Free America."

Because legats are generally located in attractive overseas capitals, the jobs are eagerly sought. Mills told anyone who would listen that being the legat in London was the best job in the FBI. At one point, he and his attractive wife, Elaine, a former Miss Maine, figured out that they had either been to dinner parties—including one at Buckingham Palace—or thrown dinner parties seventy nights in a row.

Before the FBI can open a new legat, it must obtain approval from the State Department, which is chary of sharing scarce space in American embassies with other agencies. It took three years for the FBI to obtain approval to open its newest legat, in Madrid.

"We went through two ambassadors," Guido said. "There were some State Department entities that said it is not needed. We looked at it as a location for the summer Olympics and the World's Fair. Many Americans are there. It has a high incidence of terrorist activities, and it is a key drug importer. It was a long, long struggle. The Spanish were very anxious to have us there."

Each legat covers a number of countries. The one in Rome, for example, covers not only Italy but Cyprus, Greece, Malta, the Middle East, Turkey, and much of Africa. With a new alliance between La Cosa Nostra in America and the mafia in Sicily, Walter Mangiacotti, who is legat in Rome, and his assistant, Thomas E. Bondonza, have had their hands full coordinating investigations. They worked with a key informant whose information helped convict Sicilian-born John Golotolo and eleven others for arranging in January 1988 for the Sicilian mafia, working with La Cosa Nostra, to ship thirteen hundred pounds of cocaine from Colombia to Sicily.[442]

"My job is to be a channel," said Mangiacotti in his office in Rome, his walls and tables covered with plaques and souvenir hats. "We arranged for testimony of FBI agents in Italian courts. We didn't have authority to investigate, but we were close to what was going on."

Four of the legats in Europe pursued information about Felix Bloch, the American diplomat suspected of spying for the KGB, looking for leads at posts where he had been assigned or might have engaged in spying. The legats in Brussels and London obtained information from government and banking regulatory agencies to help the FBI investigate the Bank of Credit and Commerce International (BCCI). After the U.S. military intervention in Panama, legats helped investigate murders and kidnappings of U.S. military personnel in Panama.

Of all the FBI's investigations, none has been both so massive and so wide-ranging as the case of Pan Am 103. Radiating from an international response squad in the Washington metropolitan field office, the investigation took three years, required agents to crisscross the globe, and involved extensive work by the FBI lab, including detonation of test explosive devices.

On the night of the crash, Darrell Mills dispatched Tim Dorch, an assistant legat, to fly to the scene on an Air Force jet with the American ambassador, Charles Price II. Smooth and cerebral, Mills was friends with the head of every British and Scottish police and security service. When jurisdictional battles occasionally arose—hiccups, he called them—Mills knew just the right person to call to untangle them. In the beginning, Sessions called him several times a day to keep abreast of developments and make sure he was getting the help he needed.

The morning after the crash, Neil Gallagher, head of the counterterrorism section at headquarters, came to work in shock. "Slowly we realized it was everybody who had been annihilated plus people on the ground," Gallagher said.[443]

Because the crash occurred four days before Christmas, the FBI held off a few days on interviewing families of victims.

"We hesitated because there were these families with Christmas presents under the trees for many people who were not coming home," Gallagher said. "We felt they didn't need an FBI agent coming up and asking a lot of factual questions."

Technical agents flew to Scotland and set up communications in Lockerbie so that the FBI could transmit by satellite pictures of survivors and their fingerprints. Laboratory agents led by James T. (Tom) Thurman, a renowned FBI bomb expert, worked with local authorities to organize the search for evidence.

"This was a crime scene that covered 845 square miles," Gallagher said. "The police recovered well over 90 percent of the plane with Scottish police and military lining up and going on their hands and knees. If debris fell on a farm, they [the farmers] would call the police. They wouldn't touch it."

Two days after arriving, one of the agents called FBI headquarters and said, "We saw what we came to see."

Gallagher knew that meant the agents had seen the evidence they needed to determine if an explosive device was involved. The experts had found a piece of metal from the plane with pitting and cratering that indicated it had been subjected to high-intensity explosive devices.

"You would look at it, and it would look black and charred as if there had been a fire," Gallagher said. "But to them, it meant there had been a bomb."

Investigators subsequently found a plate riveted to the inside of the baggage compartment listing the name of Boeing, the manufacturer. The pattern of pitting and cratering on the plate told the bomb experts that the device had been inside the baggage area, not in the commercial cargo area. That was a break. With twenty-one tons of commercial cargo, determining the origin of each shipment would have been even more time consuming than investigating the plane's baggage.

Embedded in the manufacturer's plate was a piece of tan plastic smaller than a fingernail. The experts recognized it as a fragment of a computer chip. They later determined that it was from a particular model Toshiba radio. That led back to the PFLP-GC (Popular Front for the Liberation of Palestine—General Command). Some of their members had just been arrested with explosive devices concealed in Toshiba radios.

For a time, the investigation focused on the PFLP-GC. But the bomb experts had recovered enough clues to lead the investigators in other directions as well. They knew, for example, that the terrorists had used a highly effective plastic explosive called Semtex. They knew from pieces found on the ground that the device had been in a packing crate inside a brown Samsonite suitcase.

"We knew the bomb was inside its original packing crate with the instructions in Arabic inside the crate," Gallagher said. "We knew it was a particular make and model Samsonite. Some twenty-three hundred of them had been made. So we had a lot of information."

With British forensic experts, the FBI lab conducted tests in Maryland to determine the size of the explosive charge. The lab packed metal containers resembling the baggage area with suitcases, detonated a charge inside, and then examined the damage. The FBI concluded that the saboteurs had used ten to fourteen ounces of plastic explosive concealed inside the radio. The tests also pinpointed in which compartment in the baggage area the suitcase containing the radio was located. This narrowed the source of the luggage to certain baggage from other airlines. Even more important, because of differences in the blast damage, the examiners were able to differentiate between clothing that had been inside the suitcase containing the bomb and clothing that had not been in the suitcase.

Focusing on the clothing from the suitcase, the experts found a fingernail-size piece of a green circuit board embedded in a fragment of shirt. Thurman determined that the board had been part of a timing device. He matched the piece to devices seized in Senegal and in Togo. Each device had been used by terrorists connected with Libyan intelligence. To make the circuit boards, a photographic negative was produced. If there was a flaw in the negative, it would appear in all the circuit boards. Every board had the same flaw.

Examining the Togo board further, Thurman found that something had been scratched out on the back. The lab raised the lettering, which said MEBO. It stood for Meister Et Bolier, a Zurich firm. Company executives disclosed that the timing device was one of twenty delivered to a Libyan official in 1985 and 1986.

"The solution came down to a bombing expert finding remnants of the device which conclusively led to the people who commissioned the device to be built," said John W. Hicks, the assistant director over the lab. "The circuit board in the shirt was found by the British. They weren't able to identify its significance. It wasn't until it was made available to the FBI lab a year later that Tom Thurman was able to associate it in a matter of two weeks with some devices that had been recovered."

Meanwhile, the FBI and Scottish police had traced the manufacturers of the clothing and the retail outlets where it might have been purchased. They wound up at a boutique in Malta called Mary's Shop.

"When we showed them the clothing, the owner told us a phenomenal story," said Gallagher, who is over counterterrorism. "He said that in December 1988, a person he described as having a Libyan accent came in and bought clothing indiscriminately, not worrying about size, shape, or color. We wondered if he was telling us what he thought we wanted to hear. But he also said he sold him a black umbrella. We went back to the British and asked if they had a black umbrella. They went back and found the black umbrella they had. They had not noticed the blast damage on it. So we were on the money."

By interviewing the shopkeeper further, the FBI determined that the man with the Libyan accent most likely came in on December 8, 1988. From the shopkeeper's recollection, the lab drew a composite sketch of the man. Having already traced the timing device to Libyans, the FBI focused on Libyan intelligence officers. Eventually, the bureau narrowed the list of suspects and showed the shopkeeper photographs. He identified Abdel Basset Ali al-Megrahii, a Libyan intelligence officer, as the man who had bought the clothing. The FBI found that he had arrived in Malta with Lamen Khalifa Fhimah, a former station manager of the Libyan Arab Airlines there, on December 20, 1988, at 5:30 P.M. Witnesses said they saw them arrive with a dark-colored Samsonite suitcase. Because he was the former station manager, Fhimah could place the luggage with the bomb on a flight without going through security checks.

Basset left for Tripoli the next day at 10:26 A.M., half an hour after Air Malta Flight KM-190 left Malta for Frankfurt. Through computer records, the FBI had already traced the bag that exploded over Lockerbie to the Malta flight, which connected in Frankfurt with Pan Am 103 bound for New York.

In November 1991, both Basset and Fhimah were indicted. Libya refused to turn them over to the FBI, creating just the situation that the Justice Department opinion on seizing suspects in foreign countries had been designed to cover. Instead of taking such drastic action, the U.S. and other countries imposed economic sanctions on Libya. Gallagher believed the bombing could have been retaliation by Mu'ammar Qaddafi for the 1986 bombing of Tripoli by U.S. warplanes.[444]

Everyone had been deeply affected by the catastrophe.

"It was so tragic to see people on Christmas looking for their daughters," said Mills, the London legat who flew to the scene on Christmas Eve. In part because of his work on the case, the FBI later named Mills to head the U.S. office of Interpol, the international police organization.[445]

Together with the British, Scottish, and German authorities, the FBI had conducted fourteen thousand interviews in fifty countries.

"The scope and complexity is probably unparalleled in international counterterrorism investigations," Gallagher said. "The Scottish police put hundreds of officers on it. A lot of the credit has to go to them. As many FBI agents as were needed we put on it. There were legal attachés around the world working it. Wherever it took us, we went."

"Major cases aren't broken overnight," said William Baker, who directed the investigation as assistant director over the criminal division. "Major cases take great amounts of effort, coordination, and patience. Pan Am 103 I believe demonstrated that."

18
Public Affairs: Selling the Image

● **Hoover created** the world's most successful public relations machine. Other law enforcement agencies might arrest armed and dangerous men, but only the FBI knew how to get the credit. Other law enforcement agencies had brave and effective officers, but only the FBI created an image of its agents as supermen. Others had chiefs as smart and as patriotic, but only Hoover fashioned a cult of personality with himself as symbol of truth, justice, and the American way.

The tool for shaping the FBI's image was called the crime records division. This was the austere-sounding name given to the public and congressional relations arm of the FBI, started in 1934. Besides handling press inquiries and dealing with Congress, the division responded to letters asking for Hoover's favorite recipes, sent out autographed photos of Hoover, and wrote angry letters to newspapers that published anything critical about the director. The division ran the public tours of FBI headquarters and the Ten Most Wanted Fugitives program. Most important, the division helped create books, movies, television and radio shows, and newspaper and magazine articles extolling Hoover and the FBI.

For that purpose, the division had on hand "interesting case memoranda." These were articles written by agents in the crime records division about the FBI's successful cases. According to these versions, the FBI never made mistakes and always got its man. Many publications ran them shortened, but otherwise unedited, under their own writers' bylines.

The crime records division gave Don Whitehead, an Associated Press reporter, access to FBI files so that he could write *The FBI Story*, then edited the manuscript to make sure the FBI's image shone brightly. The division wrote *Masters of Deceit*, then put Hoover's name on it and cut him in on the royalties. As early as 1932, a predecessor of the crime records division contributed material to the *Lucky Strike Hour*, the first radio program to dramatize FBI cases on a national network. That was followed by other radio programs concerning FBI cases, including *G-Men*, *Gangbusters*, *The FBI in Peace and War*, *This Is Your FBI*, and *I Was a Communist for the FBI*. The division helped create movies as well, including *Men of the FBI*, *Inside the FBI*, and the *FBI Front*. In 1965, the crime records division created *The FBI*, the ABC television series starring Efrem Zimbalist, Jr., as Inspector Lewis Erskine.

In all these projects, the FBI retained complete control. They were free advertisements for the bureau, with no disclosure that they were anything but objective, independent works. To an extent, the bureau controlled the press as well. The crime records division had a "special correspondents list" of reporters who could be counted on to project the bureau in a positive light. The division also had a "not to be contacted" list. The approved reporters were given cooperation and leaks from FBI files. The others were shunned and handed a stiff "no comment."

As part of its mission, the crime records division glorified Hoover. As a king might be in a foreign country, he was portrayed as all-knowing, magnanimous, and kind to animals. The few attacks on him were labeled "smears" that were "Communist inspired."

"Through its responsibility in handling all public inquiries, the importance of the FBI's image was emphasized," according to the bureau's own history of the crime records division. "Mistakes were not tolerated because they were 'embarrassing' to the FBI as stated by the director."

The role of Louis B. Nichols, who headed the crime records division, was "epitomized by his visit to a hospitalized twelve-year-old boy who idolized G-men. As a result, he received numerous letters of commendation," the history said.[446]

To a large extent, the syrupy publicity campaign helped make the FBI as effective as it is today. For image and reality are intertwined. If the public both admired and feared the FBI's agents, it would be more apt to help them. More than anyone, Hoover understood that and used it to his advantage. At the same time, by turning himself into a cult figure and the FBI into an icon, Hoover was able to conceal the bureau's abuses and inefficiency.

Even derogatory remarks made about Hoover at bridge parties or in beauty parlors were met by visits from the FBI. It was a tactic widely used by the KGB. After the owner of a beauty parlor and one of her patrons in Washington referred to Hoover as a "queer," agents visited them and told them "in no uncertain terms that such statements . . . would not be countenanced," according to a 1951 memo from Nichols, who usually orchestrated the visits. As a result of the visit by the agents, the beauty parlor's owner "fully realizes the seriousness of her accusations, and it is not believed that she will ever be guilty of such statements," Nichols assured Clyde Tolson, Hoover's companion and the associate director.[447]

After Hoover's death, the exposure of the FBI's abuses led to more accountability. Times had changed. After Watergate and the Vietnam war, Americans no longer accepted at face value what their government said. Congress became more aggressive in exercising oversight responsibility. Unlawful activities would not be tolerated.

After L. Patrick Gray and William D. Ruckelshaus served briefly as acting directors from May 1972 to April 1973, President Nixon named Clarence M. Kelley FBI director. A former FBI agent himself, Clarence Kelley, who was director from July 1973 to February 1978, was familiar with many of the bureau's warts. As police chief in Kansas City, he had developed a reputation as an honest and enlightened executive. In his effort to modernize the FBI, he ordered a more open and even-handed approach to the press.

"The press policy is not what the press office wants it to be," said Homer Boynton, who was over public affairs under Kelley and Webster. "It's what the head of the agency wants it to be. Clarence Kelley wanted it open. He did not want it to be as adversarial, and he wanted a closer working relationship."[448]

Kelley fought a never-ending battle with Hoover holdovers who could not adapt to the more open approach. It was not until Webster took over in February 1978 that the public relations function— renamed congressional and public affairs—became a sophisticated and credible operation. Under the direction of Roger S. Young and later William Baker, the division responded honestly to press inquiries from any source and became more cooperative with book authors and television and movie producers. By admitting the bureau's past mistakes and weaknesses, Young and Baker engendered trust; thus, the bureau's successes were believed.

Many FBI agents had the uninformed view that the only press officers the media liked were those who leaked information on investigations. But there was a way of working around the margins, walking a fine line between giving away investigative secrets and stiffing the press. Lane Bonner, the feisty agent who handled press inquiries on a daily basis under Young and Baker, knew how to walk that line. In doing so, he engendered goodwill for the FBI without giving away secrets. After the devastating series of disclosures about the bureau's abuses, this more open and responsive approach to both the press and Congress helped restore the FBI's credibility.

The credit goes to Webster, who understood the importance of the press and Congress and also knew how to gain their confidence.

"It just isn't enough to run the organization," Webster said. "Your ability to be supported, both with resources and in terms of public approval, depends upon being able to deal with the Congress, the press, and the outside community."[449]

While Sessions was effective at giving speeches and engendering goodwill on a personal level, he had trouble communicating that through the press office. Sessions split the FBI's press and congressional functions into two offices and downgraded their importance. No longer part of a division, each office was placed under an inspector in charge instead of an assistant director.

"Webster thought the press should be handled as a high priority, and he set up a structure to handle it that way," said Milt Ahlerich, who headed the office under Webster and Sessions. "I'm not sure Judge Sessions was entirely comfortable with that structure. There was a difference in style."

Sessions placed John E. Collingwood in charge of congressional affairs. A lawyer from Ohio, Collingwood had become an agent in 1975, three years after Hoover's death. Before taking over congressional affairs, Collingwood was a special assistant to Sessions and had his confidence. Like Baker and Young, Collingwood had a direct, honest approach. He quickly developed a reputation as an effective congressional liaison. In contrast, Sessions did not have a close relationship with Thomas F. Jones, whom he placed in charge of the public affairs office. Moreover, as symbolized by his decision to downgrade the office's importance, Sessions's view of the role of the press was more limited than Webster's. In his own interviews,

Sessions tended to preach rather than convey useful information.

"Sessions is very circumspect," said Buck Revell, the former associate deputy director. "He may inadvertently say things, but he is so guarded that generally reporters come away feeling he has said nothing."

Before being named to head the press office, Jones had been special agent in charge in Springfield, Illinois. He made no secret of his desire to become an SAC again. Although smart and personable, he did not have the touch of Collingwood, Baker, or Young. Under Jones, the press office deteriorated to the point where even media representatives in field offices and assistant directors complained about its unresponsiveness and bureaucratic approach. Because of the office's slowness, negative attitude, and insistence on controlling events, media representatives in field offices circumvented the office and did not inform it of their plans for local press conferences and interviews. When, as assistant director over the criminal investigative division, Baker asked the office to put out a booklet on the bureau's success in freeing hostages at the Talladega prison, the office took more than a month. By the time the booklet came out, the press had lost interest. Bureau officials complained that the office was even slow to coordinate award ceremonies and speeches.

Of more concern to reporters, the office lost the credibility it had developed under Webster. While some press officers continued to do an excellent job, arranging some five hundred interviews a year with FBI officials, others operated more like salesmen than press officers. They did not understand that the unctuous, formal approach of the Hoover era would not work today. Because they did not balance their glowing accounts of bureau accomplishments with the mistakes and uncertainties, what they said was not taken seriously. Because Sessions did not cut them in on his thinking, they were not valuable as sources of information.

Nevertheless, in rating the press office, the FBI's inspection division said it was "very effective and very efficient," an unusually high grade. The inspection report made no significant recommendations for improvement. Having interviewed only one of the reporters from the major newspapers and television networks that cover the bureau, the inspection division had little or no information on which to base its judgment. That reporter said he had not revealed his negative opinion of the office because he was afraid it would affect his relations with the FBI.

A reporter from a major network who was not interviewed said of the press office, "It was obviously a lot stronger under Webster.

Roger Young and Bill Baker were so close to Webster. They were so knowledgeable about the FBI. They had a real sense of the FBI's mission. Sessions downgraded that job. He didn't have people who were real close to him."

The reporter said that under Sessions, the press office no longer seemed informed on events going on within the FBI.

"When Young and Baker were there, if Kansas City was having a press conference, the day before you could call in and they would say, 'They are having one, and you ought to be there.' Now they have no idea. You frequently find out about it when it is over and too late to say the FBI did something significant," the reporter said. "My biggest criticism is, if they are doing something interesting, I'm not going to hear about it."

"Under Webster," said a reporter for a major newspaper, "they [the public affairs officers] seemed to be more important advisers. They seemed to have a lot more information and insight."

FBI media representatives in field offices, who generally understood how to handle the press, had a similarly negative view of the headquarters operation. If the inspection staff had asked for his view of the headquarters press office, Frank G. Scafidi, the media representative at the Washington metropolitan field office, said, "I would have told them they are archaic, maybe loosening up some, but they need to go a long way.

"I would tend to go for openness as much as you can, no matter what the story is—good, bad, or ugly—which down the road creates more fair treatment when you do stub your toe than if you say, 'No comment, can't help you.' "

Besides the fact that the press office had obtained a correction in the *New York Times*—no great feat if an article is wrong—the inspection staff singled out for praise the fact that the public affairs office had prepared an "abbreviated history" of the FBI. But that, too, lacked credibility. Nowhere did the account refer to anything negative in the FBI's past. Reading the twenty-page, single-spaced document, one would never know that the bureau had engaged in any abuses or illegal acts or that, as a result of congressional hearings conducted by the Church Committee, the FBI had had to implement significant reforms. The only reference to COINTELPRO—the illegal plan to disrupt antiwar protesters and other malcontents—was a defense of it. The history said that no specific guidelines had prohibited the kinds of tactics used under the program—tactics that Attorney General William Saxbe described as "abhorrent in a free society."[450]

Writing a 7,600-word history of the FBI without mentioning any abuses was like writing a history of the United States without mentioning slavery. In part, the parochialism reflected a bureau-wide attitude. So objective and factual in its investigations, the FBI as an institution was still defensive about its past. Most senior bureau officials freely acknowledge the mistakes of the Hoover era. James Greenleaf, the associate deputy FBI director, and John Collingwood, who is over public and congressional affairs, examined bureau files on FBI abuses during the Hoover era and were horrified. As part of a special Justice Department investigation of former FBI officials, Greenleaf looked into the extensive work that bureau employees had done on Hoover's home. Collingwood examined COINTELPRO files when he oversaw their release under the provisions of the Freedom of Information Act.

"That was unbelievable stuff," Collingwood said. "You thought nobody in his right mind would do those things."[451]

But most agents who were in the bureau before Hoover's death had no personal experience with the abuses. The vast majority of today's agents entered the FBI after Hoover died. In learning about Hoover, they tended to rely on oral history passed from agent to agent. According to this version, Hoover built a great institution, reflected the times, and perhaps stayed on too long. While Hoover did build a great institution, the abuses he perpetrated occurred throughout his career. They were recognized at the time as abuses, as evidenced by the fact that the press ran exposés on them when it was able to learn about them. Thus, the need for a "not to be contacted" list of reporters who had not written favorably about the bureau.

One way to set the record straight would be to take a balanced approach in the course on bureau history given to new agents. But, like the history prepared by the FBI's public affairs office, it manages to avoid any reference to abuses. Instead, through a slide show, the two-hour course runs through the same popular history that members of the public get when they tour FBI headquarters—pictures of G-Men capturing Bonnie and Clyde, Rudolf Abel, and the Rosenbergs. There is nothing about Hoover bugging, harassing, and trying to discredit Martin Luther King, acts that then Attorney General Nicholas deB. Katzenbach called "shocking" and "grossly improper" when he found out about them. There is nothing about illegal surreptitious entries, or about the bureau spying on political activities at the 1964 Democratic National Convention for the Johnson White House. There is no mention of how Hoover illegally had

FBI employees paint his house each year; build a front portico, a redwood fence, a rear deck, and a flagstone walk at his home; or install artificial turf and plant and move shrubbery outside his home. Nor is there a reference to Hoover's pocketing a portion of the royalties from *Masters of Deceit* after bureau employees wrote the book on government time. Two of the most critical differences between the old and the new bureau—the bureau's fixation during the Hoover era with statistics, and its lack of focus in the counterintelligence area—do not rate a mention either.

In teaching the course, the only hint Nicholas Landino, Jr., gave that Hoover might have been the subject of controversy was when he said, "Depending on who you are reading, he [Hoover] is either a devil or angel. You need to do some balanced reading. I encourage you to do this." He listed a range of books, including several that are quite critical of Hoover.[452]

In fact, without reading them, many agents dismiss critical books on Hoover as unfair media distortions. Photographs of Hoover dot bureau offices, and his name appears on the headquarters building. Like Richard Nixon, Hoover was responsible for a number of achievements. But the prominence of his image throughout bureau offices suggests that the FBI is insensitive to the abuses he perpetrated. Bureau officials say that as the FBI's longest-serving director, he deserves to be remembered, just as George Washington is remembered.

With Hoover dead and the crime records division reorganized, the Society of Former Special Agents of the FBI carries on the battle to perpetuate the image of Hoover as deity. Whether because they feel it legitimizes their tenure, or because they have a need to worship a strong leader, the 7,800-member society—comprised for the most part of agents who served under Hoover—devotes much of its time to glorifying the former FBI director. The society often runs articles in its newsletter about Hoover's feats. It funds awards and establishes memorials in Hoover's name. And the society encourages former agents to write critical letters to those who write unfavorably about Hoover. At one point, the society discussed pushing to install a Hoover memorial with an eternal flame at the FBI Academy, an idea that current bureau officials mocked.

To be sure, some of the recent claims about Hoover, such as that he wore dresses, are pure malarkey. Based on questionable sources, they suggest that Hoover was so open about his alleged homosexuality that mob figures knew about it. In fact, at the time, there were not even rumors of cross-dressing. While Hoover's lifestyle suggests that he likely was homosexual, no credible source has demonstrated that. Probably only the late Clyde Tolson, Hoover's longtime friend, deputy, and beneficiary of his estate, knew for sure.

From his basement office in Rockville, Maryland, Lawrence J. Heim, who was in the crime records division, edits the society's newsletter, *Grapevine*. In doing so, he obtains help from the press office. Despite his fervent admiration of Hoover, when handling inquiries from the press, Heim responds to questions honestly and professionally.

By consulting the society's directory, former agents in security or other businesses can enlist the cooperation of others in the same field. Even current agents know they will receive more cooperation from the security office of an airline if a former agent heads it. As a courtesy, a former agent may waive the formalities of requiring a subpoena to find out if a suspect was on a flight manifest, for example. Agents are aware that the society may not accept them as members if they are too critical of Hoover. So, even some high-ranking bureau officials think twice before being quoted on the record as saying anything negative about the FBI's founder.

The society objects even to the proposition that there is a "new" and an "old" bureau. Society officials look down on today's agents as less disciplined and less hardworking than they were. While the dedication and ingenuity of the agents are the same, the changes before and after Hoover have been breathtaking.

"I think there is a new bureau as opposed to the old bureau," said Caroll Toohey, the assistant director over the inspection division. "I think it started under Clarence Kelley. He brought a lot of progressive ideas and got things started in a certain direction. They were carried on by Webster and Sessions. They are totally different organizations." Toohey, who gives speeches to the society, said that if the members "came back today, they wouldn't recognize it as the FBI."

Revell compared the degree of change since Hoover's death with the amount of change that occurred after Hoover took over the corrupt Bureau of Investigation in 1924. "Those who worked with him [Hoover] become defensive and don't admit to any of the mistakes and failures," Buck Revell said. "Hoover was a man who built a fine organization and essentially kept politics out of it, but he also had his own agenda. The zenith of his effectiveness was about 1960, after which he sort of lost it."[453]

The FBI's institutional lack of objectivity about Hoover can be attributed in part to Webster and Sessions, who strenuously avoided saying anything negative about him. For the FBI as a whole to take a more realistic approach to the Hoover era would require a decision by the director.

"To denigrate Hoover would be to denigrate the careers of former agents," Webster said. "He was a symbol of what they had contributed in their time in the agency. My thinking on it was I didn't come to take sides over J. Edgar Hoover. I took sides to make sure the agency was staying relevant to the times and the challenges."

Whatever the policy from on high, many FBI agents will always be suspicious of the media. Many believe that having anything to do with the press, including acting as a media representative, will only get them into trouble.

"Our agents have seen hatchet jobs and are concerned they will be the victim of it," said Scott Nelson, who was Tom Jones's deputy in the press office. "We tell the executives it makes sense to get our story out. If you didn't get it out, then shame on you. If it's not reported properly, and you had an opportunity to deal with it, then don't complain about it."

"There are very few people who want the press job in the FBI," said Steve Ramey, who did two tours as the media representative for the Washington field office. "It takes you away from what the FBI is all about—investigating cases. You are setting yourself up to get into trouble. You should develop a sound relationship with reporters, and you can't do that by feeding them the straight bureau line. A good reporter is going to see that. When you say, 'We never make a mistake, and we handle every case professionally,' well, we do make mistakes. That's part of life. Hopefully, mistakes will be corrected or at least are not the type that will be catastrophic and get somebody killed. The media relations job just isn't pleasant."

"We have our own culture," said Collingwood, who now heads the public affairs office. "We all think like FBI people. Particularly at the headquarters level, we're all extremely proud of the bureau and that we are FBI agents. We're a little bit suspect of anyone who is not."

Nevertheless, the press office surveyed articles relating to the FBI and found them generally to be "fair," Nelson said. "We categorized articles that are negative, positive, or neutral," Nelson said. "The best articles are the neutral ones that just report facts. We found that 54 percent were favorable, 42 percent were neutral, and 5 percent were negative."[454]

If an article or a book singles out an agent for praise, it may get him in trouble. The bureaucracy works to level all players. One way or another, a way may be found to criticize an agent who maintains a high profile. In Hoover's day, even having a business card would have been unthinkable. Today, agents freely hand out business cards, but the institutional aversion to letting anyone take personal credit lingers.

Still, even the most wary agents recognize that the press can be valuable, not only in projecting a good image of the FBI—which often requires focusing on individual agents—but in helping to catch criminals. Fox Broadcasting Company's *America's Most Wanted* and NBC's *Unsolved Mysteries* have been powerful tools used by the press office for finding fugitives. *America's Most Wanted* succeeds in locating an average of thirty fugitives a year, while *Unsolved Mysteries* nabs about twenty a year.

In some instances, the cooperation of the press extends to withholding information that may harm a case or a victim. The first note from the kidnappers of Sidney J. Reso, an Exxon Corporation executive who was snatched in front of his home in Morris Township, New Jersey, warned that there should be no publicity about the kidnapping. As a result, the FBI's Newark office asked the media to call Reso's disappearance a missing-persons case.

"We told them if our guy is alive, we have to get him back," said Gary Penrith, the special agent in charge in Newark. " 'We'd appreciate it if you would do this,' and they did." In return, Penrith promised to give the press extensive details about the case once it was solved. "We said, 'We'll try and return the favor,' which we did in aces, I think," Penrith said. "The press went along with it 100 percent. They did everything they could to help."[455]

The only exception was the *New York Post*, which ran a story from a source saying that Reso had apparently been kidnapped. The paper had not checked with the FBI first. The bureau therefore did not have a chance to ask the paper to alter its story.

As it turned out, when the FBI received the first note, Reso was already dead. By watching every public phone in the area twelve hours a day, the Newark office was able to solve the case and arrest Arthur D. Seale, a former supervisor of Exxon's private security guards, and his wife, Irene. Irene Seale later pleaded guilty in federal court to two counts of extortion and agreed to testify against her husband, who then pleaded guilty himself.[456]

As in the Hoover days, the press office tried to control television programs when it could. The office has a letter of understanding with ABC's *FBI: The Untold Stories*, giving it veto power over what is shown, according to Swanson D. Carter, who is in charge of liaison with the program. While in part the agreement is to prevent sensitive methods from being disclosed, the agreement also gives the bureau the power to veto anything it considers inaccurate or that reflects poorly on it. Thus, when the program wanted to air the story of Mark S. Putnam, the FBI agent who killed the informant he had impregnated, "We discouraged it, and they agreed," Nelson said. David Buelow, one of the Arthur Company executives who deals with the FBI, said that the bureau also vetoed a show on the fatal shooting of FBI agent Robin Ahrens by her fellow agents. To make sure the FBI retains control, an agent from the Los Angeles field office sits in on the production meetings as the weekly TV shows are planned and receives a copy of the shooting schedule. Like Whitehead's The FBI Story, which was edited by Hoover executives, the show does not disclose that the bureau controls its content.[457]

"We have veto power to the extent we are made aware of the issue, and we will go to the show and let them know we don't like this, we don't like that. Change it. Then they change it," Carter said. "If they don't comply with our wishes, we can simply cut it off. We informed them by letter of the conditions."[458]

Recognizing that there were problems in the press office, Sessions eventually recombined it with congressional affairs. Naming Jones SAC in Cleveland, one of the top fifteen offices, Sessions placed Collingwood in charge of the new public and congressional affairs office. Collingwood vowed to make the combined office of 140 employees more responsive to the press. As chief of congressional affairs, Collingwood had been troubled by a response that the public affairs office had made to a letter from an elementary school student that a member of Congress had asked Collingwood to answer. To Collingwood, the answer prepared by the press office was a kiss-off; it did not answer the student's question. Using materials the press office makes available to the public, it would not have been difficult to answer the student's question properly.

"My purpose in life is to make as much information available to the media as possible without compromising investigations," Collingwood said after taking over the new office. "I will be raising the profile of the press office, get them better plugged in to things, get them plugged in to the director."[459]

Taking an innovative approach, Collingwood meshed some of the press and congressional affairs activities. An officer familiar with certain issues—like the FBI's push to make it easier for the bureau to wiretap digital telephone communications—now responds to questions both from members of the media and from members of Congress. More important, by being more open and direct, Collingwood restored the press office's most important asset: credibility.

19

The Director: Perception vs. Reality

● **According to bureau legend,** Hoover once penned these words on a memo about a fugitive: "Watch the borders." He meant that the memo as typed had not left wide enough margins for him to write his comments. But headquarters is said to have interpreted the remark as a command to watch the borders for the wanted man. Agents rushed to the Mexican and Canadian borders to carry out Hoover's instructions.

As a paramilitary organization, the FBI accords tremendous loyalty and unswerving obedience to the person who has the title of director. At the same time, agents by their nature are independent, skeptical people. They could not be good investigators otherwise. They are in the information business and enjoy passing on the latest news—or rumor. Ever since Hoover's day, the result has been a schizophrenic existence. As demonstrated by the Hoover anecdote, when the director wants something, he gets it—and fast.

"The support for the director is like nothing you have ever seen before," said John Otto, who was acting FBI director after Webster left to become director of Central Intelligence. "It's like having the ultimate jet aircraft at your control."[460]

But agents distinguish between the position of director and the person who actually has the job. They often grumble among themselves about the individual holding the office, questioning his judgment, style, direction, and taste. Like any other employees, agents' individual needs and ambitions color their perceptions of the boss.

Beyond the reality and agents' perceptions is a third layer—the public image of the director. In Washington, where power rather than money is the coin of the realm, creating the right image can be the most important part of a director's job. For the FBI is like a machine that operates quite efficiently without anyone at the controls. As long as no one tries to change its direction, it will continue to vacuum up criminals and spew them out like a giant snowblower. On the other hand, if the public sees the director as less than honest or competent, support for the bureau diminishes.

At image building, Hoover was the master. He was said to be incorruptible, fiercely loyal to his agents, a patriot, and a visionary. In fact, Hoover laid the foundation for the world's most effective crime fighting organization. By stressing careful selection and character, he built an agent cadre of unusually high quality. He was a pioneer in such areas as training, use of scientific laboratory techniques, and accurate reporting and filing of information. Long before the Supreme Court's 1966 decision in *Miranda vs. Arizona*, Hoover required FBI agents to warn suspects of their rights when they were arrested. Under Hoover, the FBI was virtually free of corruption. Agents neither engaged in brutality nor fabricated evidence. The bureau developed a well-deserved reputation for accuracy and honesty in reporting facts, for tenacity in getting its man, and for handling complex investigations.

But, like his achievements, Hoover's abuses were monumental. They ranged from illegal use of bureau employees to maintain his house to illegal break-ins and wiretaps. Through implicit blackmail techniques, Hoover set himself up as a power feared by members of Congress and presidents. He was the moral arbiter of the country, the czar of a national thought police. Through COINTELPRO, Hoover violated the rights of Americans, using the same tactics the KGB used on Soviet citizens. Because of his emphasis on quantity over quality, and because he feared corruption of his agents, Hoover ignored the important problems that only the FBI was in a position to address—organized crime, political corruption, and white collar crime. Instead, agents under Hoover wasted their time taking credit for stolen cars recovered by police. In the area of counterintelligence, Hoover had trouble distinguishing between people who engaged in espionage and those who had dissident political views, with disastrous consequences both for espionage investigations and for citizens exercising their right of free speech.

Hoover considered the bureau his child, and he ran it like an arbitrary parent. How much he actually cared about agents is open to question. According to Dana Caro, a former agent in charge of the Washington metropolitan field office, Hoover declined to attend the funeral of Terry R. Anderson, an agent who was slain in 1966 by a suspect in a kidnapping near Shade Gap, Pennsylvania.

"You can't imagine the impact that had on the agents and the bureau nationwide," Caro said. "I have never said a nice word about Hoover since then. He didn't give a shit about the FBI. He didn't care about the people. He had disdain for us." In contrast, Caro said, "Webster drove himself to exhaustion to attend the funeral for the Miami agents who were killed."[461]

As the only director who had been an agent, Clarence Kelley had a clear idea of how the bureau needed to be changed. When he became director in 1973, he immediately set out to make the FBI more progressive and effective. Kelley put a stop to the fixation on statistics. He instituted career boards composed of high-ranking FBI officials to make personnel selection more objective and fair. He demanded that investigations be opened only when there was reason to believe that a violation of law had occurred. And he began a push to hire females and minorities.

"They [the Nixon White House] thought old Clarence, who had been an FBI agent for twenty years and retired and became Kansas City police chief, would be malleable," said Buck Revell, who was in Kelley's office of planning and evaluation. "He was entirely different from that. He was very amiable but also very straight. He brought with him the concept of reorganizing the bureau that today is largely responsible for what we are doing and how we are doing it."[462]

"Kelley helped create an environment for change and innovation," said Lee Colwell, who headed what was then the planning and inspections division under Kelley and later was an associate director under Webster.[463]

Because of opposition from Hoover holdovers, Kelley had to move cautiously. He never was able to put into effect all the reforms he had in mind. "Too many people liked things the way they were," Kelley said in his book. Moreover, as a part-time director who returned to his home in Kansas City to see his sick wife every week from Thursday until Monday, Kelley was not able to devote the energy needed to make over the bureau.

Despite his achievements, Kelley's public image was that of an honest plodder, a square-jawed traditionalist who was afraid to make changes. This misperception arose because he had no feel for dealing with the media and Congress and never projected his program outside the bureau.

After Hoover, what the FBI needed more than anything was a director who would restore its credibility. Webster understood that. Like Hoover, he was a master at image building. But, unlike Hoover, there were few differences between the image he projected and the reality.

Born on March 6, 1924, in St. Louis, William Hedgcock Webster attended secondary school in Webster Groves, a suburb of St. Louis. He served as a lieutenant in the U.S. Navy during World War II and in the Korean War. After graduating from Amherst College in 1947 and from Washington University Law School in 1949, he practiced law in St. Louis. In 1960, he was appointed U.S. Attorney for the Eastern District of Missouri.

In 1961, Webster returned to the practice of law. In 1970, he was appointed a judge for the U.S. District Court for the Eastern District of Missouri. In 1973, he was named to the U.S. Court of Appeals for the Eighth Circuit. Although Webster was a Republican, President Carter appointed him FBI director in 1978.

Webster had an ageless face, thin lips, and a high forehead. His slightly graying black hair was always immaculately combed. He wore Brooks Brothers suits, monogrammed button-down shirts, and gold tie clips. After his wife Drusilla died of cancer in 1984, Webster dated a number of attractive women, from tennis pro Kathy Kemper to syndicated columnist Karen Feld. He eventually married Lynda Jo Clugston, a very attractive thirty-four-year-old blonde who had once applied to the CIA and been turned down because of a minor health problem.

A competitive tennis player, Webster recognized that "tennis diplomacy" could win more support in Washington than the most eloquent testimony before congressional oversight committees. He had played with everyone from George Bush when Bush was vice president to Zsa Zsa Gabor.

As a former federal judge, Webster came to the job with built-in credibility. While Webster never criticized Hoover, he implicitly positioned himself in a different orbit by repeatedly emphasizing the importance of adhering to the Constitution and the law.

"He was very careful not to talk about his predecessors at the FBI or CIA in ways that were disparaging," said Russell J. Bruemmer, who was his assistant at the FBI and later became his general counsel at the CIA. "It was also clear from watching him that he was making, and knew he was making, conscious decisions that were very different from Hoover's."[464]

Webster preferred that agents refer to him as "judge" rather than "director," in part to convey his independence and probity. In contrast to the cult of personality created by Hoover, "He promoted the agency rather than Bill Webster," Bruemmer said.

"I found some extraordinarily gifted and dedicated public servants who believed in their organization but were shaken by the criticisms that were heaped on them after the Church and Pike committees and the break-in [black bag] investigations," Webster said. "I wanted to get moving with them, and moving in ways the American people expected. I kept using over and over again the line I used when I was sworn in: 'We will do the work the American people expect of us in the way the Constitution demands of us.' "[465]

Webster brought in assistants with law degrees from Harvard and Yale to help evaluate proposals. As lawyers, Webster wanted his assistants to make sure bureau initiatives conformed with statutes and guidelines. But he also wanted them to look at what went on in the FBI as outsiders might have.

"He wanted us to look at it like Joe Q. Public," said Nancy D. McGregor, one of his assistants. " 'Does this make sense?' "

In material the bureau submitted to Webster, McGregor would make sure all points were covered. If she did not think he would approve it, she would send it back with the reasons. When McGregor later went to the CIA with him, she came to realize what people meant when they said the FBI was a paramilitary organization.

"The nice thing about being the judge's special assistant especially at the FBI was it is a militarily structured organization," said McGregor. "The director is like the general, not like at the CIA," which is more loosely structured.

"A lot of people [at the CIA] were resentful because we were the young Turks and outsiders," she said. "We couldn't give marching orders. We didn't have anyone working for us. It required a lot of diplomatic skill."[466]

Still, the assistants had to tread carefully.

"There is a natural aversion by the agents to any outsider," said Howard Gutman, who also was a special assistant to Webster. "No matter how good the director's background, if he didn't go to Quantico and carry a gun, there is at least initially mistrust and an 'us versus them' perception."

But Webster led forcefully. Besides increasing the numbers of blacks and women, Webster focused on improving the bureau's investigations. Under him, the bureau began aggressively to attack terrorism, white collar crime, political corruption, organized crime, drug trafficking, and espionage. Webster had John B. Hotis, an agent with a doctorate in law from Yale, develop guidelines to pinpoint exactly when an investigation could be opened. Just what elements had to be present? Sometimes defining the necessary ingredients was like a metaphysical exercise, but it was a way of restricting the bureau's power so that it would not run amok.

Webster would zero in on the minutest details of cases to make sure they would hold up in court. In the ABSCAM investigation, he made sure that no member of Congress was pressured into taking a bribe from the undercover agent pretending to be a sheik in the operation.

"We had put all these protective mechanisms into place in AB-SCAM," Webster said. " 'Don't bring anybody to the sheik who wasn't ready to deal. We're not going to sell him. Bring him if he wants to deal. We're not going to sell him. Don't try to persuade him. If he wants to leave, let him leave.' "

Webster became involved as well in the investigation of federal judge Alcee L. Hastings in Miami, this time with less beneficial results. An intermediary was supposed to take a $125,000 bribe for Hastings from an FBI undercover agent. Webster was afraid that the FBI, which had supplied the bribe money, would never see it again. So the FBI arrested the intermediary before he could give the bribe money to Hastings, weakening the government's case against the judge. Hastings was acquitted of soliciting bribes in return for favorable rulings for defendants who appeared before him. The Senate eventually impeached Hastings for engaging in a "corrupt conspiracy."[467]

Webster stressed the importance not only of obeying the law but of not *appearing* to be too intrusive in using techniques such as wiretapping.

"Anytime you deal with ultrasensitive techniques, you have to have thought through the reality and perception of your actions," Webster said. "It must not only be legal but also not be seen to be so offensive that we might lose the technique because of outrage."

When Webster thought agents were not giving him the full story, or had not done their homework, his voice became taut and his eyes steely.

"At one of the first executive conferences, they started to give Webster the dance," said William Gavin, who became an assistant director under Webster. "He didn't let them dance more than seventeen seconds before he was all over them. He would let you know with a crisp, terse statement with the blue sparks coming out of his eyes. I wouldn't want that happening to me more than once. It was like your dad when he took you to task. You didn't want to upset him again. He saw through the bureaucratic horse manure. All of a sudden, people realized, 'If we don't know the answer, say we don't know the answer.' "[468]

"Bill Webster was difficult to work for at times, but you always knew he would be fair," Buck Revell said. "He brought out the best in his people. He did an outstanding job as director and helped return the organization to favor with the Congress, the press, and the public."

If Kelley fathered the new bureau, Webster brought it into the world and shaped it into the organization it is today. For all the care he took to avoid abuses, the investigation of the left-wing CISPES organization, the intrusion symbolized by the Library Awareness Program, and the harassment of Donald Rochon occurred during Webster's watch. While disturbing, they did not rise to the level of violations of law.

Webster served as director until May 1987, when he became director of Central Intelligence. John Otto, the executive assistant director, served as acting director until November 1987. To succeed Webster, President Reagan nominated Sessions, who had been recommended by Edwin Meese III, then the attorney general. The Texas congressional delegation had brought him to Meese's attention. As a federal judge, Sessions was thought to be a clone of Webster. With white hair that framed his face, Sessions had a wide smile and riveting eyes behind round glasses. He looked like a country boy, farm raised, with enough of a Texas twang to make the stories he liked to tell sound authentic.

The son of a minister in the Disciples of Christ Church, William Steele Sessions was born on May 27, 1930, in Fort Smith, Arkansas. He graduated from Northeast High School in Kansas City, which Clarence Kelley had attended. When he was a sophomore, he met his wife, Alice, who attended the same school. She too was the daughter of a minister, but from a different church—the Reorganized Church of Jesus Christ of Latter-Day Saints. She later became a Methodist.

"Sessions was a good student and well respected," said Charlene Law, who was a friend of Alice Sessions and double dated with them after high school. "He was not high profile. He was not extremely outgoing. He was always known as one of the nice guys. Just a nice guy."

"His father always said he didn't care what he did for a living as long as he is a Christian gentleman," Alice Sessions said. "That has been the ideal he held up to him all his life."

Sessions attended the University of Kansas and Florida State University before graduating in 1956 from Baylor University and, two years later, from its law school. He served as a first lieutenant in the Air Force and, after ten years of practicing law in Waco, Texas, joined the Justice Department in 1969. There, he headed a section that prosecuted draft evasion, pornography, election fraud, and violations of the Foreign Corrupt Practices Act. Having served in 1966 as a county chairman for Senator John Tower, the Texas Republican, Sessions was connected politically. In 1971, he was named U.S. Attorney in San Antonio. Three years later, he became a judge at the U.S. District Court in San Antonio and, in 1980, chief judge.

As a judge, Sessions was known for his fairness, his toughness, and his attention to decorum.

"He sits at the edge of his seat, with a straight back," said federal judge Ed Prado. "There is no humor in his courtroom."

In person, he had a self-deprecating sense of humor and knew how to put people at ease. Despite a bout with polio when he was sixteen, Sessions was a mountain climber and made two treks up to the eighteen-thousand-foot level of Mount Everest.

Sessions gained national attention when he presided over the trials of defendants charged with assassinating U.S. District Court Judge John H. Wood. Accusing Sessions of "unspeakable evil" and the government of "Gestapo tactics," Charles Harrelson, the convicted triggerman, ranted in Sessions's courtroom in San Antonio, "I think the court should consider a charge against itself for rape and murder." Sessions never flinched. He quietly sentenced him to two consecutive life terms for murder and conspiracy to murder, to be served after he has finished a forty-year state sentence for drug trafficking.

Before recommending Sessions to succeed Webster, Meese consulted Jack Lawn, who was the FBI's SAC in San Antonio and had directed the investigation into Wood's killing. Lawn spoke highly of him.

"I thought he would be the ideal candidate for the FBI," Lawn said. "He is a people person. I thought that was important. As chief judge, he listened. I thought that would be a wonderful attribute for him to bring to FBI headquarters."[469]

After two postponements because of a still undiagnosed stomach ailment, Sessions was sworn in on November 1987. Contrary to expectations, Sessions turned out to be quite different from Webster and a man of many contradictions. Whenever it seemed that people had a handle on him, he did something to prove them wrong.

Despite advice from bureau officials that he stay at headquarters to learn how the FBI works, Sessions spent his first several years visiting all but four of the FBI's fifty-six field offices. In 1988 he gave 88 speeches and in 1989 101 speeches to the likes of the Rotary Club of Cincinnati and the El Paso Chamber of Commerce. When visiting field offices, he shook every agent's hand and made him or her feel appreciated.

After visiting the field offices, Sessions cut down on traveling but continued to give several out-of-town speeches a month. On one such trip, Sessions and his wife, Alice, flew to New York in the Justice Department's MU-2 Mitsubishi turbo prop to hand out agent awards he had instituted. Normally, Sessions flew on the FBI's Sabreliner jet, but Attorney General William Barr was using it that day.

Sessions and his wife arrived at National Airport in Washington in an FBI limousine, which drove onto the tarmac. During the plane trip, a member of Sessions's twelve-agent security detail served coffee and offered a platter of sliced fruit.

Sessions presented awards to nine agents, including Eileen J. Roemer, who received the FBI's Meritorious Achievement Medal. A pretty woman with red hair, Roemer was the daughter of retired New York agent William J. Roemer. She received the award for her part in a surveillance with another agent and two New York City detectives working an Asian organized crime case. Two neighborhood toughs, apparently unhappy that their turf was being invaded, began assaulting one of the detectives. The second detective came out of a car to help. The first detective pulled out his gun and identified himself as a police officer.

"Shoot me, shoot me! I'll make you eat that fuckin' gun," one of the men said.

The detective replaced his gun in its holster, but one of the men grabbed it. At that point, Roemer, who had been watching from inside a surveillance van, rushed the two men.

"FBI! You're under arrest," she yelled, lunging at the man who had taken the detective's gun. She got him in a choke hold, and he dropped the gun. The two men then fled, but not before Roemer had taken down their license number, leading to their arrest.[470]

As Sessions handed the medal to Roemer, he whispered congratulations in her ear. Then it was off to the University Club for a luncheon speech. It was the kind of work Sessions does best.

On the plane ride back to Washington, Sessions ate a Snickers bar and did a *New York Times* crossword puzzle.

Sessions seems to be a genuinely warm, outgoing, and decent man, and it comes across in his speeches. Like Webster, he talked about the need to adhere to the rule of law and to the Constitution. To those who remember the Hoover days, it was reassuring stuff. But while the talk at the University Club was better than most—perhaps because it was not prepared—Sessions's speeches were usually so general and full of platitudes that they sounded more like sermons than authentic communication. This contributed to his reputation among agents as a cheerleader who engages in "Sessions-speak."

"He's a cheerleader for the FBI," said Larry Lawler, who headed the Los Angeles office and was on Sessions's SAC advisory board. "He goes out and gives speeches and pumps up the FBI. 'We're doing a great job for you.' He comes into the field offices and says, 'You're doing a great job.' The agents go away very pleased. They tell their wives, 'I met the director, and he shook my hand.' So he is a good cheerleader. But telling us where we are going to be in six years? Holy Christ.

"He just babbles," Lawler added. "At the SAC conferences, there was the gibberish meter. Sessions would get up, and the meter would start beeping. He thinks he is a very good orator. He thinks he's very glib. He talks and everyone looks at each other and says, 'What the hell is he saying?' "

When Sessions talked with bureau officials, "You don't want to be impolite," Lawler said. "You can't walk away saying, 'I don't understand.' He would say, 'This guy doesn't understand me. I have to remove him.' So you say, 'Uh-huh.' There is no sense to what he says."[471]

Sessions loved the perquisites of his job. He wore his brass FBI badge pinned to his shirt at all times. He referred to himself in the third person as "your director," even when talking to retired agents. These habits annoyed some agents, who pointed out that unless going on an arrest, agents pin the badge to the inside of their credentials case.

"I'm sure it's an emotional thing that is done from his heart," one agent said of Sessions's practice of wearing his badge. "But it's not where agents wear the badge. It may be his attempt to show his love for the bureau. But he has created the wrong impression, that he has less respect for the badge because of the way he wears it."

Asked why he wore the badge on his shirt, Sessions gave an example of Sessions-speak: "The badge was given to me at the ceremony when I was sworn in. When I got it, I said to myself I would wear it. I knew that agents all have their credentials, and I knew I had my credentials. I knew I wasn't an agent. I knew I wasn't an investigator. But it's my identification really more with the bureau than anything else. I know that right now I'm on bureau business. If I go to an embassy party tonight, I'll be on bureau business."

As a former federal judge, Sessions was expected to be able to focus on complex issues. Former aides say that he assimilated complicated memos. The question is whether he wanted to. Many agents reported trying to brief him on important subjects, only to find him looking over their shoulders at his television set, which he kept tuned to CNN with the volume off, or—when traveling—interrupting to ask about the sights.

Sessions kept a neat office and was proud of the fact that he emptied his In box each day. But there was a frenetic quality to the way he ran the bureau. He constantly peppered assistant directors with questions through their electronic mail, requiring them to conduct research that was often pointless because Sessions later forgot what his questions had been.

"He will ask you a question, you'll begin the answer, and he'll walk away," said a former member of Sessions's FBI security detail, which consists of FBI agents who request the assignment.

In December 1990, Sessions traveled to Atlantic City to publicly announce, with Dick Thornburgh, then attorney general, that based on an FBI investigation, the Justice Department was filing a civil suit against the largest casino-workers union in the city. On the way, Sessions asked agents from the Newark field office to brief him on the case. In the middle of the briefing, according to two witnesses, he began singing the Brylcreem commercial—"Brylcreem, a little dab will do you. Brylcreem, you'll look so debonair."

Shocked, baffled, and hurt, the agents stopped briefing him, aware that he had not been listening to them and unsure why.

Another official who briefed Sessions in Sessions's office about an espionage case was startled to find Sessions looking over the man's shoulder at a television screen showing large pots. "Those moujahedeen do everything in those pots," said Sessions, according to a *Los Angeles Times* report by Ronald J. Ostrow. "They cook in them. They shave in them."

A few days after the start of the air war against Iraq in January

1991, Sessions met with Thornburgh and other top officials in a Justice Department room shielded to prevent electronic eavesdropping. Offhandedly, Thornburgh said he had learned about the start of the air war initially from the president. He asked how the others had learned about it. When it was his turn to speak, Sessions, sitting bolt upright, said that the information was classified, according to Ostrow. When Thornburgh pointed out that everyone in the room was cleared to receive top secret information, Sessions said stiffly that he had been asked not to talk about the air strike.

"I liken him to a shore bird who runs along the shore, looks up a little startled, dashes off in another direction, and does the same thing," said a former high-ranking bureau official.

Sessions made it clear that he saw no reason to learn the details of investigations, and he displayed little interest in them.

"Sessions is an individual who, by his own admission, says, 'I am not an investigator. You people are the career investigators. You have a wealth of experience. That's your business,' " said Floyd Clarke, the deputy director. "So he doesn't try to get into the details of the investigative process to the extent some of the directors have, especially Webster."[472]

Instead, Sessions focused on the personnel, technical, and systems aspects of the bureau, trying to improve advancement opportunities for women and minorities, modernizing the bureau's record keeping, pushing such techniques as DNA typing, closing field offices that were no longer needed, trying to change practices such as keeping paper needlessly—practices that in many cases date to Hoover's time and have become archaic. Sessions focused on such boring but important issues as how the FBI coordinates with the states what data goes into the National Crime Information Center (NCIC), the national computer network that stores data for police on stolen cars and other property.

"Webster wasn't particularly interested in the board [that coordinates with the states]," said P. J. Doyle, the Florida Department of Law Enforcement official who is chairman of the NCIC advisory board. "He came to it once and said a few words and left. Sessions sent his number-three man [James Greenleaf] to every single meeting. Sessions has come to the last two out of four. Under Sessions they want to know, 'What do these guys want?' All of a sudden, they are asking and listening. Before, if they asked, they never listened."[473]

By zeroing in on such matters, Sessions complemented Webster, who had focused more on the FBI's investigations.

Besides pushing minority advancement within the bureau, Sessions worked with Coretta King and Benjamin Hooks of the NAACP on civil rights causes, engendering goodwill in the black community. He assigned Edison U. (Ed) Horne, a black agent in the Atlanta office, to work full-time with the Martin Luther King Federal Holiday Commission to establish Martin Luther King's birthday as a holiday in every state.

After Sessions presented Hooks with an FBI award, Hooks wrote to the director, "I am proud of the relationship which has been formed and continues to evolve between the NAACP and the FBI. At a time when negative publicity continues to heighten public distrust of law enforcement officials . . . a relationship such as ours must exist to perpetuate the wheels of change."

When Sessions became director, he was appalled at how much material he was given to read and how many decisions he had to make. Pointing to his In box, he said in an interview, "I would come in routinely, and the In basket you see there would have sixteen to eighteen inches of material that would flow across my desk each day. It was flowing from three executive assistant directors, all of whom were highly energetic. I would get here at 7:30 or 7:45 A.M. They would already be here. I would leave at 7:00 to 7:30 at night, and they would still be here. I would talk to them on the weekends. I was here, and they were here or at home working."[474]

Sessions decided to force down decision levels in the bureau, giving lower-level managers more responsibility. He reorganized the top hierarchy so that instead of three executive assistant directors, he had a deputy director—Floyd Clarke—and two associate deputy directors. One, Greenleaf, oversaw the administrative divisions. The other, W. Douglas Gow, oversaw the investigative divisions.

In trying to bring about change, Sessions pushed Total Quality Management (TQM), a concept used by many companies to stress doing things right the first time. He set up a separate quality management office that reported directly to him to spread the word throughout the bureau. Because of his laid-back style, some FBI executives said they were more apt to express opinions than they were under Webster. Others interpreted Sessions's inclination to push down decision making as a lack of leadership. But John Collingwood, who was Sessions's assistant and now heads the public and congressional affairs office, said it is all part of a calculated strategy.

"He is a little bit of a cheerleader in that he tries to get people to do their best," Collingwood said. "But his personality is often mistaken for a lack of firmness or conviction. That is not the case. He is absolutely intent on accomplishing some things. He is very firm in keeping the bureau moving in the direction he wants to move it. He is bound and determined to drag us into the twenty-first century. But he does that in an interesting way. He wants the bureau management structure and administrative systems to operate in a way that accomplishes things that he wants accomplished without prodding from the top. . . . He manages by allowing wide latitude to his senior officials. I really enjoy that. I have a tremendous amount of discretion and freedom. To me, that is very exciting."[475]

In running the bureau, Sessions picked highly capable agents such as Clarke and Greenleaf. A former head of the criminal investigative division, Clarke is smart, knowledgeable, and gets along well with everyone. He made it a point not to decorate his office with FBI seals and photos of himself shaking hands with presidents.

"In terms of FBI seals and flags and all those official trappings, to me, that is not a relaxing environment," he said. "I like people to come into the office and feel comfortable about talking to me and dealing on an equal plane. I'm not trying to impress anyone with the president or attorney general or me shaking hands with some official."

Clarke worked to retain experienced bureau officials who otherwise might have retired. At Clarke's urging, Sessions got the mandatory retirement age lifted from fifty-five to fifty-seven. To keep people like Revell and Greenleaf, Clarke and Sessions let them choose where they wanted to work after they tired of headquarters. Revell chose to become SAC in Dallas, while Greenleaf eventually became the London legat.

Before becoming associate deputy director for administration, Greenleaf was an assistant director over the laboratory, the training division, and the inspection division. When Webster needed to replace William Baker as his director of public affairs at the CIA, he chose Greenleaf. A cool personality, Greenleaf is both knowledgeable and sharp.

As his other associate deputy director, Sessions chose Gow. In making such decisions, Sessions had the benefit of a career board composed of high-level bureau officials. Another board reviews candidates for lower-level jobs. The board's unanimous first choice for associate deputy director was Baker. As assistant director over congressional and public affairs, and later over the criminal investigative division, Baker was one of the most liked, experienced, and respected bureau executives. Extremely bright, he moved easily between the cloistered world of FBI agents, on one hand, and the politicians and media stars who control Washington on the other. While he held extremely powerful positions at the FBI, then at the CIA, and then back at the FBI, he never lost the touch of a street agent. He was charming, slightly roguish, and able to cut through bureaucracy like a razor blade. When agents talk about Baker, they often compare him with Thomas E. DuHadway, a loved and admired agent who headed the intelligence division until his sudden death from a heart attack in 1991. Two thousand FBI employees attended his funeral, placing a piece of black tape across their badges, a demonstration of mourning.

Instead of choosing Baker for the deputy job, Sessions selected Gow, who was not among the top three recommendations of the career board. Before joining the FBI in 1967, Gow had been a captain in the Marines. He had been SAC in Knoxville, Houston, and Washington before Sessions named him to head the intelligence division.

Like Sessions, Gow was known as a nice man who said next to nothing when being interviewed. In speeches to intelligence groups, he proudly referred to a history of the intelligence division compiled under him. The three-and-a-half-page, single-spaced document was so lacking in information and so sophomoric in tone that it could have been written by a sixth-grader. But, while the career board rated him lower than Baker, Gow was highly experienced.

"He helped me on the Reso kidnapping," said Gary Penrith, the SAC in Newark. "Gow does everything in his power to help."

In choosing Gow over Baker, Sessions said that he was influenced by Gow's experience in heading the intelligence division. He wanted to have someone in the job who was experienced in both criminal and counterintelligence investigations. Those who know Sessions said it was typical of him to weigh paper qualifications and go with the person who had the most. In weighing Baker's qualifications, his tenure at the CIA apparently counted little against Gow's experience in FBI counterintelligence.

"I could have very easily chosen Bill Baker, and he would have done an excellent job," Sessions said. "I chose to give it that kind of balance."

However, in making the choice, there was considerable evidence that Sessions had followed the advice of his wife, Alice. For reasons unknown, Alice Sessions detested Baker but liked Gow.

After Sessions selected Gow, Baker left the FBI to become a senior vice president of the Motion Picture Association of America in Los Angeles.

"I thought when Bill [Baker] was in charge of the criminal division and Tom [DuHadway] was over counterintelligence, the FBI was really in good shape," said James Fox, the assistant director over the New York field office. "Then within a few months, they were both gone. It was a tremendous loss."

If nothing else, Sessions's decision to elevate Gow rather than Baker showed that he was his own man—except when Alice decided to call the shots. When Sessions decided not to appeal the judge's decision in the discrimination lawsuit brought by Hispanic agents and not to litigate the racial lawsuit brought by Donald Rochon, agents began calling him "Con-sessions." In fact, it would have been easier for Sessions to continue to litigate, sparing him the backlash from agents.

At an executive conference breakfast attended by the author, Sessions appeared firmly in command. Over sausage and pancakes, he went around the room asking the bureau's top officials what was going on in their divisions or offices. They talked about the latest kidnapping case, technological changes, the backlog in matching fingerprints, and locations of field offices.

John Hicks, the assistant director over the laboratory, described plans to make the front of the J. Edgar Hoover FBI Building look more hospitable. One idea was to erect green granite slabs along the front and decorate them with ivy planters and bronze bands. Caroll Toohey, the assistant director over inspections, said he thought the marble would make the building look like a mausoleum. Sessions wanted to know what the costs were and if the granite could be defaced easily.

"Congress is taking steps to limit their own appropriations [for their own operations], which is unusual and a bad sign," said Collingwood, reporting on the congressional area.

"It may not be a bad sign. It may be a good sign," Sessions said.

"It depends on whether you are a taxpayer or trying to get more money to the FBI," Collingwood said.

"What if you are both?" Sessions said.[476]

While Sessions's comment made Collingwood wince, it was an example of the kind of independent outsiders' thinking he brought to the bureau.

But Sessions is a jumble of contradictions, and if he was firm in some areas, he was not in others. The best example is the way he allowed his wife, Alice, and his longtime assistant, Sarah Munford, to interfere with the bureau's work.

Alice Sessions is a down-home, just-plain-folks woman who

speaks with a nasal twang and has pretty blue eyes. Having earned a master's degree in historical costuming, she designed and made costumes for the San Antonio ballet and other dance companies. In Waco, Texas, she worked on local antidrug and antipornography efforts.

Alice Sessions saw herself as a codirector of the FBI. When referring to her husband becoming FBI director, Alice Sessions says, "When we were sworn in." Sessions saw her as his helpmate at the bureau. After describing how his wife helps him in representing the FBI, Sessions said, "So I think it's kind of a two-for-one proposition. You have a director, and you also have a director's wife—very important to the bureau."

According to Whitney North Seymour, Jr., a close friend of both, Alice Sessions "puts on a wonderful wifely air, as a nice, friendly, warm person. But through it all, I know she is tough and looking out to make sure she gives him her frank advice and good judgment and picks up for him things that she believes he should know, about how he is doing his job or things she might hear about the bureau."

Alice Sessions called herself her husband's "eyes and ears."[477]

"I learn things in the elevator," she said, referring to chitchat she hears from secretaries in the elevators at headquarters.

But just how good her judgment is and how accurate her perceptions are are open to question. In giving her opinion on Bill Baker, Alice Sessions said, "Baker was known among agents as not being bright." In fact, Baker is considered one of the smartest agents ever to hit the FBI, one who was selected by both Sessions and Webster for high-level posts both at the FBI and the CIA.

According to Alice Sessions, when President Carter asked for suggestions on candidates to replace Kelley as FBI director, she wrote a letter to Carter suggesting her husband. She said that she asked Sessions first if he would mind, but Sessions claimed he knew of no such letter.

"We are probably being recorded," Alice Sessions said during a phone conversation patched through the FBI headquarters switchboard. Asked in another interview if she believes that the FBI is intercepting all her calls or only those calls routed to her home through the headquarters switchboard, she said, "My other line often gives me indications of compromise," referring to a second line to her home. "I have no idea if they are doing it on other calls." Referring to the FBI's wiretapping capabilities, she said, "I have consulted some other people professionally about this. In fact, I had the telephone company in a year ago."[478]

When something she had told the director in their bedroom was later repeated to her, she suggested to Ronald H. McCall, then the head of the director's FBI security detail, that the bureau had placed an electronic bugging device in their bedroom. Alice Sessions said she thought the bug was in a transmitter supplied to Sessions by the bureau for coded communications.

"I began thinking that the radio was kind of funny, you know," she said.

The allegation was reported through the chain of command of the administrative services division up to the level of assistant director.

Alice Sessions freely advised her husband on matters ranging from the qualifications of bureau officials to the way maternity leave is handled. In doing so, her opinions were overwhelmingly negative —opinions she shared freely with wives of bureau officials. The bureau according to Alice Sessions is full of self-serving, inept officials with their own agendas.

"In the bureau, the saying is 'mess up, move up,' " she said. "This has come to me as Bureau-ese. The other big thing you'll hear is everybody covers ass."

A teetotaler like her husband, Alice Sessions expressed negative opinions of people she saw with drinks in their hands or whom she suspected of drinking. Referring to a successful Washington lawyer who is the wife of a bureau official, Alice Sessions said that when she talked with her at an FBI legal party, she thought she "probably had been drinking. At least I felt she had. . . . They had probably been at a party before."

Referring to headquarters officials, Alice Sessions said, "Some of them are not well educated or intellectually bright, but they are cunning. They leave no fingerprints. They have to drink to facilitate things."

Referring to criticism by bureau officials that her husband watched CNN during FBI briefings, she said, "He should watch CNN. Some of them are bores and self-serving. He can't sit there and stroke them."

According to Alice Sessions, her introduction to the bureau was rocky. Even before Sessions was confirmed, "They [bureau officials] said, 'We aren't used to having a wife involved in the FBI, and we don't intend to.' "[479]

Asked who these brave agents were, she declined to say.

"It was more than once, by more than one person, on more than one occasion," she said.

In another early experience, FBI agents told her they would pick her up at the train station in Washington so that she could attend her husband's confirmation hearings. Since she was going to be in New York, the agents told her to phone the New York field office and have the office relay her call to the appropriate people in Washington. But it didn't work quite that way. According to her, the New York office thought she was a nut and would not connect her.

"I told the FBI New York office, 'I am the wife of the man who is going to be your new director,' " she said. "They put me off to somebody who gave me a cock and bull story about 'the person you wanted was out on surveillance.' They wouldn't patch me from New York to Washington."[480]

Alice Sessions said she later complained to FBI officials.

For all the problems in New York, Alice Sessions saw headquarters as the greatest enemy. "It's the field that does the work," she said. "The FBI headquarters is three or four people who have their own agenda. When you get out to the field and see this, you see the great respect people have in the community for the FBI."

Alice Sessions's husband came in for criticism as well. According to her, the FBI director has a "fatal" flaw: He is a "Pollyanna" who is "not curious." She said, "He thinks everyone is as up front as he is."

When Bill Baker retired, Alice Sessions said that she did not go to the dinner, which was attended by five hundred people including both Sessions and Webster, because she knew the jokes would include remarks she considers offensive. She later found out from her husband that she had been right. As master of ceremonies, William Gavin, the Miami SAC, had referred to the airline stewardesses Baker had dated before marrying Robin Baker, who is herself an attractive, savvy airline stewardess. Baker was forty-six when he married her.

"I think it would have been embarrassing for me to sit in front of Robin and hear this," Alice Sessions said. "I didn't want to dignify it."

But Robin Baker said, "I laughed harder at that than anything else. I called Gavin before the party and said, 'Don't hold back on account of me.' "

Another reason why Alice Sessions did not attend Baker's dinner was that she had been offended by a skit at the retirement dinner for John Otto, who had been executive assistant director. Wearing a green mask and a big shirt, an agent from the hostage rescue team pretended to be the Incredible Hulk, a monster from a television series who changed character when he got mad. At the bureau, Otto was known for his temper and would "hulk out" when displeased.

"I was embarrassed and shocked," Alice Sessions said.

Before being told of her reaction, Otto said of the skit, "We were all very happy about the whole evening, including that part. That was a stroke of genius, I thought. I called him [the agent who did it] the next day and thanked him for being such a good sport."

What most offended Alice Sessions was that then Attorney General Barr had invited Floyd Clarke, the deputy director, and Bill Baker, the assistant director, to his home and had not invited her and her husband.

Before being named attorney general, Barr had attended a speech Sessions gave at the FBI. Barr, then an assistant attorney general, was appalled. The talk was nothing but platitudes. Ever since that first encounter, Barr had been unimpressed by Sessions. Once he became attorney general, Barr developed disdain for him. Six months into his new job, Barr learned that Sessions had been using FBI planes to see his family and friends. Invariably, Alice Sessions went along on these trips. Barr talked to Sessions about it, rebuking him for taking his wife. Barr pointed out that as attorney general, he could make up excuses to take his wife anywhere in the world, yet he had never taken her on a trip. Sessions launched into a defense that Barr found laughable: that Alice Sessions was somehow important to maintaining the morale of the FBI. Barr made it clear that he did not accept Sessions's explanation, but he never followed up to make sure Sessions was not abusing his position. Instead, Barr became convinced that Sessions had to go because he was not a good FBI director. His responses in discussions seemed bizarre, and Barr tried to avoid him. For example, when deciding how to respond to the 1992 Los Angeles riots, Sessions started talking about the FBI's hostage rescue team, as if such a small force would solve the problem.

Barr was told that his predecessor, Dick Thornburgh, was said to have had so little respect for Sessions that he generally refused his calls. It appeared to Barr that Sessions's chief concern was getting invited to the right parties, taking trips to Europe, and appearing at important ceremonial functions. In one nineteen-day period, Sessions and his wife attended nineteen parties. Barr would mock the way Sessions strutted and talked, imitating his baritone voice, mouthing bromides. Barr decided that aside from the abuses, he would like to replace Sessions for incompetence. He found President Bush was also appalled by Sessions's shallowness. When Bush wondered aloud how Barr could put up with him, Barr expressed his determination to get rid of him after the 1992 election. Bush agreed.

When Barr was an assistant attorney general, he had come to know Floyd Clarke and was impressed by his professionalism, brightness, and knowledge. He much preferred the company of Clarke and Bill Baker to that of Sessions. His failure to invite Sessions to his home was intentional. As much as possible, Barr tried to deal with Clarke at the bureau rather than Sessions. But Sessions constantly tried to interpose himself so that he would not be cut out of the loop.

Barr was also put off by the surly way Sessions and his wife treated FBI agents. Alice Sessions in particular tended to treat agents like hired help. At a reception at the Brookings Institution, she motioned toward an ambassador and said to Baker, "Get the ambassador a drink."

"As soon as I finish mine, I'd be very happy to go to the bar and get anyone refreshment," Baker replied.*

Alice Sessions routinely chastised the FBI security detail as well, which is one reason why members of the detail were warned before they started the job that they will see "outlandish, bizarre, and incredible" things. The detail consists of agents who volunteer for the job. After her husband had given out awards to agents in New York, Alice Sessions asked an agent from the security detail what had happened to the platter of sliced fruit that had been on the plane on the way up from Washington.

"It's gone," he said.

"Gone?" she snapped.

"It was just fruit," he said.

"Just fruit?" she growled, humiliating him as if he had just allowed a bank robber to escape.

"It was gone by the time I got here," he said.

Bill Sessions, meanwhile, expected agents to empty coffee cans he urinated in on long trips on FBI planes, which do not have toilets.

Alice Sessions's unconventional behavior extended well beyond treating agents like serfs. She would startle members of the security detail by asking for doggie bags at receptions given by foreign embassies. While attending a meeting of Interpol in Lyons, she, Sessions, and Interpol officials dined at Le Tour Rouge, one of France's best restaurants. She later complained to astonished FBI agents that the food was terrible.

---

* During telephone interviews, Alice Sessions several times requested that the author come to her home and help her peel wallpaper from the dining room walls.

When her husband was a judge, Alice Sessions displayed little interest in the court. When Sessions became FBI director, she saw an opportunity to enhance her own status and lifestyle. When shopping in downtown Washington, Alice Sessions routinely asked FBI security guards to park her car for her in the garage under the Hoover Building. On one occasion, she asked a startled FBI guard to park her car and look after the director's elderly father, Will, who was sitting in the car.

When she accompanied her husband to a speech in Baltimore, she had Sessions divert the procession of FBI cars to an appliance plant so that she could return a toaster. Seeing the motorcade, a guard at the plant asked, "This is necessary to return a toaster?" according to an agent who was then a member of the security detail.

When the FBI decided that the director's home off Sixteenth Street in Washington needed better security, Alice had her own ideas about it. She suggested that the security detail use Donald Munford. Then the husband of Sarah Munford, Sessions's longtime assistant, Don Munford was in the home security alarm business—not in Washington but in San Antonio. Alice Sessions recommended him because she knew him. Because she is the director's wife and is determined, the security detail acceded to her request.

"When she gets her mind set on something, she won't let it go," said an agent involved in the matter. "A month may pass, but it is in the inventory."

Don Munford proposed a system that would have cost $97,046—roughly a quarter of the $435,000 the Sessiones paid for the three-bedroom home in 1989. Higher bureau officials vetoed the proposal. If allowed to proceed, it would have violated government procurement rules because of the lack of competitive bidding. In addition, the bureau officials decided that it would have been improper to award the contract to Don Munford because of his relationship to the director's special assistant. Although he asked for considerably more, the bureau paid him $5,822 for time spent doing the survey.[481]

Alice Sessions said that she had wanted other bids to be obtained. However, both Don Munford and the bureau officials involved—Weldon Kennedy, Joe Davis, and Caroll Toohey—dispute this.

"Had I been tasked with doing it from day one, I would have done it differently," said Kennedy, the assistant director over administrative services. "I would not have hired Mr. Munford because of the relationship and the appearance. He is a businessman and did a survey which he is fully qualified to do. But it gives the appearance of favoritism, and someone could question why he was selected and not someone else."

In the end, the FBI hired another private firm to improve security, including installing a fence. So that intruders could be seen, the FBI wanted to install what is known as a security fence with vertical iron pickets, the same kind used around the White House and foreign embassies in Washington. But Alice Sessions insisted on a six-foot wooden fence with slats almost touching one another. It would give her more privacy, she said. FBI security officials objected. They said that the fence she wanted should not be paid for by the FBI because it did not provide security. Instead, they believed that Alice Sessions wanted the fence to enclose her dog, Petey. William Sessions washed his hands of the issue. He even walked out of an FBI meeting called to discuss the issue, leaving Alice Sessions in charge.

"She is the authority on security," a former member of the detail said with irony. "We don't know what we are doing."

While the Sessionses may have some say in deciding what kind of security system they want in their home, FBI regulations govern the security of the J. Edgar Hoover FBI Building. According to those regulations, anyone entering the building without an escort must have a top secret security clearance and a special building pass. No one can get a top secret clearance without a need to know, which Alice Sessions does not have, according to Martin V. Hale, who, as security programs manager, is in charge of the building's security.

Nonetheless, Alice Sessions requested and received FBI head-quarters building pass number 14592, which entitles her to the special privileges accorded an assistant director or above. The pass displays a photo of her with a gold background. Passes of agents who are not assistant directors but have top secret clearances have a blue background. Because she has the special gold pass, Alice Sessions could bring in visitors without signing them in.[482]

"This [the gold pass] means an FBI official is very trusted and would not bring anyone in this building unless they are very trusted and had a need to know," said an agent familiar with the security regulations.

On the other hand, even though they have top secret clearances, agents whose photos have blue backgrounds must sign visitors in. Alice Sessions has, in fact, brought friends into the FBI building without having to clear them through the security procedures that hundreds of visitors are forced to go through every day. Even agents from field offices outside the Washington area who have top secret clearance must check in at the escort desk and receive a temporary pass before entering the building unescorted. When headquarters employees forget their passes, their supervisors are notified in writing. But because she often forgot to bring her pass, Alice Sessions and her friends were admitted without any pass. Realizing that the director had exempted his wife from such regulations, FBI security officials were afraid to challenge her.

"The building guard [at the parking garage entrance] called me and said, 'Mrs. Sessions just went by the post with a car full of ladies. What do I do?' I said, 'Get out of the way,' " said a former member of the security detail.

Even this level of access was not enough for Alice Sessions, who asked for and received a four-digit code that allowed her access to the director's suite without going through receptionists. Entry is controlled in this way because of the extraordinarily sensitive information the suite contains. On an official's desk could be the name of a mafia informant or a spy the FBI is watching, or documents from other supersecret agencies such as the CIA or the National Security Agency (NSA). In general, only those FBI officials who work in this high-security area—known as mahogany row because of its wood paneling—have a code to enter the suite.

Asked about her special access, Alice Sessions said she did not know that a top secret clearance was required.

"Why shouldn't I be able to go in and out of Bill's office?" she asked. "[T]hey better get on to investigating me for a top secret clearance because, believe me, I hear a lot more things than the girls in the telephone room do. I'm privy to a lot more things than that."[483]

Alice Sessions said that, in any case, she had forgotten the four-digit code that gave her access to the director's suite. She said the people she has brought into the building without registering them at the escort desk have generally been her immediate family—something security officials dispute.

If Alice Sessions created concern within the bureau, Sessions's assistant Sarah Munford created even more. An attractive woman with a Texas drawl, Munford began working for Sessions in 1980, when Sessions became chief judge in San Antonio and she was deputy clerk of the court. When he became FBI director, Sessions brought her to the bureau as his special assistant in charge of scheduling.

What concerned headquarters officials the most was that, having lived in Virginia for five years, Sarah Munford continued to register her Cadillac in Texas. Virginia law requires Virginia registration after living in the state thirty days. Agents, who stand to be disci-

plined if they disobey local laws, saw Sessions's refusal to require
his assistant to comply with the law as another example of the
double standard he applies when it comes to his wife and his assistant.

Munford said that she would not comment in detail on any allegations concerning her. But she said that the Virginia Department
of Motor Vehicles had granted her permission to continue to register
her car in Texas because she is in Washington for a fixed term and
has property in Texas. However, Charles E. Murphy, the department's director of investigations in Richmond, said, "There is no
such thing as a waiver. The Virginia statute doesn't give anyone the
authority to waive anything. Even Jesus Christ doesn't have the
authority to waive the laws of the Commonwealth of Virginia. I'd
like to see it [the waiver]. As far as I'm concerned, it doesn't exist."[484]

Munford again demonstrated her belief that she is above the law
on December 24, 1991, when two Texas state troopers stopped her
and her son Glenn one mile west of San Saba, Texas, for having
tinted side windows. Too much tinting is considered a safety hazard.
Munford was on the passenger side of the 1989 Chevrolet Blazer,
which was owned by her son. According to trooper Stephen L. Boyd,
as he approached the driver's side of the car, Munford rolled down
the passenger window and displayed her FBI credentials. Although
she is a support employee, Munford has so-called soft credentials,
which look like an agent's and are kept in a credentials case. Apparently, she thought that waving the credentials out the window
would take care of the ticket. Saying that she was the assistant to
the director of the FBI and that her family was in law enforcement,
Munford told the trooper, "You go home at night, and your kids
think you are a decent person, and then you go and do something
like this."[485]

Boyd ignored her and wrote her son a ticket, explaining that the
judge would probably dismiss the case if the son mailed in a photo
showing that the tinting had been removed.

"If I'm not mistaken, there was a row about selective law enforcement with the Idaho state troopers. They were letting other troopers
go when they stopped them. The FBI did an investigation of them,"
Boyd said. "She was saying her family was in law enforcement, and
she was an FBI employee, and I should have let them go," Boyd
said. "I take my kids to church and make sure they do what is right,"
he said. "Who is this lady telling me what my kids think of me?"

Munford had attached her FBI business card to Boyd's copy of
the ticket, and the following week he decided to call the number

on the card and complain. He was quickly transferred to the FBI's Office of Professional Responsibility (OPR), which opened an investigation into Munford's actions.

"Dad-gum, I thought they ought to know about it," he said. "I felt she was abusing her position by flashing her credentials. She was wanting off just because she was an FBI employee. I thought that's not right."

When asked about the incident, Munford said, "I don't know what you are talking about." She later said she had been referring to another question but said she would not discuss the matter in any case. Nor would she provide a copy of the exemption that she said allowed her to continue registering her car in Texas.

According to the Texas court, six months after the incident occurred, the ticket—which originally was for fifty-five dollars—had not been paid. A warrant was issued for the arrest of Glenn Munford as the owner of the car. When informed of this, Don Munford, Glenn's father, said, "I'll get him to pay that. I appreciate your calling me." But a month later, the warrant was still outstanding.[486]

At the direction of the OPR, the FBI sent two agents from its San Antonio office to interview Boyd and his partner. As a result of the investigation, the administrative summary unit recommended that Munford be suspended without pay for seven days.

As scheduler, Munford's job was relatively limited. But according to bureau officials and other assistants who have worked with her, she saw her role as helping to formulate policy. They say she did not understand that as an assistant she had no line authority and must defer to bureau officials. While hardworking, her diplomatic skills were in need of sharpening.

One day she called Gavin, who was then an assistant director over the inspection division.

"She wanted to talk to me," Gavin said. "She said, 'Can you come up?' I said, 'No, you can come down.' It was done lightly, but there was a message in there someplace."

Referring to Munford, John Hicks, the assistant director over the laboratory, said, "You have an individual who doesn't have a full appreciation or understanding of how this organization functions exactly. But she has found where the special projects section is, where we do plaques and photographs. Invariably she wants things done on short notice. Many requests require reviews and approvals. She is not familiar with that."

"Some people come in and think they are FBI agents," said Wayne Gilbert, the assistant director over intelligence. "We let them know early on they are not FBI agents. 'You were not there in the streets. You did not work civil rights cases. You were not spit on and kicked. You were not in a dark room at 3:00 A.M. with the rats at your feet and scared stiff. You haven't been through that crap. So don't come on to me like you were.' "

Bill Baker found that Munford tried to refer to him people who wanted to talk about pending criminal cases, not realizing that such contacts would be improper. He ignored her.

According to former assistants who have worked closely with her, Munford often claimed that the director had asked her to take action or obtain information that the director had not, in fact, requested. Moreover, these former assistants said, Munford was in the habit of making up information.

"I would never think of calling someone and telling them the director asked me to say a certain thing, when in fact he had not done that," said John L. McKay, Jr., a lawyer who was a special assistant to Sessions. "I have seen that many times [with Munford], and I think others have. It makes him [Sessions] look bad, and that is very unfortunate." He added, "I would just say that by the time I left the FBI, I did not rely on anything she [Munford] told me."

A White House fellow who had been assigned to the FBI, McKay said that Sessions had no idea that Munford lies. "He would be absolutely appalled," he said.[487]

James J. Hogan, a veteran agent who also served as one of Sessions's special assistants, said that one Monday, Munford mentioned that she had been in working all weekend. As it happened, Hogan had been in working all day Sunday and had not seen her. Nor had his eight-year-old daughter, who had watched television in Munford's office during the day. When Hogan said that he had not seen her, Munford questioned whether *he* had been in.

"She then proceeded to tell me I wasn't in," Hogan said. "She wasn't there. It was as simple as that."[488]

In the FBI, telling the truth is a prerequisite. Not only is the FBI accountable to the courts for its veracity, but agents have to trust one another when they face danger together. Moreover, the people who work in the director's suite are entrusted with some of the most sensitive secrets in the government. Everyone who worked there has to be above reproach. While it did not involve a matter of consequence, Munford's claim that she had been in all weekend shook up Hogan. He mentioned it to Ron McCall, the head of Sessions's security detail, saying that Munford "would just make things up, and that he should be careful when dealing with her," according to Hogan.

McCall then proceeded to warn the detail to be careful around Munford.

It was not the first time the security detail had noticed such behavior. Munford would routinely misplace items that she was supposed to give to Sessions, then blame the detail for not giving them to the director on time.

"The FBI is as good as it is because there is a fundamental trust of your fellow worker, not only of his ability but of his candor," said a former member of the security detail who was familiar with some of the incidents. "You make decisions based on what coworkers say. When you can no longer function in that environment, you become apprehensive, and your ability to function is greatly diminished."

Munford and Alice Sessions would talk on the phone for hours each day, often manipulating each other and putting the security detail in the middle, according to former assistants. Because she wanted to control Sessions's schedule, Munford would periodically blame the security detail for not delivering to Alice Sessions personal invitations or copies of the director's daily and future schedules. In fact, Munford would tell the detail that she did not want some of this material to go to Sessions's wife. When the detail followed Munford's instructions and Alice Sessions complained about not getting invitations, Munford would tell her she had sent the mail with the detail. She would blame the detail for losing the mail.

"But, Director, I told them," was her refrain, according to a former member of the detail.

As scheduler, Munford arranged Sessions's travel. Sessions had made it clear that the attorney general—who was, after all, his boss—had first priority on using the Justice Department's Sabreliner jet. But Munford had different ideas about which official was more important. She wanted Sessions to get the Sabreliner all the time. So, when both officials needed to travel at the same time, Munford would instruct the security detail or FBI aviation managers to tell the Justice Department that the attorney general couldn't have the Sabreliner because it was unavailable. FBI agents refused to carry out her requests; it would have meant lying to the Justice Department and the attorney general. Nonetheless, because of Munford's intervention, confusion over who should get the Sabreliner continued. In a meeting, Sessions bawled out his staff for the continuing controversy. Munford, who was at the meeting, failed to acknowledge that she had caused it.

Because she was in the habit of delving into areas they did not consider part of her job, Justice Department officials often did not return Munford's calls. Recognizing that James Kramarsic, the FBI agent who heads the attorney general's security detail, had a lot of credibility at Justice, Munford asked him to use his influence to improve her position within the department. When he said there was nothing he could do about it, she said she was displeased with him, and that the director was displeased with him, according to agents involved. Among other reasons, she cited the fact that Kramarsic had refused to go along with her requests to tell the Justice Department that the Sabreliner was unavailable for the attorney general's use. In such circumstances, agents never knew whether Munford was speaking for the director or for herself. Kramarsic later said that he felt he had been able to keep his job as head of the detail only because of his relationship with the attorney general, who was then Dick Thornburgh. In fact, when Barr became attorney general, Sessions tried to remove Kramarsic from Barr's security detail, but Barr overruled Sessions.

"So many people have no respect for her whatsoever that she finds herself thwarted in doing anything," McKay said of Munford.

In commenting, Munford said that she is an honest person. "I'll have to hope these people get to know me better," she said.

Eventually, Sessions removed McCall from his position. An agent who is a lawyer, an FBI pilot, and an accountant, McCall subsequently found himself passed over for a promotion as well. His removal followed his warning to the security detail that Munford dissembles. When Munford heard about it, she confronted him and threatened to have him fired if he ever again called her a liar.

At about the same time, McCall gave copies of the key to the Sessionses' home to each member of the director's security detail. He felt that to protect the director if he was in trouble, the security detail needed to be able to enter his home easily. In addition, Alice Sessions periodically asked the detail to let her into her house because she had forgotten her key. For these reasons, McCall gave each member of the detail a copy of the key. But McCall's action was contrary to Alice Sessions's request that the detail have no copies or only one. Thus, McCall had crossed both Munford and Sessions's wife, and his removal became a foregone conclusion.

Some tried to attribute Munford's problems to the fact that she was an outsider and a woman. But Nancy McGregor, Webster's assistant, was widely admired by bureau officials and experienced no problems at the FBI. When Sessions replaced two of his assistants with Ray and LeRoy Jahn, two former assistant U.S. Attorneys from San Antonio, they were greeted with suspicion at first. But agents quickly accepted them as the husband-and-wife team proved themselves.

The fact that Munford continued to register her car in Texas five years after she had moved to Virginia grated on many headquarters agents, who had to follow the law when they were transferred to the Washington area from other parts of the country that have lower car insurance rates. While no one at the FBI believed her a security risk, the fact that Alice Sessions was given a special exemption from the rules simply because she was the director's wife eroded respect for Sessions if not for the rules.

In his own dealings, Sessions seemed to go out of his way to demonstrate his propriety. For example, he would return FBI paper clips attached to documents that had been sent to his home. In his courtroom, he had been a stickler for rules and procedures. In his speeches, he would talk about the importance of following regulations and laws. In an interview, he said, "If you ask people today whether the bureau operates within the law, they will say 'yes, but.' They will have that shading that maybe there are times when they [the FBI] operate outside the law. That is not acceptable. We must operate within the framework of the law. We must do what the law requires."

In other settings, however, Sessions betrayed a lack of sensitivity about the way he conducted himself. As director, he repeatedly steered his speaking engagements toward his home state of Texas. In his first four years as director, one of every five of his official trips was to his home state—an average of one trip every two months. While Sessions could justify each trip as related to business, the pattern made it clear that he was taking advantage of his position to see his family and friends and his old doctor and dentist back in Texas.

But it was not this insensitivity that concerned bureau officials. Absent more information, Sessions's proclivity for returning to his home state violated no laws or regulations. Nor did it interfere with the bureau's operations. Rather, it was Sessions's refusal to control his wife and special assistant that dismayed and infuriated FBI officials. Alice Sessions controlled her husband to such an extent that she dictated what shirts he wore. Admiring an Interpol official's blue striped dress shirt at a meeting in Uruguay, Sessions remarked that he had bought a similar shirt for himself, but he said that Alice "won't let me wear it" because it made him look "too young." Many bureau officials believed Munford and Alice Sessions responsible for Sessions's selection of bureau officials who were seen as less competent than their competition.

While it is impossible to know how spouses influence each other, many of Sessions's personnel decisions conformed with his wife's views. An example was the way he began to cut out Deputy Director Floyd Clarke—whom Alice Sessions disliked—from contact with then Attorney General Barr. Many thought that Sessions did not choose Baker as an associate deputy director because he was a close friend of Clarke. Naming Baker to the post would only have strengthened Clarke's position, the theory went.

In Alice Sessions's mind, Clarke was a symbol of the dark forces she thought were trying to undermine her husband. In fact, Clarke was loyal to Sessions to the point of failing to blow the whistle on his abuses when perhaps he should have done so. Bureau officials blamed Alice Sessions for her husband's decision to promote Douglas Gow—whom she liked—over Baker. Besides lacking Baker's polish and intelligence, Gow was slow to make decisions. After Gow took over, a malaise set in at the top echelons of the FBI.

Barr had little use for Sessions's choice. He overruled Sessions when he wanted to place Gow in charge in the aftermath of the Los Angeles riots. Barr felt that Gow did not have the acuity or forcefulness to handle such a situation. He was reluctant to appear to be micromanaging the bureau. But in this case, he thought it was necessary. He ordered Sessions to place Buck Revell in charge in Los Angeles.

At one point or another, most of the FBI's top officials, such as Clarke, Revell, Greenleaf, and Otto, had pointed out to Sessions at least some of the problems caused by Munford or Alice Sessions. Taking matters into his own hands, Revell issued standing orders that any agent in his Dallas field office who received a call from Alice Sessions or Sarah Munford was to take no action on their requests and refer them to him. Privately, Revell and the other top FBI officials speculated that Sessions could lose his directorship if the abuses got out. While the FBI director can serve no longer than ten years, the president can remove him at any time during those ten years.

Sessions was aware that Munford registered her car in Texas and that his wife had a building pass in violation of regulations. Any local police department would quickly take action against an employee who violated the law by failing to register her car in the state where she lived or who violated security regulations. Yet, Sessions turned a deaf ear, allowing Munford and his wife to do as they pleased, displaying an arrogance that conflicted with his image as a fair-minded, objective individual and making a mockery of the FBI's program of policing itself.

"The position of director carries with it so much power that people who occupy it sometimes come to think that they are entitled to perquisites they are not entitled to," said Theodore Gardner, the former SAC in Washington.

Sessions placed bureau officials in charge of these matters in an uncomfortable position: They were aware that Alice Sessions and Sarah Munford were breaking the rules and that the director must realize this, so they did not raise the issue with him for fear that he would react negatively, jeopardizing their relationship with him or their careers.

Underscoring that point, the FBI public affairs office under Tom Jones at first refused to arrange another interview by the author with Sessions to go over the abuses uncovered during the research for this book. Jones had just been named SAC in Cleveland, and the last thing he wanted to do was confront Sessions over his own wrongdoing. However, higher-level officials such as James Greenleaf intervened. They told Jones to ask the author to put in writing the issues to be discussed. Sessions could then determine if he wanted to grant another interview.

Sessions took a month and half to decide whether to accede to the request for an interview. An FBI official said that Sessions was "pondering" how to respond. When he finally agreed to a meeting, Sessions said he would not answer any of the questions raised in the June 24, 1992, letter, including whether Munford had in fact been suspended; whether he believed that allowing Alice Sessions to violate FBI security regulations created a problem; and whether he was aware of Munford's reputation for dissembling and invoking his name without authority. Instead, Sessions launched into a half-hour tongue-lashing about the fact that the author had delved into any FBI personnel matters, particularly the issues relating to his wife.

Sessions singled out for criticism the fact that this book would report that Fred Verinder, as the special agent in charge of the Columbia, South Carolina, field office, had been stopped for allegedly drinking and had avoided a ticket by calling the superintendent of state police, who drove him home. After the incident, which was reported in every paper in South Carolina, the FBI removed Verinder from his position and transferred him to headquarters. However, the bureau later promoted him to deputy assistant director.

When street agents said that there was a double standard for discipline in the FBI, one for street agents and one for high-ranking bureau officials, they invariably cited Verinder's case. They believed that for the same offense, they would have been fired. In fact, the author's investigation concluded that the bureau applies such lenient discipline across the board to street agents and high-ranking officials. But Sessions said he was "offended" and "disappointed" that such matters would be included in this book. He noted that he had thrown open the doors of the FBI for the book, making sure that everyone cooperated. Sessions said he thought that instead of covering such internal issues, the book would focus exclusively on the great work the FBI does.

Having seen drafts of parts of the book submitted by the author as a check on accuracy, Sessions also questioned why the book did not emphasize his role in calling agents to offer encouragement and ask questions as they pursued such cases as the assassination of federal judge Robert S. Vance. He even sent the author a tape of the court proceedings, apparently oblivious to the fact that his own role as the judge on the case had nothing to do with a book on the FBI. Nonetheless, Sessions at the time said he did not regret his decision to have the FBI cooperate, which he noted had never been done before to such an extent.[489]

Sessions said that his wife occupied a special and important place in the bureau. He said wives of other directors had been sick or had stayed in Kansas City, an apparent reference to the fact that Clarence Kelley's wife had been sick and never moved to Washington. Webster's first wife, Drusilla, who was widely admired and loved by the bureau, died six years after Webster became FBI director. As a Christian Scientist, she did not go to a doctor. She did not know until a few months before she died that she had breast cancer.

In stressing his own wife's importance to the FBI, Sessions did not address the fact that Alice Sessions had accused the bureau of wiretapping her calls and bugging their bedroom, or that she had a chronic negative attitude about the bureau.

Despite the questions that had been raised, FBI officials said that Sessions refused to do anything about Munford and his wife. "The one person who can do anything about it won't," said an agent.

Permitting his wife to enter the FBI building in violation of regulations and failing to require Munford to register her car in conformance with the law were the types of abuses that Congress intended inspectors general to find and rectify. But Richard J. Hankinson, who became the Justice Department's inspector general in 1990, keeps such a low profile that very few FBI agents know he exists. The *Washington Post* has mentioned Hankinson, a former Secret Service official, only once, when listing his confirmation hearing. When asked for an interview, he had an assistant reply by letter that he did not give them. According to information provided by the assistant, since Hankinson was appointed, his office has given thirty-six briefings to Justice employees about his office. Without indicating how they were distributed, the assistant also sent a booklet about the inspector general's hotline.[490]

An agent with knowledge of the abuses relating to Alice Sessions and Sarah Munford said he would not have complained to the FBI's inspection division about them because it is staffed by agents who depend on the director for advancement. "Our inspection process is far from independent," he said. "If you tell them something, it will go back to the people you are telling them about." The agent said he would complain to an independent inspector general, but, he said, the Justice Department does not have one. His lack of knowledge of Hankinson reflected the fact that, because he is so secretive, hardly anyone in the bureau below the level of assistant director knows of Hankinson's existence.

But the Justice Department has its own Office of Professional Responsibility, one that is separate from the FBI's OPR and that assumes jurisdiction when high-level FBI officials require investigation. On the grounds that the FBI is obligated to make Justice OPR aware of any specific allegations of wrongdoing by high bureau officials, high-level FBI officials first turned over to the FBI's OPR the author's ten-page, single-spaced letter summarizing the abuses Sessions had allowed to exist. The FBI's OPR then officially gave the letter to Justice's OPR. A week after the FBI's OPR received the author's letter, then Attorney General William Barr received a second, anonymous letter purportedly written by a retired FBI agent. Dated June 25, 1992, it focused on the question of whether Sessions disguised personal trips as official business. It cited one instance when Sessions diverted his security detail to perform a personal errand. The fact that the second letter was dated a day after the FBI received the author's letter suggested that the anonymous writer was aware of the author's investigation.

Based on the two letters, Justice's OPR opened an investigation into Sessions's actions and broadened the previous FBI OPR investigation into Sarah Munford's activities. The FBI agents who carried out the investigation for Justice did so in unusual secrecy. But on October 11, 1992, at the height of the presidential campaign, Sam Donaldson broke the story of the investigation on ABC-TV. Donaldson cited "sources friendly to Sessions" as claiming that the investigation had come about because the Justice Department was afraid the FBI would uncover more about whether the department limited an investigation into the Italian government's role in approving billions of dollars in fraudulent loans to Iraq by the Atlanta branch of Banca Nazionale del Lavoro (BNL). The loans, made to finance Saddam Hussein's war machine, were a constant reminder of then President Bush's policy before the Persian Gulf War of trying to pacify Iraq by promoting trade.

To those familiar with the way the FBI and Justice Department operate, the reports of Byzantine plots were laughable. Each agency is a vast bureaucracy populated for the most part of career professionals who have no political motives and would not engage in cover-ups on behalf of political appointees. In fact, it was Barr rather than Sessions who had ordered the FBI to investigate Justice's role in the BNL case. Since he could not reach Sessions one evening, he called Larry Potts, who had succeeded Baker as head of the criminal investigative division, to bring the FBI into the case. But, coming in the middle of the election campaign, the charges of political interference turned what was already a good story into one of major proportions.

Three days after Donaldson's story aired, the press reported that in addition to the ethics investigation of Sessions and Munford, Justice was conducting a preliminary criminal investigation into the question of whether Sessions had lied to avoid paying District of Columbia income taxes and whether he or Munford had made extensive personal calls on government phone lines. While Munford was known to use government lines for personal long-distance calls, the other charges had no validity. Nevertheless, the fact that the director of the FBI was being investigated for possible criminal violations magnified the story. The *New York Times* ran the story of the criminal investigation at the top of the front page of its October 14, 1992, editions. The *Times* story and others quoted extensively from the author's June 24 letter, which Donaldson had shown on the air as part of his initial story. Every television network ran interviews with the author on the question of whether the investigation was part of a political plot. Why had the story been leaked at this particular time? Why had the investigation started just as the scandal involving BNL was emerging? Who was the "Deep Throat" who had tipped the author to the abuses in the first place?[491]

In fact, there was no single source who was aware of all the abuses relating to Sessions and handed them to the author. The first tip came from a longtime source who said that Alice Sessions had been trying to get the bureau to hire Munford's then husband to install a security system in the Sessionses' Washington home. After receiving confirmation of that fact from an FBI official, the author asked Sessions about it in an interview on January 28, 1992. Sessions said it was Ron McCall, then the head of the FBI security detail, who had suggested the FBI use Don Munford to install the system.

One did not have to know anything about the FBI or the details of this particular case to appreciate the spuriousness of Sessions's claim that a low-level agent on his own had tried to steer the contract in Washington to the husband of the director's assistant in San Antonio. Sessions's effort to shift the blame led the author to look more closely at him and to listen carefully to complaints about Alice Sessions and Sarah Munford. Through dozens of interviews, the full story finally emerged. Alice Sessions unwittingly aided that effort by discussing the allegations and providing further information, such as the name of the small town in Texas where troopers had stopped Sarah Munford and her son. It was then a simple matter to track down the troopers and obtain their story. The fact that Alice Sessions derided FBI officials to the author in on-the-record interviews contributed to the impression that Sessions's leadership was seriously flawed.

Contrary to the conspiracy theories, the Justice investigation of Sessions began immediately after the department received the author's letter and the anonymous letter, well before the BNL issue heated up.

As a result of the investigation, the Justice Department put Sarah Munford on administrative leave, pending her dismissal from the FBI, for misusing her position. Among other abuses, Justice OPR found that Munford had used FBI telephone lines to make personal long-distance calls and had lied to FBI officials about her car registration. Her dismissal was also over the fact that she had flashed her FBI credentials to try to avoid a ticket for her son. In keeping with normal practice when FBI employees are fired, FBI security police escorted Munford out of the building. In taking the action, Justice had pointedly bypassed Sessions, who could do nothing to protect his longtime aide. Munford's attorneys issued a statement denying that she had misused her position and saying that she had become an "unfortunate pawn in what appears to be a high-stakes battle over the future direction and leadership of the FBI."[492]

To allay suspicions of cover-ups, Barr then named Frederick B. Lacey, a retired federal judge from New Jersey, to investigate the Bush administration's handling of the bank fraud case in Atlanta. Barr also instructed Lacey to determine if the leak of the Justice investigation into Sessions was to divert attention from the allegations that the department had been involved in covering up the bank case. Yet, the real culprit in that case was not the Justice Department but the CIA, whose general counsel, Elizabeth R. Rindskopf, admitted that she had not properly disclosed to the Justice Department CIA documents needed for a criminal prosecution. In her previous job as general counsel of the National Security Agency (NSA), Rindskopf had been rigid and uncooperative about turning over NSA documents needed for independent counsel Lawrence E. Walsh's investigation of the Iran-Contra affair. In one acrimonious meeting, Walsh accused her of misleading him about the nature of the material NSA had on the affair. Rindskopf's failure to properly disclose CIA documents was compounded by an inadequate filing system at the agency. Lacey ultimately concluded that the Justice Department had pursued the BNL investigation properly.[493]

Alice Sessions weighed in with her own analysis of the investigation of her husband. In an interview with the *San Antonio Light*, she suggested that evidence had been manufactured and that her husband "is waking up out of a stupor, realizing he's been had." Someone tacked a copy of the article to a bulletin board in FBI headquarters with the inscription, "Alice in Wonderland."

In the opinion of FBI officials, Alice Sessions's comment was almost as damaging to her husband and the FBI as was the fact that the director had created a double standard for his wife and his assistant. Beyond that, there was no easy way to categorize reactions within the bureau. Each agent put his or her own spin on the controversy. While Sessions had little popular support within the bureau, some high-ranking bureau officials saw the negative publicity as an attack on the FBI. These were the officials who distinguished between the position of the director and the actual occupant of the office. While they had little respect for Sessions personally, they resented the fact that the position of the director had been cast in a bad light. Their reaction was a holdover from the Hoover years, when the director *was* the bureau, the image of the FBI was all-important, and embarrassing the bureau publicly was seen as a worse sin than taking steps to correct the wrongdoing that had caused the embarrassment.

Other high-level FBI officials took a more objective view. As FBI agents, they had sworn faithfully to uphold the laws of the U.S. Allowing Alice Sessions and Sarah Munford to break laws and regulations was something they could not condone. Rather than defend Sessions, they fed the press even more stories of improprieties. For example, one high-ranking official said Sarah Munford had the previous year demanded that the FBI give her and Sessions their W-2 tax forms immediately, even though a computer run was planned for the following week to generate the forms. The result was a costly special run.

At the field level, agents had little sympathy for Sessions. Agents were routinely suspended without pay for up to a month for failing to register their cars properly or for having abused their positions. Why should Sessions's aide have been treated differently?

There were those who said the abuses were trivial and who questioned why the investigation had been leaked at the peak of a political campaign. Those who minimized the abuses did not have a full appreciation of the awesome power of the FBI and how important it is to keep that power in check. Only by insisting that every employee from the director on down obey the rules could the FBI itself remain accountable. The real question was not why the investigation had been leaked to the press three and a half weeks before a presidential election. It was why the FBI had been able to keep the abuses secret for so long. That went back to the issues of loyalty and image. Some agents said that the FBI on its own would have disclosed to Justice more serious abuses involving criminal conduct or abuses of rights. But the fact that high-ranking FBI officials did not themselves report the abuses to Justice remained disturbing.

As if purposely to fan the criticism of him, Sessions, at the height of the investigation into his improper use of FBI planes, flew with Alice on the Sabreliner jet on November 27, 1992, to attend a performance of the Bolshoi Ballet at the Sands Hotel & Casino in Atlantic City. Moreover, the Sands picked up the hundred-dollar tab for the tickets. After the story hit the press, there were the usual tortured explanations: The Russian ambassador, Vladimir Lukin, had invited him. They had planned to discuss the possibility of giving FBI training to Russian law enforcement personnel. Sessions thought the Russian government, not the Sands, would pay for the ballet tickets. And the ambassador was "reaching out to him [Sessions] to make official contact," according to an FBI spokesman.

The explanations sounded like the rationalizations given by John Sununu, President Bush's chief of staff, for his excessive use of military aircraft before he was laughed out of the White House. Since the end of the cold war, the Russians had been lobbying the FBI to assist them with law enforcement training. For the purpose, they simply hopped a cab from their embassy in Washington to FBI headquarters, a seven-minute ride. If Sessions wanted to hear their pleas again, he could have invited them to his office. While a Justice official approved the trip to Atlantic City, key FBI officials warned Sessions against taking it. What never came out is that the Russians had scored an even bigger coup by bringing along to the performance the resident or chief of the successor to the KGB. Thus, Sessions found himself chatting at length with the man in charge of the spies whom FBI agents track daily. American taxpayers meanwhile got stuck with a tab of $750 for each hour the plane was in use so that Sessions and his wife could attend a ballet performance. Within the FBI, the action undermined the director's credibility still further. Coming as it did in the middle of an OPR investigation, Sessions's conduct appeared self-destructive. As one FBI official put it, if he were being investigated by the OPR for misuse of the bureau plane, "You would have to drag me to get me on that plane."[494]

After all the leaks to the press, it would have been hard to imagine the Justice Department's OPR report doing much more than confirming what was already known. But when it finally came out in January 1993, the report contained so many examples of Sessions's abuses and lack of judgment that it hit like bombshell. The 161-page report, prepared by Michael E. Shaheen, Jr., the head of the office, disclosed what the *New York Times* editorially called "a seemingly endless record of chiseling and expense account padding."

The report said that Sessions had kept an unloaded gun in a locked briefcase in the trunk of his FBI limousine as part of a "sham arrangement" to avoid paying income taxes on the value of FBI transportation to and from work; he had the FBI pay for the fence around his house even though it detracted from the security of his home; he took nonofficial passengers in his limousine, in violation of regulations; he abused government travel for personal gain; he systematically used his security detail for personal purposes; and he allowed his wife to have an FBI building pass without the required clearance. Finally, Sessions refused to allow the OPR to examine the note for his home mortgage, which the OPR concluded had most likely been made at a low interest rate because of Sessions's position. When Sessions finally did allow access to the papers, the OPR found that not only was the interest rate on the low side by perhaps a point, but were it not for his position, it was unlikely that any lender would have extended the mortgage based on Sessions's income.

In another example of poor judgment, Sessions, at Alice's request, gave a ride in his FBI car to two Soviet women who were with the Kirov Ballet. Because the two dancers spoke only Russian, Sessions asked the FBI to assist the Soviets through the airport in France during a layover. Moreover, Sessions allowed his wife to use the security detail to take her to a dressmaker and to a social function in Washington, and to get her nails and hair done.

The report said that four times while he was director, Sessions and his wife took the FBI plane to San Francisco, where their daughter lives, for Christmas. There, they had the FBI generate official business to justify the trips. Indeed, Alice Sessions attended a breakfast meeting to which she had not been invited and explained to an agent that she had come because she had to justify her trip. While the report did not say so, Sessions made a similar trip for Christmas 1992, even as the report was being written. On trips to Australia and France, Sessions collected per diem reimbursement for days when he transacted no official business. Because they had so much baggage, he ordered a larger FBI plane sent to San Antonio to pick up his wife and their daughter. On another trip, Sessions had FBI agents load firewood into an FBI car and drive it from Salisbury, Connecticut, to Poughkeepsie, New York, then fly the firewood back to Washington.

As a result of an anonymous tip, the OPR also looked into the Sessionses' purchase of their home. The OPR concluded that on his salary, Sessions could not afford to buy the $435,000 house unless he had received a break from Riggs National Bank in Washington, either on the interest rate on the mortgage or on the income standards needed to qualify for such a loan. Such a "sweetheart" arrangement would have been made only because of the bank's interest in accommodating the FBI director, the report said. When asked for the mortgage document, Sessions refused, saying that the request related to an issue that was "entirely new" and came as the press was reporting leaks from the investigation. "There seemed to be no end to the search into my privacy, and in this instance it seemed totally unwarranted; certainly the reason for it was not clear," Sessions said in a statement.[495]

The irony of an FBI director making such a disingenuous argument was exquisite. Every day, FBI agents probe into the personal and financial affairs of thousands of Americans, each of whom would dearly love to brush aside the requests by saying there seems "no end" to the inquiries.

What was most revealing was the report's characterization of Sessions's attempts to obtain prior approval of his actions. When it suited his purposes, the report said, Sessions cited officials who allegedly approved his trips and other benefits in advance. When it did not, Sessions blamed authorities for not having told him that his actions would have been improper. "Yet," the report said, "when the independent review does not produce the desired opinion, he seeks another forum until he finds an acceptable answer." For example, in seeking approval for his trip to Atlantic City to attend the Bolshoi Ballet, Sessions first sought the advice of Wayne Gilbert, who headed counterintelligence, and Doug Gow, the associate deputy director. When they recommended that Sessions not take the trip, Sessions asked Lawrence S. Eagleburger, the secretary of state. "When the Secretary of State did not object, Director Sessions made the decision to go on the trip," the report said.

The OPR report concluded that the issues raised by the internal investigation were so serious that the president should decide whether Sessions should remain in office. Agreeing, Barr sent the report to President Bush. He also ordered Sessions to reimburse the government $9,890 for the fence around his property, pay taxes on the value of his FBI transportation to and from work, release his mortgage documents to the OPR, and—once the amount is determined—pay back the government for travel and per diem payments for personal trips.

"Given that you are a former U.S. attorney and federal judge, and that you are currently director of the premier federal law enforcement agency, I must conclude that there is no excuse for your conduct," Barr wrote to him.[496]

No one at Justice was able to pinpoint the source of the leak of the OPR investigation of Sessions. However, while he did not have evidence, Shaheen believed that Sessions or his people had leaked the story to Donaldson, who was the only media person listed on Sessions's Rolodex. In his report, Donaldson—citing sources friendly to Sessions—had claimed that Justice was investigating the FBI director in retaliation for the FBI's role in investigating Justice's actions in handling the BNL investigation. Sessions used the fact that the investigation had been leaked to bolster his claim that Justice was railroading him. Thus, the leak of the investigation appeared to be a preemptive strike to divert attention from the real issue, which was Sessions's conduct.

In fact, Donaldson had talked with Alice Sessions about the investigation before airing his report. He would not comment on whether she had initially been the source of his information. But she was one of the "sources friendly to Sessions" who had linked the OPR investigation of Sessions to the BNL investigation.[497]

As in his interviews with the OPR, Sessions blamed everyone but himself for his actions. If it was not FBI agents who disapproved of his racial policies who were out to get him, it was Barr, Hooverite FBI officials, or Floyd Clarke—who had loyally defended the director. Without naming him, Sessions also claimed that the OPR report had accepted uncritically the statements of Ron McCall, whom Sessions had removed as head of the security detail because of what Sessions referred to as his "conduct." In fact, the OPR report was based on the statements under oath of hundreds of FBI agents and hundreds of internal memos written contemporaneously by those agents. McCall's "conduct" had amounted to standing up to Sessions and his wife when their requests were improper.

The OPR report was released the day before Bill Clinton became president. Asked about the report, George Stephanopoulos, Clinton's spokesman, called it "disturbing." In an editorial titled "Time's Up for William Sessions," the New York Times called for his removal. The fact that Sessions had chosen to attack the bureau itself for his own wrongdoing infuriated agents and made them willing to leak even more evidence of his abuses. Many FBI officials agreed among themselves that if asked by Sessions or anyone outside the bureau for their opinion, they would say he should resign. After wrestling with the idea of going public to show their lack of support, FBI officials decided that such an action would not be appropriate or necessarily helpful. However, Weldon Kennedy, who replaced Greenleaf as associate deputy director for administration, ordered a halt, for as long as Sessions was director, to the disciplining of agents for infractions similar to Sessions's. That included unauthorized use of bureau cars—an abuse that requires a suspension of thirty days without pay. Kennedy reasoned that he could not in good conscience discipline agents for what the director was doing with impunity. Moreover, agents disciplined for what the director was getting away with could conceivably mount a successful legal challenge to their own punishment. Only if and when Sessions was replaced, Kennedy said, would normal disciplining of agents resume.

Kennedy did not tell Sessions about his action. When it hit the papers, Sessions overruled Kennedy and ordered disciplining to proceed. Sessions thus laid the groundwork for a convincing appeal by those agents who were disciplined.

Virtually the only defender of Sessions was Representative Don Edwards, the California Democrat who called him the "best FBI director ever." But even his support was feeble. A leaflet titled "Special FBI Income Tax Rules" circulating at headquarters offered this advice to agents charged with breaking bureau regulations: "Claim that you were advised by bureau lawyers to act as you did. This gets the responsibility for your actions off you."

In fact, while Sessions claimed publicly that Joe Davis, the FBI's legal counsel, had approved each of the 126 trips he took with Alice Sessions, Davis had approved only a handful of them, according to a Justice OPR analysis.

The withdrawal of Zoë E. Baird as Clinton's nominee for attorney general prolonged the controversy. Clinton wanted to name an attorney general before taking action on the FBI director. Clinton's transition team had concluded that Sessions was not a good leader of the FBI. It recommended that Sessions be allowed to leave gracefully after a year or so if the OPR report was tepid; if it was tough, he should be removed immediately. A short list of candidates to replace Sessions had been prepared.

Any question about how Clinton felt about Sessions was dispelled when the White House refused to invite Sessions to the new president's State of the Union address to Congress. Sessions had been at all four previous addresses while he was director. Miffed, he asked John Collingwood, who headed congressional affairs, to try every avenue possible to get an invitation, to no avail. Earlier, Alice Sessions, distraught at not receiving enough invitations to Clinton inauguration festivities, had accused a Sessions assistant of throwing away her mail.

For all their idiosyncrasies, both William and Alice Sessions mounted an impressive lobbying campaign, apparently convincing the usually savvy *Washingtonian* magazine that Sessions was the victim of a conspiracy, which included this author, bigoted FBI agents, Hooverites, Shaheen, and Barr, to drive Sessions from office.

"If they get Sessions," the magazine's March 1993 issue quoted a former law enforcement official, "it means you're going to have a tough time convincing the American people that the bureau can do its job independently. It's important to know the bureau can't be bought off or ordered off."[498]

In fact, it was Sessions's abuse of his position that had undermined faith in the FBI. Many agents were afraid that because of the controversy, their own credibility and effectiveness in conducting investigations had been impaired.

Thus, Sessions emerged as an enigma, not at all a clone of Webster, who would have found it unthinkable to break the rules for anyone, who would have fired any assistant who abused his or her position, and who leaned over backward to avoid creating even the appearance of impropriety. At times, Sessions appeared to be acting out a role, trying to project the kind of cheerleader image he thought an FBI director should have, but in reality he—like his wife—was mistrustful and disdainful of the bureau and its people.*

In suggesting that a book about the FBI should ignore embarrassing personnel issues, Sessions demonstrated why he became known as a cheerleader rather than a credible spokesman. For only by presenting specific, honest, and balanced information will anyone be believed—something FBI agents are sophisticated enough to know, but their director had yet to learn. If a police officer was accused of drinking while driving and then used his official position to avoid being charged, one would expect to see the story splashed across the local papers. But Sessions appeared to think that FBI agents should be immune to such exposure.

"Sessions takes the easy way out," said a former member of Sessions's security detail. He said that while Sessions was aware that his wife and Munford undermined respect for him in the bureau, the director avoided conflict and therefore would not confront such problems. "He is run by two women," he said before Munford's firing, contending that Sessions's erratic style stemmed from the stress people feel when they are in "over their heads."

Instead of the pleasant man he appeared to be, many FBI and Justice officials—including Barr—decided that Sessions was, in fact, arrogant. One example took place at a reception, where an interpreter offered to introduce Sessions to a diplomat from the People's Republic of China. Sessions told the interpreter that there would be no need for his help, since he spoke fluent Chinese. Sessions then turned to the diplomat and said, "Chop sticks. Chop suey."

Sessions's comment that wives of other FBI directors had been

---

* Sharon LaFraniere first applied the term "cheerleader" to Sessions in print on page A-1 of the December 15, 1991, *Washington Post*. According to FBI officials who discussed it with him after it appeared, the story devastated Sessions.

sick also revealed a nastiness that conflicted with his affable image.

After Clinton became president, Stuart M. Gerson briefly became acting attorney general. His opinion of Sessions was similar to Barr's. Gerson expressed his view both to the Clinton White House and to Barr's successor, Janet Reno, who was sworn in as attorney general on March 12, 1993.

As the former prosecutor in Dade County, Florida, Reno had been so careful about avoiding even the appearance of impropriety that she had refused to use restaurant discount coupons. When parking her official car at parking meters, she had fed the meters quarters. Having worked in one of the highest crime areas in the country, the Harvard Law School graduate had hands-on knowledge of the problems facing law enforcement. Prosecutors in her office respected her for her toughness, her ability to focus on complex issues, and her ramrod straight integrity.

As Gerson saw it, those were the qualities Sessions lacked.

"The issue is respect," Gerson told Reno and the White House. "Sessions doesn't have it."

Yet before Sessions left, two events occurred within two days of each other that would give the FBI one of the most resounding successes and one of the most tragic failures in its history. The FBI solved the first one—the bombing of the World Trade Center on February 26, 1993—within a matter of days. The bureau not only apprehended those believed to be responsible but also began tracing the funding for the terrorist act back to the government of Iran.

Then two days later, the Treasury Department's Bureau of Alcohol, Tobacco, and Firearms (ATF) staged a disastrous raid on a ramshackle compound in Mount Carmel, Texas, ten miles east of Waco. There, thirty-three-year-old David Koresh and his group of religious fanatics had been arming themselves with illegal machine guns and explosive devices, preparing for what Koresh said would be a bloody confrontation with nonbelievers.

Koresh was an unlikely prophet. Born Vernon W. Howell in Houston, Koresh was a high school dropout with a history of learning disabilities. As a young man, Koresh attended services of the Seventh-Day Adventists. He had a knack for interpreting the Bible's Book of Revelation and its doomsday prophecies to make any point he wished. His seventeen-hour dissertations attracted members of the Waco-based Branch Davidian sect, which had splintered from Seventh-Day Adventists in 1934. Koresh briefly lived in the sect's compound but moved in the mid-1970s to southern California, where he began recruiting for the sect.

In a fierce gun battle in 1987, Koresh returned to the compound and took it away from George Roden, who had led the sect. The two had feuded since Koresh had begun having sex with Roden's mother, then in her late sixties. Roden was injured in the gun battle, and Koresh was charged with attempted murder but acquitted.

In 1990, the charismatic leader changed his name to David Koresh—David to reflect his conviction that he was the head of the biblical House of David, and Koresh because it is the Hebrew transliteration of Cyrus, the Persian emperor who allowed the Jews being held captive in Babylon to return to Israel. With wavy hair and soft eyes, the guitar-strumming Koresh was particularly attractive to women, who flocked to his cult. By the time he had taken over the compound, Koresh was proclaiming himself the Messiah. Part con artist, part paranoid personality, part frustrated rock star, Koresh had some 120 followers whose only wish was to serve his will.

The Treasury Department's ATF first learned of the group on June 4, 1992, when a member of the local sheriff's department told an ATF agent about vast quantities of arms and explosives being shipped to the compound. Larry Gilbreath, a United Parcel Service employee, had become suspicious of the cult when a package to be delivered to the compound broke open, spilling out hand grenades. Gilbreath had told the sheriff's department that he made deliveries every few weeks to the compound. Before entering it, he had to report to another location and announce himself. Then, Branch Davidians would clear him to proceed to Koresh's seventy-acre compound on Route 7. At the compound—called Ranch Apocalypse—armed men at observation posts waved him past. He would collect for the deliveries in cash.

The ATF interviewed a number of former Branch Davidians and traced some of the shipments back to arms dealers. From these inquiries, the ATF learned that Koresh preached that by having sex with him, female members of the group would become his disciples. Koresh had already fathered at least fifteen children by different women whom he called his wives. Many of the "wives" were as young as twelve. For those who were married when they entered his cult, Koresh had a simple solution. He purported to annul their marriages and reserved the right to have sex with any of the wives himself. Their husbands were to remain celibate.

Koresh used all the mind-manipulating devices of traditional cults. He created a spartan environment, required members to surrender all their worldly possessions, and insisted on slavish loyalty. At times, the cultists subsisted for days only on popcorn or fruit.

He would ban sugar and ice cream, then for no apparent reason decided sugar and ice cream were good. At one point he decided hot dogs made with chicken were acceptable. When cultists brought him bologna made with chicken, he flew into a rage.

Koresh administered discipline by paddling children as young as eight months for as long as forty-five minutes until they bled. Adults were forced into a pit of raw sewage and not allowed to bathe afterward. Children were to call their parents "dogs," and only he was to be referred to as their father. When they were as young as eleven, girls were given a plastic Star of David to wear, signifying that they possessed "the light" and were ready to have sex with him.

Of more interest to the ATF, the firearms accumulated by the group could have held off a battalion during the Persian Gulf War. In one year, the group had spent $44,300 on such purchases as eight thousand rounds of 9-millimeter and .223-caliber ammunition, two hundred grenades, thirty pounds of potassium nitrate used for making explosives, and hundreds of parts for making machine guns. Since the Davidians had no license to make machine guns, this was a violation of federal law.

Based on the information it had gathered, the ATF obtained a warrant to arrest Koresh and seize material within his compound as evidence. Given the degree of danger and the fact that the compound held innocent women and children who could be used as hostages, it would have been foolhardy to try to arrest Koresh while he was in the compound. Koresh periodically jogged around the compound on Double EE Ranch Road or ran errands in town; that would have been the time to arrest him. Yet the ATF tried to arrest Koresh in the compound. Moreover, in any raid, surprise is critical. As a rule, such raids are conducted in the early-morning hours when people are still asleep. But, brandishing a search warrant and a warrant for Koresh's arrest, ninety-one ATF agents stormed the compound at ten A.M. on Sunday, February 28, 1993.

What was worse, ATF supervisors knew before their agents went in that the Davidians were expecting them. In an effort to burnish its image, ATF had alerted eleven media outlets of the raid. Cameramen and reporters were waiting for the ATF agents when they arrived to storm the fortress. Forty minutes before the raid, the ATF undercover agent who had managed to infiltrate the Davidians scurried out to warn supervisors that Koresh knew the ATF was coming. Yet—despite protests by some ATF agents—the ATF ordered the raid to proceed. While the ATF knew from another undercover agent who had infiltrated the group that the Davidians would be finishing their worship service then, and therefore would be away from their ammunition, they would still be alert and far more likely to present a threat than if they had been surprised in their sleep.

The ATF also knew that the Davidians had .50-caliber rifles capable of shooting a round from the White House to the Capitol, not to mention assault rifles, machine guns, and shotguns. Yet many of the ATF agents were armed only with semiautomatic weapons.

Given the almost criminally negligent planning, it was a wonder more lives were not lost. As it was, in the ensuing forty-five-minute gun battle, the Davidians killed four ATF agents and wounded or injured another fifteen. The ATF finally had to withdraw.

Later that same day, President Clinton ordered the FBI to take over. Thus from the start the bureau was at a disadvantage. From their first days at Quantico, FBI agents are taught to plan such raids thoroughly. Unlike police, FBI agents usually have the luxury of choosing the best time and place to confront suspects. Traditionally, the FBI overpowers targets with superior manpower and weapons. The ATF's fumbling had deprived the FBI of these natural advantages.

Under the direction of Jeffrey Jamar, the beefy FBI special agent in charge in San Antonio, members of the HRT began surrounding the compound on the afternoon of February 28, hoping to negotiate an end to the standoff. Over the next fifty-one days, Jamar, Bob A. Ricks, and other agents agreed to arrange a radio broadcast of a fifty-eight-minute tape of Koresh's preaching. They sent in milk for the children and typewriter ribbons for Koresh's typewriter. They also allowed his lawyers to talk with him in the compound.

Repeatedly, Koresh promised he would come out, but then he would explain that God had told him to wait. For example, on March 20, Koresh demanded that after his inevitable arrest he be allowed to preach to his followers from jail while awaiting trial. Two days later, Jamar had the FBI give Koresh a letter agreeing to the demand. But Steve Schneider, Koresh's deputy, told the negotiators that Koresh had "taken the letter, wadded it up, and thrown it in the corner."

Meanwhile, conditions within the compound were deteriorating. From several people who had chosen to leave, FBI agents learned that the Davidians were surrounded by human waste and dead bodies from the ATF raid. Koresh continued to live with his underage wives, an abuse of children, and a violation of statutory rape laws.

Since the Davidians might have chosen to attack the FBI at any time, members of the HRT had to be in a constant state of readiness, training their rifle scopes on the compound. Members of local FBI SWAT teams were brought in to relieve members of the HRT, but they were not as highly trained as HRT members. If another crisis had occurred elsewhere in the country, the HRT would have been unprepared to deal with it. Already, the FBI's presence at the compound had cost taxpayers $6 million, not including regular salary payments or the cost of repairing an FBI helicopter that crashed when it hit a power line.

Besides trying to negotiate, the FBI's strategy was to shrink the perimeter, removing a fence and sending in armored vehicles to surround the compound. The bureau also sought to make life inside the compound increasingly uncomfortable, shining searchlights into the windows at night. Through loudspeakers, the FBI blared constant noise at the compound—Nancy Sinatra songs, chants of Tibetan monks, and the sounds of rabbits being slaughtered.

But by early April, the FBI realized the strategy was not working. The last straw was when Koresh said he would come out after finishing his manuscript on the Seven Seals of the Book of Revelation. Schneider, who resented Koresh because he had taken away his wife, told the FBI Koresh was not even working on the manuscript. In an April 9 letter to the FBI, Koresh predicted calamities at the compound. He said there would be an earthquake, and a dam would burst. "I AM your God," he wrote to the FBI, "and you will bow under my feet. . . . Do you think you have the power to stop My will?" From his actions and statements, and from conversations sporadically picked up through electronic surveillance, the FBI determined that Koresh had no intention of coming out alive.

The Davidians had their own water supply and enough food for at least a year. The prospect of armed criminals who had killed four federal agents getting away with their crimes for up to a year was not cheering. At the end of the year, the Davidians could still use the children as hostages or kill them in an effort to save themselves. What's more, according to an internal FBI position paper, there was "increasing risk, as the standoff continues, of injury to federal agents, whether by accident or . . . shooting from inside the compound."

By waiting, the FBI had achieved the end of allowing thirty-four people, including twenty-one children, to leave the compound voluntarily. But by now, the defections had stopped.

Jamar proposed to step up the pressure by inserting CS gas, which is more effective than tear gas, into the compound. Jamar was aware of the possibility that the Davidians might commit mass suicide as did the religious fanatics led by Jim Jones, who in 1978 committed suicide with more than nine hundred of his followers at the People's Temple in Guyana. Former cult members had told the FBI that there had been rehearsals of mass suicide, and one cultist said Koresh had toyed with the idea of coming out of the compound with grenades strapped to himself so he could blow up both himself and the agents sent to arrest him.

In the bureau's statements after the incident, the FBI claimed the experts had said Koresh was not likely to commit suicide. That was not entirely true. Peter A. Smerick, a profiler reporting to John Douglas at Quantico, had said in a memo that was passed to the criminal investigation division that the Davidians would indeed commit mass suicide if the FBI confronted them. The fact that Smerick had made the prediction never became public. But most of the experts had taken the opposite view. Douglas, psychologists, and psycholinguistic experts consulted by the bureau said Koresh, while virulently paranoid, would not commit suicide. There was plenty of evidence to support that view. Koresh had been planning to write a book and seemed concerned about selling the rights. When FBI agents towed his black 1968 Camaro in preparation for the raid, Koresh became furious. Based on talks with his client inside the compound, Koresh's attorney Dick DeGuerin said he was sure Koresh would not commit suicide. Four times, the FBI negotiators had asked Koresh if he planned to kill himself, and four times he said he would not.

"If I wanted to commit suicide," he told the agents, "I would have done that a long time ago."

As Jamar's plan moved up the FBI hierarchy, the bureau's top officials decided this was the best way to end the standoff. No one could say with certainty what the Davidians would do if confronted. But it was clear that the status quo was not acceptable. Sooner or later, criminals must be held accountable for their crimes.

During the deliberations at headquarters, Sessions took his usual posture of letting the experts work out strategy. Unlike William Webster, who would have cross-examined FBI officials for days if such a plan had been proposed, Sessions for the most part was passive—unless he saw a chance to take another trip back home at government expense. In the middle of the standoff, Sessions decided he wanted to go to Waco, where he had once practiced law. It was not clear whether Sessions thought he would rally FBI agents in Waco or stand Koresh down Texas-style. In any case, Gerson, who was then acting attorney general, was appalled. He thought Sessions's idea was "stupid," showed poor judgment, and was probably a ploy to help him retain his job. As acting attorney general, he ordered him not to go.

On the other hand, Janet Reno, who became attorney general only a month before the FBI made its proposal, in effect substituted for the leadership that the FBI director would normally provide. On April 12, Sessions, Deputy Director Floyd Clarke, and Larry Potts, the chief of the criminal investigative division, presented the plan to Reno. Instead of accepting the bureau's recommendation on the spot, as some might have done, she asked the FBI to find out the answers to dozens of questions: Would the gas harm the children? Can anything else be done? For hours, Reno personally quizzed two army experts on the subject of CS gas. They assured her that the gas was nonlethal, would not permanently harm adults or children, and would not start a fire on delivery. On the other hand, if the FBI used an anesthetic gas, it might kill the weaker adults and children. Reno lived in fear that if the siege were to continue, she would find many children dead from disease, starvation, or beatings.

Reno would wake up at four A.M. trying to come up with some better solution. There appeared to be none. As she would later say, "In some cases, there is no right answer. What you've got to try to do is do the best you can, based on all the information you can assimilate, and then be as candid as you can."

By 7:15 P.M. on Saturday, April 17, Reno had decided to go ahead. The next evening, she called Clinton and discussed the plan for fifteen minutes. "Have you carefully considered it?" he asked. "Yes, sir, and it's my responsibility, and I think it's the best way to go," she replied. Clinton said to go ahead.

Having received approval, Jamar chose the morning of April 19 for the raid. At 5:55 A.M., when the wind had died down, the FBI warned Koresh and his followers over loudspeakers, "This is not an assault! Do not fire! Come out now and you will not be harmed!" For some, this only confirmed Koresh's predictions that the world was coming to an end. Schneider, Koresh's lieutenant, broke off communication by defiantly throwing the telephone out a front window. At 6:04 A.M., a modified M-60 tank began battering holes near the entrance to the compound and spraying a mist of CS gas through a boom on the tank. The Davidians began firing at the tanks, but agents held their fire.

At nine A.M., a tank bashed down the front door of the compound to make it easier for the occupants to leave. It also bashed a hole in the wall near the northwest corner of the compound. At noon the FBI demolished whole sections of the exterior.

No one in the FBI thought the Davidians would come out immediately. Rather, the strategy was to build up the pressure gradually until Koresh and his followers became so uncomfortable that they would give up. Over the next two days, the FBI planned to demolish the entire compound if necessary.

At 11:12 A.M., Janet Reno left the SIOC to attend a function in Baltimore. But at 12:05 P.M., a wisp of smoke followed by a small tongue of flame appeared at the southwest corner of the compound. By 12:20 P.M., fire was whipping along the west side of the compound, fanned by thirty-mile-per-hour prairie winds. Two minutes later, FBI agents climbed out of their tanks and surrounded the compound. One cult member fell from the roof, engulfed in flames. As he tried to wave them off, agents tore off his burning clothing and placed him inside an armored vehicle. A distraught woman emerged from the flames, her clothes smoking. An agent snatched her as she tried to run back into the burning compound.

The agents entered the building and tried to find children, wading thigh-deep into a concrete pit filled with water, human excrement, floating body parts, and rats.

From the FBI officials on the ground to those watching the events unfold in the SIOC command center at headquarters, everyone was stunned.

"Oh, my God, they're killing themselves!" exclaimed Ricks, whose deadpan descriptions of Koresh's religious ranting had appeared on television networks throughout the siege. In SIOC, there was silence. Danny Coulson, who had founded the HRT and now headed the violent-crimes section in the criminal investigative division, assumed Koresh was merely trying to burn firearms to destroy evidence. He was sure the mothers in the compound would get their own children out alive. But they did not come out.

The FBI had considered the possibility that fire would break out as a result of the raid; gunfights always carry that risk. But the bureau decided it would not ask fire trucks to remain at the scene because the Davidians would only try to shoot the firemen. Even if fire trucks had been on the scene, they could have done nothing. The thirty-mile-per-hour winds quickly turned the wooden structure into an incinerator, and there was something else fanning the flames. A few of the nine cultists who escaped would later claim that the fire started when the FBI's battering rams knocked over kerosene lanterns. But a local arson investigation established that the fires had been set. In addition to the obvious evidence—billowing black clouds of smoke, signifying the use of an accelerant—the FBI had infrared aerial video photography that showed at least four fires starting almost simultaneously in parts of the compound separated by half a city block. Because the material was still being analyzed, and because the FBI considered the technique to be sensitive, the bureau did not reveal the existence of the infrared photography.

Beyond the infrared photography, FBI snipers peering through the windows of the compound had seen Davidians pouring what appeared to be a liquid, seconds before the fires started. They also saw them cupping their hands as if lighting matches. Kerosene and gasoline were found on the clothes of some of the survivors who had maintained that the FBI had started the fire.

The FBI later learned after enhancing tapes of electronically bugged conversations that an hour before the blaze started, the Davidians had been discussing spreading gasoline and kerosene about the compound. The conversations had been picked up by electronic bugging devices smaller than dimes concealed by the FBI in the milk cartons and tapes sent in to Koresh. Like the infrared evidence, the FBI did not disclose this to the public because it was considered a sensitive technique.

Because the fire could have fully consumed some children, the exact toll was not known. But at least seventy-eight Davidians, including seventeen children under the age of fourteen, were killed in the fire. Seven—including Koresh—had gunshot wounds in their heads, most likely self-inflicted. Another five bodies found in the rubble were of people killed in the ATF's initial assault.

Devastated by the outcome, FBI agents faced a barrage of criticism from the media, Congress, and the families of the victims. Why couldn't the FBI have waited? Didn't the sounds of rabbits being slaughtered only toughen the resolve of the faithful? Why did the FBI choose April 19 for the raid? Why was the FBI so impatient? Didn't the FBI understand that assaulting cultists would only make them more stubborn? How could the FBI have caused the deaths of innocent children?

Having already called for the removal of Sessions for abusing his position, the *New York Times* now called for his removal over the Waco incident. At a news conference, a reporter asked Clinton if he would accept Janet Reno's resignation as well.

The frustration and anger were understandable. No one wanted to see innocent children die. But there was a difference between an avoidable mistake, such as sending in ATF agents when Koresh knew they were coming, and one over which the FBI had no control. The tragic outcome was the inevitable result of the ATF's botched planning. Besides the fact that he would lose his harem, Koresh had a morbid fear he would be homosexually raped in jail. He was not about to let the FBI take him without using his cultists as pawns. He told negotiators, "Children are like hostages because they're too young to make decisions." Whether by committing mass suicide or murder, he would have used them to save himself. If the FBI had waited, Koresh might have turned the children into human shields, threatening, for example, to kill the children if the FBI did not do as he asked.

"I was frankly—*surprised* would be a mild word—to say that anyone would suggest that the attorney general should resign because some religious fanatics murdered themselves," Clinton said when asked about Reno's resignation.

To those who accused the FBI of impatience, Jamar, the agent in charge, asked after the fire, "Where does the impatience start? Is it the sixth week? The seventh week? The negotiations were going nowhere. We could spend six more months there, and nothing would change." The authorities could continue to wait, he said, "but to what end?"

After the initial criticism, press accounts began to swing the other way. Reno immediately stated she was responsible for the decision to go in. In numerous television appearances, she articulately and candidly explained what had gone into her decision, declaring that "based on what we now know, obviously it [the decision] was wrong." At a House Judiciary Committee hearing, Reno stood her ground when Rep. John Conyers, Jr., the Michigan Democrat, suggested she resign.

"I'd like you to know that there's at least one member of Congress who is not going to rationalize the innocent deaths of two dozen children," he said.

Just as forcefully, Reno shot back, "I feel more strongly about [the death of the children] than you will ever know. But I will not walk away from a compound where ATF agents had been killed. . . . I will not engage in recriminations. I will look to the future."

In contrast, Stephen E. Higgins, director of the ATF, came off at the hearing as evasive and out of touch with events. Immediately after the raid, Higgins had insisted the ATF was not aware that Koresh knew about the planned raid. He said the ATF had made no mistakes. When reports began to filter out that Higgins's statement was false, Higgins sent a directive to the ATF's two thousand agents admonishing them not to spread rumors. Then an affadavit of Robert Rodriguez, an ATF agent who had infiltrated the compound, was unsealed in court. He quoted Koresh as saying just before the ATF raid, "Neither the ATF nor the National Guard will ever get me. . . . They are coming." Rodriguez said he ran from the compound and alerted ATF officials that Koresh knew of the raid. Ignoring the warning, the ATF moved in forty minutes later.

At the House Judiciary Committee hearing, Higgins would answer questions selectively. When he thought his answer might be embarrassing, he would claim he could not discuss the ATF raid because of a pending Treasury Department investigation. When he thought it would benefit him, he forgot about the pending investigation and answered. Rather than taking responsibility as Reno had done, Higgins came across as a crybaby, whining in the press that he was considering resigning because he was under attack.

"Who needs this?" Higgins was quoted as saying, "Is it really worth it?"

Higgins came under fire by committee members, and many questioned whether the ATF, which traced its original function of collecting federal taxes on alcohol to 1791, should be abolished. On the other hand, Jack Brooks, chairman of the committee, commented that, if anything, the FBI should have moved in sooner. Indeed, if the FBI had prolonged the standoff much longer, the press would undoubtedly have begun to criticize the bureau for allowing Koresh to get away with murder too long.

"We phrase it a thousand ways, but our single question is: Why weren't the authorities able to make a certifiably irrational man respond rationally?" columnist William Raspberry wrote in the *Washington Post.*

Public opinion supported the FBI. An ABC poll found 72 percent of Americans believed the FBI had done the right thing. The poll also found 95 percent of the public believed Koresh, not the FBI, was responsible for the outcome.

Still, the fact remained that the raid had failed in its purpose, which was to make the Davidians come out alive. The FBI had hoped that the CS gas would so disorient the Davidians that they would not be able to orchestrate a mass suicide. But because they had gas masks, because the wind was blowing strongly, and because the FBI had knocked large holes in the compound, the gas had little effect. While the bureau could have killed Koresh when he came within their sights through windows, the fact that he was not an immediate threat meant that killing him could have been considered murder. An intensive internal FBI investigation was begun to see if the tactics could have been improved.

For many of the agents involved, the outcome was a personal tragedy. Dozens received trauma counseling and had flashbacks and sleepless nights after the raid.

"The one thing we couldn't control was what Koresh would do, and that unfortunately was the deciding factor," said Buck Revell, who participated in the plan as SAC in Dallas.

Ironically, the standoff only prolonged Sessions's tenure. All along, Clinton had been reluctant to replace Sessions immediately upon taking office. While there was a consensus among Clinton's senior staff early on that he would have to go, they had wanted his removal to appear to be done by Reno. They were mindful of the legislative history behind the ten-year limit on the tenure of the FBI director. The idea was not only to prevent another FBI director from amassing the unbridled power of a J. Edgar Hoover, but also to help insulate the director from political pressures. Not realizing that the OPR report on Sessions had been prepared by career Justice Department officials and FBI agents, Clinton's aides were deeply mistrustful of the motives of what they called the Barr Justice Department. They were impressed by Sessions's record in promoting equality in the FBI and naively tended to credit his claim that he was the victim of bigoted agents who were out to get him. Instead of focusing on Sessions's abuses, they tended to be more concerned about the fact that he had lost credibility and support within the FBI. After the fiasco in Waco, the Clinton White House did not want to appear to be removing Sessions because of the FBI's performance there.

On the other hand, the fifty-one-day standoff sealed Sessions's fate with Reno. Having worked with him closely on the issue, she was unimpressed. Reno thought his manner of making pronouncements rather than discussing issues irritating. When she learned that he planned to go to Waco on May 5 to present a plaque to the mayor, she—like Gerson before her—was appalled. Sessions's grandstanding was so obvious that it was embarrassing. Moreover, Sessions again thumbed his nose at Justice by stopping off in San Antonio to give a speech at the local bar association, continuing his pattern of inventing reasons to have the government pay for his trips back home.

Meanwhile, FBI agents became increasingly bitter and demoralized as they realized they had become pawns in a political battle.

Every day, they investigated people who had abused their positions. Yet their own director had engaged in similar misconduct. Their plight appeared to be so unimportant to the politicians in the White House that they seemed willing to let the impasse drag on indefinitely. No one at the White House seemed interested in talking with any FBI agents to obtain their opinions.

There was talk in the Clinton administration of giving Sessions a lesser government job so he could preserve his pension rights. The message seemed to be that it is okay to abuse one's position so long as one is high enough in government and has perceived political support.

That message came across even more clearly when the Clinton White House, with Sessions still dangling, tried in May 1993 to get the FBI to publicly buttress its claims that career professionals in the White House travel office were corrupt. Using a blunderbuss approach, Clinton aides had fired all seven members of the travel office when an audit found that funds had not been properly accounted for. The White House asked the FBI to investigate, and the FBI confirmed to reporters who asked that it was investigating.

When the firings caused an uproar, George Stephanopoulos, the White House communications director, on May 21, 1993, asked Collingwood to meet with him in the White House. During the meeting, Stephanopoulos extracted from Collingwood the fact that the FBI believed it had a basis for conducting a criminal investigation of the matter. Knowing that the White House would likely use that statement, Collingwood the next day strengthened the FBI's own statement to be used if reporters inquired about the investigation. That same day, the White House press office, itself run by amateurs, issued the FBI statement itself—a violation of normal FBI procedures.

In the end, Collingwood had not said anything that conflicted with the facts. But the White House actions created an *appearance* of trying to use the FBI for political purposes. The fact that this happened when the FBI director was in a weakened position was but another reason the delay in dealing with Sessions was unconscionable.

"It's like waiting for David Koresh to come out," said an agent in headquarters. "We know Sessions will be leaving. The question is when."

For her part, having read the OPR report on Sessions, Reno refused Sessions' requests to meet with her on his case. After she gave a speech in the courtyard of the Justice Department on April 6, 1993,

Sessions began walking toward her, hoping to speak with her. Pointedly ignoring him, Reno walked in the other direction.

Significantly, Reno raised no objection when Larry Potts, the assistant director over the criminal investigative division, decided to go to Waco to assess the standoff with Koresh. Potts was a professional and had good reason to go. Sessions knew very little about FBI operations and appeared to want to use the incident cynically to prolong his own tenure.

If the events leading to the controversy were bizarre, the end was even more mystifying. Reno asked Sessions, who still refused to get the message, to meet with her at the Justice Department on Saturday morning, July 17, 1993. With White House Counsel Bernard Nussbaum present, Reno told Sessions that President Clinton would fire him if he did not resign by Monday.

By then, Reno had become exasperated with Sessions, who had met with her twice in a futile effort to refute the charges and was blaming others for his own conduct. Sessions and his lawyers had been trying to negotiate the terms of his resignation, demanding, among other things, that he be allowed to remain in office until a successor was confirmed so that Deputy FBI Director Floyd Clarke would not become acting director. Apparently brainwashed by his wife, Sessions had come to believe that Clarke was behind all his troubles. Reno would have none of it.

Twice, Reno had had to refuse Sessions's requests to fly on a Justice Department plane to visit his son in San Antonio and to see his daughter in San Francisco. Each time, Sessions had invented business reasons for the trips. Reno had taken to groaning each time she heard Sessions's name.

"I knew I should have stayed in Miami," she remarked one time when she heard of Sessions's latest misuse of power, saying Sessions had "brought this all on himself."

After leaving the meeting with Reno, Sessions tripped on a curb outside the Justice Department in full view of television cameras and broke an elbow. After spending the evening in a hospital, Sessions appeared outside his home to tell reporters defiantly that, as a "matter of principle," he would not resign. Beyond promoting his own self-interest, it was not clear what principle he was upholding. By ignoring Clinton's wish that he resign gracefully, Sessions had plunged the FBI into turmoil as he pointlessly battled to keep his job.

Finally, on Monday, July 19, Clinton made the announcement he should have made six months earlier. In the White House briefing room, Clinton said he had telephoned Sessions to tell him he was removing him. In a stunning blow to Sessions, Clinton then said he was naming Clarke acting director. Appearing with him at the White House, Reno said she had concluded that, as outlined by the facts contained in the OPR report, Sessions had exhibited "a serious deficiency in judgment."

Having just hired spin doctor David Gergen, Clinton tried to convey the impression that he had delayed dealing with Sessions because of his desire to weigh the evidence carefully so he would not appear to be changing directors for political reasons. But the fact was that the White House had failed to read the OPR report in detail, was indifferent to the need to have a leader who commanded the respect of FBI agents, and was unconcerned about the morale problems the delay had caused.

Before Sessions got Clinton's call at 3:50 P.M., dismissing him, Philip Heymann, the deputy attorney general, had met with Sessions in his office to warn him the call was coming. Heymann explained to Sessions what the procedures would be once he got the call. Like any agent removed from the rolls, the director would have to turn in his FBI credentials and badge and remove from his office only personal effects. Meanwhile, Clinton faxed Sessions a letter informing him of his removal. But Sessions was still in his office at 3:59 P.M. Clinton called him a second time, this time telling him his firing was to take effect "immediately."

Finally, Sessions got the message. As instructed, he handed over his FBI credentials to Heymann. Now considered a visitor, Sessions had to be escorted through the halls by his security detail. He gave a final press conference at headquarters. Saying he had been subjected to "scurrilous attacks," Sessions vowed to continue to "speak in the strongest terms about protecting it [the FBI] from being manipulated and politicized both from the inside and out."

Sessions left the building at 6 P.M., receiving one last ride home from his security detail. It was the first time an FBI director had been fired.

In fact, it was Sessions and his wife, Alice, who had engaged in scurrilous attacks. Without a shred of evidence, they had continued throughout the controversy to claim that Clarke and Ron McCall, who had been over Sessions's security detail, had engaged in an immense conspiracy to remove him. Alice Sessions constantly referred to McCall as "the one I found in my bedroom." But she had her facts confused. An FBI OPR investigation had found a previous member of the FBI security detail had entered the Sessionses' bedroom with William Sessions's permission to change the codes on the FBI director's two-way radio. Bound by bureau restrictions, McCall had to take Alice Sessions's attacks, while the OPR report remained secret.

The truth was that Clarke, fearing any divisiveness would further harm the bureau, had been so loyal to Sessions that he never said anything critical about him. McCall had been guilty of nothing more than trying to turn aside Alice Sessions's improper demands.

Within the FBI, there was jubilation, tinged with sadness that events had taken such a tragic turn. Sessions's secretary began sobbing, but other secretaries in mahogany row broke out a bottle of champagne. FBI officials and agents said they could not believe the relief they felt as the tension of the past six months finally dissipated.

With Sessions under a cloud, the Clinton administration and members of Congress had gone around him, preferring to deal with Clarke. The investigative side of the FBI had continued to thrive, symbolized by the fact that the bureau had caught Muslim extremists—some of them tied to suspects in the New York City World Trade Center bombing—in the act of mixing chemicals they intended to use to blow up the United Nations headquarters, the Lincoln and Holland tunnels, and other targets.

An equally important investigation remained secret. That was a probe by the FBI into information from a former KGB employee who had had access to KGB files. According to his account, the KGB had had many hundreds of Americans and possibly more than a thousand spying for them in recent years. So specific was the information that the FBI was quickly able to establish the source's credibility. When the FBI confronted some of the alleged spies, including military men who had had top-secret information and officials of other government agencies, one confessed, and others refused to talk until they saw their lawyers.

By the summer of 1993, the FBI had mobilized agents in most major cities to pursue the cases. A top-secret meeting was called at Quantico to plot strategy. The break came just when FBI counter-intelligence officials had concluded rather smugly that the end of the cold war had brought no great surprises about the degree to which the KGB had penetrated American secrets. While the cases were still being developed, it was clear that the intelligence division, misnamed though it was, would have enough to keep it busy into the next century.

On the other hand, every other facet of the bureau's operations—

the administrative, personnel, and budgetary sides—had become paralyzed by the standoff over Sessions. With crime increasing and the federal budget tightening, the FBI needed to restructure and streamline its operations. For months, proposals for doing so had been piling up in Sessions's office.

The day after he fired Sessions, Clinton named U.S. District Court Judge Louis J. Freeh (pronounced "free") of New York to succeed him. Whether an FBI director should come from within the agency or not is always open to debate. To overcome the stain of Hoover's legacy, presidents in recent years have preferred outsiders who are judges. On the other hand, FBI agents have become increasingly restive under judges, believing that a professional who already understands how the bureau works would do a better job. The bureau is incredibly complex, and it takes two to five years for a director to learn what the FBI is all about. Even William Webster, himself a former judge, thought it was time to consider an agent as director.

"Surely we have demonstrated the trustworthiness of the FBI during all this time," Webster said. Referring to the bureau's record since Hoover, Webster said, "There has not been a single proven case of a violation of constitutional rights. You always have people claiming it. It costs ten dollars to file a lawsuit. But there hasn't been a single one. The organization is composed of individuals, and individuals will not always be perfect. But if the training is there, if the adherence to law is there, if the understanding of the law is there, the systems are there, and the leadership is there, it's not going to happen. The bureau will stand for the protection of the rights of citizens. That's going to continue, whether it can best be fostered by someone from the outside who has to learn what goes on, or by someone inside who has been professionally trained. But an insider has to have demonstrated a clear understanding of the responsibilities of good citizenship and subservience to the law."[499]

But former acting director John Otto said, "I'm not sure you would be doing the FBI a favor by doing that. If you come from the inside, people say you've been covering up things for years."

In selecting Freeh, Clinton got both an insider and an outsider. Born in Jersey City, New Jersey, Freeh, forty-three, graduated in 1971 from Rutgers College and in 1974 from Rutgers School of Law. In 1975, he received an LL.M in criminal law from New York University School of Law.

From 1974 to 1975, Freeh was on the staff of U.S. Senator Clifford P. Case of New Jersey. He then served as an FBI agent in New York, where other agents admired the unassuming way he went about his work, drafting memos on how the relatively new RICO law could be used to fight organized crime. Working on the ground-breaking UNIRAC case, Freeh and another agent got an associate of Anthony Scotto, the president of the International Longshoreman's Union, to cooperate with the FBI, helping to break the case. Freeh was, said Frank Storey, one of his supervisors, "totally dedicated, incredibly bright, and thorough."

In 1980, Freeh was promoted to a supervisory job in organized crime at headquarters, where he chafed at its bureaucratic ways. The following year, Freeh became an assistant U.S. attorney in New York. He later was assigned to the organized-crime unit, becoming chief of the unit in 1987. He prosecuted the Pizza Connection case, a landmark in the bureau's fight against organized crime.

Freeh developed a reputation for being able to coordinate the work of often competing investigative agencies. In 1990, he was named a special federal prosecutor to coordinate the prosecution of Walter Leroy Moody, Jr., who was convicted in the bombing death of federal judge Robert Vance. Freeh worked closely with Larry Potts, now the head of the FBI's criminal investigative division. Potts had nothing but praise for the way Freeh coordinated the work of the FBI and more than a dozen other agencies and U.S. attorneys to bring about a conviction.

Finally, in 1991, Freeh was appointed a federal judge in New York. He thus could bring to the job of FBI director perspective as an FBI agent, a prosecutor, and a judge. While Freeh had no experience running a large agency, his skills at dealing with people and coordinating the work of different agencies suggested he would have no problem managing the FBI.

Twenty years after Hoover's death, the FBI could be trusted to be run by a former agent. Unlike the culture of the agency under Hoover, the institution is now firmly committed to obeying the law. In selecting a director, what is important is the character of the individual, not whether he is an outsider or insider. But the Senate Judiciary Committee should satisfy itself that any nominee understands the abuses that occurred under Hoover. For the position of FBI director is one of the most powerful in the country, and only by understanding the past can the bureau prevent such abuses from occurring again.

Despite the abuses, at least some of the improvements Sessions made in the bureau were likely to remain.

"He has caused a lot of bureau processes and procedures and methods to be reviewed and changed," said Greenleaf, whose relations with Sessions soured after he pushed him to respond to the author's letter seeking comment on his abuses. "We are doing things in a way we have never done them before."

To be sure, no director will ever make everyone in the bureau happy.

"No matter who sits there, Jesus Christ himself could come back and have the misfortune to be made director, and they would forget everything that happened during Christianity," Otto said. "It's a tough job. With our democracy as it is, it is something that is constantly in need of review. You have the ten-year limitation on that position, which is a good thing."

But by his actions, Sessions had disgraced himself, placing his personal needs above the organization's. Even Sessions's most vaunted achievement—promotion of equal rights within the bureau—was overblown. During the nearly six years Sessions was director, the number of female and minority agents added to the rolls increased at about the same rate as under Webster. Moreover, Webster had promoted a black agent—John Glover—to be directly under him. The highest-ranking black under Sessions was a special agent in charge of a field office. Finally, it was the Justice Department that had advised Sessions not to appeal the court decision favoring Hispanic agents.

It was a sad commentary that every FBI director except Webster took advantage of his position improperly. Hoover had the FBI maintain his home and build sidewalks and cabinets for it. Clarence Kelley had the FBI build and install two valances for his apartment. He also had the bureau provide him with two television sets. Kelley eventually returned the TV sets and reimbursed the FBI for the valances.[500]

Today the FBI is light-years different from the way it was under Hoover. Abuses by Sessions aside, the bureau is firmly committed to obeying the law as well as enforcing it. It focuses on the important targets. And it has opened up opportunities for minorities and women. In large part because of the FBI, the Mafia in the U.S. has been decimated; the World Trade Center bombing notwithstanding, terrorist incidents have dwindled from 100 a year to 7 a year; and spying by foreign intelligence services both during and after the cold war has been largely thwarted. White-collar crime and political corruption that would have been ignored under Hoover are being attacked aggressively. By neutralizing both right-wing and left-wing domestic terrorist groups, the FBI has diminished the fear that these groups generate. While drug trafficking continues unabated, the fact that the FBI has aimed at the top of the drug cartels means that drug money has not been allowed to corrupt the political process to any extent, as it has in other countries.

Under Hoover, not only did the bureau refuse to cooperate with local police, but he ordered agents not to cooperate with the CIA. While the CIA still occasionally fails to inform the FBI when it should about activities it conducts in the U.S., "The overall environment is one of tremendous cooperation," said Robert M. Gates when he was director of Central Intelligence.[501]

The bureau still has problems to be addressed, many stemming from its parochialism. While the rest of the country equates Hoover with abuses of individual rights, many FBI agents insist they do not know enough to judge him, or that he was misunderstood. While they do not subscribe to his methods, they proudly display Hoover's portrait on their office walls. Some agents childishly equate the director with the FBI, interpreting an attack on the director as an attack on the agency—a tendency that may be modified after agents fully understand how profoundly Sessions abused the system.

"I told agents when I was in the field they should develop a group of friends outside of the FBI," Bill Baker said. "We tend to become a totally absorbing profession. We have enough work to totally capture every spare moment. There is a tendency in law enforcement to reinforce each other and become too inward."[502]

While the rest of the country has entered the computer age, agents still perform most of their work manually, blissfully unaware of how far behind the bureau is. Marginal employees are still tolerated more than they should be. Even though everyone in the bureau thinks they will be dismissed for lying in an internal investigation or misusing files, the fact is that those infractions alone do not result in the firing of an employee. The inspection division needs to develop a way to ferret out important abuses rather than taking a vacuum-cleaner approach to its reviews. And the bureau needs to understand that the infractions agents commit and how the bureau deals with them are legitimate public concerns, not merely—as Sessions believed—the personal business of the agents involved or the private business of the FBI. Hoover's dictum—"Don't embarrass the bureau"—should not be a part of the modern FBI.

Given the bureau's monumental task, its agent force of 10,300 and its budget of $2 billion a year are relatively small. The number of agents represents only one-third of the officers in the New York City

Police Department. The annual budget is less than the cost of one Stealth bomber, now priced at $2.2 billion each. From profiling serial killers to conducting laboratory tests, the FBI needs more money to eliminate backlogs.

"People can't keep asking us to do more and more and not give us more people," said Danny Coulson, the deputy assistant director over violent crime. "We need resources. If we're going to talk about a peace dividend, where in the hell is it? We have pitiful new resources. We put fifty people on health-care fraud. The threat to our country is not from Eastern Europe. It's coming from here."[503]

In studying the FBI's future, the bureau's planning, evaluations, and audits office predicted it would need to expand its overseas offices as the world shrinks and crime becomes more international in scope. Cooperation with other law enforcement agencies will need to be augmented as well, so that the FBI serves more as an information clearinghouse. Finally, the FBI will need to step up its efforts to deal with the growing problem of computer-related crime.[504]

Despite the abuses and problems, the FBI today is an American success story.

"The organization has more competence than any single organization I have ever seen," said Lee Colwell, the former associate director. "It touches the breadth of our lives. It is probably one of the most important organizations in the country. It affects social change, social attitudes. If people feel good about the FBI, they feel good about the government."

Having survived its turbulent ride into the modern era, the FBI today is the most powerful and effective law enforcement agency in the world, one that is the envy of other nations that call upon it for help. Despite all the changes and technological advances, its strength remains its agents, who are dedicated, well trained, and professional.

For the child rescued by an agent from a kidnapper, or the target of a terrorist bombing whose life is saved because an agent had the tenacity to keep dropping in to develop an informant, the FBI means the difference between life and death. By fighting criminal cartels, the bureau maintains the sanctity of the political process. By protecting military secrets from compromise through espionage, the FBI guards American freedoms.

But the FBI can easily go off course. Americans can be proud of the FBI and the job it is doing. But they must remain vigilant to ensure that the FBI continues to do its work within the law.

The author sent this letter to the FBI's public-affairs office on June 24, 1992. The FBI turned the letter over to the Justice Department, leading to the investigation of FBI Director William Sessions.

REQUEST FOR COMMENT FROM THE DIRECTOR, FOR BOOK ON THE FBI BY RONALD KESSLER

Sarah Munford

1. According to the Texas state trooper who stopped Ms. Munford and her son Glenn on December 24, 1991, for having tinted side windows, Ms. Munford, in an effort to avoid a ticket, displayed her FBI credentials and said she was the assistant to the director of the FBI, that her family was in law enforcement, and that "you go home at night, and your kids think you are a decent person, and then you go and do something like this." As a result of an OPR investigation, a suspension of seven days has been recommended.

Ms. Munford, when asked for comment, said, "I don't know what you are talking about." She later said she was referring to the proposed seven-day suspension. She said she did not want to comment in detail on this or other allegations concerning her.

According to the Texas court, the ticket has not been paid and a warrant has been issued for the arrest of Glenn Munford as the owner of the car.

When informed of this on June 23, Don Munford, Glenn's

father said, "I'll get him to pay that. I appreciate your calling me."

QUESTION: Has a seven-day suspension of Ms. Munford been approved?*

2. After living in Virginia for nearly five years, Ms. Munford continues to register her car in Texas. Virginia law requires Virginia registration after living in the state 30 days.

Ms. Munford commented that the Virginia Department of Motor Vehicles has granted her permission to continue to register her car in Texas because she is here for a fixed term and has property in Texas.

However, Charles E. Murphy, the department's director of investigations in Richmond, said, "There is no such thing as a waiver. The Virginia statute doesn't give anyone the authority to waive anything. Even Jesus Christ doesn't have the authority to waive the laws of the Commonwealth of Virginia. I'd like to see it [the waiver]. As far as I'm concerned, it doesn't exist."

QUESTION: Would Ms. Munford provide a copy of the document giving her an exemption?

Comment: Even if Ms. Munford had special permission, the practice of continuing to register her car in Texas nearly five years after she moved to Virginia creates an appearance that she is above the law that hundreds of agents have to follow when they are transferred to the Washington area from other parts of the country that have lower car insurance rates. As a law enforcement organization, the FBI should insure that its employees—particularly one who holds such a privileged position as special assistant to the director—themselves obey the law.

3. Two of the director's former assistants have said on the record, and others who are still with the bureau and have first-hand knowledge of the events have said not for attribution, that Ms. Munford often claims that the director has asked her

---

* While the FBI does not normally discuss internal discipline, the public has a legitimate interest in knowing whether the bureau, as an agency engaged in enforcing the law, appropriately disciplines its own employees if they are believed to have abused their positions of trust.

to take actions or obtain information that the director did not, in fact, request, and that Ms. Munford is in the habit of making up information.

One of these former aides said, "I would just say that by the time I left the FBI, I did not rely on anything she [Sarah Munford] told me. It was unfortunate, but that's the way it was." He added, "[Director] Sessions had no idea that she lies. He would be absolutely appalled." A second former assistant acknowledged that he told a member of the security detail that Ms. Munford "would just make things up, and that he [the agent on the security detail] should be careful when dealing with her."

In commenting, Ms. Munford said she is an honest person. "I'll have to hope these people get to know me better," she said.

Comment: While this problem has not had any serious ramifications, it has created an atmosphere of mistrust and resentment within the top echelons of the bureau and appears to conflict with the high standards of personal integrity and candor expected of bureau employees.

4. The director has made it clear that the attorney general has first priority on the Sabreliner jet. But when both the director and the attorney general have needed to fly at the same time, Ms. Munford has instructed the security detail and/or FBI aviation managers to tell the Justice Department, so that the director would be able to use the better plane, that the attorney general cannot have the Sabreliner because it is unavailable. These requests have been refused. When the director has blamed his staff for the continuing confusion over who gets the Sabreliner, Ms. Munford has failed to acknowledge her role.

Ms. Munford commented that she has nothing to do with scheduling the plane.

5. Ms. Munford became convinced that someone in the bureau had deliberately scratched her car and, as a result, video cameras were set up in the FBI headquarters garage primarily to watch her car.

Ms. Munford commented that someone did scratch her car but the video cameras were not put up specifically to watch her car.

QUESTION: Were cameras put up as a result of the incident involving the scratch on Ms. Munford's car and primarily to watch her car?

[NOTE: The answer has turned out to be no.]

6. Ms. Munford periodically blames the security detail for not delivering to Mrs. Sessions personal invitations or copies of the director's daily and future schedules. In fact, Ms. Munford has told the detail she does not want some of this material to go to Mrs. Sessions, apparently because she doesn't want Mrs. Sessions to alter the schedule. When the detail follows Ms. Munford's instructions and Mrs. Sessions complains about not getting mail, Ms. Munford says she sent the mail with the detail, and the detail lost it.

Because Ms. Munford said she did not want to comment in detail about the allegations concerning her, I was not able to ask her about this issue. Mrs. Sessions commented that the problem is with her husband, who sometimes forgets to give her invitations that he takes home.

7. Because she was unhappy that Justice Department officials did not give her the respect she felt she was due and often did not return her calls, Ms. Munford asked James Kramarsic, the head of the attorney general's security detail, to use his influence to improve her position within the department. When he said there was nothing he could do about it, she said she was displeased with him, and that the director was displeased with him. Ms. Munford also expressed displeasure with Mr. Kramarsic because he would not go along with her requests to tell the Justice Department the Sabreliner was unavailable for the attorney general's use. Mr. Kramarsic later said he had been able to keep his job as head of the detail only because of his relationship with the attorney general.

The lack of respect Ms. Munford complained of is widespread among top bureau officials. As one former assistant put it, "So many people have no respect for her whatsoever that she finds herself thwarted in doing anything." This is in sharp contrast to the reaction to the Jahns, who are held in at least as high regard as the FBI agents who have served as the director's assistants.

In commenting, Ms. Munford denied having any disputes with Mr. Kramarsic.

Alice Sessions

1. Mrs. Sessions has requested and received an FBI headquarters building pass that entitles her to the special privileges accorded an assistant FBI director or above. Because she often forgets to bring the pass, she is admitted without any pass. This conflicts with FBI security procedures, which require a top-secret security clearance before anyone is allowed unescorted into the building. No one can get a top secret clearance without a need to know, which Mrs. Sessions does not have.

Because of the special access accorded holders of the gold building pass, Mrs. Sessions has brought friends into the FBI building without having to clear them through the security procedures that hundreds of visitors are forced to go through every day. Even FBI agents from field offices outside of the Washington area who have top secret clearance must check in at the escort desk and receive a temporary pass before entering the building unescorted. When headquarters employees forget their passes, their supervisors are notified in writing.

Mrs. Sessions has also asked for and received a four-digit code that allows her access to the director's suite without going through receptionists. Access is controlled in this way because of the extremely sensitive information the suite contains. In general, only those FBI officials who work in this high-security area have a code to enter the suite.

Mrs. Sessions commented, "Why shouldn't I be able to go in and out of Bill's office? . . . [T]hey better get on to investigating me for a top-secret clearance because, believe me, I hear a lot more things than the girls in the telephone room do. I'm privy to a lot more things than that."

Mrs. Sessions said she has forgotten the four-digit code that allowed her access to the director's suite. She said the people she has brought into the building without registering them at the escort desk have generally been members of her immediate family.

Comment: While no one believes Mrs. Sessions to be a security risk, the fact that she is given a special exemption from the rules simply because she is the director's wife appears to be an abuse that creates a lack of respect for the rules and for the director. It places bureau officials in charge of these matters in an uncomfortable position: They are aware that they are breaking the rules and that the director must realize this, so they do not raise the issue with him for fear he will react negatively, jeopardizing their relationship with him and/or their career.

2. Mrs. Sessions has told FBI agents and others that she believes the FBI may be bugging the director's bedroom or wiretapping their home telephones.

In an interview with me, she referred to the FBI and said, "We are probably being recorded." She also said that one of her phone lines "gives me indications of compromise."

When she believed information she had imparted to the director in their bedroom got back to her, Mrs. Sessions suggested to Ron McCall that the bureau had placed a bug in their bedroom. This allegation was reported through the chain of command of the administrative services division up to the level of assistant director.

In commenting, Mrs. Sessions said she did not recall the conversation with Mr. McCall. But she said, "What you are relating back to me I recently related to someone involved in my security. You are giving me back the very story I have told to them. I think that is interesting. Of course, those are the facts of the story anyway." Referring to the FBI's wiretapping capabilities, Mrs. Sessions then said, "I have no idea what their capabilities are with the telephone. I have consulted some other people professionally about this. In fact, I had the telephone company in a year ago."

3. Because she knew him, Mrs. Sessions suggested that the security detail use Sarah Munford's husband, Don Munford, to survey the director's residence to make recommendations on improving the alarm system at the director's home. Because she is the director's wife and is determined, the security detail acceded to her request. Don Munford proposed a costly system which he wanted to install. However, higher bureau officials

vetoed the proposal. If allowed to proceed, it would have violated government procurement rules because of the lack of
competitive bidding. In addition, the bureau officials decided
it would have been improper to award the contract to Mr.
Munford because of his relationship to the director's special
assistant.* Saying that the director had put her in charge of
security at the residence, Mrs. Sessions also requested copies
of all memos relating to the proposed installation, a request
that the security detail denied.

In commenting, Mrs. Sessions said that she wanted other
bids to be obtained. However, both Don Munford and the bureau officials involved dispute this. Mrs. Sessions said she does
not recall asking for documents.

4. Mrs. Sessions routinely chastises the FBI security detail
for allegedly not doing their job. It would appear that it is up
to the director, not his wife, to critique the performance of FBI
employees.

In commenting, Mrs. Sessions said she has criticized the
detail two or three times.

5. Ron McCall, who was over the director's security detail,
was removed from his position and passed over for a promotion
after he: 1) warned the detail to "be careful" when dealing with
Ms. Munford because she is a "pathological liar," and 2) in
carrying out his duties as he saw them, gave copies of the keys
to the Sessions' home to each member of the director's security
detail, contrary to Mrs. Sessions' request that the detail have
no copies or only one copy of the keys.

In commenting, Mrs. Sessions said she did not know why
Mr. McCall was removed. She confirmed that Mr. McCall had
had extra keys made against her instruction.

QUESTION: Why was Mr. McCall removed?

6. When taking Director Sessions and his wife to give a
speech in Baltimore, the security detail was diverted to an

_____

* The Munfords are now separated.

appliance plant so that Mrs. Sessions could return a toaster.

Mrs. Sessions confirmed this incident.

7. When going shopping downtown, Mrs. Sessions routinely asks FBI guards to park her car for her in the FBI garage. On one occasion, she also asked them to take care of the director's father, Will, who was sitting in the car.

Mrs. Sessions said she does not recall this incident.

8. Mrs. Sessions widely expresses negative opinions of bureau headquarters and of many of the FBI's highest-ranking officials both to people in the bureau and on an on-the-record basis to me.

Comment: While Mrs. Sessions is entitled to her opinions, and her independence is to be admired, her open criticism of people who work for her husband, which is sometimes based on an incomplete understanding of the FBI, creates resentment and apprehension about whether she reflects the director's views and, conversely, whether her views influence him.

Notes

1. Teletype of October 3, 1991, from the FBI director to all field offices and legal attachés regarding "request by author Ronald Kessler to interview FBI personnel for upcoming book."
2. Interview on May 4, 1992, with Nelson.
3. Interviews on April 4 and 18, 1992, with Tullai. Tullai estimates he prepared seven thousand agents to meet Hoover.
4. Interview on January 3, 1992, with De Sarno.
5. Interview on November 26, 1991, with McKenzie.
6. Theoharis, Athan, ed., *From the Secret Files of J. Edgar Hoover*, Ivan R. Dee, 1991, pages 346–56.
7. Department of Justice, *Report on the Relationship Between U.S. Recording Co. and the FBI and Certain Other Matters Pertaining to the FBI*, January, 1978, pages 13–14. In referring to similar practices by former Hoover aides who were then living, the report states that such practices arguably violated federal criminal statutes barring conversion of government property to personal use and misuse of federal property.
8. Interview on December 30, 1991, with DeLoach.
9. Interview on November 22, 1991, with Revell.
10. Interview on December 9, 1991, with Clark.
11. Interview on November 22, 1991, with Ramsey.
12. Interview on November 23, 1991, with Revell.

13. Interview on November 5, 1991, with Storey.
14. Interview on November 14, 1991, with Giel.
15. *New York Times*, April 25, 1982, page A-1.
16. *New York Times*, March 25, 1982, page B-8, and April 25, 1982, page A-1.
17. Interview on February 7, 1992, with Verinder.
18. Interview on November 5, 1991, with Richards.
19. Interview on November 16, 1991, with Walton.
20. U.S. Senate, Select Committee to Study Governmental Operations with Respect to Intelligence Activities (the Church Committee), volume 6, *Intelligence Activities: FBI*, U.S. Government Printing Office, 1975, page 11.
21. *Abridged History of the FBI*, Research Unit, FBI.
22. Interview on December 10, 1991, with Valiquette.
23. Interview on November 6, 1991, with Walton.
24. Interviews on November 6, 1991, with Walton, and on February 7, 1992, with Verinder; *New York Times*, December 14, 1982, page A-18.
25. *Newsweek*, October 12, 1987, page 10.
26. Interview on February 13, 1992, with Webster.
27. Interview on November 6, 1991, with Walton.
28. Interview on April 9, 1992, with Colwell.
29. Interview on November 25, 1991, with Clarke.
30. Interview on November 22, 1991, with Revell.
31. Interview on November 5, 1991, with Richards.
32. *New York Times*, June 29, 1991, page A-25.
33. Interview on December 2, 1991, with Stowe.
34. Interview on January 8, 1992, with Binney.
35. Interview on December 9, 1991, with Doran.
36. For more about the Koechers, see the author's *Spy vs. Spy: Stalking Soviet Spies in America*, Scribner's, 1988; Pocket Books edition, 1989.
37. Interview on December 10, 1991, with Fox; Garrow, David J., *The FBI and Martin Luther King, Jr.: From "Solo" to Memphis*, Norton, 1981, pages 34–43.
38. Interview on December 10, 1991, with Fox; *New York Times*, May 30, 1990, page B-2, and February 14, 1990, page B-3.
39. *New York Times*, June 14, 1991, page A-1.
40. Interview on January 13, 1992, with Flynn.
41. Interview on November 25, 1991, with Castonguay.
42. *History of the J. Edgar Hoover Building*, FBI Office of Congressional and Public Affairs, March 1987.

43. Interview on February 21, 1992, with Alice Sessions; confirmed by Seymour on February 25, 1992, and with William Sessions on June 4, 1992.
44. Interview on February 13, 1992, with Webster.
45. Interview on January 16, 1992, with Hicks.
46. Interview on March 20, 1992, with Clarke.
47. Interview on September 29, 1991, with Baker.
48. Interview on January 17, 1992, with Gallagher.
49. Interview on January 17, 1992, with Gallagher.
50. *Terrorism in the United States*, Terrorist Research and Analytical Center, FBI, 1990, page 3; interview on January 17, 1992, with Gallagher.
51. *Terrorism in the United States*, Terrorist Research and Analytical Center, FBI, 1990, page 7.
52. Interview on November 22, 1991, with Revell.
53. Interview on November 26, 1991, with McKenzie.
54. Turner, William W., *Hoover's FBI: The Men and the Myth*, Sherbourne Press, 1970, memo of May 18, 1961, reproduced in full in appendix.
55. Davis, James K., and Clarence M. Kelley, *Kelley: The Story of an FBI Director*, Andrews, McMeel & Parker, 1987, pages 298–303, confirmed on April 16, 1992, by DeBruler.
56. *Gulfport Sun Herald*, June 20, 1985, page A-10, and interview on January 15, 1992, with Kennedy.
57. Interview on November 22, 1991, with Revell.
58. The Warren Commission report, based largely on the FBI's investigation, remains an impressive marshaling of the evidence in the assassination of John F. Kennedy. In addition, *Final Disclosure: The Full Truth About the Assassination of President Kennedy*, by David W. Belin, who was counsel to the Warren Commission, effectively refutes many of the conspiracy theories about the assassination. The book was published by Scribner's in 1988.
59. Interviews on April 28, 1992, with Witschard and with Lawn.
60. Interview on April 28, 1992, with Lawn.
61. Interview on November 25, 1991, with Clarke.
62. *Washington Post*, February 16, 1985, page A-7; *San Antonio Light*, May 28, 1989, page B-1; interview on May 11, 1992, with McCormick.
63. Associated Press, October 2, 1991, and November 5, 1991.
64. Interview on April 3, 1992, with South.
65. Interview on February 5, 1992, with Baker.

66. Whitaker declined on March 6, 1992, to comment.
67. Interview on November 23, 1991, with Revell.
68. Interview on March 9, 1992, with Zopp.
69. Interview on March 9, 1992, with Evans.
70. Interview on March 9, 1992, with Ford.
71. Interview on March 9, 1992, with Zopp.
72. Interviews on March 9 and May 2, 1992, with Robinson.
73. *Baltimore Sun*, March 21, 1988, page D-1.
74. Interview on January 3, 1992, with Zopp; *Cumberland Times-News*, April 11, 1989, page 1.
75. Interview on January 5, 1992, with Rosalie Ford. Her former husband declined to be interviewed.
76. Interview on March 9, 1992, with Robinson. The incident occurred during Robinson's first assignment to Denver.
77. Interview on October 23, 1991, with Roach.
78. Interview on October 23, 1991, with Roach.
79. *Washington Post*, February 10, 1991, page A-1, and interview on January 3, 1992, with Gillham.
80. *Security Awareness in the 1980s*, Defense Security Institute, 1989, page 1990.
81. Interview on October 17, 1991, with Kirby.
82. Interview on October 24, 1991, with Barrett. At Barrett's request, only her maiden name is used here.
83. Interview on June 5, 1992, with Gardner.
84. *Employee Survey Report of Findings*, Institutional Research and Development Office, Training Division, FBI, December 1990, pages 64–65. The findings were based on a random sample of 4,172 employees, of whom 74 percent responded to the survey.
85. Interview on October 21, 1991, with Kirby.
86. Interview on November 7, 1991, with Kaiser.
87. Interview on May 31, 1992, with Depue.
88. Interviews on November 23, 1991, with Revell, and on March 17, 1992, with Geer.
89. Interview on January 28, 1992, with Sessions.
90. Theoharis, Athan, ed., *From the Secret Files of J. Edgar Hoover*, Ivan R. Dee, 1991, page 129.
91. Elliff, John T., *The Reform of FBI Intelligence Operations*, Princeton University Press, 1979, page 6.
92. Interview on November 25, 1986, with Wannall.
93. Interview on March 17, 1992, with Geer.
94. Kessler, Ronald, *Moscow Station: How the KGB Penetrated the*

American Embassy, Scribner's, 1989; Pocket Books edition, 1990, page 103.

95. For more details on some of these operations, see the author's *Spy vs. Spy* and *Inside the CIA*.

96. Interview on February 7, 1992, with Lawton.

97. *People*, January 20, 1992, page 76; *New York Times*, October 28, 1991; interview on January 17, 1992, with Neil Gallagher.

98. *History of the Intelligence Division: Brief Historical Outline*, FBI, page 3.

99. Interview on March 4, 1992, with Watson.

100. *Washington Post*, August 1, 1989, page A-1; *New York Times Magazine*, May 13, 1990, page 29.

101. Interview on September 15, 1991, with Ramey.

102. Interview on March 17, 1992, with Geer. Bloch did not respond to a March 19, 1992, letter requesting comment.

103. Interview on January 17, 1992, with Gilbert.

104. Interview on November 14, 1991, with Gow.

105. *Washington Post*, May 7, 1992, page A-12.

106. Interview on April 13, 1992, with Penrith; *New York Times*, January 18, 1992, page A-1.

107. *Briefing Book of General Information on the FBI*, FBI, 1990–1991, page 12.

108. Interview on April 10, 1992, with Garcia, and *New York Times*, April 23, 1990, page A-1.

109. Interviews on April 10, 1992, with Garcia, and on April 20, 1992, with Newport; *New York Times*, April 23, 1990, page B-10.

110. Interview on November 1, 1991, with Pledger.

111. *Firefight*, a video prepared by the FBI's training division on the Miami shootout, and *Miami Herald*, April 12, 1986, page A-1.

112. Interview on July 19, 1992, with Revell.

113. Interview on May 29, 1992, with Hanlon.

114. Interview on June 1, 1992, with McNeill.

115. Interview on February 19, 1992, with Mazella.

116. Interview on October 13, 1991, with Greenleaf.

117. *Washington Post*, September 12, 1989, page A-28. Smith & Wesson did not respond to requests for comment.

118. Interview on June 8, 1992, with Giglia.

119. Interview on February 5, 1992, with Baker.

120. Interview on February 19, 1992, with Warner.

121. Interview on February 18, 1992, with John Thompson, and

Breslin, Jack, *America's Most Wanted*, Harper, 1990, pages 285–86.

122. Interview on February 19, 1992, with Grogan.
123. Interview on February 21, 1992, with Webster.
124. Interview on November 23, 1991, with Revell.
125. Interview on February 19, 1992, with Mazella.
126. Interview on November 25, 1991, with Clarke.
127. Interview on March 3, 1992, with Lawn.
128. Class conducted on December 3, 1991, by Sirene.
129. *New York Times*, March 15, 1985, page A-1; Associated Press, November 15, 1985.
130. Interview on June 4, 1992, with Thompson.
131. *Miami Herald*, August 31, 1991, page B-2.
132. *Washington Post*, January 5, 1987, page A-4, and *Miami Herald*, January 5, 1987, page B-1.
133. Interview on May 26, 1992, with Frank Monserrate. Suzanne Monserrate, who now uses her maiden name, had no comment because she and her former husband were then appealing their dismissal.
134. Interview on February 18, 1992, with Miller.
135. Brochure of the Playhouse, Miami.
136. *Miami Herald*, January 9, 1987, page B-1.
137. FBI memo from Edwin J. Sharp to John D. Glover, July 14, 1987, page 6.
138. FBI memo from Edwin J. Sharp to John D. Glover, July 14, 1987, page 16.
139. *Miami Herald*, January 18, 1988, page C-1.
140. Interview on March 5, 1992, with Otto.
141. Interview on May 26, 1992, with Frank Monserrate.
142. FBI memo from Edwin J. Sharp to John D. Glover, July 14, 1987, page 26.
143. Interview on June 8, 1992, with Anthony Silva.
144. Interview on January 8, 1992, with Binney.
145. Interview on October 26, 1991, with King.
146. Interview on January 3, 1992, with Manning.
147. *Summary of Disciplinary Actions, Five Year Calendar Summary*, FBI, calendar 1990 figures. In calendar 1991, the bureau delegated responsibility for levying discipline for more minor infractions such as sleeping on duty or abusive language to special agents in charge of field offices. As a result, the number of inquiries handled by the administrative summary unit at headquarters dropped to 982 from 1,304. Actions were taken

on 501 of those cases, resulting in 21 dismissals, 17 demotions, and 16 suspensions for fourteen days or more. In addition, 32 employees resigned during the inquiries. The number of such adverse actions increased to 54 from 50 in calendar 1990, while the number of firings decreased to 21 from 25.

148. Interviews on January 8, 1992, with Binney, and on January 15, 1992, with Greenleaf.
149. Interview on February 21, 1992, with Webster.
150. Interview on December 19, 1991, with Minor.
151. Interviews on October 4, 1991, with Hume, and on December 19, 1991, with Minor. Tickel declined on October 19, 1991, to comment on any aspect of his cases.
152. Jury verdict in *U.S. vs. Tickel*, Case No. CR 82-269-A, U.S. District Court, Eastern District of Virginia; Case No. CT87-1287, Prince George's County Circuit Court, State of Maryland; *Washington Post*, June 19, 1987, page C-3; and interview on October 4, 1991, with Hume.
153. Interview on October 4, 1991, with Hume.
154. Case number CT87-1287, Prince George's County Circuit Court, State of Maryland, and interview on October 20, 1991, with Deborah A. Johnston, the prosecutor in the case.
155. Interview on December 19, 1991, with Minor.
156. Interviews on October 23, 1991, with Friedrick; on November 22, 1991, with Revell; and on December 19, 1991, with Minor; Neff, James, *Mobbed Up: Jackie Presser's High-Wire Life in the Teamsters, the Mafia, and the FBI*, Dell, 1989, pages 439–55; *New York Times*, December 8, 1986, page A-17; *Cleveland Plain Dealer*, December 3, 1988, page A-1.
157. *Chronological Record of the Inspection Division*, FBI, page 1.
158. Interview on January 9, 1992, with Toohey.
159. Interview on May 19, 1992, with Lumpkin.
160. Interview on May 18, 1992, with Hogan.
161. Interview on October 11, 1991, with Wagner.
162. Associated Press, January 14, 1980, and October 20, 1979.
163. Interview on April 13, 1992, with Penrith.
164. *Arizona Republic*, June 21, 1987, page A-1.
165. Interview on November 26, 1991, with McKenzie.
166. Interview on January 16, 1992, with Collingwood.
167. Interview on April 10, 1992, with Sessions.
168. Interview on January 9, 1992, with Leary.
169. Interview on December 17, 1991, with Burnett.
170. *New York Times*, September 5, 1990, page 20-A.

171. Interview on February 7, 1992, with Verinder and Associated Press, July 25, 1990.

172. Interview on February 7, 1992, with Verinder and Associated Press, July 25, 1990. Osborne declined on February 13, 1992, to comment.

173. Interview on November 23, 1991, with Revell.

174. Interview on January 15, 1992, with Greenleaf.

175. *Philadelphia Inquirer*, July 1, 1988, page 1-A.

176. Interview on April 9, 1992, with Colwell.

177. Interview on March 20, 1992, with Clarke.

178. *Quarterly Summary of Disciplinary Matters*, FBI, September 10, 1990.

179. *Philadelphia Inquirer*, December 14, 1988, page 1-A, and interview with Davis on April 30, 1992.

180. An August 6, 1991, letter from the Justice Department to Mata responding to Mata's appeal of the revocation of his security clearance said Mata admitted giving information that "certain materials purchased by the Cuban government had been altered by a government agency." The letter also said that Mata passed a polygraph test when he claimed he gave the Cubans classified information.

181. Interview on November 22, 1991, with Revell.

182. *Washington Post*, March 7, 1990, page 28-A. Mata's current lawyer, Steven Raber, had no comment on May 19, 1992.

183. Interviews on May 27, 1992, with Kennedy, and on June 10, 1992, with Davis.

184. Interview on December 10, 1991, with Dufour.

185. Interviews on December 10, 1991, with Dufour; with Kelly on May 7, 1992; and with Siano on May 13, 1992. Kelly said he wanted Dufour to be neatly groomed only if he continued to work in the Dallas office.

186. Interview on April 13, 1992, with Penrith.

187. "Reordering the Priorities of the FBI in Light of the End of the Cold War," Don Edwards, *St. John's Law Review*, winter 1991, page 72.

188. Interview on January 9, 1992, with Toohey.

189. Interview on November 23, 1991, with Revell.

190. *The FBI and CISPES*, report of the U.S. Senate Select Committee on Intelligence, July 1989, page 72.

191. Interview on November 23, 1991, with Bruemmer.

192. Interview on December 19, 1991, with Minor.

193. *Washington Post,* September 15, 1988, page A-1.
194. FBI reports of January 20, 1964, from Cleveland, and February 24, 1976, from Newark.
195. Interview on November 22, 1991, with Ramsey.
196. Interview on April 21, 1992, with Duffin.
197. Interview on November 22, 1991, with Temple.
198. *Report on Applications for Orders Authorizing or Approving the Interception of Wire, Oral, or Electronic Communications,* Statistics Division, Administrative Office of the U.S. Courts, January 1, 1990–December 31, 1990, page 8.
199. Interview on November 22, 1991, with Torres.
200. Interview on November 22, 1991, with Collins.
201. Interview on November 22, 1991, with Revell.
202. Interviews on November 22, 1991, with Revell, and on December 19, 1991, with Minor.
203. Interview on November 22, 1991, with Revell.
204. Interview on January 3, 1992, with Gillham.
205. Interview on January 3, 1992, with Gillham, and letter of March 11, 1992, from Siller.
206. *Dallas Morning News,* April 8, 1992, page A-29.
207. Interviews on November 5, 1992, with Revell, and on October 30, 1992, with Siano; *New York Times,* October 27, 1992, page A-1, and April 19, 1992, page A-10; *Newsweek,* November 9, 1992, page 24.
208. Interview on February 21, 1992, with Webster.
209. Interview on January 15, 1992, with Greenleaf.
210. Interview on January 15, 1992, with Greenleaf.
211. Swearing in on December 2, 1991.
212. Desing white-collar-crime class on December 3, 1991.
213. Interview on December 3, 1991, with Cibulas.
214. Sirene ethics class on December 3, 1991.
215. Interview on November 7, 1991, with Yates.
216. Interview on November 1, 1991, with Stowe.
217. Interview on November 26, 1991, with McKenzie.
218. Interview on June 4, 1992, with Stowe.
219. Kavina sensitivity class on December 6, 1991.
220. *Stress Management in Law Enforcement,* FBI, James T. Reese. Quotes from Reese, Beccaccio, and Tully are from interviews the author conducted at the FBI Academy in 1983, when he was with the *Washington Post.* They were updated for this book on May 29 and June 1, 1992.

221. Interview on May 29, 1992, with Reese.
222. Interviews on October 23, 1991, with Davis, and on September 10, 1992, with Miller.
223. Interview on October 15, 1991, with Depue.
224. Interview on November 1, 1991, with Pledger.
225. Interview on November 26, 1991, with McKenzie.
226. Interview on December 2, 1991, with Jones.
227. FBI case summary of *Christine A. Hansen v. FBI*, EEOC complaint number 033-079-X-3070.
228. Hogan's Alley was viewed on November 1 and December 3, 1991. Events from both days are combined.
229. Graduation on December 6, 1991.
230. Interview on February 4, 1992, with Parsons.
231. Interview on February 4, 1992, with Lawler.
232. Interview on February 4, 1992, with Rehder.
233. Interview on January 9, 1992, with Toohey.
234. Interview on January 28, 1992, with Schwein.
235. Interview on December 16, 1991, with McKenzie.
236. Interview on Dec. 30, 1991, with Walsh, and *Daily Herald*, Mount Prospect, Illinois, December 19, 1986; *Chicago Tribune*, September 5, 1985, page 8, and *Chicago Sun-Times*, December 11, 1986, page 38.
237. *Bank Crime Statistics, Federally Insured Financial Institutions*, FBI, 1991, pages 2–6.
238. Interview on February 4, 1992, with Thornton.
239. Interview on February 4, 1992, with Gardner.
240. *Washington Post*, January 12, 1986, page A-1.
241. Interview on March 5, 1992, with Otto.
242. *Los Angeles Times*, December 26, 1991, page B-1, and *Washington Post*, December 27, 1991.
243. Interview on February 4, 1992, with Gardner.
244. Interview on October 18, 1991, with Minor.
245. Interview on October 16, 1991, with Gallagher.
246. Interview on October 21, 1991, with Bates.
247. *Detroit News*, June 10, 1990, page A-1.
248. AP, December 11, 1990.
249. Interview on February 4, 1992, with Jones.
250. *Los Angeles Times*, January 9, 1992, page B-3.
251. Interview on January 23, 1992, with Brekke.
252. *Washington Post*, August 6, 1992, page A-1.
253. *Los Angeles Times*, March 13, 1992, page B-11.
254. Interview on February 4, 1992, with Marino.

255. See the author's *Spy vs. Spy: Stalking Soviet Spies in America,* Pocket Books, 1988, page 176.
256. Interview on February 5, 1992, with Baker.
257. Interview on June 2, 1992, with Watson.
258. Interview on December 19, 1991, with Minor.
259. *Security Awareness in the 1980s,* Defense Security Institute, 1990, page 191, and *Time,* February 18, 1991, page 45.
260. *Time,* October 15, 1984, page 34.
261. Interview on December 2, 1991, with Douglas.
262. Interview on July 13, 1992, with York.
263. Interview on April 10, 1992, with Sessions.
264. Interview on October 30, 1991, with Teten.
265. Interview on January 2, 1992, with Mullaney.
266. Interview on June 8, 1989, with Depue.
267. Interview on June 12, 1992, with Depue.
268. Ressler, Robert K., with Tom Shactman, *Whoever Fights Monsters,* St. Martin's Press, 1991, pages 47–48, and interview on December 4, 1991, with Depue.
269. Interview on December 6, 1991, with Campbell.
270. Interview on October 31, 1991, with Bryant.
271. Interview on June 8, 1989, with Depue.
272. Interview on June 16, 1992, with Douglas.
273. Ressler, Robert K., Burgess, Ann W., and Douglas, John E., *Sexual Homicide: Patterns and Motives,* Lexington Books, 1988, page 122.
274. *Washington Post,* May 2, 1992, page A-7.
275. Interview on June 12, 1992, with Zopp.
276. Interview on December 2, 1991, with Douglas.
277. Interview on June 16, 1992, with Lano.
278. *Baltimore Sun,* March 15, 1992, page A-14; *Wilmington News Journal,* November 24, 1989, page A-1; and interview on June 12, 1992, with Zopp.
279. Interview on December 6, 1991, with Hagmaier.
280. Newton, Michael, *Hunting Humans: An Encyclopedia of Modern Serial Killers,* Loompanics Unlimited, 1990, page 28.
281. Associated Press, August 23, 1982, and *St. Louis Post-Dispatch,* August 18, 1982, page A-1.
282. Interview on July 21, 1992, with Strentz.
283. Interview on February 7, 1992, with Schultz.
284. H. Paul Jeffers, *Who Killed Precious?,* Pharos Books, 1991, pages 169–171.

285. *Washington Post,* October 18, 1991, page A-1, and interview on January 16, 1992, with Hicks.
286. Interview on December 2, 1991, with Hazelwood.
287. Ressler, Robert K., Burgess, Ann W., and Douglas, John E., *Sexual Homicide: Patterns and Motives,* Lexington Books, 1988, page x, and interviews on October 30, 1991, with Teten, and on December 16, 1991, with Douglas.
288. Interview on December 2, 1991, with Brennan.
289. This quote is from the author's article in the *Washington Post,* February 20, 1981, page A-1.
290. *New York Times,* May 3, 1992, page A-50.
291. Interview on September 29, 1991, with Baker.
292. Interview on January 22, 1992, with Potts.
293. *New York Times,* July 20, 1990, page A-8.
294. Interview on June 16, 1992, with Erwin.
295. *FBI Bomb Summary,* FBI, 1990, page 9.
296. *Philadelphia Inquirer,* June 6, 1990, page A-8.
297. *Philadelphia Inquirer,* June 20, 1991, page A-11, and interview on January 22, 1992, with Potts.
298. *New York Times,* November 22, 1990, page A-24.
299. *Washington Post,* June 29, 1991, page A-4, and August 21, 1991, page A-6.
300. *Washington Post,* February 10, 1985, page H-1, and February 28, 1982, page A-1.
301. Interview on January 9, 1992, with Toohey.
302. Interview on July 7, 1992, with McComas.
303. *Atlanta Journal-Constitution,* August 30, 1987, page A-1.
304. Interview on January 16, 1992, with Hicks.
305. *FBI Law Enforcement Bulletin,* March 1984, by Harold A. Deadman, page 13, and May 1984, page 17, and interview on June 19, 1992, with Deadman.
306. *Us,* October 13, 1981, page 10.
307. Interviews on November 22, 1991, with Revell; on December 2, 1991, with Douglas; on December 19, 1991, with Minor; and on January 16, 1992, with Hicks.
308. Interview on July 31, 1992, with Glover.
309. Associated Press, June 29 and July 7, 1981.
310. Interview on November 7, 1991, with Lloyd.
311. Associated Press, June 29, 1981, and interview on June 20, 1992, with Blakeney.
312. Interview on January 16, 1992, with Hicks.

313. Interview on June 26, 1992, with Hicks.

314. Interview on September 11, 1991, with O'Donnell.

315. Interview on June 25, 1992, with O'Donnell; *Los Angeles Times*, June 18, 1989, page A-2; *People*, June 19, 1989, page 69; and *Washington Post*, April 13, 1990, page A-10.

316. Interview on September 11, 1991, with Gleason, and *Washington Post*, August 8, 1990, page C-1.

317. Interview on November 25, 1991, with Clarke.

318. *Polygraph Errors in the FBI: A Critical Events Study*, FBI Inspection Division, December 1987, page 9.

319. *New York Times*, March 5, 1987, page A-27; interview on December 19, 1991, with Minor; and letter of January 7, 1992, from McFarlane.

320. *New York Times*, October 7, 1988, page A-1, and September 27, 1988, page A-1; Robert D. McFadden, et al, *Outrage: The Story Behind the Tawana Brawley Hoax*, Bantam Books, 1990; and interview on November 5, 1991, with Doran.

321. Interview on January 16, 1992, with Hicks; *Miami Herald*, August 8, 1990, page 1-B; and *Washington Times*, August 22, 1990, page B-1.

322. Interview on December 27, 1991, with Lano.

323. FBI teletype of June 17, 1972.

324. Interview on December 27, 1991, with Lano; FBI teletype of June 17, 1972; Sussman, Barry, *The Great Coverup: Nixon and the Scandal of Watergate*, Seven Locks Press, 1992, pages 3–39; *Washington Post*, June 14, 1992, page A-1; and Bernstein, Carl, and Woodward, Bob, *All the President's Men*, Simon & Schuster, 1972, pages 13–26.

325. Interview on September 5, 1991, with Lill.

326. Interview on December 1, 1992, with Walters.

327. Interview on December 30, 1991, with Mahan.

328. Interview on December 30, 1991, with Mahan.

329. Interview on December 29, 1991, with Shoffler.

330. Interview on December 30, 1991, with Silbert.

331. Interview on January 9, 1992, with Leary.

332. Associated Press, June 15, 1992.

333. Interview on May 21, 1992, with McCall.

334. Interview on October 24, 1991, with Wagner.

335. Kessler, Ronald, *Spy vs. Spy: Stalking Soviet Spies in America*, Scribner's, 1988, pages 159–67.

336. Interview on June 22, 1992, with Mack.

337. See the author's *Escape from the CIA: How the CIA Won and Lost the Most Important KGB Spy Ever to Defect to the U.S.,* Pocket Books, 1991.

338. While preparing *Escape from the CIA,* about Vitaly Yurchenko's defection and redefection, the author investigated Yurchenko's tip about former *Washington Post* Moscow bureau chief Dusko Doder in 1990 and concluded that it was unfounded. The allegation therefore did not appear in the book.

339. Interview on October 14, 1991, with Yablonsky.

340. Interview on October 30, 1991, with Teten.

341. Interview on September 5, 1991, with Lill.

342. Interview on February 21, 1992, with Webster.

343. Interview on February 7, 1992, with Hake; *Chicago Tribune,* June 28, 1987, page A-14, and *Los Angeles Times,* December 15, 1989, page A-1.

344. Interview on October 9, 1991, with Zigrossi, and *Washington Post,* February 14, 1991, page E-3.

345. Interview on December 8, 1991, with Bassett.

346. Interview on June 7, 1992, with Coulson.

347. Interview on January 7, 1992, with Johnson.

348. Interviews on August 20, 1990, and on March 13, 1991, with Francis D. Carter, Younis's lawyer.

349. *Talladega Prison Uprising,* FBI, Office of Public Affairs, 1991.

350. *New York Times,* August 31, 1991, and interview on June 7, 1992, with Baker.

351. Interview on November 22, 1991, with Revell, and *Legal Times,* September 9, 1991, page 6.

352. Interview on February 20, 1992, with Mullen, and Associated Press, May 16 and November 11, 1983.

353. Interview on January 3, 1992, with De Sarno.

354. Interview on February 20, 1992, with Mullen.

355. *Washington Post,* May 17, 1978, page A-6, and April 15, 1978, page A-4.

356. *Washington Post,* September 7, 1991, page A-6, and *New Orleans Times Picayune,* June 19, 1991, page A-1.

357. Interview on January 23, 1992, with Brekke.

358. Interview on December 19, 1991, with Minor.

359. Interview on November 25, 1991, with Clarke.

360. Interview on January 16, 1992, with Wade; Associated Press, October 1, 1990; and *New York Times,* August 29, 1992, page 33.

361. *Washington Post,* May 5, 1990, page A-1, and *New York Times,* January 19, 1990, page A-28.

362. Interview on February 7, 1992, with Gardner.

363. Interview on February 13, 1992, with Gardner.

364. *Washington Post,* December 29, 1983, page A-5.

365. *Washington Post,* September 14, 1992, page A-1.

366. Interview on October 31, 1991, with Bryant.

367. Interview on October 31, 1991, with Parsons.

368. Interview on December 30, 1991, with DeLoach.

369. *U.S. Intelligence Agencies and Activities: Domestic Intelligence Programs: Part 3,* Select Committee on Intelligence, House of Representatives, November 18, 1975, page 1067.

370. Theoharis, Athan, ed., *From the Secret Files of J. Edgar Hoover,* Ivan R. Dee, 1991, page 67.

371. Theoharis, Athan, ed., *From the Secret Files of J. Edgar Hoover,* Ivan R. Dee, 1991, page 82.

372. Elliff, John T., *The Reform of FBI Intelligence Operations,* Princeton University Press, 1979, page 31.

373. Theoharis, Athan, ed., *From the Secret Files of J. Edgar Hoover,* Ivan R. Dee, 1991, pages 255–56 and 264.

374. Sullivan, William C., with Bill Brown, *The Bureau: My Thirty Years in Hoover's FBI,* W.W. Norton & Co., 1979, pages 197– 98.

375. Interview on December 18, 1991, with Heim.

376. *New Yorker,* December 14, 1992, page 90.

377. Interview on January 23, 1992, with Christensen.

378. Interview on June 22, 1992, with Kallstrom.

379. Interview on July 14, 1992, with Saunders.

380. Interview on February 4, 1992, with Lawler.

381. Interview on February 4, 1992, with Lawler.

382. Interview on December 23, 1991, with Bayse.

383. *The FBI's Automatic Data Processing General Controls,* Justice Department, Office of the Inspector General, September 1990, pages i–ii and 42.

384. Interview on April 10, 1992, with Sessions.

385. Interview on April 21, 1992, with Duffin.

386. Interview on January 31, 1992, with Christensen.

387. Interview on October 22, 1991, with Stoops.

388. Interview on January 23, 1992, with Christensen.

389. Affidavit of July 12, 1989, of Cleary, and interview on February 26, 1992, with Cleary.

390. Interview on July 13, 1992, with Cleary; *Terrorism in the U.S.: 1990,* FBI, Counterterrorism Section, page 5; *Reader's Digest,* March 1991, pages 65–71; BBC documentary; and opening statement on May 1, 1990, of Stearns in *U.S. vs. Richard Clark Johnson,* et al.

391. Interview on July 17, 1992, with King.

392. Interview on March 5, 1992, with Otto, and Associated Press, November 22, 1978; June 20 and 22; and May 24, 1979.

393. Interview on March 6, 1992, with Jordan.

394. *Boston Herald,* July 4, 1991, page A-1, and *Cleveland Plain Dealer,* March 28, 1990.

395. *Providence Journal,* March 27, 1990, page A-1, and *Boston Herald,* March 27, 1990, page A-1, and July 4, 1991, page A-1.

396. *Boston Globe,* January 23, 1992, metro page 1, and June 18, 1992, page A-18.

397. Interview on July 13, 1992, with Hughes.

398. Interview on February 26, 1992, with Hughes.

399. Interview on October 22, 1991, with Greenleaf.

400. Interview on October 24, 1991, with Wagner.

401. *FBI Law Enforcement Bulletin,* October 1987, page 7; *New York Times,* December 14, 1991, page A-28; September 27, 1984, page B-3; November 9, 1984, page A-1; and May 22, 1987, page A-14; *USA Today,* October 2, 1985, page A-3.

402. Dimura, on July 16, 1992, and Prince, on July 16, 1992, said they would have no comment.

403. Interview on July 17, 1992, with Hughes. The next day, the *Boston Herald* published a story by Shelley Murphy on page 1 revealing the incident.

404. Interview on January 15, 1992, with Kennedy.

405. Sullivan, William C., with Bill Brown, *The Bureau: My Thirty Years in Hoover's FBI,* W.W. Norton & Co., 1979, pages 104–105. Eventually, Sullivan and Hoover came to blows. Sullivan openly criticized Hoover and suggested he should resign for the good of the bureau. Instead, Hoover forced Sullivan to retire.

406. Davis, James K., and Kelley, Clarence M., *Kelley: The Story of an FBI Director,* Andrews, McMeel & Parker, 1987, pages 36–37.

407. Interview on April 9, 1992, with Colwell.

408. *Grapevine,* November 1991, page 32, quoting Hoover's testi-

mony before the House Appropriations Committee on February 10, 1966.

409. Interview on February 21, 1992, with Webster.
410. *Washington Post*, November 11, 1990, page B-1.
411. Interview on August 12, 1992, with Revell.
412. Interview on December 20, 1991, with Bernardo Matias (Mat) Pérez.
413. *Washington Post*, March 23, 1988, page C-1.
414. Interview on December 2, 1991, with Jones.
415. Equal Employment Opportunity Commission, statement of findings, filed August 8, 1988, with Civil Action 87-3008, U.S. District Court, Washington, pages 18–21 and 24–25.
416. Interview on November 22, 1991, with Siller.
417. *Donald and Susan Rochon vs. Thomas Dillon*, et al, filed in Civil Action 87-3008, U.S. District Court, Washington, D.C., pages 24–35.
418. Interview on June 25, 1992, with Ahlerich.
419. Interview on November 22, 1991, with Revell.
420. Interview on October 23, 1991, with Davis.
421. *Washington Post*, August 24, 1991, page A-4.
422. Interview on January 8, 1992, with Carter.
423. Interview on October 22, 1991, with Greenleaf.
424. *Employee Survey Report of Findings*, FBI, Institutional Research and Development Office, Training Division, December 1990, pages 36–63. The findings were based on a random sample of 4,172 employees, of whom 74 percent responded to the survey.
425. Interview on January 7, 1992, with James R. Pérez.
426. Interview on April 13, 1992, with Penrith.
427. Interview on December 7, 1990, with Johnson.
428. Interview on February 4, 1992, with Langberg.
429. Interview on December 9, 1991, with Clark.
430. Interview on October 23, 1991, with Davis.
431. The *Washington Post* of August 1, 1992, page A-2, reported on brain differences between homosexual and heterosexual males.
432. Interviews on October 6, 1991, and July 22, 1992, with Buttino.
433. *Washington Post*, October 10, 1991, page A-20.
434. *Frank Buttino vs. FBI*, U.S. District Court, San Francisco, February 11, 1992, page 22.
435. Interview on January 28, 1992, with Sessions.

436. Interview on July 31, 1992, with Glover.

437. *Washington Journalism Review*, July/August, 1992, page 40, and *Wall Street Journal*, January 22, 1992, page B-8.

438. Interview on April 10, 1992, with Green.

439. *Los Angeles Times*, November 26, 1991, page A-1.

440. Interview on October 6, 1992, with Mills.

441. Interview on February 1, 1992, with Guido.

442. Interviews on March 27, 1992, with Mangiacotti and Bondonza, and *New York Times*, November 5, 1990.

443. Interview on January 17, 1992, with Gallagher, and on July 28, 1992, with Marquise.

444. *New York Times*, November 15, 1991, page A-1 and *Time*, November 25, 1991, page 62.

445. Interview on April 8, 1992, with Mills.

446. *FBI Public Affairs: An Early History*, FBI Office of Congressional and Public Affairs, Research Unit, August 1985, pages 1 and 6.

447. Theoharis, Athan, ed., *From the Secret Files of J. Edgar Hoover*, Ivan R. Dee, 1991, pages 348–55.

448. Interview on December 23, 1991, with Boynton.

449. Interview on February 21, 1992, with Webster.

450. Elliff, John T., *The Reform of FBI Intelligence Operations*, Princeton University Press, 1979, page 5.

451. Interview on January 16, 1992, with Collingwood.

452. Landino class on May 4, 1992.

453. Interview on November 22, 1991, with Revell.

454. Interview on May 4, 1992, with Nelson.

455. Interview on July 24, 1992, with Penrith.

456. *New York Times*, July 1, 1992, pages A-1 and B-4, and September 9, 1992, page A-1.

457. Interviews on June 2, 1992, with Buelow, and on February 4, 1992, with Gardner.

458. Interview on January 23, 1992, with Carter.

459. Interview on July 28, 1992, with Collingwood.

460. Interview on March 5, 1992, with Otto.

461. Interview on November 19, 1991, with Caro.

462. Interview on November 22, 1991, with Revell.

463. Interview on April 9, 1992, with Colwell.

464. Interview on December 6, 1990, with Bruemmer.

465. Interview on February 13, 1992, with Webster.

466. Interview on November 6, 1990, with McGregor.

467. *New York Times*, December 31, 1981, page A-8, and *Wash-*

ington Post, February 8, 1983, page C-3, and June 10, 1992, page A-7; and interviews on November 2, 1991, with Revell, and on February 13, 1992, with Webster. Because a Senate committee rather than the full Senate tried Hastings, U.S. District Court Judge Stanley Sporkin in Washington reversed Hastings's impeachment on September 17, 1992. Sporkin's decision is being appealed.

468. Interview on February 18, 1992, with Gavin.
469. Interview on March 3, 1992, with Lawn.
470. Award ceremony on February 6, 1992, and interview on March 2, 1992, with Roemer.
471. Interview on February 4, 1992, with Lawler.
472. Interview on November 25, 1991, with Clarke.
473. Interview on June 22, 1992, with Doyle.
474. Interview on January 28, 1992, with Sessions.
475. Interview on January 16, 1992, with Collingwood.
476. Executive conference meeting on June 4, 1992.
477. Interview on February 6, 1992, with Alice Sessions.
478. Interviews on May 20 and June 22, 1992, with Alice Sessions.
479. Interviews on February 6 and May 21, 1992, with Alice Sessions.
480. Interview on February 6, 1992, with Alice Sessions.
481. Interviews on January 30 and June 4, 1992, with Kennedy; on April 29 and June 10, 1992, with Davis; on January 23, 1992, with Toohey; on June 8, 1992, with McKay; on January 15, 1992, with Greenleaf; on March 20, 1992, with Clarke; on January 28, 1992, with Sessions; on February 14 and 21 and June 22, 1992, with Alice Sessions; and on June 23, 1992, with Don Munford. Also, Justice Department OPR report, January 12, 1993, page 50.
482. Interview on June 18, 1992, with Hale.
483. Interview on June 22, 1992, with Alice Sessions.
484. Interview on June 23, 1992, with Murphy.
485. Interview on May 21, 1992, with Boyd.
486. Interviews on June 23, 1992, with the clerk of the San Saba, Texas, court, and on July 29, 1992, with Judge Tom Dean.
487. Interview on June 1, 1992, with McKay.
488. Interviews on June 2, 1992, with Hogan, and on June 1, 1992, with McKay.
489. Interview on August 7, 1992, with Sessions, responding to a June 24, 1992, letter from the author asking for comment on issues relating to Alice Sessions and Sarah Munford.

490. Letters on June 5, 1992, from Hankinson, and on June 17, 1992, from Allen J. Vander-Staay.

491. *New York Times, Washington Post, Los Angeles Times,* October 4, 1992, page A-1.

492. *Washington Post,* October 16, 1992, page A-1, and January 12, 1993, page A-5.

493. *New York Times,* October 8, 1992, page A-1, and *Washington Post,* March 19, 1990, page A-1.

494. Interview on December 10, 1992, with Collingwood, and Ronald J. Ostrow's story on page A-6 of the December 11, 1992, *Los Angeles Times.* The GAO's June 1990 report, *Government Civilian Aircraft,* says the FBI in 1990 estimated the incremental cost of operating the Sabreliner at $750 per hour, while a trade publication estimated the cost at $1,362 per hour, including depreciation.

495. Justice OPR report of January 12, 1993, page 134, and Sessions's statement of January 19, 1993, page 2.

496. Barr memo of January 15, 1993, to Sessions, page 3.

497. Alice Sessions, on March 4, 1993, declined to comment.

498. *Washingtonian,* March 1993, page 97.

499. Interview on February 21, 1992, with Webster.

500. Department of Justice, *Report on the Relationship Between U.S. Recording Co. and the FBI and Certain Other Matters Pertaining to the FBI,* January 1978, page 18.

501. Interview on January 31, 1992, with Gates.

502. Interview on October 21, 1991, with Baker.

503. Interview on June 7, 1992, with Coulson.

504. *Law Enforcement Views on Future Policing Issues,* FBI Office of Planning, Evaluation and Audits, January 1990.

Selected
Bibliography

Davis, James K., and Clarence M. Kelley. *Kelley: The Story of an FBI Director*. Andrews, McMeel & Parker, 1987.

DeToledano, Ralph. *J. Edgar Hoover: The Man in His Time*. Arlington House, 1973.

Demaris, Ovid. *The Director: An Oral Biography of J. Edgar Hoover*. Harper's Magazine Press, 1975.

Elliff, John T. *The Reform of FBI Intelligence Operations*. Princeton University Press, 1979.

Felt, W. Mark. *The FBI Pyramid: From the Inside*. G.P. Putnam's Sons, 1979.

Jeffers, H. Paul. *Who Killed Precious?* Pharos Books, 1991.

Newton, Michael. *Hunting Humans: An Encyclopedia of Modern Serial Killers*. Loompanics Unlimited, 1990.

Garrow, David J. *The FBI and Martin Luther King Jr.: From "Solo" to Memphis*. Norton, 1981.

Gentry, Curt. *J. Edgar Hoover: The Man and the Secrets*. W.W. Norton & Co., 1991.

Kessler, Ronald. *Inside the CIA: Revealing the Secrets of the World's Most Powerful Spy Agency*. Pocket Books, 1992.

————. *Escape from the CIA: How the CIA Won and Lost the Most Important KGB Spy Ever to Defect to the U.S.* Pocket Books, 1991.

————. *The Spy in the Russian Club: How Glenn Souther Stole America's Nuclear War Plans and Escaped to Moscow.* Scribner's, 1990; Pocket Books edition, 1992.

————. *Moscow Station: How the KGB Penetrated the American Embassy.* Scribner's, 1989; Pocket Books edition, 1990.

————. *Spy vs. Spy: Stalking Soviet Spies in America.* Scribner's, 1988; Pocket Books edition, 1989.

Pistone, Joseph D. *Donnie Brasco: My Undercover Life in the Mafia.* Signet, 1987.

Powers, Richard Gid. *Secrecy and Power: The Life of J. Edgar Hoover.* The Free Press, 1987.

Ressler, Robert K., with Tom Shactman. *Whoever Fights Monsters.* St. Martin's Press, 1991, pages 47–48.

Ressler, Robert K., Ann W. Burgess, and John E. Douglas. *Sexual Homicide: Patterns and Motives.* Lexington Books, 1988.

Robins, Natalie. *Alien Ink: The FBI's War on Freedom of Expression.* Morrow, 1992.

Sullivan, William C., with Bill Brown. *The Bureau: My Thirty Years in Hoover's FBI.* W.W. Norton & Co., 1979.

Theoharis, Athan, ed. *From the Secret Files of J. Edgar Hoover.* Ivan R. Dee, 1991.

Turner, William W. *Hoover's FBI: The Men and the Myth.* Sherbourne Press, 1970.

Welch, Neil J., and David W. Marston. *Inside Hoover's FBI: The Top Field Chief Reports.* Doubleday & Co., 1984.

Ungar, Sanford J. *FBI: An Uncensored Look Behind the Walls.* Atlantic–Little, Brown Books, 1975.

U.S. Department of Justice, FBI. *Briefing Book of General Information on the FBI.* 1990–1991.

U.S. Senate, Select Committee to Study Governmental Operations with Respect to Intelligence Activities (the Church Committee), volume 6. *Intelligence Activities: FBI.* U.S. Government Printing Office, 1975.

Significant Dates

July 26, 1908   Attorney General Charles J. Bonaparte ordered the existing special agent force within the Justice Department to report to Chief Examiner Stanley W. Finch. This order is considered the formal beginning of the agency that in 1935 became the FBI.

March 16, 1909   Attorney General George Wickersham, Bonaparte's successor, named the force the Bureau of Investigation.

August 1, 1919   The General Intelligence Division was created within the bureau to collect evidence and data on revolutionary and radical movements. It was placed under the direct administrative supervision of J. Edgar Hoover, who had joined the Justice Department on June 26, 1917. Later that year he was placed in charge of a unit of the Enemy Alien Registration Section.

August 22, 1921   William J. Burns, who headed a private detective agency, became director of the bureau, and Hoover was named assistant director.

May 10, 1924   Attorney General Harlan F. Stone designated J. Edgar Hoover acting director of the bureau and appointed him director on December 10, 1924; however, Hoover's tenure as director is considered to have started on May 10, 1924.

July 1, 1924   The bureau set up its identification division after Congress authorized "the exchange of identification records with officers of the cities, counties, and states."

January, 1928   The bureau instituted a theoretical and practical training course for new agents.

June 11, 1930   Congress authorized the bureau to collect and compile uniform crime statistics for the entire United States.

October 25, 1932   The *Lucky Strike Hour* became the first radio program to dramatize FBI cases on a national network. Later radio programs concerning FBI cases included *G-Men, Gangbusters,* and *This Is Your FBI.*

May 18, 1934   Congress gave the bureau authority to investigate robberies of national banks and member banks of the Federal Reserve System.

July 1, 1935   The date traditionally designated for the official use of the term Federal Bureau of Investigation is the beginning of fiscal 1936. The change was approved by the president on March 22, 1935.

July 29, 1935   The FBI established the forerunner of the FBI National Academy.

August 25, 1936   President Franklin D. Roosevelt, through Secretary of State Cordell Hull, gave the FBI authority to conduct investigations of subversive activities.

March 14, 1950   The FBI initiated its Ten Most Wanted Fugitives program.

September 19, 1965 *The FBI,* the first such television series on a national network, premiered on ABC. Actor Efrem Zimbalist, Jr., played the central character, FBI Inspector Lewis Erskine. The show ran until 1974.

January, 1967   The National Crime Information Center became operational.

May 2, 1972   J. Edgar Hoover died.

May 3, 1972   President Nixon appointed L. Patrick Gray III to be acting director.

May 8, 1972   The new FBI Academy was opened on the U.S. Marine Corps Base at Quantico, Virginia.

July 17, 1972   The first female agents in recent years were appointed. A handful served early in bureau history.

April 27, 1973   William D. Ruckelshaus was appointed acting director of the FBI by President Nixon following the resignation of L. Patrick Gray.

July 9, 1973   Clarence M. Kelley was sworn in as director of the FBI. Nominated on June 7 by President Nixon, he was confirmed by the Senate on June 27, 1973.

July 9, 1973   The first FBI Special Weapons and Tactics (SWAT) training was held.

September 30, 1975   The J. Edgar Hoover FBI Building was formally dedicated during ceremonies attended by President Gerald R. Ford and other guests. FBI headquarters units began moving into the new building in October 1974.

March 10, 1976   Attorney General Edward H. Levi issued guidelines for FBI intelligence activities. On April 5, 1976, Levi issued guidelines for FBI domestic security activities. These were superseded on March 21, 1983, by guidelines issued by Attorney General William French Smith.

February 23, 1978   William H. Webster took the oath of office as FBI director. Webster, judge of the Eighth Circuit, U.S. Court of Appeals, was appointed by President Carter on January 19, and confirmed by the Senate on February 9, 1978. He served until May 26, 1987, when he became director of Central Intelligence.

January 1983   The first members of the hostage rescue team began their training program. The team became fully operational in August 1983.

November 2, 1987   Former federal judge William Steele Sessions was sworn in as director of the FBI. On September 25, 1987, he was confirmed as FBI director by the Senate 90 to 0. He was nominated on July 24, 1987, by President Reagan.

July 19, 1993   President Clinton removed William Sessions as FBI director after Attorney General Janet Reno concluded he had exhibited "serious deficiencies in judgment." Clinton named Deputy Director Floyd Clarke acting director.

July 20, 1993   President Clinton nominated U.S. District Court Judge Louis J. Freeh, a former FBI agent and federal prosecutor, as FBI director.

Source: FBI Office of Public and Congressional Affairs

Glossary

ADIC—See *assistant director*; pronounced ay-dick.

Airtel—An FBI communication requiring immediate attention but of lower priority than a teletype.

Assistant director—An FBI official who oversees one of the ten headquarters divisions or, in the case of New York, the New York field office.

ASAC—See *assistant special agent in charge*; pronounced ay-sack.

Asset—In counterintelligence, any human or technical resource available for operational or informational purposes.

Assistant special agent in charge (ASAC)—Assistant special agent in charge of a field office.

Balloon—To take off for the afternoon, signing out at the end of office hours but leaving early.

Beach Time—Suspension.

Betty Bureau—A female support employee who has worked for the FBI all her life and is "married to the bureau."

Brick agent—An agent who works cases in a field office. Also known as street agent.

Brush contact—In counterintelligence, a discreet, prearranged momentary contact between intelligence personnel when information or documents are passed.

Bucar—Bureau car. Also called Buc; pronounced bu-see.

Bubird—Bureau airplane.

Bureau—FBI or, depending on context, headquarters.

Bureau name—The name the FBI chooses to use for an agent. If there are two Patrick Richard Watsons in the bureau, the FBI will tell one agent to use "Patrick R. Watson" and the other "P. Richard Watson."

Busteed—Bureau car; pronounced bu-steed.

Case agent—The agent in charge of a case.

Clagent—A derisive term for an agent who began as a clerk or support employee.

Cover—A guise used by an individual, organization, or installation to prevent discovery of intelligence activities.

Counterintelligence—Actions undertaken to counter the intelligence, espionage, and sabotage operations of foreign governments.

Creds—Short for credentials.

Dead drop—In counterintelligence, a location where communications, documents, or equipment can be left by an individual and picked up by a second individual without meeting.

Defection—In counterintelligence, abandonment of loyalty, allegiance, duty, or principle to one's country.

Division—Normally referring to one of the ten headquarters divisions, *division* also refers to the territory covered by a field office.

Double agent—In counterintelligence, an agent who is cooperating with a foreign intelligence service on behalf of and under the control of an intelligence service and/or security service of another country.

Dry cleaning—Any technique used to detect surveillance; a usual precaution that intelligence personnel take when actively engaged in an operation.

Espionage—Intelligence activity aimed at acquiring classified information through clandestine means.

False flag recruitment—Occurs when an individual is recruited believing that he is cooperating with an intelligence service of a particular country. In fact, he has been deceived and is cooperating with an intelligence service of yet another country.

First Office Agent—An agent who is assigned to his first office after finishing new-agent training.

Four Bagger—Internal discipline consisting of censure, transfer, suspension, and probation.

HBO—High bureau official.

Headquarters city—A field office as opposed to a resident agency or satellite of that office.

Illegal—In counterintelligence, an officer or employee of an intelligence service dispatched abroad with no overt connection to the intelligence service that sent him or to the government operating the intelligence service.

Intelligence officer—In counterintelligence, a professionally trained member of an intelligence service.

KMA—Short for "kiss my ass," refers to agents who are eligible for retirement and do not have to put up with guff from the bureau.

Legal attaché (legat)—An overseas FBI agent or office that performs liaison with foreign law enforcement and intelligence agencies.

Legend—In counterintelligence, a coherent and plausible cover story, including an individual's background, living arrangements, employment, daily activities, and family given by a foreign intelligence service to (an) agent. Often the legend will be supported by fraudulent documents. See *cover*.

Ninjas—SWAT team members in full garb.

Office of origin—The office that originated an investigation and has the case agent who is in charge of it.

Office of preference—An office requested by an agent who signs up on a waiting list until a transfer is granted.

Offsite—A covert FBI site away from a field office where agents engage in activities such as physical surveillance or highly sensitive undercover investigations.

Picket surveillance—Placement of surveillance personnel at locations that encircle an area being watched. Also known as perimeter surveillance.

Recruitment—In counterintelligence, the process of enlisting an individual to work for an intelligence or counterintelligence service.

Recruitment in place (RIP)—In counterintelligence, a foreign official who overtly continues to work for his government and covertly provides the U.S. with information of intelligence value.

RA—See *resident agency*.

Rent-a-goons—Agents from other field offices assigned to help out temporarily on inspections.

Resident agency (RA)—A smaller satellite office of a field office consisting of one to fifteen or twenty agents. Agents assigned to an RA are called resident agents.

Roscoe—A gun.

SA—See *special agent*.

Safehouse—In counterintelligence, a location controlled by an intelligence or counterintelligence service that provides a secure meeting place for individuals engaged in intelligence operations.

Seat of government—Under Hoover, a term used by the bureau to refer to headquarters.

Section—A headquarters component that is larger than a unit and smaller than a division.

Set up—To conduct surveillance on a suspect or target.

Soft credentials—Credentials that look similar to agents' credentials but are issued to support employees who deal with the public.

Soundman—A technical agent who installs electronic bugging devices, arranges court-authorized wiretaps, and uses other covert means to conduct technical surveillance or to intercept conversations.

Special agent (SA)—An FBI agent.

Split tails—Female agents, also known as "skirts" and, in California, "breast-feds."

Street agent—See *brick agent*.

Subject—The target of a criminal or background investigation.

Special agent in charge (SAC)—The agent in charge of a field office.

Squad—A unit within a field office composed of four to more than twenty agents assigned to particular types of cases or targets.

SAC—See *special agent in charge;* pronounced ess-ay-see.

Three B's—The offenses most likely to get agents in trouble—booze, broads, and Bucars.

Too-Hard Box—A mythical box between the In box and Out box for matters that are too difficult to handle.

UACB—Unless advised to the contrary by the bureau.

Unit—The smallest headquarters component, equivalent to a squad in the field.

Unsub—An unknown subject of an investigation.

Walk-in—In counterintelligence, an individual who voluntarily offers his services or information to a foreign government.

Terms are from the FBI's *List of Terminology Used in Foreign Counterintelligence and Counterespionage Investigations,* the FBI's *Manual of Administrative Operations and Procedures,* and interviews with agents.

Index

Abbott, James M., 12, 13
Abdel Rahman, Sheik Omar, 25
Abel, Rudolf, 2, 64, 368
Abouhalima, Mahmud, 25
ABSCAM, 7, 21, 280–81, 286, 379
Abu Nidal terrorist organization,
    70–71
Abuses (FBI), 2–3, 65, 71, 149–50,
    364, 365, 367–69, 380
    under Hoover, 126, 368–69, 375
    by Sessions, 404–11, 412–18,
    429, 430
Academy Group Inc., 234
Administrative division, 326–51
Administrative services division,
    326–51
Aerospace industry, 210, 213
Affirmative action, 134, 331, 343,
    345
Agent misconduct, 100–10, 112–
    23, 128, 129–31, 134–36, 137,
    197, 300–01
    see also Marginal employees
Agents, 1, 11, 85
    applicant tests, 342

background, 166, 168, 170
demoralization, 429–30
and directors, 374–75, 376, 382,
    383–84, 406, 411, 417
discretion, 162
dropping out, 175–76
power of, 5–6
prosecution of, 126–28
racial discord, 345–46
recruiting, 169, 183, 350–51
work of, 152–53
    see also Marginal employees
Ahlerich, Milt, 335–36, 365
Ahrens, Robin, 61, 130, 373
Alcohol, Tobacco and Firearms Bu-
    reau (ATF), 24, 240, 241, 242,
    418–21, 426, 427–28
Americans for a Competent Federal
    Judicial System, 237
America's Most Wanted (TV pro-
    gram), 35, 93, 256, 257, 372
Anderson, William R., 298, 299
Andress, Beverly, 273, 324
Appearance, emphasis on, 1, 11,
    18, 47, 141–42, 294

Artificial intelligence systems, 302
ASAC, 325
Assassinations, assassins, 40, 43,
    222–23, 236–37
Atlanta field office, 152, 193, 236–
    51
Attorneys general, 68, 69, 163, 238,
    401–02
Ault, Richard L., Jr., 223, 232–33
Automation, 216–17, 301–02,
    305–08
Aviation unit, 159, 272, 274, 275,
    276, 277

Background investigations, 37, 271,
    285–89, 291
BADGE (black agents organization),
    343, 345
Baker, William, 23, 32–34, 35, 45,
    53, 92, 94, 115–16, 129, 168,
    207, 237, 238, 285, 321, 361,
    364–65, 366, 367, 387–89,
    394, 400
  and prejudice issue, 341
  retired, 250
  SAC, Los Angeles, 211
  Alice Sessions and, 389, 390,
    392–93, 404
Baltimore field office, 46–63
Bandidos (gang), 140–48, 261
Bank fraud, 161, 324
Bank of Credit and Commerce In-
    ternational (BCCI), 92, 358
Bank robbery(ies), 53–56, 73, 93,
    94, 259
  Los Angeles, 189–96
Barker, Bernard L., 266, 267
Barnes, Scott, 162
Barnhart, Bryant L., 165–66, 185
Barr, William P., 53, 163, 208, 209,
    285, 312, 325, 382, 393–94,
    402, 404, 407, 408, 410, 414,
    415, 416, 417, 418, 429
Barrett, Kathy, 60–61, 62
Barry, Marion, 282, 293
Basset al-Megrahii, Abdel, 361

Bayse, William A., 116, 140, 301–
    02, 305, 306, 307, 308
Beccaccio, Livio A., 178
Behavioral science services unit,
    223, 224, 231–32, 248, 309,
    339
Bell, Griffin B., 66, 246
Berkowitz, David, 223, 225
Bernstein, Carl, 269–70
Biaggi, Mario, 133
Binney, David G., 19, 20, 102, 111,
    113, 126, 131, 272, 280
Birmingham, Ala., field office, 11,
    45, 237
Bittaker, Lawrence S., 214–15,
    230–31, 235
Black agents, 137–38, 168, 169,
    170, 187, 329–30, 333–37,
    339, 341, 345, 378
  class-action suit, 343
  promoted, 240, 331
  proportion of, 350
Black bag jobs, 65, 344, 378
Blackmail files, 296–300, 301, 310,
    375
Blacks, 65, 342
Blakeney, Leon H., 249–50
Bland, Jerry, 44
Bloch, Felix S., 72–73, 357–58
Bombs, bombings, 16, 237–45, 323,
    344
Bonner, Lane, 88, 365
Bonney, Lawrence A., 169
Boss of Bosses (O'Brien and
    Kurins), 27
Boston office, 311–25
Boyce, Christopher J., 210
Branch Davidians, 418–29
Braver, Rita, 18, 124
Brawley, Tawana, 262–63
Break-ins, illegal, 65, 344, 375
Brekke, Tron W., 209, 211
Brennan, Tom, 234
Brown, Robert B., 132
Bruemmer, Russell J., 150–51,
    377–78

Brussel, James A., 221
Bryant, Robert M., 224–25, 292–93
Budget, 16, 33, 75, 234–35, 264
Bugging devices, 116, 301, 303–05, 344, 426
Bundy, Ted, 173, 230
Bunton, Lucius D., 332, 341
Burnett, James T., 131
Bush, George, 35, 163, 294, 325, 377, 393–94, 408, 414
Bush administration, 343, 410
Buttino, Frank, 347–49
Byrd, Robert C., 217

Campbell, John H., 224
Canedo, Blás Fernando, 85
Career board, 387, 388
Carjacking, 291–92
Caro, Dana E., 163, 376
Carter, Jimmy, 291, 377, 390
Carter, Jimmy C., 326–27, 338–41, 350–51
Casey, William, 277
Castonguay, Roger T., 29
CAT-COM, 78–83
Cavanagh, Thomas P., 210
Central Intelligence Agency (CIA), 6, 32, 35, 65, 66, 68, 71, 72, 92, 148, 151, 260, 264, 277, 278, 353, 355, 388, 410
  electronic snooping, 304–05
  information storage, 301, 307, 309
  moles in, 22
  and Watergate, 266, 267, 268
Chagra, Jamiel (Jimmy), 40–43, 261
Chaplin, Charlie, 3
Chicago field office, 281
Chin, Lawrence Wu-Tai, 71, 271
Christensen, G. Norman, 308, 309, 310
Church, Frank, 4
Church Committee, 66, 300, 367, 378
CISPES, 124, 140, 148–51, 380

Civil rights, 11, 37, 340–41, 386
  see also Rights violations
Civil Rights Act of 1964, 37, 201, 208
Civil rights and special inquiry section, 33
Civil rights cases, 209, 245
Civil rights workers, Philadelphia, Miss., 2, 40, 338
Clancy, Tom, 157
Clarke, Floyd I., 18, 31, 41, 43, 53, 97–98, 134, 137, 260, 285, 295
  deputy director, 288–89, 290, 304, 341, 344–45, 386, 387, 393, 394, 404, 415, 424
  on polygraphing, 260
  on Sessions, 385
Cleary, Brendan O., 311, 313–18
Clinton, Bill, 349, 415, 416, 418, 421, 424, 426, 427, 429, 430
Coast Guard, 80, 81, 82–83
Cocaine, 77, 78–83, 92, 95–96, 208, 292, 354, 357
COINTELPRO, 15, 65, 150, 299, 367, 368, 375
Cold war, end of, 22, 73, 75, 212–13, 353
Collingwood, John E., 131, 307, 365, 366, 368, 371, 373, 386–87, 389, 416, 430
Collins, Nancy J., 157
Collins, Robert F., 287–88
Colombian drug trade, 77, 78, 353, 354
Colwell, Lee, 18, 134, 329, 376
"Commission" case, 7
Committee for the Re-Election of the President, 266, 271
Computer Analysis and Response Team (CART), 258
Computer crimes, 290, 433
Computer sketches, 255–57
Computers, 188, 216–17, 242, 254, 258, 259
  in information storage, 301–02
  in investigations, 289–90

Computers (*cont.*)
lack of, 305–08
Congress, 2, 11, 21, 36, 365, 377
and background investigations, 286, 287
and FBI budget, 16, 75
FBI files on, 296–98, 300, 310
investigations of, 280–81
oversight responsibility, 364
Congressional and public affairs division, 364–65
Conner, Terry Lee, 193–94
Corruption, 2, 3, 17, 93–94, 100–01, 375
police, 312, 319–20, 323
political, 375, 379
public, 21, 38–39, 132–33
Costellano, Paul, 21, 27
Coulson, Danny O., 53, 93, 207, 283, 424
Counterintelligence, 16, 64–65, 74, 75, 212–13, 309, 310, 369, 375
see also Intelligence division
Counterintelligence cases, 18, 21–23, 32, 271, 272, 279, 304
Counterterrorism, 34, 37, 74, 155, 361
Counterterrorism section, 26, 33, 35–36, 70, 263
COURTSHIP, 68
Credentials, 99, 108, 384, 398–99
showing, 5, 6, 27, 28, 114, 128, 154, 178
soft, 398–99
Credibility (FBI), 365–67, 373, 377
Crime records division, 362–63, 369
Crime scene(s), 217–18, 220, 221, 225, 226, 254
Pan Am 103, 358–59
Crime-scene evidence, 252, 264
Crime-scene patterns, 218, 219
Criminal cases, 74, 94–95, 155, 291
Criminal division, 17, 18, 29–45, 159
sections of, 33
Criminal investigations

Washington office, 279–80
Criminal investigative analyses, 227
Criminal investigative division, 224, 250–51, 310
Criminal justice information services division, 216, 309
Crisp, John, 242

Dahmer, Jeffrey L., 226–27
Dallas office, 140–64
Daniels, Anthony E., 169
Davis, Joseph R., 137–38, 179, 336, 346–47, 394, 416
Davis, Wayne G., 331, 336
Deadman, Harold A., Jr., 247–48
DeBruler, Wilbur K., 38–39
Decision making, 386–87, 431
Defense Department, 271, 289, 290, 348, 349, 354–55
Defensive tactics, 183–84
DeLoach, Cartha D., 65, 296, 297, 299
Democratic National Committee, 163, 266, 268, 368
Denman, Warren, 54
Dennedy, Margot D., 20–21
Depue, Roger L., 63, 176, 179–80, 219
and prejudice, 326–27, 332, 337–38, 339–41, 351
and profiling, 222–23, 225, 234
De Sarno, James V., Jr., 2, 287, 293
Desing, Philip, 171–72
Detroit office, 17–18
Dillinger, John H., 1, 10, 161, 185, 186, 259
DiMauro, Catherine A., 227–28, 229
Dimura, Paul M., 324–25
Director (FBI), 374–430
power of, 434
Discipline, 110, 113, 115–16, 118, 126–27, 130, 151
double standard for, 406, 415–16
fairness of, 131–39
FBI Academy, 167–68

of Hoover, 328–29
new agents, 182–83
statistics on, 113
Discrimination, 104, 137–38
lawsuits claiming, 109–10, 326,
332–37, 341, 343, 346, 349,
389
DNA analysis, 188, 230, 254–55,
301, 385
Doder, Dusko, 278–79
Doherty, Vincent P., 185
Donaldson, Sam, 408, 414–15
Donovan, Raymond J., 285–86
Doran, William Y., 21, 26
Dos Passos, John, 3
Dougherty, Joseph W., 193–94
Douglas, John E., 214–15, 217,
222–23, 224, 225–26, 227,
228–30, 234, 248, 424
Dove, Jerry, 85, 86–88, 91, 180
Doyle, Sir Arthur Conan, 218
Drug cartels, 79–80, 84, 96, 98
Drug Demand Reduction Program,
293
Drug Enforcement Administration
(DEA), 23, 78, 96–97, 98, 148,
291, 349, 354, 355
agents, 166, 167–68
Drug trafficking, 353, 354–55, 379,
432
Drug section, 33
Drugs, drug cases, 2, 23, 37, 77–83,
93, 95–98, 196, 206, 293
and agent corruption, 100–01
Duffin, Andrew J., 154, 308
Dufour, Dennis L., 141–48

Echeverra, Carlos Mario, 84, 85
Edwards, Don, 149, 307, 416
Electronic surveillance, 19, 68, 155
see also Bugging devices
Eliot, T. S., 3
Elliot, Jane, 177–78
Ellis, Shirley, 227, 229
Embarrassment to bureau, 2, 39,
53–54, 96, 221, 312, 363, 433
agent espionage, 210–13

Boston office, 324–25
Emergency Vehicle Operation
Course, 155, 178
Engineering Research Facility, 302
Engineering section, 302, 303–05
Equal employment opportunity af-
fairs office, 328, 341–42
Equal Employment Opportunity
Commission, 109–10, 183,
333, 334, 335, 337
Equal Employment Opportunity
laws, 104
Espionage, 37, 64, 66, 67, 71, 74,
75, 223, 375, 379, 432, 434
agents in, 115, 189, 210–13
cases, 73, 94, 231
economic, 354
prevention of, 74
prosecuting, 67
Ethics training, 173–74
Evans, Courtney, 299
Evans, Van E., 48, 49, 51, 52
Evidence, 73, 252, 253, 264
Excepted service, 115–16
Executive conference, 23, 292

Faulkner, David E., 73, 138–39
Faulkner, William, 3
FBI, The (TV series), 170, 203, 330,
363
FBI: The Untold Stories (TV series),
4, 372–73
FBI Academy, 58, 100, 101, 165–
68, 181–82, 196, 215, 222, 227,
234, 253, 310, 337, 338
FBI Agents Association, 131, 343–
44, 345
FBI National Academy, 100, 166
teaching profiling at, 218–19,
220, 221
FBI Police, 36, 328
FBI Story, The (Whitehead), 363,
373
Federal Bureau of Investigation
changes in, 4, 37–39
as family, 104, 178–79, 348
headquarters building, 29–32

Federal Bureau of Investigation
  (*cont.*)
  history of, 367–69
  new, 29, 127, 148, 239, 347, 369,
    370, 380
  old, 39–40, 65–66, 238, 369, 370
  as paramilitary organization, 374,
    378
  reforms, 376, 431
  successes/failures, 2, 43–45, 56–
    57, 65, 85–86, 362–63, 365
Federal crimes, 37
Federal Deposit Insurance Corporation (FDIC), 195
Felt, W. Mark, 344
Female agents, 20, 57, 59–63, 110,
    127–28, 130, 134, 187, 294,
    378, 385
  hiring, 58–59, 329, 376
  physical training requirements,
    183
  prejudice against, 326–27
  proportion of, 350
  recruitment of, 183, 330, 331
  training, 168
  undercover work, 101–05
Ferrell, Paul W., 48–52
Fhimah, Lamen Khalifa, 361
Field Office Information Management System (FOIMS), 307–08
Field offices, 8, 9, 11, 56, 385
  inspection division examination
    of, 122–23
  largest, 236
  and profilers, 227
  security devices, 152
  support employees, 157
  and terrorism, 35–36
  Webster visiting, 382
Files, 65, 296–310
Fingerprint identification division,
  216–17
Firearms, 86, 89–90, 152, 259
Firearms tests/training, 58, 59, 178,
  180–81
Firearms training unit, 86, 89, 282,
  283

First Amendment, 71
Flanagan, Dan, 148, 150
Florez, Carl P., 81–82, 83
Floyd, "Pretty Boy," 1, 161, 259
Flynn, Eugene J., 85
Flynn, Kevin D., 27–28
Foran, Patrick J., 165, 185, 186–87
Ford, Catherine D., 47–52
Ford, Richard, 48, 49, 52
Ford, Rosalie, 47–48, 52
Foreign counterintelligence (FCI),
  37, 64, 75, 94–95, 155
Foreign intelligence program, 67–
  68
Foreign Intelligence Surveillance
  Act of, 1978 (FISA), 68–69, 70
Foreign Intelligence Surveillance
  Court, 273, 313, 314, 315
Foreign offices. *See* Legal attachés
  (legats)
Forensic examination, 254–55,
  359–60
Forensic lab. *See* Laboratory
  division
Forensic Science Research and
  Training Center, 253
Fox, James M., 7, 14, 21, 22–26,
  129, 389
Fraud cases, 161
Free expression, 65–66, 375
Freedom of Information Act, 310,
  368
Friedrick, Robert S., 121–22

Gacha, José Rodriguez, 84
Gallagher, Neil J., 35–37, 70, 200,
  317–18, 358–59, 360, 361
Gallagher, Richard J., 166, 204
Gangs, 291, 292, 354
  Los Angeles, 180, 206, 207–8,
    209
Garcia, Amando, 197–98, 199
Garcia, Richard T., 78–83
Gardner, Karen E., 103–04, 196–
  206
Gardner, Theodore M., 196–97,
  291, 295, 405

Gavin, William A., 31, 77, 85, 92, 95, 98–100, 150, 345–46, 379–80, 392, 399

Geer, James H., 67, 71, 73, 74

General Services Administration (GSA), 56, 274

Gerson, Stuart M., 418, 423–24, 429

Giel, Kenneth A., 8, 10–13

Giglia, Michael, 91, 305–06

Gikman, Reino, 72

Gilbert, Wayne R., 74–75, 76, 399–400, 414

Gillham, Bobby R., 54, 161

Ginsburg, Douglas H., 288–89

Gleason, Robert L., 255, 259

Glover, John J., 249, 250, 331, 349–50

Gonzalez, Anthony M., 92

Gonzalez, Manuel J., 95–96, 97, 306, 346

Gotti, John, 21, 301, 304

Government, 271, 289–90

Gow, W. Douglas, 75, 295, 386, 387, 388–89, 404, 414

Gray, L. Patrick, III, 57, 268–69, 330, 364

Gray, William H., III, 18

Greenleaf, James, 90, 91, 113, 116, 119, 133, 137, 164, 234–35, 368, 385, 404, 405
   associate deputy director, 386, 387, 415
   assistant director, training division, 167–68
   on files, 308, 309
   head, Boston office, 323
   head, laboratory division, 251
   head, training division, 340–41

GREYLORD, 281

Grogan, Benjamin P., 85, 86–88, 91, 180

Grogan, Michael D., 94–95

GRU, 67–68, 71, 94, 272, 276–77, 303–04

Guibilo, Michael, 101–04

Guido, John E., 355, 356, 357

Gunther, John, 3

Hagmaier, William E., III, 230

Hake, Terrence, 281–82

Hanafi Muslims, 282

Hanlon, John F., 88–89

Hansen, Christine A., 183

Harper, James Durward, 210

Harrelson, Charles V., 42, 43, 381

Harris, Rick, 144

Hartwig, Clayton M., 232–33

Hauptmann, Bruno Richard, 254

Hazelwood, Robert R., 226, 232–33, 234, 248

Headquarters, 34, 268

Headquarters city(ies), 11

Headquarters divisions, 8, 122–23

Health-care fraud, 75, 209

Hearst, Patricia, 204–05, 232

Heim, Lawrence J., 300, 370

Held, Richard W., 307, 349

Hemingway, Ernest, 3

Hicks, John W., 31, 240, 247, 254–55, 264, 360, 389, 399

Higgins, Stephen E., 427–28

Hill, Anita, 271, 288

Hinshaw, William L., 241, 244, 251

Hispanic agents, 137, 168, 187, 332, 341, 350, 389

Hodgson, Dudley F. B., 73

Hogan, James J., 126, 400

Homicides, 234

Homosexuals, 347–49

Hoover, J. Edgar, 8, 10, 23, 29, 30–31, 39–40, 47, 96, 100, 122, 127, 151, 166, 181, 206, 297, 337–38, 353, 370, 429
   abuses under, 126, 368–69, 375
   alleged homosexuality, 369–70
   blackmail files, 296, 297, 299–300
   criticism of, 363, 364, 369–70
   cult of personality, 362, 363, 364, 368, 378, 410–11
   death of, 37–38, 93, 140, 268, 279

Hoover, J. Edgar (*cont.*)
  discipline under, 138–39, 179
  FBI under, 1–4, 9, 11, 14–15, 54,
    66, 71, 74, 110, 111–12, 113,
    114, 118, 141, 149, 159, 163,
    218–19, 221, 238, 271, 294,
    296, 344, 368, 371–72, 375–76
  filing system, 301
  image building, 362–63, 374, 377
  image of, 369, 370–71
  and laboratory division, 253–54
  and National Academy, 166, 167
  Official and Confidential files,
    297
  personnel policy, 327, 328–30,
    332
Hostage rescue team (HRT), 159,
  253, 272, 282–85, 290, 393,
  421–22, 424
  and attack on Branch Davidians,
    421–22
Hostages, 231–32, 236, 249–50
House, Fred, 179–80
Howard, Edward Lee, 71–72, 75,
  277
Hughes, Thomas A., 321, 322–23,
  325, 347
Hume, John P., 117, 118, 119
Hunt, E. Howard, 267, 268
Hunter, Robert W., 273, 324

Identification division, 309
Illegal practices, 65, 66
  see also Abuses (FBI)
ILLWIND, 289–90
Image (FBI), 4, 11, 47, 176, 410–11
  of director, 375, 376–77
  Hoover and, 330, 362–63, 374,
    377
  selling, 362–73
Informants, 20–21, 78, 262, 263,
  357
Information division, 296–310
Information management division,
  310
Information storage and retrieval,
  301–02, 309

Innovative techniques, 39–40
Inspection division, 106–07, 111–
  39, 149, 150, 260, 407, 432
Inspectors, inspections, 122–23,
  124–26, 131, 237–38
Intelligence division, 32, 35, 64–
  76, 309, 310, 353, 388
"Interesting case memoranda,"
  362–63
International crime, 353–56
Interpol, 6, 353, 355, 361, 394
Interviews, interviewing, 183, 231
Investigations, 151, 159, 378–79
  limits on, 300–01
  OPR, 126–31
Investigations, internal, 100, 102–
  03, 104, 138, 151, 260
  Branch Davidian raid, 429
  lying during, 121–22
Investigative support unit, 33, 227
Iran-Contra affair, 291, 410
Iraq, 35, 36, 37, 384–85, 408
Isa family, 69–71

J. Edgar Hoover Building, 302, 389,
  396–97
Jamar, Jeffrey, 421, 422–23, 424,
  427
Jameson, Joe D., 40
Jeter, Mel, 179
Johnson, Emanuel, Jr., 343
Johnson, Richard C., 311–18
Jones, Ray E., 182–83, 333
Jones, Robert L., 207–08
Jones, Thomas F., 336, 350, 365–
  66, 371, 373, 405
Jordan, Charles, 93–94
Jordan, Robert J., 319–20
Juan Garcia Abrego gang, 161
Junior G-Man Program, 293–94
Jurisdiction, 96–97, 246, 353, 354,
  355–56
Justice Department, 1, 31, 37, 66,
  70, 97, 117, 160, 206, 258, 307,
  332, 333, 356, 360, 384, 401–
  02
  and civil rights program, 208–09

and counterintelligence, 67, 68
and FBI, 238, 239, 346, 368
guidelines, 163, 201
internal security section, 318
Office of International Affairs,
355
Office of Professional Responsibility, 407–08, 409–10, 412–
15, 416, 429
prosecution of spies, 271

Kaiser, Catherine M., 62, 179
Kallstrom, James K., 302–03, 304,
305
Kavina, James A., 176–78
Kelley, Clarence, 38–39, 65, 126,
163, 329
as director, 10, 45, 58, 111, 166,
250, 294, 300, 376–77, 390
fathered new bureau, 380
on Hoover, 329
innovations, 204
press relations, 364
reform of bureau, 204, 370,
380
Kelly, Thomas C., 141–42
Kemper, Edmund E., III, 223, 230
Kennedy, John F., 40, 140, 151,
157, 158, 162, 216, 299, 329,
330
Kennedy, Robert F., 299, 330
Kennedy, Weldon L., 38, 39, 115,
118–19, 187–88, 210–11, 347,
350, 394–95
associate deputy director, 415–
16
on discipline, 136, 137–38
and personnel policy, 327–28,
330
KGB, 2, 22, 57, 65, 66, 67–68, 71,
72, 73, 74, 75–76, 94, 211,
212, 261, 275, 278, 279, 364
bugging cars of, 303–04
successor to, 354, 412
and Walker, 276–77
King, Allan A., 318, 319
King, Martin Luther, 2, 40, 216,
281, 293, 296, 299, 337–38,
339, 368, 386
King, Phillip M., 111–12
King, Rodney, 37, 163, 173–74,
189, 206, 208–09
Kirby, Pat, 57–63
Kitzmiller, Pamela, 48, 49, 50
Koresh, David, 418–20, 421–29
Kunkel, Robert G., 266, 267, 294,
295
Kurins, Andris, 27

LA COLORS (case), 208
Laboratory division, 8, 252–64, 301
Lamp, Jacqueline, 214–15, 230,
231, 235
Langberg, Larry W., 212, 344, 345
Lanier, J. H., 132
Lano, Angelo J., 265–68, 269, 270
Lano, Renée C., 228–29
Law, rule of, 377, 379, 383
Law enforcement, professionaliza-
tion of, 166
Lawler, Larry G., 190, 205, 207,
306, 337, 383
Lawn, Jack, 40–42, 96–98, 381
Lawson, Carrie Smith, 43–45
Lawson, Earl, Jr., 43–45
Lawton, Mary C., 68, 69, 70, 314–
15, 318
Leaks, 262, 269, 271, 296, 297
Leary, Edward R., 131, 136, 270
Lee, W. Richard, 132
Legal attachés (legats), 352–53,
355–58
see also London legal attaché
Legal division, 123, 346–47
Levi, Edward H., 66, 300
Liberation Army Fifth Battalion,
25–26
Library Awareness Program, 71,
124, 380
Lill, Robert E., 115, 163, 268, 269,
279, 280
Linares, Luis, 79, 81, 85
Lindbergh, Charles A., Jr., 2, 253–
54

List, John E., 257
Local law enforcement, 207, 216, 224, 291
London legal attaché, 352–61
Los Angeles office, 123, 189–213
Los Angeles police, 37
Los Angeles riots, 163, 206, 209, 393, 404
Los Angeles Times, 124, 196, 199, 200–01

McFarlane, Robert C., 262
McGrath, William J., 248–49
McKay, John L., Jr., 337, 400, 402
McKenzie, James D., 2, 38, 88, 130, 175, 181–82, 183, 194, 283, 339, 340
McNeill, Gordon G., 89
Mafia, 10, 12, 19, 21, 74, 161, 320, 322, 353–54, 357
  secret induction, 312, 319, 320–22
Maguire, Peter E., 313, 314, 315, 318
Mahan, Daniel C., 269, 270
Management, 100, 113, 131, 133, 340, 341, 342, 386–87
Mann, Thomas, 3
Manning, Andrew S., 112
Marginal employees, 115, 211, 212, 334, 349
Marino, Mary Jo, 61, 197, 210
Martin, John L., 66–67
Masselli, William, 286
Masters of Deceit (Hoover), 3, 363, 369
Mata, Fernando E., 137
Matix, William R., 86–88
Mazella, Chris R., 89, 97, 104, 329
Medellin cartel, 78, 79, 84, 85, 208
Media, 107, 113, 123, 124, 189, 196, 201–02, 365
  relations with, 371, 373, 377
  and Watergate, 269–70
Media, Pa., resident agency, 15

Media representatives, 124, 152, 189, 196–206, 366, 367, 371
Meese, Edwin, III, 238, 380, 381
MEGAHUT, 68–69
Meisel, Alvaro, 78–83
Metesky, George, 221
Miami office, 77–110, 345–46
Miller, Henry, 3
Miller, Paul L., 92, 105–06
Miller, Richard W., 115, 116, 189, 210–13, 263, 349
Mills, Darrell W., 352, 354, 357, 358, 361
Minor, Paul K., 117, 119–21, 122, 151, 158, 211–12, 262, 263, 288
Minorities, 58, 293
Minority agents, 124, 329–30, 331–47, 349–50
  advancement of, 342, 376, 385, 386
  hiring, 376
  Miami office, 345–46
  prejudice against, 326–27, 329–30
  promotion of, 349
  proportion of, 350
  recruitment of, 330, 331
Mireles, Edmundo, Jr., 87–88
Miron, Murray S., 204–05
Mitrione, Dan A., Jr., 100–01, 116, 119, 173
Monaco, James R., 104
Money laundering, 354, 355
Monserrate, Frank, 105–10
Monserrate, Suzanne, 105–10
Moody, Susan McBride, 242–43, 244, 245
Moody, Walter Leroy, Jr., 239–45
Motley, Earlington H., Jr., 56
Movies about FBI, 362, 363
Mullaney, Patrick J., 221–22
Mullen, Francis M., 285–86
Mumford, Lewis, 3

Munford, Sarah, 389, 395, 397–403, 404, 405, 406–07, 408, 409–10, 411, 417

NAACP, 237, 386
National Center for the Analysis of Violent Crime, 227, 309
National Crime Information Center (NCIC), 193, 216, 259, 385
National priority program targets, 37
National Security Agency (NSA), 68, 69, 264, 410
National Security Threat List, 74
National Stolen Art File, 259
Naval Investigative Service (NIS), 289
Nelson, Scott, 371, 373, 431
New Agent Review Board (NARB), 175
New York office, 5–28
  Operations and Command Center, 21–22
New York Times, 124, 262, 349, 367, 408, 412, 415, 426
Nichols, Louis B., 363, 364
Nixon, Richard, 4, 66, 267, 269, 299–300, 364, 376
Norfolk office, 27, 274
Norris, Roy L., 215, 230–31, 235

Oberwetter, Jim, 162
O'Brien, Joseph F., 27
Ochoa, Jorge, 79, 85
O'Donnell, Gene J., 256–57
Office of Planning and Evaluation, 37
Office of Professional Responsibility (OPR), 102–03, 104, 107–08, 109, 111, 114, 117, 119, 120, 121, 122, 126–31, 325, 347–48, 399, 407
Office of public affairs, 124–25
"Offsites," 18–19, 69, 155
Ogorodnikov, Svetlana, 211–12
O'Keefe, William P., 275, 276–77

Omnibus Crime Control and Safe Streets Act of 1968, 155
Operation Safe Streets, 207, 291, 293
Organized crime, 37, 94–95, 304, 353, 354, 375, 379
  New York, 2, 8–10, 12, 13, 18, 20, 21
Organized crime families, 7, 13, 21
Organized-crime section, 33
Ostrow, Ronald J., 124, 200, 384, 385
Oswald, Lee Harvey, 158, 216
Otto, John E., 109, 200, 295, 318, 319, 374, 380, 392–93, 404

Pan Am 103, 34, 272, 352, 358–61
Parker, Phillip A., 272–73, 295
Parsons, Charlie J., 124, 189–90, 196, 197–98, 199, 206, 208
Parsons, Mildred C., 294–95
Patriarca, Raymond J., 319, 320–22
Pearson, Bill, 158
Peel, Harry L., 119–21
Pelton, Ronald W., 56, 59, 71, 73, 138, 271, 277
Pennell, Steven P., 229–30
Penrith, Gary L., 129, 130, 148–50, 151, 342–43, 372, 388
Pérez, Bernardo Matias, 327, 332, 333, 337, 341, 350
Pérez, James R., 61, 341–42
Performance standards, 181–82, 183
Perot, Ross, 162, 163
Perpetrators, categorization of, 226
Persian Gulf War, 34, 36, 56–57, 408
Personality, organized/disorganized, 226–27, 228
Personnel policies, 327–33, 376
Petras, Barbara, 104
PFI Inc., 279
Philadelphia field office, 39–40, 192, 193
Pistone, Joseph D., 21, 143–44

Pizza Connection (case), 20
Platt, Michael, 86–89
Pledger, James R., 86, 90, 91, 180–81
Polar Cap (case), 354
Police, 57–58, 93, 166, 209
  cooperation with, 3, 9, 15, 190
  as information source, 166
  relations with, 57–58
  see also Local law enforcement
Political dissent, 2, 15, 149, 375
Political scandals, 290–91
Politics, 298–99, 408–09, 411, 414–15, 429–30
Pollard, Jonathan J., 71, 271
Polygraph, computerized, 263–64
Polygraph unit, polygraphing, 51, 119, 120–21, 253, 259–63
Positive intelligence, 353
Potts, Larry A., 238–45, 250–51, 408, 424
Prejudice, 177–78, 326–51
  see also Discrimination
Presidents, 2, 66, 290–91, 296, 297
Press, 363, 364–67, 371–72, 373
  see also Media
Press office, 365, 366–67, 370, 372–73
  control of television programs, 372–73
Presser, Jackie, 121–22
Prince, Walter B., 324–25
Priority cases, 11, 33, 37
Proactive approach, 10, 67–68
Profiles, profiling, 49–51, 62–63, 214–35, 247, 280
Provisional Irish Republican Army (PIRA), 311, 312–18, 319
Psychopaths, 220–21
Public affairs, 362–73
Public affairs office, 124–25, 367, 371, 405
Public relations function, 364–65
Public trust, 17, 136, 138, 173–74
Putnam, Mark S., 116, 373

Qaddafi, Mu'ammar, 361
Quality-management office, 124
Queen, David D., 62–63
Quigley, Martin, 311–18

Race, racism, 177–78, 326–27, 337–38, 340–41, 345–46, 347
  see also Minority agents
Racketeer Influenced and Corrupt Organizations Act (RICO), 12, 320, 321
Radio shows about FBI, 362, 363
Ramey, J. Stephen, 73, 167, 371
Ramsey, Donald W., 7, 152–53
Ray, James Earl, 216, 222
Reagan, Ronald, 232, 262, 291, 334, 380
Reese, James T., 178
Rehder, William J., 190–92, 195
Reid, Christina L., 314, 315, 318
Reno, Janet, 418, 424, 425, 426, 427, 429, 430–31
Reporters, 124–25, 199, 363, 366–67, 368, 371
  see also Media; Press
Resident agencies (RAs), 11, 15, 19, 46–47, 50, 53
Reso, Sidney J., 372, 388
Ressler, Robert K., 222, 223
Revell, Oliver B. (Buck), 3, 10, 18, 37–38, 40, 45, 64, 88, 122, 150, 182, 224, 246, 356, 404
  and air force, 272
  on Branch Davidian raid, 429
  collection of plaques, 98, 140, 160, 161
  on discipline, 133, 136, 137
  on drug cases, 78, 97
  on extraterritorial jurisdiction, 356
  on Hoover, 294
  and hostage rescue unit, 282–83, 285
  on Kelley, 376
  and intelligence, 66, 72
  and Los Angeles riots, 209

and minority lawsuits, 332, 334–35, 336
on reform of FBI, 370
SAC, Dallas office, 140, 157–64, 387
on Sessions, 366
and VANPAC, 237–38
on Webster, 380
Rezza, Anthony P., 136
Rich, James T., 123
Richards, Donald S., 14, 19
Ricks, Bob A., 421, 425
Rights, warning suspects of, 72, 73, 172, 375
Rights violations, 2–3, 149, 375
Roach, Edward J., 6, 7, 32, 53–56
Roberts, Morris E., Jr., 249–50
Robinson, Everett A., III, 46–47, 49–50, 51, 52
Robinson, Robert E., 237, 245
Rochon, Donald, 327, 332, 333–37, 380, 389
Rodriguez, Pablo Correa, 85
Roemer, Eileen J., 382–83
Rogers, Richard M., 284
Rogers, Robert F., 183–84
Roosevelt, Franklin D., 66, 352–53
Rosenberg, Ethel, 64, 368
Rosenberg, Julius, 64, 368
Rotton, Alan H., 127
Rowan, Carl, Jr., 333–34, 336
Ruckelshaus, William D., 364
Russian Republic, 73–74, 75
Russo, Joseph A., 320, 321, 322

SACs. See Special agent(s) in charge
Salary (agent), 26, 188, 344
Santimauro, Michael J., 185, 333, 335
Savage, Nancy L., 92
Schneider, Steve, 421, 422, 424
Schuler, Ruby, 210
Schultz, Carl A., 231–32
Scientific analysis section, 254
Scientific crime analysis, 253–54
Secret Service, 223, 267

Security clearance, 72, 287
Security devices, 152
Sensitivity training, 176–78, 337, 339–41
Serbian nationalist terrorists, 318–19
Serial bandits, 190–91
Serial killers/killings, 215, 217–18, 223–24, 230, 255, 258
black Atlanta schoolchildren, 236, 245–49, 250
personality characteristics, 225–27, 228
Serial rape, 222, 223, 255, 258
Sessions, Alice, 356–57, 380, 381, 382, 388, 389–93, 394–97, 401, 402, 403–04, 405, 406, 407, 409, 410, 411, 412, 413, 415, 416, 417
Sessions, William, 33, 43, 163, 295
an affirmative action, 343
as director, 17, 30, 35, 45, 64–65, 71, 90, 113, 124, 125, 151, 179, 196, 206, 209, 238, 285, 291, 293, 309, 321, 344, 346–47, 356–57, 358, 380–89, 390, 392, 393–94, 398, 400, 401–18
and discipline, 134
equality in employment, 327
and intelligence, 74, 75
investigation of abuses by, 407–11, 412–15, 429
and laboratory division, 254, 255
and minority agents, 331–32, 337, 350
and OPR, 130–31
and prejudice, 341–42
and public relations, 365–67, 373
reform of bureau, 370
and technology, 306, 307, 308
tenure, 429–31
and Waco raid, 423–24, 426, 429
Sex-related crimes, 217–18, 234
Sexism, 326–27, 337–38, 341
Seymour, Whitney North, Jr., 30, 390

Shaheen, Michael E., Jr., 412, 414, 416
Sheer, Thomas L., 8–10, 13–14, 100, 133
Shields, Michael L., 205–06
Siano, James J., 144
Silbert, Earl J., 269, 270
Simple schizophrenia, 219–21, 226
Sirene, Walt H., 101, 173–75, 176
Smith, William French, 96, 291
SOARU (Special Operations and Research Unit), 309
Society of Former Special Agents of the FBI, 30, 369–70
SOLO, 23
Special agent(s) in charge (SACs), 9, 99, 159, 181
  and discipline, 126–27, 133
  and media, 196
  minority, 350
Special Intelligence Service, 352–53
Special Operations Group (SOG), 18, 155–56, 303
Special Support Group (SSG), 18, 274–75
Speck, Richard, 218, 223
SPIDERWEB, 303–04
Spies, 64–76, 210
  see also Espionage
Spinelli, George, 194
Star stalker crimes, 189, 202–04, 205–06
State Department, 36, 70, 72, 73, 356
Statistics, 37, 92–93, 113, 376
  deemphasized, 37, 376
  on discipline, 113
  emphasis on, 2, 11, 15, 38, 369
Steinbeck, John, 3
Sting operations, 163, 271, 279
Stockholm Syndrome, 231–32
Stolen cars, 2, 15, 375
Stone, Harlan F., 298–99
Storey, Frank J., 9–10, 16
Stowe, Walter B., Jr., 20, 176
Strategic Information Operations

Center (SIOC), 34–35, 159, 317, 425
Strentz, Thomas, 231–32
Stress, 178–80
Subversion, 2, 37, 66
Sullivan, William C., 65, 299–300, 328–29
Support employees, 157, 249–50
Surveillance, 18–19, 71–72, 73, 152, 303
  aerial, 272, 274, 275, 276, 277
  illegal, 15
  of Walker, 273–74, 275
  see also Electronic surveillance
Surveillance squad (Dallas), 155–56
SWAT teams, 33, 91, 148, 152, 154–55, 199–200, 249–50, 253, 282, 285, 422

Talladega, Ala., federal prison, 253, 285, 366
Technical agents, 303
Technical services, 302
Technical services division, 116, 305
Technical Support Squad (TSS), 303
Technology, 301, 306, 307, 308
  theft of, 213
Television networks/programs, 124, 362, 363, 372–73
Temple, George B., 154–55
Ten Most Wanted Fugitives program, 198, 362
Terminology, 309–10
Terrorism, terrorists, 2, 35–37, 70–71, 284–85, 353, 355, 379
Teten, Howard D., 217–21, 222, 231, 234, 338
Thomas, Clarence, 37, 271, 285, 287, 288
Thompson, John H., 94
Thompson, Linda C., 101–05
Thornburgh, Richard, 70, 321, 384, 385, 393, 402
Thornton, Earl, 116–17

Thornton, Jerry D., 195–96
Thurman, James T., 358, 360
Tickel, H. Edward, Jr., 116–19
Tolson, Clyde, 3, 364, 370
Toohey, D. Caroll, 118, 123, 124,
  138, 150, 192, 193, 195, 246,
  389, 394
  on personnel policy, 332
  on reform of FBI, 370
Top Ten fugitives, 197
Torres, Ralph A., 155–56
Total Quality Management (TOM),
  386
Tower, John, 271, 286–87, 381
Tradebom (case), 24–26
Training division, 166–68, 216,
  340, 341
Training programs, 1, 11, 165–66,
  168–69, 170–79, 180–86, 188
Travis, Stephen S., 127
Tullai, Simon, 1, 11
Tully, Edward, 183

Undercover operations, 2, 10, 12–
  13, 20, 141–48, 279–82
  female agents, 59, 101–05
  organized crime, 10
Undercover review board, 33
Undercover review committee, 33,
  280
Uniform Crime Reporting Program,
  310
UNIRAC (case), 10
United Freedom Front, 312, 323
Unsolved Mysteries (TV series), 35,
  256, 372
U.S. Attorney(s), 113, 174, 238

Valiquette, Joe, 14, 16, 201–02
Vance, Robert S., 236–45, 251, 406
VANPAC (case), 237–45, 250
Varelli, Frank, 148–49, 150–51
Verinder, Fred B., 13–14, 131–33,
  405–06
Video support unit, 257–58
Videotape, 225, 252, 257–58
Vietnam war, 4, 15, 65, 364

Violent crime, 37, 75, 91, 161,
  291–93
  as priority, 206–07
Violent crime and major offenders
  section, 33

Wagner, John C., 126–27, 273,
  323–24
Walker, John A., Jr., 64, 71, 85–86,
  271, 272–77, 324
Walsh, Robert E., 28, 194
Walters, Leonard M., 268–69
Walton, Kenneth P., 14–18
Wannall, W. Raymond, Jr., 66
Warfield, William, 272–73, 295
Warner, Steven B., 93, 94
Washington (D.C.) office, 265–95
Washington metropolitan field of-
  fice (WMFO), 271–72, 290,
  291, 303, 309
Washington Post, 124, 269, 271,
  278, 291, 293, 307, 349, 407
Watergate, 4, 265–71, 295, 364
Watson, R. Patrick, 72, 75, 211
Weapons, 87, 89–91, 154–55, 156,
  180
  see also Firearms
Weather Underground, 18, 344
Webster, William, 32–33, 88, 115,
  122, 130, 163
  and dealing with Congress, 286
  as director, 8, 13, 17, 18, 30, 40,
  45, 58, 67, 116, 118, 124, 125,
  150–51, 158, 159, 181, 206,
  250, 278, 281, 283, 291, 300,
  302, 306, 377–80, 385, 417,
  423
  director, Central Intelligence,
  160, 200, 374, 380
  discipline under, 134, 136
  on drugs, 96, 97
  on Hoover, 371
  and intelligence programs, 71
  and minority agents, 330–31
  and public relations, 364, 365,
  366–67
  reform of bureau, 370

Webster, William (*cont.*)
    relations with agents, 376
Wedtech case, 133, 238
Weinstock, Daniel, 75
Wells, William, 108
Whitaker, Allen C., 43, 45
White agents, 342–43, 345, 349
White collar crime, 2, 37, 196,
    209–10, 258, 289–90, 375, 379
White-collar crime section, 33
White House, 4, 267, 268, 269, 287,
    430
WHITE MARE, 23
Whitehead, Don, 363, 373
Williams, Chester, 105
Williams, David, 24–25
Williams, Wayne B., 224, 246–49,
    250
WIND FLYER, 273–77
Wiretaps, 2, 12–13, 65, 68, 116,
    127, 150, 155, 208, 305, 375
    illegal, 2, 375
Witschard, Walter A., 40–41
Wolfe, Thomas, 3

Wolfinger, Joseph R., 272, 273, 274
Wood, John H., 40, 42, 236, 237,
    261, 381
Woodward, Bob, 269–71, 291
World Trade Center (New York
    City), 23–26, 37, 418

Yablonsky, Joe, 279, 280
Yates, Robert E., 175
York, Lawrence K., 216
Young, Robert S., 364–65, 366, 367
Younis, Fawaz, 284–85, 354, 355
Yurchenko, Vitaly, 277–79

Zakharov, Gennadiy F., 21–22
Zevallos, Hector, 231–32
Zevallos, Rosalie, 231–32
Zigrossi, Norman A., 282, 295
Zimbalist, Efrem, Jr., 170, 203, 330,
    363
Zimbalist, Stephanie, 202–04,
    205–06
Zopp, James L., 47, 49, 50, 51, 228

12/93

YOU CAN RENEW
BY PHONE!
623-3300

GAYLORD M